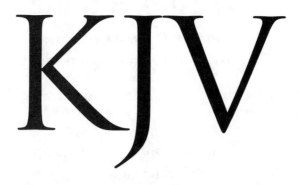

KJV

STANDARD LESSON
COMMENTARY®

2004–2005

International Sunday School Lessons

Edited by

Ronald L. Nickelson

Published by
STANDARD PUBLISHING

Jonathan Underwood,
Senior Editor, Adult Ministry Resources

Douglas Redford,
Contributing Editor

Carla J. Crane,
Production Manager

Fifty-second Annual Volume

©2004
STANDARD PUBLISHING
A division of STANDEX INTERNATIONAL Corporation
8121 Hamilton Avenue, Cincinnati, Ohio 45231
Printed in U. S. A.

In This Volume

Artists

TITLE PAGES: James E. Seward

Cover design by DesignTeam

Lessons based on International Sunday School Lessons © 2002 by the Lesson Committee.

CD-ROM AVAILABLE

The *Standard Lesson Commentary®* is available separately in an electronic format. This compact disk contains the full text of the King James *Standard Lesson Commentary®* and *The NIV Standard Lesson Commentary®*, a variety of preparation resources powered by the Libronix Digital Library System, and a collection of presentation helps that can be projected or reproduced as handouts. Order #06005.

System Requirements: Windows XP/2000/ME/98/95; Pentium 133 MHz processor (300MHz recommended), 64 Meg RAM (128 recommended); 60 Meg Available Hard Drive Space; 2x or better CD-ROM drive.

Index of Printed Texts, 2004-2005

The printed texts for 2004-2005 are arranged here in the order in which they appear in the Bible. Opposite each reference is the number of the page on which it appears in this volume.

How to Say It

The following pages list some of the names and other hard-to-pronounce words used in the lessons of this edition of the *Standard Lesson Commentary*® along with a phonetic pronunciation guide for each. In each lesson is an abridged version of this list that includes only the words used in that lesson.

A

ABANA. *Ab*-uh-nuh or Uh-*ban*-uh.
ABBA. *Ab*-uh.
ABINADAB. Uh-*bin*-uh-dab.
ABRAHAM. *Ay*-bruh-ham.
ABRAM. *Ay*-brum.
ABSALOM. *Ab*-suh-lum.
ACHAIA. Uh-*kay*-uh.
ADAM *(Hebrew)*. uh-*dahm*.
AGRIPPA. Uh-*grip*-puh.
AHAB. *Ay*-hab.
AHAZ. *Ay*-haz.
ALCMENE. Alk-*mee*-nee.
ALPHEUS. Al-*fee*-us.
AMMONITE. *Am*-un-ite.
AMORITES. *Am*-uh-rites.
AMOS. *Ay*-mus.
AMOZ. *Ay*-mahz.
ANATHEMA. Uh-*nath*-uh-muh.
ANNAS. *An*-nus.
ANTIOCH. *An*-tee-ock.
ANTIPAS. *An*-tih-pus.
APHRODITE. Af-ruh-*dite*-ee.
ARABIA. Uh-*ray*-bee-uh.
ARAMAIC. Air-uh-*may*-ick.
ARIMATHEA. *Air*-uh-muh-*thee*-uh (strong accent on *thee* as in *thin*).
ARISTOPHANES. A-ris-*tof*-a-neez.
ARTEMIS. *Ar*-teh-miss.
ASAPH. *Ay*-saff.
ASHER. *Ash*-er.
ASSYRIANS. Uh-*sear*-e-unz.
ATHENA. Uh-*thee*-nuh.
ATHENS. *Ath*-unz.
AUGUSTINE. *Aw*-gus-teen (strong accent on *Aw*) or Aw-*gus*-tin.

B

BAAL. *Bay*-ul.
BABYLON. *Bab*-uh-lun.
BABYLONIANS. Bab-ih-*low*-nee-unz.
BARNABAS. *Bar*-nuh-bus.
BAR-THOLAMI. Bar *Thal*-uh-me.
BARTHOLOMEW. Bar-*thahl*-uh-mew.
BARTIMEUS. *Bar*-tih-*me*-us (strong accent on *me*).
BASHAN. *Bay*-shan.
BATH-SHEBA. Bath-*she*-buh.
BENEDICTUS. *Ben*-eh-*dik*-tus (strong accent on *dik*).
BEN-HADAD. Ben-*hay*-dad.
BETHEL. *Beth*-ul.

BETHLEHEM. *Beth*-lih-hem.
BETHSAIDA JULIAS. Beth-*say*-uh-duh *Joo*-lee-ahs.
BETHUEL. Be-*thu*-ul.
BEZALEEL. Bih-*zal*-ih-el.
BLASPHEMER. *blas*-feem-er.
BLASPHEMY. *blas*-fuh-me.
BOLSHEVIK. *Bol*-shuh-vik.
BUDDHA. *Bew*-duh.

C

CAESAREA. Sess-uh-*ree*-uh.
CAIAPHAS. *Kay*-uh-fus or *Kye*-uh-fus.
CANA. *Kay*-nuh.
CANAAN. *Kay*-nun.
CANAANITES. *Kay*-nun-ites.
CAPERNAUM. Kuh-*per*-nay-um.
CARPE DIEM *(Latin)*. kar-pay *dee*-um.
CENTURION. sen-*ture*-ee-un.
CEPHAS. *See*-fus.
CHALDEANS. Kal-*dee*-unz.
CHALDEES. *Kal*-deez.
CHEBAR. *Kee*-bar.
CHEMOSH. *Kee*-mosh.
CHILION. *Kil*-ee-on.
CHINNERETH. *Kin*-e-reth or *Chin*-ne-reth.
COLOSSIANS. Kuh-*losh*-unz.
CORINTHIANS. Ko-*rin*-thee-unz.
CORNELIUS. Cor-*neel*-yus.
CYRUS. *Sigh*-russ.
CZARIST. *Tsar*-ist.

D

DALMANUTHA. Dal-muh-*new*-thuh.
DAMASCUS. Duh-*mass*-cus.
DECAPOLIS. Dee-*cap*-uh-lis.
DENARII. dih-*nair*-ee or dih-*nair*-eye.
DENARIUS. dih-*nair*-ee-us.
DERBE. *Der*-bee.
DEUTERONOMY. Due-ter-*ahn*-uh-me.
DIDYMUS. *Did*-uh-mus.
DISPUTATIONS. dis-pyoo-*tay*-shunz.
DISSIMULATION. dis-sim-you-*lay*-shun.

E

EBAL. *Ee*-bull.
ECCLESIASTES. Ih-klees-ee-*az*-tees.
ECZEMA. *ek*-zuh-muh.
EDEN. *Ee*-den.
EGYPT. *Ee*-jipt.
ELIAB. Ee-*lye*-ab.

ELIJAH. Ee-*lye*-juh.
ELIMELECH. Ee-*lim*-eh-leck.
ELISHA. E-*lye*-shuh.
ELOHIM *(Hebrew)*. el-o-*heem*.
EMMAUS. Em-*may*-us.
EPHESIANS. Ee-*fee*-zhunz.
EPHESUS. *Ef*-uh-sus.
ESAU. *Ee*-saw.
ESSENES. *Eh*-seenz.
ETHIOPIAN. Ee-thee-*o*-pea-un.
EUPHRATES. You-*fray*-teez.
EUSEBIUS. You-*see*-be-us.
EZEKIEL. Ee-*zeek*-ee-ul or Ee-*zeek*-yul.
EZRA. *Ez*-ruh.

G

GADARENES. *Gad*-uh-reens.
GADITES. *Gad*-ites.
GAIUS. *Gay*-us.
GALATIANS. Guh-*lay*-shunz.
GALILEAN. Gal-uh-*lee*-un.
GALILEE. *Gal*-uh-lee.
GAULS. Gawlz.
GENNESARET. Geh-*ness*-uh-ret (G as in get).
GENTILES. *Jen*-tilez.
GERASENES. *Gur*-uh-seenz.
GERIZIM. *Gair*-ih-zeem or Guh-*rye*-zim.
GETHSEMANE. Geth-*sem*-uh-nee (G as in *get*).
GIBEAH. *Gib*-ee-uh (G as in *get*).
GIULIANI. Joo-lee-*ahn*-ee.
GOLGOTHA. *Gahl*-guh-thuh.
GOLIATH. Go-*lye*-uth.
GOMORRAH. Guh-*more*-uh.
GUYANA. Guy-*ah*-nuh.

H

HABAKKUK. Huh-*back*-kuk.
HAGAR. *Hay*-gar.
HAI. *Hay*-eye.
HANNAH. *Han*-uh.
HARAN. *Hair*-un.
HEBREWS. *Hee*-brews.
HERCULES. *Her*-kew-leez.
HEROD. *Hair*-ud.
HEZEKIAH. Hez-ih-*kye*-uh.
HITTITES. *Hit*-ites or *Hit*-tites.
HIVITES. *Hi*-vites.
HOREB. *Ho*-reb.
HOSEA. Ho-*zay*-uh.
HOSHEA. Ho-*shay*-uh.

I

ICONIUM. Eye-*coe*-nee-um.
ISAAC. *Eye*-zuk.
ISAIAH. Eye-*zay*-uh.
ISCAH. *Is*-ka.
ISHMAEL. *Ish*-may-el.

ISHSHAH *(Hebrew)*. ish-*shaw*.
ISIS. *Eye*-sis.
ISRAEL. *Iz*-ray-el.

J

JACOB. *Jay*-kub.
JAIRUS. *Jye*-rus or *Jay*-ih-rus.
JEBUSITES. *Jeb*-yuh-sites.
JEHOIACHIN. Jeh-*hoy*-uh-kin.
JEHOIAKIM. Jeh-*hoy*-uh-kim.
JEHOSHUA. Je-*hosh*-you-uh.
JEREMIAH. Jair-uh-*my*-uh.
JERICHO. *Jair*-ih-co.
JERUSALEM. Juh-*roo*-suh-lem.
JESSE. *Jess*-ee.
JETHRO. *Jeth*-ro.
JEZEBEL. *Jez*-uh-bel.
JORDAN. *Jor*-dun.
JOSEPHUS. Jo-*see*-fus.
JOSES. *Jo*-sez.
JOSHUA. *Josh*-yew-uh.
JOTHAM. *Jo*-thum.
JUDAH. *Joo*-duh.
JUDAISM. *Joo*-day-iz-um.
JUDAIZERS. *Joo*-day-eye-zers.
JUDAS ISCARIOT. *Joo*-dus Iss-*care*-e-ut.
JUDEA. Joo-*dee*-uh.

K

KERIOTH. *Kee*-rih-oath.
KETURAH. Keh-*too*-ruh.
KORINTHIAZESTHAI *(Greek)*. ko-rin-thee-*adz*-ess-thai
(*th* as in *thin*).

L

LAMENTATIONS. Lam-en-*tay*-shunz.
LASCIVIOUSNESS. luh-*siv*-ee-us-ness.
LAZARUS. *Laz*-uh-rus.
LEBBEUS. Leh-*bee*-us.
LEVI. *Lee*-vye.
LEVITE. *Lee*-vite.
LEVITICUS. Leh-*vit*-ih-kus.
LEX TALIONIS *(Latin)*. leks tal-ee-*oh*-niss.
LYSTRA. *Liss*-truh.

M

MACCABEES. *Mack*-uh-bees.
MACEDONIA. Mass-eh-*doe*-nee-uh.
MAGDALENE. *Mag*-duh-leen or Mag-duh-*lee*-nee.
MAGNIFICAT. Mag-*nif*-ih-cot.
MAHLON. *Mah*-lon.
MALACHI. *Mal*-uh-kye.
MANASSEH. Muh-*nass*-uh.
MARTYRS. *mar*-turz.
MELCHIZEDEK. Mel-*kiz*-eh-dek.
MESOPOTAMIA. *Mes*-uh-puh-*tay*-me-uh (strong
accent on *tay*).

MESSIAH. Meh-*sigh*-uh.
MESSIANIC. mess-ee-*an*-ick.
MICAH. *My*-kuh.
MIDIAN. *Mid*-ee-un.
MILCAH. *Mil*-kuh.
MOABITES. *Mo*-ub-ites.
MOJAVE. Moh-*hah*-vee.
MOREH. *Moe*-reh.
MOSES. *Mo*-zes or *Mo*-zez.

N

NAAMAN. *Nay*-uh-mun.
NAHOR. *Nay*-hor.
NAOMI. Nay-*oh*-me.
NATHAN. *Nay*-thun (*th* as in *thin*).
NATHANAEL. Nuh-*than*-yull (*th* as in *thin*).
NAZARETH. *Naz*-uh-reth.
NEBUCHADNEZZAR. *Neb*-yuh-kud-*nez*-er (strong
    accent on *nez*).
NEHEMIAH. *Nee*-huh-*my*-uh (strong accent on *my*).
NICODEMUS. *Nick*-uh-*dee*-muss (strong accent on *dee*).
NUN. None.
NUNC DIMITTIS *(Latin)*. Nunk Dih-*mit*-us.

O

OMRI. *Ahm*-rye.
ORPAH. *Or*-pah.
OSHEA. O-*shay*-uh.

P

PARTHENON. *Par*-thuh-non (*th* as in *thin*).
PARTHENOS *(Greek)*. par-*then*-ahss (*th* as in *thin*).
PEREA. Peh-*ree*-uh.
PERIZZITES. *Pair*-ih-zites.
PHANUEL. Fuh-*nyoo*-el.
PHARAOH. *fair*-o or *fay*-roe.
PHARISEES. *Fair*-ih-seez.
PHARPAR. *Far*-par.
PHILIPPI. Fuh-*lip*-eye or *Fill*-uh-pie.
PHILIPPIANS. Fih-*lip*-ee-unz.
PHILISTINES. Fuh-*liss*-teenz or *Fill*-us-teenz.
PHOENICIA. Fuh-*nish*-uh.
PISGAH. *Piz*-guh.
PISIDIAN. Puh-*sid*-ee-un.
PONTIUS PILATE. *Pon*-shus or *Pon*-ti-us *Pie*-lut.
PROPITIATION. pro-*pih*-she-*ay*-shun (strong accent
    on *ay*).
PROSELYTE. *prahss*-uh-light.
PSORIASIS. suh-*rye*-uh-sis.

R

RABBI. *Rab*-eye.
RACA. *Ray*-kuh or Ray-*kah*.
RAMAH. *Ray*-muh.
REBEKAH. Reh-*bek*-uh.
REUBENITES. *Roo*-ben-ites.
RUAH *(Hebrew)*. rue-ah.

S

SADDUCEES. *Sad*-you-seez.
SALOME. Suh-*lo*-me.
SAMARIA. Suh-*mare*-ee-uh.
SAMARITAN. Suh-*mare*-uh-tun.
SAMARITANS. Suh-*mare*-uh-tunz.
SANHEDRIN. *San*-huh-drun or San-*heed*-run.
SARAI. *Seh*-rye.
SARAPIS. Suh-*rap*-is.
SATAN. *Say*-tun.
SEPTUAGINT. Sep-*too*-ih-jent.
SEPULCHRE. *sep*-ul-kur.
SERGIO GUTIERREZ. *Sar*-jyo Goo-*tar*-ez (*a* as in *air*).
SHECHEM. *Shee*-kem or *Shek*-em.
SHEMA *(Hebrew)*. shih-*mah*.
SICHEM. *Sigh*-kem.
SIERRA LEONE. See-*air*-uh Lay-*own*.
SIHON. *Sigh*-hun.
SILAS. *Sigh*-luss.
SILVANUS. Sil-*vay*-nus.
SIMEON. *Sim*-ee-un.
SINAI. *Sigh*-nye or *Sigh*-nay-eye.
SIRACH. *Sigh*-rak.
SODOM. *Sod*-um.
SOLOMON. *Sol*-o-mun.
STRABO. *Stray*-bow (*bow* as in rain*bow*).
SYCHAR. *Sigh*-kar.
SYNAGOGUE. *sin*-uh-gog.
SYRIA. *Sear*-ee-uh.

T

TERAH. *Tair*-uh.
TETRARCH. *Teh*-trark or *Tee*-trark.
THADDEUS. Tha-*dee*-us.
THESSALONIANS. *Thess*-uh-*lo*-nee-unz (strong
    accent on *lo*; *th* as in *thin*).
TIBERIAS. Tie-*beer*-ee-us.
TIGRIS. *Tie*-griss.
TIMOTHY. *Tim*-o-thee (*th* as in *thin*).
TITUS. *Ty*-tus.
TYRE. Tire.

U

UR. Er.
UZZIAH. Uh-*zye*-uh.

V

VLADIMIR LENIN. *Vlad*-ih-meer *Len*-in.

Z

ZACCHEUS. Zack-*key*-us.
ZAREPHATH. *Zair*-uh-fath.
ZEBEDEE. *Zeb*-eh-dee.
ZECHARIAH. *Zek*-uh-*rye*-uh (strong accent on *rye*).
ZEDEKIAH. Zed-uh-*kye*-uh.
ZELOTES. Zeh-*low*-teez.
ZEUS. Zoose.

A Tribute to
Orrin Root

by Shawn McMullen

Standard Publishing employees, Sunday school teachers, and Bible students around the world recently lost a dear friend, teacher, writer, editor, and mentor. Orrin Root died May 13, 2003 at the age of 98.

Mr. Root began his ministry with Standard Publishing in 1945. His early responsibilities included editing *Bible Teacher and Leader*, the adult Sunday school curriculum, and three age levels of youth curriculum.

In the June 26, 1949 issue of *The Lookout*, editor Guy P. Levitt introduced Mr. Root as the new writer of the magazine's Sunday school lesson commentary. First under the title, "Untying Some Knots," and later, "Background and Commentary," Mr. Root maintained this vital ministry to Sunday school teachers and students for more than half a century. His insightful commentary and polished writing have helped Bible students around the world understand and apply God's Word to their lives.

In 1953 Mr. Root, as editor-in-chief of Standard Publishing's Sunday school materials, oversaw the production of the first STANDARD LESSON COMMENTARY. As editor and as writer, he has been instrumental in the production of the COMMENTARY each year. His name appears in every issue except one as either editor or writer. This year marks the thirty-third consecutive issue in which he was writer or co-writer of one full quarter of verse-by-verse exposition of the Scripture text.

Mr. Root left his post as Standard Publishing's editor-in-chief to retire in 1970. When editor Jay Sheffield died, Mr. Root was called out of retirement to serve as editor "pro tempore" of *The Lookout* from August of 1975 to September of 1976.

Even in retirement, Mr. Root's influence at Standard Publishing continued to be felt through his ministry as a freelance writer and editor. His regular visits to the office to deliver manuscripts and receive new assignments were welcomed by everyone. His gentle spirit, quick wit, charm, and humility endeared him to us all.

His mastery of the English language combined with a concise and accurate writing style made him an "editor's editor." Mr. Root worked ahead and never missed a deadline. With his family's permission, we will use the material he wrote for "Background and Commentary" through October of 2003. If my calculations are correct, this means that Mr. Root wrote 2,826 consecutive weekly Scripture commentaries for *The Lookout* magazine.

Orrin Root, 1905-2003

I know few people who have served God with greater purpose, passion, and steadfastness. *Christian Standard* editor Mark Taylor and I visited Mr. Root in the hospital a few days before his death. Weakened physically but still focused and thoughtful, he told us he had informed the hospital staff that he needed to get home right away because he had a great deal of writing to do.

I had been editing only a few months when I paid a visit to Mr. Root at the Mt. Healthy Christian Home in Cincinnati, Ohio. We talked about writing, editing, and ministry. Among the many helpful things he said to me, I fondly remember two. I asked what advice he could give me as a new editor. He said, "Write and edit not only to be understood, but also not to be misunderstood." Near the conclusion of our visit he said, "I read your material. You're a good writer." I'll hold onto those words as long as I live.

Upon hearing of Mr. Root's death, I thought, *What does an editor like Mr. Root do in Heaven?* He worked so long and hard and faithfully in this life to help men and women understand and apply God's Word. Now he lives where there are no mistakes to correct, no misunderstandings to set right, no puzzling thoughts to clarify. Then it occurred to me. Whatever else Mr. Root is doing in Heaven, he is enjoying a well-deserved rest.

Then I heard a voice from heaven saying to me, "Write: 'Blessed are the dead who die in the Lord from now on.'" "Yes," says the Spirit, "that they may rest from their labors, and their works follow them" (Revelation 14:13, *NKJV*).

Lesson Planning Page

Reproduce this outline and then fill it in each week to plan your lesson.

Lesson Aims

List the aims here, either directly from the lesson or revised to suit your individual needs.

Getting Started

Begin with an illustration from the beginning of the lesson, the "Into the Lesson" activity from the Learning by Doing section, a discussion question, or some other appropriate opener.

Lesson Development

List in order the activities you will use. These include key points from the commentary section, discussion questions, and activities from the Learning by Doing section.

I.

II.

III.

Conclusion & Application

How will you bring the lesson to a climax, stressing the key point and desired action steps?

Closing Activity

Dismiss the class with an activity that reinforces the Bible lesson.

Fall Quarter, 2004

The God of Continuing Creation

Lessons

About These Lessons

"Newness" holds a fascination for us all. New cars, new careers, and new houses cause excitement! But are we as excited about the "newness" that comes from God? This quarter's lessons teach us why we should be.

Sep 5

Sep 12

Sep 19

Sep 26

Oct 3

Oct 10

Oct 17

Oct 24

Oct 31

Nov 7

Nov 14

Nov 21

Nov 28

Starting Again, for the First Time

THOSE WHO HAVE EXPERIENCED the entire six-year cycle of International Sunday School Lessons that just ended are in for a treat: it's time to start over! This observation is not meant to be flippant, but recognizes the fact that there's always more to learn.

Each time we work through our Bibles we do so with "new eyes" because our life situations are always changing. For instance, those who have come to Christ only recently will relate to the idea of being a "new creation" somewhat differently than will the long-time Christians. Those who have recently lost the "community" of an earthly family through divorce, death, etc., will value the idea of a "Christian community" rather differently than someone who has never experienced an unstable home life.

Our "new eyes" should notice something else as well: the six-year cycle of the past is now a three-year cycle, as the chart below reveals. The themes for each quarter are interesting, aren't they? We begin with two surveys. The first focuses on what we might call "God's actions" as we see Him moving to create and re-create in various ways. The second may be thought of as "God's expectations" as it explores God's call to the community of faith to live out its purpose.

The two surveys then give way to considerations of specific themes in specific books. Some will challenge our thinking about doctrine. Others will move us to change our behavior. Still others will convict us in our hearts and spirits. All will draw us closer to God.

A feature continued from the old six-year cycle is the high value placed on both Old and New Testaments. Neither Testament can be fully understood without reference to the other. God's Word forms a unity that must not be broken.

As we work through our new three-year plan, may we never forget that both Testaments ultimately point to Jesus. From the very beginning, Jesus was involved in our creation (Colossians 1:16). From the very beginning, He was part of the plan of our redemption (Genesis 3:15b). He is the One who promises to return for us (Revelation 22:20).

When Jesus does return, will He find us serving and ready as He expects? (See Matthew 24:36-51.) This new cycle of lessons will help ensure that He does.

International Sunday School Lesson Cycle
September, 2004—August, 2007

YEAR	FALL QUARTER (Sept., Oct., Nov.)	WINTER QUARTER (Dec., Jan., Feb.)	SPRING QUARTER (Mar., Apr., May)	SUMMER QUARTER (June, July, Aug.)
2004-2005	The God of Continuing Creation (Bible Survey)	Called to Be God's People (Bible Survey)	God's Project: Effective Christians (Romans, Galatians)	Jesus' Life, Teachings, and Ministry (Matthew, Mark, Luke)
2005-2006	"You Will Be My Witnesses" (Acts)	God's Commitment— Our Response (Isaiah; 1 and 2 Timothy)	Living in and as God's Creation (Psalms, Job, Ecclesiastes, Proverbs)	Called to Be a Christian Community (1 and 2 Corinthians)
2006-2007	God's Living Covenant (Old Testament Survey)	Jesus Christ: A Portrait of God (John, Philippians, Colossians, Hebrews, 1 John)	Our Community Now and in God's Future (1 John, Revelation)	Committed to Doing Right (Various Prophets, 2 Kings, 2 Chronicles)

"Creation"	"Call"	"Covenant"	"Christ"	"Community"	"Commitment"

God's Continuing Creation

by Orrin Root

SEPTEMBER, OCTOBER, AND NOVEMBER of 2004 bring us a new cycle in the International Sunday School Lesson series. This cycle is an innovative one, including only three years instead of the customary six; but this three-month introduction follows the usual pattern. By considering events widely separated in time, it creates an awareness of the whole scope of Bible history in which all the lessons of the three-year cycle will find their places.

This time our introductory series of thirteen lessons follows the theme of creation through the Bible. Beginning with the creation of man, it leaps to the new beginning after the great flood, then to the creation of a chosen nation, Israel, to maintain faith in God in a pagan world.

Along the way we shall be led to think of the creation of intangible things like hope and trust. Later we shall consider the importance of being new creatures in Christ Jesus and to anticipate the new spiritual bodies that will be ours when we are raised from the dead. The thirteen lessons of this quarter fall into three units corresponding to the months of September, October, and November.

Unit 1. September
Created for a Purpose

The unit title suggests that we look for God's purposes. Why did He make us in His own image? When human behavior proved to be unsatisfactory, why did He start again with the same kind of people? Perhaps the lesson texts will not state God's purpose as plainly as we would like to see it all along the way, but the question does make us think.

Lesson 1. From the Dust of the Ground. Our first lesson comes from the second chapter of Genesis and centers attention on the creation of Adam and Eve. When we read of a new man with a new wife at home in a garden newly created from God's hand, we see a wonderful opportunity to live happily ever after. But there is a touch of foreboding here. The mention of one prohibition indicates that from the beginning there was the possibility of disobedience and disaster.

Lesson 2. Beginning Again. It is a long leap from the creation to Noah's new beginning after the flood, but Genesis itself provides a three-and-a-half chapter background for lesson 2. Adam and Eve did disobey the only prohibition in the world and lost their home in the garden. Genera-

tion after generation then became worse and worse. Looking at the human race, God saw that "every imagination of the thoughts of his heart was only evil continually" (Genesis 6:5). So He cleansed the earth with a great flood.

But God didn't overlook the glimmer of righteousness. He saw one good family in an evil world, and so eight people survived the flood in the ark.

Lesson 3. God Raises Up a Deliverer. Like Adam's descendants, Noah's descendants kept getting worse and worse in their character and action. This time God did not destroy the evil people, but instead chose one man of faith, Abraham, to be the father of a good nation.

Abraham's family numbered about seventy people when it moved to Egypt to escape a famine in Palestine. In Egypt it prospered and increased, perhaps until it numbered in the millions. Eventually a new king made slaves of Abraham's people and tried to work them to death, but still they increased. So the hostile king ordered that all their boy babies must be put in the river.

Moses was one of those babies, but his thoughtful mother put him in a tiny boat that floated among the reeds near the bank. There the king's daughter found him. Moved by sympathy, she reared him as her own son, a prince of Egypt.

At the age of forty, this prince killed a slave driver who was abusing a Hebrew slave. Moses escaped retribution by fleeing to Midian. Lesson 3 takes up the story forty years later. God sent this eighty-year-old man back to Egypt to lead the Hebrew slaves to freedom.

Lesson 4. Becoming God's People. This time the gap between lessons is only about forty years. God and Moses did lead the Hebrew slaves to freedom; but because they lacked faith and refused to obey, the older generation had to die off during forty years in the desert before the younger generation could have the promised land. Lesson 4 brings us some of what Moses said to them as they stood ready to go forward as God's people and take that promised land as their own.

Unit 2. October
God's Creativity Continues

Again we leap across a gap of centuries. The people of Israel captured the promised land and lived there for hundreds of years. Then, for reasons that seemed good to them, leaders decided to make their country into a monarchy. God consented without approving. Saul became the first king, and David the second.

Lesson 5. Creating a New Dynasty. David was Israel's great empire-builder. He captured Jerusalem from the pagans and made it his capital. He brought the ark of the covenant there and proposed to house it in a magnificent temple.

David wanted to build a splendid house for God, but God sent a prophet to dissuade him. God said His house should be built by David's son; but God would build for David a house: that is, a household, a family, a dynasty of kings that would rule forever. The text of lesson 5 records David's prayer in response to that surprising promise.

Lesson 6. Creating a Redeemed People. Again we leap across a wide span of time between lessons. David's son Solomon built a temple as God had predicted. He also brought Israel to the peak of power and glory.

After Solomon's death, Israel split into two weaker nations that swiftly lost their power and glory. Isaiah was a prophet in Judah, the south part of divided Israel. He wrote of events to come as if they were past, for already they were determined in the mind of God. Clearly the prophet foretold Judah's captivity in Babylon (Isaiah 39:5-7). In lesson 6 we shall see that he foretold the end of that captivity just as clearly. God would redeem His captive people and send them home.

Lesson 7. Creating a New Covenant. Jeremiah was God's prophet in Judah before and during Judah's captivity in Babylon. He predicted that Babylon's rule of Judah would end after seventy years. Then he looked further into the future and predicted a new covenant that would feature the forgiveness of sins. That is the Christian covenant under which we live today.

Lesson 8. Creating a New Hope. Ezekiel was one of the captives in Babylon. God gave him a fantastic vision to create new hope in the minds and hearts of his fellow captives.

Lesson 9. Creating a Renewed Trust. Now we turn back through centuries to the time of David. Asaph, a psalmist and musician, found his faltering trust in God renewed by a time of worship. Anyone whose trust is faltering may find a like renewal in a time of sincere worship.

Unit 3. November
A New Creation

November brings us to the New Testament part of these studies that introduce our new cycle of lessons. We are now at the time of the new covenant foretold by Jeremiah (lesson 7), the time when God's plan allows us to become new creations (2 Corinthians 5:17).

Lesson 10. A New Approach. Jesus fulfilled the Old Testament laws. He reaffirmed their original meaning by reasserting their application to thoughts and motives as well as to actions. What a guide for every Christian's self-control!

Lesson 11. A New Body. This lesson moves us to anticipate the trumpet that will call the dead to be raised incorruptible. When that happens, we will enjoy a change from natural bodies to spiritual bodies that are fitted for eternity. What joy!

Lesson 12. A New Creature in Christ. Even while we wear our natural bodies we are new creatures. What an incentive to guide these natural bodies in spiritual ways!

Lesson 13. A New Relationship. When we are children of God we are brothers and sisters of all of God's children. Aren't we glad we are part of the family of God?

From our hearts we sing with the psalmist, "Thy word is a lamp unto my feet, and a light unto my path" (Psalm 119:105). At the end of the stanza, we sing also the resolution of each heart: "I have inclined mine heart to perform thy statutes always, even unto the end" (v. 112). As we study the thirteen lessons of this introductory series, we shall find in each some guidance on life's pathway. If we give attention also to the long periods of time between the lessons, we shall refresh our concept of the whole scope of Bible history. As we go on through the three-year cycle of lessons, we shall be able to fit each one into that concept of the whole. Happy learning!

Answers to Quarterly Quiz
on page 8

Lesson 1—1. dust of the ground. 2. eat of the tree of the knowledge of good and evil. 3. false. **Lesson 2**—1. grieved. 2. false. **Lesson 3**—1. take off his shoes. 2. affliction, cry. **Lesson 4**—1. true. 2. Reubenites, Gadites, and the half-tribe of Manasseh. 3. a covenant with the Lord. **Lesson 5**—1. God did them for His word's sake and according to His own heart. 2. Israel. **Lesson 6**—1. water and fire. 2. way, rivers. **Lesson 7**—1. false. 2. He would write it in their hearts. **Lesson 8**—1. breath. 2. hope. **Lesson 9**—1. the prosperity of the wicked. 2. being cast into destruction. 3. heaven, earth. **Lesson 10**—1. true. 2. love them, bless them, do good to them, pray for them. **Lesson 11**—1. the natural. 2. the trumpet shall sound. 3. victory. **Lesson 12**—1. true. 2. reconciliation. **Lesson 13**—1. the blood of Christ. 2. false.

The World of Moses

The God of Continuing Creation

Created for a Purpose	God's Creativity Continues	A New Creation
From the Dust of the Ground: Adam and Eve Genesis 2	Creating a New Dynasty: King David 2 Samuel 7	A New Approach: Attitudes and Actions Matthew 5
Beginning Again: The Flood Genesis 6–9	Creating a Redeemed People: Israel's Savior Isaiah 43	A New Body: Our Resurrection 1 Corinthians 15
God Raises Up a Deliverer: Moses and the Exodus Exodus 3	Creating a New Covenant: Looking Toward Jesus Jeremiah 29, 31	A New Creature in Christ: Reconciled to God 2 Corinthians 5
Becoming God's People: Covenant Promise Deuteronomy 29	Creating a New Hope: Life From Death Ezekiel 37	A New Relationship: Community in Christ Ephesians 2
	Creating a Renewed Trust: Looking Upward Psalm 73	

Four Issues of Humanity

by Ronald L. Nickelson

ORIGIN, CONDITION, SALVATION, AND DESTINY. Ravi Zacharias, one of the most profound Christian thinkers of our time, points out that all religions must address these four issues when it comes to grasping truth about humanity. Ultimately, it is only Christianity that offers coherent and verifiable truth across all four areas.

But other religions certainly do try to provide answers! Indeed, the wide variety of approaches that we see to these four areas boggles the mind. When we think about all the work that it will take to separate truth from error, we may be tempted to give up and say, "I just believe in Jesus, and that's good enough for me." But such thinking is very dangerous because it leaves us susceptible to false doctrine. Such a mind-set also leaves us unable to help others see the problems with their own false viewpoints. So let the struggle begin!

Origin

The issue of origin asks, "Where did humanity come from?" Quite apart from the secular idea of evolution, we see a variety of religious answers. Many of those answers do not firmly separate humans from God.

Some devout people believe, for instance, that our forefather Adam was created with "a spark of the divine" that was wrapped within a physical body. Another viewpoint, called pantheism, proposes that everything (including humans) somehow "is" God.

But the Bible teaches us that God is our uncreated Creator. He has existed from eternity past, and it is He who called us into being. This is important because it means that we are accountable to Him.

Condition

The issue of the human condition asks, "What is our standing before God?" In other words, how are we doing in His eyes?

Some think that all of humanity is essentially "okay," and that God's love means that no one is truly lost for eternity. Somehow, someway even Hitler, Stalin, and Hussein are to find places in Heaven. This viewpoint can hold sway in circles that believe sin to be only an illusion.

The Bible, of course, teaches otherwise. Sin is real. Its presence places our eternity in jeopardy. Sin means that we are lost and need salvation.

Salvation

The issue of salvation asks, "How is our lost condition remedied?" For many religious viewpoints, the answer is "by works." Some devout people think that these works may come about through numerous lifetimes of reincarnation. Others propose that we can tap in to the "extra" works of very godly people who died long ago.

But the Bible teaches none of this! The apostle Paul is especially clear that we are saved by the grace of God, not by human works. God's grace is possible because Jesus paid the sin penalty as He suffered and died on the cross.

Destiny

The issue of destiny asks two questions: "What are we saved *from?*" and "What are we saved *to?*" Of the fanciful answers to these questions there seems to be no end! One religion proposes three "layers" to Heaven, each reserved for those achieving a certain level of obedience to God. Other religions propose that there simply is no Hell. Still another viewpoint thinks there to be neither Heaven nor Hell, and that the ultimate destiny of everyone is "nothingness."

But the Biblical truth is that there is a Heaven to be gained and a Hell to be avoided. Those in either place spend an eternity there. Our only chances to avoid Hell come in our earthly life.

"It's All Important!"

A cultural expression that came into vogue a few years ago was "it's all good!" This phrase reveals, among other things, a postmodern outlook that doesn't want to promote one viewpoint at the expense of another. But the false ideas that we have explored so briefly above are not "all good"—in fact, quite the opposite! But they are indeed "all important."

They are important because eternity is at stake. A wrong conclusion in any of the four areas can lead us away from God, who wants us to be with Him for eternity. Preachers spend much time in Bible college and seminary learning how to help people avoid error in these and other areas. We can train ourselves as we allow our lessons to be something of a "Bible college" for us. As we begin a new three-year cycle, let us resolve to study to show ourselves approved (2 Timothy 2:15).

Quarterly Quiz

The questions on this page may be used in several ways: as a pretest at the beginning of the quarter; as a review at the end of the quarter; or as a review after each lesson. The questions are based on the Scripture text of each lesson (King James Version). ***The answers are on page 4.***

Lesson 1

1. What did God use to form Adam? (ooze from the ocean, clay from the garden, dust of the ground?) *Genesis 2:7*
2. What was the one thing Adam was forbidden to do? *Genesis 2:17*
3. Adam and Eve gave names to every living creature. T/F *Genesis 2:19, 20*

Lesson 2

1. When God saw the wickedness of mankind, he felt _____ in his heart. *Genesis 6:6*
2. Noah was instructed to take only two of each animal into the ark. T/F *Genesis 7:2*

Lesson 3

1. When God spoke to Moses from the burning bush, what did He command him to do? (cover his face, take off his shoes, fall to the ground?) *Exodus 3:4, 5*
2. God said He had seen His people's _____ and heard their _____. *Exodus 3:7*

Lesson 4

1. During their forty years of wandering in the wilderness, the Israelites found that their clothes and shoes did not wear out. T/F *Deuteronomy 29:5*
2. Which tribes received land after the Israelites defeated Sihon and Og? *Deuteronomy 29:7, 8*
3. What did Moses encourage the Israelites to enter into? (the promised land, a truce with Egypt, a covenant with the Lord?) *Deuteronomy 29:12*

Lesson 5

1. What two reasons did David give for the great things God did for him? *2 Samuel 7:21*
2. In his prayer to God David said, "Thou hast confirmed to thyself thy people _____ to be a people unto thee for ever." *2 Samuel 7:24*

Lesson 6

1. From what two things would the Lord protect the Israelites? (water and fire, famine and pestilence, death and destruction?) *Isaiah 43:2*
2. God said that He would make a _____ in the wilderness, and _____ in the desert. *Isaiah 43:19*

Lesson 7

1. The Lord said the Israelites would be exiles in Babylon for one hundred years. T/F *Jeremiah 29:10*

2. What covenant did God make with the Israelites concerning the law? (the law would pass away, they would keep it perfectly, He would write it in their hearts?) *Jeremiah 31:33*

Lesson 8

1. When Ezekiel prophesied over the dry bones and they came together with sinews, flesh, and skin, the only thing missing was _____. *Ezekiel 37:7, 8*
2. What had the Israelites lost, as indicated by the dry bones? *Ezekiel 37:11*

Lesson 9

1. What did the psalmist see that almost caused his steps to slip? *Psalm 73:2, 3*
2. What will be the end of the ungodly? (receiving more riches, being cast into destruction, seeing the godly prosper?) *Psalm 73:17, 18*
3. The psalmist declares, "Whom have I in _____ but thee? and there is none upon _____ that I desire besides thee." *Psalm 73:25*

Lesson 10

1. Jesus said that not one jot or tittle of the law would pass away before the law is fulfilled. T/F *Matthew 5:18*
2. What four actions did Jesus teach His followers to take toward their enemies? *Matthew 5:44*

Lesson 11

1. Which comes first—the spiritual or the natural? *1 Corinthians 15:46*
2. What happens immediately before the dead are raised incorruptible and we are all changed? *1 Corinthians 15:52*
3. Complete this saying: "Death is swallowed up in _____." *1 Corinthians 15:54*

Lesson 12

1. Since Christ died for all of us, we should not live unto ourselves but unto Him. T/F *2 Corinthians 5:15*
2. What ministry has God given to us? (reconciliation, admonition, dedication?) *2 Corinthians 5:18*

Lesson 13

1. What is it that helps us who were once far off to draw nigh to God? *Ephesians 2:13*
2. We are strangers and foreigners in the household of God. T/F *Ephesians 2:19*

From the Dust of the Ground

September 5
Lesson 1

DEVOTIONAL READING: Psalm 150.

BACKGROUND SCRIPTURE: Genesis 2.

PRINTED TEXT: Genesis 2:4-7, 15-25.

Genesis 2:4-7, 15-25

4 These are the generations of the heavens and of the earth when they were created, in the day that the LORD God made the earth and the heavens,

5 And every plant of the field before it was in the earth, and every herb of the field before it grew: for the LORD God had not caused it to rain upon the earth, and there was not a man to till the ground.

6 But there went up a mist from the earth, and watered the whole face of the ground.

7 And the LORD God formed man of the dust of the ground, and breathed into his nostrils the breath of life; and man became a living soul.

. . . .

15 And the LORD God took the man, and put him into the garden of Eden to dress it and to keep it.

16 And the LORD God commanded the man, saying, Of every tree of the garden thou mayest freely eat:

17 But of the tree of the knowledge of good and evil, thou shalt not eat of it: for in the day that thou eatest thereof thou shalt surely die.

18 And the LORD God said, It is not good that the man should be alone; I will make him a help meet for him.

19 And out of the ground the LORD God formed every beast of the field, and every fowl of the air; and brought them unto Adam to see what he would call them: and whatsoever Adam called every living creature, that was the name thereof.

20 And Adam gave names to all cattle, and to the fowl of the air, and to every beast of the field; but for Adam there was not found a help meet for him.

21 And the LORD God caused a deep sleep to fall upon Adam, and he slept; and he took one of his ribs, and closed up the flesh instead thereof.

22 And the rib, which the LORD God had taken from man, made he a woman, and brought her unto the man.

23 And Adam said, This is now bone of my bones, and flesh of my flesh: she shall be called Woman, because she was taken out of Man.

24 Therefore shall a man leave his father and his mother, and shall cleave unto his wife: and they shall be one flesh.

25 And they were both naked, the man and his wife, and were not ashamed.

GOLDEN TEXT: The Lord God formed man of the dust of the ground, and breathed into his nostrils the breath of life; and man became a living soul.—Genesis 2:7.

The God of Continuing Creation
Unit 1: Created for a Purpose
(Lessons 1-4)

Lesson Aims

After participating in this lesson, each student will be able to:

1. Tell briefly about the origin of life on earth, especially human life.

2. Explain how the Genesis 2 account reveals the special place men and women have in God's creation.

3. Suggest a way to live consistent with that special place in some specific area.

Lesson Outline

INTRODUCTION
    A. Various Answers
    B. Lesson Background
  I. HOME FOR MAN (Genesis 2:4-7)
    A. Habitation (vv. 4-6)
    B. Inhabitant (v. 7)
      Reproducing Creation
 II. INSTRUCTIONS FOR MAN (Genesis 2:15-17)
    A. Location and Occupation (v. 15)
    B. Permission and Prohibition (vv. 16, 17)
III. COMPANION FOR MAN (Genesis 2:18-25)
    A. Man's Condition (v. 18)
    B. God's Creatures (vv. 19, 20)
    C. Man's Companion (vv. 21, 22)
    D. Man's Comment (v. 23)
      Proof of the Designer's Skill
    E. God's Comment (v. 24)
    F. Comfortable Nakedness (v. 25)
CONCLUSION
    A. The Message to Us
    B. Prayer
    C. Thought to Remember

Introduction

Where do babies come from? Parents are likely to be challenged by that question from their first-born when a second child is born into the family. It is not easy to frame an accurate answer for a three-year-old, so parents resort to a variety of subterfuges.

A. Various Answers

From a land where storks perch on rooftops beside wide chimneys has come a tradition that storks bring new babies by way of those chim-

neys. That, of course, is patently preposterous. If even a two-year-old accepts it, he or she probably will abandon it before age six. But the fiction is so charming that it has a firm place in popular culture—even in places where no stork has been seen since the creation of the world.

More sober minds explain our origin via rational theories of evolution. Through countless millennia, we are told, microscopic living things developed into fish, and fish developed into birds, etc., etc., until monkeys finally became human.

But if that theory is true, then why aren't people developing into something else? We are, we are told; but the change is too slow to be observed in a lifetime, or even by the techniques of modern science. Again, we are left to wonder.

When the question of origin is broadened to include all the things we see in earth and sky, it engages the attention of not only our greatest scientists but also that of the average person on the street. Where did everything come from? All the power of human intellect is engaged in the search for rational answers that do not include God, for God is not seen even with our most powerful telescope.

The authentic answer is written in the first two chapters of Genesis: God made them. He created the basic stuff of which stars and planets are made. With or without a "big bang," He put each where He wanted it to be. He shaped each one according to His will. He fashioned all living things, and gave them life.

How did the ancient writer know so many facts that modern researchers seem unable to discover? God revealed those facts—sometimes directly to the ancient writer and sometimes through creation itself (Psalm 19:1-6). In the first two chapters of Genesis we have God's own report of His own creation. Nothing can be more authentic than that.

B. Lesson Background

Easily we see that in Genesis 1 and 2 we have two reports of creation. Some students conclude that those two reports were written by different authors, but that is not a necessary conclusion.

Chapter one may be called a diary of creation. The days are counted one by one, and there is a brief summary of what God did each day. Then it seems most probable that the same author (Moses) wrote chapter two, adding some interesting and important details.

This week we take our lesson from Genesis 2. Naturally its background is seen in Genesis 1. Learners will find this lesson more meaningful if they first read Genesis 1 and the first three verses of Genesis 2.

I. Home for Man
(Genesis 2:4-7)

We begin with two things of importance to us. First, the new earth of our text is the same earth (now grown old) upon which we live and move and have our being. Second, the new man of our text is the father of us all, the primary provider of the genes that make us who and what we are. We are not only investigating the origin of things, we are investigating the origin of ourselves.

A. Habitation (vv. 4-6)

4. These are the generations of the heavens and of the earth when they were created, in the day that the LORD God made the earth and the heavens.

In the antique English of the *King James Version,* the word *generations* means something like "account" or "record." This record tells us that there was a *day* when *the Lord God made the earth and the heavens.* This brief statement of fact draws our attention back to the fuller account in Genesis 1:1-5. [See question #1, page 16.]

5. And every plant of the field before it was in the earth, and every herb of the field before it grew: for the LORD God had not caused it to rain upon the earth, and there was not a man to till the ground.

Again we may be confused by the phrasing, this time because the word *before* is used in a way unknown to us. To get the meaning, we can substitute the idea of "not yet" for the two instances of *before it.* Thus we see that there was not a single plant on *the earth* on that first day of creation.

Then comes the word *for,* meaning "because." That word directs us to look for explanations as to why there were no plants, and two reasons are given: a lack of *rain* and a lack of manpower. The next two verses tell how these two issues were resolved, thus opening the way for vegetation to flourish.

6. But there went up a mist from the earth, and watered the whole face of the ground.

The exact meaning of the word *mist* is a bit uncertain. This word may be used here as part of a description of the weather cycle that produces rainfall. If so, then it means that as water evaporated *there went up a mist from the earth* (especially that part of the earth that was covered with expanses of water) into the cooler temperature of the upper atmosphere. There the mist or vapor condensed into clouds, then into rain, *and watered the whole face of the ground.*

On the other hand, *mist* may be translated as the "streams" that bubbled up from below the earth's surface. In either case, it is God causing the natural irrigation so that the earth will be ready for vegetation.

B. Inhabitant (v. 7)

7. And the LORD God formed man of the dust of the ground, and breathed into his nostrils the breath of life; and man became a living soul.

The second reason for the absence of plants was that there was not a *man* to till the ground (v. 5). Now there is a man. True, God made the plants before He made the man, but only three days before (Genesis 1:11-13). The man was there in plenty of time to do the needed tillage.

Although man's body was formed *of the dust of the ground,* it was the very breath of God that transformed that dust into living flesh. At this point in our Bible text we should not think that the phrase *a living soul* means that man was a being different from the animals and above them. Genesis 1:30 translates the same Hebrew phrase as *life* and indicates that all the animals have it. Genesis 1:26-28 makes it plain that humans are indeed different from the animals and superior to them. [See question #2, page 16.] But in the text at hand the phrase *a living soul* asserts man's similarity to the animals, not his difference from them.

REPRODUCING CREATION

You can be in touch with a celebrity! How about owning Edgar Allen Poe's hackberry tree or Orville and Wilbur Wright's red cedar tree or, for a *real* historical contact, how about owning George Washington's tulip poplar tree?

You can't actually own those specific trees, of course, but you can own a seedling started from them. American Forests is an organization that collects seeds from trees owned by famous people and grows them as seedlings to sell for the historical interest and also as a way of promoting the planting of trees for ecological reasons.

But how about owning a *really* historic tree? Actually, every tree or plant we have in our yards and gardens can in some way trace its lineage back to those trees God created in the beginning. Within those plants God placed the reproductive power that would perpetuate the image of His creation for millennia to come.

How to Say It

ADAM (Hebrew). uh-*dahm.*
CORINTHIANS. Kor-*in*-thee-unz (*th* as in *thin*).
EDEN. *Ee*-den.
EUPHRATES. You-*fray*-teez.
ISH (Hebrew). ish.
ISHSHAH (Hebrew). ish-*shaw.*
TIGRIS. *Tie*-griss.

And, of course, the same is true of humans. We continue to reproduce the image of our first ancestors, Adam and Eve. More important, since they were created in God's image we also continue to reproduce that image. The question for each of us is whether we are striving to replicate the untarnished image of the God who made us, or are we satisfied merely to reflect the sin-blemished image of the first parents of our race?

—C. R. B.

II. Instructions for Man (Genesis 2:15-17)

When a boy is born, those around him do not think of him as a man until he reaches a certain age (depending on the culture). Through his pre-adult years he is taught, guided, and disciplined by his parents, teachers, and other authority figures. After becoming a man in the sense of being an adult, he has more freedoms.

It seems that the first man was an adult as soon as he was animated by the breath of life, but he had no more experience than a newborn baby. Almost immediately "God commanded the man" (v. 16). Then did God give him the gift of language in a miraculous way, or did it take two years for the man to learn to talk? We have no information about that, but some items of God's instruction are suggested.

A. Location and Occupation (v. 15)

15. And the LORD God took the man, and put him into the garden of Eden to dress it and to keep it.

Gardening can truly be called "the world's oldest profession," since man's first job was the care of the garden that God had prepared as man's home (vv. 8, 9, not in today's text). We are left to wonder about how much instruction God gave to the man in this regard. Did He tell the man to plant wheat in the autumn, or did the man learn that by experience? Did God say grapevines should be pruned? And how did the man or his descendants ever learn to make a pruning knife?

For such questions we have no answers. What is important is the bigger picture: God is our Cre-

VISUALS FOR THESE LESSONS

The visuals pictured in each lesson (e.g., page 13) is a small reproduction of a large, full-color poster included in the *Adult Visuals* packet for the Fall Quarter. The packet is available from your supplier. Order No. 192.

ator. It was in this garden that the first humans were to have fellowship with Him (Genesis 3:8).

B. Permission and Prohibition (vv. 16, 17)

16. And the LORD God commanded the man, saying, Of every tree of the garden thou mayest freely eat.

Man's food is described more completely in Genesis 1:29. There, herbs and seeds are mentioned along with the fruit of trees, but there is no mention of meat. It seems that God prescribed a vegetarian diet in the beginning. But when there was a new beginning of mankind after the great flood, the Lord authorized the eating of meat as well (Genesis 9:3). Permission to *eat* of the fruit *of every tree of the garden* is mentioned to prepare us for the one exception in the next verse.

17. But of the tree of the knowledge of good and evil, thou shalt not eat of it: for in the day that thou eatest thereof thou shalt surely die.

In the description of the Garden of Eden, two trees are given special mention: the tree of life and *the tree of the knowledge of good and evil* (Genesis 2:9). Dwellers in that garden can live as long as they continue to eat from the tree of life, but they must *not eat* from the tree of the knowledge of good and evil. To eat from that tree, God says, will bring death.

We wonder what the word *die* means to the man at this point. Is it possible that a predator-prey relationship exists among the animals in the Garden of Eden, so that man can see firsthand what death is? In any case, man begins to learn about death all too soon.

Genesis 3 records that the man and his wife ignore God's one prohibition and eat from the forbidden tree. Thus by personal experience the first two people gain the knowledge of evil and its consequences. For this disobedience the man and his wife will be banished from the garden, with the tree of life "off limits" (Genesis 3:22, 23; Revelation 22:2). In that day the process of dying will set in, and in the course of years it will be complete. (See Romans 5:12.)

III. Companion for Man (Genesis 2:18-25)

Wherever the man looks there is beauty, "every tree that is pleasant to the sight" (Genesis 2:9). Abundant food is in the reach of his hand. He is in the Garden of Eden, and the word *Eden* means *delight!* What more could a man need?

If you have ever been desperately lonely, you know what that solitary person needed. In the midst of delight he was alone, all alone, the only one of his kind.

A. Man's Condition (v. 18)

18. And the LORD God said, It is not good that the man should be alone; I will make him a help meet for him.

Perhaps the man does not know what he needs, but *the Lord God* knows! The Creator Himself has built into that man the need for companionship and now the Creator determines to supply that need. The antique word *meet* means "suitable, appropriate."

In all the new world there is no suitable companion for that lonely man. But that situation is about to change. Centuries later the apostle Paul will offer some important reflections on why some people should remain unmarried (1 Corinthians 7). Those cases, however, are the exceptions rather than the rule. *It is not good that . . . man should be alone.* [See question #3, page 16.]

B. God's Creatures (vv. 19, 20)

19. And out of the ground the LORD God formed every beast of the field, and every fowl of the air; and brought them unto Adam to see what he would call them: and whatsoever Adam called every living creature, that was the name thereof.

The Lord God had made the animals before He made man, so we can take *formed* to mean "had formed." Now God brings to *Adam* the animals He had previously created, and the man gives them their names. [See question #4, page 16.] Speaking of names, here for the first time we see the name *Adam* in our *King James Version* of the Bible. (Other translations put the first use of Adam in v. 20, next.) In the original Hebrew, the same word appears in 2:5, 7, 8, 15, 16, and 18 where it is translated as the general term *man.* Thus "the man" is literally "Adam."

20. And Adam gave names to all cattle, and to the fowl of the air, and to every beast of the field; but for Adam there was not found a help meet for him.

All kinds of animals and birds are viewed and named, but not one of them is fit to be man's companion. The process of naming seems also to involve a process of searching for such a companion. Man is a special creation. He is unique. But that uniqueness makes him alone.

Today we may keep dogs, cats, birds, ferrets, and hamsters as pets. But none of these can come close to substituting for human companionship. The person who wears a T-shirt that says, "The more people I meet, the more I prefer my cat" needs some Biblical counseling!

C. Man's Companion (vv. 21, 22)

21. And the LORD God caused a deep sleep to fall upon Adam, and he slept; and he took one of his ribs, and closed up the flesh instead thereof.

Humorists like to describe this as the world's first surgery with anesthesia. Perhaps it was, but the surgeon was the almighty Creator performing a slight alteration on one of His own creatures. It seems that our popular English versions agree that God took a rib from Adam, and that fits well with the phrase that follows: God took a bone and filled its space with *flesh.* The Hebrew word that is translated *ribs* is much more often translated "side," but this difference scarcely affects the meaning here.

22. And the rib, which the LORD God had taken from man, made he a woman, and brought her unto the man.

Whatever it is that God takes from Adam—a *rib* in particular or part of his side in general—the companion He fashions for the man is not only suitable, but fascinating as well. We may safely conclude that when Adam opens his eyes, he opens them wide!

D. Man's Comment (v. 23)

23. And Adam said, This is now bone of my bones, and flesh of my flesh: she shall be called Woman, because she was taken out of Man.

Adam had been in deep sleep during the surgery, but he knows what has happened. Perhaps God tells him, either before or after the operation. Now Adam realizes that what he is seeing is a part of himself. [See question #5, page 16.] Obviously she is more like him than any animal is, but how delightfully she is different from him as well!

The word at the very end of the verse translated *Man* is not the Hebrew *adam* that we have seen before, but rather is the word *ish.* In designating his new companion, Adam simply adds the feminine suffix to this word and we translate

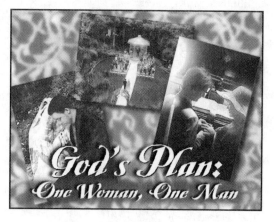

Visual for lesson 1. *Use these images to remind your learners of God's unchanging design for marriage.*

the resulting *ishshah* as *Woman*. The word *ishshah* is the generic name of all the female members of humanity. To his own personal companion Adam will gave the name *Eve*, which means *life*, "because she was the mother of all living" (Genesis 3:20).

PROOF OF THE DESIGNER'S SKILL

In the summer of 1908 at the Brooklands racetrack near London, England, three Cadillacs were disassembled into their more than six thousand separate parts. Royal Automobile Club officials intermixed the parts, then selected eighty-nine of those pieces and locked them away so they could not be used. The replacements were taken from standard spare parts stock.

The cars were then reassembled from this jumble of pieces, so that the "new" vehicles were a combination of parts from the three original cars. Mechanics were not allowed to change or manipulate any of the pieces to make them fit together in their new environments. Following this reassembly, each car was driven five hundred miles on the racetrack. All three cars passed the test, proving that precision mass production had become a reality.

The creation narrative of today's text tells us that after God had made one "model" of a human being, He took a part of it and created another whole new being. Although this new person was slightly different from the original, she was similar enough to him that she and the man from whom she had been made would each portray the image of God. Upon seeing his new companion Adam could exclaim, "At last, here is someone like me!" These two specimens of the Creator's skill were so perfectly matched that the human race still thrives thousands of years and "millions of miles" later!   —C. R. B.

Home Daily Bible Readings

Monday, Aug. 30—Praise the Lord (Psalm 148:1-6)

Tuesday, Aug. 31—Let All the Earth Praise God (Psalm 148:7-13)

Wednesday, Sept. 1—God's Creation Is Good (Genesis 1:26-31)

Thursday, Sept. 2—God Created Man (Genesis 2:4b-9)

Friday, Sept. 3—The Garden Is Watered by Rivers (Genesis 2:10-14)

Saturday, Sept. 4—Man Is Placed in the Garden (Genesis 2:15-20)

Sunday, Sept. 5—God Creates a Helper for Man (Genesis 2:21-25)

E. God's Comment (v. 24)

24. Therefore shall a man leave his father and his mother, and shall cleave unto his wife: and they shall be one flesh.

This cannot be a continuation of Adam's comment in verse 23. What did Adam know about *father* and *mother*? He was just beginning to know about *wife*! Furthermore, Jesus attributed the comment in verse 24 to God, and regarded it as God's statement against divorce (Matthew 19:4-6).

F. Comfortable Nakedness (v. 25)

25. And they were both naked, the man and his wife, and were not ashamed.

In their innocence the new *man and his wife* are unclothed and unashamed. Too soon that innocence will be gone, with the two gripped by shame and fear and an urgent need to hide from the God who created them (Genesis 3). But that issue belongs to the Background of next week's lesson.

Conclusion

This series of lessons deals with God's beginning and His new beginnings, His creation and His re-creations. So the drama of His first recorded creation ends on a high note of triumph. God set the stage and provided the persons for a drama that ought to end "they lived happily ever after." When unhappiness invaded the drama, it was the fault of the creatures, not the Creator.

A. The Message to Us

Today's lesson reminds us that God is Creator and that all good things come from Him. Living in the shadow of our Creator means that men and women should bow in humble submission, realizing in wonder the special place we have in His creation. This week, how will you live in a way that is consistent with these facts?

B. Prayer

Father in Heaven, holy and mighty, hallowed be Your name! Thank You for making the pleasant and productive world we live in. Thank You for stretching around it the ever-changing and always beautiful sky. Thank You for giving Adam firm guidelines in the beginning. Thank You for giving us firm guidelines in Your written Word. Today we pledge ourselves anew to do Your will, and we look to You for wisdom and strength to keep our pledge. In Jesus' name, amen.

C. Thought to Remember

Remember your Creator.
Know His goodness.

Learning by Doing

This page contains an alternative lesson plan emphasizing learning activities.
Classes desiring such student involvement will find these suggestions helpful.

Learning Goals

After participating in this lesson, each student will be able to:

1. Tell briefly about the origin of life on earth, especially human life.

2. Explain how the Genesis 2 account reveals the special place men and women have in God's creation.

3. Suggest a way to live consistent with that special place in some specific area.

Into the Lesson

Prepare a large balloon filled with bits of paper, flat and rolled into small balls. Inflate the balloon to capacity. As class begins, take a sharp object and puncture it. As the class reacts, say, "This is a picture of the Big Bang theory of the origin of the universe."

Say, "Here are some questions we could ask someone who believes that the universe began without God's help: (1) 'From where did the balloon—that is, original substance—come?' (2) 'From where did the energy for the explosion come?' (3) 'How did new substances find direction, speed, revolutions, and order?'"

While the popular "Big Bang theory" and the creation account agree that the universe began at a specific point in time, they differ on the cause of that beginning. Today we study the creation account as revealed by God in Genesis 2 and discover mankind's unique place in that creation.

Into the Word

The first chapter of Genesis must be reviewed, if only briefly, before the verses in our text in chapter two. Consider an oral reading of the entire chapter by one of your outstanding readers (or a professionally recorded version).

Remind the class, "Our task is not to explain God's method. Surely it is sufficient to trust the Word and accept the fact that God created in His own way. It is enough to believe that God created in His own timelessness and in His own omniscient, omnipotent way."

From a map showing the current courses of the Tigris and Euphrates rivers identify what is generally believed to have been the approximate location of the Garden of Eden—in the southern Mesopotamian valley of modern Iraq. Note, "Some suggest that the cataclysmic changes at the flood obliterated the possibility of knowing certain exact locations (and even precise chronologies)."

Make copies of today's text and give one to each learner. Provide highlighters or pens to each. Assign the following words/phrases to four groups respectively: *LORD God* to those born in the first eight days of a month; *created, made, formed* to those born from the ninth to the sixteenth; *man* to those born the seventeenth to the twenty-fourth; *Adam* to the remaining. Direct the groups to highlight/circle their word(s) in the text and count how many times each appears. (The count is 9, 5, 11, 6, respectively.) Note that, "This count reflects the significant characters and acts in the text, and the relationship between God and man. No other creature 'gets as much press'; no other creature gets the face-to-face interaction with God nor receives God's special attention. Humans are special."

Give the class this list (without the references) and ask them to identify a verse or verses in chapters one or two of Genesis that reveal and confirm each: (1) Man is given moral choice—2:16, 17; (2) Man is given dominion over the earth—1:26; (3) Man is assigned specific responsibility—2:15; (4) Man is given a privilege that belongs to God: naming creatures—2:19b; (5) Man has the possibility of shame—2:25; (6) Man is created in God's image—1:26, 27.

Into Life

Give your learners a work sheet with five headings: "Man's Purpose," "My Purpose," "Things I Have Done for God in the Past," "Things I Am Doing Now for God," and "Things I Could Do in the Future for God."

Ask the group, "What is man's purpose? Why was he created?" Have them fill in the agreed answers. Say, "God gave Adam the task of naming the animals and tending the garden." Suggest they write a statement to answer, "What is your task or purpose in this life?"

Finally, direct them to respond to the other stimulus headings, either in class or at home in their own study and devotional times: "Make a list of all the things you believe God has created you to do. You may include things you have done in the past as well as what you are doing now and what you could do in the future. How do your accomplishments and your interests help you determine your spiritual gifts?"

Let's Talk It Over

The questions on this page are designed to promote discussion of the lesson by the class and to encourage application of the lesson Scriptures. The answers provided are only discussion starters. Let your class talk it over from there.

1. What does the recognition that God is the Maker of Heaven and earth mean for us? How should Christians order their lives, thinking, and worship to reflect this fact?

Just as we realize that our money and our time are gifts from God and that we are to be stewards of them, we realize that the earth is also God's gift to us. Our stewardship will include, among other things, taking environmental and resource conservation concerns seriously.

On a personal level, believers realize that the Creator God is the God of our "re-creation" as well. Though He created the entire universe, His main concern is for the individuals created in His image—us! When you think of ways that God cares for your life and your church, you will come to realize how important you are in His eyes.

2. How would you answer someone who sees no real difference between people and animals?

Think about all the things that humans can do that animals cannot. Just two examples include the ability to make moral judgments and the capability to build hospitals, etc. This is evidence of intelligent design. The argument that "intelligent design requires an intelligent designer" is powerful!

It is important to understand that persuading people with such an argument requires time and patience. Years of humanistic teaching may have to be undone in the mind of the hearer. Discussion as to why the other person came to hold his or her view could be useful.

3. The marriage of one man to one woman for life is God's ordained plan. How can the church lead people back to God's plan for marriage?

The church can make sure its teaching program includes instruction on Biblical principles regarding marriage. Small groups for newlyweds, a mentoring program to link newlyweds with older married couples, marriage enrichment seminars, and mandatory premarital counseling can be useful.

But as the church seeks to have a godly influence, it must first recognize the reality of divorce and the presence of divorced people in her midst. Instead of treating divorce as an "unpardonable sin," the church should develop ways to extend God's grace to the hurting.

The church can also recognize the special needs of the "blended families" that result from divorce and remarriage. This is not God's ideal plan for family formation, but divorce and remarriage *does* happen. People in these families need the grace of Christ as much as anyone else.

4. God, in a sense, chose to make Himself "dependent" on man when calling upon Adam to name the animals. What are some other ways God has made Himself dependent on us, and how can we fulfill our role in this partnership?

God has given the church the Great Commandment (Matthew 22:37-39) and the Great Commission (Matthew 28:19, 20). Obeying God in these areas of ministry and evangelism allow God to use us to advance His kingdom.

There are many other examples. For instance, a study of the many "one another" commands of the New Testament reveals Biblical principles of the work to which God has called His people. Church leaders who maintain the purity of the church through church discipline also are partnering with God. Ephesians 3:10 declares that it is through the church that God demonstrates to the world His manifold wisdom. Brainstorm ways in which you can partner with God by using Biblical principles in these and other ways.

5. Adam saw in his newly formed wife a part of himself. When Paul spoke of the church, he used the imagery of husband and wife (Ephesians 5:22-24). How can our church do a better job of reflecting this imagery of the bride of Christ to her Groom?

Unity and submission are key qualities for the church to hold in order to demonstrate that she is truly the bride of Christ. As Eve was part of the body of Adam, the church is the body of Christ. Submission of the wife to the husband is a model of the submission that God desires the bride of Christ to have toward Him.

This is difficult to do in a world that is fragmented with special-interest groups demanding their "rights." Yet the church is to stand in stark contrast by being a body where individual rights are surrendered voluntarily so that we might obey and submit to Christ. The church must constantly monitor her ministry and activity to see that she is demonstrating this quality.

Beginning Again

DEVOTIONAL READING: Genesis 9:8-17.

BACKGROUND SCRIPTURE: Genesis 6:5–9:17.

PRINTED TEXT: Genesis 6:5-8, 13, 14; 7:1-5, 17, 23; 8:14-16; 9:1.

Genesis 6:5-8, 13, 14

5 And GOD saw that the wickedness of man was great in the earth, and that every imagination of the thoughts of his heart was only evil continually.

6 And it repented the LORD that he had made man on the earth, and it grieved him at his heart.

7 And the LORD said, I will destroy man whom I have created from the face of the earth; both man, and beast, and the creeping thing, and the fowls of the air; for it repenteth me that I have made them.

8 But Noah found grace in the eyes of the LORD.

.   .   .   .

13 And God said unto Noah, The end of all flesh is come before me; for the earth is filled with violence through them; and, behold, I will destroy them with the earth.

14 Make thee an ark of gopher wood; rooms shalt thou make in the ark, and shalt pitch it within and without with pitch.

Genesis 7:1-5, 17, 23

1 And the LORD said unto Noah, Come thou and all thy house into the ark; for thee have I seen righteous before me in this generation.

2 Of every clean beast thou shalt take to thee by sevens, the male and his female: and of beasts that are not clean by two, the male and his female.

3 Of fowls also of the air by sevens, the male and the female; to keep seed alive upon the face of all the earth.

4 For yet seven days, and I will cause it to rain upon the earth forty days and forty nights; and every living substance that I have made will I destroy from off the face of the earth.

5 And Noah did according unto all that the LORD commanded him.

.   .   .   .

17 And the flood was forty days upon the earth; and the waters increased, and bare up the ark, and it was lifted up above the earth.

.   .   .   .

23 And every living substance was destroyed which was upon the face of the ground, both man, and cattle, and the creeping things, and the fowl of the heaven; and they were destroyed from the earth: and Noah only remained alive, and they that were with him in the ark.

Genesis 8:14-16

14 And in the second month, on the seven and twentieth day of the month, was the earth dried.

15 And God spake unto Noah, saying,

16 Go forth of the ark, thou, and thy wife, and thy sons, and thy sons' wives with thee.

Genesis 9:1

1 And God blessed Noah and his sons, and said unto them, Be fruitful, and multiply, and replenish the earth.

GOLDEN TEXT: The bow shall be in the cloud; and I will look upon it, that I may remember the everlasting covenant between God and every living creature of all flesh that is upon the earth.—Genesis 9:16.

The God of Continuing Creation
Unit 1: Created for a Purpose
(Lessons 1-4)

Lesson Aims

After participating in this lesson, each student will be able to:

1. Recite the account of God's punishment of sin and giving the world a new start in the time of Noah.

2. Express confidence in God's willingness to give second chances today.

3. Identify a personal area of sin and ask for God's help in making a fresh start.

Lesson Outline

INTRODUCTION

    A "The Devil Made Me Do It"

    B Lesson Background

  I. SITUATION AND GRIEF (Genesis 6:5-8)

    A. Continual Evil (v. 5)

      A Band-Aid® Remedy

    B. God's Grief (v. 6)

    C. God's Remedy (v. 7)

    D. One Exception (v. 8)

 II. PLAN AND INSTRUCTION (Genesis 6:13, 14)

    A. Announcement of Disaster (v. 13)

      Carriers of a Dread Disease

    B. Way of Escape (v. 14)

III. COMMAND AND OBEDIENCE (Genesis 7:1-5)

    A. Invitation Offered (vv. 1-3)

    B. Invitation Explained (v. 4)

    C. Invitation Accepted (v. 5)

IV. THE OLD AND THE NEW (Genesis 7:17, 23; 8:14-16; 9:1)

    A. End of the Old (7:17, 23)

    B. Beginning of the New (8:14-16; 9:1)

CONCLUSION

    A. Chances

    B. Prayer

    C. Thought to Remember

Introduction

A. "The Devil Made Me Do It!"

In the early 1970s, comedian Flip Wilson (1933–1998) became known for his line, "The devil made me do it!" People began to pick up that line and quote it to excuse certain behaviors. Of course no one really believed it, not even the comedian who originally said it. It was a quip, a joke. The devil cannot make us do anything un-less we cooperate with him. He does not compel, he persuades. And it is not very hard to persuade people to do wrong if they have a heart that is inclined toward evil.

By the power of God you can beat the devil every time (1 Corinthians 10:13). James urges us to "Resist the devil, and he will flee from you" (James 4:7). It is your own fault if you give in to the devil and do wrong. It will be because you have not done your best to resist him.

B. Lesson Background

Last week's lesson reminded us that God made earth, sky, plants, and animals. God crowned His creation with human beings who would be in charge over the things on earth. For the home of the humans God planted the Garden of Eden, which may be translated "the garden of delight." Beauty was everywhere, food was abundant, and only one kind of fruit was forbidden.

But there was a snake in the garden. To Eve the snake praised that forbidden fruit. Since you and I have never heard a snake talking, we easily conclude that the devil was making this one his mouthpiece. Poor Eve! She had never heard anything but truth before. Too easily she was fooled. Rashly she ate some of the forbidden fruit, and rashly her husband shared it with her.

The results were tragic. Suddenly the two were ashamed of their nakedness and tried to cover themselves in crude garments of leaves. When they heard the voice of God, they tried to hide from Him. Worse yet, they were banished from the garden and had to battle weeds to produce food from the ground. Worst of all, they could not eat from the tree of life, so they must die. You can read all of this in Genesis 3.

After the tragic loss of the garden, you might think that the growing race of humanity would be careful to do what was pleasing to God. But no—one of Adam's sons killed his brother "because his own works were evil, and his brother's righteous" (1 John 3:12). See Genesis 4.

Then in the opening verses of Genesis 6 we read what happened as the human race continued to multiply: "The sons of God saw the daughters of men that they were fair; and they took them wives of all which they chose." This tells us about what may be called the normal state of affairs between the time of Adam and Eve's sin and the great flood that was to come. Perhaps it indicates that people didn't have much of a clue about God's coming wrath. "For as in the days that were before the flood they were eating and drinking, marrying and giving in marriage, until the day that Noah entered the ark, and knew not until the flood came, and took them all away" (Matthew 24:38, 39).

I. Situation and Grief
(Genesis 6:5-8)

Many centuries after the time of creation, the people of the world had come to the sorry state described in the opening verse of our text.

A. Continual Evil (v. 5)

5. And God saw that the wickedness of man was great in the earth, and that every imagination of the thoughts of his heart was only evil continually.

What a world! Most of the people had not even one good thought to brighten the darkness of sin. And just as Adam had been unable to hide his sin from the Lord, now not one sin of multiplied thousands can be hidden from His sight. We may be certain that God is just as able to see all sins today.

A BAND-AID® REMEDY

The close of the twentieth century brought significant advances in our understanding of the human body. In December 1999 scientists announced that they had broken the genetic code of human chromosome number twenty-two. This chromosome is thought to contain genetic information that affects immunity, heart disease, and several cancers and types of mental illness. The project was able to discover the order in which the thirty-three million chemical components are put together in the DNA that makes up the chromosome. It would take a very large telephone book to hold the information!

Scientists think that this knowledge may enable us to predict illnesses such as cancer, arthritis, and heart disease. The next step, of course, would be to find ways to treat and eventually to prevent such problems. Whether that day will ever come we do not know.

What we *do* know from Scripture is that these imperfections are the result of the sin that entered the human race in Genesis and had become full-blown by Noah's time. Even God's drastic action in the flood could not change the human heart, so we should not expect our modern genetic manipulations to do much more than put a Band-Aid® on a problem requiring an even greater solution. The spiritual problem was much harder to solve and would have to wait until Christ came to redeem us.   —C. R. B.

B. God's Grief (v. 6)

6. And it repented the LORD that he had made man on the earth, and it grieved him at his heart.

Imagine God's grief, if you can. He had made a bright new world with new plants and animals and people, "and God saw every thing that he had made, and, behold, it was very good" (Genesis 1:31). But over the course of hundreds of years, God has seen that same world with its multitudes of people grow progressively bad. God is at the point of regretting that He had created humanity in the first place. [See question #1, page 24.]

C. God's Remedy (v. 7)

7. And the LORD said, I will destroy man whom I have created from the face of the earth; both man, and beast, and the creeping thing, and the fowls of the air; for it repenteth me that I have made them.

What a disappointment! God had made *man* in His own image and appointed humanity to have dominion over the lesser creatures. Now, centuries later, God is looking at vast numbers of that man's descendants. They look more like images of the devil than images of God. They are not even fit to rule themselves with decency and honor. What is there to do but *destroy* them all! So the Lord proposes to wipe them out, along with all the rest of the living creatures.

D. God's Exception (v. 8)

8. But Noah found grace in the eyes of the LORD.

In a world of wicked people there is one exception. "*Noah* was a just man and perfect in his generations and Noah walked with God" (v. 9). With incredible strength of character, Noah continues that walk when no one else walks by his side. Noah is a "preacher of righteousness" (2 Peter 2:5). In him the image of God is bright in a world of darkness, and he keeps it so for hundreds of years (Genesis 7:6; 9:29).

No less remarkable, he married a woman of his own kind. Or perhaps he taught an unrighteous woman to be holy. And, wonder of wonders, this peerless pair has brought up three sons who are worth saving when others on earth are fit only for destruction. Here is a family worthy of starting to repopulate the world, a good family toughened by long years of godly living in a godless world.

How to Say It

ABRAHAM. *Ay*-bruh-ham.
ABRAM. *Ay*-brum.
CORINTHIANS. Kor-*in*-thee-unz (*th* as in *thin*).
HARAN. *Hair*-un.
HEBREWS. *Hee*-brews.
UR. Er.

II. Plan and Instruction
(Genesis 6:13, 14)

Of course God does not intend to destroy that one good family along with the wicked. He means to preserve it for a new start, but Noah will have a big part in saving himself and his extended family.

A. Announcement of Disaster (v. 13)

13. And God said unto Noah, The end of all flesh is come before me; for the earth is filled with violence through them; and, behold, I will destroy them with the earth.

First, the Lord tells *Noah* what is going to happen: God will *destroy* the people of earth because they are so wicked. Apparently there is no hope of reclaiming them. The wicked are determined to remain wicked. The Lord also says that the means of destruction will be a great flood (v. 17).

It may be surprising and puzzling to see the words *with the earth* at the end of verse 13, for the earth itself is going to survive the coming disaster. Perhaps we should understand this to mean that the earth as people know it for their habitation will be destroyed. Noah and his family will survive, but they will find no house to live in, no growing crop, no flock of sheep. They will have to "start from scratch" to make a home on the renewed earth.

CARRIERS OF A DREAD DISEASE

"Typhoid Mary" is a name many of us recognize, but most people probably don't know why the woman was famous. She was Mary Mallon (1869–1938), an immigrant from Ireland who found work in America as a cook.

Although Mary was immune to typhoid herself, she was a carrier of the disease—eventually infecting about fifty people (and killing at least three) through the food she prepared. An investigator traced several typhoid outbreaks over seven years to Ms. Mallon. In 1907 she was quarantined for three years. After promising never to work as a cook again, she was released in 1910. But eventually a 1915 epidemic was also traced to her. This time she was isolated for twenty-three more years until her death.

The people of Noah's time did not realize how deadly was the disease that afflicted them. They went on sinning, unaware of the terrible fate that awaited—"infecting" others with the spiritual malady that would soon destroy almost everyone. It would remain for God to "quarantine" the disease by means of the flood.

Unfortunately, Noah and his family members, even though they were comparatively righteous people themselves, would turn out to be "carri-ers" of the dread disease of sin, and the process of infection would begin again. May we never forget that even though we as Christians are relatively healthy spiritually, we also carry the disease.

—C. R. B.

B. Way of Escape (v. 14)

14. Make thee an ark of gopher wood; rooms shalt thou make in the ark, and shalt pitch it within and without with pitch.

An ark is a box, a chest. Our translators did not know what kind of wood is called *gopher* in Hebrew, so they simply wrote the Hebrew word in English letters. Some scholars think it was cypress wood, but we cannot be sure.

The ark is described further in verses 15 and 16 (not in today's text). The next part of our text takes up the story when the ark is complete.

III. Command and Obedience
(Genesis 7:1-5)

Every reader who is accustomed to handling animals must have wondered how Noah got all of those beasts aboard the ark. The domestic animals would have been difficult enough, but there were wild animals, too.

Do you suppose the assembling and loading of those animals was one of the most spectacular miracles ever done? Do you suppose that each beast obeyed the unspoken will of God as if it were instinct? Do you suppose that all those creatures actually paraded into the ark in orderly pairs, as our artists like to picture them? We can only conjecture. The record gives no information—but it gives no hint of difficulty, either.

A. Invitation Offered (vv. 1-3)

1. And the LORD said unto Noah, Come thou and all thy house into the ark; for thee have I seen righteous before me in this generation.

This *ark* is the haven of life in the presence of death. *Noah* and his family are invited to enter because they are *righteous*. This may be seen as an analogy to our own future entrance into Heaven. Christians will be able to enter that place of eternal security because they have been counted righteous through the blood of Christ. God will have nothing to do with unrighteousness.

2. Of every clean beast thou shalt take to thee by sevens, the male and his female: and of beasts that are not clean by two, the male and his female.

Clean animals are suitable as food for people on earth and as sacrifices to God in Heaven (Genesis 8:20, 21); unclean animals are not. For example, cattle and sheep are clean, but rabbits and camels aren't. Obviously the distinction is well known in Noah's time. Centuries later it will be recognized in the law given at Sinai (Leviticus 11). When Jesus comes, He will declare all foods to be clean (Mark 7:19).

3. Of fowls also of the air by sevens, the male and the female; to keep seed alive upon the face of all the earth.

The law to be given at Sinai will make a distinction between clean and unclean birds (Leviticus 11:13-19). But we see no such distinction in our text, and no explanation is given.

B. Invitation Explained (v. 4)

4. For yet seven days, and I will cause it to rain upon the earth forty days and forty nights; and every living substance that I have made will I destroy from off the face of the earth.

The invitation is given a week before the *rain* starts. This advance notice is probably necessary because it will take most of that time for all the animals and birds to come aboard, find their places, and get settled for a long stay.

C. Invitation Accepted (v. 5)

5. And Noah did according unto all that the LORD commanded him.

Noah counts the animals as they board the ark. Ample food already has been loaded (Genesis 6:21). The ark and its cargo and its passengers are ready for the coming storm as Noah continues his pattern of obedience (Genesis 6:22; Hebrews 11:7). [See question #2, page 24.]

IV. The Old and the New (Genesis 7:17, 23; 8:14-16; 9:1)

The ark rests on solid ground before the flood. Within it the people and animals are in their proper places. Outside, the people go about their business and their pleasures (Luke 17:27). No doubt they are loud in their ridicule of Noah and his big box. The time frame is given precisely: "In the six hundredth year of Noah's life, in the second month, the seventeenth day of the month" (Genesis 7:11). Then comes the deluge!

A. End of the Old (7:17, 23)

17. And the flood was forty days upon the earth; and the waters increased, and bare up the ark, and it was lifted up above the earth.

Forty days is not the entire time of *the flood*—rather, it is the duration of the rainfall (Genesis 7:12). The rain is so heavy that it is described as "the windows of heaven" being opened (7:11). Still, the flood is not due to rain alone since "the fountains of the great deep [were] broken up" (again, 7:11). Vast quantities of ocean water must be flowing out onto the land.

Remember the Everlasting Covenant

Visual for lesson 2. *Use this interesting visual as you discuss the various ways that God uses to remind us of His covenants.*

23. And every living substance was destroyed which was upon the face of the ground, both man, and cattle, and the creeping things, and the fowl of the heaven; and they were destroyed from the earth: and Noah only remained alive, and they that were with him in the ark.

The flood accomplishes God's purpose. The wicked people of earth die, one and all. With them die the living creatures that walk or crawl on the ground. The birds can fly above the flood, of course, but they cannot fly continually without food for five months (7:24). Utterly exhausted, they sink one by one from air to water, where they die. Ducks and geese can swim, but they cannot dive to the bottom of that flood for food (v. 20). *Noah only remained alive, and they that were with him in the ark.* [See question #3, page 24.]

B. Beginning of the New (8:14-16; 9:1)

14. And in the second month, on the seven and twentieth day of the month, was the earth dried.

It was also *in the second month* that the rain began (Genesis 7:11), but that was the six hundredth year of Noah's life. Now we are reading of the following year (8:13), and of a time just a year and ten days after "the windows of heaven were opened" for forty days of torrential rain. Inside the ark is the entire population of the world: eight people. For more than a year, not one of the eight has been able to go out for a walk.

But now once again the ark rests on solid *earth* (Genesis 8:4). Now again one can look out the window and see dry ground. The eight must be impatient, but God has shut them in (7:16). No one moves to open the door until God gives the word.

15, 16. And God spake unto Noah, saying, Go forth of the ark, thou, and thy wife, and thy sons, and thy sons' wives with thee.

God now gives the welcome order! It is time for the people to leave *the ark,* and to take the animals with them (8:17). The order is obeyed promptly (8:18, 19). Once outside, the first act of the grateful people is to build an altar and worship the Lord (8:20). The Lord responds with a promise that He will never again punish the evil of earth as He has done (8:21, 22).

There will be other beginnings, as we shall see in future lessons, but never an ending like the one just past. The rainbow would become the symbol of that promise (9:8-17). Even so, unrepentant people will be caught off guard as in the days of Noah when the Son of Man returns (Matthew 24:38, 39).

9:1. And God blessed Noah and his sons, and said unto them, Be fruitful, and multiply, and replenish the earth.

Like Adam and Eve many centuries before (Genesis 1:27, 28), the survivors of the flood receive God's blessing along with instructions to produce children. Those children, in turn, will produce other children in numbers increasing in generation after generation until the earth has a suitable population. [See question #4, page 24.] Like Adam and Eve, the survivors are given dominance over the animal creatures (9:2).

Conclusion

A. Chances

On the basis of this week's Scripture text and of many other passages, some students have described the Lord as "the God of second chances." What a chance for happiness our original parents had! Faced with every opportunity for joy forever, they chose the one slim chance of misery. Warned that disobedience meant death, they defied the only prohibition in the world, and humanity's chance for perfect happiness was gone.

Instead of learning from their parents' experience, the children of Adam and Eve followed their parents' example of wrong. Century after century, people wandered in the way of unrighteousness. To a God of absolute holiness, that was intolerable. Rottenness had to be discarded, evil had to be cleansed. Yet there was one family worthy of respect, an island of decency in a world of corruption. That family had to be preserved. So in the family of Noah God gave humanity a second chance.

As water flows downhill, the natural course of humanity seems to be downward, away from God and goodness. Through centuries the descendants of Noah followed that course until most of them had forgotten God and were worshiping gods of their own invention.

But in Ur, and later in Haran, lived a man whose faith in God was steadfast. God chose Abram (later known as Abraham) to be the father of a nation to be faithful to God, a nation to show the world that it is good and profitable to serve God alone. But that chosen nation followed the downward course of willful sin until its leaders contrived to have God's Son crucified. Soon after that, the nation of Abraham's people was crushed under the Roman boot and scattered.

While the nation of Abraham's children was crumbling, God's ambassadors were sounding His call to the kingdom of Heaven. Today that call still sounds in a world of sinners, and sinners are still responding. Men and women are repenting and being baptized for the remission of sins, and are receiving the gift of the Holy Ghost (Acts 2:38). In something of a parallel, the waters of baptism form a dividing line between saved and unsaved, as did the flood waters of Noah's day (1 Peter 3:18-21). [See question #5, page 24.] This, however, is the last chance.

Like the rest of humanity, we Christians have felt the pull of the downward way. But in Christ our sins have been forgiven. Praise the Lord!

B. Prayer

Dear God, how we humans have offended You from the beginning! How shamefully we ourselves have disappointed You! Forgive us, we pray, and give us wisdom and strength and courage to cling to Christ. In the Son's name we pray, amen.

C. Thought to Remember

"Be thou faithful unto death, and I will give thee a crown of life" (Revelation 2:10).

Home Daily Bible Readings

Monday, Sept. 6—The Wickedness of Humans Is Great (Genesis 6:5-12)

Tuesday, Sept. 7—God Has Noah Build an Ark (Genesis 6:13-22)

Wednesday, Sept. 8—Noah Enters the Ark (Genesis 7:1-16)

Thursday, Sept. 9—The Flood Comes (Genesis 7:17—8:5)

Friday, Sept. 10—Noah Leaves the Ark (Genesis 8:6-19)

Saturday, Sept. 11—God Blesses Noah and His Family (Genesis 8:20–9:7)

Sunday, Sept. 12—God Makes a Covenant (Genesis 9:8-17)

Learning by Doing

This page contains an alternative lesson plan emphasizing learning activities.
Classes desiring such student involvement will find these suggestions helpful.

Learning Goals

After participating in this lesson, each student will be able to:

1. Recite the account of God's punishment of sin and giving the world a new start in the time of Noah.

2. Express confidence in God's willingness to give second chances today.

3. Identify a personal area of sin and ask for God's help in making a fresh start.

Into the Lesson

Bring in some borrowed children's building blocks for this brief statement and demonstration. Say, "Many preschoolers love to play with building blocks. They work diligently to erect whatever structure is in their minds, and then at one fell swoop they knock them down with a squeal of delight." (Demonstrate by building some kind of structure with building blocks and suddenly knock them over with a yell of delight.)

"Then they are unhappy. With some encouragement they begin a reconstruction project." (Demonstrate by building up the structure again.)

"Today's lesson is a dramatic story of beginning again. This is a story of God's frustration with His perfect creation that succumbed to the temptation offered by Satan. Sins continued and multiplied. There were apparently no written instructions about worshiping God or avoiding sin and wickedness. How did the people know what was right and wrong?" Let the class suggest answers.

Finish by saying, "In God's holiness and exasperation, He set about to destroy His entire creation—with the exception of one man and his family. Noah found favor with God because of his righteousness."

Into the Word

Display two large flash cards: one with the word *GOD* and one with the word *MAN*. Say, "The Bible answers the two most significant questions that can be asked: one, 'Who is God and what is He like?' and two, 'Who is man and what is he like?'"

Provide blank paper and pens to each class member and ask them to fold the sheet lengthwise, putting "God" at the top of one half, "man" at the top of the other. Direct the class to exam-ine today's text for answers to the basic questions above. For example, "God is a God who sees" (6:5); "God is a God of grace" (6:8); "Man is capable of evil" (6:5); and "Man can choose righteousness even in a wicked time and place" (6:9). Note to the class that it is possible to develop a rather complete "Biblical theology" from today's texts and story.

Give the class a few minutes, then collectively make a list of truths for both *God* and *Man*. If no one suggests this truth, add it at the end: "God gives second chances."

Say, "The flood was a catharsis or cleansing of the earth of its evil. Like in the beginning when Adam sinned, the animals and the plant life suffered from his guilt. All of God's creation is interrelated. When God destroyed the earth for humanity's wickedness in the flood, all nature suffered as well.

"The New Testament uses the figure that as in Christian baptism the old man dies and a new man arises in Christ, the flood brought death to the old life on the earth and in Noah a new life began." Have someone read 1 Peter 3:20, 21 and Romans 6:1-4. "God gave the earth and mankind a second chance, as He still will."

Into Life

God gave the world a second chance beginning with the life of Noah and his sons who were charged with repopulating the earth. Would man now be pure or once again return to wickedness? Of course, the latter is true. That is why God sent His Son to rectify our awful plight. He became the sinless second Adam.

Ask, "What are the steps one must go through to achieve a second chance at rebuilding life?" Draw a simple stairway graphic, put the earlier flashcards on the stairway—MAN at the bottom and GOD at the top, and ask, "What are the steps one must climb to achieve a second chance at rebuilding life? What can you do to help a person 'get back on top'?"

Have copied and ready to distribute pieces of paper with two words, one atop the other: CHANCE over CHANCE. Draw an arrow toward the lower one. When all have a copy, ask if anyone can identify the symbolism (each has a "second chance"). Suggest that they carry this slip for a time as a ready reminder that all who are in Christ are living God's life of "a second chance."

Let's Talk It Over

The questions on this page are designed to promote discussion of the lesson by the class and to encourage application of the lesson Scriptures. The answers provided are only discussion starters. Let your class talk it over from there.

1. One of the saddest comments in all of Scripture is that God was grieved because He made man (Genesis 6:6). How do we keep from grieving God today?

The main thing that grieves God today, as in Noah's time, is *sin*. This is because God is holy and desires that His people be holy (1 Peter 1:16). God is also grieved when we try to walk by our own power instead of in His power (Zechariah 4:6) and when we walk by sight instead of by faith (2 Corinthians 5:7). God is further grieved when we allow our genuine concern for the things of this life to deteriorate into worry and anxiety (Philippians 4:6).

In today's church God is grieved when people focus more on self than on Him—for instance, when our comfort, our preferences, and our agendas take priority over God's will for the church. We see this happening when programs take precedence over people's needs, and when maintaining buildings and balancing budgets replace outreach and ministry. Though programs, buildings, and budgets are important, to focus on them to the neglect of ministry to people must grieve the heart of God. Challenge your class to consider some of the things your church can do to maintain a proper balance in these areas.

2. Just as Noah did everything according to God's plan, God desires similar obedience from His people now. What are some specific things your church can do to accomplish God's will today?

Answers to this question will be highly individual. As a general observation you can point out that too often people look at the instructions in God's Word as nice-sounding ideas, but "not realistic" in the world in which we live. There are those who half-jokingly say that we have turned the Ten Commandments into the ten suggestions. But God's instructions are not optional! Individual Christians and the church as the body of Christ must follow God's plan.

God's plan includes evangelism (Matthew 28:19, 20), exhibiting wisdom (Ephesians 3:10), living holy lives (1 Peter 1:16), and modeling a certain lifestyle (Colossians 3:1-17). The church's task, in many cases, is to teach Christians to be ready to apply God's general expectations to new and surprising circumstances.

3. Some people ask how a loving God could destroy people in the wholesale manner seen in our text. How would you answer this very real concern—a concern that hinders some from coming to faith in God and Christ?

The teaching that God is love is a truth that must be continually upheld (1 John 4:8). But it must be understood and taught that God is also holy (1 Peter 1:16). Being perfectly holy means that God is totally pure. Sin is against His nature and must be dealt with. God's holiness results in wrath (Romans 1:18).

Part of your response to an unbeliever should include mention of both the love and holiness that we see in Christ's death on the cross at Calvary. Jesus' death satisfies God's holy requirement that sin be punished. Jesus, in love, voluntarily takes the punishment that belongs to us (1 John 4:10). Helping people refocus on John 3:16 and Romans 5:8 is a necessary step in their understanding God's full nature.

4. After the flood God blessed Noah and his family, telling them to be fruitful and multiply. How can we do a better job at going forth and being fruitful in a spiritual sense today?

The gift of salvation is a gift to be shared, and God has given to His church the task to "go into all the world." Going into the world begins right outside your own door! Christians can fulfill this commission through opening their homes for discussions with unchurched people on basic questions of life. Knocking on doors and simply asking "Is there anything I can pray about for you?" can be a powerful starting point for evangelism.

5. The water of Christian baptism is a dividing line—it is a point in time when we move from lost to saved, from death to life, from life without the Spirit to life filled with the Spirit. How does (or should) this new nature affect the life of the Christian?

The Christian must "bring forth . . . fruits worthy of repentance" (Luke 3:8). The "fruit," of course, will be somewhat different from person to person, depending on the individual gifts of the Spirit. Even so, admonitions such as turning the other cheek, feeding the hungry, clothing the naked, and visiting those in prison are general means of living out the Christian faith.

God Raises Up a Deliverer

September 19
Lesson 3

DEVOTIONAL READING: Exodus 3:13-17.

BACKGROUND SCRIPTURE: Exodus 3–4.

PRINTED TEXT: Exodus 3:1-12.

Exodus 3:1-12

1 Now Moses kept the flock of Jethro his father-in-law, the priest of Midian: and he led the flock to the back side of the desert, and came to the mountain of God, even to Horeb.

2 And the angel of the LORD appeared unto him in a flame of fire out of the midst of a bush: and he looked, and, behold, the bush burned with fire, and the bush was not consumed.

3 And Moses said, I will now turn aside, and see this great sight, why the bush is not burnt.

4 And when the LORD saw that he turned aside to see, God called unto him out of the midst of the bush, and said, Moses, Moses. And he said, Here am I.

5 And he said, Draw not nigh hither: put off thy shoes from off thy feet; for the place whereon thou standest is holy ground.

6 Moreover he said, I am the God of thy father, the God of Abraham, the God of Isaac, and the God of Jacob. And Moses hid his face; for he was afraid to look upon God.

7 And the LORD said, I have surely seen the affliction of my people which are in Egypt, and have heard their cry by reason of their taskmasters; for I know their sorrows;

8 And I am come down to deliver them out of the hand of the Egyptians, and to bring them up out of that land unto a good land and a large, unto a land flowing with milk and honey; unto the place of the Canaanites, and the Hittites, and the Amorites, and the Perizzites, and the Hivites, and the Jebusites.

9 Now therefore, behold, the cry of the children of Israel is come unto me: and I have also seen the oppression wherewith the Egyptians oppress them.

10 Come now therefore, and I will send thee unto Pharaoh, that thou mayest bring forth my people the children of Israel out of Egypt.

11 And Moses said unto God, Who am I, that I should go unto Pharaoh, and that I should bring forth the children of Israel out of Egypt?

12 And he said, Certainly I will be with thee; and this shall be a token unto thee, that I have sent thee: When thou hast brought forth the people out of Egypt, ye shall serve God upon this mountain.

GOLDEN TEXT: I will send thee unto Pharaoh, that thou mayest bring forth my people the children of Israel out of Egypt.—Exodus 3:10.

The God of Continuing Creation
Unit 1: Created for a Purpose
(Lessons 1-4)

Lesson Aims

After participating in this lesson, each student will be able to:

1. Retell, in his or her own words, the story of God's call to Moses.

2. Estimate honestly his or her own abilities and how they can be used in Christian service.

3. Engage in service suited to his or her abilities.

Lesson Outline

INTRODUCTION
  A. The Making of a Leader
  B. Lesson Background
 I. STRANGE FIRE (Exodus 3:1-3)
  A. Shepherd (v. 1)
  B. Surprise! (v. 2)
  C. Scrutiny (v. 3)
 II. HOLY GROUND (Exodus 3:4-8)
  A. Awe-inspiring Identification (vv. 4-6)
    A Voice in the Desert
    Aware of God's Presence
  B. Awe-inspiring Mission (vv. 7, 8)
 III. BREATHTAKING CALL (Exodus 3:9-12)
  A. Moses' Mission (vv. 9, 10)
  B. Moses' Protest (v. 11)
  C. God's Answer (v. 12)
    What Trust Can Do
CONCLUSION
  A. Modern Search
  B. Ancient Method
  C. Prayer
  D. Thought to Remember

Introduction

A. The Making of a Leader

In reviewing the book *Leadership* by Rudolph "Rudy" Giuliani, Stephen Wolter poses an age-old question: "Does the man make the times, or do the times make the man?" Giuliani was elected mayor of New York City in 1993 and re-elected in 1997.

During his tenure as mayor, Giuliani seemed destined to be remembered by history as an effective administrator, as one who dramatically lowered his city's crime rate, and as someone whose style and politics polarized his constituents. But then came the terrorist attacks of September 11, 2001, and Giuliani's true leadership skills became obvious to the entire world.

We often pause to wonder about what we do not know. As we read our Bibles, do we see God finding people naturally fitted to lead and shape their times, or does God design and create such leaders through the trials they undergo? Or is it a little of both? Noah, Abraham, Joseph, Moses, David, John the Baptist, Paul—so many great leaders, so many unanswered questions about them! We meet one of these leaders today.

B. Lesson Background

Many centuries after Noah's descendants were wandering away from God, the Lord called Abraham to be the father of a great nation. That nation would show the rest of the world what it means to be holy. All this must have seemed very mysterious to Abraham, but "he went out, not knowing whither he went" (Hebrews 11:8). As a result the chosen family was planted in the land of Canaan, or Palestine as it came to be called.

Jacob, grandson of Abraham, had twelve sons. One was Joseph, who became a ruler in Egypt through an interesting series of events (Genesis 37, 39–41). God worked through human weakness (Jacob's foolish favoritism toward Joseph, and the jealousy of Joseph's brothers) to bring about a deliverance that saved a people from famine.

Then came disaster. After Joseph's death, a new Egyptian king became frightened when he saw all those foreigners living in his land (Exodus 1:1-10). What if they joined forces with a foreign country against Egypt? So the new king made slaves of the Hebrews and worked them under brutal overseers. When the Hebrew people continued to increase in number, the king decreed that every boy born among them should be thrown in the river (Exodus 1:22). This is the situation in which God moved to prepare His people to leave Egypt for the land that He had promised long before (Genesis 28:10-14).

Moses was one of the babies born in the days when the king was insisting that every baby boy of the Hebrews must be thrown into the river. Moses' mother did indeed put him there, but she protected him with a watertight basket that would float on the surface.

The princess found the floating baby, and her motherly instincts were stirred. She took him home and reared him as her own. So the Hebrew baby became a prince of Egypt, trained in all the knowledge and wisdom of that culture (Exodus 2:1-10).

When Moses was forty years old, he happened to see a merciless overseer beating one of the Hebrew slaves. Angered by that treatment, Moses killed the overseer. Such behavior was not to be tolerated, even in a prince. The king meant to have Moses executed, but Moses fled eastward across the desert to Midian.

There Moses joined the retinue of a priest and sheep grower named Jethro, married one of Jethro's daughters, and settled down to be a shepherd for the rest of his life (Exodus 2:11-22; Acts 7:23-29). For the next forty years (Acts 7:30) Moses enriched his wisdom of Egyptian culture with the lore of nomadic tribes and knowledge of desert living. Thus he was about eighty years old when God interrupted his life in a profound way.

I. Strange Fire
(Exodus 3:1-3)
A. Shepherd (v. 1)

1. Now Moses kept the flock of Jethro his father-in-law, the priest of Midian: and he led the flock to the back side of the desert, and came to the mountain of God, even to Horeb.

The land of *Midian* is named after one of Abraham's sons (Genesis 25:1-6). It is a large area without definite boundaries, perhaps one hundred fifty miles to the southeast of Egypt. Moving his *flock to the back side of the desert* likely means that *Moses* is traveling into *Horeb* or Sinai, toward Egypt. Pasture is so scarce that the sheep have to move far and wide to get enough to eat.

A certain mountain in Horeb is known as *the mountain of God,* as this record is written many years after the fact. We do not know whether or not it has that name when Moses first goes there. We do know, however, that this is not the last time that Moses will visit this place (Exodus 17:6; 33:6).

B. Surprise! (v. 2)

2. And the angel of the LORD appeared unto him in a flame of fire out of the midst of a bush: and he looked, and, behold, the bush burned with fire, and the bush was not consumed.

It is very strange to see a *fire* in that remote place, and as Moses stares at the *flame* he sees something stranger still: *the bush* is *not consumed.* No branches are vanishing in the fire. What kind of fire could this be?

Moses has forty years of experience in desert environments—he knows what is out of the ordinary when he sees it. But this event is not just out of the ordinary, it is a miracle. The God who is "a consuming fire" (Hebrews 12:29) has created a fire that does not consume!

C. Scrutiny (v. 3)

3. And Moses said, I will now turn aside, and see this great sight, why the bush is not burnt.

How to Say It

ABRAHAM. *Ay*-bruh-ham.
AMORITES. *Am*-uh-rites.
CANAAN. *Kay*-nun.
CANAANITES. *Kay*-nun-ites.
EGYPT. *Ee*-jipt.
GIULIANI. Joo-lee-*ahn*-ee.
HITTITES. *Hit*-ites or *Hit*-tites.
HIVITES. *Hi*-vites.
HOREB. *Ho*-reb.
JEBUSITES. *Jeb*-yuh-sites.
JETHRO. *Jeth*-ro.
JOSHUA. *Josh*-yew-uh.
MIDIAN. *Mid*-ee-un.
MOJAVE. Moh-*hah*-vee.
PERIZZITES. *Pair*-ih-zites.
PHARAOH. *fair*-o or *fay*-roe.
SINAI. *Sigh*-nye or *Sigh*-nay-eye.

Probably *Moses* says these words to himself; it is unlikely that anyone is with him. We might conclude that natural human curiosity "gets the best of him" and he can't resist stepping aside from his normal tasks to investigate what he sees. [See question #1, page 32.]

II. Holy Ground
(Exodus 3:4-8)
A. Awe-inspiring Identification (vv. 4-6)

4. And when the LORD saw that he turned aside to see, God called unto him out of the midst of the bush, and said, Moses, Moses. And he said, Here am I.

If *Moses* is moving toward the burning *bush,* the sound of a voice in the desert stillness stops him short. Or perhaps he has not yet started toward the bush. Perhaps the audible voice replies to his private thoughts, riveting him to the spot where he stands.

If the fire is surprising, this voice must be doubly so. Moses may be trembling, but nonetheless he answers *Here am I.*

A VOICE IN THE DESERT

The "Mojave Phone Booth" stood for years in the desert between Los Angeles and Las Vegas. It had been installed in that lonely place in the 1960s for the benefit of miners in the area. Much later it became famous when information about its existence and location was put on a Web site. Soon callers from around the world were dialing its number.

As a result the phone booth became something of a shrine. People came from long distances just to experience the uniqueness of hearing a human voice in the midst of a desert. People camped out by the phone for days, answering each call as it came in. One person reported taking seventy-two calls in one four-and-a-half-hour period.

Moses' experience in the desert was rather different from this! The voice he heard was that of God Himself. And to receive a "call" through a burning bush is unusual, to say the least. Moses responded as he should have; the rest, as they say, is history.

On May 17, 2000, Pacific Bell removed the "Mojave Phone Booth" that had been in service for more than thirty years; the voice in the desert disappeared. After thousands of years, the original bush that Moses saw is long gone. But that doesn't mean that God's voice is silenced! God still issues calls to repentance, forgiveness, and service today. Those calls come through His written Word as that Word is read and preached. As you hear God's call through that Word, are you ready to "pick up the phone"?   —C. R. B.

5. And he said, Draw not nigh hither: put off thy shoes from off thy feet; for the place whereon thou standest is holy ground.

The command to *draw not nigh hither* puts a quick stop to Moses' thought of stepping up for a closer look at that incredible fire. We may assume that when he hears the command to bare his *feet* he does so—and quickly!

Moses is looking at holy fire, fire so holy that even at this distance he is standing on *holy ground*. A place where sheep and goats walk is now holy because of the presence of God. [See question #2, page 32.]

AWARE OF GOD'S PRESENCE

September brings with it the reds and golds of autumn leaves in many parts of the world. This is particularly so in southern Canada and the northern tier of American states from New England west to the Rocky Mountains. In these places the terrain comes alive with the fiery hues of autumn foliage. For many people, autumn's beauty makes it their favorite season, even though the frigid days of winter are sure to follow quickly.

A wonderful image of earth's autumnal beauty (as well as the human tendency to use God's creation without recognizing Him in it) is summoned up by Elizabeth Barrett Browning (1806–1861) in her poem "Aurora Leigh":

> Earth's crammed with heaven,
> And every common bush afire with God;
> But only he who sees, takes off his shoes;
> The rest sit round it, and pluck blackberries.

At the burning bush Moses finally took notice of the presence of God that seemed suddenly to have entered his life. (God had been there all along, but He had to use this extraordinary means to arrest Moses' attention!) How many of us are oblivious to God's presence in our daily lives? Surely the beauty of changing seasons (wherever we may live) should awaken our souls to the evidence all around us of God's loving care. And how sad is our soul's plight if we ignore Him—except, of course, to eat the "blackberries" He has provided!   —C. R. B.

6. Moreover he said, I am the God of thy father, the God of Abraham, the God of Isaac, and the God of Jacob. And Moses hid his face; for he was afraid to look upon God.

Now *Moses* knows: it is *God* who is speaking— God the Creator, God the Commander, God the Keeper, God the Almighty. Perhaps Moses drops to his knees as he buries his face in his hands. Surely he knows that God is more than any fire, but he is *afraid* even *to look* at the symbol of God. (See also Acts 7:30-33.)

B. Awe-inspiring Mission (vv. 7, 8)

7. And the LORD said, I have surely seen the affliction of my people which are in Egypt, and have heard their cry by reason of their taskmasters; for I know their sorrows.

Moses has been away from *Egypt* for forty years, apparently content with his life as a shepherd. But who knows how much his mind and heart are burdened with the memory of his people's misery? Does he feel a nagging frustration day by day because he can do nothing to help them? We are not told, but *the Lord* speaks as if Moses is well aware of his people's distress. The Lord himself is even more keenly aware of the situation. No *affliction* or *cry* or *sorrows* escape His notice (cf. Matthew 10:29; Acts 7:34).

8. And I am come down to deliver them out of the hand of the Egyptians, and to bring them up out of that land unto a good land and a large, unto a land flowing with milk and honey; unto the place of the Canaanites, and the Hittites, and the Amorites, and the Perizzites, and the Hivites, and the Jebusites.

How the heart of Moses must leap! Already the Lord has *come down;* already God's campaign is in operation. The Lord is going to rescue His people from the terrible slavery and cruelty that has oppressed *them* all through the eighty years of Moses' life, and for some years before that.

The Lord is going to lead His people out of Egypt to *a good land*—a land so *large* that it is currently occupied by at least six other nations. Its description as being *a land flowing with milk and honey* is so profound that that phrase almost becomes a proverb (Exodus 3:17; 13:5; 33:3; etc.).

When God keeps this promise, He will be fulfilling a prophecy that is hundreds of years old. And the heart of Moses must be saying, "Amen."

III. Breathtaking Call (Exodus 3:9-12)

A. Moses' Mission (vv. 9, 10)

9, 10. Now therefore, behold, the cry of the children of Israel is come unto me: and I have also seen the oppression wherewith the Egyptians oppress them. Come now therefore, and I will send thee unto Pharaoh, that thou mayest bring forth my people the children of Israel out of Egypt.

From the future triumph declared in verse 8, God turns to face again the depressing present. God's *people* in Egypt are suffering terribly and crying for help.

How many of us feel our hearts leaping when we read the triumphant announcement that in the end "The kingdoms of this world are become the kingdoms of our Lord, and of his Christ; and he shall reign for ever and ever" (Revelation 11:15)? But then how many of us feel our hearts sinking when we read what God expects us to do in the meantime: "Go ye therefore, and teach all nations, baptizing them in the name of the Father, and of the Son, and of the Holy Ghost" (Matthew 28:19)? So likewise Moses' heart probably sinks at God's personal call to him. No wonder Moses protests (v. 11, next).

B. Moses' Protest (v. 11)

11. And Moses said unto God, Who am I, that I should go unto Pharaoh, and that I should bring forth the children of Israel out of Egypt?

Who am I? is a natural question. Back in Egypt *Moses* is a murderer sentenced to death. He is alive only because he fled to another country. It would be dangerous even to go to *Egypt,* even secretly. But to *go* boldly to *Pharaoh* with an unwelcome demand—wouldn't that be a demand for Moses' own death? [See question #3, page 32.]

On top of all that Moses may be thinking, "I'm eighty years old and have spent the last half of my life herding sheep." But Moses will discover as events unfold that he will need some herding skills to guide and push an obstinate people forward. [See question #4, page 32.]

C. God's Answer (v. 12)

12. And he said, Certainly I will be with thee; and this shall be a token unto thee, that I have sent thee: When thou hast brought forth the people out of Egypt, ye shall serve God upon this mountain.

Visual for lesson 3. *Use this visual all quarter long to help your learners "get their bearings" from lesson to lesson.*

What better promise can God give than *I will be with thee*? It will not be humans alone who go to Pharaoh to demand freedom for the Hebrews; God will be there as well. When Pharaoh says "no" to Moses, he will be saying "no" to God, too. But God has ways of enforcing His demands. Moses will not be able to mistake the hand of God in all of this when he serves God upon the very *mountain* where God is now speaking (again, Exodus 17:6; 33:6). Until then Moses must go in faith.

The rest of the story is well known to Bible readers. Pharaoh refuses to set God's people free, but God persuades that ruler with a series of plagues so terrible that at last both king and people urge the Hebrews to get out of Egypt, and get out quickly. Then for forty years Moses proves his skills as a leader as this people makes its way toward the promised land.

WHAT TRUST CAN DO

Hulda Crooks began climbing mountains at the age of fifty-three. She climbed 11,502-foot Mount San Gorgonio in Southern California twenty times. At age sixty-six she made the first of twenty-four ascents of California's 14,495-foot Mount Whitney, the highest peak in America's forty-eight contiguous states. Her last ascent was at age ninety-one! She is also the oldest person to climb Mount Fuji, the highest mountain in Japan.

Hulda started jogging when she was seventy-two, saying, "it made climbing so much easier." She also backpacked the two hundred and twelve-mile John Muir Trail in the Sierra Nevada, set a Senior Olympics world record in her age group for fifteen hundred meters, and hiked to the bottom of the Grand Canyon.

Before she died in 1997 at age one hundred and one, Hulda—a Christian—expressed the guiding principle of her life: "When you have faith in a supreme power that you believe is love and kindness and justice and has a care for you, you're not under tensions [like other people]. You develop a habit of trusting."

Trusting: so easy to say, so hard to do. At first, Moses had trouble trusting God. He had questions about his ability to do what God asked. In the end, it was Moses' trust in God's promise, "I will be with you," that made the difference. When trust in God took hold in Moses' life, he began to accomplish things he never would have imagined doing before. Do you suppose the same could be true for the rest of us?   —C. R. B.

Conclusion

A. Modern Search

When we need someone to teach a Sunday school class, or sponsor a youth group, or manage the nursery, or be on the finance committee, we do not have the privilege of starting with an unborn baby to build the person we need. So we look for a person already qualified by nature, training, and/or experience. If we see no one as well qualified as God thought Moses to be, then perhaps we choose the best person available and pray that he or she will learn on the job.

Our search for leaders would be easier if we would take more care to have leaders in training. Mary Weber is known as the best teacher in the Primary Department of her Sunday school. The children love her and the class. They are eager to learn. Mary likes to have an assistant in her class, not so much because she needs assistance but rather because the Sunday school needs to have teachers in training.

At first Mary's helper may do little more than check attendance, take care of the offering, and distribute crayons. But soon Mary asks her assistant to lead the children in their songs, or to prepare a simple object lesson.

Seldom does Mary keep an assistant for as much as a year. The assistant learns the teacher's skill and is requested for another class that needs a teacher. The kingdom of God moves forward as a result.

B. Ancient Method

Mary Weber is a good mentor, but Mary isn't perfect. Even after all these years she still makes an occasional mistake. Moses was a good leader, a great leader, a magnificent leader, but on one important occasion his leadership failed (Numbers 20:1-12; Deuteronomy 32:50, 51). That failure didn't stop him from being a good mentor to Joshua, however. Undoubtedly Joshua saw Moses' failure and learned something from it.

Joshua was a "minister" for Moses (Exodus 24:13). Here, of course, the word *minister* does not mean a preacher. It means a servant or helper. Joshua went along with Moses for a forty-day stay with the Lord in a cloud of glory on Mount Sinai, and Joshua came back with Moses as well (Exodus 32:15-17). Apparently Joshua was Moses' constant companion.

When Moses died at the border of the promised land, it was Joshua who stepped into his place to lead Israel (Joshua 1:1-9). Years of wandering were followed by years of warfare. But when the wars were over, the influence of Joshua was still strong. The people were loyal to the Lord until the death of that great leader, and loyal even beyond that time (Joshua 24:31; Judges 2:7).

All this has something to say to us today about the importance of mentoring and cultivating new leaders. Pause right now to take a close look at the age of your church's leaders. Are they all in their fifties, sixties, and seventies? Are they mentoring others? If not, that could be a big problem! When those leaders pass on, who will take their places? [See question #5, page 32.]

C. Prayer

Dear Father of us all, we thank You for the witness of Your leaders that speaks to us from the pages of the Bible. Noah, Abraham, Moses, Joshua, David, Nehemiah, Peter, and Paul all have something to teach us from both their successes and their failures. May all our leaders and all our followers be united in following You. In Jesus' name, amen.

D. Thought to Remember

The leader's call: "Be ye followers of me, even as I also am of Christ" (1 Corinthians 11:1).

Home Daily Bible Readings

Monday, Sept. 13—God Speaks to Moses (Exodus 3:1-6)
Tuesday, Sept. 14—God Calls Moses to Lead (Exodus 3:7-12)
Wednesday, Sept. 15—God Gives Moses Instructions (Exodus 3:13-22)
Thursday, Sept. 16—God Gives Moses Special Powers (Exodus 4:1-9)
Friday, Sept. 17—Moses Still Feels Inadequate (Exodus 4:10-17)
Saturday, Sept. 18—Moses Returns to Egypt (Exodus 4:18-23)
Sunday, Sept. 19—The Israelites Believe Moses (Exodus 4:24-31)

Learning by Doing

This page contains an alternative lesson plan emphasizing learning activities.
Classes desiring such student involvement will find these suggestions helpful.

Learning Goals

After participating in this lesson, each student will be able to:

1. Retell, in his or her own words, the story of God's call to Moses.

2. Estimate honestly his or her own abilities and how they can be used in Christian service.

3. Name a specific ministry in which he or she is using those abilities—or will use them—in the Lord's work.

Into the Lesson

Begin this class on the development of leaders (deliverers) with the following statement: "Adolf Hitler, who wanted to be the world's greatest leader, has gone down in history as one of the world's most wicked people. One of his goals was to create a superior race.

"Others are now attempting to unite the sperm and eggs of brilliant scholars and leaders in order to raise up outstanding children of unique mental ability and physical appearance. Still others are studying the possibility of the cloning of people. Question to ask are, 'What does it require to develop outstanding leaders? What qualities are necessary? Do circumstances play a part? To what degree does God's input play in developing a leader?'"

Let your class members suggest their answers.

Note that God is able to take someone seemingly insignificant and unknown and mold him or her into a mighty force for Him. Examples include Gideon, Deborah, David, and Peter.

Into the Word

Make this observation: "Occasionally some CEO who is tired of the commercial rat race decides to move to the mountains or sail around the world to live a more serene life.

"Moses, the 'CEO of Egypt,' was reared from infancy in the palace. Brought up as the adopted son of the princess of Egypt and trained by the greatest minds of Egypt, he may have been in line to become the next pharaoh.

"But God's training of Moses was incomplete. He needed to learn another lifestyle and another worldview. So by God's providence, he will end up in the nomadic desert."

Divide your class into three smaller groups and give them the discussion assignments that follow.

Group 1: Relate as much as you can about Abraham, Jacob, Joseph, and Moses relative to their leadership traits. What specific deeds testify to their leadership abilities?

Group 2: Summarize the outstanding events of the three forty-year phases of Moses' life. (First forty, in Pharaoh's palace; second forty, as a shepherd in Midian; third forty, as a leader of the Israelites.)

Group 3: Describe how God shaped and developed Moses (1) from birth until he ran to Midian; (2) during his life in the desert; (3) during his leading the Israelites to the promised land.

Have each group make a brief summary of its conclusions.

Into Life

Display these scrambled words of several people who helped in Moses' development into the outstanding leader whom he became: CEINPRSS, EHOMRT, EHJORT, AAHHOPR. (The *princess* who rescued him and kept him in the royal palace; his own *mother*, who was his early nurse-maid; *Jethro*, his father-in-law, who was a priest of Midian; *pharaoh*, who gave him all the education Egypt could offer.)

Ask the students to identify significant people who played important roles in their own personal development. A teacher? A preacher? A parent? A grandparent? Others? (This activity is included in the student book.)

Ask, "Have you thanked those people?" Provide paper or note cards for each to write a short letter of thanks to one who helped him or her. If the one chosen has died, direct the class member to write as if the person were still alive.

Note to the class: "God provided the church as a leadership-training institution. How can we, both as a class group and as individuals, help in the leadership development of young people and other adults in our church and in our community?" Try to get the group beyond such activities as teaching a Bible school class or serving as a Scout leader.

Give each person an index card with the following imprinted (or to be written on as you write it on the class board): "Believing that I can be used by God to help another grow in leadership ability in His kingdom, I will, with God's empowering Spirit. . . . " Encourage those who want to share their answers to do so.

Let's Talk It Over

The questions on this page are designed to promote discussion of the lesson by the class and to encourage application of the lesson Scriptures. The answers provided are only discussion starters. Let your class talk it over from there.

1. What "burning bushes" are there in your life or church today where God demonstrates His presence and His power?

At certain times in history God has revealed Himself through miraculous signs. But more often God works through the "still, small voice" or in the ordinary things of life. God's presence is often seen in the comforting word of a friend offered in a time of need, the encouragement received through a message from God's Word, or the godly peace that comes in the midst of sorrow. Seeing a new soul won to Christ or a prodigal returning to the local church are times to stop and marvel at God's mighty presence and power.

In a world oriented so heavily toward tasks and results, it is necessary to take time out to reflect and meditate upon God's Word as well as His creation. When we do, God's presence will be unmistakable.

2. When God is present, holiness abounds. How can you show the proper respect due to God as you "stand on holy ground"?

From the strut of the football player who just scored a touchdown to the sneer of the CEO defending unjust business practices, pride and arrogance are evident all around us. In the midst of such a culture the Christian is sometimes tempted to "strut his or her stuff" as well. Bragging about church attendance, huge offerings, and square footage of buildings can deny God as being the giver of all of these things.

A few years ago a lady remarked with excitement in her eyes about the presence of a certain basketball star in her church's worship services. An onlooker quipped, "Yes, and God was here, too." Take time to stop and remember that after all is said and done, it is all about God. When we do, we demonstrate an attitude of humility.

3. Being called by God to serve Him is a humbling and awe-inspiring experience. How should we respond when we sense God calling us into His service?

A feeling of inadequacy when called of God is not a reason to reject or ignore the call. A study of those God used throughout Scripture reveals a feeling of inadequacy time and again. Moses, Gideon, Isaiah, and Jeremiah all felt they were not up to the task. But it is when we recognize our inadequacy, our weakness, that God is able to work (cf. 2 Corinthians 12:9).

Humbly accepting the call of God begins with realizing we are unworthy. We then realize that in our own power we are too weak for the task. When we recognize our unworthiness and our weakness, then we are fit vessels for God to use.

4. God spent eighty years training Moses in "the school of life" to prepare him for the ministry he was to perform. How has God been training you for a particular ministry in the church? What ministry could you do in your church as a result of this training?

Answers will be highly individual since "God's training school" involves a wide variety of practical life experiences. When we are struggling, God is preparing us to trust Him. As we deal with people in their various life experiences, God could be teaching us patience. When we have victories in our service, He is teaching us to be confident in ministry. When others correct or rebuke us, we learn humility. That difficult person we encounter may be God's way to teach us the art of practicing unconditional love.

An additional important principle in this lesson from Moses is that there is no retirement age in service to God. The wisdom of age is greatly needed for the maturing of the church.

5. Realizing that the church is always one generation away from extinction, how can your church prepare leaders for the next generation?

There must be the continual infusing of new leadership for the church to continue, but it is difficult sometimes to find people who want to accept leadership roles in the church. Some don't want to assume leadership roles because of improper and unchristian ways past leaders have been treated by church members. Others avoid leadership because of poor role models.

One way to raise up new leaders is to hold current leaders accountable to godly standards. Modeling proper respect and submission to current leadership is another way to encourage others to step up and accept leadership roles. Mentoring new leaders is vital. Your church can also help mold the next generation of leaders by "talking up" the importance of Bible college education for specialized areas of Christian service.

Becoming God's People

DEVOTIONAL READING: Deuteronomy 30:15-20.

BACKGROUND SCRIPTURE: Deuteronomy 29:1-29.

PRINTED TEXT: Deuteronomy 29:1-15.

Deuteronomy 29:1-15

1 These are the words of the covenant, which the LORD commanded Moses to make with the children of Israel in the land of Moab, besides the covenant which he made with them in Horeb.

2 And Moses called unto all Israel, and said unto them, Ye have seen all that the LORD did before your eyes in the land of Egypt unto Pharaoh, and unto all his servants, and unto all his land;

3 The great temptations which thine eyes have seen, the signs, and those great miracles:

4 Yet the LORD hath not given you a heart to perceive, and eyes to see, and ears to hear, unto this day.

5 And I have led you forty years in the wilderness: your clothes are not waxen old upon you, and thy shoe is not waxen old upon thy foot.

6 Ye have not eaten bread, neither have ye drunk wine or strong drink: that ye might know that I am the LORD your God.

7 And when ye came unto this place, Sihon the king of Heshbon, and Og the king of Bashan, came out against us unto battle, and we smote them:

8 And we took their land, and gave it for an inheritance unto the Reubenites, and to the Gadites, and to the half tribe of Manasseh.

9 Keep therefore the words of this covenant, and do them, that ye may prosper in all that ye do.

10 Ye stand this day all of you before the LORD your God; your captains of your tribes, your elders, and your officers, with all the men of Israel,

11 Your little ones, your wives, and thy stranger that is in thy camp, from the hewer of thy wood unto the drawer of thy water:

12 That thou shouldest enter into covenant with the LORD thy God, and into his oath, which the LORD thy God maketh with thee this day:

13 That he may establish thee today for a people unto himself, and that he may be unto thee a God, as he hath said unto thee, and as he hath sworn unto thy fathers, to Abraham, to Isaac, and to Jacob.

14 Neither with you only do I make this covenant and this oath;

15 But with him that standeth here with us this day before the LORD our God, and also with him that is not here with us this day.

GOLDEN TEXT: Enter into covenant with the LORD thy God, . . . that he may establish thee today for a people unto himself.—Deuteronomy 29:12, 13.

The God of Continuing Creation
Unit 1: Created for a Purpose
(Lessons 1-4)

Lesson Aims

After participating in this lesson, each student will be able to:

1. Summarize the details of the covenant Moses rehearsed with the Israelites at the border of the promised land.

2. Explain how keeping God's covenant was best for Israel and is best for us.

3. Express a commitment to live within God's covenant.

Lesson Outline

INTRODUCTION
 A. A Thirty-Year Waste
 B. Lesson Background
 I. REMEMBER EGYPT (Deuteronomy 29:1-4)
 A. What the Lord Says (v. 1)
 B. What You Saw (vv. 2, 3)
 Creating a Family Identity
 C. How You Resist (v. 4)
 II. REMEMBER THE WILDERNESS (Deuteronomy 29:5-9)
 A. Decades of Care (vv. 5, 6)
 B. Victory Over Enemies (vv. 7, 8)
 C. Advice to Heed (v. 9)
 III. HONOR THE COVENANT (Deuteronomy 29: 10-15)
 A. Assembled People (vv. 10, 11)
 B. Awe-inspiring Purpose (vv. 12, 13)
 C. Additional People (vv. 14, 15)
 Blessings of the Covenant
CONCLUSION
 A. Two Important Principles
 B. Prayer
 C. Thought to Remember

Introduction

A. A Thirty-Year Waste

On March 10, 1974, World War II finally ended for Second Lieutenant Hiroo Onoda of the Imperial Japanese Army. Lieutenant Onoda had been drafted into his country's army in 1942, and, evading capture, had survived in a remote part of the Philippines since the war ended in 1945.

For the next three decades, Lieutenant Onoda refused to believe any evidence that the war was over. The authorities knew his general location, and tried dropping leaflets, magazines, and newspapers to convince him to give up. Nothing worked. Finally, Lieutenant Onoda's former commanding officer arrived on the scene and personally ordered him to surrender. What should have been two or three years of service to his country turned into a thirty-year waste of time. Onoda's pointless war was finally over.

Such blindness is nothing new, is it? Just after Jesus' resurrection, He chastised some disciples on the road to Emmaus when He said, "O fools, and slow of heart to believe all that the prophets have spoken" (Luke 24:25). They had the prophecies, they had the fulfillments, they had the miracles, they had the evidence. Yet they still doubted—just like their forefathers in the desert (Numbers 14:11). Today's lesson is about a people struggling to establish an identity as they recover from forty years of blindness.

B. Lesson Background

Last week we saw God call Moses from the pastureland of Midian to go to Egypt and free the Hebrew slaves. God had a place for those slaves to be free and to be His own people. It was the very place to which God had led Abraham long before. It was "a land flowing with milk and honey" (Exodus 3:8). In that place God would prepare that nation to usher in the Messiah.

So Moses took his request to the king of Egypt. Brusquely the king refused, but he changed his mind when God sent a series of plagues. After the death of their firstborn, all Egypt joined the king in urging the Hebrews to get out of Egypt. So after four hundred and thirty years (Exodus 12:40, 41), the Hebrews left the valley of the Nile to begin forty years of life in the wilderness.

Forty years was certainly a long time to make a trip that at most should have totaled no more than three hundred and fifty miles! The travelers actually came to the border of the promised land in a little less than two years, although they camped at Sinai for nearly a year while on the way (Exodus 19:1; Numbers 10:11-13).

Pausing at the edge of the promised land, the Hebrews sent twelve scouts to study the countryside and plan an invasion (Numbers 13:1-25). Ten of the twelve came back with a frightening report: the cities of that land were fortified, and the warriors who defended them were giants. The other two scouts disagreed. With God's help, they said, the land could surely be taken.

But the majority report prevailed and the people refused to go forward (Numbers 14:1-4). For that failure of faith, God said they must live in the desert for thirty-eight more years (Deuteronomy 2:14). During those years they were not travelers moving toward a goal; rather, they were herdsmen moving about the desert to find pasture for their livestock.

When God allowed those wilderness wanderers to approach the promised land again, they did so by way of the eastern side of the Dead Sea and the Jordan River. Then there was a pause, for that was the end of the road for Moses. Now one hundred and twenty years old (Deuteronomy 34:7), Moses was to die east of the Jordan, leaving Joshua to lead the people to cross the river and conquer the larger part of the promised land (34:9). This week our text brings us a bit of what Moses said to his people before he left them and climbed up Mount Pisgah, never to return.

I. Remember Egypt (Deuteronomy 29:1-4)

Of those listening to Moses, only two had left Egypt as adults some forty years earlier. The rest of the adults who had begun the trip died in the desert (Numbers 14:29-35; Deuteronomy 2:14, 15). Many of Moses' hearers had left Egypt as teenagers and younger children; many others had been born during the desert wanderings.

Moses, therefore, is very wise to begin his address by recalling the last days of Israel's long stay in Egypt. A reminder of those days sets the context for what Moses says afterward.

A. What the Lord Says (v. 1)

1. These are the words of the covenant, which the LORD commanded Moses to make with the children of Israel in the land of Moab, besides the covenant which he made with them in Horeb.

This verse may be called a title of the part of Moses' discourse that follows. See how it resembles the title in Deuteronomy 1:1. Nearly forty years have passed since God had made a *covenant* (a contract, an agreement) with His people *in Horeb,* or Sinai (1:6; 4:10, 15). That former covenant fills large parts of Exodus, Leviticus, and Numbers.

Now, *in the land of Moab,* which is east of the Jordan River (1:5), *the Lord* is commanding another covenant. Of course this is not to replace the earlier covenant. Rather, it is a supplement, consisting largely of instructions to abide by the former agreement.

B. What You Saw (vv. 2, 3)

2. And Moses called unto all Israel, and said unto them, Ye have seen all that the LORD did before your eyes in the land of Egypt unto Pharaoh, and unto all his servants, and unto all his land.

Moses is referring to the famous ten plagues that God had used to persuade the Egyptians to release their Hebrew slaves. Among the hearers those under age forty had been born since their parents had left *Egypt.* Although they had not seen the plagues personally, the others in the assembly could well remember the furor in Egypt.

3. The great temptations which thine eyes have seen, the signs, and those great miracles.

Moses continues to speak of the ten plagues. Probably "trials" is a better translation than *temptations* to give the idea of difficulties that bring distress. The plagues are also *signs* of God's power, and all of them, without doubt, were *great miracles.* [See question #1, page 40.]

CREATING A FAMILY IDENTITY

Joe Mountain and his family have a unique family reunion each year. Joe, a bus driver, takes the proverbial "busman's holiday" by chartering a bus to take his family on a vacation trip. Recently, the vacation included forty-one relatives who shared a twelve-day, twenty-eight-hundred-mile reunion through the American Southwest. Another year it was a three-thousand-mile trip to the Pacific Northwest.

One year the bus broke down; on another occasion a family member was left behind for a short while before he was missed. The mishaps add color to the story as they are remembered later. And remembering is a large part of what these trips are all about. The mishaps, the adventures shared, and the marvelous sights they've seen all contribute to the family identity passed on to the next generations.

Moses' speech to Israel in today's text serves somewhat the same purpose as the Mountain family vacations. Moses reminds Israel of the marvelous sights they have seen as God brought them freedom and provided sustenance on their journey from Egypt. He reminds them of the miracles and signs of God's power they saw, as well as the "mishaps" along the way in which some got "left behind"—permanently.

To Israel's experiences we can add our own. In so doing, we find a growing awareness of God's care and of our community with the family of God in every age.　　　　—C. R. B.

C. How You Resist (v. 4)

4. Yet the LORD hath not given you a heart to perceive, and eyes to see, and ears to hear, unto this day.

The Israelites certainly have "head knowledge" about God's miraculous intervention, but such knowledge does not always convert easily into *"heart* knowledge." After all the signs and great miracles God has done on their behalf, the people should be perceptive enough to realize that God is on their side and that He will give

How to Say It

ABRAHAM. *Ay*-bruh-ham.
BASHAN. *Bay*-shan.
EMMAUS. Em-*may*-us.
GADITES. *Gad*-ites.
HOREB. *Ho*-reb.
ISAAC. *Eye*-zuk.
JACOB. *Jay*-kub.
JEREMIAH. Jair-uh-*my*-uh.
MANASSEH. Muh-*nass*-uh.
MIDIAN. *Mid*-ee-un.
MOAB. *Mo*-ab.
MOABITES. *Mo*-ub-ites.
MOSES. *Mo*-zes or *Mo*-zez.
PISGAH. *Piz*-guh.
REUBENITES. *Roo*-ben-ites.
SIERRA LEONE. See-*air*-uh Lay-*own*.
SIHON. *Sigh*-hun.
SINAI. *Sigh*-nye or *Sigh*-nay-eye.

them success when they obey Him. But at their first approach to the promised land, those people had turned back in terror instead of trusting God and going forward. Why hadn't they provided their own *ears to hear* and *eyes to see* and hearts *to perceive,* instead of waiting for God to provide them with perceptions as well as doing great miracles for them?

In Romans 11:8 Paul uses this passage (along with Isaiah 29:10) to criticize the people of his own day. Jesus makes a similar observation in Matthew 13:13-15. Human nature doesn't seem to change much, even across hundreds or thousands of years! [See question #2, page 40.]

II. Remember the Wilderness (Deuteronomy 29:5-9)

Those who remember what great things God had done for them in Egypt ought to be ready to trust Him and obey Him without fear. But events in the wilderness had been even more encouraging: God had led His people and provided for them all the way.

A. Decades of Care (vv. 5, 6)

5. And I have led you forty years in the wilderness: your clothes are not waxen old upon you, and thy shoe is not waxen old upon thy foot.

All through those *forty years in the wilderness* God led His people, going before them in a pillar of cloud by day and a pillar of fire by night (Exodus 40:38; Numbers 14:14). The miraculous preservation of their clothes and shoes shows us that God is concerned about the Israelites' physical needs on top of their spiritual welfare.

6. Ye have not eaten bread, neither have ye drunk wine or strong drink: that ye might know that I am the LORD your God.

For forty years God's people planted no seed, harvested no wheat, picked no grapes, pressed no wine, and made no beer. Rather, each day they picked up their food ("manna") from the desert floor, food such as was never seen before or since. For forty years they drank clear water (Exodus 15:22-27; 17:1-7). Every helpful favor and every benevolent miracle is evidence that the One who did it is *the Lord your God.*

B. Victory Over Enemies (vv. 7, 8)

7. And when ye came unto this place, Sihon the King of Heshbon, and Og the king of Bashan, came out against us unto battle, and we smote them.

Sihon and *Og* had been kings of two small nations east of the Dead Sea and the Jordan River, the very area where God's people now have their camp. Each of those kings had come *out* with an army to drive the invading Israelites away; but God helped the invaders, and the defenders were defeated (Numbers 21:21-35).

8. And we took their land, and gave it for an inheritance unto the Reubenites, and to the Gadites, and to the half tribe of Manasseh.

The few enemies who survived the battles had to flee from their lands, leaving them to the victorious Israelites (Deuteronomy 2:24–3:11). That area is notable for the rich grass that makes it a splendid place for cattle. The tribes of *Reubenites* and *Gadites,* and part of the tribe *of Manasseh* have many cattle, so they had asked Moses to let them have that area as their share of the land.

Moses granted that request, with the provision that the men of those tribes would not settle down on their new land until they had crossed the Jordan River and helped the other tribes capture the land on the western side (Numbers 32).

C. Advice to Heed (v. 9)

9. Keep therefore the words of this covenant and do them, that ye may prosper in all that ye do.

Now Moses offers advice based on the facts he has been reviewing: the people must be faithful to the *covenant* now being made. As indicated in the comments to verse 1 above, this is not a different covenant to replace the one made at Sinai nearly forty years earlier. Rather, it is a ratification and renewal of that former covenant.

With one voice, those present at Sinai had said, "All that the Lord hath said will we do, and be obedient" (Exodus 24:7). Now Moses invites his current audience to make the same pledge. Clearly, that is the way to be assured *that ye may prosper in all that ye do.* Every miracle of the past forty years is evidence that nothing is impossible with God. So how can God's people be intimidated by walled cities and tall men? "Trust and obey" is the advice of Moses. Forty years of history prove that it is good advice.

III. Honor the Covenant (Deuteronomy 29:10-15)

A covenant with God is not an alliance of equals. It recognizes that God is supreme and we are His servants. Our duty and our pleasure is to do His will, and that is for our good. Moses stresses that God's people must accept the fundamental principle that God is Number One in the covenant. They must shape their lives in accord with that principle.

A. Assembled People (vv. 10, 11)

10, 11. Ye stand this day all of you before the LORD your God; your captains of your tribes, your elders, and your officers, with all the men of Israel, your little ones, your wives, and thy stranger that is in thy camp, from the hewer of thy wood unto the drawer of thy water.

Notice the wide spectrum of people who are present! God's covenant is not just for the leaders, but for everyone—oldest to youngest, male and female. *Stranger* refers to the non-Israelites within the assembly. The covenant is for them as well. Another designation for such "resident aliens" is *hewer of thy wood . . . drawer of thy water* (see Joshua 9:21, 23, 27). In the case at hand, these may be Moabites, since the Israelites are on the east side of the Jordan River.

It may seem a bit surprising that foreigners can be welcomed into the promises of the Jewish nation since the Jews are not commanded to "evangelize" such people. In fact God requires the Israelites to avoid intermingling with non-Jews (Deuteronomy 7:1-6). But foreigners can participate in the covenant if they wish (Exodus 12:48, 49; Numbers 15:26; 19:10). The Israelites are not to oppress these resident aliens because the Jews themselves know what it was like to be in that position (Exodus 23:9; Deuteronomy 10:19). [See question #3, page 40.]

B. Awe-inspiring Purpose (vv. 12, 13)

12. That thou shouldest enter into covenant with the LORD thy God, and into his oath, which the LORD thy God maketh with thee this day.

The people meet for the purpose of entering into the *covenant* that is being offered. By that covenant the Israelites have the added assurance that they are God's people. God intends to keep *his oath*—will they keep theirs? [See question #4, page 40.]

13. That he may establish thee today for a people unto himself, and that he may be unto thee a God, as he hath said unto thee, and as he hath sworn unto thy fathers, to Abraham, to Isaac, and to Jacob.

Here the provisions of the covenant are summarized very briefly. The people entering into the covenant are to be God's *people*. That means they agree to obey all the commandments of the lengthy covenant that had been made nearly forty years earlier. God, in turn, will give them the blessings promised to *Abraham, Isaac*, and *Jacob* (all three now having been dead for hundreds of years), and the blessings promised in the covenant made at Sinai. Deuteronomy 28:1-14 briefly describes those blessings, while 28:15-68 sets forth the sobering penalties for failure.

C. Additional People (vv. 14, 15)

14, 15. Neither with you only do I make this covenant and this oath; but with him that standeth here with us this day before the LORD our God, and also with him that is not here with us this day.

Here is another mild surprise: the *covenant* is to be made with others besides those to whom Moses is talking. Verses 10 and 11 make it plain that the meeting is intended to include everyone in the camp of Israel, including foreigners. But what about *him that is not here with us?*

This sounds too important to refer merely to a few Hebrews who may be out hunting deer and are not in the meeting at the moment. The proper interpretation is that this covenant is for Israelites of future generations, not just the ones currently alive. Again we note that verses 10 and 11 offer us a hint that people who are not Hebrews may find a place in God's covenant.

Enter into covenant with the Lord thy God.
—Deuteronomy 29:12

Visual for lesson 4. *Use these three images to start a discussion on the importance of covenants, both God's and ours.*

Acts 2:39 also points to those future generations that may be included in the new covenant. Since our lesson title is "Becoming God's People," will not our study of that topic be most helpful if it includes some thoughts on being God's people in our own time? We turn our minds in that direction as we conclude this lesson. [See question #5, page 40.]

BLESSINGS OF THE COVENANT

In March, 2000, a replica of the schooner *Amistad* was launched in Mystic, Connecticut. The original ship had a sobering history. In 1839 this vessel was bringing slaves to the Americas from what is now Sierra Leone, Africa.

During the trip the slaves revolted and took control of the ship near Cuba. The vessel sailed north, to be eventually captured by the U.S. Navy near Long Island, where the slaves were arrested. While the slaves were imprisoned, students from (then Christian) Yale University taught them the Christian faith.

Former President John Quincy Adams took up the cause of the slaves, and in 1841 a ruling by the U.S. Supreme Court freed them. A year later the surviving thirty-five freedmen returned to Africa, where they began schools and churches. The faith of the "Christian" nation that had imprisoned them became the means to better the lot of people in their homeland. Even so, another twenty-five years would have to pass before American slaves would be freed by a civil war and President Lincoln's "Emancipation Proclamation."

When God established the nation of Israel thousands of years ago, He told His people that the disenfranchised and powerless—women, children, aliens, and even the unnamed people who were yet to be among them—were to be considered members of the covenant, with all the blessings that that promise brought with it. In the era of the new covenant, it has taken us far too long to realize that God's compassion and offer of salvation extends to all people, not just the powerful or "chosen few."   —C. R. B.

Conclusion

A. Two Important Principles

The covenant mentioned in today's text is definitely according to the earlier covenant, the one made at Sinai just after God brought His people out of Egypt. But in Jeremiah 31:31-34 we read God's promise of a new covenant that is not according to that covenant made in Sinai. That new covenant is promised to the house of Israel and the house of Judah: those two houses made up the descendants of Abraham, and now faithful Christians have replaced them as Abraham's children (Galatians 3:7-9). Lesson 7 of this series will bring us more thoughts about Jeremiah's prophecy of a new covenant, and lessons 10 to 13 will be drawn from the New Testament itself.

For the present, however, let us take note of two principles that belong to all of the covenants that God has made with humanity. Our *first principle* is that God is Number One in every instance. He commands us, we do not command Him. He instructs us, we do not instruct Him. He leads, and we follow; He sends, and we go. He is the potter, we are the clay.

The *second principle* is that the covenant is for our good. Keeping it does us good; breaking it does us harm. The blessings and curses described in Deuteronomy 28 may seem extreme, but they are verified in centuries of Israel's experience.

Today we do well to ask ourselves, "If the word spoken by angels was steadfast, and every transgression and disobedience received a just recompense of reward; how shall we escape, if we neglect so great salvation?" (Hebrews 2:2, 3). Sin promises to pay, and in the short term it may seem to be paying. May we never forget, however, that we have a covenant with God. Sin has no place in this covenant that leads us into life eternal.

B. Prayer

Our Father in Heaven, we know that You alone are God. We know You are wiser and stronger than we are. Thank You for Your Word, the sure guide in the right way of the new covenant. Forgive our foolish wandering from that way, we pray, and help us to wander no more. In Jesus' name, amen.

C. Thought to Remember

Focus on the promised land of Heaven!

Home Daily Bible Readings

Monday, Sept. 20—Moses Reminds the Israelites (Deuteronomy 29:2-9)

Tuesday, Sept. 21—The Israelites Join the Covenant (Deuteronomy 29:10-15)

Wednesday, Sept. 22—Moses Warns the Israelites (Deuteronomy 29:16-21)

Thursday, Sept. 23—The Reason for Devastation (Deuteronomy 29:22-29)

Friday, Sept. 24—God Will Forgive Those Who Return (Deuteronomy 30:1-5)

Saturday, Sept. 25—God Will Prosper Those Who Believe (Deuteronomy 30:6-10)

Sunday, Sept. 26—Obey God and Choose Life (Deuteronomy 30:11-20)

Learning by Doing

This page contains an alternative lesson plan emphasizing learning activities. Classes desiring such student involvement will find these suggestions helpful.

Learning Goals

After participating in this lesson, each student will be able to:

1. Summarize the details of the covenant Moses rehearsed with the Israelites at the border of the promised land.

2. Explain how keeping God's covenant was best for Israel and is best for us.

3. Express a commitment to live within God's covenant.

Into the Lesson

Say, "In 1620 Puritans landed at Plymouth Rock on the barren, cold coast of Massachusetts near Cape Cod Bay. They were in search of a new life and religious freedom. The journey had been perilous with several deaths and sickness on board. But their spirits were high and their hope outstanding. Their new beginning is similar to that of the Israelites who came to the Jordan River and were led by Joshua into the promised land."

Ask your class to list some of the factors the Puritans overcame in starting a colony in the New World. (Cold, lack of food and medicine, houses to build, illness, death, loneliness.) What allowed them to persevere? (Faith, determination, will of God.)

Note that Moses gave the children of Israel a huge challenge as he offered his final instructions to them before he died.

Into the Word

For a review of Israel's history from the exodus to the time of today's text—as Moses does in the text—ask the following questions to your class:

(1) How many years did Israel wander in the wilderness before going into the promised land? *(forty, v. 5)*; (2) Since it took only a few days to reach Canaan from Egypt (including a day to worship God), why did they not go in and take the land immediately? *(They sent in twelve spies who returned with a mixed report. Ten of the spies reported that an invasion would be impossible, for the giants in the land and walled cities would prevent their taking the land.)*; (3) Which two spies recommended that they go in and take the land with God's help? *(Joshua and Caleb)*; (4) Who died on the forty-year journey? *(All adults who left Egypt except two men)*; (5) Who were the ex-ceptions? *(Joshua and Caleb)*; (6) Why were they spared when the other adults died? *(They were the two spies who gave the good report that expressed confidence in God's presence and power.)*; (7) What other benefits were the Israelites given on their wilderness trek? *(God provided good water as they needed it. Neither their clothes nor shoes wore out for the forty years. Also they went to battle and defeated two kings—Og, King of Bashan, and Sihon, King of Heshbon. Lands east of the Jordan ruled by pagan kings were given to the Reubenites, the Gadites, and half of the tribe of Manasseh.)*; (8) When Moses gave this new covenant, what was the reaction of the people? *(Eager anticipation)*

Into Life

Get an artistic class member to render simple line drawings of a house under construction and of a traditional church building on a single sheet. Copy and distribute each sheet and say, "This house represents Israel. Write in the spiritual foundation for the house (Mosaic covenant including the Ten Commandments). Walls are built of the continuous teaching of the Word of God. (Write the names of some of the prophets of the Old Testament on the studs of the walls.) The windows provide light to the interior of the house. The windows represent God's message by prophecies as they looked forward to the time of Messiah. (Write a messianic prophecy in the windows.) The roof is God's protection. (Write an incident when God protected them from enemies, such as at the Red Sea.)"

Now turn to the simple drawing of a church building. Ask the group to identify the foundation (Jesus Christ), the walls (Christians), the windows (light via the Word of God), the roof (the protection of God's Holy Spirit).

Remind the class, "The church is not the building, but rather the people committed to Jesus Christ, who worship in the building dedicated for that purpose. Ask, "What is the one thing that holds the church together?" The key is the power and providence of God and the relationship between the members. Ask, "What is the 'glue' that solidifies the church in relationship?" The Bible identifies the relationship as love for one another. This is a key to good relationships and for an effective church. Ask, "How is this different from the 'glue' of the Israelites?"

Let's Talk It Over

The questions on this page are designed to promote discussion of the lesson by the class and to encourage application of the lesson Scriptures. The answers provided are only discussion starters. Let your class talk it over from there.

1. We often forget the many ways that God has blessed us. What are some things we need to do to remember what God has done for us? Why is this important?

A secular culture teaches us that we are self-sufficient. When things go well and we have success (whether financially, educationally, in business, or any other area) it's easy to feel that we have accomplished these goals on our own. But truly grateful servants of God realize that our Father is the source of all goodness (James 1:17).

We can remember our giving Father in many ways. Prayer at meals is one example. It has been said that if you have a roof over your head, one change of clothing, food in the refrigerator, and twenty dollars in your pocket, then you are more blessed than 80 percent of the people in the world. Truly we are blessed!

2. The people of God seem to forget rather quickly God's gracious leading in the past. Why is this, and what can we do to keep in remembrance the leading of God?

Always "looking forward" without stopping to take an inventory of the past leads to a failure to remember God. It destroys spiritual discernment. When Jesus healed ten lepers, only one took time to come back and give Him thanks (Luke 17:11-19). In celebrating their new status they apparently forgot the past life of leprosy and the One who had cleansed them.

Remembering the past (but not "living in" it) is essential for being able to give God the glory for His leading. Brainstorm some ways to do this.

3. God does not show preference toward one group of people over another. How should this attitude of God affect how we view others?

Each generation seems to have its own sources of prejudice or unhealthy pride. The early church was no exception. Paul confronted Peter because of the prejudice he displayed against Gentiles (Galatians 2:11-13). This was after God already had revealed to Peter that no one was to be considered unclean (Acts 10:9-15)! See also Galatians 3:28.

When it comes to accepting others into our local churches, it is imperative to have the heart of God. No distinctions based on appearance, status, race, background, nationality, or gender can be permitted or tolerated. See James 2:1-9.

4. All of the covenants that God established with Abraham, with Moses and the nation of Israel, and with David find their ultimate fulfillment in the new covenant that God made in Christ (Acts 13:32, 33). How does the significance of God's new covenant affect you today?

The foundation to any answer we can give is the realization that we have eternal life only within and because of the new covenant. God established this covenant relationship with His people (the church) through the shedding of the blood of His Son. Another important foundation to grasp is that God takes the making and breaking of covenants very seriously.

Being included in God's new covenant has many implications. For one, we are to live lives of holiness (1 Peter 1:15, 16). For another, Christians are not to enter into covenant relationships with non-Christians (2 Corinthians 6:14-16). This includes business and marriage relationships. Encourage your learners to give other examples of how Christians can take these general principles and apply them to specific situations.

5. When salvation was offered on the Day of Pentecost, it was stated that this covenant would continue into future generations (Acts 2:39). How can our church be sure that the covenant that God established continues on to our children and to all who "are afar off"?

Just before Jesus ascended into Heaven, He commissioned His followers to be His witnesses in Jerusalem, Judea, Samaria, and to "the uttermost part of the earth" (Acts 1:8). Often when Christians think of this commission they focus on "the uttermost part of the earth" and forget their own Jerusalem—that is, their own city, neighborhood, and family. They forget their own Samaria, which includes crossing racial and ethnic lines with the gospel.

To make sure that all have access to the new covenant, we need to reach out to everyone with the gospel message. Training members in lifestyle evangelism and beginning a strong prayer outreach ministry are effective ways to begin to reach a local community with the gospel.

In addition, a genuine concern for "the uttermost part of the earth" is needed. You can also encourage members of your church to take part in short-term mission trips to see the need firsthand.

Creating a New Dynasty

DEVOTIONAL READING: 2 Samuel 7:10-17.

BACKGROUND SCRIPTURE: 2 Samuel 7.

PRINTED TEXT: 2 Samuel 7:18-29.

2 Samuel 7:18-29

18 Then went king David in, and sat before the LORD, and he said, Who am I, O Lord GOD? and what is my house, that thou hast brought me hitherto?

19 And this was yet a small thing in thy sight, O Lord GOD; but thou hast spoken also of thy servant's house for a great while to come. And is this the manner of man, O Lord GOD?

20 And what can David say more unto thee? for thou, Lord GOD, knowest thy servant.

21 For thy word's sake, and according to thine own heart, hast thou done all these great things, to make thy servant know them.

22 Wherefore thou art great, O LORD God: for there is none like thee, neither is there any God besides thee, according to all that we have heard with our ears.

23 And what one nation in the earth is like thy people, even like Israel, whom God went to redeem for a people to himself, and to make him a name, and to do for you great things and terrible, for thy land, before thy people, which thou redeemedst to thee from Egypt, from the nations and their gods?

24 For thou hast confirmed to thyself thy people Israel to be a people unto thee for ever: and thou, LORD, art become their God.

25 And now, O LORD God, the word that thou hast spoken concerning thy servant, and concerning his house, establish it for ever, and do as thou hast said.

26 And let thy name be magnified for ever, saying, The LORD of hosts is the God over Israel: and let the house of thy servant David be established before thee.

27 For thou, O LORD of hosts, God of Israel, hast revealed to thy servant, saying, I will build thee a house: therefore hath thy servant found in his heart to pray this prayer unto thee.

28 And now, O Lord GOD, thou art that God, and thy words be true, and thou hast promised this goodness unto thy servant:

29 Therefore now let it please thee to bless the house of thy servant, that it may continue for ever before thee: for thou, O Lord GOD, hast spoken it: and with thy blessing let the house of thy servant be blessed for ever.

GOLDEN TEXT: Thine house and thy kingdom shall be established for ever before thee: thy throne shall be established for ever.—2 Samuel 7:16.

The God of Continuing Creation
Unit 2: God's Creativity Continues
(Lessons 5-9)

Lesson Aims

After participating in this lesson, each student will be able to:

1. Describe, using David's prayer, the blessings that God had bestowed on David and his people.

2. Explain how one's relationship with God can affect future generations.

3. Evaluate the effect of his or her life on others in the family.

Lesson Outline

Introduction

A. Rises and Falls

Sports fans seem to be always on the alert for the next "dynasty" to come along. Just a passing mention of the Green Bay Packers of the 1960s, the Pittsburgh Steelers of the 1970s, the San Francisco 49ers of the 1980s, or the Dallas Cowboys of the 1990s is guaranteed to start a conversation with someone who follows professional football closely. The existence of dynasties—whether in sports, politics, or business—causes us to envy, to admire, or to grimace in distaste.

The collapse of a dynasty can cause us to mourn or to breathe a sigh of relief, depending on our viewpoint. And human dynasties do in-deed tend to collapse and disappear over time! In 1982 *Forbes* magazine began its annual list of the four hundred wealthiest Americans. By 2002, just twenty years later, only sixty-four (or 16 percent) of the original "Forbes 400" remained on the list.

The ancient dynasty of King David is unique, however. Just before today's text begins, Scripture notes that the Lord had promised that David's throne would be established forever (2 Samuel 7:13, 16). But before we consider what all this means, we need a brief review of how history has moved in the three hundred or so years since we saw the Israelites camped on the border of the promised land in last week's lesson.

B. Lesson Background

After the death of Moses, Joshua led the Israelites across the Jordan River into the promised land and into conflict. This conflict continued for years. When the men of Israel had as much land as they thought they needed, they disbanded the army and settled down to peacetime living. All this and more is recorded in the book of Joshua.

Grateful to God for His help in their campaign, and guided by the strong hand of Joshua, the people were loyal to the Lord for years. But then Joshua passed away at the age of one hundred and ten (Joshua 24:29; Judges 2:8). One by one the leaders associated with him passed away as well. Israel became a nation of people with no personal remembrance of the miracles that had given birth to the nation and had brought it to independence and prosperity (Judges 2:10).

Then a common human tendency set in: a tendency to drift away from God. His law was still the law of the land; but there was no strong national government to enforce it, and local enforcement was feeble or absent. Lying, cheating, and stealing increased, followed by mayhem and murder.

When Israel's sin became intolerable in the sight of God, punishment followed. God allowed pagan bands to invade the land, driving off livestock, stealing the grain of harvest, and killing anyone who got in the way. Now unarmed and unorganized, Israel was helpless.

In poverty and misery, Israel had enough memory of God to realize what was wrong. The people stopped their wickedness and begged God for help. God responded by raising up among them talented leaders who rallied them to defeat the oppressors and drive them away. So peace returned, and prosperity followed.

For about three hundred years that cycle was repeated over and over: prosperity was followed by sin, sin by punishment, punishment by re-pentance, and repentance by renewed prosperity. This is told briefly in Judges 2:6-19 and recorded in detail in the rest of that book.

Samuel was one of the greatest of Israel's judges. After freeing the country from oppressors, he established a circuit court to administer justice (1 Samuel 7:16). His decisions were respected, for they were according to the law. When Samuel was old, he appointed his two sons to be judges as well. Those young men turned out to be evil. Leading men of Israel could see that when Samuel died, justice would be dead, too. So they asked Samuel to appoint a king for Israel. Neither God nor Samuel was pleased with that idea, but God said to let the people have their way (1 Samuel 8:6-9).

As a result, Saul became the first king. He started his reign in a splendid way, but later became arrogant and disobedient to God. God rejected him and then sent Samuel to anoint David to be king (1 Samuel 9–15). When Saul ended his own life in battle, David took the throne (1 Samuel 31; 2 Samuel 5). [See question #1, page 48.]

Instead of letting David build a house for Him, God said He would build for David a house—that is, a household, a family, a ruling dynasty. God said that people of David's family would continue to rule forever if they kept God's law (1 Chronicles 28:7). To that message David responded with the prayer we have taken for the text of this lesson.

I. The King and His Lord (2 Samuel 7:18-22)

If David is disappointed because he is not allowed to build the temple, his disappointment is lost in the grandeur of what God has done for him. Greater still is the grandeur of what God promises to do in the future.

A. Modest King (vv. 18-20)

18. Then went king David in, and sat before the LORD, and he said, Who am I, O Lord GOD? and what is my house, that thou hast brought me hitherto?

The year is roughly 1000 B.C. The phrase *then went king David in, and sat before the Lord* probably means that David is sitting before the ark of the covenant inside a tent (2 Samuel 6:17).

Over the course of the years, God has transformed David from being a young shepherd of the fields into being the king of a great nation. What was there in that shepherd to merit such a transformation? Certainly his family had not been prominent, influential, or wealthy enough to make their boy a king.

As a matter of fact, David himself had much to do with his own advancement. As a shepherd he showed daring and strength in hand-to-paw combat with wild animals (1 Samuel 17:34-37). He showed like courage and skill in his conflict with Goliath, the Philistine giant who intimidated the whole army of Israel (1 Samuel 17).

David also showed restraint and respect for authority when he spared the life of King Saul when the king was trying to kill him (1 Samuel 24, 26). As an officer in Saul's army, David was so successful in war that he became a national hero (1 Samuel 18:5-7). David seems to be a natural leader. But this modest king gives all the credit to *God.* [See question #2, page 48.]

19. And this was yet a small thing in thy sight, O Lord GOD; but thou hast spoken also of thy servant's house for a great while to come. And is this the manner of man, O Lord GOD?

Most of us may think making a king out of a shepherd is a pretty big thing. But David recognizes that this is *a small thing* compared with what God intends to do next: God promises that David's descendants will continue to rule *for a great while to come,* in fact, "for ever" (vv. 16, 29).

In the Hebrew, the line *and is this the manner of man, O Lord God?* is a puzzle to translators. Perhaps it means something like, "Is this the usual way you deal with people, O Lord God?" If this idea is correct, then David's rhetorical question is intended to express amazement.

20. And what can David say more unto thee? for thou, Lord GOD, knowest thy servant.

The *Lord God* knows David—knows what is in his mind and heart. Actually, there is no need for David to go on expressing his humble gratitude for the great things the Lord has done because the Lord knows David's heart thoroughly. Still, David cannot refrain from praising the Doer of those great things, as we see in the next verses.

How to Say It

ABRAHAM. *Ay*-bruh-ham.
DEUTERONOMY. Due-ter-*ahn*-uh-me.
EGYPT. *Ee*-jipt.
GOLIATH. Go-*lye*-uth.
GUYANA. Guy-*ah*-nuh.
ISRAEL. *Iz*-ray-el.
JEREMIAH. Jair-uh-*my*-uh.
JOSHUA. *Josh*-yew-uh.
MOSES. *Mo*-zes or *Mo*-zez.
NATHAN. *Nay*-thun (th as in *thin*).
NEHEMIAH. *Nee*-huh-*my*-uh (strong accent on *my*).
PHILISTINE. Fuh-*liss*-teens or *Fill*-us-teen.
UR. Er.

GRACE TO THE HUMBLE; DEATH TO THE PROUD

Jim Jones was a man who rose from obscurity to a position of influence over other people. Fame and power turned his head and heart, and evil took over his life. Jones ministered to a church in a poorer area of San Francisco. That church was meeting the needs of the people in a significant way. However, in 1977 reports of physical and sexual abuse came to the attention of civic authorities.

Jones ordered his church members to go with him to Jonestown, his jungle compound in Guyana, where he could continue to control their lives. Continuing reports of abuse prompted Congressman Leo Ryan and several reporters to fly to Jonestown. On November 18, 1978, the day they were to return to the United States, Ryan and three reporters were murdered. That same day more than nine hundred people in the cult were either killed or committed suicide by drinking a poisoned beverage. Jones was found shot to death, perhaps a suicide.

David also came from a humble background. It is true that he succumbed at one point to the lust connected with power, an all too common occurrence. But David had a penitent heart, and God promised him a dynasty that exists today, with Jesus, His Son, still reigning. If we are wise, we will heed the striking difference between David and the Jim Joneses of the world. God gives grace to those who remain humble (Proverbs 3:34).

—C. R. B.

B. Glorious Lord (vv. 21, 22)

21. For thy word's sake, and according to thine own heart, hast thou done all these great things, to make thy servant know them.

David's modesty is still evident. He knows God had done *great things* to make him king. (See also the parallel version of this passage in 1 Chronicles 17:16-27, as well as David's praise in Psalm 145:6.) [See question #3, page 48.] It is God who has decreed David to be a ruler (1 Samuel 16:1-13).

For the *sake* of God's own Word, the Lord has done all that is needed to bring this kingship about. David adds that what God has done is according to God's *own heart*—it is just what God wanted to do. God did not do it reluctantly, as when He gave in to the people's request for a king in the first place (1 Samuel 8:7, 22).

The phrase *to make thy servant know them* is part of David's acknowledgment that there is no guesswork about how all this has come to be. The evidence is clear: God's hand is behind everything. Realizing that, David will try very hard to make sure that God is not disappointed with his kingship.

22. Wherefore thou art great, O LORD God: for there is none like thee, neither is there any God besides thee, according to all that we have heard with our ears.

The great things that *God* has done are proof that God himself is *great*. Not only is there no other God *like* Him, there is no other God *besides* Him. He is the one and only real and living God. When David reflects on *all that we have heard with our ears*, he is undoubtedly thinking about God's mighty acts in Israel's history, as passed from generation to generation.

II. The Lord and His Nation (2 Samuel 7:23, 24)

Thinking about the greatness of God leads to thinking about the greatness of the nation that God claims as His own. God has chosen that populous nation to emerge from only two people, namely Abraham and his wife.

God had taken those two away from the moon worshipers in Ur and planted them in the very land where David is now king. God has given that growing nation His providential and miraculous care through centuries, and now its people number in the millions.

A. The Redeemed Nation (v. 23)

23. And what one nation in the earth is like thy people, even like Israel, whom God went to redeem for a people to himself, and to make him a name, and to do for you great things and terrible, for thy land, before thy people, which thou redeemedst to thee from Egypt, from the nations and their gods?

God is incomparable: there is no other like Him. Likewise, His *nation* is incomparable: there is not another like it. When it fell into slavery in Egypt, God did not abandon it. He rescued it *from Egypt*, protected it from other nations, and took it back to the promised land where He had first taken Abraham. The "redemption" of God's people is an important Old Testament theme (see Deuteronomy 7:8; 9:26; 13:5; 15:15; 21:8; 24:18; Nehemiah 1:10; and Jeremiah 31:11).

Just previously in 2 Samuel 7:9, the Lord had promised that David's name would be great. Now, in abject humility, David recognizes the greatness of the Lord's *name*. By His mighty acts, God has made for Himself that name through having a reputation for possessing irresistible power. The *great* and *terrible* things that the Lord has done include, of course, the ten plagues in *Egypt* and the defeat of pagan nations in the promised land. Israel is not the biggest of nations or the richest, but it is God's own nation. It is ruled by David, the king of God's own choosing.

MANIFEST DESTINY

In 1845 journalist John L. O'Sullivan coined the phrase *manifest destiny* to describe a concept that has existed throughout history. From time immemorial kings who wished to expand their borders claimed it to be God's will (or the will of the gods, as the case may be). In Western civilization—from the Crusades of the Middle Ages (with their motto *deus lo vult* or "God wills it"), to the great empires of Europe of the sixteenth through the nineteenth centuries (Portugal, Spain, and England)—it was the same.

In the nineteenth and twentieth centuries—and this is what O'Sullivan was referring to—the United States developed this same sense that God had destined its expansion from the Atlantic to the Pacific. As many see it, manifest destiny *created* American history.

David saw the same principle at work in ancient Israel, but with this vital difference: through miraculous events there was *no doubt* that God indeed had played an active and intimate role in the history of Israel, His own people under the old covenant. It was a unique role in all of human history. Occurring in one era and in one place, it is a role never to be repeated with any other nation.

Today, God has covenant people in every nation. They are called Christians. Manifest destiny now calls for the continuous expansion of Christ's realm until He returns.   —C. R. B.

B. The Confirmed Nation (v. 24)

24. For thou hast confirmed to thyself thy people Israel to be a people unto thee for ever: and thou, LORD, art become their God.

Israel is God's nation because He is the One who created it. The one who creates is the one who has ownership rights! God *confirmed* that ownership by redeeming Israel from Egypt, by defending it against other countries, by giving it the promised land, and by making David its king.

III. Prayer for the Future
(2 Samuel 7:25-29)

The first verse of our printed text begins, "Then went King David in, and sat before the Lord." All the rest of the text records what David said to the Lord. Now we come to the part of his prayer that makes requests for the future. It is notable that this modest king asks only for what God already has promised. Truly David is a man after God's own heart (1 Samuel 13:13, 14).

A. For David's House (v. 25)

25. And now, O LORD God, the word that thou hast spoken concerning thy servant, and con-

cerning his house, establish it for ever, and do as thou hast said.

See God's promise in verse 16 of this chapter. David is now asking God to keep that promise, to *do as* He has *said* He will do.

This means that David's kingdom will be established and his descendants will continue to rule. That certainly is pleasing to David, but also of great concern is God's reputation, as the next verse shows.

B. For God's Name (v. 26)

26. And let thy name be magnified for ever, saying, The LORD of hosts is the God over Israel: and let the house of thy servant David be established before thee.

Again the glory of God's *name* and the glory of David's *house* are tied together. Again *David* gives first place to the glory of God's name. In verses 25-29 of this prayer, David refers to himself as *servant* seven times.

C. Revelation and Prayer (v. 27)

27. For thou, O LORD of hosts, God of Israel, hast revealed to thy servant, saying, I will build thee a house: therefore hath thy servant found in his heart to pray this prayer unto thee.

Countless nations have risen and fallen; some have been forgotten. Countless dynasties have had their years of power and have ceased to be. Is it presumptuous and arrogant for the king of Israel to pray that his own dynasty might rule forever? It could be, if eternal rule is the king's own idea.

To this king, however, the Lord Himself has already *revealed* that this dynasty will continue forever. The grateful king is only saying, "*O Lord of hosts,* Your will be done." As we labor in God's everlasting kingdom, may we say the same thing.

Home Daily Bible Readings

Monday, Sept. 27—God's Steadfast Love Is Great (Psalm 86:8-13)

Tuesday, Sept. 28—David Moves the Ark of God (2 Samuel 6:1-5)

Wednesday, Sept. 29—David Brings the Ark to Jerusalem (2 Samuel 6:11-15)

Thursday, Sept. 30—God Sends a Message to David (2 Samuel 7:1-9)

Friday, Oct. 1—God Makes a Covenant With David (2 Samuel 7:10-17)

Saturday, Oct. 2—David Prays to God (2 Samuel 7:18-22)

Sunday, Oct. 3—David Seeks God's Blessing (2 Samuel 7:23-29)

D. Promise and Plea (vv. 28, 29)

28. And now, O Lord GOD, thou art that God, and thy words be true, and thou hast promised this goodness unto thy servant.

The phrase *thou art that God* seems intended to emphasize David's belief that the God to whom he prays is the one and only true God. There is no other god. What God says is true because there is no other god to contradict Him.

And what *goodness* has the truthful God promised to David? He has promised David a house—not a building of stone, but a household, a family. And God has promised that men of that family will continue to rule among God's people forever (2 Samuel 7:12-16). [See question #4, page 48.]

29. Therefore now let it please thee to bless the house of thy servant, that it may continue for ever before thee: for thou, O Lord GOD, hast spoken it: and with thy blessing let the house of thy servant be blessed for ever.

Again we hear David asking God only to do what God already has promised to do. But if God is going to do what David knows that God will do, whether or not David asks for it, then is this request merely a waste of words? Far from it! With this request David is expressing his submission to God and gratitude for what God is going to do.

As he prays, does David understand that the last and greatest of his ruling descendants will be the Son of God as well as a son of David? Does David realize that there will be one King eternal, the crucified Savior, risen to die no more, enthroned at the right hand of God in Heaven? Probably not.

Perhaps instead King David envisions a long line of his descendants, one by one enthroned in

Visual for lessons 5 and 10

This visual can be a discussion starter for the question, "How is Jesus 'the fulfillment'?"

Jerusalem and ruling the nation of Israel from that day forward, as long as they "be constant to do my commandments" (again, 1 Chronicles 28:7). But on the other hand, we know the Spirit of the Lord is with David (1 Samuel 16:13). Perhaps the Spirit has revealed to David far more than he learned from God's message spoken by Nathan in 2 Samuel 7:5-16.

Whether David knew it or not, today we certainly know that the King eternal is the crucified Savior who gave His life to redeem us. No less than David, we can be grateful for the providence of the God who invites us to live eternally. [See question #5, page 48.]

Conclusion

A. Modesty and Duty

David could have claimed credit for his rise to the throne, for all the reasons listed in the discussion of verse 18. But David chose to give all the credit to God. God had chosen him to be king; God had sent the prophet to anoint him; God had arranged the circumstances and events that had contributed to his rise.

David's modesty has appeared plainly in this lesson, and certainly it was part of the attraction of this Biblical hero. He was a doer, not a boaster. Even so, he did not carry his modesty to a counterproductive extreme. It seems that he graciously accepted the plaudits of a multitude in victory celebration. He did not mar the joy of the occasion by frowning or shrinking away, even though King Saul was obviously annoyed (1 Samuel 18:8).

Our challenge is to have the same balance. To be a "glory grabber" in the church is distasteful and ungodly; it is a violation of Romans 12:3. Christ is our model of humility (Mark 10:45). Even so, there is also such a thing as being overly modest. We see this problem arise in people who have skills and talents but pretend that they don't. This is false humility. May God deliver us from both extremes.

B. Prayer

Heavenly Father, we are grateful for the example set before us by Your noble people, ancient and modern. Along with the precepts of Your Word, their godly lives guide us in godly ways. And if we see in their lives some things less than godly, may we realize that these too are for our learning. By Your grace may we be led in ways that are right, and by Your grace may our sins be forgiven. In Jesus' name, amen.

C. Thought to Remember

Choose a good example, and make it better.

Learning by Doing

This page contains an alternative lesson plan emphasizing learning activities.
Classes desiring such student involvement will find these suggestions helpful.

Learning Goals

After participating in this lesson, each student will be able to:

1. Describe, using David's prayer, the blessings that God had bestowed on David and his people.

2. Explain how one's relationship with God can affect future generations.

3. Evaluate the effect of his or her life on others in the family.

Into the Lesson

During the week ask four people to prepare a short synopsis of a portion of the historical review in the lesson commentary. Give or send each student a copy of the appropriate page of the commentary. Also prepare a visual with the following outline points, that you will uncover or write in as each person reports.

FROM MOSES TO DAVID

A. Taking the Promised Land

B. Backsliding and Repentance

C. Becoming a Monarchy

D. David the King

Ask, "For what would you like to be remembered after you die?" Ask the class to jot down answers. They can share these with two or three people or with the entire class.

After the reports have been given, make the transition to Bible study by telling the class, "King David wished to build a house or temple for God. But God said that He would build David a house—that is, a household or family that would rule forever. David's response is today's text. It is a prayer that reveals how God would create a whole new dynasty that would change the world forever.

"We'll learn something about how to live as we see how God worked in David's life."

Into the Word

Hang signs from the ceiling, each with one of the following headings: "David's Prominent Descendants," "The Modest King," "A Redeemed Nation," "Praying for the Future." The signs should be separated enough for small groups to gather under. Add duplicate signs for larger classes. Ask class members to choose one and to move under that sign. Give the following assignments, poster board, and markers to each group.

David's Prominent Descendants: Read 2 Samuel 7:11b-16. (1) Where do you see a promise of Solomon in this passage? A promise of Jesus? (2) Also read Matthew 1:1-17 and tell how Jesus, the Messiah, is the Son of David. List your answers on the poster board.

The Modest King: Read 2 Samuel 7:18-29, then focus on verses 18-21. (1) As David looks back, for what would he be thankful about God's work in his personal life? (2) What does this text imply about how God works in everyday life? List answers on the poster board.

A Redeemed Nation: Read 2 Samuel 7:18-29. Now focus on verses 22-24. (1) Make a list of the special, and sometimes miraculous, ways God worked in Israel's history. (2) Discuss and list lessons any nation should learn from how God worked in the nation of Israel.

Praying for the Future: Read 2 Samuel 18-29. Focus on verses 25-29 and write answers to the following: (1) Why do you think David asks God to do what God already has promised to do? What does this say about David's heart? (2) List David's requests from God (see verses 25, 26, 29). (3) Would David have any idea that the last of his ruling descendants would be the Son of God as well as a son of David?

Ask the groups to report their conclusions.

Into Life

Bring the group back together. Prepare the following instructions and questions on paper. Use the following heading: "Stick-Man Art and Application." Instructions include "Draw stick art to represent how you would answer or apply the following assignments":

1. David was a great man in history. Using him as an example, illustrate how one's relationship with God can affect future generations.

2. We live in an uncertain world. What assurance about God's dynasty or kingdom do we find in David's prayer? Illustrate with stick art.

3. Thankfulness is an important element in human relationships with God. Sketch one thing for which you are especially thankful to God.

4. Use stick art or a word picture to answer the following. For what would you like to be most remembered when you die? What would you like on your tombstone to represent your values or your contribution to society? (A similar activity is in the student book activity page.)

Ask people to share their answers with one person and to pray together for each other.

Let's Talk It Over

The questions on this page are designed to promote discussion of the lesson by the class and to encourage application of the lesson Scriptures. The answers provided are only discussion starters. Let your class talk it over from there.

1. The path Saul took is, unfortunately, the same that many others take as well. Why do some leaders who begin well seem to finish so poorly? How can we help them avoid failure?

Many who rise to places of leadership do so because they have demonstrated certain qualities. But sometimes these folks place more confidence in themselves than in the power and ability of God.

We must remember that the world makes judgments based on external things, but we should guard against having this type of thinking leak over into the church. Someone might say, "Joe would be a good elder for our church because he's a proven leader in his company." Scripture reminds us, however, that God looks on the heart (1 Samuel 16:7). We would do well to do the same, to the greatest extent that we can, when we evaluate the qualities and qualifications of potential church leaders. This can help us minimize the possibility of leadership failure in the church. We must also pray for our leaders!

2. David knew that in and of himself he did not deserve to be king. Why do you think that God chooses to use those whom the world often sees as weak to accomplish His purposes? How should this affect our own thinking?

God intends that His name be glorified above all else. God does not desire to use people who feel adequate of their own strength, but those who recognize that it is by God's power that success is achieved. (See Zechariah 4:6.)

Just as God chose the weak things to advance His cause in the past, so the church today should do the same. Are there people who are being overlooked for ministry in our church because we consider them weak in some way? Let us make sure we don't overlook their potential for service! (See 1 Corinthians 1:26-29.)

3. Often we take for granted so much of what God has done in us and through us and for us. Why are we so quick to forget the great things God has done? How can we make sure we remember these great things?

In the hectic pace at which we live, we no longer finish one task or project before we begin another. But as a *Wall Street Journal* article of February 27, 2003, noted, such "multitasking" (trying to manage two or more mental tasks at once) ends up making us "stupid." Multitasking doesn't allow time for reflection. This is one problem that can pull us away from remembering that it really is God who has done the great thing, not we ourselves.

Remembering the great things that God has done in your life will help you overcome fear and face trials. Now could be a good time to recall some of the great things God has done for you and for your church—things that prepare you to face tomorrow.

4. God made promises to His people because He placed His trust in people to seek His face. We in turn make promises to God because of the faith we have in Him. How can we make promises—to God and to others—that we can keep?

To make a promise requires carefully thinking through the situation in advance. In the final analysis, a promise is a covenant. When promises are made, there should be benefits to both parties in the promise (covenant) relationship.

Consider some promises you have made to God and to others. How are you doing at keeping these promises? Is there a need for repentance in this area? What can you do to renew promises that you may have broken? Promises are not made to be broken once things do not go our way.

5. As Christians we often pray for God's blessing upon our lives and our church. How can we play a part in the answer to this prayer?

For God to bless, we must put ourselves into a position that God *can* bless. If we pray for God to bless us financially yet we refuse to be good stewards as Scripture teaches us, how can we expect God to honor our prayer and grant that blessing? We sometimes pray a prayer for forgiveness, yet will not forgive one who has sinned against us. Jesus teaches that this is a prayer God will not honor (Matthew 6:15).

To be blessed by God means that we must do those things that God blesses. In your life and in your church, look and see what God is already blessing and doing, then get involved with Him in His work and pray for His continued blessing in that work. Surely this is a prayer that God will bless.

Creating a Redeemed People

October 10
Lesson 6

DEVOTIONAL READING: Isaiah 42:5-13.

BACKGROUND SCRIPTURE: Isaiah 43.

PRINTED TEXT: Isaiah 43:1-3a, 10-19.

Isaiah 43:1-3a, 10-19

1 But now thus saith the LORD that created thee, O Jacob, and he that formed thee, O Israel, Fear not: for I have redeemed thee, I have called thee by thy name; thou art mine.

2 When thou passest through the waters, I will be with thee; and through the rivers, they shall not overflow thee: when thou walkest through the fire, thou shalt not be burned; neither shall the flame kindle upon thee.

3a For I am the LORD thy God, the Holy One of Israel, thy Saviour.

· · · · · · · · · · · · ·

10 Ye are my witnesses, saith the LORD, and my servant whom I have chosen; that ye may know and believe me, and understand that I am he: before me there was no God formed, neither shall there be after me.

11 I, even I, am the LORD; and beside me there is no saviour.

12 I have declared, and have saved, and I have showed, when there was no strange god among you: therefore ye are my witnesses, saith the LORD, that I am God.

13 Yea, before the day was I am he; and there is none that can deliver out of my hand: I will work, and who shall let it?

14 Thus saith the LORD, your Redeemer, the Holy One of Israel; For your sake I have sent to Babylon, and have brought down all their nobles, and the Chaldeans, whose cry is in the ships.

15 I am the LORD, your Holy One, the Creator of Israel, your King.

16 Thus saith the LORD, which maketh a way in the sea, and a path in the mighty waters;

17 Which bringeth forth the chariot and horse, the army and the power; they shall lie down together, they shall not rise: they are extinct, they are quenched as tow.

18 Remember ye not the former things, neither consider the things of old.

19 Behold, I will do a new thing; now it shall spring forth; shall ye not know it? I will even make a way in the wilderness, and rivers in the desert.

GOLDEN TEXT: Fear not: for I have redeemed thee, I have called thee by thy name; thou art mine.—Isaiah 43:1.

The God of Continuing Creation
Unit 2: God's Creativity Continues
(Lessons 5-9)

Lesson Aims

After participating in this lesson, each student will be able to:

1. Recall some great nationwide movements that God predicted through Isaiah.

2. Understand what caused Israel's disaster and what caused its recovery.

3. Trust God and obey Him.

Lesson Outline

INTRODUCTION
  A. "Twice Mine!"
  B. Lesson Background
 I. PRESERVATION BY GOD (Isaiah 43:1-3a)
  A. Reassurance (v. 1)
     What's in a Name?
  B. Safety (v. 2)
  C. Identity (v. 3a)
 II. WITNESSES FOR GOD (Isaiah 43:10-13)
  A. Servants Who Know (vv. 10, 11)
  B. Evidence That Proves (v. 12)
  C. God Who Is (v. 13)
III. WORK OF GOD (Isaiah 43:14-19)
  A. The Doom of Babylon (v. 14)
  B. The Lord and His Power (vv. 15-17)
  C. The Coming New Thing (vv. 18, 19)
     What God Is Doing Now
CONCLUSION
  A. Trust and Obey
  B. Thought to Remember

Introduction

A. "Twice Mine!"

Jimmy's favorite toy was a little boat that he made himself. It started with a piece of driftwood that he found by the river. In Dad's workshop he put it in the vise and used chisels to hollow it out. In the little reflecting pool in Mom's garden, the little boat floated neatly, right side up. Jimmy fitted it with mast and sail. He brought the big fan from Dad's workshop, and it blew the boat all the way across the pool.

When the family had a picnic in the park by the river, Jimmy's boat went along. But there was no fan to make it go in the little pool there, so Jimmy took it down to the river itself. Near the bank the water was only a few inches deep and

moving slowly. The little boat rode sedately down the stream for a hundred feet.

Then Jimmy peeled off his shoes and socks and waded in to get his boat for another trip. This time he let it go a little farther downstream. There a log in the edge of the water turned the current away from the bank. Before Jimmy realized what was happening, his boat was out in deep water and moving swiftly. Poor Jimmy! He could only watch the river carry his favorite toy out of sight.

The family went to town some time later. Mom liked to stop at the little store where the sign said, "Antiques and Oddities." There among other oddities Jimmy saw his little boat.

"Look, Dad," he said. "That's my boat!"

"Not anymore," Dad informed him. "Now it belongs to whoever got it out of the river."

The owner of the store was listening nearby. Jimmy asked him, "How much is the little boat?"

The man rubbed his chin thoughtfully. "I guess I'd have to have a quarter for that."

So Jimmy paid a quarter and went home with his favorite toy. He hugged it tight before he put it in the reflecting pool. "Now you're twice mine," he told it. "You're mine because I made you and you're mine because I bought you."

This week we read about a nation that was like Jimmy's little boat. It belonged to God twice: first because God made it, and then because God bought it. We read about this nation in the book of Isaiah.

B. Lesson Background

As we open today's study from Isaiah 43, time has moved forward more than three hundred years since last week's lesson about King David. Various kings have come and gone, the nation of Israel sadly has split herself into two parts. The Jewish people have been through various cycles of sin and repentance.

The opening verse of the book of Isaiah tells us that what follows is a record of "the vision of Isaiah the son of Amoz, which he saw concerning Judah and Jerusalem in the days of Uzziah, Jotham, Ahaz, and Hezekiah, kings of Judah." History gives good reports of three of these kings, but Ahaz "did not that which was right in the sight of the Lord his God" (2 Kings 16:2). It is hard to be certain about many dates in Old Testament history, but we shall not be far off if we say that these four kings ruled from 790 to 695 B.C., or about ninety-five years altogether.

In chapter 39 of Isaiah we read a little of what Isaiah said to King Hezekiah. Very plainly the prophet foretold captivity in Babylon, which would begin about a century later (Isaiah 39:5-7). Then chapter 40 begins what some students call

"The Book of Comfort." Clearly it promises the pardon of sinful Israel and the end of the punishing captivity (40:2). Less clear is the prophecy of John the Baptist (40:3), but its meaning is revealed when it is fulfilled (Matthew 3:1-3). To comfort the captives there is much more about the limitless power of God and His unfailing care for His people. Our text is part of it.

For the immediate background of the first part of our text, the last two verses of Isaiah 42 tell us that Israel's troubles were punishment imposed by the Lord because of Israel's sins. In Isaiah's own time the northern nation of Israel was defeated, and its people were scattered in foreign lands (2 Kings 17:5, 6). Isaiah foretold the captivity of Judah, the southern nation (Isaiah 39:5-7). Both of these disasters are punishment for the long-continued sins of the Jewish people.

Just so we don't get too confused by terminology, we should point out that sometimes the word *Israel* in the book of Isaiah means only the northern kingdom of that name, as distinct from the southern kingdom of *Judah*. At other times, however, the word *Israel* refers to all the Jewish people in both northern and southern kingdoms together. The context will tell us what is meant at any one time. We also do well to remember that a prophet's vision is not a meaningless dream; it is God's revelation.

I. Preservation by God (Isaiah 43:1-3a)

The last verses of Isaiah 42 speak of the fury of God's anger, of the scattering of north Israel, of the coming captivity of Judah. Why, then, does anyone call this part of Isaiah "the Book of Comfort"? Read on! Even in His anger the Lord is merciful and gracious. Israel will not be wiped out.

A. Reassurance (v. 1)

1. But now thus saith the LORD that created thee, O Jacob, and he that formed thee, O Israel, Fear not: for I have redeemed thee, I have called thee by thy name; thou art mine.

The opening words *but now* create a link with chapter 42, but also signal a sharp contrast between what goes before and what follows. Isaiah 42:25 speaks of furious anger and punishment, but we read of these no more. An opposite message is given, and notice how emphatic it is.

First, the Lord identifies Himself as the Creator. He stresses that announcement by repeating it in different words after the fashion of Hebrew poetry. Notice that the statement *the Lord that created thee, O Jacob* is really the same as *he that formed thee, O Israel*. The names *Jacob* and *Israel* are two designations of the same man (Genesis

How to Say It

AHAZ. *Ay*-haz.
AMOZ. *Ay*-mahz.
BABYLON. *Bab*-uh-lun.
CHALDEANS. Kal-*dee*-unz.
CYRUS. *Sigh*-russ.
HEZEKIAH. Hez-ih-*kye*-uh.
ISAIAH. Eye-*zay*-uh.
ISRAEL. *Iz*-ray-el.
JORDAN. *Jor*-dun.
JOTHAM. *Jo*-thum.
JUDAH. *Joo*-duh.
UZZIAH. Uh-*zye*-uh.

32:28). In our text they are two names of the same nation, the nation descended from that one man. The words *created* and *formed* are synonyms, so the declaration that the Lord is the Creator is repeated with simplicity and power.

Next comes the substance of God's message: *Fear not*. These two words stand alone, clear and bright as a trumpet call. (See also v. 5, not in today's text.)

Then God explains why Israel should not fear. He makes that emphatic by heaping up three reasons, different but related. First, *I have redeemed thee*. The Lord owned Israel because He created her. But Israel had been captured and enslaved by her own sin. So the Lord *redeemed* her, or bought her back. Although Babylonian captivity is still in the future, the Lord's rescue is so certain that He speaks of redemption in the past tense.

Second, God has *called thee by thy name*. There could be no question about whom God redeemed. Third, God states the result, or effect, of His redemption: *Thou art mine*. How, then, can Israel be afraid of anything? [See question #1, page 56.]

WHAT'S IN A NAME?

It's a question dating back at least four hundred years to the time of Shakespeare: "What's in a name?" The issue, of course, is philosophical. But it's also practical, as when a name helps us to identify a specific person. Think about what happens when we hear our first name over the loudspeaker in a public place. Our brain filters out all background noise and we pay attention to that set of sounds—at least until the last name of the person being paged is spoken. Then we go back to ignoring it.

Another practical use of names has been discovered by the FBI. Its agents give nicknames to serial bank robbers, usually on the basis of the physical characteristics or habits of the criminals. For example, the "Gentleman Bandit" always said "please" and "thank you." The "Bourgeois Bandit" made his getaway in a limousine. The "Bad Breath Bandit" was noted for his halitosis. The nicknames give the public and the officers a "handle" by which to identify people on the wanted list.

God comforted Israel through Isaiah by noting that He called them by name. Their name means "he strives with God" or "God strives" (Genesis 32:28; 35:10). As we know, the nation of Israel did not often live up to its namesake! The question for us is whether the character we show the world merits the name *Christian*—"one who belongs to Christ."   —C. R. B.

B. Safety (v. 2)

2. When thou passest through the waters, I will be with thee; and through the rivers, they shall not overflow thee: when thou walkest through the fire, thou shalt not be burned; neither shall the flame kindle upon thee.

When Israel was young as a nation, God used miracles to bring His people *through* the Red Sea and the flooded Jordan River (Exodus 14; Joshua 3). It was not likely that they ever would need such miracles again, or a miracle to keep them safe in literal *fire.* God is using figurative language to promise to keep them safe in whatever dangers they may face. [See question #2, page 56.]

But read carefully! This is not a promise to keep them from experiencing fire, whether literal or figurative. Rather, this is a promise to keep them safe as they *walkest through the fire.* Also, God does not promise to keep them safe and unpunished if they again turn away from Him and sell themselves to sin as they do prior to their captivity in Babylon.

C. Identity (v. 3a)

3. For I am the LORD thy God, the Holy One of Israel, thy Saviour.

In verse 1 we saw that the Lord identified himself as the Creator and Redeemer and Owner of His people. In verse 3 He stresses that He is their *God,* their *Holy One,* their *Saviour.* The message isn't new, but it does bear repeating.

II. Witnesses for God
(Isaiah 43:10-13)

The assurance we saw in verses 1-3a is continued in verses 4-9, which are not included in our printed text. God affirms His love for His people; He promises to gather again those who are scattered; He challenges the pagan world to produce witnesses to prove that anyone among them has foretold future events as God has done. Then God names His own witnesses, as we see next.

A. Servants Who Know (vv. 10, 11)

10. Ye are my witnesses, saith the LORD, and my servant whom I have chosen; that ye may know and believe me, and understand that I am he: before me there was no God formed, neither shall there be after me.

The Lord's people are His *witnesses.* Both by His unfailing care and by foretelling the future, He gives them ample evidence that He is *God,* the real God, the only God.

The people of Israel are not only His witnesses, but their nation as a whole is also His *servant.* The behavior of the Israelites ought to demonstrate to the rest of the world that He is the only God. The devotion of the Jewish people should look back to the wonderful miracles and prophecies that prove He is God.

11. I, even I, am the LORD; and beside me there is no saviour.

The pagan world is full of false gods (e.g., 2 Kings 23:13). Over and over, the Jewish people find themselves seduced by these idols, so God announces again that He is *the Lord.* And this time He adds that He is the one and only *saviour* of His people. Long before Isaiah's time, God had saved them from Egypt, from starvation in the wilderness, and from strong nations in the promised land.

In Isaiah's time God saved the southern kingdom of Judah from the Assyrians, who defeated and scattered their kinsmen to the north in 722 B.C. After Isaiah's time God will save His people from the Babylonian exile that is to begin in 586 B.C. His witnesses should testify to all of these facts by their right behavior and worship.

B. Evidence That Proves (v. 12)

12. I have declared, and have saved, and I have showed, when there was no strange god among you: therefore ye are my witnesses, saith the LORD, that I am God.

Put the first and last phrases of this verse together: *I have declared . . . that I am God.* Between those two phrases we see ample evidence that the Lord is indeed the only true God. Time after time He has *saved* His people from powerful forces.

In this way He has *showed* that He is God, more powerful than all pagan earthly forces or make-believe gods in Heaven. He did this *when there was no strange god among you*—when His people were giving Him their undivided devotion. But when the people turned away from the Lord and looked to fictitious gods, they were defeated. The captivity of northern Israel proves it. God's people have seen the evidence: they are *witnesses.* Again, their right behavior and worship ought to be testifying to these facts.

C. God Who Is (v. 13)

13. Yea, before the day was I am he; and there is none that can deliver out of my hand: I will work, and who shall let it?

Thus the Lord gives the conclusion drawn from the evidence presented. *Before the day was I am he* means that the Lord was God before the creation of the world, and He has been God ever since. No one *can deliver* anyone from His power, for He is all-powerful (cf. John 10:27-29). He will do what He ought to do, and no one can prevent it. [See question #3, page 56.]

The word *let* is an example of how our language has changed since the *King James Version* of the Bible was translated. Today the word *let* means "permit, allow"; however, when this version was made, the word *let* meant "hinder, prevent." No one or no thing in the world will keep the Lord from doing what He chooses to do. He is God! His people are witnesses of this. May their actions testify!

III. Work of God (Isaiah 43:14-19)

The last part of verse 13 assures us that God will go on with His work, and no one will prevent it. Now the final part of today's text tells a little about what He will do. To assure us of His ability, He also reminds us of what He has done in the past.

A. The Doom of Babylon (v. 14)

14. Thus saith the LORD, your Redeemer, the Holy One of Israel; For your sake I have sent to Babylon, and have brought down all their nobles, and the Chaldeans, whose cry is in the ships.

As in verses 1 and 10, the announcement begins by making it plain that it comes from God, not from Isaiah. God is going to bring down the haughty *nobles* of *Babylon* and end their oppression. God revealed this and Isaiah wrote it many years before the captivity even began! But God can put it in the past tense because in His mind it is already "a done deal." His plan is complete, and nothing is going to keep Him from carrying it out. (*Chaldeans* is another name for Babylonians.)

The word *cry* is understood in different ways. Some take it to be the mariners' outburst of pride in their *ships;* others take it to be a wail of distress because they are forced to get in the ships and flee from the Persian invaders who ultimately conquer their territory.

B. The Lord and His Power (vv. 15-17)

15. I am the LORD, your Holy One, the Creator of Israel, your King.

Visual for lesson 6

Ask your learners what these titles tell about the One who is really "in charge."

Again comes the reminder of who is speaking. *Lord, Holy One, Creator, King*—such a list of titles! Can anyone in Israel be so foolish as to turn a deaf ear?

16, 17. Thus saith the LORD, which maketh a way in the sea, and a path in the mighty waters; which bringeth forth the chariot and horse, the army and the power; they shall lie down together, they shall not rise: they are extinct, they are quenched as tow.

To anyone who knows Israel's history, this brief verse is a reminder both of God's power and of His favor to His people. As we noted with verse 2 above, He had made a road through the Red Sea for them to escape from Egypt; He had made *a path* through the raging Jordan for them to enter the promised land.

Egypt's army had charged into the dry bed of the Red Sea in pursuit of God's fleeing people, ignoring the walls of water on its right and left. That was the end of *the army,* as men and horses died together (Exodus 14:26-28). *Tow* is fiber used to make a wick for a lamp. As the flame of a wick is put out by a puff of breath, so the life of Egypt's army was put out by the water of the sea as it returned to its usual place. How can Israel not know that God will protect them from every danger?

C. The Coming New Thing (vv. 18, 19)

18. Remember ye not the former things, neither consider the things of old.

How's that again? Has the Lord used verses 16 and 17 to remind us of great events in the past, only to tell us to forget them? Not at all. What the Jewish people are to *remember . . . not* is the old order of *things* such as their slavery in Egypt. What is important is to wake up and realize what God is doing now. See the next verse.

19. Behold, I will do a new thing; now it shall spring forth; shall ye not know it? I will even make a way in the wilderness, and rivers in the desert.

To dwell on the hardships of days gone by is pointless. To cherish the record of what God did in the ancient past to overcome those hardships is valuable, but is not a stopping point. What's most important is the *new thing* that God is doing and will be doing right before their very eyes. [See question #4, page 56.]

God's ancient leadership of His people for forty years *in the desert* was no less remarkable than the spectacular crossings of the Red Sea and the Jordan River. But thinking ahead to the end of captivity in Babylon, God is laying the foundation for another journey to the ancient homeland. This future trip will lead the people there directly; they will not wander for a generation in a desert. God will keep them all the way.

WHAT GOD IS DOING NOW

In 1633 Galileo "confessed" to being a heretic: he believed that the earth orbits the sun. The church prohibited him from discussing this Copernican view of the solar system. In 1874 John William Draper, a scientist and son of a Wesleyan clergyman, published his influential *History of the Conflict Between Religion and Science.* And so it went until the late twentieth century: science and religion (particularly Christianity) were thought to be mortal enemies.

But the times are changing, and scientists are "getting religion." The Massachusetts Institute of Technology offers Bible study courses; Carnegie Mellon Institute (whose engineering and computer science programs are rated in the top five in the country) offers a minor in religious studies; UC–Berkeley has a Center for Theology and

---

Home Daily Bible Readings

Monday, Oct. 4—Our God Is the Everlasting God (Isaiah 40:25-31)

Tuesday, Oct. 5—Give Glory to God (Isaiah 42:5-13)

Wednesday, Oct. 6—Israel Is Redeemed (Isaiah 43:1-7)

Thursday, Oct. 7—God Is Our God and Savior (Isaiah 43:8-15)

Friday, Oct. 8—God Will Bring Salvation (Isaiah 43:16-21)

Saturday, Oct. 9—Israel Is Still on Trial (Isaiah 43:22-28)

Sunday, Oct. 10—The One God Blesses Israel (Isaiah 44:1-8)

Science; and Caltech now has a course in New Testament.

God urged Israel to look to the future, saying to Isaiah, "I will do a new thing." God is doing a new thing in our time: He is helping a scientific world realize there is more to life than science. Some Christians are still living in the past, fighting old enemies. We would do better to help the world to see that "all truth is God's truth" and winsomely persuade it of the importance of the things of the spirit.   —C. R. B.

Conclusion

A. Trust and Obey

What we have been reading in Isaiah was given as prophecy. It was given in the past tense because it was fully established in the mind of God: it surely was to come to pass, but not in the time of Isaiah. God promised captivity in Babylon for His people (Isaiah 39:5-7). That captivity served as punishment for long-continued sin. But God also promised the defeat of Babylon (43:14). He named the Persian king, Cyrus, who would lead the conquerors (44:28). God even promised to redeem Israel by giving the Persians three countries in Africa as ransom (43:3b, 4).

After citing great things He had done in the past, God promised to provide a way by which His people would be able to return to their ancient homeland (Isaiah 43:15-19). Truly God can say that the Israelites are "twice mine" as He keeps all of these promises recorded by Isaiah.

Today God can say that Christians are "twice mine" as well. This is true because He first created us, then He purchased our salvation through the blood of His Son. Because of those facts, our task is clear: we are to be "faithful unto death" so that we will receive "a crown of life" (Revelation 2:10).

We maintain our faithfulness when we trust Him and obey Him. We must listen to the Word of God. [See question #5, page 56.] When we do, our obedience will be a natural outflow of our love for Him (John 14:15, 23, 24). That is the way to be happy now and forever.

B. Prayer

Father in Heaven, while we stand in awe of Your majesty and power and knowledge, we take delight in Your love and goodness. Thank You for the Bible and the strong but gentle way it guides us in this confusing world. Give us understanding as we read, and give us courage to obey. In Jesus' name, amen.

C. Thought to Remember

Only redeemed people have hope!

Learning by Doing

This page contains an alternative lesson plan emphasizing learning activities. Classes desiring such student involvement will find these suggestions helpful.

Learning Goals

After participating in this lesson, each student will be able to:

1. Recall some great nationwide movements that God predicted through Isaiah.

2. Understand what caused Israel's disaster and what caused its recovery.

3. Trust God and obey Him.

Into the Lesson

Unscramble the letters. Give each of eleven students a sheet of copier paper with one word printed on it in large letters. Four students should receive one of the following four words printed on blue paper (or color of your choice): *I have redeemed thee.* The remaining seven pieces of paper should be a different color. One of each of the following words should be printed on each: *Ye are my witnesses saith the Lord.* Distribute these sheets randomly to students as they enter the room.

Begin the class by having the four students with blue (or whatever color you chose) paper stand in front of the class, unscramble the words, and stand in the correct order. After they have done so, ask them to remain in place while the second team does the same with their words.

Make the transition to Bible study by explaining, "These are two key statements by God to His people in the Old Testament. But these are certainly statements He could repeat to Christians. We'll find these concepts as we study Isaiah."

Into the Word

Activity #1: Minilecture. Prepare a short lecture introducing Isaiah's book and the Lesson Background by using the notes in the lesson commentary.

Activity #2: Question and Answer. Prepare a visual of this three-point outline to use as structure for the remainder of the Bible study.

    I. God's Redemption (Isaiah 43:1-3a)

    II. Israel's Responsibility (Isaiah 43:10-13)

    III. God's Mercy (Isaiah 43:14-19)

Ask the following discussion questions as you highlight or uncover each point of the outline. Use the notes in the lesson commentary to clarify concepts and answer questions the students may raise.

I. God's Redemption. Have a student read verses 1-3. Then ask the following questions. (1)

The word *but* is important in verse 1, since it signals a change. As you scan chapter 42, what is the stark contrast you see in today's printed text? (2) What are some of God's blessings that have or will come to Israel through their Redeemer? If this language could be figurative about future blessings, what may those blessings include? (3) Also scan verses 4-9, not in our printed text. What compliment(s) to Israel do you find?

II. Israel's Responsibility. Ask a student to read verses 10-13. Questions to ask include the following: (1) Notice the double call to be witnesses in verses 10 and 12. To what was Israel to be witness? What could or should be included in Israel's testimony? (2) Verse 11 echoes verse 3 and is later pronounced again in verse 15. Why do you think God placed a triple emphasis on this principle? (3) Notice the wonderful comfort to Israel in verse 13. How does this assurance give comfort to believers in verse 13? How does this assurance give comfort to believers in 2004?

III. God's Mercy. Read verses 14-19 and ask these questions: (1) Verses 18 and 19a are the key to this passage. Why did God make this statement to Israel? (2) How does it contrast with verses 16-18? (3) How will this encourage Israel?

Into Life

Introduce the following activity by reminding the class of God's infinite knowledge. God knows what will happen tomorrow, next week, and a hundred years to come. And God not only *knows* the future, He *holds* the future in His hands.

Divide the class into small groups. Give each group one of the following assignments, a piece of poster board, and a marker pen.

Task #1: Remember how God declared, "Ye are my witnesses" to Israel. Jesus echoed that command and brought it into Christian life when He said, "Ye shall be witnesses unto me" (Acts 1:8). List ways that Christians can fulfill this command in life today.

Task #2: Reread the assurances given in verses 13, 15, and 19. Discuss how this security brings hope to a Christian facing crisis.

Task #3: Reread verses 13, 15, and 19 yet again. Discuss how this hope affects a believer's view of death and eternity. Then, write lines from hymns or songs that reflect this hope.

Ask someone in advance to prepare a prayer on the theme of hope. Close with that prayer.

Let's Talk It Over

The questions on this page are designed to promote discussion of the lesson by the class and to encourage application of the lesson Scriptures. The answers provided are only discussion starters. Let your class talk it over from there.

1. God is our Creator; God is our Redeemer. How should the knowledge of these two ideas affect our daily lives?

The opening illustration "Twice Mine!" captures the principles of God's work of creation and redemption. God owns us completely, and He owns His church completely. All that we do needs to glorify God as Creator and Redeemer.

We can fail to give God glory if we serve Him with wrong motives. If we grow our Sunday school class just to win a contest, then that's a problem! It is good to read the Bible, but if we read it merely to be able to say that we've read it, then we have missed the point. Motives are important. (See Colossians 3:17.)

2. God is not only our Creator and Redeemer (Isaiah 43:1), He is also our Protector. Why is this knowledge important to you as you go through tough times?

We all pass through deep waters, rushing rivers, and intense fires of life through trials and persecutions. Daniel and his friends knew what it meant to have God's protection (Daniel 3:26, 27; 6:22). Peter knew God was his protector when he was miraculously released from prison (Acts 12:11, 12). Paul also experienced God's care on numerous occasions (2 Corinthians 11:23-28).

The One who protected them also promises to protect His people today. But we must remember that this is primarily *spiritual* protection. Many Christians have been martyred whom God kept spiritually safe nonetheless. Jesus' prayer was that His followers be protected from the evil one (John 17:15). Now is a good time to reflect upon some of the spiritually rough times when you, your family, or your church received God's protection.

3. Because of the fact that the God of the Bible is the one true God, He has all power to deliver His people. In what ways has God delivered you? In what areas do you still need God's deliverance?

Verse 13 of our text is quite similar to Deuteronomy 32:39. The promise is that those under God's protection cannot be taken away from Him. Since there is only one God, there is in reality no other god that can entice you to follow after him. Neither is there any other god who is able to deliver you from your trials of life.

Our most important deliverance, of course, is from the bondage to sin through the death of His Son. As we follow Jesus, He continues to deliver us from the evil one as He guides us in paths of righteousness. (See John 16:33.)

4. God's desire is that we be made new, continually renewed, in our relationship with Him. How will the knowledge of God's continuing work of renewal in your life cause you to face life differently this week?

The apostle Paul spoke of forgetting what was behind and straining toward what was yet ahead (Philippians 3:13). Paul could have "rested on his laurels" in remembering past victories; on the other hand, he could have wallowed in his failures to the point where he couldn't function. Instead, he chose to focus on his future.

All of us have things from our past that we are proud of. But we can't dwell on these things. We rejoice in them, we learn from them, and we move on. In the same way each of us have things from our past that we are ashamed of. Again, dwelling on the past will not advance us in the present or the future. There are lessons to be learned from these situations, but there is a time to move on.

The realization that spiritual victories are from God's hand keeps us from becoming smug and inactive. The knowledge that God is a God of new beginnings and continual renewal helps us deal with past sin and its guilt as we move to higher levels of spiritual life and growth.

5. Like Israel, sometimes we are slow to hear and act. At other times we fail to learn from the past. What are some areas in your life where you need to be a better listener and learner?

Answers here will be highly individual, so expect a free-flowing discussion. Remind your learners that failure to learn from the past is a sure recipe for disaster in the future. God demonstrated His patience time and again with Israel. He does the same with us.

One day, however, the time of His patience will end and the day of His judgment will begin. It is vital that we have learned the lessons and made the necessary corrections before that time! Also remind your learners that we commit sin when we think we know better than God does.

Creating a New Covenant

DEVOTIONAL READING: Jeremiah 30:18-22.

BACKGROUND SCRIPTURE: Jeremiah 29–31.

PRINTED TEXT: Jeremiah 29:10-14; 31:31-34.

Jeremiah 29:10-14

10 For thus saith the LORD, That after seventy years be accomplished at Babylon I will visit you, and perform my good word toward you, in causing you to return to this place.

11 For I know the thoughts that I think toward you, saith the LORD, thoughts of peace, and not of evil, to give you an expected end.

12 Then shall ye call upon me, and ye shall go and pray unto me, and I will hearken unto you.

13 And ye shall seek me, and find me, when ye shall search for me with all your heart.

14 And I will be found of you, saith the LORD: and I will turn away your captivity, and I will gather you from all the nations, and from all the places whither I have driven you, saith the LORD; and I will bring you again into the place whence I caused you to be carried away captive.

Jeremiah 31:31-34

31 Behold, the days come, saith the LORD, that I will make a new covenant with the house of Israel, and with the house of Judah:

32 Not according to the covenant that I made with their fathers, in the day that I took them by the hand to bring them out of the land of Egypt; which my covenant they brake, although I was a husband unto them, saith the LORD:

33 But this shall be the covenant that I will make with the house of Israel; After those days, saith the LORD, I will put my law in their inward parts, and write it in their hearts; and will be their God, and they shall be my people.

34 And they shall teach no more every man his neighbor, and every man his brother, saying, Know the LORD: for they shall all know me, from the least of them unto the greatest of them, saith the LORD: for I will forgive their iniquity, and I will remember their sin no more.

**Oct
17**

GOLDEN TEXT: This shall be the covenant that I will make with the house of Israel;
After those days, saith the LORD, I will put my law in their inward parts,
and write it in their hearts; and will be their God, and they shall be
my people.—Jeremiah 31:33.

The God of Continuing Creation
Unit 2: God's Creativity Continues
(Lessons 5-9)

Lesson Aims

After participating in this lesson, each student will be able to:

1. Tell what God promised for the future of the Jewish exiles, including a return to their homeland and the making of a new covenant.

2. Explain how the gospel of Jesus Christ fulfills Jeremiah's prophecy of a new covenant.

3. Describe the future that awaits those who enter into a covenant relationship with God.

Lesson Outline

INTRODUCTION
  A. Fortune-tellers, Then and Now
  B. Lesson Background
I. LONG-TERM PROMISE (Jeremiah 29:10-14)
  A. The Lord's Plan, Part 1 (vv. 10, 11)
  B. The Spiritual Result, Part 1 (vv. 12-14)
    The Long Road Home
II. LONGER-TERM PROMISE (Jeremiah 31:31-34)
  A. The Lord's Plan, Part 2 (vv. 31, 32)
  B. The Spiritual Result, Part 2 (vv. 33, 34)
    All Brain and No Heart?
CONCLUSION
  A. Review and Preview
  B. Prayer
  C. Thought to Remember

Introduction

A. Fortune-tellers, Then and Now

The fortune-teller's tent was a fascinating spot at our state fair. Unlike our camping tent of white canvas, this one was a riot of color. It rose to a lofty peak, from which a scarlet pennon fluttered in the fitful breeze. When the fortune-teller herself appeared in the doorway, her brunette beauty was enhanced by heavy makeup, big earrings, and a glittering tiara. Her long robe was solid black, but it, too, glittered as she moved.

A timid child at the age of nine, I watched from the other side of the midway. Fascinating as they were, that woman and her tent seemed somehow evil, dangerous, frightening. Bolder than I, a little bevy of high-school girls sat in the waiting area; yet they were prim and silent, and I knew they felt a bit of the fear that kept me on the other side of the busy midway.

Afterward I asked some of the girls about the fortune-teller. They said she promised each one a rosy future: every hope would be realized, every fear would prove to be unfounded.

Did ancient fortune-tellers also contrive to be mystical and half-frightening? No doubt some of them did. Why else would they "peep" and "mutter" instead of speaking clearly (Isaiah 8:19)? And certainly they continued to say what the people wanted to hear, regardless of truth. Else why would they say Israel would not be subject to Babylonian rule (Jeremiah 27:9, 10)?

B. Lesson Background

God's real prophets spoke the truth that God gave them, whether anyone wanted to hear it or not. In last week's Lesson Background we noted that the prophet Isaiah had foretold captivity in Babylon (Isaiah 39:5-7). But no one wanted to hear that message.

Jeremiah, prophesying many decades after Isaiah, said Jerusalem would be destroyed. The hearers wanted to kill him for bringing that message (Jeremiah 26:8-11). But the southern kingdom of Judah did indeed become captive in Babylon, and Jerusalem was indeed destroyed. These disasters could have been averted if God's people had listened to God's truth in time.

The Babylonian dominance over Judah can be seen in terms of three phases. *Phase 1* began about 605 B.C. when the Babylonian army approached Jerusalem. In short order, King Jehoiakim (reigned 609–598 B.C.) gave up without a struggle and was forced to pay tribute. Daniel and a few other outstanding young men were taken captive (Daniel 1:1-6).

In a few years Jehoiakim revolted and refused to pay tribute. The Babylonian army was busy elsewhere. But Babylon then controlled several small nations near Judah, and those nations harassed Judah until Nebuchadnezzar returned with his army (2 Kings 23:36–24:2).

Phase 2 began about 597 B.C. when the Babylonian army again arrived on the scene at Jerusalem. King Jehoiakim had died recently, and his son Jehoiachin had taken his place. Following his father's example, the new king surrendered to the enemy.

This time the Babylonians took ten thousand captives, including civil and military leaders, blacksmiths skilled in making weapons, and probably the prophet Ezekiel. Zedekiah was left to rule Judah and pay tribute to Babylon (2 Kings 24:8-17).

Phase 3 began about 588 B.C. when Zedekiah revolted and the Babylonian army returned a third time. After besieging Jerusalem for a year and a half, that army broke through the wall and captured the starving city in 586 B.C. The city and its temple were leveled, and most of the surviving people were taken to Babylon (2 Kings 25).

This week's lesson belongs in Phase 2 of the Babylonian domination. Ten thousand Jewish captives have been taken to Babylon, but this does not include the prophet Jeremiah, who remains in the city. From Jerusalem he writes a letter to give God's message to his ten thousand countrymen who are being held against their will in Babylon.

I. Long-term Promise
(Jeremiah 29:10-14)

In Jeremiah's letter, the Lord advises the captives in Babylon to settle down and live normal lives. They are to work for the peace of Babylon so the captives, too, would be at peace.

The Lord also warns them not to be fooled by self-proclaimed prophets who are not telling the truth (Jeremiah 29:1-9). The next part of the letter begins our text.

A. The Lord's Plan, Part 1 (vv. 10, 11)

10. For thus saith the LORD, That after seventy years be accomplished at Babylon I will visit you, and perform my good word toward you, in causing you to return to this place.

Seventy years, a round number, is the total time assigned for *Babylon* to rule Judah (Jeremiah 25:11). It includes all three phases listed in the Lesson Background.

Of the people of Judah, only Daniel and a few others are at Babylon all of that time (Daniel 1:3-7). Those who receive this letter from Jeremiah have nearly sixty years ahead of them to spend in Babylon. At the end of that time, and not before, the Lord will bring about their liberation and their return *to this place,* Jerusalem (cf. Jeremiah 27:22). [See question #1, page 64.]

The prophet Daniel will be an eyewitness to the overthrow of Babylon in 539 B.C. Daniel even will make a prophecy about it (Daniel 5). As events will unfold, Daniel himself comes to understand Jeremiah's prophecy regarding the seventy years (Daniel 9:2).

11. For I know the thoughts that I think toward you, saith the LORD, thoughts of peace, and not of evil, to give you an expected end.

The Lord is quite sure about His thinking. He has planned captivity for His people because they have been sinning. But captivity is causing them to change their ways. Now the Lord is planning their liberation. False prophets are promising a quick end to the captivity (Jeremiah 28:1-4, 10, 11). The Lord's plan, however, is the one that offers the *expected end* of true hope.

B. The Spiritual Result, Part 1 (vv. 12-14)

12. Then shall ye call upon me, and ye shall go and pray unto me, and I will hearken unto you.

Before the captivity, the people and officials of Judah often ignore God's prophets. Sometimes the prophets are persecuted (e.g., Jeremiah 26:20-23). But, homesick in Babylon, many of the people and officials will have ample time to rethink their attitudes.

Perhaps while in captivity they will realize that the Lord is "merciful and gracious, long-suffering, and abundant in goodness and truth" (Exodus 34:6). Perhaps while in captivity some wise teacher will remind them how important it is to *pray.*

God would rather pardon than punish the wayward. God ultimately will listen to the prayers of His penitent people. Even so, the most severe part of the captivity—including the destruction of Jerusalem—will make even Jeremiah wonder if God is listening (Lamentations 3:8, 44). [See question #2, page 64.]

13. And ye shall seek me, and find me, when ye shall search for me with all your heart.

God had not been hiding from His people in those years before the captivity. Rather, it is they who had been hiding from Him. Happy with His gifts, they saw no need of the Giver. Now a precious gift—their liberty—is gone and in grief they will look for the Giver.

But there is a condition attached to being able to find the Lord: they must *search for* him *with all* their hearts. Only then will they find the Lord. Only then will He restore their liberty. When God restores their liberty, some hearts will rejoice at the gain while others will sorrow over

---

How to Say It

ABRAHAM. *Ay*-bruh-ham.
BABYLONIAN. Bab-ih-*low*-nee-un.
CORINTHIANS. Kor-*in*-thee-unz (*th* as in *thin*).
EGYPT. *Ee*-jipt.
EZRA. *Ez*-ruh.
ISAIAH. Eye-*zay*-uh.
JEHOIACHIN. Jeh-*hoy*-uh-kin.
JEHOIAKIM. Jeh-*hoy*-uh-kim.
JEREMIAH. Jair-uh-*my*-uh.
JERUSALEM. Juh-*roo*-suh-lem.
LAMENTATIONS. Lam-en-*tay*-shunz.
NEBUCHADNEZZAR. *Neb*-yuh-kud-*nez*-er (strong accent on *nez*).
THESSALONIANS. *Thess*-uh-*lo*-nee-unz (strong accent on *lo; th* as in *thin*).
ZEDEKIAH. Zed-uh-*kye*-uh.

what need not have been lost in the first place (Ezra 3:10-13). [See question #3, page 64.]

14. And I will be found of you, saith the LORD: and I will turn away your captivity, and I will gather you from all the nations, and from all the places whither I have driven you, saith the LORD; and I will bring you again into the place whence I caused you to be carried away captive.

What a striking list of events will happen when the captives seek the Lord with all their hearts! First, they will find Him; they will be on His side again; they will really be His people. Second, He *will turn away* their *captivity*—He will reverse it, setting them free.

Third, He will gather them *from all the nations, and from all the places* to which He has driven them. As a result He will bring all those people back to the land from which they had been taken.

The forthcoming return will be to the ancient homeland, back to the promised land to which the Jewish people had gone from Egypt. It will be a return to the land promised to Abraham and his descendants centuries earlier.

THE LONG ROAD HOME

Long-haul truckers have been called "road warriors" and "the last cowboys." They have a lonely job that takes them far from home for long periods at a time.

But temptations lurk at many stops along the road. That's why Truckstop Ministries began in the 1980s. The chapels are tractor-trailer rigs at some sixty locations in about one-half of the United States. Some of the volunteer ministers wish they could have been truckers themselves; some are former truckers. All want to share their faith.

A typical service may have a "crowd" ranging from none to several; an occasional motorist may even attend. A woman who had a flat tire in Hesperia, California, attended a trucker's service, saying, "I just wanted to talk to God." However, the primary goal is to help truckers find God and get their lives headed down the right road. No matter where their load of freight has to go, finding God is the most important thing.

Jeremiah told Judah that turning to God would bring their lonely captivity to an end. If they repented, God would put them on the long road home and bring them safely there. We Christians are on the road to a Heavenly home where temptation and loneliness will be banished forever. Although our destination is different from Judah's, God's promise to us is the same: our home awaits us if we let God take us there.

—C. R. B.

II. Longer-term Promise (Jeremiah 31:31-34)

Chapters 30 and 31 of Jeremiah indicate that the promise of return is not made just to the captives in Babylon, but to all the scattered tribes of Israel (cf. 2 Kings 17:5, 6). The Lord specifies both "Israel and Judah" (Jeremiah 30:3) and "all the families of Israel" (Jeremiah 31:1). As great as that will be, it is only preparatory for something better still: a new covenant.

A. The Lord's Plan, Part 2 (vv. 31, 32)

31. Behold, the days come, saith the LORD, that I will make a new covenant with the house of Israel, and with the house of Judah.

We notice three things in this verse. First, the Lord promises to *make a new covenant* to replace the old one He had made with Israel at Mount Sinai more than eight hundred years previously. For this reason, some students consider Jeremiah 31:31-34 to be one of the most important sections in the entire Old Testament!

Second, the Lord promises to make it *with the house of Israel, and with the house of Judah,* not just with the people of Judah who are captives in Babylon. The prophet Isaiah had earlier prophesied that the new covenant would be for the rest of the world, too (Isaiah 42:6; 49:6).

Third, the Lord does not make the new covenant at the time of this writing, but promises to make it later, or in *the days to come.* Historical hindsight tells us that the Lord is predicting something that will not occur for more than five hundred years. But it will indeed occur!

32. Not according to the covenant that I made with their fathers, in the day that I took them by the hand to bring them out of the land of Egypt; which my covenant they brake, although I was a husband unto them, saith the LORD.

In our lesson for September 26 we read that God spoke of making a covenant as His people ended their forty years of wandering in the desert (Deuteronomy 29:1, 9, 12). Evidently that covenant was mostly a reaffirmation of the one made forty years earlier at Mount Sinai. Now, however, we are reading God's promise of a new covenant that is very different from the one made at Mount Sinai.

It seems evident that a new covenant is needed, because the people have broken the old one so flagrantly and frequently. That is why north Israel has been scattered in foreign places and south Judah has suffered captivity in Babylon. Their breaking of the covenant is inexcusable, for God has been *a husband unto them* (cf. Jeremiah 3:14, 20). That means that He has generously provided all they needed, both in their wilderness wandering and in the promised land itself. [See question #4, page 64.]

B. The Spiritual Result, Part 2 (vv. 33, 34)

33. But this shall be the covenant that I will make with the house of Israel; After those days, saith the LORD, I will put my law in their inward parts, and write it in their hearts; and will be their God, and they shall be my people.

We are startled to see the people of Israel breaking God's law in such an "in your face" way! Certainly one reason for this problem is that they do not know God's law by heart, so *their hearts* are not "in tune" with it.

In their defense we must note that the ancient Jews do not have Bibles in every home. How much of Leviticus would you know if your only way of learning were your parents' teaching by word of mouth? It would take persistent and consistent teaching to give children a working knowledge of Old Testament law, and incessant teaching was just what the law required (see Deuteronomy 6:6, 7).

The New Testament, for its part, is less than a third the length of the Old Testament, and we do have Bibles in every home today. We do tell Bible stories to our children and send them to Sunday school. Yet we are ashamed because neither we nor the children know Christian teaching as well as we should.

It takes effort on our part as well as on God's part to have His words really written in our hearts as they should be if we are God's *people.* And it should be obvious that He will write the new covenant only on willing hearts. To a person who stubbornly resists, that new covenant will be no more effective than was the old covenant when it was broken.

ALL BRAIN AND NO HEART?

Parking meters came to town on July 16, 1935, in Oklahoma City. Today there are at least five million of them in the United States alone. Promoted as a way to discourage day-long parking in business districts, meters have proven to be good sources of municipal income—by one estimate $1,250,000 per day in the U.S.!

But the meters' original purpose was defeated when wily motorists began feeding the meter just before time ran out. This circumvented both the "Meter Maids" as well as the spirit and purpose of the law.

Now, electronic "smart" meters will not accept constant feeding. They will also reset to zero when a car moves away in order to deny any remaining time to the next car to park. As one report said of the new meters, they "have a brain, but no heart."

Visual for
lesson 7

I will put my law . . .
in their hearts.

The law of God in our hearts calls us to serve in many ways. How will you heed that call today?

Spiritual scofflaws, who were all brain and no heart, thought that "feeding the meter" of the old covenant with sacrifices and offerings allowed them to keep just barely on "the right side of the law." Jeremiah says that there will be no doubt that the new covenant is to be based on the heart of the individual.

To stay technically on the right side of God's law is no longer an option (it never was, really). Instead, a true righteousness of the heart is fostered by our new relationship with God. Living for Christ involves our whole being: with the brain we affirm the covenant, with the heart we obey with right motives.   —C. R. B.

34. And they shall teach no more every man his neighbor, and every man his brother, saying, Know the LORD: for they shall all know me, from the least of them unto the greatest of them, saith the LORD: for I will forgive their iniquity, and I will remember their sin no more.

According to the old covenant, each descendant of Abraham enters the covenant at birth. According to the new covenant, a person does not become one of God's people by being born to parents who have a certain biological heritage. Rather, he or she becomes one of God's people by being born again (John 1:12, 13).

In the time of the new covenant, *teach no more* means that people will have direct access to God without needing to go through the human intermediaries—the priests of the levitical system—that are a feature of the old covenant (cf. Isaiah 54:13; John 6:45; Hebrews 4:16; 10:19-22).

To remind us of these facts, the writer of Hebrews quotes from this section of Jeremiah in Hebrews 8:8-12 and 10:16, 17 (see also Romans 11:27 and 1 Thessalonians 4:9). Of course, a teaching function still exists under the new covenant as the New Testament makes clear (1 Corinthians 12:28, 29; Ephesians 4:11, 12). [See question #5, page 64.] When Christ returns, all Christians will *know* Him in the fullest sense of Jeremiah's prophecy.

An outstanding feature of this new covenant is God's permanent plan of forgiveness through the blood of Christ. Here is the Christian's hope! The Christian does not imagine that he or she is sinless. But forgiveness is certain nonetheless (see 1 John 1: 8, 9). Because Christ takes the sin penalty upon Himself, God takes away the sins of His people. He forgives and forgets.

Conclusion

A. Review and Preview

Looking back at our seven lessons thus far, we see that God's good beginning is followed by the growth of evil again and again. In the beginning the Lord put Adam and Eve in a garden of delight, with light and easy chores to do and with an opportunity for unending happy life. But those two chose to do as they pleased instead of obeying God. They lost their garden home, they had to sweat to make a living, and death reared its ugly head.

Instead of learning from their parents' experience, the children and grandchildren of Adam and Eve also chose to do as they pleased. They became so evil in the course of centuries that God determined to wipe out sinners with a tremendous flood. Yet godly Noah and his family were saved to start a brave new world.

As more centuries passed, Noah's descendants learned to do as they pleased and the world grew wicked again. This time God did not wipe out the sinners, but chose to let them go their own way. The solution to sin this time was to come through the man Abraham. He was to be the father of a godly nation that would show the whole world what it meant to obey and fear the one true God.

When Abraham's family grew to be a nation, God sent Moses to lead it from Egypt to a country of its own, as we saw in two of our lessons. But through centuries the leaders and people ignored God's leading, and disaster came. The nation was divided. Both parts eventually ended up in exile, by God's decision.

We cannot conclude that God was like a scientist conducting experiments and hoping to learn by trial and error what to do. Rather, He was demonstrating His desires and His power for our learning. By Bible history and all other history, by our observation and experience, we are driven to the conclusion that Paul states so bluntly in Romans 3:23: "All have sinned, and come short of the glory of God."

What could be done about that? God knew before the world began. God's Son could give His life to pay the sin-penalty for humanity. Then forgiveness would be possible. So when God announced the coming of the new covenant He said, "I will forgive their iniquity, and I will remember their sin no more."

The new covenant is thus established through the birth, life, death, burial, and resurrection of Jesus Christ, the sinless Son of God. On the Day of Pentecost the apostle Peter stated firmly and simply what is required to enter into the new covenant and receive its blessings: "Repent, and be baptized every one of you in the name of Jesus Christ for the remission of sins" (Acts 2:38). The apostle Paul explains the significance of the new covenant in Romans 3:21-26. May the Word of God guide us in understanding!

B. Prayer

Holy Maker of all humanity, how wonderfully You have cared for Your people through the centuries! We are grateful even for the painful punishment that sometimes has turned Your straying people back to the duty and privilege of behaving as creatures made in Your image.

Knowing that all have sinned, we confess our guilt. We are grateful for the new covenant by which sins are forgiven and forgotten. In the name of Jesus we pray for wisdom and courage to avoid sin and walk daily in the good ways indicated in Your Word, amen.

C. Thought to Remember

Learn from the old covenant, embrace the new covenant.

Home Daily Bible Readings

Monday, Oct. 11—God Will Restore the Exiles (Jeremiah 29:10-14)

Tuesday, Oct. 12—After Judgment Will Come Freedom (Jeremiah 30:2-9)

Wednesday, Oct. 13—Restoration Will Bring Abundance and Happiness (Jeremiah 30:18-22)

Thursday, Oct. 14—God Is Always Faithful (Jeremiah 31:1-6)

Friday, Oct. 15—The Exiles Will Return With Joy (Jeremiah 31:7-14)

Saturday, Oct. 16—God Restores All Who Are Responsible (Jeremiah 31:23-30)

Sunday, Oct. 17—God Makes a New Covenant (Jeremiah 31:31-34)

Learning by Doing

This page contains an alternative lesson plan emphasizing learning activities.
Classes desiring such student involvement will find these suggestions helpful.

Learning Goals

After participating in this lesson, each student will be able to:

1. Tell what God promised for the future of the Jewish exiles, including a return to their homeland and the making of a new covenant.

2. Explain how the gospel of Jesus Christ fulfills Jeremiah's prophecy of a new covenant.

3. Describe the future that awaits those who enter into a covenant relationship with God.

Into the Lesson

Prepare and display a poster that says, "I enjoy going back home because. . . ." Open the class by asking where some of your class members were born and reared. Then ask a few students to respond to the statement on the poster by completing the sentence.

Make the transition to Bible study by saying, "It is natural to have warm spots in our hearts for our homeland. History has seen deported or exiled peoples and nations struggle to return home. Being forced to be away brings heartache and a yearning for home. Such is the case of the Israelites. Today, as God speaks to their longing to return home, He makes a promise that will impact all of history and our very own lives."

Into the Word

Minilecture. Early in the week ask a class member who enjoys history to use the Lesson Background materials to prepare a five-minute "snapshot" summary of Israel's history. Suggest the following outline for the lecture.

  I. Deterioration of Israel
  II. Babylonian Captivity
    A. Phase 1
    B. Phase 2
    C. Phase 3

Explain to the class that today's text comes from Phase 2 of this section of history.

Making Notes. Distribute photocopies of today's printed text with a wide margin for notes. Class members may work in pairs or alone.

Activity #1: Ask the class to read Jeremiah 29:10-14 and circle every word or phrase that would offer hope or encouragement to this exiled people. After a few moments, ask class members to share findings as a "scribe" jots their findings on the board under the heading "Hope." Then ask why God would delay completing this

promise for such a long time (v. 10). What was God's purpose for delay?

Activity #2: Read Jeremiah 31:31-34 for the class. Then ask the teams or individuals to locate and identify the following: (a) the key verse that summarizes it all (v. 31) and (b) the eternal promise (v. 34b). Then ask two discussion questions: (a) "When and how will this promise be fulfilled?" (b) "How would the promised new covenant be different from the old covenant?" (vv. 32-34). See the lesson commentary for ideas to stimulate and supplement the discussion.

Into Life

Activity #1: Tell the class, "The covenant of forgiveness is one of the outstanding and wonderful features of the new covenant, the Christian covenant. Brainstorm and list some of the imagery God used in the Old Testament and New Testament to illustrate the depth and wonders of God's forgiveness. A great example is in our text: God will remember their sin no more (31:34)." Other answers may include "sin is covered" (Psalm 32:1), sins are removed as far as the east is from the west (Psalm 103:12), our sins will be like snow or wool (Isaiah 1:18), we are washed (1 Corinthians 6:11). If the students need ideas, ask them to read the Scriptures noted.

Activity #2: Ask and discuss the question, "Why and how do these passages about forgiveness bring great peace to today's Christians?"

Remind the class that an adult may sometimes feel that he or she has permanently broken his or her relationship with God. Is that possible? How does Israel's experience speak to this concern?

Concluding activity: The review part of the "Review and Preview" in the lesson commentary is an excellent summary of the last few lessons. Give a minilecture using material from this review. Display and use the following outline:

  I. Adam and Eve   III. Moses—a Nation
  II. Abraham   IV. A New Covenant

Conclude with small-group prayers. Ask one person in each group to thank God for His work in history, especially in the life of Israel. Another should focus on forgiveness, praising God for having the authority and power to forgive. A third person may pray for the ability to accept and enjoy the peace that comes through knowing that God has chosen to forgive when we are not deserving.

Let's Talk It Over

*The questions on this page are designed to promote discussion of the lesson
by the class and to encourage application of the lesson Scriptures. The answers
provided are only discussion starters. Let your class talk it over from there.*

**1. God promised that the captives in Babylon
would be returned to their homeland after seventy years. Compare that promise with Jesus'
promise to return at some future date. How does
each promise inspire hope? What does each
promise do to inspire faithfulness in the waiting
period?**

The main difference, obviously, is the time period affixed to the earlier promise. The captives
could predict their return (Daniel did just that in
Daniel 9:1-3). We do not know when the Lord
will return (Matthew 24:36-39).

Still, the fact that He has promised to return
excites in us a hope even as it did for the exiles
in Babylon. The fact that the exiles did indeed return makes the promise to us even surer. God
keeps His word. We see it in the return from
exile, and we anticipate it in the return of Christ.
While we wait, we cultivate our relationship
with the Lord. We want to be pure and spotless
for Him when He comes!

**2. God promised to hear His people when they
called out to Him. Do you ever doubt that God
hears your prayers? If so, when? Why? How can
you reassure yourself or another that God truly
does hear even when you are suffering?**

Adults can experience a variety of trying circumstances, each one with the potential to make
them question the substance of their faith. The
kind of faith required to chase away such doubts
cannot be gained in a moment. It must be nurtured over a lifetime through prayer, Bible study,
and Christian service. Mature Christians need to
set an example of faith for others.

Bible teachers and preachers, for their part,
can focus on such passages as Romans 8:28;
James 1; and 1 Peter 4:12-18. If these passages are
to be helpful, they need to be firmly understood
and believed before encountering trials.

**3. Suppose a non-Christian neighbor has
come to class with you this morning. As we read
verse 13, he says, "I don't know how to find
God. I searched for Him when I was out of
work, and I couldn't find Him. It took me eighteen months to find work—and God had nothing
to do with it." How would you respond?**

If someone really does have such a neighbor
with him or her today, the class member might
want to discuss the issue privately with that person on the way home or over dinner. But the
class can suggest some ideas on how to share
with unbelievers.

Of great importance is the clause, "When ye
shall search for me with all your heart." Searches
for God that are based on a financial need are
self-centered searches. Many unbelievers search
for God on their own terms, hoping to get something from God that He has not promised. What
the prophet promises in verse 13 is a response
from God when people turn to Him without conditions, but wholeheartedly yield to Him in total
submission. Those who seek God according to
the promises in His Word will find Him.

**4. In verse 32 God uses the image of a loving
husband to describe His relationship with His
people. What other images describe this relationship? Which image is most significant to
you? Why?**

Another family relationship is that of father.
We address God as our Heavenly Father when we
pray (cf. Matthew 6:9). We recognize that God
disciplines us as a loving father disciplines his
children (Proverbs 3:11, 12; Hebrews 12:5-11).

Another popular image is that of the shepherd
with his sheep (Psalm 23; John 10:11-18). Untold
numbers of believers have taken comfort in the
picture of Jesus as the good shepherd. Your class
will suggest other images as well.

**5. In spite of the fact that the Bible is so readily
available, we still see a good deal of ignorance
about what it says—even in Christian homes.
Why is that? What can be done about it? What
will result if churches do not address this issue?**

It takes effort on our part to have His words
written in our hearts as they should be if we are
God's people. To put forth that effort requires that
we make it a priority. The same kind of teaching
in the home that Deuteronomy 6:6-9 prescribes
ought to characterize Christian homes today.

The church and the Sunday school are no substitutes for parental involvement. But they can
supplement the parents' activities. Children's
ministries ought to include help for parents. This
can include resources, ideas, and other support
to help parents bring their children up in the
nurture and admonition of the Lord.

Creating a New Hope

DEVOTIONAL READING: Ezekiel 37:24-28.

BACKGROUND SCRIPTURE: Ezekiel 37.

PRINTED TEXT: Ezekiel 37:1-14.

Ezekiel 37:1-14

1 The hand of the LORD was upon me, and carried me out in the Spirit of the LORD, and set me down in the midst of the valley which was full of bones,

2 And caused me to pass by them round about: and, behold, there were very many in the open valley; and, lo, they were very dry.

3 And he said unto me, Son of man, can these bones live? And I answered, O Lord GOD, thou knowest.

4 Again he said unto me, Prophesy upon these bones, and say unto them, O ye dry bones, hear the word of the LORD.

5 Thus saith the Lord GOD unto these bones; Behold, I will cause breath to enter into you, and ye shall live:

6 And I will lay sinews upon you, and will bring up flesh upon you, and cover you with skin, and put breath in you, and ye shall live; and ye shall know that I am the LORD.

7 So I prophesied as I was commanded: and as I prophesied, there was a noise, and behold a shaking, and the bones came together, bone to his bone.

8 And when I beheld, lo, the sinews and the flesh came up upon them, and the skin covered them above: but there was no breath in them.

9 Then said he unto me, Prophesy unto the wind, prophesy, son of man, and say to the wind, Thus saith the Lord GOD; Come from the four winds, O breath, and breathe upon these slain, that they may live.

10 So I prophesied as he commanded me, and the breath came into them, and they lived, and stood up upon their feet, an exceeding great army.

11 Then he said unto me, Son of man, these bones are the whole house of Israel: behold, they say, Our bones are dried, and our hope is lost: we are cut off for our parts.

12 Therefore prophesy and say unto them, Thus saith the Lord GOD; Behold, O my people, I will open your graves, and cause you to come up out of your graves, and bring you into the land of Israel.

13 And ye shall know that I am the LORD, when I have opened your graves, O my people, and brought you up out of your graves,

14 And shall put my Spirit in you, and ye shall live, and I shall place you in your own land: then shall ye know that I the LORD have spoken it, and performed it, saith the LORD.

**Oct
24**

GOLDEN TEXT: [I] shall put my Spirit in you, and ye shall live, and I shall place you in your own land: then shall ye know that I the LORD have spoken it, and performed it, saith the LORD.—Ezekiel 37:14.

The God of Continuing Creation
Unit 2: God's Creativity Continues
(Lessons 5-9)

Lesson Aims

After participating in this lesson, each student will be able to:

1. Describe the details of Ezekiel's vision and its application of hope to the captives from Judah.

2. Suggest some circumstances or situations of today in which a word of hope is needed.

3. Make a plan of action to inject the hope of Christ into one of those situations.

Lesson Outline

Introduction

A. Revelations—Meaningful and Otherwise

Carl was in love. He couldn't help it. Carla was so cute, so charming, and her smile was the most beautiful one on earth. Besides, her name was almost like his. Didn't that mean they were meant for each other?

Carl and Carla worked in the same big office. One day Carl went out alone to lunch. Purely by chance, he entered a little neighborhood restaurant just as Carla was seating herself at a little table built for two. Putting a hand on the vacant chair, Carl asked, "Is this seat taken?"

"Not unless you're taking it," Carla responded with her dazzling smile. So Carl began watching Carla as lunchtime drew near. If she went out alone, he followed a few minutes later. Often they enjoyed delightful lunches at that same table for two.

One Saturday night, Carl had a vivid dream. He was sitting in a kitchen, and Carla was serving him breakfast. Carl believed in dreams because one had led him to the job he liked so well. So it was clear to him that this dream meant it was time to push his courtship. So the very next Monday he asked Carla for a date for the coming Friday. Carla looked straight across the table without her usual smile. "Thank you, Carl, but no."

Carl was surprised. Could his dream have misled him? "How about the next Friday?" he asked.

"That's no, too," Carla shook her pretty head.

Carl was crushed. "Does that mean you don't ever want a date with me?"

"I wouldn't put it that way," Carla said with half a smile. "It's my husband. He doesn't want me to date other men."

Now Carl doesn't believe in dreams anymore. He thinks that cozy kitchen dream deceived him cruelly. Perhaps you don't trust dreams to guide you either. I know I don't.

Still, there have been dreams full of meaning. God has used them as one way to present His messages to His people and to others. Pharaoh's dreams were a valuable warning of a famine (Genesis 41). Nebuchadnezzar's dreams revealed future world-history (Daniel 2). Dreams sent the wise men home by a secret way instead of giving information to Herod (Matthew 2:12). And the visions of the prophets, whether they can be called dreams or not, were used to give God's messages in picturesque ways, as we see today.

B. Lesson Background

Last week's Lesson Background discussed the three phases of the Babylonian captivity. This week's lesson puts us into Phase 3 of that time of distress. The prophet Ezekiel, who was probably one of the ten thousand captives taken to Babylon in Phase 2, received messages from the Lord for his fellow captives. Some of the messages were given in visions (Ezekiel 1:1-3).

We take one of those visions as our text. As we begin our lesson from Ezekiel 37, we realize that we are now in Phase 3 of the exile because the city of Jerusalem has fallen (see Ezekiel 33:21).

I. Vision and Question (Ezekiel 37:1-3)

Ezekiel 1:1 indicates that Ezekiel's home while in captivity is with a colony of captives "by the river of Chebar." Many think that that was not a natural river, but one of the big man-made canals used for irrigation and navigation. The "land of the Chaldeans" or Babylonians (Ezekiel 1:3) is modern-day Iraq.

A. Dry Bones Revealed (v. 1)

1. The hand of the LORD was upon me, and carried me out in the Spirit of the LORD, and set me down in the midst of the valley which was full of bones.

The hand of the Lord, God's own power, takes control of Ezekiel and transports him to another place. The phrase *in the Spirit of the Lord* suggests that the Holy Spirit takes charge of Ezekiel's mind for the purpose of imparting some revelation to that prophet. Ezekiel seems to be saying that the Lord's hand carries him through the air and sets him down at his destination. Does Ezekiel's body go along on that trip, or only his mind and spirit?

We also have questions about the destination, a certain *valley which was full of bones.* Is this a real valley with bones visible to normal eyesight? Or is the whole scene a vision put into Ezekiel's mind by the Holy Spirit? As interesting as such questions are, we should not allow them to delay us in uncovering what message the Lord is giving to His prophet.

B. Dry Bones Examined (v. 2)

2. And caused me to pass by them round about: and, behold, there were very many in the open valley; and, lo, they were very dry.

The Lord leads the prophet about to inspect the entire floor of this *open valley.* It looks as if a terrific battle had been fought there in the long-ago time when Assyrians and Babylonians had battled for supremacy.

Apparently, thousands of dead bodies had been devoured by wild beasts and birds, or perhaps just reduced to dust by a century of decay. What Ezekiel sees is countless thousands of scattered bones, dried and bleached as if exposed to the harsh rays of the sun for years and years. [See question #1, page 72.]

C. Ezekiel Questioned (v. 3)

3. And he said unto me, Son of man, can these bones live? And I answered, O Lord GOD, thou knowest.

Perhaps we are surprised to see Ezekiel referred to as *Son of man,* since Jesus uses that phrase of Himself many times in the Gospels. In the book of Ezekiel, however, this phrase points to that prophet's mortality. It is not a reference to deity here.

When God asks the question *can these bones live?* it does not mean that He is seeking information. Rather, the question is designed to start a conversation and to gauge Ezekiel's outlook. Accustomed as we are to the ordinary course of events, we might answer God's question, "No way!" But Ezekiel is God's prophet, and obviously God is setting the stage for something extraordinary. Wisely the prophet gives the answer he is sure of: *O Lord God, thou knowest.* [See question #2, page 72.]

"FAREWELL, DEATH VALLEY"

Few North Americans set foot in Death Valley National Park in the summertime, but that's when many European tourists want to visit it. They are drawn to the adventure of going to the hottest, driest place on the continent! Much of the park is below sea level; "Badwater" is the lowest (at –282 feet) as well as the hottest.

The legend of how the valley got its name comes from the days of the gold-seekers who headed west in the mid-nineteenth century to find their fortune in the Sierra Nevada. One party of pioneers (including several families) sought to cross a very deep and wide valley in eastern California. Many in the party died from lack of fresh water. As the survivors finally made their way out of the valley—where the bodies and eventually the bones of those who died would lie—one of the fortunate ones is said to have remarked, "Farewell, Death Valley."

Ezekiel was transported in a dream to a place of death—a valley full of bones. In this place filled with symbols of death, the prophet is asked the question the human race has always asked: Can the dead live again? That question may explain in part the fascination that modern travelers have with Death Valley. Our technology can help us survive such a place; but even the most advanced technology cannot bring the dead back to life. Whether physically or spiritually, that can be accomplished only by God.   —C. R. B.

II. Death and Life (Ezekiel 37:4-10)

In the first lesson of this series, we read that "the Lord God formed man of the dust of the ground." The dust had no life in it, and neither did the man who was formed from it. But God "breathed into his nostrils the breath of life; and man became a living soul" (Genesis 2:7). Anyone who knows of that fact can hardly doubt that God can use dead bones and lifeless dust to create another person, or a multitude of people.

A. Instruction (v. 4)

4. Again he said unto me, Prophesy upon these bones, and say unto them, O ye dry bones, hear the word of the LORD.

God neither had nor needed a prophet to relay His word when He created Adam. But now God chooses to honor Ezekiel by having him speak *the word* for the *dry bones*. So God instructs, and His prophet obeys.

B. Promise (vv. 5, 6)

5. Thus saith the Lord GOD unto these bones; Behold, I will cause breath to enter into you, and ye shall live.

Just like the "mountains of Israel" that Ezekiel prophesies to in 36:1, the *bones* have neither ear to hear nor mind to understand. But God's prophet obediently gives them God's promise. Ezekiel himself can hear, understand, and be impressed when the promise is kept, and so can we.

6. And I will lay sinews upon you, and will bring up flesh upon you, and cover you with skin, and put breath in you, and ye shall live; and ye shall know that I am the LORD.

To those bare bones God intends to give *sinews* and *flesh* and *skin*—yes, and we may presume livers and lungs and brains as well. When God infuses *breath* into them, they will have all they need for new life. And with their new minds they will know that He is *the Lord*.

C. Action! (vv. 7-10)

7. So I prophesied as I was commanded: and as I prophesied, there was a noise, and behold a shaking, and the bones came together, bone to his bone.

As Ezekiel begins to speak to *the bones* as the Lord had told him to do, the response is prompt. But it is hard for us to know exactly what the prophet hears and sees. The *noise* mentioned here may very well be a rattling sound as dry bones in motion click against one another. Whatever details of sound and motion we choose to imagine, the result seems clear: countless disconnected bones join themselves together to form thousands of complete human skeletons.

8. And when I beheld, lo, the sinews and the flesh came up upon them, and the skin covered them above: but there was no breath in them.

How to Say It

ASSYRIANS. Uh-*sear*-e-unz.
BABYLON. *Bab*-uh-lun.
BABYLONIANS. Bab-ih-*low*-nee-unz.
CHALDEANS. Kal-*dee*-unz.
CHEBAR. *Kee*-bar.
EZEKIEL. Ee-*zeek*-ee-ul or Ee-*zeek*-yul.
EZRA. *Ez*-ruh.
ISAIAH. Eye-*zay*-uh.
RUAH (Hebrew). *rue*-ah.

Ezekiel watches as ligaments tie the bones together at every joint, as muscles appear and are joined by tendons to the proper bones. Easily we imagine what is not mentioned in the text: hearts, lungs, and other internal organs taking their proper places before *skin* is wrapped around a completed body. In other words, Ezekiel watches while thousands of complete human skeletons become complete human bodies. But they are bodies with *no breath* of life *in them*.

9. Then said he unto me, Prophesy unto the wind, prophesy, son of man, and say to the wind, Thus saith the Lord GOD; Come from the four winds, O breath, and breathe upon these slain, that they may live.

In this verse and the next, we see some differences in our English versions. The Hebrew word *ruah* can mean *wind* or *breath* or spirit, depending on context. When we see *the wind* or the *breath* invited to *come from the four winds*, we have to understand that *the four winds* are the four directions—north, south, east, and west. When the *ruah* is invited to come from everywhere and blow on those lifeless bodies in the valley, we naturally translate it *wind*. But when the *ruah* enters those bodies, one version calls it *breath* and another calls it *spirit*—and who can say that either of them is wrong?

So we see Ezekiel, directed by God, calling the wind, or the breath, to come from all directions and blow or breathe on those lifeless bodies *that they may live*. Whatever of wind that enters those bodies will be breath or spirit or both, and with it God Himself will supply life. The entire picture is one of God's great power. [See question #3, page 72.]

10. So I prophesied as he commanded me, and the breath came into them, and they lived, and stood up upon their feet, an exceeding great army.

Life from death! Instead of a valley full of skeletal remains there is now a standing *army*, and it is *exceeding great*.

This imagery leaves us with some questions, however. Is it real and literal, this standing army suddenly raised from the bones of men long dead? Or is it just a vision given to the prophet? Is there actually a sudden army of the unemployed looking for jobs in a time when jobs are scarce and pay is low because all those captives from Judah have to take whatever work they can get at whatever pay is offered? Are the dry bones and the living men seen only by Ezekiel? Look at chapter one of Ezekiel's book. Obviously it describes a fantastic vision. Perhaps what we have been reading describes another.

In the final analysis, this lesson is not really about the dead bones that become living men.

Rather, it is about Jewish captives in a foreign land. The story of the dead bones that become living men is an illustration designed to show how great the change will be when those hopeless, despairing captives will be restored to liberty in their homeland. The last part of our text is part of God's message to those captives.

III. Explanation and Future (Ezekiel 37:11-14)

The captives now have been in Babylon for between twelve and twenty-five years (compare Ezekiel 33:21 with 40:1). Homesickness grows worse instead of better. Each morning the captives look out at the flat plain and long for the hills of home. Each evening their loneliness deepens as the sun sets behind a foreign horizon (e.g., Lamentations 2:11).

Visual for lesson 8. *Use this sobering visual to remind your learners of a question that each of us must answer.*

A. Situation as Is (v. 11)

11. Then he said unto me, Son of man, these bones are the whole house of Israel: behold, they say, Our bones are dried, and our hope is lost: we are cut off for our parts.

Now we have answers to the questions we raised in the commentary for verse 10. The Lord explains that the dry *bones* represent all captive Israelites (not just the Judeans in Babylon) as they see themselves. They are dead to family, friends, and country, as dead as those bleached bones in the valley (cf. Lamentations 3:6).

Even when they had been at home with their countrymen in Jerusalem, the Judeans had been too weak to resist the conquering army of Babylon. Now that Jerusalem has fallen, they see no hope of ever being released. Perhaps when the captives say *we are cut off* they are remembering the prophecy of 1 Kings 9:6-9.

What our translators mean by that phrase *for our parts* is a bit of a mystery. Perhaps the entire phrase *we are cut off for our parts* should be taken to mean something like "we are cut off to ourselves." The captives are out of contact with their homeland, their temple (now destroyed), and all that they hold dear. Undoubtedly, they think they will live and die in that condition (Lamentations 5:2, 3).

B. Situation to Come (vv. 12-14)

12, 13. Therefore prophesy and say unto them, Thus saith the Lord GOD; Behold, O my people, I will open your graves, and cause you to come up out of your graves, and bring you into the land of Israel. And ye shall know that I am the LORD, when I have opened your graves, O my people, and brought you up out of your graves.

The captives in Babylon think they are dead to home and country. But things are not really as they seem to be! The restoration to come will have two aspects. We see the first one mentioned in the verse before us: a physical renewal of Israel as a nation.

This renewal comes about when God brings the Persian army to defeat Babylon and free the captives (Ezra 1:1-4; Isaiah 44:28; 45:1, 13). When that happens, those former captives will know that it is God's doing because God's prophet has told them about it in advance. [See question #4, page 72.] When it happens, the Jews will again give close attention to God and His law. This will inaugurate the second aspect of the renewal, as our next verse shows. [See question #5, page 72.]

GETTING OUT OF THE GRAVE

There's an old joke about a fellow who left a bar late one night after having spent the whole evening drinking. Although quite drunk, he still had enough awareness of his situation to know that he should walk home, rather than drive. However, home was a long way off, and his normal path would take him around the perimeter of a very large cemetery.

After contemplating this for a long time—his consumption of alcohol having slowed his thinking processes greatly—he decided to take a short-cut through the graveyard. Stumbling along in the dark, he fell into a new grave that had just been opened the previous afternoon. Little did he realize that another drunk had fallen into the grave and was lying there waiting for morning to come.

The subject of our story then started clambering for hand- and toeholds that would enable him to escape the grave. That's when the voice of the other man startled him from the darkness: "You'll never get out of here." But he did!

Israel's sin had placed many of them in graves in a foreign land. The graves were literal for those who died there, and figurative for those who felt themselves to be as good as dead. But as God spoke to the exiles through Ezekiel, His voice was reassuring: "I'll bring you up out of your graves and you shall live again in the place I have given to you." God's promise through Christ to people of all nations is the same: "I'll raise you from the dead and bring you to the eternal place that I am preparing for you." Do we really have faith that this will happen as He promised?   —C. R. B.

14. And shall put my Spirit in you, and ye shall live, and I shall place you in your own land: then shall ye know that I the LORD have spoken it, and performed it, saith the LORD.

The second aspect of Israel's restoration is spiritual renewal. Free in their own country and knowing that it is *the Lord* who has made it so, the people will be ready to be led by His *Spirit.* Ezra 3 shows us the receptive attitude of the people upon their return.

Conclusion

A. Hope—Theirs and Ours

Never was there a people more hopeless than those held captive in Babylon. In their own estimation they were as good as dead—dead as bones that had been bleached by the harsh sunshine of many decades. But God did not want them to be captives forever. He wanted them to be free in their own land, serving Him exclusively.

Yet God did not allow the captives to have hope in their own power. They were thoroughly intimidated by the might of Babylon's army.

Home Daily Bible Readings

Monday, Oct. 18—God's Name Was Profaned (Ezekiel 36:16-22)
Tuesday, Oct. 19—God Will Give a New Heart (Ezekiel 36:23-32)
Wednesday, Oct. 20—The People Shall Know God (Ezekiel 36:33-38)
Thursday, Oct. 21—Ezekiel Sees the Dry Bones (Ezekiel 37:1-6)
Friday, Oct. 22—The Dry Bones Live and Breathe (Ezekiel 37:7-14)
Saturday, Oct. 23—Two Nations Shall Become One (Ezekiel 37:15-23)
Sunday, Oct. 24—God Will Bless the New Nation (Ezekiel 37:24-28)

They could have no hope in the few remaining countrymen back home. Those folks had no more power than did the captives themselves. So for the captives God created hope in Himself. He did it with a promise, a promise of liberty and of return to homeland (also Jeremiah 30:3).

God had a long record of promises kept. To Adam He promised death for disobedience, and Adam died. To Noah He promised life for building an ark, and Noah lived. To Israelites enslaved in Egypt He had promised freedom and a land of their own, and they had lived in that land for centuries. To sinners in that land the Lord promised captivity in Babylon, and that promise was being kept in the lives of these captives. So when God promises a return to their own land, they can live in hope until they are home again.

Yet the captives do not pack their bags and set out for home as soon as they hear God's promise from Ezekiel. For several decades they will continue to live in Babylon, and in hope. We wonder how much their hope is dimmed when Phase 3 of the captivity begins, and Jerusalem and the temple are burned and battered to the ground. To the captives already living in Babylon, it must seem that there is no home to go back to.

But the holy hill of Zion is still there, and so is God's earlier promise. So hope has the potential of burning brightly in the hearts of the captives until the seventy years of Babylonian rule is complete. With love of God and love of country pushing them forward, God's people will go back to rebuild temple and town.

Hope in God is the best kind of hope! And to those of us who have put our trust in Jesus the Savior, Peter writes, "who by him do believe in God, that raised him up from the dead, and gave him glory; that your faith and hope might be in God" (1 Peter 1:21). Hope does not die easily when it rests in God. "In the world ye shall have tribulation," said Jesus (John 16:33), and sometimes we have it year after weary year. "But be of good cheer," Jesus goes on, "I have overcome the world."

So we look forward, taking to ourselves Jesus' own promise: "Be thou faithful unto death, and I will give thee a crown of life" (Revelation 2:10). Praise God for such a Savior!

B. Prayer

Our Father and our God, we know that You are eternal and that Your promises can never fail. Thank You for the bright hope they create to guide us and to energize us in the way everlasting. In Jesus' name, amen.

C. Thought to Remember

God is dependable. Are you?

Learning by Doing

This page contains an alternative lesson plan emphasizing learning activities.
Classes desiring such student involvement will find these suggestions helpful.

Learning Goals

After participating in this lesson, each student will be able to:

1. Describe the details of Ezekiel's vision and its application of hope to the captives from Judah.

2. Suggest some circumstances or situations of today in which a word of hope is needed.

3. Make a plan of action to inject the hope of Christ into one of those situations.

Into the Lesson

Option #1: Have three or four unassembled models of simple human skeletons available on tables. As students enter, ask them to attempt to set up the skeletons. You may choose to play the song "Dem Bones" during the activity. Make the transition to Bible study by saying, "What opportunities for the future does a skeleton hold? Does it have any hope? Today's study includes an unusual vision that tells how God used human bones to demonstrate hope in a hopeless and desperate world. He offers such hope to believers who find themselves in desperate circumstances."

Note: If a model of a skeleton is not available, simply hold up a bone and ask the same questions and make the same transition.

Into the Word

Activity #1: Writing Newspaper Headline Stories. Ask teams of four or five to read today's printed text and outline a story suitable for publication in a newsletter. Their outline should include (1) a headline that captures attention, (2) a list of facts to be included, (3) items to include in a section that emphasizes the unusual visual and audio scene Ezekiel witnessed. Give each team a sheet of paper and a marker to make notes. After the activity ask teams to share the headlines they chose. Mention that most of the other information is probably similar in each team's list. Make the transition to the next activity by mentioning the uniqueness and wonder of this vision. Say, "Maybe it would be helpful to have a firsthand impression from Ezekiel himself."

Activity #2: An Interview with Ezekiel. Have a class member or guest portray Ezekiel. Give the person the following questions to be used. Include the suggested items he or she may choose to talk about under each. Give this actor a photocopied article about "Ezekiel" from a Bible dictionary and an article introducing the book of Ezekiel from a Bible handbook for study. Ezekiel's costume may be as simple as wearing a name tag. A cloak and actor's beard may add flavor. Questions (and suggested material for answers) follow:

1. Tell us about yourself, Ezekiel. Who are you? Where did you come from? *(Mention his prophet and priest background, time that he lived, what was going on in his world at the time.)*

2. What was the occasion for writing your book? What is its purpose? *(A snapshot of Israel and Judah's captivities, what the Babylonians were like, how the book differs from and complements Jeremiah's prophecies, and what Ezekiel is communicating to Judah's captives. Emphasize the hope that God offers His people.)*

3. Your book is full of visions and vivid imagery. Tell us about some of these visions. Also, tell us how you felt when you saw the miracle in the valley of dry bones. *(Ezekiel may tell about two or three of his visions before focusing on the shock and wonder of the dry bones story.)*

4. What did you personally discover about the character and will of God in this bizarre vision or event? *(Ezekiel can talk about God's supernatural power, His yearning for peace for His people, His insistence on holy living, patience in waiting for God's timing, and the hope He offers to people who are feeling hopeless.)*

Thank your "Ezekiel" as he leaves the room. Make transition to application by reminding the class of the hopeless feelings among the people of Judah. Yet, Ezekiel came offering hope. There are lessons here for people in extremely difficult circumstances today.

Into Life

Ask the class to identify circumstances in today's world that bring a sense of hopelessness. Examples: dysfunctional marriage relationships, financial hardships, terminal illnesses. List these.

Next, ask members to imagine that they are Judeans who lived through the Babylonian captivity and heard Ezekiel's prophecies. Ask, "What advice would you give from your experience to people suffering hardships like those listed?" List these answers.

Third, note that there are Christian people in seemingly hopeless circumstances today. Challenge all to be ready to be God's encouraging Word to them.

Let's Talk It Over

The questions on this page are designed to promote discussion of the lesson by the class and to encourage application of the lesson Scriptures. The answers provided are only discussion starters. Let your class talk it over from there.

1. The valley of dry bones must have been a hopeless sight for the prophet. It may have caused a feeling of despair or anxiety. Have you ever been in a hopeless valley of "dry bones"? What did you do to maintain your faith?

It was clear that many, many people had lost their lives in this valley. The presence of death often brings fear and anxiety. But other losses can also put us in the valley of dry bones. We quarrel with someone in the family, a good neighbor moves away, our job is eliminated, credit card debt gets out of control—these and countless other issues may have at one time or another put some of your learners into a dry valley. Have them tell of Scripture passages that encouraged them, or of supporting brothers and sisters in Christ. These stories will be great testimonies, and may encourage other class members who might even now be in such a valley.

2. The lesson writer notes that we might have answered, "No way!" to the question, "Can these bones live?" We might also have expected God's prophet to answer confidently, "Of course, they can!" When is it proper to affirm faith in a positive outcome to a situation, and when should we, like Ezekiel, simply say, "God knows"?

We should be very careful about assuring people in the surgical intensive care unit that "everything will be okay; your loved one is going to recover." Yes, God *can* heal, but we are in no position to know that He *will*. Faithful people have seen their prayers answered "yes" and have had their loved ones restored; equally faithful people have had to learn to live with "My grace is sufficient for thee."

We can be assured that God's grace will sustain us whatever the outcome. We can be confident that God loves us no matter what. We know that not a sparrow falls without His notice, but sometimes they do fall. As a popular Christian song of a few years ago affirmed, sometimes He calms the storm; at other times He calms His child.

3. It was an amazing sight! Dry bones had become human bodies, covered in flesh and skin. By itself, that would have been an awe-inspiring miracle. But of course, the miracle was not complete. Had the prophet left the val-

ley right then, he would have missed the greater good God was doing. How do we sometimes miss out on God's blessings because we assume God is finished when He is not?

First, we need to advise caution in stating too confidently "what God is doing." We often see His providence much better in hindsight. Still, as we walk by faith we are sure that God is present with us and is guiding us through His Word, through His people, and through His indwelling Spirit. In the course of things, perhaps our church launches a capital expenditures drive to erect a new facility. People pray about it and give money or commitments to see it built.

As a result the program is a success, and we have a lovely new edifice. But two years later it's too small! Perhaps our vision of what God wanted to do with us two years earlier was itself too small—perhaps we did not allow God to do what He really wanted because our plan was too easy to accomplish in our own strength.

4. The Jewish captives thought their situation was hopeless. Ezekiel was sent to tell them otherwise. What hopeless situation needs a word of comfort from you or your church?

Of course, the biggest need is that of salvation. Outside of Christ people are without hope for eternity. But there may be some "earthly" issues that your class can address as well. Are there single mothers in your church facing a seemingly hopeless struggle to make ends meet? How can you help them? Is there a seemingly hopeless racial division in your city? How can you help bring reconciliation?

5. What "grave" has God brought you out of? How did He do it? How can your story help to lift up someone else?

Again, the issue of salvation ought to come up first. God has raised us from eternal death to eternal life in Christ Jesus.

But many of your learners have been "in the depths" since their salvation. Times of stress and anxiety, financial hardship or physical ailments, have brought them low. But God is faithful, and He has seen them through those trials and raised them up. Encourage these folks to share their testimonies in an effort to encourage and lift up others.

Creating a Renewed Trust

DEVOTIONAL READING: Psalm 91:1-10.

BACKGROUND SCRIPTURE: Psalm 73.

PRINTED TEXT: Psalm 73:1-3, 12, 13, 16-18, 21-26.

Psalm 73:1-3, 12, 13, 16-18, 21-26

1 Truly God is good to Israel, even to such as are of a clean heart.

2 But as for me, my feet were almost gone; my steps had well-nigh slipped.

3 For I was envious at the foolish, when I saw the prosperity of the wicked.

· · · · · · · · · · ·

12 Behold, these are the ungodly, who prosper in the world; they increase in riches.

13 Verily I have cleansed my heart in vain, and washed my hands in innocency.

· · · · · · · · · · ·

16 When I thought to know this, it was too painful for me;

17 Until I went into the sanctuary of God; then understood I their end.

18 Surely thou didst set them in slippery places: thou castedst them down into destruction.

· · · · · · · · · · ·

21 Thus my heart was grieved, and I was pricked in my reins.

22 So foolish was I, and ignorant: I was as a beast before thee.

23 Nevertheless I am continually with thee: thou hast holden me by my right hand.

24 Thou shalt guide me with thy counsel, and afterward receive me to glory.

25 Whom have I in heaven but thee? And there is none upon earth that I desire besides thee.

26 My flesh and my heart faileth: but God is the strength of my heart, and my portion for ever.

Oct 31

GOLDEN TEXT: My flesh and my heart faileth: but God is the strength of my heart, and my portion for ever.—Psalm 73:26.

The God of Continuing Creation
Unit 2: God's Creativity Continues
(Lessons 5-9)

Lesson Aims

After participating in this lesson, each student will be able to:

1. Tell the reasons why Asaph's trust in God was lost and how it was restored.

2. Explain why we can trust God even when evil seems to prosper.

3. Identify a personal area of struggle and make a statement of trust in God to help him or her deal with it.

Lesson Outline

INTRODUCTION
    A. Myopic Mike Murphy
    B. Lesson Background
  I. ASAPH'S ENVY (Psalm 73:1-3, 12, 13)
    A. Goodness from Above (v. 1)
    B. Peril from Below (vv. 2, 3)
    C. Error from Within (vv. 12, 13)
      Feeling Like Asaph
 II. ASAPH'S UNDERSTANDING (Psalm 73:16-18, 21, 22)
    A. Success in the Sanctuary (vv. 16, 17)
    B. End of Envy (v. 18)
      Not Always as They Seem
    C. Victory Through Self-examination (vv. 21, 22)
III. ASAPH'S APPRECIATION (Psalm 73:23-26)
    A. Presence and Guidance (v. 23)
    B. Now and Later (v. 24)
    C. Weakness and Strength (vv. 25, 26)
CONCLUSION
    A. Ancient Example
    B. Modern Example
    C. Our Decision
    D. Prayer
    E. Thought to Remember

Introduction

A. Myopic Mike Murphy

Mike Murphy was a friendly man, and he made new friends quickly when he came to our town to be manager of the supermarket. The Rotary Club welcomed him eagerly, and the PTA gave a like welcome to him and his wife.

But Mike's wife and children came to church without him. That was a surprise, for some of us knew Mike had been a leader in the church in his former town. To many invitations he answered, "I tried that. What does it get you?"

Mike was such a good friend that we didn't want to give up our efforts to get him back to church. With lots of information from him and his wife and other sources, we pieced together the story of his leaving the church.

Mike had owned a store—not a very profitable one, but he had made a comfortable living. He was proud of being a successful merchant, and he gave God credit for his success. "If you're true to God, He will be true to you," he said frequently.

Then a chain of supermarkets had put a store in Mike's town. It dwarfed Mike's store. Its stock was vastly larger, and its prices were lower. Month after month Mike faced loss instead of profit. So he closed his store and sold the building to pay his debts. "If that's the way God takes care of His people," he thought, "I'm through with God." [See question #1, page 80.]

The next day the very chain that had put Mike out of business looked him up to hire him and sent him to manage the store in our town. Strangely, it never occurred to Mike that God had anything to do with that. He never went to church again until his brother's family came for a weekend visit. Not going to church was unthinkable to that family, as it was to Mike's own wife and children.

Almost by force, the two families took Mike to church with them. Members of the choir later testified that Mike never put his handkerchief back into his pocket. He just kept wiping his eyes through the whole service. At the front door the minister gripped Mike's hand and said, "I hope we'll see you again next Sunday."

Struggling to find his voice, Mike managed to gulp, "You know, I had forgotten how good it is to worship."

Mike has been seen in church every Sunday since that time. In a discussion he likes to say, "Be true to God, and He will be true to you." If a friend twits him about losing his store and being through with God, he says, "Only in December did my store make as much as my monthly pay is now. God will take care of you if you take care to do right."

B. Lesson Background

Asaph was a man who never stopped going to worship services, as Mike had. Indeed, Asaph's business *was* worship. But like Mike, Asaph inquired, "What's in it for me?"

For a time he was discontent with the remuneration he received. But Asaph did not have complete freedom in choosing his work, for he was born in the tribe of Levi. That means he was dedicated from his birth to help with the religious life of Israel. In the tribe of Levi some were destined to be priests while others helped out in many ways, with duties ranging from janitor work to sacred music. (See Numbers 3:17-37; 4:4-15; 7:4-9; 1 Chronicles 6:1-48.)

Asaph was a musician, being one who sang psalms in the services of worship (1 Chronicles 15:16, 17). When the orchestra was performing, Asaph was one who handled cymbals (15:19). That may seem to be a minor part, but Asaph was made chief of the musicians (16:4, 5), so he must have been skilled.

Asaph was a songwriter, too. Psalms 50 and 73–83 are his work. Asaph's work was apparently so profound that he established what we might call a "school of music" that endured even after the return from exile (see Nehemiah 7:44). (Just so we don't get confused, three other Asaphs are mentioned in 2 Kings 18:18; Nehemiah 2:8; and 1 Chronicles 26:1.)

Last week we read how a new hope was created in despondent captives in Babylon. This week we look to a time several hundred years earlier to see how Asaph's trust was restored. King David was beginning to expand his empire. He had taken Jerusalem from the pagans, made it his capital city, and installed the ark of the covenant there in its special tent. Asaph was a leader among the musicians who served in ceremonies of worship there.

As David continued to press his campaign against the pagans, the wartime economy provided many businesses an opportunity to get rich quickly. Even so, Asaph and his fellow musicians found no corresponding increase in their income. Asaph was disturbed.

The brief line printed above Psalm 73 says, "A Psalm of Asaph." No doubt that simple byline names the writer of the song. But in this case it happens also to name the subject. This is a song *about* Asaph as well as *by* him.

This psalm is thus a personal song, recording thoughts, feelings, and reflections of the writer, including his shame. To thoughtful readers it therefore becomes a didactic (teaching) song, instructing us and moving us to avoid such feelings as the writer abandoned. It propels us to cling to such thoughts and feelings as Asaph cherished in his conclusion.

I. Asaph's Envy
(Psalm 73:1-3, 12, 13)

The first notes of the song sound a sharp contrast between the beautiful harmony of God's goodness and the threatening peril of Asaph's nearly misguided walk.

A. Goodness from Above (v. 1)
1. Truly God is good to Israel, even to such as are of a clean heart.

God certainly is *good* to His people. Haven't all of us noticed that? *A clean heart* attracts God's favor as a magnet attracts steel (cf. Matthew 5:8). Matters of the heart are very important to Asaph (see Psalm 73:7, 13, 21, 26). [See question #2, page 80.]

When we start to count our blessings, it's safe to say that the blessings we overlook are more than those we count. *God is good.* This essential truth stands like a rock at the beginning of the song. Beware of anything that seems to contradict it!

B. Peril from Below (vv. 2, 3)
2, 3. But as for me, my feet were almost gone; my steps had well-nigh slipped. For I was envious at the foolish, when I saw the prosperity of the wicked.

The phrase *but as for me* signals a discord, something out of harmony with the fact of God's goodness that we saw in verse 1. What follows pictures a walker or hiker on a hazardous path. That unstable path for Asaph is to develop attitudes of envy and covetousness when seeing the *prosperity of the wicked.* So Asaph seems to speak of two "masters" who compete for his allegiance. Surely "God is good" (v. 1), but the path of the wicked seems to be very pleasant as well! [See question #3, page 80.]

With refreshing candor, Asaph is one who freely admits his error in this regard. But Asaph's problem brings up an age-old question: if God is good, how can He give *prosperity* to the *wicked?* (See also Job 21:7-15.) Verses 4-11 tell more about the wealthy wicked, but we can bypass that for this lesson. We already know enough about people who seem to prosper with impunity through less-than-ethical dealings, don't we?

C. Error from Within (vv. 12, 13)
12. Behold, these are the ungodly, who prosper in the world; they increase in riches.

Thus the psalmist sums up what he has been saying about the wealthy wicked. The fact that they are *ungodly* is a commentary on their dishonesty and lack of ethics. This is a problem throughout Israel's history (e.g., 1 Samuel 8:1-3; Jeremiah 6:13; 22:17; Ezekiel 22:12, 23-31; Hosea 12:7; Amos 8:4-6). The temptation to join them is always there.

FEELING LIKE ASAPH

The final issue of *U.S. News & World Report* for 2002 had a ten-page article detailing—as it called them—the "actions of corporate honchos

[that] horrified the nation." The lead page of the article mimicked another newsmagazine's red border and headline with the words, "Rogue of the Year," showing the picture of a former CEO of a large corporation who was charged in 2002 with stealing six hundred million dollars from his company.

The article also named thirteen other executives who had been charged variously with fraud, money laundering, conspiracy, mismanagement, insider trading, and—in at least one case—causing the bankruptcy of his firm with a loss of one hundred and forty *billion* dollars in market value! A few did some jail time, some were fined heavily; but most had protected themselves so that they could continue their lavish lifestyles even though thousands of their employees had lost jobs, health insurance, and pensions.

In the pages of the Psalms, Asaph reminds us that such behavior and outcome is nothing new. The world always has been full of selfish schemers who have no regard for others. We sometimes feel just like Asaph, don't we? Fortunately, there is another side to the story that our lesson makes clear. *That's* what we need to hear when we feel as Asaph did. —C. R. B.

13. Verily I have cleansed my heart in vain, and washed my hands in innocency.

Asaph has been careful to keep himself clean and pure, both in the motives of his *heart* as well as what he has done with his *hands.* But at some point he came to think that such holiness was all *in vain.* His prosperity did not match that of the crooks. It wasn't fair! What was the use of being good and doing good? Asaph had indeed envied the wicked (v. 3). By the time he gets around to writing this song, he knows that that attitude was a mistake.

Home Daily Bible Readings

Monday, Oct. 25—Sing for Joy to God (Psalm 84:1-7)

Tuesday, Oct. 26—Trust in God (Psalm 84:8-12)

Wednesday, Oct. 27—God Is Our Refuge (Psalm 91:1-10)

Thursday, Oct. 28—The Wicked People Prosper (Psalm 73:1-9)

Friday, Oct. 29—Is Our Faith in Vain? (Psalm 73:10-14)

Saturday, Oct. 30—The Prosperous Ones Are Destroyed (Psalm 73:15-20)

Sunday, Oct. 31—Faith in God Renewed (Psalm 73:21-28)

II. Asaph's Understanding (Psalm 73:16-18, 21, 22)

Asaph must have done a lot of thinking about the situation that troubles him. He will not think the Lord to be unfair, but he cannot think the situation itself is fair. God is all-powerful. Asaph knows that. Then why does God let His faithful servants be underpaid while every crooked businessman in Israel gets richer and richer?

A. Success in the Sanctuary (vv. 16, 17)

16. When I thought to know this, it was too painful for me.

The more Asaph *thought* about the situation— the more he struggled to reconcile the apparent inconsistency—the more *painful* it became. Is God content with the unfair lot of His people? That seems incredible. Is He unable to do anything about it? That seems illogical. So Asaph agonizes, as have others (cf. Habakkuk 1:2-4.)

17. Until I went into the sanctuary of God; then understood I their end.

Finally the musician carried his discord *into the sanctuary of God,* to worship with the assembled people. Perhaps he sang in the choir; perhaps he sounded his cymbals in the orchestra. No doubt the familiar forms of worship brought happiness to him as they brought it to Mike Murphy in the Introduction of this lesson. No doubt the melody of well-known psalms was soothing to his troubled soul. [See question #4, page 80.]

Perhaps special inspiration brought understanding to God's musician, and with understanding came peace. Specifically, says Asaph, *then understood I their end.* Asaph knows that the inequitable situation that troubles him is not permanent. The wealthy wicked are ecstatic now, but *their end* will be disaster (cf. Psalm 37).

B. End of Envy (v. 18)

18. Surely thou didst set them in slippery places: thou castedst them down into destruction.

The wealthy wicked feel secure, but the ground under them is more *slippery* than they realize. At the proper time a nudge from the Lord will send them hurtling *down into destruction.* Asaph no longer envies them. Not for the world will he change places with one of those doomed souls. "The same shall receive greater damnation" (Luke 20:47). Asaph has more to say about the fate of the wicked in Psalm 75:8.

NOT ALWAYS AS THEY SEEM

NASA's Viking I spacecraft was orbiting the planet Mars in 1976, taking photographs of possible landing sites. One of the pictures it relayed to earth showed what looked like a giant head rising from the Martian plain. NASA scientists jokingly called it the "Face on Mars," and released the picture to the media, hoping to increase public interest in America's space efforts.

Some people saw the "face" as evidence that the red planet had been inhabited by an intelligent civilization in the past. Some thought it to be like the Sphinx in Egypt, surrounded by other evidence of a lost civilization, including pyramids, cities, and even a sewage plant!

In 1998 NASA's Mars Global Surveyor took more pictures on two occasions, using improved technology that two decades had brought into existence. These pictures demonstrated that the "face" was nothing more than an eroded mesa on the planet's surface. But that didn't satisfy the operator of at least one Web site, who still claims to see "evidence" where few others see it.

As Asaph got a better look at things, he realized that his earlier view had been skewed by his envy of, and anger at, evil people. Things are *not* always as they seem, and we often need to take a clearer look at the situation. Looking through the eyes of God is often a cure for our mistaken perceptions of life. —C. R. B.

C. Victory Through Self-examination (vv. 21, 22)

21. Thus my heart was grieved, and I was pricked in my reins.

Asaph's *heart was grieved*, not so much for the fate of the wicked as for his own recent envy of them. Now that understanding has come, Asaph is ashamed for ever allowing envy into his *heart*.

After the fashion of Hebrew poetry, *pricked in my reins* repeats the line before it, *my heart was grieved*. The ancients thought, as we do, that the heart is responsible for emotions such as grief and joy. But, unlike us, they thought that responsibility to be shared by the other internal organs. Literally, *reins* are kidneys (cf. Psalm 7:9). [See question #5, page 80.]

22. So foolish was I, and ignorant: I was as a beast before thee.

In the light of his new outlook, Asaph makes a sobering estimate of his previous understanding. He had been so *foolish* and *ignorant* that he was no better than a donkey or a dog. Such honesty!

III. Asaph's Appreciation (Psalm 73:23-26)

When Asaph was foolish and ignorant enough to envy the wealthy wicked, that envy overshadowed his appreciation for the many blessings he already had. But when understanding comes and envy departs, Asaph can count his blessings with redoubled appreciation.

Visual for lesson 9

This visual shows one way to find God's strength. What other ways can your learners suggest?

A. Presence and Guidance (v. 23)

23. Nevertheless I am continually with thee: thou hast holden me by my right hand.

What a privilege! To be continually with God is better than all the riches gathered by all the wicked through the ages. And God holds Asaph by his *right hand.* That implies God's guidance and support as being constant in His presence. Asaph is in good company!

B. Now and Later (v. 24)

24. Thou shalt guide me with thy counsel, and afterward receive me to glory.

Divine guidance is emphasized again, and one who trusts God's *counsel* will never be led astray by it. To this singer of sacred songs, God's guidance no doubt includes inspiration of his writing. We wonder if inspiration makes him aware of future *glory* in Heaven that at the time of Asaph is not yet revealed to most of humanity. But God's counsel can lead one to have respect and honor even on this earth, and that, too, may be called *glory*. [See question #6, page 80.]

C. Weakness and Strength (vv. 25, 26)

25. Whom have I in heaven but thee? And there is none upon earth that I desire besides thee.

Family and friends are good to have. They give encouragement, companionship, and practical help. But no one on earth can compare with our Helper *in heaven*, and in Heaven we have no helper but God.

26. My flesh and my heart faileth, but God is the strength of my heart, and my portion for ever.

Flesh is mere human tissue; *heart* is mere human courage, fortitude, and determination. Neither is adequate for the needs of godly living in an ungodly world. But God supplies what we lack if what we have is truly committed to Him. And He does it *for ever!*

Conclusion

A. Ancient Example

For Asaph trust faded with the coming of envy. Wicked people were getting richer and richer. That couldn't be right, could it? If it is, why should anyone be good?

At first glance we may think Asaph to be a mercenary wretch, greedy for gold. But the matter was not so simple. Didn't God's own honor and prestige demand that one of His chief musicians be rewarded more richly than some common crook? How could children be taught that honesty is the best policy if God's people plodded on weary feet while the wealthy wicked rode in gilded chariots?

So who can say what concerned Asaph most? Was it God's prestige or Asaph's income? His job was secure enough, and the people's tithes kept the Levites from poverty. Could it be that Asaph was merely coveting a gilded chariot of his own? Did Asaph's envy arise from simple greed, or was it based in his zeal for God? Probably it came from some combination of the two, for a human being is not a simple creature.

Whatever the cause of Asaph's envy and the fading of his trust in God, the cure was found in the sanctuary. Perhaps some godly teacher there reminded choir and audience that the destination is more important than the journey. Perhaps some Scripture reading emphasized the assurance that wickedness must lead to disaster and misery. Perhaps a song of the choir focused on God's eternity and reminded the singer that truth and righteousness are eternal, too.

For some reason or combination of reasons, Asaph rose above the short-sighted thinking that made him agitated with the status of the wealthy wicked. Taking the long view, he again rested secure with a steadfast trust in God's eternal goodness.

How to Say It

AMOS. *Ay*-mus.
ASAPH. *Ay*-saff.
BABYLON. *Bab*-uh-lun.
EZEKIEL. Ee-*zeek*-ee-ul or Ee-*zeek*-yul.
HABAKKUK. Huh-*back*-kuk.
HOSEA. Ho-*zay*-uh.
JEREMIAH. Jair-uh-*my*-uh.
NEHEMIAH. *Nee*-huh-*my*-uh (strong accent on *my*).

B. Modern Example

Now think again of Mike Murphy, the genial fellow from the Introduction to this lesson. When he lost his business, he thought God had let him down. He retaliated by turning his back and refusing to speak to God.

As a matter of fact, the loss of Mike's business was no financial loss at all. He sold his building for twice as much as he had paid for it a few years earlier. An entrepreneur was eager to make it into an entertainment complex near the new supermarket. Mike had taken a small loss during the last few months of his operation, but the profit on the building more than compensated.

So what did Mike really lose? He lost some pride. He had been proud to be an independent, successful businessman in competition with larger stores. Now he was "only an employee." His employment was more profitable than his business had been, but he lost the pride in what he had been doing formerly. He felt humiliated and he blamed the Lord. Who else was there to blame?

Like Asaph, Mike found restoration in the sanctuary. He went there unwillingly at first; but once there, he knew he had long been homesick for that place and the people who met there and the God who was worshiped there. His full heart overflowed in tears, tears of mingled regret and joy. Then did Mike trust God again? You know he did.

C. Our Decision

How is your trust in God? Has it faltered because God does not always do what you wish He would do? Have you stopped expecting help from Heaven because sometimes you do not get just the help you want in the way you want it? Are you a Mike Murphy? He wanted a business of his own. God gave him instead a position that brought him more money with less responsibility and less risk. Therefore Mike turned way from God, but kept the profitable position.

If we have followed Mike in turning away from God, let's be quick in following him back. Asaph, too, found truth and reason in the sanctuary, and so can we. Let us not neglect "the assembling of ourselves together" (Hebrews 10:25).

D. Prayer

We do trust You, Father—even when we are disappointed we trust You still. From a thousand evidences we know You love us and want us to have what is good for us. So forgive our misunderstanding and our selfish wishes, and love us still. We pray in Jesus' name, amen.

E. Thought to Remember

Come back to God; stay with Him.

Learning by Doing

This page contains an alternative lesson plan emphasizing learning activities. Classes desiring such student involvement will find these suggestions helpful.

Learning Goals

After participating in this lesson, each student will be able to:

1. Tell the reasons why Asaph's trust in God was lost and how it was restored.

2. Explain why we can trust God even when evil seems to prosper.

3. Identify a personal area of struggle and make a statement of trust in God to help him or her deal with it.

Into the Lesson

Prepare a huge poster by taping pieces of poster board together or by unrolling a long sheet of table paper and taping it to the wall. At the top print, "Why Do the Wicked Prosper?" Bring a large stack of newspapers and/or newsmagazines to class, several rolls of transparent tape, and numerous pairs of scissors. As students arrive, ask them to cut out articles or photos that illustrate unfair situations in the world today. These could include oppression, illegal monetary gains, profits from sin, courtroom injustice, and more. Ask them to tape the clippings to the poster.

Make the transition to Bible study by saying, "Many injustices in today's world may make us angry, even with God. Today's study is of a little-known man who will help us understand injustice, show us a model for handling unfairness, and teach us a lesson in trusting God."

Into the Word

Minilecture: Introduce Asaph by giving a brief lecture based on the Lesson Background beginning on page 74. Prepare a poster as a visual aid, including the following notes. Have each line covered with pieces of paper that you will remove as you lecture on that point.

ASAPH: Musician (1 Chronicles 15:16, 17); Handled Cymbals (1 Chronicles 15:19); Chief of Musicians (1 Chronicles 16:4, 5); Songwriter (Psalms 50, 73-83); Asaph's Discontent; A Personal Song.

Scripture Search: Give individuals or small groups a piece of paper with headings noted below. Students are to look for lines, phrases, or words that describe the heading's themes. They are to write these lines and the Scripture text under the appropriate headings. The headings: "Asaph's Discontent," "Asaph Sees His Error," and "Asaph's Trust Restored." Examples follow.

Asaph's Discontent: Envied the foolish, v. 3; Envied the prosperity of the wicked, v. 3; Saw the ungodly prosper, v. 12; Considered his clean heart and hands to be in vain, v. 13; His heart was grieved, v. 21.

Asaph Sees His Error: Feet almost slipped, v. 2; Was foolish and ignorant, v. 22; Was dumb as an ox ("beast"), v. 22.

Asaph's Trust Restored (Where and how?): Went into the sanctuary, v. 17; Understood the end of the wicked, v. 17; The wicked will slip and fall, v. 18; Is always with God, v. 23; God holds his hand, v. 23; God's counsel and guidance, v. 24; God's strength, v. 26.

After the study ask groups or individuals to report what they found for each section.

Into Life

Ask the following two discussion questions to prepare for the group activity: (1) "How do you feel when an unjust or unfair situation continues over a long period?" (2) "What does Asaph's experience teach us about trusting God when evil seems to prosper?"

Ask the class to work in groups of three or four to prepare a worship service based on lessons from Psalm 73. Distribute a work sheet with the following guidelines for the worship service. Leave adequate space between segments. (A similar activity is in the student book Learning by Doing page.)

A Worship Service Based on Psalm 73
(Theme: Trusting God While Evil Prospers)
Appropriate Songs to Sing:
New Testament Scripture Reading:
Prayer Theme:
Communion Theme/Scripture:
Sermon Title: Learning To Trust Again
Sermon Points:
Song of Commitment:

After the groups have completed their worship service, ask what Scripture readings were selected. Then ask what sermon points need to be made. Finally, ask what songs were selected.

Conclude the class by asking class members to identify a personal struggle where this lesson of trust may apply. Pray for your class members' struggles, asking God to help them as He did Asaph in learning to trust Him completely. After the prayer, sing one of the worship songs suggested by the class.

Let's Talk It Over

The questions on this page are designed to promote discussion of the lesson by the class and to encourage application of the lesson Scriptures. The answers provided are only discussion starters. Let your class talk it over from there.

1. If Mike were your friend, how would you have counseled him when he lost his store and his faith?

Maybe some of your learners have encountered friends or family members who have had experiences similar to Mike's. What did they say? How did things turn out? What might they do differently if they could do it over again?

When people are in Mike's situation, we must not minimize their hurt. Quips and platitudes like, "Cheer up! It will all work out eventually" do little to help the hurting person. Even Scriptures like Romans 8:28 may not be very comforting at the moment. Sharing the hurt is more important than "saying the right thing" or giving advice. In some manner, however, hurting believers need to be encouraged to stay the course.

2. If "God is good to Israel, even to such as are of a clean heart," doesn't that imply that those who are having a hard time must not be "of a clean heart"? How would you convince someone otherwise who applied that reasoning to his or her own troubles or was pointing a finger at someone else?

This is the error of Job's friends. It is also the error of Jesus' disciples in John 9:1, 2. These passages may be instructive in trying to help someone see the fallacy of such thinking. The main issue is understanding what it means for God to be good. If He allows trials and testing to strengthen us (James 1), isn't that a good thing?

3. Have you ever felt envious of people who seemed to get ahead by unscrupulous means? Why? What helped you to get over such feelings?

It's hard to watch other people get what you think you deserve—especially if you're convinced they got it unfairly. How do you deal with the co-worker who lies about you to get promoted ahead of you? What about the shopper in the express checkout line ahead of you—the one with three items more than the posted limit?

The important thing is to focus on what really matters. This world is temporary. Our jobs, our houses and cars, our shopping carts are all destined for destruction. Only our relationship with the Lord and His people is eternal. When we focus on that, our envy about earthly advantages will fade.

4. What is it about worship that helps you get a right perspective? What would you change—if you were in charge of the church's worship services—to make sure that that happened more regularly?

Worship should help us appreciate the presence of the Eternal. That appreciation will strip away all the issues of our temporary world. It reminds us that God is in control and that things are not always as they seem.

As you discuss changes to your church's worship service, you probably will note that different people appreciate different things. The leadership's unenviable task is in balancing these so that all the worshipers have an opportunity to worship in a manner that best suits each one. (Be careful with entertaining ideas about how to change the worship service. If your church is in danger of splitting over this issue, you may want to skip over the second part of the question.)

5. Asaph realized he had been wrong to envy the wicked, and it grieved him. How do people today react when they have been wrong? If they are not moved to sorrow for their sin, then what? Why?

In a culture that has a hard time accepting the fact of sin, this is difficult. Many people get defensive when their errors are exposed. They try to blame someone or something else. Others simply dig in and refuse to admit they are wrong.

Others react very differently. Overwhelmed by sorrow, they begin to doubt their own worth. They become depressed. We need to commit ourselves to a godly response—to a godly sorrow that leads to repentance (2 Corinthians 7:10, 11). Only in that will we find forgiveness and the grace to go on.

6. How can we focus more on the truth that God will one day "receive [us] to glory"? What difference will it make?

Keeping this focus will help us live pure lives (1 John 3:3). It will help us establish our priorities (Colossians 3:1-4). It will help us endure when we are treated cruelly (Hebrews 12:1-3). Regular participation in worship is important. Christian friends can help us keep our focus as well—even as we help them in return.

A New Approach

DEVOTIONAL READING: Matthew 5:1-12.

BACKGROUND SCRIPTURE: Matthew 5.

PRINTED TEXT: Matthew 5:17, 18, 21, 22, 27, 28, 31-35, 38, 39, 43-45, 48.

Matthew 5:17, 18, 21, 22, 27, 28, 31-35, 38, 39, 43-45, 48

17 Think not that I am come to destroy the law, or the prophets: I am not come to destroy, but to fulfil.

18 For verily I say unto you, Till heaven and earth pass, one jot or one tittle shall in no wise pass from the law, till all be fulfilled.

· · · · · · · · · · · ·

21 Ye have heard that it was said by them of old time, Thou shalt not kill; and whosoever shall kill shall be in danger of the judgment:

22 But I say unto you, That whosoever is angry with his brother without a cause shall be in danger of the judgment: and whosoever shall say to his brother, Raca, shall be in danger of the council: but whosoever shall say, Thou fool, shall be in danger of hell fire.

· · · · · · · · · · · ·

27 Ye have heard that it was said by them of old time, Thou shalt not commit adultery:

28 But I say unto you, That whosoever looketh on a woman to lust after her hath committed adultery with her already in his heart.

· · · · · · · · · · · ·

31 It hath been said, Whosoever shall put away his wife, let him give her a writing of divorcement:

32 But I say unto you, That whosoever shall put away his wife, saving for the cause of fornication, causeth her to commit adultery: and whosoever shall marry her that is divorced committeth adultery.

33 Again, ye have heard that it hath been said by them of old time, Thou shalt not

forswear thyself, but shalt perform unto the Lord thine oaths:

34 But I say unto you, Swear not at all; neither by heaven; for it is God's throne:

35 Nor by the earth; for it is his footstool: neither by Jerusalem; for it is the city of the great King.

· · · · · · · · · · · ·

38 Ye have heard that it hath been said, An eye for an eye, and a tooth for a tooth:

39 But I say unto you, That ye resist not evil: but whosoever shall smite thee on thy right cheek, turn to him the other also.

· · · · · · · · · · · ·

43 Ye have heard that it hath been said, Thou shalt love thy neighbor, and hate thine enemy.

44 But I say unto you, Love your enemies, bless them that curse you, do good to them that hate you, and pray for them which despitefully use you, and persecute you;

45 That ye may be the children of your Father which is in heaven: for he maketh his sun to rise on the evil and on the good, and sendeth rain on the just and on the unjust.

· · · · · · · · · · · ·

48 Be ye therefore perfect, even as your Father which is in heaven is perfect.

Nov 7

GOLDEN TEXT: Think not that I am come to destroy the law, or the prophets: I am not come to destroy, but to fulfil.—Matthew 5:17.

The God of Continuing Creation
Unit 3: A New Creation
(Lessons 10-13)

Lesson Aims

After participating in this lesson, each student will be able to:

1. Give examples from the text of how Jesus corrected misunderstandings of the Old Testament law.

2. Explain why the law of love should be our guide in interactions with others.

3. Commit to Jesus one specific area in which he or she will choose to be more loving.

Lesson Outline

INTRODUCTION
    A. The Greatest Preacher
    B. Lesson Background
I. RESPECT FOR GOD'S WORD (Matthew 5:17, 18)
    A. Jesus' Purpose (v. 17)
    B. Indestructible Law (v. 18)
      Good Advice, While It Lasted
II. EXAMPLES OF BEHAVIOR (Matthew 5:21, 22, 27, 28, 31-35, 38, 39, 43-45)
    A. Murder (vv. 21, 22)
    B. Adultery (vv. 27, 28)
    C. Divorce (vv. 31, 32)
    D. Oath-taking (vv. 33-35)
    E. Violence (vv. 38, 39)
    F. Love (vv. 43-45)
      An Untold Wealth of Information
III. CHALLENGE TO GROW (Matthew 5:48)
CONCLUSION
    A. Excuses or Reasons?
    B. Prayer
    C. Thought to Remember

Introduction

A. The Greatest Preacher

From my childhood I remember what a stir there was when a famous preacher came to town to address a meeting every night for two weeks. Most of the churches and both of the daily papers helped to spread the news in advance.

No auditorium in town was big enough for the expected crowd, so the baseball field was rented. Extra hitch racks were provided to tether the many horses that would arrive with carriages loaded with listeners. Most of the bicycle racks in town were borrowed and taken to the ball field. Extra streetcars were lined up because everyone wanted to hear the famous Gypsy Smith.

About eighty years later I witnessed a similar stir in a bigger town with a bigger grandstand. The name of Gypsy Smith was replaced by that of another famous preacher, the streetcars were replaced by buses, the hitch racks were replaced by parking lots, and no provision was made for bicycles. Otherwise the two campaigns were very much alike. Together they bear witness to the power of preaching.

By far the greatest preacher of all time is Jesus of Nazareth. He is the most famous, the most popular, the most influential. No newspapers heralded His coming, but word-of-mouth advertising was better. No rival churches joined forces to promote His program. Most of the hearers came on their own feet, and some came quite a distance (Matthew 4:25).

Jesus found no baseball field or grandstand to hold His listeners. Nowhere in town was there room for them (Mark 1:45). He led them to open spaces in the countryside, or to the beach by the Sea of Galilee, or to a sloping hillside that served as a grandstand.

Two things set Jesus apart from other teachers and attracted huge audiences. First, His miracles were amazing and obviously genuine (John 2:23; 6:2). Second, His teaching was also amazing, and strikingly different from that heard every Sabbath in the synagogues (Matthew 7:28, 29; Mark 1:22).

B. Lesson Background

Jesus' famous Sermon on the Mount was spoken during the second year of His ministry, His "year of popularity." At that time great crowds gathered wherever He went.

It was a time to speak of the nearness of the kingdom of Heaven (Matthew 4:17). But so that there would be no misunderstanding, much of Jesus' Sermon on the Mount focused on the true nature of that kingdom. This was primarily for His disciples, but multitudes also were listening (Matthew 5:1, 2).

I. Respect for God's Word (Matthew 5:17, 18)

As our printed text opens, Jesus is about to say some things that sound, on first impression, to be quite different from the bits He will quote from the Old Testament. But He does not want anyone in that Jewish audience to think He means to deny or contradict God's Word, so He begins by declaring His respect for the Scriptures and His relationship to them.

A. Jesus' Purpose (v. 17)

17. Think not that I am come to destroy the law, or the prophets: I am not come to destroy, but to fulfil.

Many Old Testament prophets had predicted some of the things Jesus would do, but their messages are not complete until Jesus actually does those predicted things. Each prophecy and fulfillment demonstrates that God knows the future as well as the past. So many prophecies have been fulfilled that we ought to have complete confidence in those that are to be fulfilled in the future. *The prophets* point to Jesus!

Some of the events recorded in the Old Testament's five books of *law* (Genesis through Deuteronomy) function as prophecies, too. For example, the Passover law directed that a spotless lamb be sacrificed by each family of Israel. That was not only a memorial of the long-ago time when Israel was saved from slavery in Egypt; it also foreshadows the later time when Jesus, the spotless lamb of God, would be sacrificed to rescue God's people from slavery to sin (cf. 1 Corinthians 5:7, 8). [See question #1, page 88.]

The apostle Paul acknowledges that the law and the prophets have always looked forward to something beyond themselves (Romans 3:21; Galatians 3, 4). That "something" is Jesus. This bears repeating!

B. Indestructible Law (v. 18)

18. For verily I say unto you, Till heaven and earth pass, one jot or one tittle shall in no wise pass from the law, till all be fulfilled.

Jot (or *yod*) is the name of a Hebrew letter. It is the smallest letter in the Hebrew alphabet, but a *tittle* is smaller still. It is only a part of a letter. Compare the English letters C and G. The tiny stroke of the pen that distinguishes one from the other is a *tittle.*

Jesus is saying that not even the tiniest part of the law will pass *till all be fulfilled.* In other words, *the law* will not fail to accomplish its purpose in pointing to the Christ, and in pointing people *to* the Christ. "The law was our schoolmaster to bring us unto Christ, that we might be justified by faith" (Galatians 3:24).

When people are brought to Christ and justified by faith, part of the law is fulfilled when those new Christians "are no longer under a schoolmaster" (Galatians 3:25). The law will not reach its complete fulfillment until Christ returns. That will be the time when *heaven and earth pass* away (Revelation 6:12-14).

GOOD ADVICE, WHILE IT LASTED

"Wear sunscreen." Those were the opening words of an alleged commencement address that

Visual for lessons 5 and 10

Use this visual as you ask how ancient prophecy establishes that Jesus is "the fulfillment."

made the rounds on the Internet a few years ago. It was attributed to author Kurt Vonnegut, among others. Actually it was part of a newspaper column written by Mary Schmich for the *Chicago Tribune* and was never given as a commencement address.

Some of the other advice included, "Sing. . . . Don't be reckless with other people's hearts. . . . Floss. . . . Remember compliments, forget insults. . . . Keep old love letters. Throw away old bank statements. . . . Be kind to your knees. You'll miss them when they're gone. . . . Get to know your parents. You never know when they'll be gone. . . . Be nice to your siblings. . . . Respect your elders. . . . Don't mess too much with your hair, or by the time you're forty it will look eighty-five." And the "speech" closed with the words, "But trust me on the sunscreen."

Some advice is timeless; some fits one time and place and may be irrelevant to another. Jesus said it was so even with the law. It was divinely inspired, but its purpose will be fully served when everything it points to has been accomplished. Christ is indeed that realization, and we look forward to the law's ultimate fulfillment when He returns. Until that time comes, it's still a good idea to remember the sunscreen! —C. R. B.

II. Examples of Behavior (Matthew 5:21, 22, 27, 28, 31-35, 38, 39, 43-45)

Now that Jesus has made His relationship to the law clear, He moves to a discussion of how the law actually should be applied. In what follows Jesus will not be "pouring additional meaning" into the Old Testament law. Rather, He will stress the true meaning that was there all along, but had been lost over the centuries.

Those in Jesus' audience have a lot of misunderstandings that they must abandon! Jesus will clear up those misunderstandings with His *ye have heard it said . . . but I say to you* technique.

A. Murder (vv. 21, 22)

21. Ye have heard that it was said by them of old time, Thou shalt not kill; and whosoever shall kill shall be in danger of the judgment.

This is the sixth of the Ten Commandments (Exodus 20:13). Everyone in Israel has heard of it. Some English versions have *murder* instead of *kill*. That is closer to the real intent, for God prescribes capital punishment for various crimes (Genesis 9:6; Acts 25:11; Romans 13:4). That is indeed "killing" but it is not "murder." A murderer is *in danger of* being judged, condemned, and executed. A devout Jew in Jesus' day will not disagree with this.

22. But I say unto you, That whosoever is angry with his brother without a cause shall be in danger of the judgment: and whosoever shall say to his brother, Raca, shall be in danger of the council: but whosoever shall say, Thou fool, shall be in danger of hell fire.

Jesus points to the fact that the action of murder (v. 21, above) has its roots in the attitude of anger. This has been true since the very first murder (Genesis 4:5-8). Why have the people apparently forgotten this?

There is such a thing as anger that results in righteous outrage. That is not sinful (cf. Matthew 21:12, 13; Mark 3:1-5). But angry, murderous attitudes that result from personal slights (real or imagined) are condemned (1 John 3:15). [See question #2, page 88.]

It is notable that many English translations leave out the phrase *without a cause*. They leave it out because it is not found in many of the most ancient manuscripts. Since Jesus Himself had proper cause to be angry in some circumstances, the *without a cause* idea is probably correct in any case.

Actually, an angry person is in some danger even if he or she has a good reason for being

angry. Such a person still has to exercise self-control to be sure that the anger does not lead to personal vengeance. The angry person had better control his or her tongue as well, because contemptuous, insulting talk may feed the anger and lead to criminal acts. *Raca* is an insult comparable to *idiot* or *bonehead*.

The word translated *thou fool* in our text probably is even more malicious than that. Jesus referred to some people as fools on at least one occasion (Matthew 23:17). The fact that He did not sin in doing so shows us, again, the vital distinction between expressing righteous outrage and expressing personal offense. In any case, an expression of anger through labels, characterizations, and name-calling invites the same in return.

B. Adultery (vv. 27, 28)

27. Ye have heard that it was said by them of old time, Thou shalt not commit adultery.

This is the seventh of the Ten Commandments (Exodus 20:14). It forbids a physical act that is just as wrong in the New Testament era as it was in the Old Testament era. But in the next verse Jesus explains this Commandment's true depth.

28. But I say unto you, That whosoever looketh on a woman to lust after her hath committed adultery with her already in his heart.

As murder has its roots in anger, so adultery has its roots in lustful thoughts. People who lived as far back as Job realized the nature of the lustful thought process (see Job 31:1), and Jesus brings this ancient knowledge back to life. People today who think they can drool over pornography and still be right with God just as long as they don't "actually" commit adultery are sadly mistaken! (See Psalm 101:3.) [See question #3, page 88.]

C. Divorce (vv. 31, 32)

31. It hath been said, Whosoever shall put away his wife, let him give her a writing of divorcement.

The law allowed a man to divorce *his wife*. If she lost favor in his eyes because he found some uncleanness or indecency, all he had to do was to give her a written statement that he was divorcing her (Deuteronomy 24:1). But the requirement to find uncleanness or indecency apparently has been "lost" in Jesus' day.

32. But I say unto you, That whosoever shall put away his wife, saving for the cause of fornication, causeth her to commit adultery: and whosoever shall marry her that is divorced committeth adultery.

If we take a close look at Deuteronomy 24:1-4, we see Jesus reaffirming a part of the law that somehow has been ignored. The complicated

---

How to Say It

CORINTHIANS. Kor-*in*-thee-unz (*th* as in *thin*).

DEUTERONOMY. Due-ter-*ahn*-uh-me.

EZEKIEL. Ee-*zeek*-ee-ul or Ee-*zeek*-yul.

GALATIANS. Guh-*lay*-shunz.

JEREMIAH. Jair-uh-*my*-uh.

LEVITICUS. Leh-*vit*-ih-kus.

LEX TALIONIS (Latin). leks tal-ee-*oh*-niss.

RACA. *Ray*-kuh or Ray-*kah*.

conditions of that passage should have served to put the brakes on hasty divorces, and Jesus intends the same. Jesus will have more to say on this subject in Matthew 19:3-12. [See question #4, page 88.]

D. Oath-taking (vv. 33-35)

33. Again, ye have heard that it hath been said by them of old time, Thou shalt not forswear thyself, but shalt perform unto the Lord thine oaths.

What the people *have heard* in regard to oath-taking is an accurate summary of Exodus 20:7; Leviticus 19:12; Numbers 30:2; and Deuteronomy 23:21-23. The problem is that the religious leaders of Jesus' day have developed very intricate rules regarding oaths that "counted" vs. oaths that "didn't count" (see Matthew 23:16-22). Jesus intends to put a stop to such quibbling.

34, 35. But I say unto you, Swear not at all; neither by heaven; for it is God's throne: nor by the earth; for it is his footstool: neither by Jerusalem; for it is the city of the great King.

Jesus' plain instruction is to *swear not at all.* It is not fitting for us to swear (take oaths) by things that belong to God. We ought to be able to tell the truth and keep our promises without swearing oaths (Matthew 5:37; James 5:12). This straightforward plan affirms the intent of the Old Testament law that the Jewish leaders had set aside with their convoluted reasoning.

Even so, some students like to point out that Jesus Himself, when on trial for His life, will be sworn in by the high priest to answer a question under oath (Matthew 26:63, 64). Therefore they think Jesus does not intend to forbid formal oath-taking in the most serious situations. (See also 2 Corinthians 11:31; Galatians 1:20; and Hebrews 6:16.) At least we can be sure that Jesus does not want us to join in uttering the frequent and reckless "I swear to God"-type of oaths that are so common today.

E. Violence (vv. 38, 39)

38. Ye have heard that it hath been said, An eye for an eye, and a tooth for a tooth.

If you want to know the Latin term for this kind of justice, it is *lex talionis.* This means, roughly, "law of equal and direct retribution." For physical injury the legal punishment is the same kind of injury in return, according to Exodus 21:24; Leviticus 24:19, 20; and Deuteronomy 19:21. That kind of justice, strictly speaking, is "fair." The prospect of such punishment might keep an angry person from injuring an opponent.

39. But I say unto you, That ye resist not evil: but whosoever shall smite thee on thy right cheek, turn to him the other also.

In Jesus' day a strike on the *cheek* is more of an insult than an outright attack. Jesus advises a nonviolent response, a response that goes against the natural wish to strike back. This is the quickest way to stop the confrontation from escalating.

This attitude speaks to what our hearts should look like in the kingdom of God. The ancient prophets had predicted a new heart for God's people (Jeremiah 31:31-34; 32:39; Ezekiel 36:26). This is all part of the fulfillment that Jesus brings.

F. Love (vv. 43-45)

43. Ye have heard that it hath been said, Thou shalt love thy neighbor, and hate thine enemy.

Love thy neighbor is plain in Leviticus 19:18. Jesus recognizes the importance of this command (Matthew 22:35-39), and so do Jewish students of the law (Luke 10:25-27).

But *hate thine enemy* is not found anywhere in God's law. Even so, God's people sometimes were ordered to destroy whole nations of enemies, killing men, women, and children without mercy (Deuteronomy 7:2; 1 Samuel 15:3). It is not surprising that Jewish teachers interpreted such orders as orders to hate those enemies. The command to hate enemies is found in the Dead Sea Scrolls, written by a very conservative Jewish sect that existed just before the time of Christ.

44. But I say unto you, Love your enemies, bless them that curse you, do good to them that hate you, and pray for them which despitefully use you, and persecute you.

This is one of our Lord's more difficult commands. Quite naturally, we do not love our enemies. We do this only with diligent effort. Sternly we repress our inclinations to say or do anything to hurt an enemy.

Jesus requires that we look for opportunities to help an enemy. We even set about to create such opportunities. When we do, we fulfill Old Testament requirements found in Exodus 23:4, 5 and Proverbs 25:21. This really isn't anything new! [See question #5, page 88.]

45. That ye may be the children of your Father which is in heaven: for he maketh his sun to rise on the evil and on the good, and sendeth rain on the just and on the unjust.

It isn't easy to love our enemies. It takes thought, effort, and time. Sometimes it even costs money. Yet God sends the goodness of *sun* and *rain* on *evil* and *unjust* people, so why shouldn't we have a similar attitude?

It's our nature to be like God, and He is One who helps His enemies. They give Him no thanks, no honor, no recognition; but still He helps them. Your duty, your pleasure, your desire is to be like your Father in Heaven.

AN UNTOLD WEALTH OF INFORMATION

A ninety-year-old man was talking with his son one day about the astounding leaps that technology has taken during the father's lifetime. He had been born two years after the first electric starter appeared on automobiles, in the same year that the head of the U.S. Patent Office is said to have proposed closing down the department because "everything has been invented"!

The man's son was explaining how computers work and was showing his father how one can access the Internet and find an untold wealth of information—some of which is actually true! They talked of how every eighteen months or so the power of computers doubles, or the price of the old computer is cut in half. In what became something of a litany, the father said with each succeeding revelation, "I was born thirty years too soon!"

Most of us who use computers for our living still don't completely understand them or take full advantage of their wealth of features. Jesus' explanation of the law said, in effect, "There is an untold wealth of information here; you don't completely understand it, so you can't take full advantage of its benefits."

Many in Jesus' audience saw the law only as an external force placing limits on their lives. They could not appreciate the freedoms God offers to those who let his words become an intrinsic motivator in their hearts! Are we repeating their error?

—C. R. B.

III. Challenge to Grow (Matthew 5:48)

We now come to the conclusion of the matter. What follows next is Jesus' summary of all of His *ye have heard it said . . . but I say to you* statements to this point.

Home Daily Bible Readings

Monday, Nov. 1—Jesus Teaches About Blessings (Matthew 5:1-12)

Tuesday, Nov. 2—We Are to Obey God's Will (Matthew 5:13-20)

Wednesday, Nov. 3—A Teaching About Anger (Matthew 5:21-26)

Thursday, Nov. 4—Teachings About Adultery and Divorce (Matthew 5:27-32)

Friday, Nov. 5—A Teaching About Taking Oaths (Matthew 5:33-37)

Saturday, Nov. 6—A Teaching About Non-violent Resistance (Matthew 5:38-42)

Sunday, Nov. 7—A Teaching About Loving Enemies (Matthew 5:43-48)

48. Be ye therefore perfect, even as your Father which is in heaven is perfect.

Now wait a minute, Jesus, please! I do want to be like God. I realize that I ought to be like Him. But I'm only human. Isn't perfection too much to ask? "Nobody's *perfect*" is an axiom of our hearts; it is our excuse for all our imperfections. We are frightened by a blunt command to be perfect, and doubly frightened when the perfection demanded is like that of God himself.

Jesus knows, of course, that we can't be perfect in this life. But that fact should not keep us from trying. Jesus' command is nothing new, since Leviticus 19:2 says almost the very same thing, with "holy" instead of "perfect." (See also Deuteronomy 18:13.)

As children of our Heavenly *Father*, we strive to be more and more like Him every day. That's a vital part of our new heart that we have as members of the kingdom of God!

Conclusion

A. Excuses or Reasons?

Our lesson title directs our attention to "A New Approach," and the Sermon on the Mount leads our thoughts along that line. Readily we agree that we cannot be as great and good as God is; but just as readily we agree that we can be better than we are. Then why aren't we? With so many years of Christian living behind us, why aren't we closer to perfection? Some reasons (excuses, really!) are clearly seen.

First, when we notice some imperfection in our character or life, we shrug it off with the cliché, "Nobody's perfect." Often we just don't try very hard to be better than we are.

Second, we often find that our time is fully occupied with things we like to do. It takes time and effort to do good to our enemies, for example. So we just don't get around to it.

Third, we never have done those good things that we are not doing now. A sense of inertia keeps us from improving. Maybe we should listen to the more mature Christians who say, "Try it—God commands it." If we can be a hundred-watt lamp, why be content with sixty watts?

B. Prayer

Father in Heaven, thank You for being perfect, and thank You for sending Your Son, Your perfect sacrifice for sin. Forgive our easy self-satisfaction, we pray, and help us to be better than we are in all the ways that glorify Jesus. In His name we pray, amen.

C. Thought to Remember

May our obedience to Christ honor Him.

Learning by Doing

This page contains an alternative lesson plan emphasizing learning activities. Classes desiring such student involvement will find these suggestions helpful.

Learning Goals

After participating in this lesson, each student will be able to:

1. Give examples from the text of how Jesus corrected misunderstandings of the Old Testament law.

2. Explain why the law of love should be our guide in interactions with others.

3. Commit to Jesus one specific area in which he or she will choose to be more loving.

Into the Lesson

Prepare a handout with the following hidden message puzzle. (You may also include the activities suggested in "Into the Word" and "Into Life" in this handout.) The heading for this portion of the handout should read "Changing Our Thinking." Instructions should read: "Delete the letters of the words found in Matthew 5:17. The remaining letters will spell a theme from today's lesson, a guide for our lives. Enter those in the blanks below.

THIANKNNOTTHEATIWAMCOA
METOPDESTPROYTHRELAOWOR
ATCHEHPROPHETS:AITTIATUM
DENSOTARECAOSMEIMPTOODE
RSTTRAONYTBASUTTOACFTUL
IFOILNS.

— ——— ————————:
————————— ——— ——
————————— ——
————————.

Answer: A new approach: Attitudes are as important as actions. (This activity is included in the student book.)

Say, "We have been studying how God created a special people and offered them a new dynasty. Today's lesson begins a series that reminds us we are new creations in Christ, bound to live within His will. Today's study addresses our attitudes as well as our actions. In the broad range of topics addressed, you will find Jesus touching a need in your life."

Into the Word

You may choose to do the following exercise as a whole class or in small groups. Include the following instructions on a handout, or if doing this exercise as a whole class, on four pieces of poster board side by side on the wall. The headings for four columns (or sheets) should read:

"Subject Discussed"; "Old Testament Law"; "A New Approach"; "Why Is This Better?"

Ask the learners to identify and list in the first column the six subjects Jesus addressed. *(Answers: Murder, Adultery, Divorce, Swearing Oaths, Retaliation, Love)*

Next, they are to summarize the Old Testament law for each in the second column and write Jesus' approach in the third column.

After completing the study of the first three columns, ask the following questions and write responses in the "Why . . . Better" column.

Murder: Explain the word *Raca* before asking: (1) "Why would name-calling bring one dangerously close to Hell?" (2) "How is Jesus' approach a better approach?"

Adultery: (1) "Why is Jesus' way a better approach?" (2) "What are some ways this temptation comes to us today?" (3) "What 'tips' can we list to help minimize the impact of such temptations in our lives?"

Divorce: See the lesson commentary to explain or clarify the meaning of this passage, and then ask why Jesus' way is a better way.

Swearing Oaths: (1) "If one key phrase summarizes this teaching in verses 33-35, what would it be?" ("Swear not at all.") "Why is this new approach better than the Law?"

Retaliation: "Why is a nonviolent response to violence better?" "On what everyday occasions are adults tempted to break this teaching?"

Love: "Why is this new approach so difficult?" "How is this a better approach to life?"

Into Life

Distribute a handout with the heading: "Attitudes and Actions." In a left column print the following phrases: "Murder and Name-Calling," "Adultery and 'Just Looking,'" "Divorce and Remarriage," "To Swear or Not to Swear," "Violence and Retaliation," "Loving Our Enemies."

After each of these headings, print the following four self-evaluation levels: No Problem, Sometimes Tempted, At Risk, I Need Help.

Invite students to circle the most appropriate answer for each of the six subjects. Afterward, ask each to select one area that needs attention. Ask each student to determine one immediate step to take to complete this commitment. Example: not to retaliate when someone cuts him or her off on the highway.

Let's Talk It Over

The questions on this page are designed to promote discussion of the lesson by the class and to encourage application of the lesson Scriptures. The answers provided are only discussion starters. Let your class talk it over from there.

1. Paul says we are to "keep the feast . . . with the unleavened bread of sincerity and truth" (1 Corinthians 5:7, 8). Why is it difficult to live in consistent "sincerity and truth"? How can we get better at doing that?

By and large, people are not convinced that honesty is always a good thing. Even Christians give in to the temptation to lie to avoid embarrassing themselves or someone else. As a result, we are divided in our minds. We want to do what is right, but we don't want to offend anyone.

We need a recommitment to the truth. Jesus' speech and actions were consistent with each other and with the Scriptures. He tempered the truth with love, however. Thus, the common people flocked to Him. Even sinners found Him a friend—even though He denounced sin in no uncertain terms.

2. Anger is altogether too common in our culture. Road rage, gang violence, political protests, spouse abuse—they all speak of anger in our society. How much of a problem is anger within the church? What can we do about it?

Christians are not immune to anger. To a certain degree anger is healthy (Ephesians 4:26). Taking that into account, we understand Jesus was talking about uncontrolled anger, but that is small comfort.

We Christians do not always control our anger properly, otherwise there would never be a church split! The church needs to work harder on building healthy relationships within the body. We need to learn to value people over things and personal preferences. The unity of the church is important (see 1 Corinthians 3:17). We need to be more forgiving when others are insensitive. Uncontrolled anger is not consistent with the fruit of the Spirit (Galatians 5:22-26).

3. How serious is the problem of lust in the church? What needs to be done to address it?

Visual images are powerful stimulants for men and some women, and modern culture is happy to provide such stimulation. Sex sells—and sexually stimulating images are used in marketing almost everything.

To be "sexy" is understood as a positive thing, so people dress and otherwise present themselves in a provocative manner that invites lust.

Print media add many more such images, and not just in magazines that get the label of pornography. Fashion and entertainment magazines cover just enough skin to avoid being labeled pornography, but they incite lust just the same.

All this indicates that we live in a society in which the temptation to lust is very great. It is a problem in the church because the church is in the world. Entertain as many ideas for countering this problem as your learners can come up with.

4. Why is divorce such a problem in the church today? What can the church do to address this problem?

There are many reasons for the prevalence of divorce today, and different people attach greater or lesser significance to each one. One problem is the pace of modern society. Ten- and twelve-hour workdays, high stress and pressure on the job, juggling the schedules of two working parents, and arranging child care are wearing people out. They don't have the energy to build relationships. They are exhausted, and exhaustion tries the patience.

Your learners will suggest other problems. Be sure to spend time also on solutions. How can your church foster healthy relationships for couples? What about premarital counseling—is enough being done? Do couples in crisis know where to turn—other than to the divorce lawyers?

5. When have you had occasion to return good to someone who deliberately did something to harm you or your reputation? What was the result?

Returning good for evil is unnatural; it takes a deliberate act of the will. Even in the church it is rare. When someone harms us, we seem to think we are being more than generous to let it slide but to sever the relationship with the person. We don't return hurt for hurt, but we do not return good either.

If someone has gone out of his or her way to bring a blessing to an antagonist, that story will be instructive. Did it soften the antagonist, or was the good deed received with cynical mistrust? Was the relationship restored? What about the person who did good—how did he or she feel, knowing that he or she had acted according to God's will?

A New Body

DEVOTIONAL READING: 1 Corinthians 15:1-11.

BACKGROUND SCRIPTURE: 1 Corinthians 15.

PRINTED TEXT: 1 Corinthians 15:42-57.

1 Corinthians 15:42-57

42 So also is the resurrection of the dead. It is sown in corruption, it is raised in incorruption:

43 It is sown in dishonor, it is raised in glory: it is sown in weakness, it is raised in power:

44 It is sown a natural body, it is raised a spiritual body. There is a natural body, and there is a spiritual body.

45 And so it is written, The first man Adam was made a living soul; the last Adam was made a quickening spirit.

46 Howbeit that was not first which is spiritual, but that which is natural; and afterward that which is spiritual.

47 The first man is of the earth, earthy: the second man is the Lord from heaven.

48 As is the earthy, such are they also that are earthy: and as is the heavenly, such are they also that are heavenly.

49 And as we have borne the image of the earthy, we shall also bear the image of the heavenly.

50 Now this I say, brethren, that flesh and blood cannot inherit the kingdom of God; neither doth corruption inherit incorruption.

51 Behold, I show you a mystery; We shall not all sleep, but we shall all be changed,

52 In a moment, in the twinkling of an eye, at the last trump: for the trumpet shall sound, and the dead shall be raised incorruptible, and we shall be changed.

53 For this corruptible must put on incorruption, and this mortal must put on immortality.

54 So when this corruptible shall have put on incorruption, and this mortal shall have put on immortality, then shall be brought to pass the saying that is written, Death is swallowed up in victory.

55 O death, where is thy sting? O grave, where is thy victory?

56 The sting of death is sin; and the strength of sin is the law.

57 But thanks be to God, which giveth us the victory through our Lord Jesus Christ.

Nov
14

GOLDEN TEXT: O death, where is thy sting? O grave, where is thy victory?
—1 Corinthians 15:55.

Lesson Aims

After participating in this lesson, each student will be able to:

1. Describe the resurrection bodies in which believers will rise when Jesus returns to earth.

2. Explain why Jesus' resurrection gives us hope that we will receive a new eternal body.

3. Compose words of hope and encouragement to someone grieving the death of a Christian friend or family member.

Lesson Outline

INTRODUCTION
   A. Our Hope Is Not Lost
   B. Lesson Background
 I. FOUR CHANGES (1 Corinthians 15:42-44)
   A. From Corruption to Incorruption (v. 42)
     A Futile Project
   B. From Dishonor to Glory (v. 43a)
   C. From Weakness to Power (v. 43b)
   D. From Natural to Spiritual (v. 44)
 II. TWO ADAMS (1 Corinthians 15:45-49)
   A. Stark Contrast (v. 45)
   B. Evident Order (vv. 46-49)
III. ONE MYSTERY (1 Corinthians 15:50-53)
   A. Flesh Limited (v. 50)
   B. Flesh Changes (vv. 51-53)
IV. FINAL VICTORY (1 Corinthians 15:54-57)
   A. End of Death (v. 54)
   B. End of Death's Power (vv. 55, 56)
     Removing the Sting
   C. Eternal Gratitude (v. 57)
CONCLUSION
   A. Our Work Is Not Finished
   B. Prayer
   C. Thought to Remember

Introduction

A. Our Hope Is Not Lost

Many years ago in a Western town there was a little congregation that irreverent neighbors called "the happy church." Its every meeting was a joyous celebration. Happiest of all was the preacher, though his health was frail. Cheerfully he told the congregation he would die soon, but would rise on the third day as Jesus had done. Members of the church trusted the preacher. He never had told them anything but truth, and no one thought of doubting his promise.

So there was no mourning when the preacher died, and no funeral. His body was laid on a couch on the speaker's platform in the little church building, and an honor guard attended him day and night. On the third day the congregation assembled before daylight and continued the meeting until midnight, but the preacher never stirred.

In the dark hours after midnight the disappointed congregation decided that their beloved preacher must have misunderstood the message. Perhaps he was to rise on the thirtieth day instead of the third. So he was left and guarded on his couch for a month, but still he never stirred.

Finally the county health officer obtained a court order, and the rotting corpse was buried without ceremony. Then there was a long period of mourning because a "godless" government had prevented the promised resurrection.

Every member of that long-ago congregation has passed away by now. Each in turn has been buried and mourned with genuine sorrow. But in every case the sorrow has been lightened by the steadfast hope that the dead will rise again (John 5:28, 29). That is the promise of Jesus.

B. Lesson Background

Worse than the belief that a dead friend will rise in three days is the belief that he or she will not rise at all—ever. That is the belief of millions of non-Christians today, and perhaps it is the belief of some members of your church. It was the belief of some in the church at Corinth (1 Corinthians 15:12). This false belief was also held by some Jewish leaders of the day (Luke 20:27).

As proof that the dead do rise, Paul pointed to the resurrection of Christ. There can be no doubt that He really had been dead. The spear thrust into His side would have killed Him if He had not been dead already (John 19:31-34). And Jesus really returned to life. That is proved in at least three ways: (1) an abundance of reliable witnesses (1 Corinthians 15:3-8), (2) the failure of Jewish authorities to produce a corpse to refute the claims of a resurrection, and (3) the willingness of the disciples to die martyrs' deaths for their belief in a risen Lord. It is Jesus' resurrection that sets the stage for our own.

I. Four Changes
(1 Corinthians 15:42-44)

Since the fact of Jesus' resurrection was proven beyond doubt, some skeptics want to confuse the issue by quibbling about just how resurrection is accomplished and what the risen body looks like (1 Corinthians 15:35). Paul answers with an analogy. When you plant a grain of wheat, the plant that grows from it is very different from the seed itself (15:36-38). Likewise the body that rises from the dead may be very different from the body that died.

In verses 39-41 Paul goes on to point out the great variety of things in earth and sky: different kinds of flesh on earth, and sun and moon and many different stars in the sky. Then he moves to his summary or application.

A. From Corruption to Incorruption (v. 42)

42. So also is the resurrection of the dead. It is sown in corruption; it is raised in incorruption.

The two words *so also* cause us to look back to the analogy in verses 37, 38. As a plant that grows is different from the seed that was planted, so also the body that rises from the dead is different from the body that died and was buried. The text goes on to point out some of the differences.

We marvel at the undertaker's art that makes our departed friend look so natural, as if he or she were sleeping and might wake and speak at any minute. But we know that the person's body is *dead*. That is why we bury it in the ground or seal it in a tomb where it returns to dust. But the final trumpet (v. 52, below) will call from that grave or tomb a body forever alive, never again to be touched by decay or *corruption* (cf. 2 Timothy 1:10).

A FUTILE PROJECT

Vladimir Lenin died in 1924. Most of us have seen pictures of his body lying interred in Moscow's Red Square, maintaining a fairly lifelike appearance. Throughout the Communist era in the old Soviet Union, the Communist leadership kept the body on view—with no apparent decomposition of the tissues—as a symbol of the supposed immortality of the Communist political and economic philosophy.

To accomplish this feat, embalming specialists inspect the body twice a week. From time to time, the face is treated with a solution that prevents breakdown of the tissues, and about every year-and-a-half the body is soaked in a bath of preservatives. (An irony of Lenin's fate is that since the fall of Communism the group entrusted with preserving his body has had to engage in capitalism: they have sold the secret embalming methods to the rest of the world in order to fund their work.)

How futile is this project in symbolizing a failed system of government! Even if Lenin's body could somehow retain its lifelike appearance for a millennium, it would still be a dead body, nothing more! How much better is the promise Paul

makes to us that our natural bodies—physical, weak, and subject to decomposition—will someday be raised alive in the spiritual realm. Then we will live forevermore as symbols of a divine cause that shall *never* fail.   —C. R. B.

B. From Dishonor to Glory (v. 43a)

43a. It is sown in dishonor, it is raised in glory.

We honor a departed friend with mounds of flowers, with glowing eulogies, and with words of honor carved in stone. But we know that the body we lay to rest is dishonored by death and will be dishonored by decay.

Even so, we know that dishonor to be only temporary. The "vile" body (Philippians 3:21) will rise to *glory* grander than any seen on earth when the last trumpet sounds. [See question #1, page 96.]

C. From Weakness to Power (v. 43b)

43b. It is sown in weakness, it is raised in power.

What a sharp contrast! The effects of sin weaken our bodies as we live. At death the body is weaker still: utterly helpless and inert. But the coming resurrection will change all that. We cannot even imagine the *power* that will attend a body raised from the dead.

D. From Natural to Spiritual (v. 44)

44. It is sown a natural body; it is raised a spiritual body. There is a natural body, and there is a spiritual body.

We know much about *a natural body* since each of us lives in one and sees others. But what do we know about *a spiritual body*? This has been an area of many scholarly debates! From this lesson we know that the new body will be incorruptible, glorious, and powerful. We can also conclude that it will be a real, literal body; God intended from the beginning that humans should be a combination of body and spirit.

Much remains for us to learn about the nature of our new bodies. Our knowledge will be complete only when we are actually "in" them.

II. Two Adams
(1 Corinthians 15:45-49)

As we learn from Genesis, Adam became the father of the entire human race. Adam brought sin into the world very early in human history, and death followed. So death passed to the whole human race (Romans 5:12). Over the centuries all humanity has been burdened and handicapped by sin.

Then came Jesus, who never sinned. He suffered the agony of the cross to pay the sin price for others. Thus He became another Adam, the beginning of a new race of people, of people forgiven, and therefore not burdened and handicapped by sin. In the next part of our text, Paul compares and contrasts the first Adam, the Adam of Genesis, with the last Adam, namely Jesus Christ.

A. Stark Contrast (v. 45)

45. And so it is written, The first man Adam was made a living soul; the last Adam was made a quickening spirit.

In Genesis 2:7 *it is written* that *the first man Adam* was formed of lifeless dust and so was a lifeless being until God breathed into his nostrils the breath of life and *made* him *a living soul.* By contrast Jesus, *the last Adam,* has existed from eternity past (John 1:1).

Not only has Jesus always lived, He is also *a quickening spirit*—that is, a life-giving spirit, for all things were made by Him, including all living things (John 1:3). But in another way He became a life-giving spirit when He gave His life to pay the price for our sins. Thus He won our forgiveness and gave life to those who were dead in trespasses and sins (Ephesians 2:1). Every Christmas we praise Him as the "Second Adam from above" in the last stanza of "Hark! the Herald Angels Sing."

B. Evident Order (vv. 46-49)

46. Howbeit that was not first which is spiritual, but that which is natural; and afterward that which is spiritual.

It is plain to all that the first Adam lived his *natural* life in his natural body long before the last Adam arrived on the scene. That last Adam is Jesus Christ our Savior. He is the One who gives new *spiritual* life to people who are dead in their sins.

47. The first man is of the earth, earthy: the second man is the Lord from heaven.

Now we see a contrast in origin, which tells us something about the order or hierarchy of creation. *The first man,* Adam, is the one who is *earthy.* He was formed of dust, and lifeless as dust till God breathed into him the breath of life.

How to Say It

CORINTH. *Kor*-inth.
CORINTHIANS. Kor-*in*-thee-unz (*th* as in *thin*).
HOSEA. Ho-*zay*-uh.
ISAIAH. Eye-*zay*-uh.
MARTYRS. *mar*-turz.
PHILIPPIANS. Fih-*lip*-ee-unz.
VLADIMIR LENIN. *Vlad*-ih-meer *Len*-in.

The second man, Jesus, is the one *from heaven.* There He lived with Father and Holy Spirit through countless millennia of unending time before the world was made.

In the order of appearance in visible form on earth, Adam is first and Jesus is second. But the phrases *of the earth* and *from heaven* reveal the true hierarchy. Also in our own experience the natural comes before the spiritual. [See question #2, page 96.]

48. As is the earthy, such are they also that are earthy: and as is the heavenly, such are they also that are heavenly.

Earthy people are like Adam. You are, I am. *Heavenly* people are like Jesus (1 John 3:2). You will be, I will be—if we are Christians.

49. And as we have borne the image of the earthy, we shall also bear the image of the heavenly.

We have borne the image of the earthy, and we bear it still: we look very much like Adam (cf. Genesis 5:3). In our graves these natural bodies will come to look more like the dust from which Adam was formed. But the last trumpet will call us out, and we shall look neither like dust nor like Adam nor like our present natural bodies. We shall rise as spiritual bodies, and we shall look very much like Jesus in His glorified body (Philippians 3:20, 21). Wonderful!

We shall look something like Jesus, but that does not mean we shall be identical, like so many peas in a pod. In our natural bodies we all look much like Adam, but see how varied we are. Some are tall and some are short; some are thin and some are muscular. We cannot imagine what variety we will see in our spiritual bodies, but we can expect to be pleased.

III. One Mystery (1 Corinthians 15:50-53)

Only partly do we understand these natural bodies in which we are spending our lives on earth. Even with all our modern technology and diagnostic tools there is still much to learn!

Sometimes our bodies surprise us with their vigor and endurance; sometimes they frighten us with their weakness or illness. But the spiritual bodies that will be ours will be amazing; only dimly can we imagine them now. "It doth not yet appear what we shall be" (1 John 3:2).

A. Flesh Limited (v. 50)

50. Now this I say, brethren, that flesh and blood cannot inherit the kingdom of God; neither doth corruption inherit incorruption.

Flesh and blood are what our natural bodies are made of. In these bodies we do indeed experience a foretaste of *the kingdom of God* when we make God our King; but it is only a foretaste. The fullness, the perfection, of that kingdom awaits our spiritual bodies. Immortal and forever incorruptible, we will be able to appreciate the perfection of God's rule when we have those new bodies.

B. Flesh Changes (vv. 51-53)

51. Behold, I show you a mystery; We shall not all sleep, but we shall all be changed.

In the vocabulary of the New Testament, *a mystery* is not a puzzle that we can solve by clever detective work. A mystery is something we will never know unless someone tells us. Paul proposes to tell us this one.

Here the word *sleep* is a figure of speech, as it is in John 11:11-14. In literal English we would say, "We shall not all die." However, the word *sleep* is an appropriate figure, for Paul is about to emphasize the fact that literal death is not permanent. That is in the next verse; here in verse 51 we read that not everyone will die. Some will still be living in their natural bodies when the last trumpet sounds.

Those natural bodies that have not died will be changed into spiritual bodies along with those who will be raised from the dead. See also 1 Thessalonians 4:13-17. [See question #3, page 96.]

52. In a moment, in the twinkling of an eye, at the last trump: for the trumpet shall sound, and the dead shall be raised incorruptible, and we shall be changed.

The forthcoming change will not be a long, drawn-out process. It will be complete before the sound of *the trumpet* dies away. People long dead and people never dead will stand together, lost in the wonder of it all. See also Matthew 24:31 and Revelation 11:15.

53. For this corruptible must put on incorruption, and this mortal must put on immortality.

In a bit of a repeat from verse 42, Paul summarizes that which is best about the spiritual bodies: they are immortal, never to die. And they are incorruptible—they will not even be sick or subject to weakness. Paul says nothing about how handsome, intelligent, strong, skillful, or useful they are. But we cannot imagine that any one of them is deficient in any way. See also 2 Corinthians 5:4.

IV. Final Victory
(1 Corinthians 15:54-57)

"The last enemy that shall be destroyed is death" (1 Corinthians 15:26). When God's people rise triumphant over death, that will indeed be the final victory. The conflict between good and evil, wide as the world and long as human his-

tory, will be over. So our text ends with a brief song of victory.

A. End of Death (v. 54)

54. So when this corruptible shall have put on incorruption, and this mortal shall have put on immortality, then shall be brought to pass the saying that is written, Death is swallowed up in victory.

Paul is alluding to Isaiah 25:8. A glance at that passage shows us that the victory over death is God's doing, not our own: "He will swallow up death in victory; and the Lord God will wipe away tears from off all faces."

We think also of John 3:16: "For God so loved the world, that he gave his only begotten Son, that whosoever believeth in him should not perish, but have everlasting life." God gave His Son, and His Son gave His life. His death paid the price for all our sins, and Christians have everlasting life. So the victory belongs to God, and we give Him all the glory. But the benefits belong to us.

B. End of Death's Power (vv. 55, 56)

55. O death, where is thy sting? O grave, where is thy victory?

Now Paul draws his thoughts from Hosea 13:14. *Death* has been scaring people ever since Adam and Eve, but it should hold no terror for Christians. Why should we be afraid to turn loose of these frail bodies when we know we shall receive incorruptible bodies in exchange? Death is an enemy, to be sure, but it is a defeated enemy. [See question #4, page 96.]

56. The sting of death is sin; and the strength of sin is the law.

What makes us afraid of *death?* Our sins do. We know we have earned eternal condemnation

Visual for lesson 11. *Ask your learners what loved ones who have passed on are they most anticipating being united with at the resurrection.*

instead of everlasting life. And *the law* gives our sins the power to terrify us, because the law makes our sins so plain, so undeniable.

Yet we are not terrified. We are Christians. We are forgiven. Our sins are taken away. We are not in line for the wages of sin, but for the gift of God. Eternal life is ours (Romans 6:23).

REMOVING THE STING

Humans have long been fascinated with the idea of defying death. Some do it today by participating in the so-called "extreme sports." More traditionally, people have experienced the thrill of challenging death vicariously. Perhaps the most famous person to be connected with the concept is Harry Houdini (1874–1926). He was known for defying death by jumping into rivers while handcuffed or by being buried alive.

Many have imitated Houdini. For example, in 1999 David Blaine gained fame by spending seven days in a transparent coffin buried six feet into the ground in New York City. A three-ton tank of water covered his see-through coffin in which he had only six inches of headroom and two inches of room on either side. Like Houdini, Blaine survived this stunt and others, but also like Houdini (and the rest of us), Blaine will one day die.

But not being able to escape death through either technological means or any amount of "magic" or trickery is only part of death's sting. The more significant part is, as Paul says, *sin*. It, too, is something we cannot avoid, and it is responsible for the fact of death. But we can thank God for the sacrifice of Christ. When He conquered death by His resurrection, He gave us hope and assurance of our own!   —C. R. B.

Home Daily Bible Readings

Monday, Nov. 8—Paul Reviews the Resurrection Tradition (1 Corinthians 15:1-11)

Tuesday, Nov. 9—Doubts Concerning Resurrection (1 Corinthians 15:12-19)

Wednesday, Nov. 10—The Significance of Christ's Resurrection (1 Corinthians 15:20-28)

Thursday, Nov. 11—Arguments to Support Belief in Resurrection (1 Corinthians 15:29-34)

Friday, Nov. 12—Paul Deals with Physical Resurrection (1 Corinthians 15:35-41)

Saturday, Nov. 13—Paul Explains the Spiritual Body (1 Corinthians 15:42-50)

Sunday, Nov. 14—Have Confidence in the Resurrection (1 Corinthians 15:51-58)

C. Eternal Gratitude (v. 57)

57. But thanks be to God, which giveth us the victory through our Lord Jesus Christ.

We have seen that the victory is God's, not ours (comments on v. 54). Now we see that it is ours, too—not in the sense that we won it, but because God gives it to us *through our Lord Jesus Christ*. So *thanks be to God!* [See question #5, page 96.]

Conclusion

A. Our Work Is Not Finished

With verse 57 our text ends in triumph. Thanks to God, *victory* is ours! But let us read one more verse, for verse 58 tells us what to be doing here and now in addition to speaking our thanks to God: "Therefore, my beloved brethren, be ye steadfast, unmovable, always abounding in the work of the Lord, forasmuch as ye know that your labor is not in vain in the Lord."

Verse 58 thus gives us our job assignment for this week, the one following, and all the weeks afterward. And as we labor we constantly think forward to the day when Jesus will come back to earth, in person and visible (1 Thessalonians 4:16, 17).

Can you imagine that wonderful day when our own spiritual bodies will soar aloft along with those of all of God's saints? Yet the blessed saints are not the only dead ones who will return to life at the trumpet blast and Jesus' shout. A great many will be aroused to hear the sad sentence, "Depart from me, ye cursed, into everlasting fire, prepared for the devil and his angels" (Matthew 25:41). Their sins are noted in Revelation 21:8. Their lack of concern for others and failure to do anything good is stressed in Matthew 25:41-46. What a sobering thought!

So let our conclusion still be 1 Corinthians 15:58: "Be ye steadfast, unmovable, always abounding in the work of the Lord."

B. Prayer

Thank You for hope, dear Father in Heaven, for the hope generated by the promises of our God who never has broken even the least of His promises. Thank You for the assurance of spiritual bodies and life everlasting, for the assurance of an end to death and its power, for the assurance of eternal victory.

By Your grace we rest secure in the assurance of Heaven and eternity; by Your grace may we here and now be always abounding in the work of the Lord. In Jesus' name, amen.

C. Thought to Remember

Be faithful in the work of the Lord.

Learning by Doing

This page contains an alternative lesson plan emphasizing learning activities. Classes desiring such student involvement will find these suggestions helpful.

Learning Goals

After participating in this lesson, each student will be able to:

1. Describe the resurrection bodies in which believers will rise when Jesus returns to earth.

2. Explain why Jesus' resurrection gives us hope that we will receive a new eternal body.

3. Compose words of hope and encouragement to someone grieving the death of a Christian friend or family member.

Into the Lesson

Say, "Few people talk openly about death and dying. However, today we will face it head-on." Ask the class to cite and define contemporary views of what happens to people after death. List the responses on a board under the heading "After Death?" The list may include reincarnation (Buddhism, Hinduism), various "New Age" views of becoming one with the universe, the Jehovah's Witnesses' view of a very limited number of people in Heaven with the rest remaining on earth, the idea that there is no life after death, and others.

Afterward, ask people to cite what they think happens after death. Of course, most of these responses will have a Christian perspective. List these in a second column on the board under the heading, "Our Beliefs." Make the transition to Bible study by reminding the class, "The Christian has strong evidence of life after death and a wonderful experience ahead for all believers."

Into the Word

This activity will require at least five groups for study. Large classes can duplicate the group assignments. Before class begins, have five different signs posted on the walls in different places in the classrooms, each with one of the following headings: "Death: Before and After—Part I," "Death: Before and After—Part II," "Unpacking a Mystery," "Happy Endings," and "Death's Dark Side."

Appoint a group leader for each of the discussion teams. As these leaders move to the sign and topic assigned, ask class members to choose and join them. (All groups must have at least three people.) Give the group leaders a marker, poster board, photocopies of the lesson commentary on the appropriate verses, and a piece of paper with the following instructions:

Death: Before and After—Part I. Your team is to study 1 Corinthians 15:42-44. Make a list with two columns, contrasting our present bodies with our resurrected bodies. Be ready to explain the significance of these contrasts. The lesson commentary attached may be helpful.

Death: Before and After—Part II. Your team is to study 1 Corinthians 15:45-49. Make a list with two columns, contrasting the first and second "Adam." Be ready to explain the significance of these contrasts. The lesson commentary attached may be helpful.

Unpacking a Mystery. Your team is to find and study 1 Corinthians 15:50-53. Make a list with two headings. The first will be the "limitations of the flesh" and the second will be "the process of change." Be ready to explain the significance of what is in your lists. The attached commentary may be helpful.

Happy Endings. Your group's task is to study 1 Corinthians 15:54-57. Make a list of key phrases and be ready to explain them. The attached commentary notes may be helpful.

Death's Dark Side. While the rest of the class reviews the wonderful joys of life beyond death for the believer, your task is to give a brief report of some of the things awaiting the unsaved. See Matthew 25:41-46; John 5:28, 29; and other Scriptures. Attached notes from the conclusion of today's lesson commentary may be helpful.

After the study groups have completed their work, ask the team leader from each group to report their findings.

Into Life

Ask the class to help you pull these teachings into contemporary life. Ask them to imagine you are writing a friend who is mourning the death of a Christian family member or Christian friend. What are the concepts and thoughts to include in the letter? Ask a class member to note these remarks on your marker board. After the exercise, remind the class that mourning is not limited to just a few months after the death of a loved one. Mourning is especially strong at holidays. Thanksgiving Day is less than two weeks away. Ask them to consider sending a Thanksgiving card to someone this year who will be experiencing mourning. The card should include why you are thankful for the deceased, as well as a reminder of our Christian hope.

Let's Talk It Over

The questions on this page are designed to promote discussion of the lesson by the class and to encourage application of the lesson Scriptures. The answers provided are only discussion starters. Let your class talk it over from there.

1. Knowing the body will be raised in incorruption, power, and glory, why are we so distraught when we bury a loved one? What encouraging words do you say to the family of a departed believer?

While we know what the future holds, that future has a far-off feel. The immediate future looks like one of loneliness, as we have to go on without the company of our loved one. It is not a grief of hopelessness, but one of separation. The loss of our loved one means we have lost one who shared our dreams, our interests, and our responsibilities. Our lives will be different, so we are anxious about the change.

Of course we talk of the future hope when we visit at the funeral home. We talk of Heaven, of rest from labor, and of respite from suffering. But we also admit the loss, and we agree that the person has a right to feel sorrow. We celebrate the earthly life, we mourn the loss, and we anticipate the resurrection. Sorrow and joy mix, and both are genuine and appropriate.

2. As Paul contrasted Adam and Jesus, he could have used strictly parallel terms: "of the earth" and "from heaven." Instead, he added that Jesus is "the Lord from heaven." What is significant about noting the lordship of Christ?

We share common features with Adam simply by virtue of our birth. We have no control over it. But whether or not we share in the traits of the second Adam depends on our faith. If we make Jesus Lord of our lives, then we can expect to share in the resurrection.

Perhaps Paul was hoping to get the Corinthians to reaffirm their commitment to Jesus as Lord. Recall that the church suffered from a divisive spirit (see 1 Corinthians 1:10-13). Encourage your learners to focus on their own need to reaffirm a commitment to submitting to Jesus as Lord of their lives.

3. Do you expect the Lord to return before your own death? Why, or why not? How does your belief affect how you live your life?

Ever since the Lord departed, Christians have lived with a sense of the imminent return of Christ. But whether the Lord returns before we die or we die before He returns, our ultimate future will be the same. Thus we live our lives in view of the reality of His return and the consummation of His Heavenly kingdom. We want to be a part of it, so we live in faithfulness.

Many believers have an expectation that the Lord's return must be near because of the prevalence of sin in the world. Surely we want to see the reign of Satan come to an end, so we long for the Lord's return. But we simply do not know how long it will be until He returns. We must remain faithful until He does.

4. We know that death holds no terror for us as Christians. How terrifying ought we portray it to unbelievers? What is the proper place for discussion of death and eternal punishment as we talk to unbelievers?

Various preachers of years past became known for their "fire and brimstone" sermons. But manipulating people by playing to their fears is a very questionable tactic. Even so, we do need to tell people the bad news of sin and judgment if they are to appreciate the good news of forgiveness and salvation. Accepting Christ must be a total commitment of mind and heart.

Many people today fear death because of the pain that may come with it or because they have dreams and plans to accomplish. But they do not realize that they are lost without Christ. We need to inform them and urge them to share in Christ's victory over death.

5. God gives us victory through Jesus. What specifically do you thank Him for in giving you this victory?

The thrust of this lesson is the victory of the resurrection. Certainly the idea of spending eternity in Heaven in glorified bodies ought to fill our hearts with gratitude to God.

We can also thank Him for the sense of purpose He gives us. Knowing that this life is not all there is to our existence fills us with meaning. Knowing that we can help to lead others to share in this victory gives us a mission as well. We are grateful for the fellowship of believers that we are part of and for the encouragement those believers give us.

Finally, we thank God that someone cared enough to share with us the good news of this victory. Because someone cared, we can be included. With whom will we share it?

A New Creature in Christ

DEVOTIONAL READING: **2 Corinthians 4:16–5:5.**

BACKGROUND SCRIPTURE: **2 Corinthians 5:11-21.**

PRINTED TEXT: **2 Corinthians 5:11-21.**

2 Corinthians 5:11-21

11 Knowing therefore the terror of the Lord, we persuade men; but we are made manifest unto God; and I trust also are made manifest in your consciences.

12 For we commend not ourselves again unto you, but give you occasion to glory on our behalf, that ye may have somewhat to answer them which glory in appearance, and not in heart.

13 For whether we be beside ourselves, it is to God: or whether we be sober, it is for your cause.

14 For the love of Christ constraineth us; because we thus judge, that if one died for all, then were all dead:

15 And that he died for all, that they which live should not henceforth live unto themselves, but unto him which died for them, and rose again.

16 Wherefore henceforth know we no man after the flesh: yea, though we have known Christ after the flesh, yet now henceforth know we him no more.

17 Therefore if any man be in Christ, he is a new creature: old things are passed away; behold, all things are become new.

18 And all things are of God, who hath reconciled us to himself by Jesus Christ, and hath given to us the ministry of reconciliation;

19 To wit, that God was in Christ, reconciling the world unto himself, not imputing their trespasses unto them; and hath committed unto us the word of reconciliation.

20 Now then we are ambassadors for Christ, as though God did beseech you by us: we pray you in Christ's stead, be ye reconciled to God.

21 For he hath made him to be sin for us, who knew no sin; that we might be made the righteousness of God in him.

Nov 21

GOLDEN TEXT: If any man be in Christ, he is a new creature: old things are passed away; behold, all things are become new.—2 Corinthians 5:17.

Lesson Aims

After participating in this lesson, each student will be able to:

1. Summarize the message of the "ministry of reconciliation" that Paul describes in the text.

2. Note specific evidence for the need of this ministry in his or her own community.

3. Suggest one specific way he or she can participate in this ministry of reconciliation in the coming week.

Lesson Outline

INTRODUCTION
  A. Old Reputations
  B. Lesson Background
 I. PAUL'S EFFORT (2 Corinthians 5:11-13)
  A. Outward and Inward (vv. 11, 12)
    Beauty Isn't *Only Skin Deep*
  B. Insanity or Sanity (v. 13)
 II. LOVE'S CONTROL (2 Corinthians 5:14, 15)
  A. Fact of Death (v. 14)
  B. Effect of Death (v. 15)
III. RECONCILIATION'S RESULTS (2 Corinthians 5:16-21)
  A. New Outlook (v. 16)
  B. New Status (v. 17)
  C. Newness From God (v. 18)
  D. Message of Newness (v. 19)
  E. Messengers of Newness (v. 20)
    An Unlikely Role
  F. Method of Newness (v. 21)
CONCLUSION
  A. Reputations Count
  B. Prayer
  C. Thought to Remember

Introduction

A. Old Reputations

Bigtown and Smalltown are in such close proximity that they would be one and the same town if it were not for the state line that runs between them. Bigtown is an ordinary American city. It has a university, a symphony orchestra, an art museum, and many other embellishments of "culture." Smalltown is a typical suburb, with a new shopping center frightening the established businesses.

Back in the first half of the twentieth century, Smalltown was nicknamed Sin City. Its Palace Theatre changed its name to Sensation and began showing pornographic films.

The Bear Club opened its doors the same year. This was a showplace with a bar. There a cocktail was priced at thirty dollars, even during the Great Depression. A man who came in alone was greeted by a pretty hostess who asked him to buy a drink for her, too. Of course her drink sold elsewhere for a nickel in those days, but at the Bear Club it cost thirty dollars. The show itself was "free."

The Sensation and the Bear Club advertised in Bigtown and both promptly became popular with convention visitors wanting to "unwind," business visitors ready for a "holiday" after finishing their business, and hundreds of residents having plenty of money and looking for a "good time."

Reputations can be hard to live down! Yet both people and cities can change. But even if cities as a whole don't change, God still holds individuals accountable.

B. Lesson Background

Corinth in the first century A.D. was a city that combined the attractions of Bigtown with those of Sin City. It was a busy crossroads of culture and commerce. The streets were full of restless sailors on leave, thrill-seekers looking for excitement, and merchants willing to pander to all.

Writing about four hundred years before the time of Christ, the playwright Aristophanes used the Greek word *korinthiazesthai*—which means "to act like a Corinthian"—as a reference to sexually immoral behavior. What a reputation Corinth had! The Romans destroyed the city in 146 B.C., but its reputation for immorality came back when it was reestablished in 44 B.C.

In Paul's day a popular place in Corinth was the great temple of Aphrodite, the goddess of love. The geographer Strabo, writing just before the time of Christ, claims that a thousand priestesses who doubled as prostitutes staffed this temple.

In his first letter to the Corinthian church, Paul lists some of the sins that may well have given Corinth the reputation of being Sin City. But Paul also said that such things were not acceptable in the kingdom of God (see 1 Corinthians 6:9, 10).

When the Corinthians came out of such gross paganism to become Christians, it is not surprising that they were slow in learning Christian ways. Paul's first letter to them was unsparing in pointing out errors and urging correction. After sending such a critical letter, Paul naturally wondered how the Corinthians would receive it.

Would they acknowledge their mistakes and correct them, or would they merely be resentful and angry? He had to wonder for a long time, but finally he reconnected with Timothy (2 Corinthians 1:1), who had been in Corinth to see how the letter was received (Acts 19:21, 22; 1 Corinthians 4:17; 16:10).

The news Timothy brought was encouraging, as the content of 2 Corinthians shows. Most of the Corinthians took the criticism seriously and were making improvements. Only a minority was resentful and angry. Even they acknowledged that Paul wrote a good letter, but they insisted that in person he was weak and his speech was contemptible (2 Corinthians 10:10).

With that information Paul wrote his second letter to the Corinthians. Grateful for the progress that was being made at Corinth, he made a modest defense of himself and, more importantly, a defense of the Christ whose ambassador he was. Paul declared that he himself was truthful (2 Corinthians 4:2), but said he proclaimed Christ, not himself (4:5). God had enlightened Paul with the knowledge of Jesus (4:6).

If Paul was unworthy to carry such a treasure, as a fragile clay jar is unworthy to hold a material treasure, that only served to emphasize the power of God that was in the message (4:7). Paul, the one who had persecuted the church (1 Corinthians 15:9), was now being persecuted for this message (2 Corinthians 4:9). His old reputation had given way to a new reputation because of that very message.

I. Paul's Effort
(2 Corinthians 5:11-13)

Above all, Paul says, he is working to be acceptable to Christ, because Christ is the Judge before whom all must appear to receive a just sentence for what they have done (2 Corinthians 5:9, 10). Now verses 11-13 continue the description and discussion of Paul's ongoing effort.

A. Outward and Inward (vv. 11, 12)

11. Knowing therefore the terror of the Lord, we persuade men; but we are made manifest unto God; and I trust also are made manifest in your consciences.

In twenty-first century English, we would understand *terror* to mean *fear* in this context. Paul is thinking in terms of the final judgment (2 Corinthians 5:10, just previous). Such a thought should terrify anyone who is not obeying God. But Paul, as a Christian, faces the thought of judgment without terror. Instead, he has a deep reverence that usually is referred to as "the fear of God" (e.g., 2 Corinthians 7:1).

How to Say It

APHRODITE. Af-ruh-*dite*-ee.
ARISTOPHANES. A-ris-*tof*-a-neez.
COLOSSIANS. Kuh-*losh*-unz.
CORINTH. *Kor*-inth.
CORINTHIANS. Kor-*in*-thee-unz (*th* as in *thin*).
GALATIANS. Guh-*lay*-shunz.
HEBREWS. *Hee*-brews.
ISAIAH. Eye-*zay*-uh.
KORINTHIAZESTHAI (Greek). ko-rin-thee-*adz*-ess-thai (*th* as in *thin*).
PHILIPPIANS. Fih-*lip*-ee-unz.
SERGIO GUTIERREZ. *Sar*-jyo Goo-*tar*-ez (*a* as in *air*).
STRABO. *Stray*-bow (*bow* as in rain*bow*).

It is in this light that Paul continually is trying to *persuade* people of certain things. These things include the truth of the gospel as it speaks of the need to be reconciled to God (v. 20, below).

Paul also tries to persuade people of the purity of his own motives (2 Corinthians 1:12) and of the soundness of his credentials (4:1-6). Such facts are *manifest* (evident, well known) to God, and Paul hopes they are equally manifest in the minds, hearts, and *consciences* of the Christians in Corinth. [See question #1, page 104.]

12. For we commend not ourselves again unto you, but give you occasion to glory on our behalf, that ye may have somewhat to answer them which glory in appearance, and not in heart.

Paul may be thought of as commending himself when he declares his honesty and truthfulness (2 Corinthians 4:2) or when he speaks of his authority as an apostle (10:8; 11:5). But actually he is only trying to help the genuine Christians of Corinth. They want to defend him against the barbs of the critics who take pride in *appearance* rather than what is in the *heart.*

Such critics ridicule Paul's personal appearance and his speech (10:10). No doubt some of them are taller, handsomer, and more eloquent than he. But none is as honest and truthful, and none has been called by Jesus to be an apostolic witness for Him. Paul is the one who had received such a calling (Acts 26:13-16). By this time the devout Corinthians should be able to defend Paul on their own against such critics (2 Corinthians 12:11). [See question #2, page 104.]

BEAUTY *ISN'T* ONLY SKIN DEEP

We've all heard the saying, "Life begins at forty." Someone more cynical than most of us has rephrased it, "Life begins at forty . . . to start going downhill." By the time we have reached the end of our fourth decade we cannot deny that age (and gravity) are changing our appearance. One middle-ager said, "I weigh the same as I did when I was twenty; my weight's just shaped different now than it was then!"

To combat the effects of aging, cosmetic surgery has become a growth industry. In a recent year, 7.4 million cosmetic procedures were performed in America, up 198 percent from a decade earlier. Facelifts, eyelid lifts, chemical peels, cheek implants, hair transplants, and collagen injections are all used to get rid of the inevitable wrinkles and to disguise thinning tissue where we don't want to be thin.

Then there is liposuction, which takes away the fatty tissue where we don't want to be fat. Perhaps the strangest treatment is the injection of botulism toxin (botox) to counteract wrinkles. Some people even become addicted to cosmetic surgery!

It could be argued from all of this that modern culture is guilty of the sin that Paul alludes to: placing more emphasis on outward appearance than on character. There's nothing wrong with *looking* good—at least as good as we can! But our value to the world, and simply as persons, is far greater if we place our focus on *being* good.

—C. R. B.

B. Insanity or Sanity (v. 13)

13. For whether we be beside ourselves, it is to God: or whether we be sober, it is for your cause.

Paul received the gospel he preached from Jesus (Galatians 1:11, 12). And Paul received those things after Jesus died, rose, and ascended to Heaven.

Hearing of such things, opponents of Paul say that he is *beside* himself, out of his mind, crazy (e.g., Acts 26:24). In response, Paul points out that the things that cast doubt on his sanity are between him and *God*. When Paul talks with his fellow humans, his talk is *sober*, reasonable, with no indication of insanity. For example, when he tells of Jesus' resurrection he points to credible witnesses (1 Corinthians 15:1-8).

Paul's preaching is plain and direct. He simply presents the gospel, the good news, and urges the hearers to accept the opportunity it offers. That is what makes sense!

II. Love's Control
(2 Corinthians 5:14, 15)

Jesus Himself said to His disciples, "Greater love hath no man than this, that a man lay down his life for his friends" (John 15:13). Christ loved Paul with this kind of love, even when Paul was a bitter enemy trying to destroy the church.

When Paul realized his error, he knew he was obligated to do what he could for Christ. The following verses explain the reasoning that bring Paul to that conclusion.

A. Fact of Death (v. 14)

14. For the love of Christ constraineth us; because we thus judge, that if one died for all, then were all dead.

Christ indeed *died for all* sinners (cf. Romans 5:8). As a result, *all* people ought to be *dead* to sin, separated from it forever, no longer sinning. But we know that not everyone will accept the meaning of Christ's death, and as a consequence not everyone will die to sin. Paul must preach this message! [See question #3, page 104.]

B. Effect of Death (v. 15)

15. And that he died for all, that they which live should not henceforth live unto themselves, but unto him which died for them, and rose again.

Sinners are enslaved and controlled by sin (John 8:34). When they respond to Christ's love by dying to sin, they should not think themselves free to do whatever they please. In gratitude they should live for Jesus, who *died for them* (cf. Romans 14:7, 8). Paul must preach this message!

III. Reconciliation's Results
(2 Corinthians 5:16-21)

To become a Christian is to become a different person. A slave of sin changes to become a slave of God and Christ and righteousness (Romans 6:18). Sometimes the change is described as being born again (John 1:12, 13; 3:3-5). But in our text we have read, "If one died for all, then were all dead" (2 Corinthians 5:14). Thus the figure here is like that in Romans 6:1-4. There we see that becoming a Christian is dying to sin, being buried in baptism, and rising to a new life. This new life of being reconciled to God brings certain changes with it.

A. New Outlook (v. 16)

16. Wherefore henceforth know we no man after the flesh: yea, though we have known Christ after the flesh, yet now henceforth know we him no more.

A whole person is "spirit and soul and body" (1 Thessalonians 5:23). To know someone *after the flesh* is to know that person superficially from appearance and what he or she is seen to do. Paul's opponents make a mistake when they glory "in appearance, and not in heart" (2 Corinthians 5:12).

Paul's own mistake had been to think of *Christ* as an enemy of God and of God's people. But Paul resolved to make that mistake no more. Really knowing anyone involves acquaintance with that person's thoughts and feelings, values and ambitions, as well as desires and motives.

B. New Status (v. 17)

17. Therefore if any man be in Christ, he is a new creature: old things are passed away; behold, all things are become new.

Whether we think of a Christian as born again or as dead to sin and risen to new life, the point is that he or she is *a new creature*—a different person, a saint instead of a sinner. Love of sin and bondage to sin *are passed away;* the person's whole nature and way of life *are become new.* Compare also Romans 8:1, 10; Galatians 6:15; and Revelation 21:5. [See question #4, page 104.]

C. Newness From God (v. 18)

18. And all things are of God, who hath reconciled us to himself by Jesus Christ, and hath given to us the ministry of reconciliation.

The *all things* that *are of God* refers to our new outlook and new status according to verses 16 and 17, above. The verse now before us speaks of the change as being reconciled to God, and it is God *who hath reconciled us to himself by Jesus Christ.* By our sinning we made ourselves to be God's enemies (Colossians 1:21). We could not end our enmity, but God could. He sent Jesus, who died to pay sin's penalty. As a result, God could forgive us.

So our redemption and reconciliation are God's work, not ours. But don't miss the next two verses! They reveal that we do have a part in changing people from being sinners to being saints. That revelation is begun in the last clause of the verse before us: to Paul and other Christians, God has given *the ministry of reconciliation,* the work of presenting to God's enemies the opportunity to be reconciled to God.

D. Message of Newness (v. 19)

19. To wit, that God was in Christ, reconciling the world unto himself, not imputing their trespasses unto them; and hath committed unto us the word of reconciliation.

This is the message that was and still is delivered to the sinners of the world: because Jesus took to Himself the punishment that was due sinners, God can forgive the sinners, no longer holding them accountable for the wrongs they have done. Thus He reconciles to Himself the sinners who have been His enemies (Romans 3:24, 25; Colossians 1:19, 20). God *committed* that message to Paul and other preachers to be

Visual for lesson 12

*Use this visual to ask your learners how their "newness" in Christ is real **right now**.*

delivered to sinners, and Christians are delivering it yet today.

E. Messengers of Newness (v. 20)

20. Now then we are ambassadors for Christ, as though God did beseech you by us: we pray you in Christ's stead, be ye reconciled to God.

Because God committed to Paul and other preachers the message of reconciliation and newness, those preachers have become His *ambassadors,* His representatives, His spokesmen to all the sinners of the world (also Ephesians 6:20). [See question #5, page 104.] Speaking for Christ, they said and still are saying to sinners, *be ye reconciled to God.*

This makes it very plain that each sinner decides whether he or she will be reconciled to God or not. God is eager to forgive, and thereby to justify and reconcile; but a sinner can choose to remain unforgiven.

AN UNLIKELY ROLE

Sergio Gutierrez is a Roman Catholic priest in Mexico, but he is better known for his unlikely role as a professional wrestler. Gutierrez-the-priest is also "Fray Tormenta," who has a passionate following among wrestling fans in his country. His two roles in life are incongruous, and many people come to his matches just to see if he will actually fight.

Others come to give him money for use in another role that Gutierrez has: running an orphanage near Mexico City. The eighty-plus orphans who live there rely almost totally on his wrestling earnings for their physical needs. Many were rescued from among the thousands of parentless children roaming the streets of Mexico City. "Fray Tormenta" is more than an entertainer or sports figure; he sees himself as an ambassador who shows Christ's love and reconciliation to children who might otherwise never experience it. (Even after a wrestling victory, "Fray Tormenta" goes to his knees to ask forgiveness for any "overenthusiastic" holds that he may have used in the match!)

In the person of Jesus, God came to earth in an unlikely role—one diametrically opposed to who He really was. The sinless Son of God became sin personified so that we who have been "orphaned" by sin could be reconciled to God and experience His love and care. Some who knew Jesus in the flesh were scandalized by the idea that a man could also be God (or vice versa). But scandal or not, the dual roles Jesus played have become the means of salvation for us all.   —C. R. B.

F. Method of Newness (v. 21)

21. For he hath made him to be sin for us, who knew no sin; that we might be made the righteousness of God in him.

All are sinners (Romans 3:23). God wants to make us into new creatures (2 Corinthians 5:17). How does He go about it? First, He sent His Son to be one of us, but without *sin* (Hebrews 4:15; 1 Peter 2:22). Second, God laid the penalty for our sins on that guiltless One (Isaiah 53:6; Galatians 3:13). Since the penalty for our guilt is gone, we can have God's *righteousness* as our own, if we want it (1 Corinthians 1:30; Philippians 3:9).

Of course we are not interested in that offer unless we believe it to be genuine, unless we believe that Jesus really did die for our sins, and that we really can be (and need to be) forgiven. Even if we believe in Jesus the Savior, God will not make us new if we prefer to go on sinning— we must repent. When we repent and are bap-

tized (Acts 2:38), then we are new creatures. We have died to sin and have risen to walk in newness of life (Romans 6:3, 4).

Then it must be our intent to be free from sin throughout our lives. But sometimes we fail to live up to our intention. Every Christian can sin. The apostle Paul did (Romans 7:19-25), and not many of us are better than he! But we can praise God for His continuing forgiveness (1 John 1:9).

Conclusion

A. Reputations Count

From my long-ago youth I remember my first date with Louise. Her mother was a charming and vivacious lady. With almost no help from me, she kept up a sparkling conversation while Louise went upstairs for her coat. As we were leaving, her mother gave her daughter a quick hug and said, "Now don't forget who you are."

That instruction intrigued me. As we drove away I asked Louise, "Who are you?"

"I'm a Hampton," she said with a smile. "I guess you might call Mom a snob. She thinks everybody named Hampton is super-good."

"And your mom was afraid I might get you into something dishonorable?"

"No, not you. Somebody else at the party, maybe. When I asked her about dating you, she said, 'Sure, Honey. I know his mother and father.' So I guess I'm not the only one with a proud family name to live up to."

It's important to have an honorable family name, isn't it? And it's good to add honor to that name by what we do. This is especially true for those of us in "the family of God" (cf. Mark 3:35).

Christians are privileged to have both eternal life and the chance to offer that privilege to others. But the example we set is important to the credibility of our message. The way we "live down" a sinful past is to "live up" to the high standards of being a new creature in Christ. Are you making progress in this regard?

B. Prayer

We do love You, Father, and we love our brothers and sisters in Your family. We treasure the companionship, the joy, the learning, the help, and the encouragement that we find in our association with the church.

Help us to make our witness for the church reflect the benefits we receive—even the benefit of eternal life. May we guard the worthy reputation that Christ has given us. In His name, amen.

C. Thought to Remember

"Live down" your past
by "living up" to God's Word.

Home Daily Bible Readings

Monday, Nov. 15—Christ's Ministers Act Boldly (2 Corinthians 3:12-18)

Tuesday, Nov. 16—Paul Serves for God's Glory (2 Corinthians 4:1-15)

Wednesday, Nov. 17—We Must Live by Faith (2 Corinthians 4:16—5:5)

Thursday, Nov. 18—Serve God with Confidence (2 Corinthians 5:6-10)

Friday, Nov. 19—Paul Serves God Faithfully (2 Corinthians 5:11-15)

Saturday, Nov. 20—Paul's Ministry of Reconciliation (2 Corinthians 5:16-21)

Sunday, Nov. 21—Now Is the Day of Salvation (2 Corinthians 6:1-10)

Learning by Doing

This page contains an alternative lesson plan emphasizing learning activities.
Classes desiring such student involvement will find these suggestions helpful.

Learning Goals

After participating in this lesson, each student will be able to:

1. Summarize the message of the "ministry of reconciliation" that Paul describes in the text.

2. Note specific evidence for the need of this ministry in his or her own community.

3. Suggest one specific way he or she can participate in this ministry of reconciliation in the coming week.

Into the Lesson

Option #1: Write the words *New Beginnings* on the board. Say, "We often experience new beginnings in life, such as in a new job. What other 'new beginnings' do people experience?" Examples include new homes, marriage, new locations, new car. After compiling the list, tell the class, "The greatest new beginning one can enjoy is revealed in today's Scripture. However, with this new beginning comes a new responsibility."

Option #2: Write the word *ambassador* on the board. Ask, "What does an ambassador to other countries do?" Then ask, "To which country would you enjoy being an ambassador? Why?" Ask members to share answers with two others. Make the transition to Bible study by saying, "Christians have been called to be ambassadors. Today we'll discover why, where, and what we are to do as ambassadors."

Into the Word

Begin the Bible study with a brief lecture based on the commentary notes on Corinth and the Lesson Background. Prepare a visual with the following words to be used as an outline.

Corinth—korinthiazesthai

Aphrodite

First Letter to Corinth

Second Letter to Corinth

Give the following handout to teams of no more than five people. The heading should read "Reconciled and Reconciling!"

1. Underline 2 Corinthians 5:17. Discuss what Paul means when he says old things are passed away and all things are become new.

2. Clarify Paul's statement when he uses the words *beside ourselves* and *sober* (v. 13).

3. Discuss and explain "the righteousness of God" in verse 21. What is it? Why are we to become the righteousness of God?

4. Paul assumes that our reconciliation with God leads to reconciliation with one another. Review today's text and find clues as to why he affirms that this should happen.

5. How would you define a ministry of reconciliation? What is its purpose? What should we be doing?

6. How do the teachings of verse 16 help us keep our focus in performing this ministry?

Encourage teams to work quickly. After they are finished, ask team leaders to review their conclusions. If you have large numbers of teams, form clusters of three teams to share their conclusions with each other.

Into Life

(Similar activities to the following are included in the student book.)

Activity #1: Remind the class that Paul calls us "ambassadors" in verse 20. Ask the class to brainstorm the characteristics and mission of a Christian ambassador and list these in a column headed "Christian Ambassadors" on the board.

Activity #2: Remind the class that Paul also calls believers to a ministry of reconciliation. Ask the class how this ministry and the concept of a Christian ambassador are related. Why does Paul include both? Make a second column on the board. Ask the class to brainstorm a list of the needs for a ministry of reconciliation in your community and ways to help in this ministry.

Activity #3: Before class, prepare a Thanksgiving card to God to be distributed to each class member. Use a standard letter-size sheet of paper, folded once. On the front cover print the words, "My Thanksgiving Card to God." You may include a simple piece of Thanksgiving artwork. On the left inside page print the words, "Lord, in my community I am especially thankful for. . . ." Ask class members to list things in their community for which they are grateful. This may include such matters as values, opportunities, places, relationships, and people.

On the second inside page, print the words "Lord, in order to be an ambassador of reconciliation I will. . . ." Ask class members to respond by writing at least one thing they intend to do to complete this commitment. Also include a signature line at the bottom of this page.

Conclude with a prayer asking God's blessing on these commitments.

Let's Talk It Over

The questions on this page are designed to promote discussion of the lesson by the class and to encourage application of the lesson Scriptures. The answers provided are only discussion starters. Let your class talk it over from there.

1. Paul believed his integrity ought to be evident to the Corinthians. How can we be sure our faithfulness is evident without "blowing our own horns"?

Integrity is a quality that proves itself over the long haul. The person with integrity is genuine; he or she is the same person no matter who is around. Such a one does not worry about being noticed, but about being true. It is the kind of consistent living that Peter says will silence our critics and make them ashamed (1 Peter 3:16). It is the kind of living that Jesus urges in His Sermon on the Mount (see Matthew 6:1-4). Even if people do not notice our righteousness, Jesus assures us that it will be noticed by God—and that is what really counts.

2. We all have known leaders or others who "glory in appearance." What is it that eventually gives them away? How can we be careful to spot them early so they do not lead us astray?

The example of the people of Berea is key to this. Upon hearing Paul preach, "they received the word with all readiness of mind, and searched the Scriptures daily, whether those things were so" (Acts 17:11). We will not be led astray, even by the most eloquent speaker, if we immerse ourselves in the Word. That is what will expose the false teacher—false doctrine will not hold up under the scrutiny of the Word.

Of course, some teachers who "glory in appearance" teach truth for the most part, but with impure motives. Paul was aware of some of them as he wrote to the church at Philippi (see Philippians 1:14-18). With Paul we can rejoice that such teachers are preaching Christ even if we are disappointed in their motivation. The important thing remains the preaching of the Word (2 Timothy 4:1, 2).

3. How many believers feel the constraint that Paul describes in verse 14? What can be done to lead disciples to know that same compulsion to live and testify for Christ?

Too often the church has been content to get decisions and not disciples. The Great Commission calls us to go, teach, baptize, and then teach some more (Matthew 28:19, 20).

That teaching of the new disciples needs to include instruction that disciples are followers, followers of their Master. The Master came to seek and to save the lost, and He calls us to join in that same ministry. It is the same compulsion to which Paul appeals in Romans 12:1, 2. It is a reasonable service to give our lives to the One who gave His for us.

4. What is "new" for you as a Christian? What change in your life are you most grateful for?

The longer we are Christians, the more we tend to take for granted the new life that is ours. This question calls your learners to recall the intensity with which they first came to know Christ and the dire consequences they would have suffered if they had not come to Him.

As your learners ponder how their lives are different for knowing Christ, encourage them to use the awareness as motivation to greater discipleship. This includes walking by faith day by day and leading others out of the darkness they once knew and into the light (1 Peter 2:9).

5. The lesson writer points out that, specifically, the commission of ambassador was to Paul and other preachers like him. To what extent do you share in this "ministry of reconciliation"? Why?

Many believers think the task of evangelism is for paid preachers only. They see themselves as "off the hook." But the New Testament example is that of all believers sharing the gospel (Acts 8:4).

Paul earlier described his compulsion to share the gospel as coming from the fact of Christ's atoning death (2 Corinthians 5:14). Peter urges believers in general to "show forth the praises of him who hath called you out of darkness into his marvelous light" (1 Peter 2:9).

Of course, Paul and other preachers have opportunities and responsibilities not common to every believer. Encourage your learners to discover specific ways to support such workers. While discussing these possibilities, also stress that while we don't all have the same responsibilities as full-time preachers, the foundational task is the same for everyone: we are all ambassadors to one extent or another. Also remind your learners that in a culture that grows ever more hostile to Christianity, it is imperative for individual believers to take the gospel to their places of work and play to reach those who are lost.

A New Relationship

DEVOTIONAL READING: Ephesians 2:4-10.

BACKGROUND SCRIPTURE: Ephesians 2:11-21.

PRINTED TEXT: Ephesians 2:11-21.

Ephesians 2:11-21

11 Wherefore remember, that ye being in time past Gentiles in the flesh, who are called Uncircumcision by that which is called the Circumcision in the flesh made by hands;

12 That at that time ye were without Christ, being aliens from the commonwealth of Israel, and strangers from the covenants of promise, having no hope, and without God in the world:

13 But now, in Christ Jesus, ye who sometime were far off are made nigh by the blood of Christ.

14 For he is our peace, who hath made both one, and hath broken down the middle wall of partition between us;

15 Having abolished in his flesh the enmity, even the law of commandments contained in ordinances; for to make in himself of twain one new man, so making peace;

16 And that he might reconcile both unto God in one body by the cross, having slain the enmity thereby:

17 And came and preached peace to you which were afar off, and to them that were nigh.

18 For through him we both have access by one Spirit unto the Father.

19 Now therefore ye are no more strangers and foreigners, but fellow citizens with the saints, and of the household of God;

20 And are built upon the foundation of the apostles and prophets, Jesus Christ himself being the chief corner stone;

21 In whom all the building fitly framed together groweth unto a holy temple in the Lord.

GOLDEN TEXT: Ye are no more strangers and foreigners, but fellow citizens with the saints, and of the household of God.—Ephesians 2:19.

The God of Continuing Creation
Unit 3: A New Creation
(Lessons 10-13)

Learning Aims

After participating in this lesson, each student will be able to:

1. Describe the new relationship between Jews and Gentiles that made their differences unimportant in Ephesus.

2. Mention groups in today's church that are drawn together by a similar relationship.

3. Use his or her influence for unity and peace in the church.

Lesson Outline

INTRODUCTION
    A. Vanishing Walls
    B. Lesson Background
  I. FOREIGNERS (Ephesians 2:11-13)
    A. That Was Then (vv. 11, 12)
    B. This Is Now (v. 13)
     Christ and Culture: The Necessary Choice
 II. PEACEMAKER (Ephesians 2:14-18)
    A. Destruction (vv. 14, 15a)
    B. Construction (vv. 15b, 16)
    C. Instruction (vv. 17, 18)
III. TEMPLE (Ephesians 2:19-21)
    A. One Household (v. 19)
    B. One Foundation (v. 20)
     Cornerstones and Time Capsules
    C. One Building (v. 21)
CONCLUSION
    A. The Church's Unity
    B. Prayer
    C. Thought to Remember

Introduction

A. Vanishing Walls

The church in a certain hot-weather town was generous in giving its new preacher a vacation. "You may as well take the whole month of August," he was told. "The town practically closes down then. Half the people go to the mountains and the other half go to the beach. Those who are left just have Communion and Sunday school."

So when August came the preacher and his wife gratefully went back home to visit parents and old friends. When they again drove up to the parsonage at sunset on the last day of August, they saw that the long-vacant house across the

street was now occupied. A younger man was mowing the lawn; a woman of comparable age was operating an edger along the walk. Instead of entering the parsonage, the preacher and his wife went across the street to get acquainted.

Quickly they learned that the newcomers were Jim and Jane Meyers, that Jim was the new custodian at the nearby school. He had been working overtime to get the place ready for the first day of classes, and he hoped never to see a hotter place to work!

To that wordy introduction the preacher responded, "I'm the minister of that church over there." He pointed with a wave of his hand toward the spire. "We hope to see you there on Sunday."

"I don't know about that." Jim's voice was morose, but there was a gleam of fun in his eye. "It can't be much of a church. We watched last Sunday. They didn't have even a handful of people."

"That won't be the case next Sunday," the preacher promised. "Come and see. Come to Sunday school at nine-thirty."

Jane spoke up then, with an edge to her voice. "Those people don't want us over there. We've been here nearly a week, and not one of them has come near us."

"They don't know you're here," the preacher countered. "They don't live across the street. We do, and we came over as soon as we saw you. We want you in church. There's not one person in the congregation who doesn't want you there. Come and see."

The preacher and his wife soon went home, but they made some telephone calls before they unpacked their suitcases. Before darkness fell, two couples stopped to greet Jim and Jane, chat a little, and invite them to church.

Each evening that week, two or three more couples came over. Women stopped by while Jim was at work. They were eager to help Jane get settled in her new home. When Jim and Jane came to Sunday school at nine-thirty, they were greeted happily by friends. Never again did Jane suspect they were not wanted. The walls had come down.

B. Lesson Background

Jews of the first century often presented a strange contrast, almost a self-contradiction. Many became merchants as they scattered from their homeland in Palestine to all the countries around the Mediterranean Sea. Swiftly they learned the languages and business customs of the countries where they settled. As they made friends they also embraced some of the foreign cultural practices.

At the same time, the Jews fiercely maintained their Jewish identity. Many of them traveled long distances to attend the religious festivals at Jerusalem. They built synagogues so that they could worship separately in most of the cities where they lived.

These practices of the Jews occasionally caught the attention of others around them. In those days some pagans were losing faith in the imaginary gods of their ancestors. When they went to synagogue meetings they were welcomed, and many were attracted by the teaching about the one true God. Some were converted to the Jewish faith, becoming circumcised and taking the law of Moses as their own.

This was the situation when Paul (a Jew who became a Christian) arrived in Ephesus in about A.D. 53 to teach in the synagogue (Acts 19:8). Both Jews and Gentiles heard his message. When the hostility of some Jews drove him from the synagogue, he probably had even more Gentile listeners as he taught in another place (Acts 19:9, 10). Consequently both Jews and Gentiles became Christians. And when they became Christians, the wall between Jew and Gentile vanished.

Paul wrote a letter to the Ephesian church about five years later. In that letter he reaffirmed that Christians are new creatures (Ephesians 2:1-10). This is just as true of the Gentile Christians as it is of the Jewish Christians. The truth still stands: there is no longer a wall between them.

I. Foreigners
(Ephesians 2:11-13)

In verses 8-10, just before our lesson text, Paul reminds the readers that they did not make themselves into new creatures. Rather, they are God's workmanship, "created in Christ Jesus unto good works." Paul has more to say about Christians as new creatures as our text begins.

A. That Was Then (vv. 11, 12)

11. Wherefore remember, that ye being in time past Gentiles in the flesh, who are called Uncircumcision by that which is called the Circumcision in the flesh made by hands.

Although the Ephesian church is a mixture of Jews and *Gentiles,* Paul specifically addresses the latter here. Two important thoughts loom before us. First, the verse refers to *time past,* meaning the time before the Ephesian Gentiles became Christians. Second, in that past time the Jews had been immensely proud to call themselves *the Circumcision* and immensely scornful in calling the Gentiles *Uncircumcision.*

But circumcision is only *in the flesh,* a physical thing administered *by* human *hands.* It does not in and of itself make any difference in the spirit (cf. 1 Corinthians 7:19; Galatians 5:6; 6:15;

Colossians 2:11). What really counts with God is a circumcision of the heart (Romans 2:29). This has always been the case (Deuteronomy 10:16; 30:6; Jeremiah 4:4).

12. That at that time ye were without Christ, being aliens from the commonwealth of Israel, and strangers from the covenants of promise, having no hope, and without God in the world.

At that time, meaning the time before they became Christians, the Gentiles in the Ephesian church truly were alienated from God. Those Gentiles who previously attended the synagogue had had, at most, a tenuous connection with *the commonwealth of Israel* and *the covenants of promise.* Even so, all the Gentiles in Ephesus had been *without Christ,* by whose blood some were later made near (v. 13, below).

What a hopeless existence that previous condition was! In their previous spiritual state, these Gentile Christians had worshiped many gods. Undoubtedly these included Artemis (also known as Diana; see Acts 19:28). Perhaps they also worshiped the gods Sarapis, Isis, Aphrodite, Zeus, and a dozen others. But even though they had worshiped all these gods, in truth they had been *without God in the world.* [See question #1, page 112.]

B. This Is Now (v. 13)

13. But now, in Christ Jesus, ye who sometime were far off are made nigh by the blood of Christ.

But now things have changed! The Gentiles whom Paul addresses are *in Christ*—they are Christians. It is *the blood of Christ* that has

---

How to Say It

APHRODITE. Af-ruh-*dite*-ee.
ARTEMIS. *Ar*-teh-miss.
BOLSHEVIK. *Bol*-shuh-vik.
COLOSSIANS. Kuh-*losh*-unz.
CORINTHIANS. Kor-*in*-thee-unz (*th* as in *thin*).
CZARIST. *Tsar*-ist.
DEUTERONOMY. Due-ter-*ahn*-uh-me.
EPHESIANS. Ee-*fee*-zhunz.
EPHESUS. *Ef*-uh-sus.
GALATIANS. Guh-*lay*-shunz.
GENTILES. *Jen*-tiles.
HEBREWS. *Hee*-brews.
ISAIAH. Eye-*zay*-uh.
ISIS. *Eye*-sis.
JEREMIAH. Jair-uh-*my*-uh.
MICAH. *My*-kuh.
SARAPIS. Suh-*rap*-is.
SYNAGOGUE. *sin*-uh-gog.
ZEUS. Zoose.

bridged the gap. Paul has already stressed this in this letter (Ephesians 1:7) as he does in other letters (e.g., Colossians 1:20).

Only through Christ can people be *made nigh* to God. In fact the Gentile Christians at Ephesus are now much nearer to Him than are the devout non-Christian Jews who still rely solely on the covenants of promise that were made before Christ appeared. The Christian Gentiles now have the assurance of being God's people along with those Christian Jews who also acknowledge *the blood of Christ* as payment for their sins.

CHRIST AND CULTURE: THE NECESSARY CHOICE

Before the 1917 Bolshevik Revolution brought atheistic Communism to Russia, the Orthodox Church was the state church and the keeper of Russian culture. With the coming of Communism, however, religion was suppressed and thousands of churches closed. The Orthodox Church was able to stay feebly alive by accommodating itself to the limitations that the Soviet state placed upon it. As a result, the church lost its power to influence the culture.

When Communism fell in 1989, Russian Orthodoxy again found freedom. With that freedom came a renewed closeness to Russian culture. But a new problem has since developed: the Orthodox Church now has gained so much power in its closeness with the current culture that other denominations and sects fear a revival of the repressive treatment of non-Orthodox Christians as in Czarist Russia of old.

How aghast Paul would be were he to see this situation! Notice how he speaks of Gentile Christians who had once been part of pagan culture, but now have turned from paganism to a close relationship with the living God. In so doing, they left behind the closeness they once had had with a pagan culture that was steeped in idolatry.

Paul commends this principle to us: the church is always faced with the task of distinguishing between what God wants and what our culture expects. Sometimes cultural expectations are radically opposed to God, and sometimes they are not. But the distinction between the two always must be maintained. If we fail to make this distinction, then how will we know how or when to make godly choices?   —C. R. B.

II. Peacemaker
(Ephesians 2:14-18)

For centuries the Jews, proud of being God's people, had scorned the Gentiles, who did not share that privilege. For centuries the Gentiles had responded with enmity of their own, scorning the scorners. Now in the city of Ephesus

some of the Jews are God's people in a different way: they have been born again.

They are new creatures. They are children of God in a way they had never been before. Now some Gentiles also are born again—born anew in the same way. They, too, are new creatures. They, too, are children of God. All God's children are brothers and sisters. There is no room for scorn, no room for enmity.

A. Destruction (vv. 14, 15a)

14. For he is our peace, who hath made both one, and hath broken down the middle wall of partition between us.

Sometimes *peace* comes about only when something is first destroyed. Christ is the One who *is our peace* (Micah 5:5) because He has destroyed the work of the devil (Hebrews 2:14; 1 John 3:8).

In bringing us peace with God in this way, Jesus performed another act of destruction at the same time when He broke *down the middle wall of partition* that had existed between Jew and Gentile for centuries (cf. 1 Corinthians 12:13). Jews are still Jews and Gentiles are still Gentiles in a biological sense, but now all Christians stand as equal before God (Galatians 3:28). [See question #2, page 112.]

15a. Having abolished in his flesh the enmity, even the law of commandments contained in ordinances.

As we saw in lesson 10, Jesus, in His Sermon on the Mount, said that His purpose was not to destroy *the law*, but to fulfill it (Matthew 5:17). Additional light is cast on that statement by Paul's comment that, "The law was our schoolmaster to bring us unto Christ, that we might be justified by faith. But after that faith is come, we are no longer under a schoolmaster" (Galatians 3:24, 25). The law was thus to guide the Jews until they came to Christ.

But Jewish Christians are now no longer under the law (Romans 3:19-21). What Jesus did *in his flesh* served to destroy the enmity between God and sinner that had come about because people had broken that law. Thus Paul can speak of Christ's work as "blotting out the handwriting of ordinances that was against us, which was contrary to us, and took it out of the way, nailing it to his cross" (Colossians 2:14).

B. Construction (vv. 15b, 16)

15b, 16. For to make in himself of twain one new man, so making peace; and that he might reconcile both unto God in one body by the cross, having slain the enmity thereby.

Both Jews and Gentiles are sinners. Their sins make them enemies of God (Colossians 1:21).

But because of *the cross*, reconciliation between God and all those created in His image is now possible.

All reconciled people form *one body*, one group. They are the family of God, for all of them were born again as His children. This is an important New Testament theme (Mark 3:35; 1 Corinthians 12:12-27; Ephesians 3:6; 4:4). [See question #3, page 112.]

C. Instruction (vv. 17, 18)

17. And came and preached peace to you which were afar off, and to them that were nigh.

Those who *were afar off* are the Gentiles, while *them that were nigh* are the Jews. The message of Jesus to both groups (in other words, to everyone) is that *peace* with God is now possible. See also Isaiah 57:19. [See question #4, page 112.]

18. For through him we both have access by one Spirit unto the Father.

Jesus said, "I am the way, the truth, and the life: no man cometh unto the Father, but by me" (John 14:6). It is *through him* and Him alone that all Jews and Gentiles in the world can *have access . . . unto the Father.* If we choose this path, God's Holy *Spirit* leads us every step of the way. We must allow ourselves to be led by the Spirit in all things (Romans 8:14; Galatians 5:18).

III. Temple
(Ephesians 2:19-21)

If the body of each Christian may be called a temple where the Spirit dwells (1 Corinthians 6:19), how much more may the church—the whole assembly of Spirit-filled Christians—be described as a temple where the Spirit dwells! All the "little temples" like you and me are brought together in one holy and magnificent edifice. That is the grand thought that climaxes and completes our text today.

A. One Household (v. 19)

19. Now therefore ye are no more strangers and foreigners, but fellow citizens with the saints, and of the household of God.

In times past the Gentiles had been *strangers and foreigners*, left out of all the gracious providence of God for His special people. That was the thought that began our text (vv. 11, 12), but the status of pagan Gentiles changed when they became Christians.

Taking the one true God as their King, they have been naturalized into His kingdom and have become *fellow citizens with the saints.* They are born again and are members of God's household, His family. They are brothers and sisters of the Jewish believers who have been reborn in the

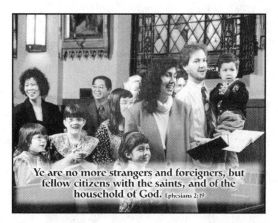

Ye are no more strangers and foreigners, but fellow citizens with the saints, and of the household of God. Ephesians 2:19

Visual for lesson 13. *Use this photograph to allow your learners to reflect on the ways that they were once "strangers" and "foreigners" to God.*

same way. Elsewhere Paul describes Gentile believers as branches of a wild olive tree that have been grafted in among the branches of a cultivated tree (Romans 11:17).

B. One Foundation (v. 20)

20. And are built upon the foundation of the apostles and prophets, Jesus Christ himself being the chief corner stone.

Modern builders have learned to leave a hole in a wall so a cornerstone can be inserted during a ceremony when the building is completed. But in ancient times the building began with the cornerstone. That stone was squared precisely and laid in exactly the right place. Then the other foundation stones were lined up with it, and the stones of the walls were placed on the foundation.

In the church Christ is *the chief corner stone* (Isaiah 28:16; 1 Corinthians 3:11; 1 Peter 2:6). He is exactly right in every respect. Inspired by the Holy Spirit, *the apostles and prophets* took positions that lined up precisely with Christ (Matthew 16:18; Revelation 21:14). Church leaders of every age must resist the temptation to follow their own fancies. They must build securely on the one true *foundation.* The consequences of doing otherwise are dire indeed (cf. Matthew 7:24-27).

CORNERSTONES AND TIME CAPSULES

Cornerstones have fallen on hard times. As our lesson writer tells us today, at one time the cornerstone was the most important stone in the building, since it was the basis for all that was built upon and around it. In recent times their primary uses have been ceremonial, informative, and, on occasion, as receptacles for time capsules.

Yet even the latter use has declined. As a result many time capsules have been lost. Back in the 1970s a time capsule was buried in Fillmore, California, to preserve the memory of the culture of that decade. Now no one can remember exactly where or even *when* it was buried.

In 1986 an attempt was made in Los Angeles to retrieve seventeen time capsules from the 1930s. Concrete was dug up all around the Civic Center, but not a single one was found. The International Time Capsule Society reports that most of the world's ten thousand or so time capsules have been lost, and with them much valuable information.

Christ is the cornerstone of the church, and the New Testament is the "time capsule" that helps us to remember Him. If we ignore the reminder of His role that the New Testament provides for us, or if we attempt to build the church of today without regard for the fundamental place Christ and His teachings should have in it, then we will have lost an essential tie with the past. In that case the church will neither be square with the truth nor stand tall against falsehood and heresy.   —C. R. B.

C. One Building (v. 21)

21. In whom all the building fitly framed together groweth unto a holy temple in the Lord.

Let every church leader take note of the three words *fitly framed together*. Those who would build the church in a spiritual sense must take care not only to build securely on the right foundation, but also to build well with "materials" that will stand the test of time (1 Corinthians 3:10-15).

Consequently, let no one be enrolled in the church until he or she is a real Christian, truly born again, a genuine child of God and a brother or sister of other Christians. However, let us not expect newborn Christians to be mature Christians. Everyone knows that newborn babies need special care. If you have any newborn Christians in your congregation, don't let them die of neglect (Ephesians 4:15, 16). [See question #5, page 112.]

Conclusion

A. The Church's Unity

In the twenty-first century not many churches have both Jews and Gentiles in their membership. But every church has different kinds of people. Churches need to plan their evangelism to reach all peoples, not just "targeted demographics." Every church needs to plan its programs carefully so that no one is left out or left behind.

For example, every growing church has old-timers and newcomers. This was considered briefly in the Introduction of this lesson. Blessed is the church where the newcomers are neither too hasty nor too slow about finding their places of service! And blessed is the church where the old-timers are neither too hasty nor too slow in helping them find those places!

We may also pause to consider the relationship between the young(er) and old(er) members of the church. The work of the church is very impressive in providing Christian education that is nicely adapted to learners of all ages. Allied with the Sunday school in many churches are graded youth programs. The Sunday school is for teaching, some educators say, and the youth groups are for learning by experience. With wise adult counselors to guide, young people meet with those their own age to discuss and debate questions of Christian doctrine or Christian living. Still with wise adult counselors, they carry out Christian service projects. From the "oldest" youth group, young adults move easily and capably into the adult life of the church.

Today many churches have more than one service on Sunday morning to appeal to differing worship styles and preferences. It is good to serve and be served as well as possible, but in so doing let care be taken to preserve the unity of the church as a holy temple in the Lord.

B. Prayer

Our Father, thank You for Your church that unites Your people in happy fellowship and earnest work and cordial love. May we nobly do our part to increase and improve it. In Jesus' name, amen.

C. Thought to Remember

Cherish the unity of the church—
and work to maintain it.

Home Daily Bible Readings

Monday, Nov. 22—We Have Received Grace Through Christ (Ephesians 1:3-12)

Tuesday, Nov. 23—One in Christ (Ephesians 4:1-6)

Wednesday, Nov. 24—Growing Together in Christ (Ephesians 4:11-16)

Thursday, Nov. 25—Alive Together with Christ (Ephesians 2:4-10)

Friday, Nov. 26—Once Apart, Now Together (Ephesians 2:11-16)

Saturday, Nov. 27—No Longer Strangers and Aliens (Ephesians 2:17-22)

Sunday, Nov. 28—Rooted and Grounded in Love (Ephesians 3:14-19)

Learning by Doing

This page contains an alternative lesson plan emphasizing learning activities. Classes desiring such student involvement will find these suggestions helpful.

Learning Goals

After participating in this lesson, each student will be able to:

1. Describe the new relationship between Jews and Gentiles that made their differences unimportant in Ephesus.

2. Mention groups in today's church that are drawn together by a similar relationship.

3. Use his or her influence for unity and peace in the church.

Into the Lesson

Set up the classroom with physical barriers between chairs. Cluster small groups of chairs facing you with barriers made of cardboard, tables on their sides, blankets over sawhorses. After the class is seated in these clusters, say, "The church often has barriers between its people. These barriers keep us from knowing each other well and keep us from working together. They may breed hostility, jealousy, or anger."

Ask the class to name barriers between people that churches experience. Examples include disabilities, race, economic status, age, traditions. As the students name these, affirm their answers as you remove the barriers you had built. Example: "Yes, newcomers often have a hard time adjusting to a new church setting. The church must work to understand and respond to their needs."

Make the transition to Bible study by saying, "Barriers separating Christians is not a new problem. It was a problem in the first days of the church. Fortunately, God gives us some powerful teaching about how to overcome this problem."

Into the Word

Display a picture or diagram of Herod's temple. If neither is available, simply describe the temple and its four walled courts, each more exclusive than the one outside it. The outer court, Court of the Gentiles, was as far as non-Jews were allowed, even if they believed in God. Inner courts included the Court of Women, as far as female Jews were allowed. Then there was the Court of Israel, available to Jewish men only, and the Court of Priests. Point out the divisive nature of these courts. In Jewish history and in the New Testament church, there was a very real racial barrier that caused division and needed healing.

Hand out copies of today's printed text. Explain the Lesson Background, and then read the text. Ask students to review verses 11-13 and underline every divisive word or phrase they find. Let a "scribe" write the findings on a poster with a heading, "Division and Tension." Use the commentary to explain the following terms as students cite them: "Aliens from the commonwealth" (v. 12) and "far off are made nigh" (v. 13). (A similar activity is included in the student book.)

After this list is complete, remind the class that the early church had a problem accepting Gentile Christians. God used powerful lessons to teach that, in spite of backgrounds, nationality, and gender, we are all united in Christ's body.

Next, ask the class to review verses 14-21 and circle terms that indicate the unity believers are to enjoy. After a few minutes, ask class members to share their findings as the "scribe" writes answers on another poster board with the heading, "The Church United." As in the previous exercise, you may need to explain a few terms or phrases such as "Make in himself of twain one new man" (v. 15) and "reconcile" (v. 16).

Into Life

Activity #1: Remind the class of the opening discussion about barriers that divide the church. Recall these and list them on a marker board.

Activity #2, Small Groups: Give the following instructions, poster board, and marking pens to groups of 4-6 people.

Group 1: Discuss and list why practicing unity with fellow believers and breaking down barriers to that unity is important to the church today.

Group 2: Name things or values that bind a church together in spite of barriers or differences that stand between us. List these on the poster board provided.

Group 3: Select one or two barriers to Christian unity in your congregation and offer ways to break them down so the church can stand united. List your suggestions on the poster board.

Encourage groups to work quickly. Allow each group to report its findings.

Activity #3: Give each class member an index card. Direct, "Identify a believer who has a different background (racial, economic, a newcomer) and make a commitment to get acquainted with that person. Write that person's name on the index card and two ways your goal may be achieved."

Let's Talk It Over

The questions on this page are designed to promote discussion of the lesson by the class and to encourage application of the lesson Scriptures. The answers provided are only discussion starters. Let your class talk it over from there.

1. In Paul's day, the division was between Jew and Gentile. Even in the church it seems that some Jews thought Gentiles were beyond God's saving grace. What groups are excluded from our church—not by command but in practice? How can we demonstrate the reconciliation that Christ offers?

We all would surely affirm that everyone is welcome at our church. But in most churches it is apparent that not everyone believes it. Most churches are very homogenous (and many church growth experts say that they must be so in order to grow). What are you doing to reach out to those in a lower economic bracket from most of your members—or to those who are wealthier? Are there racial barriers at your church? If so, what specific ideas can your class suggest to take them down? Is there much diversity of ages in your church? Is your church actively programming for all ages? What more can be done?

2. If Christ has broken down the "wall of partition," why do so many people not want to be a part of the church? How do we reach people who do not care to be reconciled to God?

In a culture that has lost sight of absolutes, being reconciled to God is a foreign concept. Far too many people have no concept of sin, so they do not realize that sin separates them from God. They believe that God, if He exists at all, is accessible through many routes. They see the church as irrelevant. In fact, if a church preaches that people are guilty of sin and need a one-and-only Savior, that church is seen as narrow and bigoted.

Christian people must work harder than ever to build bridges of relationships with people. Secular people want a sense of belonging. Individually we need to demonstrate an acceptance of people as they are. Without seeming superior, we then need to let them know how we found peace with the Lord and that they need this same peace—and that it is available to them.

3. Some people want to claim Jesus as Savior, but they want nothing to do with the church— His "body." How would you try to convince such a person that the church is important?

For many people the church is nothing more than a social organization with a variety of programs. To them the church exists for its own sake. Yet Paul makes clear the body is God's instrument for reconciliation of people to Himself and to each other.

Have your students suggest ways the church can demonstrate to nonmembers that it exists for their sake, not merely its own. How can the church show that it is interested in making people whole and restoring a sense of community with all who will come to the Lord?

4. If the church's message is one of peace, then what happens to the church's witness and credibility when church members fight and quarrel with one another? How can we prevent internal differences of opinion from destroying our church's witness?

If God's instrument of reconciliation (the church) demonstrates a problem with irreconcilable differences, then its credibility is lost. Church members need to understand just how important their relationships with others in the church really are. We need to learn to put others' interests ahead of our own (Philippians 2:3, 4). Unless we can do that, we have not truly learned to love one another.

Of course, church members will have differences of opinions from time to time. Church unity does not demand agreement on every issue, but unity of purpose. Still, we need to be careful not to air those differences outside the church. We need to be sure differences of opinion do not become rifts between people. If we can discuss issues without getting personal, then we can have diversity in the midst of our unity.

5. What is your role in building God's "holy temple"? How did you decide this role was what God wanted you to do?

This will be a good time for your learners to tell about their own ministries and the burden each one feels for his or her work for Christ. Some of your learners work in the church nursery, and perhaps others help provide food and/or clothing for those in need. Whatever ministry each member has, discuss how each one helps in reaching out to those who are lost to "fitly frame them together" into the Lord's "holy temple." If some of your learners are not involved in ministry, encourage them to find a role to fill.

Winter Quarter, 2004-2005

Called to Be God's People

About These Lessons

When the telephone rings at dinnertime, we often assume it's just a telemarketer calling. But we dare not jump to such an indifferent conclusion when God calls to us from the pages of His Word! God will be calling you to greater service in His kingdom through the lessons of this quarter. As you study, will you "pick up" or merely "let the machine get it"?

Dec 5
Dec 12
Dec 19
Dec 26
Jan 2
Jan 9
Jan 16
Jan 23
Jan 30
Feb 6
Feb 13
Feb 20
Feb 27

Quarterly Quiz

The questions on this page may be used in several ways: as a pretest at the beginning of the quarter; as a review at the end of the quarter; or as a review after each lesson. The questions are based on the Scripture text of each lesson (King James Version). **The answers are on page 116.**

Lesson 1

1. What relation was Lot to Abram? (his brother, his nephew, his cousin?) *Genesis 11:27, 31*
2. After the Lord appeared to him, Abram built an altar to the Lord. T/F *Genesis 12:7*

Lesson 2

1. The Lord told Samuel that one of the sons of ____ would be king. *1 Samuel 16:1*
2. What did the Lord look at when choosing a king? (his heart, his appearance, his height?) *1 Samuel 16:7*

Lesson 3

1. The same number of generations passed between Abraham and David, David and the Babylonian captivity, and the captivity and Christ. How many generations were in each group? (ten, fourteen, forty?) *Matthew 1:17*
2. Who told Joseph to name the baby "Jesus"? *Matthew 1:20, 21*

Lesson 4

1. According to Old Testament law, every first-born son was ____ to the Lord. *Luke 2:23*
2. It was by random chance that Simeon happened to be in the temple when Jesus was brought there by his parents. T/F *Luke 2:27*
3. How did Anna spend most of her time in the temple? (fasting and praying, gossiping and visiting, cleaning and polishing?) *Luke 2:37*

Lesson 5

1. Who were the four fishermen called to follow Jesus? *Mark 1:16-20*
2. What title did the possessed man use when he addressed Jesus? (Son of Man, Rabbi, Holy One of God?) *Mark 1:24*

Lesson 6

1. What two groups ate with Jesus and His disciples at Levi's house? (Pharisees and Sadducees, Greeks and Romans, publicans and sinners?) *Mark 2:14, 15*
2. The scribes and Pharisees criticized Jesus for His choice of dinner companions. T/F *Mark 2:16*

Lesson 7

1. When Jesus ordained His twelve disciples, He gave them power to ____ and to ____. *Mark 3:14, 15*

2. What were the apostles to do as a testimony against people who would not listen to their message? (run away, shake the dust off their feet, fast and pray?) *Mark 6:11*

Lesson 8

1. Some people thought Jesus was John the Baptist. T/F *Mark 8:28*
2. Jesus said that anyone who wanted to come after Him would have to ____ himself, take up his ____, and follow Him. *Mark 8:34*

Lesson 9

1. Which two disciples asked to sit at Jesus' right and left hand? (James and John, Peter and Andrew, Matthew and Thomas?) *Mark 10:35-37*
2. Jesus came to earth to give His life as a ____ for many. *Mark 10:45*

Lesson 10

1. After Naomi's sons died, she wanted her daughters-in-law to stay with her permanently. T/F *Ruth 1:8, 9*
2. Ruth promised to remain with Naomi until one of them remarried. T/F *Ruth 1:16, 17*

Lesson 11

1. Who first suggested that Naaman could be healed by Elisha? (Naaman's wife, an Israelite maid, the king of Syria?) *2 Kings 5:2, 3*
2. What was Naaman told to do in order to be healed? (wash, give alms to the poor, offer sacrifice?) *2 Kings 5:10*
3. According to Naaman, the God of Israel was the only God in all the earth. T/F *2 Kings 5:15*

Lesson 12

1. Why did Nicodemus believe Jesus was "a teacher come from God"? *John 3:2*
2. Jesus told Nicodemus that a man cannot enter God's kingdom unless he is born of ____ and of ____. *John 3:5*

Lesson 13

1. What did Jesus ask the Samaritan woman to give Him? (bread, meat, a drink?) *John 4:7*
2. According to Jesus, true worship takes place in ____ and in ____. *John 4:23, 24*
3. Jesus told the woman that He was the Messiah. T/F *John 3:25, 26*

The Caller

by Thomas D. Thurman

WHEN I WAS A HIGH SCHOOL BOY, I got a job one summer working for the Louisville and Nashville Railroad. My duties were few and simple. I worked the graveyard shift, and when a particular train was to leave on a run, I had to locate the engineer and the fireman and inform them of the schedule.

The railroad yards were just across the street from a couple of cheap hotels where many of the railroad men slept while waiting to be called. On the corner near the hotels was a little all-night restaurant, and there, in that restaurant, I spent my working hours. When men were to be called, I was notified by phone, left the restaurant for a few minutes, located and informed them of the situation, and returned to the restaurant. It was really a plush job for a high school boy.

I wore the glamorous title of "calling boy." Well, maybe it wasn't so glamorous, but it was certainly accurate. It described the exact nature of my work—I called people.

So does God. I suppose we could give Him the title, "The Calling God," but I prefer just "The Caller."

From the beginning of time, God has been calling people. He began to do so in the Garden of Eden. After Eve had eaten of the forbidden fruit and given it to Adam, they "heard the voice of the Lord God walking in the garden in the cool of the day." He "called unto Adam, and said unto him, Where art thou?" (Genesis 3:8, 9).

Thus began God's role as The Caller, a role seen in both the Old and New Testaments. A classic example is the case of Elijah the prophet. "What doest thou here, Elijah?" God asked His despondent prophet, who had taken up residence in a cave in Mount Horeb (1 Kings 19:9).

Elijah had been waiting for just such an opening, and he lost not a minute in pouring out his complaints to God. "I have been very jealous for the Lord God of hosts: for the children of Israel have forsaken thy covenant, thrown down thine altars, and slain thy prophets with the sword; and I, even I only, am left; and they seek my life, to take it away" (1 Kings 19:10).

In effect, Elijah was saying, "I've had it, Lord. I'm tired and weary, despondent and discouraged. I'm ready to quit."

Having listened patiently to Elijah's gripes, God spoke up and said, "Go forth, and stand upon the mount before the Lord" (1 Kings 19:11). When the prophet obeyed, "a great and strong wind rent the mountains, and brake in pieces the rocks before the Lord; but the Lord was not in the wind: and after the wind an earthquake; but the Lord was not in the earthquake: and after the earthquake a fire; but the Lord was not in the fire: and after the fire a still small voice" (1 Kings 19:11, 12). God was in that still small voice.

Perhaps you will hear God's voice through the pages of Scripture this quarter as we learn the meaning of being "Called to Be God's People." This theme will tie our thirteen lessons together. It is a theme that must be kept before the class throughout the quarter if your learners are to keep the "big picture" about what it is that we're trying to accomplish. During this time we will examine several situations where The Caller spoke to His people.

Unit 1: December
God Calls a People

Our unit of lessons for December offers us four examples of how God called people to help Him bring about His magnificent and long-range plan of redemption. **Lesson 1** concerns God's call to Abram: "Get thee out of thy country, and from thy kindred, and from thy father's house, unto a land that I will show thee" (Genesis 12:1). That seventy-five-year-old man obeyed! His faithful response to a call must resonate with us today.

In **Lesson 2** we will journey with the prophet Samuel to Bethlehem. There we will hear The Caller say concerning Jesse's youngest son, David, "Arise, anoint him: for this is he" (1 Samuel 16:12). In this anointing of a future king, Samuel learns that God considers inner qualities to be more important than outward appearance. This is a lesson that those of us who live in a mass-media-driven culture need to learn and relearn.

For **Lesson 3** we'll examine again the thrilling account of God's call to the earthly stepfather of Jesus: "Joseph, thou son of David, fear not to take unto thee Mary thy wife, for that which is conceived in her is of the Holy Ghost" (Matthew 1:20). This lesson will challenge us to consider how unexpected circumstances often present a possibility for responding to God in trust.

Lesson 4 will be about an old man named Simeon. God had communicated "that he should not see death, before he had seen the Lord's Christ" (Luke 2:26). We also will meet an elderly woman named Anna, who "spake of him to all them that looked for redemption in Jerusalem" (Luke 2:38). We will celebrate with these two the hope that Christ's birth brought to the world.

Unit 2: January
Jesus Calls His Followers

The five lessons for January are from the Gospel of Mark. In **Lesson 5** we'll hear Jesus' call to Simon and Andrew (and a similar call to James and John), "Come ye after me, and I will make you to become fishers of men" (Mark 1:17). As the early disciples were challenged to spread the good news, so shall we be.

Lesson 6 introduces us to the tax collector Levi (Matthew) and Jesus' call to him to "Follow me" (Mark 2:14). This lesson will challenge us to identify ways that we can reach out to people whom others may think are "unacceptable" in some way.

Lesson 7 allows us to witness the call of Jesus to twelve of His disciples to "be with him," and to be available so "that he might send them forth to preach" (Mark 3:14). Their call is, in a sense, our call as well. As we consider our call, we shall also identify our own ministry roles in the church and how Jesus equips us to serve.

The final two studies for January are **Lessons 8 and 9.** These will allow us to examine some important considerations in our response to Jesus' call. In Lesson 8 we'll hear Jesus say, "Whosoever will come after me, let him deny himself, and take up his cross, and follow me" (Mark 8:34). This is a call to total commitment. In Lesson 9 we'll learn of the necessity to be ministers and servants in imitation of His example. In so doing we will learn to avoid reaching for "greatness" as culture defines that idea.

Unit 3: February
Whosoever Will—Come!

The four lessons for February will acquaint us with individuals who had to overcome personal obstacles in order to answer God's call. We look first to the ancient story of Ruth in **Lesson 10**. In the midst of personal loss and tragedy, Ruth reached out to support her mother-in-law, whose own loss was greater still. God still calls His people to have the faith and commitment of Ruth.

Lesson 11 comes from 2 Kings 5. There we will see a prideful man known as Naaman seeking a cure for a skin disease. To find healing for his disease, this non-Jew had to overcome his pride in following the command of God's prophet. Our exploration of this man's situation will remind us of the dangers of pride. Our walk with God is in jeopardy if we let pride dominate our thoughts and dictate our actions.

Nicodemus, Jesus' nighttime visitor, will be the subject of **Lesson 12.** Our study will focus upon this man's need to reevaluate his thinking regarding the requirements for admission to the kingdom of God. Once again we'll hear Jesus' famous words, "Except a man be born again, he cannot see the kingdom of God" (John 3:3). What joy for those who indeed have been born again!

Lesson 13 concludes both the unit and the quarter. This will be a study of Jesus' encounter with the woman of Samaria to whom He testified, "God is a Spirit: and they that worship him must worship him in spirit and in truth" (John 4:24). Jesus had to overcome more than one barrier to reach this person. His example calls us to identify barriers that bias and prejudice create today and to consider ways to break down those barriers.

The Caller, the Called, and the Calling

Remember, The Caller is still active today as He invites men and women to come out of the world and into His kingdom. To answer that call is vital! Eternal destinies depend on it.

But while we anticipate eternity with the Master, we must remember that God calls us to serve in the here and now. Like Timothy, Christ calls us to holiness (2 Timothy 1:9). Like those at Corinth, we are "called . . . to peace" (1 Corinthians 7:15). Like those in Galatia, we are "called unto liberty" (Galatians 5:13). As we meet these challenges, may we "walk worthy of the vocation wherewith [we] are called" (Ephesians 4:1). Expect God's rich blessings as you and your learners embrace your calling through this quarter's studies!

Answers to Quarterly Quiz
on page 114

Lesson 1—1. his nephew. 2. true. **Lesson 2**—1. Jesse. 2. his heart. **Lesson 3**—1. fourteen. 2. the angel of the Lord. **Lesson 4**—1. holy. 2. false; the Holy Spirit led him there. 3. fasting and praying. **Lesson 5**—1. Simon, Andrew, James, and John. 2. Holy One of God. **Lesson 6**—1. publicans and sinners. 2. true. **Lesson 7**—1. heal sicknesses, cast out devils. 2. shake the dust off their feet. **Lesson 8**—1. true. 2. deny, cross. **Lesson 9**—1. James and John. 2. ransom. **Lesson 10**—1. false. 2. false; until death separated them. **Lesson 11**—1. an Israelite maid. 2. wash. 3. true. **Lesson 12**—1. because of the miracles He had done. 2. water, the Spirit. **Lesson 13**—1. a drink. 2. spirit, truth. 3. true.

Jesus Calls Us

To Follow in Faith . . .   like Abraham

To Lead with Integrity . . .   like David

To Respond with Grace . . .   like Joseph

To Hope in Christ . . .   like Simeon

To Fish for Men . . .   like the Disciples

To Repent from Sin . . .   like Matthew

To Tell Good News . . .   like the Twelve

To Give 100% . . .   like Jesus

To Become as a Child . . .   like the Disciples

To Overcome Grief . . .   like Ruth

To Overcome Pride . . .   like Naaman

To Overcome Doubt . . .   like Nicodemus

To Overcome Prejudice . . .   like the Samaritan Woman

Receiving God's Call

He Can't Be Put on Hold

by Ronald G. Davis

GOD'S CALL has come to men and women in a variety of ways, from the direct address to Adam and Eve in the garden to the indirect call of the written Word. What ultimately matters regarding His call is our response. Creatures of willful response, all must decide: run and hide as Adam and Eve tried, or pack up and follow as the seaside fishermen did.

Calling in the Twenty-first Century

One marvel of the twenty-first century is the discovery of God's secrets of creation. From magnetic digital patterns to electrons "floating" through the air, humanity has discovered and established dominion over the science God put into place at creation. Many calls now come through wireless phones and cyberspace e-mails.

As one strategy for helping learners attend to and internalize the lessons of this quarter, develop an e-mail or text messaging "chain" for sending a weekly preview of the following Sunday's study. This would need to be in place by November 29, so you could begin sending the weekly statements for the December 5 lesson. Consider the following weekly messages:

December 5—"Abram was called to leave his 'comfort zone.' Could you do it?" *December 12*—"David was called to replace one who was a moral failure. Could you do it?" *December 19*—"Joseph was called to set aside initial impressions and planned reactions. Could you do it?" *December 26*—"Simeon and Anna were called to wait. Could you do it?"

January 2—"The first disciples were called to leave successful vocations. Could you do it?" *January 9*—"Matthew was called to leave a position of privilege and prosperity. Could you do it?" *January 16*—"Twelve were called to fill specific servant ministries. Could you do it?" *January 23*—"All disciples are called to change their central focus: from self to Christ. Can you do it?" *January 30*—"James and John were called to leave behind their ideas of self-aggrandizement for submission and service. Could you do it?"

February 6—"Ruth was called to set aside pagan idolatry; Naomi was called from tragedy and self-pity. Could you do it?" *February 13*—"Naaman was called to show faith in God rather than pride in self-accomplishment and nationality. Could you do it?" *February 20*—"Nicodemus

was called to admit his own inadequate knowledge and understanding. Could you do it?" *February 27*—"The woman at the Samaritan well was called to face and admit her sins. Could you do it?"

For review, reinforcement, and personalization, provide each learner with a folder (either pocket or three-ring). Get a class member with calligraphic skill to pen labels for each folder reading, "Called to Be God's People." Each week, as your group study-time is nearing its end, hand the learners a sheet with the appropriate statement from the preceding list. Direct them, each week, to use the statement for a time of personal meditation and decision. If you choose, you could add other thought material on the sheets; for example, consider the following for week one: "What would have been intrinsically uncomfortable about Abram's comfort zone in Ur? What is intrinsically uncomfortable about my comfort zone in [name of community]?"

Telephone Calls from Heaven

Stand-up comedians have used the concept of "one-sided" telephone calls with great success. To contemporize God's call to the people who are a part of these studies, consider developing a "script" for one or more of these lessons. You may have a class member who would delight in such an opportunity. Here are three examples:

"Hello, this is Abram. Who is this calling? [pause] Yahweh? [pause] You want me to go where? [pause] Oh, You will show me when I need to know. [pause] Leave my people behind? Uh huh. [pause] Great nation? Uh huh. [pause] Great name? Oh, sure. [pause] Great blessing? But Lord, I feel blessed right here. [pause] All the families of the earth. How many is that, Lord? [pause] I wouldn't believe it? [pause] Trust You? Uh huh. Can I take anyone with me, Lord? [pause] Sarai, good! [pause] My nephew? Okay. [pause] Canaan? Where's Canaan? [pause] Oh, okay, Lord. I'll see. Uh huh" [click].

"Matthew, CTC—Certified Tax Collector—How may I help you? [pause] Well, I'm kind of busy today, Jesus. [pause] This is my opportunity, Jesus? Today? This is a pretty successful business I've got here, Lord. [pause] Well, yes, it does have its downside—hatred, resentment, and all that. [pause] Uh huh. That's true, Lord. Your kingdom *is* more important than Rome's. [pause] Right now, Lord? Can we discuss this over dinner? I'll invite a few friends. [pause] 'Follow first, feast later,' You say? [pause] Let me shut down my office and hand in my commission, Lord. See you at my house. [hangs up] What have I done?"

"Hey there, this is Samarielle. Who is this? [pause] Jesus? I don't know any Jesus. [pause] A Jew from Nazareth? How did you get my number? [pause] You have *everyone's* number? Sure. [pause] Does this have something to do with my business? [pause] It has *everything* to do with my business and life? [pause] You want me to meet you out at Jacob's well? [pause] How will I know which one you are? [pause] You'll ask me for a drink of water? [pause] [chuckle] That's a novel idea beside a well. Well, give me a few minutes. What did you say your name was?"

Any one of these, or one developed for another lesson, could be an effective attention-directing activity to begin a class. Be sure to have a desk phone available as a prop. And at the end of the "call," be certain to discuss how accurately or inaccurately each portrays the Biblical occasion (for example, the Biblical account reveals no hesitancy on the part of Matthew to follow).

Calls Against Lifetime Longings

In the first lesson of this study, have your class develop an acrostic for the phrase, "Call from God." Put the letters of these words vertically down a sheet that you can post for the extent of the quarter; it can have week-to-week use.

Ask the class to suggest single words that begin with each of the letters that also characterize the call of God. It will be best if no two are relatively synonymous. Here are possibilities (but note that there are possible synonymous terms included): *challenging, cryptic, clear, abrupt, answerable, life-changing, liberating, frequent, far-reaching, repeated, revolutionary, open-handed, open-ended, mysterious, majestic, magnetic, gracious, gifted, oral, demanding.*

Each week when you are ready to move from the "Into the Word" segment of the study, ask your class to look at their list of characteristics as a checklist for the person(s) and the call(s) being studied. Go entry to entry. For example, for Lesson 1 on the call of Abram, if the word for *C* were *cryptic*, the question would be, "In what sense, if any, did God's call to Abram carry any sense of puzzlement?"

If the word for *G* was *gifted*, the question could be, "In what way(s) did God enable ("gift") Abram to answer His call, as the difficulties arose?" Obviously, God left many of Abram's questions initially unanswered, but He supplied the wisdom and the means to meet any challenge to his obe-

dience. Each week it is a simple matter of replacing the name to the person under consideration.

As an alternate way of dealing week-to-week with the characteristics of God's call, consider a tabular chart; make the left column a list of statements about God's call and the columns across the top (thirteen—one for each lesson) to carry the identification of each week's subject. Such affirmations as the following could be included to the left: *God's call often comes as a sudden surprise; God's call sets high but reasonable expectations; God's call may not be fully understood initially; God's call demands response—He can't be left "on hold"; God's call comes to good people and to bad.* Distribute copies in the first session of the quarter. Then each week have the learners pull out their charts and fill in the name(s) of the person(s) under consideration; then run through the list of statements for a discussion of how each is (or isn't) relevant.

For the visually-oriented class, you might display the following images in consecutive weeks, with the words *God's Call* superimposed. **For Abram,** a picture of a comfortable home, to represent his call from home and family; **for David,** a newspaper front page headlining corruption in high places, to represent a call to moral integrity; **for Joseph,** a daily planner, to represent God's call to change one's immediate and long-term plans; **for Simeon and Anna,** a calendar, to represent their long wait for God's revelation; **for the first disciples,** a classified ads page for jobs wanted, to represent a call from one job to another; **for Matthew,** play money, to represent his call from a lucrative job; **for the Twelve,** a picture of mountain backpackers with heavy loads, to represent the opposite of the Twelve's accoutrements; **for all disciples,** a decorative cross, to represent the ultimate call for self-sacrifice; **for James and John,** a large letter *I*, to represent their self-centeredness; **for Ruth and Naomi,** slices of bread, to represent God's daily provision for them; **for Naaman,** several national flags, to represent his national pride; **for Nicodemus,** a college diploma, to represent his dependence on his learnedness; **for the woman** at the Samaritan well, a group of magazines dealing with our ungodly culture, to represent her call to leave a lifestyle behind.

At some point in each week's class time, stop to ask if someone can identify the relationship of the image to the study of the day.

Whatever teaching and learning activities the teacher chooses for this lesson series, the goal is simple: we want every learner to know that God's call continues to this day and to every person. This is a call to the blessings of a relationship with Him in His Son.

Called to Follow in Faith

December 5
Lesson 1

DEVOTIONAL READING: Jeremiah 1:4-10.

BACKGROUND SCRIPTURE: Genesis 11:27–12:9.

PRINTED TEXT: Genesis 11:27–12:9.

Genesis 11:27-32

27 Now these are the generations of Terah: Terah begat Abram, Nahor, and Haran; and Haran begat Lot.

28 And Haran died before his father Terah in the land of his nativity, in Ur of the Chaldees.

29 And Abram and Nahor took them wives: the name of Abram's wife was Sarai; and the name of Nahor's wife, Milcah, the daughter of Haran, the father of Milcah, and the father of Iscah.

30 But Sarai was barren; she had no child.

31 And Terah took Abram his son, and Lot the son of Haran his son's son, and Sarai his daughter-in-law, his son Abram's wife; and they went forth with them from Ur of the Chaldees, to go into the land of Canaan; and they came unto Haran, and dwelt there.

32 And the days of Terah were two hundred and five years: and Terah died in Haran.

Genesis 12:1-9

1 Now the LORD had said unto Abram, Get thee out of thy country, and from thy kindred, and from thy father's house, unto a land that I will show thee:

2 And I will make of thee a great nation, and I will bless thee, and make thy name great; and thou shalt be a blessing:

3 And I will bless them that bless thee, and curse him that curseth thee: and in thee shall all families of the earth be blessed.

4 So Abram departed, as the LORD had spoken unto him; and Lot went with him: and Abram was seventy and five years old when he departed out of Haran.

5 And Abram took Sarai his wife, and Lot his brother's son, and all their substance that they had gathered, and the souls that they had gotten in Haran; and they went forth to go into the land of Canaan; and into the land of Canaan they came.

6 And Abram passed through the land unto the place of Sichem, unto the plain of Moreh. And the Canaanite was then in the land.

7 And the LORD appeared unto Abram, and said, Unto thy seed will I give this land: and there builded he an altar unto the LORD, who appeared unto him.

8 And he removed from thence unto a mountain on the east of Beth-el, and pitched his tent, having Beth-el on the west, and Hai on the east: and there he builded an altar unto the LORD, and called upon the name of the LORD.

9 And Abram journeyed, going on still toward the south.

GOLDEN TEXT: The LORD had said unto Abram, Get thee out of thy country, and from thy kindred, and from thy father's house, unto a land that I will show thee.—Genesis 12:1.

Called to Be God's People
Unit 1: God Calls a People
(Lessons 1-4)

Lesson Aims

After participating in this lesson, each student will be able to:

1. Describe the historical situations of Abram as he and his family obeyed the call of God to leave Ur and then Haran.

2. Evaluate the faith of Abram through his positive responses to God's call to venture into the unknown.

3. Make changes personally in order to conform to the call of God as given in His Word.

Lesson Outline

INTRODUCTION
  A. The Tensions of Travel
  B. Lesson Background
 I. PEOPLE OF ABRAM (Genesis 11:27-32)
  A. Designating the Men (vv. 27, 28)
    Genealogy
  B. Describing the Women (vv. 29, 30)
  C. Departing from Ur (v. 31a)
  D. Delaying in Haran (vv. 31b, 32)
 II. PROMISES TO ABRAM (Genesis 12:1-3)
  A. Reminder to Continue (v. 1)
  B. Rehearsal of the Promises (vv. 2, 3)
III. PILGRIMAGE OF ABRAM (Genesis 12:4-9)
  A. Resuming the Journey, Part 1 (vv. 4-6)
  B. Receiving the Promise of Land (v. 7a)
  C. Reverence Demonstrated (vv. 7b, 8)
    Landmarks
  D. Resuming the Journey, Part 2 (v. 9)
CONCLUSION
  A. The Supporting Cast
  B. Prayer
  C. Thought to Remember

Introduction

A. The Tensions of Travel

The questions most frequently heard on an extended family trip in an automobile are probably the following: "How much longer?" "Are we there yet?" "Do you know where you are going?" "Are we lost?" "How long till we reach a rest area?" "When can we eat?" Such questions demonstrate the personality traits of impatience, a lack of trust in the driver's navigational abilities, and a compulsion to meet physical needs or wants.

When my daughter arranged a vacation trip for her family, she planned so that such tensions would be minimized. This involved researching and securing the best prices for airlines, car rentals, and motels. Upon their return it was announced that everything had gone just as it had been planned, without tensions or adjustments. In one sense this demonstrates what Jesus said about planning and counting the cost before undertaking a project (Luke 14:28).

The lesson for today tells of a different type of journey, a trip to an unknown destination. In a sense it demonstrates a tension with the well-planned trip described above. At times it is essential to organize carefully. But advance planning can go only so far. Certain tasks, however, involve the unexpected and the unknown by their very nature. Trust in God is required to secure the outcomes God has intended.

B. Lesson Background

The early chapters of the Book of Genesis move quickly from creation to an emphasis on events that involve *all humanity:* the making of the first man and woman, the consequences of sin that culminate in the flood, an explanation for the many languages, and how all this led to the formation of nations.

The lesson text for today is transitional in Genesis, for it marks the beginning of God's working with selected *individuals.* God's ultimate purpose is the redemption of every tribe, tongue, and nation, but this is made possible through a selective process that begins with Abram.

Abram (later called Abraham) is one of the heroes of the faith. His name is mentioned about three hundred times in the Bible, in twenty-seven of the sixty-six books. There are more verses about him in the New Testament's "faith chapter" than any other person listed there (Hebrews 11:8-19, or twelve verses). The apostle Paul says that Abraham is the father of all who have a genuine faith (Romans 4:16). He is the first person in Scripture of whom it is said that he "believed in" God (Genesis 15:6).

The lesson for today gives the beginnings of Abram's journey of faith. Biblical data reveal that it was about 2091 B.C. when he entered the land of Canaan.

I. People of Abram
(Genesis 11:27-32)

The verse previous to the beginning of our text concludes a genealogical listing that begins with Shem, Noah's son, in Genesis 11:10. This grouping ends by noting Terah, Abram's father.

A. Designating the Men (vv. 27, 28)

27. Now these are the generations of Terah: Terah begat Abram, Nahor, and Haran; and Haran begat Lot.

The word *generations* in the *King James Version* can be understood in modern English as "account," "history," or "descendants." It is a very important word in the book of Genesis, for it indicates that a new section is beginning. The word is from a root that means to beget or bring forth children. It therefore implies that an account of the descendants of *Terah* is ready to begin.

Terah, in addition to being the father of *Abram,* is usually remembered for a statement that Joshua made about him as being one of Israel's ancestors who worshiped other gods on the other side of the Euphrates River (Joshua 24:2). Some attempt to soften this statement by citing Genesis 31:53, which states that the God of Abram and *Nahor* was also "the God of their father" Terah. It is then suggested that Terah's departure from the land of Ur was his break with idolatry.

GENEALOGY

In his book *Midnight in the Garden of Good and Evil,* author John Berendt contrasts three Georgia cities. He says that a newcomer to Atlanta is always asked about his business. A newcomer to Macon is asked where he goes to church. A newcomer to Augusta is asked, "What was your grandmother's maiden name?" This reveals a concern for ancestry.

Why are we told the name of Lot's father and the name of his grandfather? Why are we told where Abram (Abraham) was born? It is to convey to us that these are real persons. They are not just names from a book or characters in a story.

We can relate to Abram because we share many of his experiences. Like Abram, many of us have moved to a strange place or have dealt with the sorrow of being childless. Like Abram, we have had domestic difficulties, faced danger, and been tempted to lie.

If Abram was like us in so many ways, then we can be like him in return. We can have the same unquestioning obedience. We can have the same stubborn faith. Three times in Hebrews 11 the writer begins a reference to this man with the words "by faith." Truly he is "the father of the faithful"! Being his spiritual descendants means that we walk by faith, not by sight.   —R. C. S.

28. And Haran died before his father Terah in the land of his nativity, in Ur of the Chaldees.

It is not the natural order of things for a child to predecease a parent. This marks the first such recorded incident after the great flood. The narrative that follows suggests that Abram began to serve as the father figure for Lot after *Haran died* (see Genesis 12:4).

Ur of the Chaldees is usually associated with a city that is about one hundred and twenty miles southeast of Babylon (cf. Genesis 15:7; Nehemiah 9:7). Ur is a progressive city with well-arranged streets and a sewer system. It is a trading center, so it is considered a desirable place to live. It is also a city of much idolatry.

B. Describing the Women (vv. 29, 30)

29. And Abram and Nahor took them wives: the name of Abram's wife was Sarai; and the name of Nahor's wife, Milcah, the daughter of Haran, the father of Milcah, and the father of Iscah.

The *wives* of the two surviving brothers are mentioned. *Abram's wife Sarai* later becomes "Sarah" (or "princess") in Genesis 17:15. Genesis 20:12 states that Sarai is also Abram's half-sister, having had a different mother. Over six hundred years later, God's instructions for the nation of Israel will prohibit marrying someone who is closely related (see Leviticus 18:6; 20:17). But at this time there is no such restriction.

How to Say It

ABRAHAM. *Ay*-bruh-ham.
ABRAM. *Ay*-brum.
BETH-EL. *Beth*-ul.
BETHUEL. Be-*thu*-ul.
CANAAN. *Kay*-nun.
CANAANITES. *Kay*-nun-ites.
CHALDEES. *Kal*-deez.
ESAU. *Ee*-saw.
EUPHRATES. You-*fray*-teez.
HAI. *Hay*-eye.
HARAN. *Hair*-un.
ISAAC. *Eye*-zuk.
ISCAH. *Is*-ka.
ISHMAEL. *Ish*-may-el.
KETURAH. Keh-*too*-ruh.
MELCHIZEDEK. Mel-*kiz*-eh-dek.
MESOPOTAMIA. *Mes*-uh-puh-*tay*-me-uh (strong accent on *tay*).
MILCAH. *Mil*-kuh.
MOREH. *Moe*-reh.
NAHOR. *Nay*-hor.
REBEKAH. Reh-*bek*-uh.
SARAI. *Seh*-rye.
SHECHEM. *Shee*-kem or *Shek*-em.
SICHEM. *Sigh*-kem.
TERAH. *Tair*-uh.
TIGRIS. *Tie*-griss.
UR. Er.
ZECHARIAH. *Zek*-uh-*rye*-uh (strong accent on *rye*).

Nahor, for his part, marries *Milcah.* She is one of the two daughters of *Haran,* the brother who had died. Milcah is mentioned in Genesis 22:20-24 as having eight sons. Bethuel, her youngest son, becomes the father of Rebekah, who will later marry Isaac, Abram's only son through Sarai.

30. But Sarai was barren; she had no child.

The fact that *Sarai* is *barren* becomes a major factor in the developing faith of Abram. The factor of temporary barrenness also plays an important part later in the lives of Rebekah (Isaac's wife), Rachel (wife of Jacob, Isaac's son), and, in the time of Jesus, Elisabeth (Zechariah's wife).

C. Departing from Ur (v. 31a)

31a. And Terah took Abram his son, and Lot the son of Haran his son's son, and Sarai his daughter-in-law, his son Abram's wife; and they went forth with them from Ur of the Chaldees, to go into the land of Canaan.

The fact that it is *Terah* who is in charge of this move indicates that he is still the head of the family. *Abram* and the others, therefore, have had many years of being in submission to Terah. Respect for parental authority is often entwined with a spiritual faith that respects God's authority.

The real factor behind Terah's decision is that God called Abram while the family was still in the land of Mesopotamia, an area between the Tigris and Euphrates Rivers (Acts 7:2). Genesis 12:1; Acts 7:3; and Hebrews 11:8 reveal that at this time Abram does not know that the ultimate destination is *Canaan.* [See question #1, page 128.]

Abram's experiences thus far are the early steps in a life that will be counted among the great examples of faith. There are some events in his life over which he has no control, but he does not permit them to move him from the path of righteousness. Abram's life to this point includes the death of a brother, the reality of having a barren wife, and leaving behind everything that was familiar. [See question #2, page 128.]

D. Delaying in Haran (vv. 31b, 32)

31b. And they came unto Haran, and dwelt there.

For some unknown reason the family stops at *Haran.* The name of this town is the same in English as the name of the deceased brother, but the first letter is different in Hebrew.

Some have pointed out that both Ur and Haran are centers of worship for the same moon god and goddess. It is speculation, however, to assert that this is the reason for the pause in the journey.

32. And the days of Terah were two hundred and five years: and Terah died in Haran.

If the text provides any reason for the family's stopping *in Haran,* it may have been the final illness and death of *Terah.* Stephen's comments about this event say that Abram left Haran after his father had died (Acts 7:4). Genesis 12:4 states that Abram was seventy-five when he left Haran.

II. Promises to Abram (Genesis 12:1-3)

The Lord plans to separate Abram from the other members of his family. We can only guess as to why this is done. It would seem that his faith is stronger than theirs, and the challenges ahead of Abram do not need any negative influences.

A. Reminder to Continue (v. 1)

1. Now the LORD had said unto Abram, Get thee out of thy country, and from thy kindred, and from thy father's house, unto a land that I will show thee.

Scholars debate whether this call refers back to the first call at Ur, or if this is a restatement of that original call. One thing is certain: the call indicates that a drastic change is about to take place. Each phrase becomes more demanding as Abram is told to depart from his *country,* his relatives, and the familiar surroundings of his father's dwelling.

The call of Abram causes other thoughts. To our knowledge, this is the first definite message from God since the flood in the time of Noah. Several hundred years have passed since that event. What are people thinking during those days? Is there a restlessness without a sure word from God? We know that there is faith in the earth, for Melchizedek is a good example of such (Genesis 14:18-20). The larger question may be this: why do so many people today live as if they are unaware that God has spoken through His Son (Hebrews 1:1, 2)?

B. Rehearsal of the Promises (vv. 2, 3)

2. And I will make of thee a great nation, and I will bless thee, and make thy name great; and thou shalt be a blessing.

This verse begins a series of seven special promises. God has called a man having no children, a man who is just the unknown son of Terah, and a man who seems not to have any land of his own. Now God makes promises that

---

VISUALS FOR THESE LESSONS

The visuals pictured in each lesson (e.g., page 125) is a small reproduction of a large, full-color poster included in the *Adult Visuals* packet for the Winter Quarter. The packet is available from your supplier. Order No. 292.

involve both present and future blessings that will change his situations dramatically.

The first promise is that Abram will now become the progenitor of *a great nation*. Abram will realize instantly that this demands many descendants and much time. God, however, provides comfort by emphasizing His part in the fulfillments: the expression *I will* occurs or is implied over and over throughout these verses.

These thoughts lead naturally into the following promise that God will *bless* Abram. If God is the One who calls, then it is His task to provide the blessings as He determines. Some form of the word *bless* occurs five times within two verses.

Abram will also have a *name* that is *great*. As noted earlier, his name is one of the most frequently mentioned in God's Word. His faith and obedience have been the subjects of many sermons and books throughout the centuries.

Abram is also assured that he will *be a blessing*. In Abram's case, this has spiritual implications, but it also lends itself to another thought: everyone should want to live so that his or her life is a blessing to others. This includes being a spiritual example and benefit to family, friends, employers, neighbors, etc.

3. And I will bless them that bless thee, and curse him that curseth thee: and in thee shall all families of the earth be blessed.

Individuals who are "sold out" to God draw different responses from those whom they encounter. Some feel prompted to want to *bless* such dedication. Others, perhaps because they are forced to admit their own spiritual lacks, are inclined to *curse* the one who compels them to do a spiritual self-assessment.

The seventh promise by God finds its ultimate fulfillment in the Messiah. It is interesting that the first verse of the New Testament states that Jesus Christ is a son of David and a son of Abraham.

God gave the same or similar promises to each of the three great patriarchs: in six different chapters to Abram (Genesis 12:1-3, 7; 13:14-18; 15:4, 5, 13-18; 17:1-8; 18:17-19; 22:15-18), twice to Isaac (26:4, 23, 24), and twice to Jacob (28:14, 15; 35:9-12).

III. Pilgrimage of Abram (Genesis 12:4-9)

Earlier it was Terah who had moved the family. This time it is Abram leading in this regard.

A. Resuming the Journey, Part 1 (vv. 4-6)

4. So Abram departed, as the LORD had spoken unto him; and Lot went with him: and Abram was seventy and five years old when he departed out of Haran.

Visual for lesson 1. *This map to help your students visualize where the events of today's lesson—and several lessons this quarter—took place.*

This is no longer just the travels of a family. It has become a spiritual pilgrimage, and Abram acts decisively. Abram is a man who is looking "for a city which hath foundations, whose builder and maker is God" (Hebrews 11:10). [See question #3, page 128.]

The presence of *Lot* with Abram indicates a personal decision for him to accompany his uncle. We can only speculate whether this is a religious conviction or a concern for a favorite uncle who had attained such an age.

5. And Abram took Sarai his wife, and Lot his brother's son, and all their substance that they had gathered, and the souls that they had gotten in Haran; and they went forth to go into the land of Canaan; and into the land of Canaan they came.

The separation from other family members must be an emotional moment, but that is concealed for us only to imagine. *Abram* now has the responsibility of leading, encouraging, and meeting the needs of the entire group.

The childless state of Abram and *Sarai* can produce either a greater closeness or a falling apart. The choice is theirs. These two may have moments of frustration as well as curiosity as to how God will make a great nation through them.

The one who penned these words originally was Moses, and he also experienced a call from God. One wonders if he reflected on the parallels and differences between himself and Abram as each of them start from opposite directions to lead a group to *Canaan*.

6. And Abram passed through the land unto the place of Sichem, unto the plain of Moreh. And the Canaanite was then in the land.

The journey from Haran to *Sichem* (or Shechem) is almost four hundred miles. There are no conveniences of travel that we take for granted. Sichem and its environs will later become special places for Abram's descendants. (See Genesis 33:18-20; Joshua 24:32; etc.)

B. Receiving the Promise of Land (v. 7a)

7a. And the LORD appeared unto Abram, and said, Unto thy seed will I give this land.

The word *seed* reaffirms that *Abram* will have children, and it is added that his descendants will possess the *land*. Restrictions on the promise will be given in the future, for the land-promise in view here does not extend to the descendants of Ishmael, Abram's son through his wife's handmaid. Neither does it include Abram's sons by Keturah (his wife after Sarai dies; cf. Genesis 25:1, 2) nor the descendants of grandson Esau (the twin brother of Jacob).

C. Reverence Demonstrated (vv. 7b, 8)

7b. And there builded he an altar unto the LORD, who appeared unto him.

Abram makes a bold statement by building *an altar* to *the Lord*, for pagan altars are already in existence in this place. Abram is not called to compromise the one true faith, but to express it.

8. And he removed from thence unto a mountain on the east of Beth-el, and pitched his tent, having Beth-el on the west, and Hai on the east: and there he builded an altar unto the LORD, and called upon the name of the LORD.

Abram continues his journey to the south by traveling another twenty miles to a site between *Beth-el* and *Hai* (or Ai). Having *pitched his tent,* he again erects *an altar* for worship. His worship involves invoking *the name of the Lord*. In this way he sets an example for anyone who moves from location to location but ignores or defers the spiritual aspects of life. [See question #4, page 128.]

Home Daily Bible Readings

Monday, Nov. 29—God Calls Isaiah (Isaiah 6:1-8)

Tuesday, Nov. 30—God Calls Jeremiah (Jeremiah 1:4-10)

Wednesday, Dec. 1—Jesus Calls the First Disciples (Luke 5:4-11)

Thursday, Dec. 2—God Calls Saul (Acts 9:1-9)

Friday, Dec. 3—Abram and Sarai Live in Haran (Genesis 11:27-32)

Saturday, Dec. 4—God Calls Abram (Genesis 12:1-9)

Sunday, Dec. 5—God Makes a Covenant with Abram (Genesis 15:1-6)

LANDMARKS

A visitor to Zimbabwe was shown an aeronautical map of that African country. He noticed that the most frequent landmarks on the map were mission stations. In a land where most villages look alike and where there are few modern roads or structures, the mission stations became the landmarks by which pilots could navigate.

Notice that when Abraham pitched his tent, he built altars. In effect Abraham marked his journey by those altars. Centuries later they still serve as mental reference points by which we can retrace his journey of faith.

This leads us to consider the marks of faith that we will leave on the landscape of life. Fame is fleeting. Wealth vanishes. Human accomplishments are soon surpassed. But the footprints of faith remain. That is the greatest legacy we can leave. Abraham didn't just travel through life pitching his tent here and there, and neither should we.   —R. C. S.

D. Resuming the Journey, Part 2 (v. 9)

9. And Abram journeyed, going on still toward the south.

The Hebrew word for *south* is "negev." Other versions leave this Hebrew word untranslated, turning it into the proper noun "the Negev," which is a particular desert region. Although we might like to know more about Abram's continued journey on to this area, the most important thing is that he follows in faith when God calls. [See question #5, page 128.]

Conclusion

A. The Supporting Cast

When people view a drama, there is a tendency to identify with the leading characters rather than the members of the supporting cast. Without the latter, however, the fame that is achieved by the heroes would never become a reality.

Most of those studying this lesson today will never see their "names in lights" like Abram. What is important is that they faithfully fulfill whatever God has called them to do by the precepts and principles of His Word. In the end, having your name in the Lamb's book of life means much more than having it "in lights."

B. Prayer

Thank You, Lord, for the example of Abram, who waited, struggled, and slowly matured in his faith. Like him, we sometimes fail, but we give thanks that You never do. In Jesus' name, amen.

C. Thought to Remember

Expect stages and crises in your growth of faith.

Learning by Doing

This page contains an alternative lesson plan emphasizing learning activities.
Classes desiring such student involvement will find these suggestions helpful.

Learning Goals

After participating in this lesson, each student will be able to:

1. Describe the historical situations of Abram as he and his family obeyed the call of God to leave Ur and then Haran.

2. Evaluate the faith of Abram through his positive responses to God's call to venture into the unknown.

3. Make changes personally in order to conform to the call of God as given in His Word.

Into the Lesson

Ask students to think about people they trust, then ask whether they trust you. When several students have nodded their heads in agreement, ask for a volunteer to come up to the front of the room. Tell the class that this student is going to demonstrate his or her trust in you.

Have the student stand behind you, placing a hand on one of your shoulders. Then have the student close his or her eyes, and follow you wherever you go. Emphasize no peeking! Lead the student on a simple course throughout the room. Make sure you take the student around several obstacles. (If your classroom has a small platform with stairs, so much the better!) Sometimes you'll want to warn the person that an obstacle is coming. Other times, simply walk around it and have the person follow you.

End the activity after about two minutes. Send the student back to his or her seat with a round of applause for being such a good sport. Then ask a few general questions for the whole class. "Would you be willing to go through a day this way?" "What would make it hard to do?" "What would make it less difficult?"

Close the activity by summarizing the activity and the discussion. It's hard to trust someone completely, but it's less difficult when the person is completely trustworthy. Then say, "Today we'll learn about Abram's trust in God. God told him to leave his home, and he obeyed—even though he had no idea where God would lead him."

Into the Word

Using the lesson commentary, relate the story of Abram's journey from Ur to Canaan. Have your learners trace Abram's movements on either a classroom map or a map in the back of their Bibles. Note each place along the way: Ur, Haran, Sichem (or Shechem), and Beth-el. Have them jot down the main events that happened at each place. (Be sure to emphasize the provisions of God's covenant, which was given while Abram was in Haran. Your learners can use space in the student book to jot down the seven promises God made to Abram in this covenant.)

After leading students through today's text, ask your learners to share what they've noted for each place. Here are some possible answers:

Ur: Starting point. Haran died there.

Haran: Terah dies. God calls Abram. God makes a covenant with Abram. (Review the provisions of the covenant.)

Sichem (or Shechem): God appears to Abram again. God renews the promise of the land. Abram builds an altar to the Lord.

Beth-el: Abram builds an altar to the Lord.

Toward the south: No information about Abram's activities there.

Conclude this review by asking, "Why is Abram called a man of faith?" Ask students to share responses. Be supportive of any reasonable answer, but make sure that you emphasize that Abram followed God to a place where he (Abram) had never been. Also mention the fact that Abram built altars to God. He was showing his dependence upon God and identifying himself with God's purposes.

Into Life

Ask: "Have any of you had an experience of trusting God's direction, even though you didn't know what would happen?" This could be a decision relating to career, relocation, finances, family matters, or a number of other issues. Give opportunity for several students to share briefly their experiences.

Divide the class into groups of three or four. Ask students to share a major decision they're facing now, if they feel free to do so. Then have students pray for one another in their groups. Ask them to pray for insight into what God wants them to do and courage to follow His leading.

(Note: Your learners can use their student books to write down their commitment to follow God's leading. If your students have the book, have them do this now.)

Close the class with prayer, asking God to help your students develop the faith of Abraham—to obey God and trust him for the results.

Let's Talk It Over

The questions on this page are designed to promote discussion of the lesson by the class and to encourage application of the lesson Scriptures. The answers provided are only discussion starters. Let your class talk it over from there.

1. What are some things we may need to "leave behind" in order to answer God's call or to follow His leading?

What people "leave behind" will vary greatly. Timing, needs, and lifestyle will all affect the specifics, so we must be careful about generalizing concerning personal sacrifices.

Some have been called away from places of employment because they were expected to engage in business ethics that were incompatible with their faith. Others believed God to be calling them away from most of their familiar surroundings and securities in order to train for specialized Christian service or to go minister in a faraway place or in a different cultural setting.

There are also certain relationships that we must cease or avoid from the beginning (see 2 Corinthians 6:14-16). Any relationship that hurts our Christian witness should be evaluated very carefully (cf. 1 Peter 2:9-12). Particular habits that hinder our growth or faithfulness as a disciple of Jesus will also need to be changed.

2. The lesson writer noted that even in this early account of Abram's life he faced several significant challenges: the death of a brother, a wife unable to bear children, and leaving behind everything that was familiar. How might God use similar situations in our lives to prepare us to serve Him in the future?

Such experiences help us to be realistic about living in a fallen world. We should not be quickly knocked off our feet by the shock of a sudden diversion or crisis. We can also learn the importance of depending upon God and others for strength, support, or guidance.

In negative circumstances God can teach us patience as we learn to wait on His timing and trust that He has the wisdom and power to sustain and bless us. One of the most important preparations for serving God anywhere or in any way is to learn, as Abram surely did, not to become too attached to particular people, places, or things.

3. Abram demonstrated his faith in God by his prompt obedience to God's call to leave everything behind to go to a new land and a new life. What can we learn from the first four verses of Genesis 12 that will help us respond to God today with the same trusting obedience?

These verses clearly remind us that when God calls us to a task, He also promises to do His part in the endeavor. Immediately after God issued His call to Abram, He repeatedly used the expression "I will" to remind Abram that His own hand would be actively involved in the process.

Too often we focus more on the difficulty of a particular challenge than on the ability of God to bring His blessing in the situation. When we focus our attention on the "I will" promises of God, we will be much more ready to respond with a clear "I will go" when God calls us.

4. What can we learn from the fact that Abram built an altar to God each place he moved? In what ways can we do the same thing today?

Obviously God does not expect us to construct stone altars at each place we live, work, and carry out our daily lives. However, Abram was demonstrating to his family and all other observers that God was the center of his life and the motivating force behind his journeys and actions.

It is often easy for us to move from place to place and activity to activity and leave God out of the process. We build altars in our lives like Abram by maintaining a faithful devotional life of prayer, meditation, Bible reading, and fasting. We build altars at work and in social settings by consistently demonstrating God-centered priorities, attitudes, and decisions. We also build and maintain altars for God through our active involvement with other believers in worship, Bible study, fellowship, and service. When we "pitch our tent" in a new location, it is crucial that we quickly establish each of these patterns.

5. How can we maintain our faith in God as we face detours and obstacles on the journey of life?

We must remember that this life is temporary and that God is leading us to a place that is eternal (see Hebrews 11:8-16). As we do, we trust His love and faithfulness (even though we may not see His hand working at the moment). We also treasure the fact that it is along the detours of life that we usually grow stronger and learn the most valuable lessons. God's grace is always sufficient and His power is most evident in our times of weakness and uncertainty (2 Corinthians 12:9, 10).

Called to Lead With Integrity

DEVOTIONAL READING: 2 Samuel 7:18-29.

BACKGROUND SCRIPTURE: 1 Samuel 16:1-13;
2 Samuel 7:8-16.

PRINTED TEXT: 1 Samuel 16:1-13.

1 Samuel 16:1-13

1 And the LORD said unto Samuel, How long wilt thou mourn for Saul, seeing I have rejected him from reigning over Israel? fill thine horn with oil, and go, I will send thee to Jesse the Bethlehemite: for I have provided me a king among his sons.

2 And Samuel said, How can I go? if Saul hear it, he will kill me. And the LORD said, Take a heifer with thee, and say, I am come to sacrifice to the LORD.

3 And call Jesse to the sacrifice, and I will show thee what thou shalt do: and thou shalt anoint unto me him whom I name unto thee.

4 And Samuel did that which the LORD spake, and came to Bethlehem. And the elders of the town trembled at his coming, and said, Comest thou peaceably?

5 And he said, Peaceably: I am come to sacrifice unto the LORD: sanctify yourselves, and come with me to the sacrifice. And he sanctified Jesse and his sons, and called them to the sacrifice.

6 And it came to pass, when they were come, that he looked on Eliab, and said, Surely the LORD's anointed is before him.

7 But the LORD said unto Samuel, Look not on his countenance, or on the height of his stature; because I have refused him: for the LORD seeth not as man seeth; for man looketh on the outward appearance, but the LORD looketh on the heart.

8 Then Jesse called Abinadab, and made him pass before Samuel. And he said, Neither hath the LORD chosen this.

9 Then Jesse made Shammah to pass by. And he said, Neither hath the LORD chosen this.

10 Again, Jesse made seven of his sons to pass before Samuel. And Samuel said unto Jesse, The LORD hath not chosen these.

11 And Samuel said unto Jesse, Are here all thy children? And he said, There remaineth yet the youngest, and, behold, he keepeth the sheep. And Samuel said unto Jesse, Send and fetch him: for we will not sit down till he come hither.

12 And he sent, and brought him in. Now he was ruddy, and withal of a beautiful countenance, and goodly to look to. And the LORD said, Arise, anoint him: for this is he.

13 Then Samuel took the horn of oil, and anointed him in the midst of his brethren: and the Spirit of the LORD came upon David from that day forward. So Samuel rose up, and went to Ramah.

GOLDEN TEXT: The LORD seeth not as man seeth; for man looketh on the outward appearance, but the LORD looketh on the heart.
—1 Samuel 16:7.

Called to Be God's People
Unit 1: God Calls a People
(Lessons 1-4)

Lesson Aims

After participating in this lesson, each student will be able to:

1. Share with others the purpose and results of Samuel's journey to Bethlehem.

2. Understand that integrity in the hearts of leaders at all levels of society is pleasing to God.

3. Resolve to honor God, whether leading or following.

Lesson Outline

INTRODUCTION
    A. Lead with Integrity
    B. Lesson Background
 I. CONVERSATION WITH GOD (1 Samuel 16:1-3)
    A. Command to Samuel (v. 1)
    B. Concern by Samuel (v. 2)
       The Only Safe Place
    C. Commission for Samuel (v. 3)
 II. CONVOCATION AT BETHLEHEM (1 Samuel 16: 4, 5)
    A. Concern by the Elders (v. 4)
    B. Consecration for All (v. 5)
III. CONSIDERING JESSE'S SONS (1 Samuel 16:6-13)
    A. Contrasting Standards (vv. 6, 7)
       Telegenic
    B. Continuing the Review (vv. 8-10)
    C. Calling for David (vv. 11, 12)
    D. Confirming God's Chosen (v. 13)
CONCLUSION
    A. The Prayers of Leadership
    B. Prayer
    C. Thought to Remember

Introduction

A. Lead with Integrity

The politician was "working the crowd" at the state fair, looking for votes among his constituents. Just as he entered a livestock area, one of the show horses was startled and reacted by trying to get loose. The trainer grabbed the politician and asked him to take the halter for the other horse while he tried to calm the horse that was in fright. The politician said, "Sir, I am a member of your state legislature, and . . . "—but the trainer quickly said, "Just take the halter; I'll trust you anyway."

Is it true that the words *business* and *ethics* no longer can be used in the same context, unless it is being stated that good ethics have all but disappeared? The scandals of recent years have served notice that the breakdown of morals has affected homes, schools, the courts, and governments. It often seems that those elected to public office are the ones who have the least amount of mud still clinging to them on election day.

But certain questions must be considered. Which is more important, political survival or integrity? How long can a godless society survive? How did the business world reach the place that balance-sheet falsification is common?

Just as important is to ask what it will take to reverse the process. What responses are appropriate for a Christian, especially one in leadership? Does morality have to be sacrificed in order to get ahead? Is it really worth it to "gain the whole world" in exchange for one's soul? (See Matthew 16:26.)

The title of the lesson for today seems to stand in stark contrast with the demonstration of leadership as it is portrayed by many of the business and world leaders of today. God, however, has always desired integrity for every leader, from the home to the highest levels of government.

B. Lesson Background

One millennium plus another sixty years—that is the period of time between the call of Abram in about 2091 B.C. in last week's lesson to the lesson for today. During that time God worked with two types of leaders to accomplish His purposes: family leaders and national leaders.

Family leaders. In the book of Genesis the three great patriarchs are Abram, his son Isaac, and grandson Jacob. The final fourteen chapters of Genesis give the thrilling account of how Jacob and his family went to Egypt from Canaan because of famine. In Egypt the family experienced a population explosion. During that period of four hundred and thirty years (see Exodus 12:40, 41), it is assumed that the heads of families continued their leadership roles.

National leaders. Moses became the first leader of Israel as a whole as it grew into a mighty nation in Egypt. After forty years Moses turned the leadership over to Joshua. His task was to conquer the land that God had promised to Abram over six hundred years previously.

When Joshua died, the only national leaders were the high priests. Each tribe had its leaders during the sojourn to Canaan, and that system remained in place after the conquest of the land. The Lord had promised abundant blessings if the people would obey His law. But the people did not resist the temptations of idolatry that are often combined with immorality. God punished Israel with periods of oppression. Then He raised up judges as deliverers.

Samuel is considered to be the last such judge in Israel. His sons were not worthy successors, so the people asked for a king. God then had Samuel anoint Saul as the first king of Israel. Saul began well, but his faith faltered in two critical situations (see 1 Samuel 13 and 15).

Samuel may have felt that much of his life had been a failure: his sons were dishonest judges (1 Samuel 8:3), and Saul's disobedience caused him to be rejected by the Lord.

I. Conversation with God (1 Samuel 16:1-3)

The Lord can see the big picture, involving both the past and the future. It has been over eight hundred years since Jacob gave the prophecy that the scepter of royalty would belong to the tribe of Judah, Jacob's fourth son (Genesis 49:10). The fulfillment is ready to begin, and it will extend into the future so as to include the everlasting reign of the Messiah, the Son of David (Revelation 5:5).

A. Command to Samuel (v. 1)

1. And the LORD said unto Samuel, How long wilt thou mourn for Saul, seeing I have rejected him from reigning over Israel? fill thine horn with oil, and go, I will send thee to Jesse the Bethlehemite: for I have provided me a king among his sons.

Through a reprimand and a command, *the Lord* prompts *Samuel* to action. The reprimand involves Samuel's mourning *for Saul*. God understands that a period of mourning is normal and necessary in many situations, but there is a time for the grief to end. Spiritual maturity demands that Samuel accept the fact that the Lord has *rejected* Saul. [See question #1, page 136.]

The command is for Samuel to take a *horn with oil* in order to anoint a new *king* from among the *sons* of *Jesse*. But the people present

---

How to Say It

ABINADAB. Uh-*bin*-uh-dab.
ABSALOM. *Ab*-suh-lum.
BETHLEHEM. *Beth*-lih-hem.
ELIAB. Ee-*lye*-ab.
GIBEAH. *Gib*-ee-uh (G as in *get*).
HEROD. *Hair*-ud.
JESSE. *Jess*-ee.
NAOMI. Nay-*oh*-me.
RAMAH. *Ray*-muh.

---

at the anointing will not necessarily know that the anointing is to a kingship. Jesse is in the lineage of Judah (Matthew 1:2-5).

B. Concern by Samuel (v. 2)

2. And Samuel said, How can I go? if Saul hear it, he will kill me. And the LORD said, Take a heifer with thee, and say, I am come to sacrifice to the LORD.

Some have criticized *Samuel* for his seeming reluctance, and he has therefore been compared with others such as Moses (Exodus 3:11; 4:10, 13) or Gideon (Judges 6:15). Samuel, however, has valid reasons to be concerned. He has already informed *Saul* that the Lord is seeking "a man after his own heart" (1 Samuel 13:14). If Saul discovers the purpose of Samuel's trip, it could be construed as treason. That would give Saul a valid reason to *kill* Samuel.

The Lord resolves Samuel's concern by telling him that he should also engage in one of his normal functions by taking a *heifer* as a *sacrifice to the Lord*. Samuel's response to any queries will be truthful, but he will not tell everything he plans to do. This is in accord with the advice given in Proverbs 12:23: "A prudent man concealeth knowledge: but the heart of fools proclaimeth foolishness."

The use of a heifer indicates that this will be a peace or fellowship offering as prescribed in Leviticus 3. This will be an enjoyable occasion of feasting.

THE ONLY SAFE PLACE

A man was serving a small-town church in a peaceful community when there came a call to go to Africa and teach in an emerging Bible college. That particular African country was going through a very unsettled time, and tensions were high. Someone asked him, "Is it really safe for you to go?" He replied, "The only safe place is where God wants you to be."

To do our duty in the face of danger is always honorable. It is especially praiseworthy when it is God who calls us. While we cannot expect to have a call as explicit as had Abraham, Moses, Samuel, or Paul, we can have a sense that God wants us in a certain place for a certain purpose. When we have that conviction, we must respond.

Of course, faith does not demand foolishness. We are not condemned for being prudent and careful. God does not expect us to take unnecessary risks. We can be faithful without being foolhardy. We can trust without trying to parade our faith. God was not angry when Samuel expressed reservations about his assignment. Instead, God provided a solution that calmed Samuel and still sent him on his way to do God's work.

To be daring in order to prove or flaunt our faith is a mistake. But to trust God means that we do what we are convinced He wants us to do. It's reflected in so many of our hymns: "Trusting Jesus," "Trust and Obey," and "Under His Wings." God understands our insecurity and our fears, but He does expect our unqualified obedience.   —R. C. S.

C. Commission for Samuel (v. 3)

3. And call Jesse to the sacrifice, and I will show thee what thou shalt do: and thou shalt anoint unto me whom I name unto thee.

Samuel's commission also includes calling *Jesse to the sacrifice.* Jesse seems to be a man for whom no further identification is needed. It is customary in the Bible to designate a person with a reference to his father or other ancestors, but this is not done in Jesse's case.

God does not reveal to Samuel which of Jesse's sons (16:1) is to be anointed as the next king. Some people want to know all the answers "up front," but God is deliberately planning to provide a lesson in leadership for Samuel and for us.

The examples of Scripture are that three groups of people receive special anointing: prophets (1 Kings 19:16b), priests (Exodus 30:30), and kings (as here). It has been suggested that those who witness David being anointed may assume that Samuel is anointing him to become a prophet. David also receives a gift of the Holy Spirit (1 Samuel 16:13). This special inspiration enables him to write many of the psalms. Peter will later say that David was a prophet (Acts 2:30).

II. Convocation at Bethlehem (1 Samuel 16:4, 5)

Samuel is probably in his hometown of Ramah as he prepares for his journey (see 1 Samuel 16:13). Ramah is a few miles north of Jerusalem, and the usual way for Samuel to travel to Bethlehem would take him through Gibeah, Saul's hometown and capital (10:26; 15:34). It is interesting to speculate whether Samuel took another route or left early enough not to be noticed.

A. Concern by the Elders (v. 4)

4. And Samuel did that which the LORD spake, and came to Bethlehem. And the elders of the town trembled at his coming, and said, Comest thou peaceably?

Samuel provides an example of obedience to the Lord's call. His valid question to God has been answered, and he acts promptly.

In this month of December, it is fitting to mention other people in the Bible who make *Bethlehem* journeys. They include Ruth (an ancestress

of David) and Naomi (Ruth 1:19), plus soldiers of David (2 Samuel 23:15, 16). Of course, most of us know about Joseph and Mary, the shepherds who heard the angelic announcement (Luke 2:10-12), the wise men, and soldiers of Herod.

Samuel's arrival is reported quickly to *the elders of the town,* and they tremble as they come together to inquire about the purpose of this visit. To have God's prophet suddenly appear on the scene is a matter of great concern!

B. Consecration for All (v. 5)

5. And he said, Peaceably: I am come to sacrifice unto the LORD: sanctify yourselves, and come with me to the sacrifice. And he sanctified Jesse and his sons, and called them to the sacrifice.

Samuel's answer is positive. His arrival is peaceful in its intent, and it even includes having a sacrificial meal for everyone to enjoy. The nature of the occasion also demands a spiritual emphasis that includes ceremonial cleansing to be *sanctified.* This requires a washing of clothing and the body (Exodus 19:10; Numbers 8:21).

Special mention is made of Samuel's participation in the consecration of *Jesse and his sons.* Samuel's commission makes it imperative that they be present. This also provides him an opportunity to become better acquainted with them, to discern the attitudes within the family, and to begin to determine which one would be chosen by the Lord.

III. Considering Jesse's Sons (1 Samuel 16:6-13)

At this point the elders of Bethlehem drop from the narrative. The emphasis shifts to the sons of Jesse.

A. Contrasting Standards (vv. 6, 7)

6, 7. And it came to pass, when they were come, that he looked on Eliab, and said, Surely the LORD's anointed is before him. But the LORD said unto Samuel, Look not on his countenance, or on the height of his stature; because I have refused him: for the LORD seeth not as man seeth; for man looketh on the outward appearance, but the LORD looketh on the heart.

Samuel initially judges *Eliab* by two things: his height and his looks. Samuel is confident that *the Lord's anointed is before him;* the Lord, however, has an entirely different assessment!

The two qualities cited above can be a positive advantage to someone who is chosen to be one of God's leaders, but the Lord is much more concerned with a person's *heart.* The standards of acceptance for the Lord's leaders demand that extra dimension of the inner self. As the lesson title says, God requires integrity of those who would lead His people.

It is especially true in ancient times that *height* is a desirable attribute for a king (cf. 1 Samuel 9:2). First, there is the assumption that a person who is tall is more competent. Second, in hand-to-hand combat the person with long arms has a distinct advantage. Third, a king who is tall can be seen more easily by his soldiers whenever battles are fought; they will know to continue fighting if they see that their king is still present with them.

It also seems that these genetic features of height and handsomeness are frequent in David's family. David's son Absalom later leads a rebellion against his father, and his handsomeness is noted in 2 Samuel 14:25, 26. An extra dimension is added for him—that of his abundant hair. (In recent years some election results have led to the conclusion that men with the greater amount of hair are more likely to win! This may explain why some candidates go to stylists who fluff the hair to a pleasing fullness.)

Contemporary publications on leadership may feature the "Top Ten Traits of Trailblazers and Trendsetters." But remember that God stresses the most important factor of all: a person with a pure heart. [See question #2, page 136.]

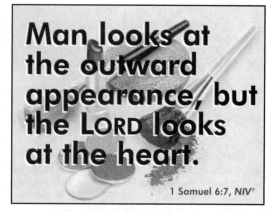

Visual for lesson 2. *Use today's visual to spark a discussion of how much concern for "outward appearance" is appropriate in view of today's text.*

TELEGENIC

The word *telegenic* entered our vocabulary in 1939. It refers to someone who looks good on television. Nowadays, successful political candidates need to be telegenic. Many who were elected to high office in the past would not even be considered as candidates today because of their appearance. Abraham Lincoln comes to mind!

Samuel was warned against making a person's looks a criterion for leadership, and we need the same warning now. In an age of superficiality, when so many never see beyond the outward appearance, it is important for believers to judge by a different standard. Some of our greatest preachers did not really look the part. The apostle Paul was not impressive in his physical appearance (2 Corinthians 10:10).

We all have had the experience of meeting someone who seemed unattractive until we got to know him or her. Then we thought that person to be very appealing. We all have known someone who gave the appearance of holiness, only to discover that it was outward and not inward.

While we cannot look at the heart in the way that God does, there are windows into every person that give us a glimpse of what is "really in there." We need to value what we see through these windows. Our challenge is to value charac-

ter over appearance, and spiritual stature as more significant than physical stature. —R. C. S.

B. Continuing the Review (vv. 8-10)

8. Then Jesse called Abinadab, and made him pass before Samuel. And he said, Neither hath the LORD chosen this.

Many people tend to hurry by this verse in order to reach the discussion about the *chosen* son. But we may pause to wonder about the reactions of the first two sons who did not "pass inspection." Are they disheartened or dismayed at being rejected, or do they experience a sense of relief that they will not have to make the changes that Samuel may require?

How a person handles not being accepted for leadership in the church is very revealing. Some have reacted in anger or even abandoned the fellowship of believers. This speaks volumes about whether such people are really qualified spiritually to lead others. Mature individuals may be disappointed, but their faith and faithfulness will not be diminished. Such reversals can become very important in a person's spiritual and emotional development. [See question #3, page 136.]

9, 10. Then Jesse made Shammah to pass by. And he said, Neither hath the LORD chosen this. Again, Jesse made seven of his sons to pass before Samuel. And Samuel said unto Jesse, The LORD hath not chosen these.

The third son of *Jesse* is the final named son in these verses until David is mentioned. *Samuel*, however, has learned his lesson well. He no longer judges by outward appearances. He simply makes his pronouncements, and the people in attendance can only wonder why the (apparently) finest young men in Bethlehem are not *chosen* by *the Lord.*

A minor concern is with the phrase that says *seven* of Jesse's *sons . . . pass before Samuel* before David makes his appearance. The alert student may be aware that the genealogy of this family in 1 Chronicles 2:13-15 says that David is the seventh. The usual reconciliation is to assume that one son died early in life, and he is not listed in the official records. The rate of infant mortality is very high in the ancient world.

C. Calling for David (vv. 11, 12)

11. And Samuel said unto Jesse, Are here all thy children? And he said, There remaineth yet the youngest, and, behold, he keepeth the sheep. And Samuel said unto Jesse, Send and fetch him: for we will not sit down till he come hither.

The absence of David is often explained by saying that the role of caring for *the sheep* falls to the youngest son. Others conclude that David is about ten years old, making him too young to be considered. It is a hasty action to dismiss young people as unimportant, for one never knows which ones will become great leaders for God and humanity.

To mention the fact that David is a shepherd is a reminder that he is also the author of Psalm 23, a favorite of many. David's most famous descendant, Jesus Christ, said of Himself, "I am the good shepherd" (John 10:11).

12. And he sent, and brought him in. Now he was ruddy, and withal of a beautiful countenance, and goodly to look to. And the LORD said, Arise, anoint him: for this is he.

The word *ruddy* is usually interpreted to mean that there is a reddish cast to David's hair or skin. David may have been young, but the blending of all his features demonstrates that he already has some of the qualities that are desired in leaders.

The selection process has come to an end as the Lord commands Samuel to *anoint* young David. This anointing of Israel's second king occurs approximately twenty years before David actually takes on his special, kingly role in God's plan in about 1010 B.C. During many of those years, he will be a fugitive from Saul. But David behaves with honor as he waits patiently for the time when he will become the king of Israel. [See question #4, page 136.]

D. Confirming God's Chosen (v. 13)

13. Then Samuel took the horn of oil, and anointed him in the midst of his brethren: and the Spirit of the LORD came upon David from that day forward. So Samuel rose up, and went to Ramah.

Samuel's task is finished. Josephus, a Jewish historian of the first century A.D., reflects a tradition of his time by writing that Samuel whispers into David's ear that he will become a king. It is not known what the onlookers think. As indicated above, they may wonder if David is being anointed to become a prophet. It is doubtful that they make any assumptions about his becoming a king, for simply being present for such an event could put all their lives in jeopardy.

The shepherd boy, with the help of *the Spirit of the Lord,* grows to become ancient Israel's most famous king. His accomplishments will be many, and his name will be used by later prophets to foretell the coming kingdom that God will establish with the Son of David as King of kings and Lord of lords.

Conclusion

A. The Prayers of Leadership

One of the famous remarks of Samuel is that it would be a sin if he did not pray for Israel (1 Samuel 12:23). The apostle Paul encouraged people to pray for him (1 Thessalonians 5:25). Prayer is therefore a mutual obligation for those who lead and those who follow.

The leaders in spiritual projects especially need prayer, for souls are involved. The spiritual implications are sobering. In the church there are the extra meetings, people with problems, plus the added stresses on the families of the leaders. Pray for your leaders at all levels—and for their spouses and families! [See question #5, page 136.]

B. Prayer

Lord, bless with wisdom, courage, and endurance the leaders of this nation, the church, and especially those who have the fearful tasks of preaching and teaching. In Jesus' name, amen.

C. Thought to Remember

Lead and follow with integrity.

Home Daily Bible Readings

Monday, Dec. 6—God Will Protect (Psalm 3)
Tuesday, Dec. 7—God Makes the Way Straight (Psalm 5:1-8)
Wednesday, Dec. 8—God Is a Rock and Fortress (Psalm 18:1-6)
Thursday, Dec. 9—God Rejects Saul as King (1 Samuel 15:10-19)
Friday, Dec. 10—Samuel Visits Jesse and His Sons (1 Samuel 16:1-5)
Saturday, Dec. 11—David Is Anointed King (1 Samuel 16:6-13)
Sunday, Dec. 12—David Joins Saul's Court (1 Samuel 16:14-23)

Learning by Doing

This page contains an alternative lesson plan emphasizing learning activities.
Classes desiring such student involvement will find these suggestions helpful.

Learning Goals

After participating in this lesson, each student will be able to:

1. Share with others the purpose and results of Samuel's journey to Bethlehem.

2. Understand that integrity in the hearts of leaders at all levels of society is pleasing to God.

3. Resolve to honor God, whether leading or following.

Into the Lesson

Make three columns on the board. The first column is headed "Category." Underneath the heading list the categories of movie actor/actress, musician, television personality, business leader, politician, and athlete. The second column is headed "Name." The third column is headed "Why?" Ask: "Who do you think is 'number one' in each of these categories? Why?" As you read each category in turn, ask two or three students to give their answers to that category. Be sure each one gives a reason for the choice.

When you've gone through all the categories, ask students to look over all the answers they wrote in the "Why?" column. Ask: "What does it take to be 'number one' today?" Many of the answers will relate to characteristics we value in our celebrities: good looks, attractiveness, achievement, talent, power, wealth, and so on.

Now ask: "How important is integrity in rating someone 'number one'?" Tell them that today's lesson will present God's criteria for leadership.

Into the Word

Lecture. Following the commentary notes, talk about the events in 1 Samuel 16:1-5. This will provide background for the next verses, which form the core of today's lesson.

Before reading 1 Samuel 16:6-13, tell students that in these verses God will inform Samuel which of Jesse's sons is to be anointed king. Have them pay attention to Samuel's thoughts and expectations, and then God's choice.

After reading verses 6-13, ask: "What kind of man did Samuel expect God to choose?" Note that Samuel looked at physical size and appearance. Perhaps he was expecting another Saul (see 1 Samuel 9:2).

"How was God's perspective different from Samuel's?" God looked on the heart. Spiritual qualifications are more important than physical ones.

Ask: "What clues do these few verses provide about David's qualifications for leadership?" Since God was looking at the heart (v. 7) we can assume that David passed that examination by God. In addition students may mention the fact that he was a shepherd and that working in that capacity may indicate that he would be a servant leader.

Ask: "What effect do you think this event had on David, especially since it would be twenty years before he became king over all Israel?" The text tells us he was filled with the Holy Spirit. This affected his thinking and his actions, preventing him from taking revenge on Saul, for one thing.

Into Life

Ask students to think about the areas of their lives in which they are called to lead. They might mention a position of responsibility at work, a ministry in the church, a position of leadership in the community, membership in an organization, and so on.

Now ask them to think about their own qualifications for leadership in these areas. Why were they selected for that position? How is their leadership evaluated? How will they know if they're successful in that position?

Write on the board the following quotation from General Norman Schwarzkopf: "Leadership is a combination of strategy and character. If you must be without one, be without the strategy." If your class is large, you can break them into small groups for a few minutes to allow your learners to discuss this statement among themselves.

Next, ask one or more of the following questions: "Why do you think the general would say something like this? Why is integrity important in military campaigns? What could be some consequences of acting without integrity? What would tempt a person to violate his or her personal integrity?"

After a time of discussion, close the class in a period of prayer. Ask students to pray for each other, that they will be men and women of integrity in the leadership roles to which God has called them. Also ask them to pray for their leaders—in civil government and in the church—that those people would perform their responsibilities with integrity. Pray also for God's help in realizing that integrity in leadership begins with integrity of "followership."

Let's Talk It Over

The questions on this page are designed to promote discussion of the lesson by the class and to encourage application of the lesson Scriptures. The answers provided are only discussion starters. Let your class talk it over from there.

1. The lesson writer points out the need for a period of mourning at times, but also that there is a time to move on with life. What factors should we consider in determining when it is time to go on to other responsibilities?

The timing will vary according to the reason for mourning, since some situations take a much heavier emotional toll on us. Generally, we can find guidance by asking and answering a few questions: Is continuing to focus on the particular situation still serving a valid emotional or spiritual purpose? Am I beginning to use this time of mourning as an escape from other necessary responsibilities? Am I now ready to use the lessons I have learned from this experience to help others and serve God more effectively? Is God now calling me as a newly-equipped leader to some special form of ministry for someone else?

2. How can we train ourselves to see people as God sees them, focusing on the heart instead of outward appearance?

Through prayer we can begin to adjust our thinking so we can look at the wonderful Biblical pattern of God choosing and using people who seemed unlikely or unlovely to others. We will begin to know and understand people's hearts better when we make the time to listen to them and share life with them. However, as long as we continue simply to glance at people as we quickly pass by them we will make judgments by mere appearances.

3. We are not told in the text how the older sons of Jesse handled the fact that they were not chosen, but it does prompt us to ask ourselves the question: "How should we respond to such a rejection?"

Not being selected for some responsibility or position can become a valuable time to evaluate ourselves. We can ask ourselves if there are things we need to learn or areas we need to develop for future service. The need for further training or mentoring may also become obvious.

The most destructive reaction is to respond with bitterness, anger, jealousy, or criticism. This type of response will simply reinforce to others that we are not ready to lead, and may even destroy relationships in the process. On the other hand, encouraging and affirming those who have been selected will have positive implications and will earn the respect of others as well.

4. The lesson writer said that David behaved with honor as he waited for the time that he would become the king of Israel. What can we learn from David's example about waiting on God's timing for our opportunity to lead?

Throughout the two decades following his anointing by Samuel, David served faithfully in many capacities where God could further prepare him. He used his musical abilities to play for the one who was already king. He gained military experience in numerous battles. He continued tending his father's sheep in preparation to shepherd God's people with integrity (see Psalm 78:70-72).

David twice rejected the urgings of his friends to kill King Saul, waiting instead on God's timing. He followed the leading of the Holy Spirit and wrote many of the psalms, which reflected his deep devotion to God and his spiritual development during his long, lonely detour to the throne. We, too, would do well simply to continue serving with all our heart wherever God leads us as He equips us for the future along the detours of life.

5. If we are to have leaders in the church who are filled with integrity, we must pray for them with passion and consistency. What are some of the things about which we should pray? Are any of these things more important than any of the others? Why, or why not?

We must ask God to fill our leaders with wisdom, grace, humility, and integrity. We should pray for them to respect the authority of the Bible and the lordship of Jesus, and ask that they would love and live the Word of God. We need to pray for them to have a spirit of harmony and teamwork in their efforts to fulfill the mission of Christ's church.

Let's pray also that they will avoid pettiness, self-centeredness, pride, and other destructive thinking. Let's pray that God would help us encourage them to be like Jesus, and that we would demonstrate humility and submission as they guide us to be like Jesus. We must also pray for a healthy, Biblical process of selecting, training, and equipping future leaders.

Called to Respond With Grace

DEVOTIONAL READING: Luke 1:26-32.

BACKGROUND SCRIPTURE: Matthew 1.

PRINTED TEXT: Matthew 1:17-25.

Matthew 1:17-25

17 So all the generations from Abraham to David are fourteen generations; and from David until the carrying away into Babylon are fourteen generations; and from the carrying away into Babylon unto Christ are fourteen generations.

18 Now the birth of Jesus Christ was on this wise: When as his mother Mary was espoused to Joseph, before they came together, she was found with child of the Holy Ghost.

19 Then Joseph her husband, being a just man, and not willing to make her a public example, was minded to put her away privily.

20 But while he thought on these things, behold, the angel of the Lord appeared unto him in a dream, saying, Joseph, thou son of David, fear not to take unto thee Mary thy wife: for that which is conceived in her is of the Holy Ghost.

21 And she shall bring forth a son, and thou shalt call his name JESUS: for he shall save his people from their sins.

22 Now all this was done, that it might be fulfilled which was spoken of the Lord by the prophet, saying,

23 Behold, a virgin shall be with child, and shall bring forth a son, and they shall call his name Immanuel, which being interpreted is, God with us.

24 Then Joseph being raised from sleep did as the angel of the Lord had bidden him, and took unto him his wife:

25 And knew her not till she had brought forth her firstborn son: and he called his name JESUS.

GOLDEN TEXT: Then Joseph being raised from sleep did as the angel of the Lord had bidden him, and took unto him his wife.—Matthew 1:24.

Learning Aims

After participating in this lesson, each student will be able to:

1. Recount the events that led to Joseph's gracious response to Mary's pregnancy.

2. Explain how Joseph's obedience to God's command revealed his character.

3. Make a commitment to respond with obedience to God's leading in a specific life situation.

Lesson Outline

INTRODUCTION
   A. Dreams and Dreamers
   B. Lesson Background
  I. BACKGROUND TO BIRTH (Matthew 1:17)
 II. PROBLEM TO SOLUTION (Matthew 1:18-21)
   A. Sticky Situation (vv. 18, 19)
   B. Remarkable Resolution (vv. 20, 21)
     The Dreamtime
III. FULFILLMENT TO OBEDIENCE (Matthew 1:22-25)
   A. Predictions (vv. 22, 23)
   B. Actions (vv. 24, 25)
     The Greatest Event
CONCLUSION
   A. Joseph's Hard Obedience
   B. Prayer
   C. Thought to Remember

Introduction

A. Dreams and Dreamers

People have dreams all the time, don't they? You may have had one just last night. Perhaps it was so "wild and woolly" that you couldn't wait to tell someone about it after you awoke. When you did, everyone had a good laugh. Then you just forgot about it and went on with your day.

In the ancient world, however, dreams were enormously important. They were seen as providing divine guidance and knowledge. In the Bible such dreamers are rare. There are only eighteen people who receive dreams from God in Scripture. Five are in the New Testament: Joseph, the wise men (assuming there were three), and Pilate's wife. Joseph is therefore in select company! He is important enough for God to use a direct and dramatic mode of communication. [See question #1, page 144.]

B. Lesson Background

Joseph, the man in our text this week, is the "father" of Jesus. We know at least six important things about Joseph. First, Matthew 1:19 calls him "a just man." In the ancient context, this means he was an upstanding, respected citizen who feared God and kept God's commandments. We see this in his obedience to the expressed will of God twice in Matthew (1:24; 2:21).

Second, Matthew 13:55 tells us that Joseph was a carpenter, a skilled tradesman in his community. Third, Matthew indicates that Joseph became the father of a large family. Four brothers are listed for Jesus, and Matthew 13:55, 56 indicates at least three sisters. Fourth, we know from both Matthew 1:20 and Luke 1:27 that Joseph was a descendant of King David, and thus from the tribe of Judah.

Fifth, Joseph was a resident of Nazareth, a small town in Galilee approximately sixty-five miles north of Jerusalem (see Luke 2:4, 39). Sixth, we learn that Joseph was a dreamer. He was not a dreamer in a negative sense—one who lives in a dreamland and refuses to face the realities of life. Rather, he was one who received messages from God in his dreams.

Matthew presents the birth circumstances of Jesus in a surprising way. Jesus has all the right credentials to be the Messiah, as Matthew shows in the genealogy (Matthew 1:1-17). Jesus is the descendant of Abraham and the descendant of David. A major agenda in Matthew, then, is to show how Jesus fulfills the prophesied expectations for the Messiah. Why must he do this?

The reason is that many other details about Jesus' birth are not what the ancient Jews would have expected. His parents come from Nazareth, a tiny village in Galilee. Shouldn't the anointed king's parents be from the grand and ancient city of Jerusalem? Shouldn't they be rich, famous, well educated, and influential? No, they are simple, rural people.

To make matters worse, there is some messiness involved in their marriage. Mary is pregnant before the marriage is consummated! Wedding customs of that day required that a marriage be arranged months or years before the couple actually lived together as husband and wife. Normally, the husband would pay a "bride price" to the father of the bride at the time of this arrangement.

After this, the woman was promised to this man, and any activity with other men was considered adulterous (see Deuteronomy 22:23, 24). Mary's pregnancy signaled to all the gossips of little Nazareth a violation of her commitment to Joseph. What was Joseph to do? Our lesson today is the story of his response, a response of grace and righteousness.

I. Background to Birth
(Matthew 1:17)

17. So all the generations from Abraham to David are fourteen generations; and from David until the carrying away into Babylon are fourteen generations; and from the carrying away into Babylon unto Christ are fourteen generations.

Matthew explains the purpose and structure of the genealogy given in 1:1-16. The list is broken down into three sections of *fourteen generations.* This employs two significant numbers for the Jewish readers (who loved numbers!). Fourteen is double seven, the number of creation and perfection (Genesis 2:3). Three is a number of reverence and holiness (Isaiah 6:3). Further, the letters of David's Hebrew name add up to fourteen. This isn't some kind of secret "Bible code," but is a simple memory device.

Matthew also highlights the most important people in the genealogy: *Abraham* and *David.* Two thousand years earlier, God had promised that Abraham would bless the earth, presumably through a descendant (Genesis 12:3). Matthew 21:15 presents Jesus as the "Son of David," an obvious messianic title. Jesus is the fulfillment of the promise to David of an eternal kingdom (2 Samuel 7:13).

One might ask why the genealogy of Joseph is given if Jesus is not really the son of Joseph. Matthew does make it clear in the following story that Joseph is not the biological father of Jesus. However, in the ancient world an adopted son is a rightful heir and, in effect, inherits the genealogy of his father.

II. Problem to Solution
(Matthew 1:18-21)

A. Sticky Situation (vv. 18, 19)

18. Now the birth of Jesus Christ was on this wise: When as his mother Mary was espoused to Joseph, before they came together, she was found with child of the Holy Ghost.

Mary already has been committed to the first stage of marriage *to Joseph* by the time he receives the disappointing news that his future wife is pregnant. Unlike many today, they are not living together nor have they had any sexual relationship. Matthew explains that Mary's *child* is *of the Holy Ghost.*

There are several Old Testament accounts of births that took place as a result of divine intervention, including Isaac (Genesis 18:11-14) and Samuel (1 Samuel 1:4-20). There is nothing like this in the Old Testament, however, where the child is conceived without a human father.

This text is perhaps even more remarkable for what it doesn't contain. There is no hint of a deity having sexual intercourse with a human woman, a story oft repeated in the ancient world (e.g., Zeus impregnating Alcmene, the mother of Hercules). This conception is not the work of a naughty god; rather, it is a miracle of the true God.

19. Then Joseph her husband, being a just man, and not willing to make her a public example, was minded to put her away privily.

We are comforted by the fact that despite the devastating news of apparent infidelity, Joseph is *a just man.* Other translations render this as "a righteous man." The meaning of this description, however, is often unclear to many readers. If he is such a righteous man, then why doesn't he follow the letter of the law and have Mary punished as an adulteress?

Matthew explains the character of Joseph's righteousness by noting that he is *not willing to make her a public example.* Instead, he decides to break the marriage agreement in private. He does not let his disappointment turn into anger. To say that Joseph is a *just* man is to say that Joseph is a *good* man. [See question #2, page 144.]

The phrase *put her away* can also be translated "divorce." The Greek word that is behind this idea is the same word used of dissolution of marriage elsewhere (see Matthew 5:31; 19:3). This is more than breaking an engagement. Joseph is legally obligated to wed Mary, and she is legally promised to him. Joseph is considering

---

How to Say It

ABRAHAM. *Ay*-bruh-ham.
ALCMENE. Alk-*mee*-nee.
ATHENA. Uh-*thee*-nuh.
ATHENS. *Ath*-unz.
BABYLON. *Bab*-uh-lun.
DEUTERONOMY. Due-ter-*ahn*-uh-me.
GALILEE. *Gal*-uh-lee.
HERCULES. *Her*-kew-leez.
HOSHEA. Ho-*shay*-uh.
ISAAC. *Eye*-zuk.
JEHOSHUA. Je-*hosh*-you-uh.
JERUSALEM. Juh-*roo*-suh-lem.
JOSHUA. *Josh*-yew-uh.
MESSIAH. Meh-*sigh*-uh.
NAZARETH. *Naz*-uh-reth.
NUN. None.
OSHEA. O-*shay*-uh.
PARTHENON. *Par*-thuh-non (*th* as in *thin*).
PARTHENOS (Greek). par-*then*-ahss (*th* as in *thin*).
PILATE. *Pie*-lut.
ZEUS. Zoose.

making arrangements for Mary to stay in her father's household, have the baby, and, perhaps, never marry.

But this arrangement can never do for God's chosen Messiah. To lose Joseph as legal father would mean throwing the Davidic lineage into doubt. It would mean that the sinless One would grow up and be perceived as having been conceived in sin. It would mean that Mary, God's chosen vessel, would live all her life as a disgraced adulteress. It would mean that God's plan to bless the earth through a son of Abraham and to establish an eternal King through a son of David had been tragically derailed. A different resolution is needed!

B. Remarkable Resolution (vv. 20, 21)

20. But while he thought on these things, behold, the angel of the Lord appeared unto him in a dream, saying, Joseph, thou son of David, fear not to take unto thee Mary thy wife: for that which is conceived in her is of the Holy Ghost.

Joseph now gets his first divinely-inspired *dream*, his first experience of God's miraculous intervention in his life. The child is not the product of adultery. His beloved Mary is not a tramp or a rape victim. God gives him a little push to do what his heart wants to do: take Mary as his full-fledged wife.

Surely Joseph does not understand all of this. He cannot possibly know that two thousand years later there will be two billion followers of Mary's child. But he takes to heart the command of the angel in the dream: *fear not!* When he obeys, "Joseph the righteous" and "Joseph the gracious" become "Joseph the fearless"! He goes ahead with the marriage. He claims his divinely-ordered destiny.

THE DREAMTIME

The aborigines of Australia have many stories from the past that have been passed down for generations. These stories embody their myths and legends about the time of the creation of the world and the beginning of their people. They call this period the Dreamtime.

We use the word *dream* rather differently! While one should be cautious about interpreting dreams, psychologists may ask their patients about their dreams because the subconscious mind is allegedly important in understanding the conscious mind. When we can remember a dream when we wake up, we usually realize that its content was ludicrous, logically impossible, or downright laughable.

But God has a right, of course, to use dreams for His own purposes. We are glad that Joseph took seriously God's message to him in this dream, and the later one that led the family to escape to Egypt. Today we have the full revelation of God for the New Testament era in Scripture. We do not need to sift through any "dreamtime" to figure out the past or to know what God wants us to do next.

The apostle Paul says that the revelation we have in Scripture is just what we need (2 Timothy 3:16, 17). And the apostle Peter put the word of the prophets above personal experience (2 Peter 1:19-21). Surely it is a dangerous vanity to expect God to speak with individuals in unique and personal ways when He has already revealed His will to everyone!   —R. C. S.

21. And she shall bring forth a son, and thou shalt call his name JESUS: for he shall save his people from their sins.

This is the climactic verse in this section, and one of the most important verses in Matthew. Long before ultrasound was invented, the gender of the unborn child is revealed by the angel. It is to be a boy, *a son!*

The angel also gives Joseph the correct name for the boy: *Jesus.* This name is actually the Greek version of the famous Hebrew name *Joshua.* This was the name of several men in the history of Israel, but the most recognized was Joshua, the son of Nun, the protégé of Moses. Numbers 13:16 tells us that Moses changes the name of Oshea (or Hoshea) to Jehoshua (or Joshua). This is a very slight spelling change in Hebrew—the addition of a single, small letter at the beginning of the name. It is an enormous change in meaning, however. Hoshea simply means "salvation," but Joshua means "Yahweh is salvation."

Jesus, then, is clearly identified as the promised Savior of His people. His mission of salvation is given from the beginning. But He is not the type of Savior that the Jews expect. He is not a military messiah, a secular savior who will deliver them from the hated Roman overlords. His mission is far more important than that.

Jesus is to be a spiritual Savior—one who will deliver His people from their sins. Only in this way can He be the son of Abraham, to bless the whole of humanity. Only as a spiritual Savior can He reign eternally on the everlasting throne of David. Part of Matthew's job from here on is to explain to the Jews what kind of Messiah God has sent.

III. Fulfillment to Obedience (Matthew 1:22-25)

A. Predictions (vv. 22, 23)

22, 23. Now all this was done, that it might be fulfilled which was spoken of the Lord by the

prophet, saying, Behold, a virgin shall be with child, and shall bring forth a son, and they shall call his name Immanuel, which being interpreted is, God with us.

For the first time, Matthew shows us one of his major agendas and its associated method. The agenda is to demonstrate that Jesus is truly God's intended Messiah, the Savior promised to the Jews. The method is to use the Jewish Scriptures (our Old Testament) in a selective way to explain God's prophesied intentions. A dozen times Matthew uses some form of the formula, "this was done, that it might be fulfilled." This is how Matthew relates the Old Testament prophecy to Jesus.

In this case the prophesied event is the creation of a child in the uterus of a virgin woman. The prophecy is found in Isaiah 7:14. Matthew uses the Greek word for virgin here, *parthenos*. This is the root word for the famous Greek temple in Athens, the Parthenon. This was a shrine to Athena, the virgin goddess of mythology.

Matthew does not intend a pagan reference here, but uses a word that everyone in the ancient world knows to represent an unmarried young woman who has not engaged in sexual intercourse. To describe Mary at this point seems to be stating a self-contradiction: a pregnant *virgin*. It is the paradoxical double truth of being a virgin and being pregnant at the same time. It is important to notice why Matthew emphasizes Mary's virginity. He tells us that Jesus' conception in the womb of a virgin is a miraculous sign, a fulfillment of prophecy. It marks Jesus as unique.

This phenomenon is further explained by Isaiah's prophesied name for the child: *Immanuel*. Jesus is not given this title as a personal name. His given, personal name is Jesus, not Immanuel. Matthew's point is in the meaning of the title. Immanuel means *God is with us.*

Isaiah's prophecy takes a marvelous turn at this point. A mighty miracle is here, and God is showing that He is the Creator, the Master of the biological universe. A baby is created where there should be no baby. We cannot help but conclude: surely, God is here with us! The further truth is that God will continue to be with us. [See question #3, page 144.]

B. Actions (vv. 24, 25)

24, 25. Then Joseph being raised from sleep did as the angel of the Lord had bidden him, and took unto him his wife: and knew her not till she had brought forth her firstborn son: and he called his name JESUS.

Now we see the character of Joseph displayed in a powerful way. He is both fearless and obedi-

Visual for lesson 3

This visual points out that obedience can require hard choices. Discuss how that is true today.

ent. He completes the marriage, brushing aside any potential criticism that his wife is "damaged goods." [See question #4, page 144.]

The phrase *and knew her not* means that Joseph honors the sacred child that Mary is carrying by having no sexual relationship with his new wife until after the birth. He completed his obedience by faithfully giving his new son the *name* given by the angel: He is *Jesus!* [See question #5, page 144.]

THE GREATEST EVENT

Many years ago, twenty-eight historians and journalists were asked to name the most significant events in human history. Columbus's discovery of America came in first. The invention of the printing press was second. There was a tie for third through thirteenth places among eleven events. After those came the writing of the U.S. Constitution, the discovery of anesthesia, the discovery of the X-ray, and the invention of the airplane. The birth of Jesus came *after* all these!

In fact nothing since creation even approaches the significance of the birth of Jesus Christ. It is more than mere convenience that divides history into B.C. and A.D. There are stiff-necked unbelievers who have changed B.C. (before Christ) to B.C.E. (before the Common Era); they have changed A.D. (*anno Domini*—in the year of the Lord) to C.E. (Common Era). Though they refuse to acknowledge the name of the Lord Jesus Christ, they cannot escape the fact that history is dated from His birth, even with their new designations.

Civil rights activist and 1950 Nobel Peace Prize-winner Ralph J. Bunche (1904–1971) said, "If you want to get across an idea, wrap it up in a person." God knew the truth of this idea long before Bunche did! God expressed His love for the world in the person of Jesus Christ. His entry into the world forever changed the world. He interrupted history and forever set it on a new path.

More specifically, in bringing the love and grace of God, Jesus brought eternal life. Thus His arrival, life, death, and resurrection were the greatest events of history. How does this fact affect the way you live your life each day?

—R. C. S.

Conclusion

A. Joseph's Hard Obedience

We may think that Joseph's situation is unlike ours. We may be tempted to admire him at first, and then dismiss him as a remote hero of olden days. But Joseph was very much like us. He was a simple man living an honest life. He had plans to marry a girl from his village, raise a family, and enjoy life.

It didn't turn out that way for Joseph. God called him to a ministry under cloudy circumstances. The plan of God stepped on Joseph's plans. He was not to have a traditional wedding nor the joy of a long-anticipated wedding night. He was called to make a difficult decision. He was called to a difficult obedience.

We must remember that Joseph's obedience was no sure thing. He could have rejected Mary and her child to follow a safe course. He easily could have found another wife, another family, another life. He didn't. He obeyed God. He gave family stability and a Davidic heritage to Jesus.

Before ending this lesson time, examine your own heart and ask yourself questions that Joseph had to answer. First, *has God given me a "dream" about what He wants me to do?* We're not talking about the appearance of an angel in a dream. Remember: even in the Bible there are few people who received this type of dream. But God is alive and active in our lives; He cares about you.

Maybe the dream was planted by a speaker at a camp or retreat many years ago. Maybe the dream is the desire to serve in some type of missions capacity. There are many short-term missions opportunities for people of all ages today. Your dream may be fulfilled by serving as a forwarding agent for a missionary and visiting him or her every year. It may be volunteer assistance in fund-raising for a ministry of compassion and benevolence. Rekindle your dream, or ask God to give you a new one!

Second, *am I willing to obey God's call in spite of public disapproval?* When the demand of God was clarified for Joseph, he obeyed. Those who obey God's leading are often criticized, even inside the church. If you are a senior willing to take a short-term missions trip, your children, your doctor, and your friends might all say that you are crazy. Imagine this, though: how would you like to write a letter asking for funds for your trip and send it to your grandchildren!? That would be a turn of the tables, and you may be surprised at how willing they are to help and how proud they will be of you.

Third, *how long will I wait?* Today's Scripture seems to tell us that Joseph began to act as soon as he woke up. He did not spend days in doubt. His obedient heart pushed him to act faithfully and boldly, no matter the consequences.

The older we get, the more we realize that life is short and many opportunities slip by us. We are often in no position to know the importance of our acts of obedience in the larger picture of the kingdom of God. Joseph probably saw himself doing the right thing in a small-town drama, a family matter. Yet his obedience was a key part of God's plan for the Messiah. God honors obedience to all ministries, great and small. May we honor them, too!

B. Prayer

Mighty God, who formed Jesus in the body of Mary, who revealed the circumstances to Isaiah seven hundred years earlier, who chose the faithful Joseph to rear Your own Son, to You we offer our amazement, our wonder, and our praise. May we be more like Joseph, acting with courage and grace to do Your will. In the name of Jesus we pray, amen.

C. Thought to Remember

Obedience to God
is never a mistake.

Home Daily Bible Readings

Monday, Dec. 13—Our God Is a Powerful God (Isaiah 40:3-11)

Tuesday, Dec. 14—A Sign of Reassurance (Isaiah 7:10-17)

Wednesday, Dec. 15—An Angel Speaks to Mary (Luke 1:26-38)

Thursday, Dec. 16—Jesus Is a Descendant of Abraham (Matthew 1:1-6a)

Friday, Dec. 17—Jesus Is a Descendant of David (Matthew 1:6b-11)

Saturday, Dec. 18—Jesus' Ancestry Is Traced Through Joseph (Matthew 1: 12-16)

Sunday, Dec. 19—Jesus Is Born and Named (Matthew 1:17-25)

Learning by Doing

This page contains an alternative lesson plan emphasizing learning activities. Classes desiring such student involvement will find these suggestions helpful.

Learning Goals

After participating in this lesson, each student will be able to:

1. Recount the events that led to Joseph's gracious response to Mary's pregnancy.

2. Explain how Joseph's obedience to God's command revealed his character.

3. Make a commitment to respond with obedience to God's leading in a specific life situation.

Into the Lesson

Before class begins, write on the board in large letters, "News We Don't Want to Get." Just below it write in smaller letters, "What is the worst news you can imagine?" Your learners should naturally begin thinking and talking about this question as they arrive.

After class begins, encourage responses from those who are interested in sharing their answers. Typical answers will include news of a death in the family, a diagnosis of cancer, etc.

Then tell your learners that in today's lesson Joseph gets the message he dreads most about his fiancée, Mary. Challenge your learners to put themselves in Joseph's place as you begin the study of today's text.

Into the Word

Joseph's reactions. Inform the class that you want them to think about three questions before you read the text: (1) "What did Joseph think when he found out Mary was pregnant?" (2) "What did he plan to do?" and (3) "What did his plan say about his character and integrity?" (Write these questions on the board. You may instead distribute individual pieces of paper with the questions preprinted on them.)

Next, read today's text aloud, pausing after verse 19. Then ask your learners to respond to the three questions. Take time to discuss issues that may come up. (The lesson commentary will prepare you for this discussion.)

Then read through verses 20-25. Ask for responses to the same questions. (Options: allow time to write answers down, or discuss them in small groups if your class is large.) Some possible answers to the questions include "Joseph thought Mary had been unfaithful to him," "He planned to divorce her quietly," "He loved her too much to disgrace her; he cared more for her welfare than for his own reputation."

Angel message. Conclude the discussion by noting that the angel said that the baby Mary was carrying was conceived by the Holy Spirit in fulfillment of Isaiah's prophecy. The baby would one day save His people from their sins.

Since this type of birth hadn't happened before, Joseph probably had no idea what the angel's message meant. He took Mary as his wife, as the angel had told him to do. Stress that Joseph was a man of faith. He obeyed the word of the Lord, even though he didn't necessarily understand it.

Into Life

Remind your class of the words of William Cowper: "God moves in a mysterious way His wonders to perform." This was certainly the case in the conception of Jesus, and Joseph no doubt struggled to understand this "mysterious way" of getting a child. God is still a God of surprises today.

Divide your class into small discussion groups of three or four, if your seating arrangement allows for this. Pose this question to the groups: "When did God surprise you in a life-changing way?" Allow time for several learners to offer answers. Some may say that it was in their choice of spouse, school, or occupation. Others may mention discovering a spiritual gift that was unexpected. Perhaps it was the birth of a child. Perhaps it was a difficult situation, such as a serious illness or the death of a loved one.

Ask: "How might God surprise you in the next five years?" In a sense this is a rhetorical question, since no one can predict the future. However, the answers to the previous question may suggest some possibilities.

Next, encourage your learners to think about how they would respond if God were to surprise them in one of the ways that they previously mentioned. Would they be resentful because their previous plans had been upended? Would they obey, but only grudgingly? How would they know that it was really God who was leading them into such and such a path, and not mere human desire or the natural course of life?

Close the class with an exhortation to respond to God's surprises the way Joseph did—in faith and obedience. Move to a time of prayer, asking God to prepare your learners for the future surprises that He will bring into their lives.

Let's Talk It Over

The questions on this page are designed to promote discussion of the lesson by the class and to encourage application of the lesson Scriptures. The answers provided are only discussion starters. Let your class talk it over from there.

1. What are some ways God may guide us or give us reassurance when we are thrust into unexpected circumstances?

The lesson writer points out that even in the Bible record there are not a lot of times when God spoke to individuals in dreams. However, God is not limited to certain methods of leading us. God may give us guidance and reassurance through the advice or timely comments from a Christian friend. He may bring to our remembrance a relevant Bible passage at just the right time. The opening and closing of certain doors is sometimes God's way of making His will clear, although these can be hard to interpret properly. He may even allow us to see certain blessings and benefits as a situation unfolds, making it clear that we are on the right path.

2. What characteristics in Joseph's life should we strive to develop as parents today?

Verse 19 describes Joseph as "just." Apparently he was a man who sought to do the right thing in all circumstances. Our world needs more people of integrity and strong character.

Joseph's decision to handle the situation decisively yet quietly shows not only great gentleness and compassion but also a determination to follow God's law. At such a time of confusion and hurt it would have been easy for him to react with anger and revenge.

Ephesians 5:22-33 sets forth what should be the primary goals of godly husbands and wives in a self-centered world that cares little for God. Joseph's humility, trust in God, and unwavering obedience also sets a powerful example for parents who would become quiet life-changers.

3. To some people the names and titles of Jesus and the doctrine of the virgin birth may seem like dry theological facts. In what ways should these things actually play a meaningful role in our life and obedience?

Verses 21-23 are the heart of this entire Bible story. At stake is the whole issue of Biblical unity and authority. All through the Old Testament, God had prophesied a Savior who would be born of woman (Genesis 3:15), be a descendant of Abraham (Genesis 22:18) and David (2 Samuel 7:12-16; Psalm 89:29), and be born of a virgin (Isaiah 7:14).

The name "Jesus" reminds us that He came to save us, and the title "Immanuel" assures us that God also wants to be "with us" in our struggles. The virginal conception helps establish that Jesus is fully God and fully human, and helps prove that God truly came to be with us. If God didn't care for us, why would He go to so much trouble?

4. Joseph probably invited scorn from the people in his community by following through with his marriage to the pregnant Mary. How can we respond to God's calls in our lives without being intimidated by peer pressure and public perception?

Having a heart that seeks the heart and will of God above all else is vital! When we seek first His kingdom and His righteousness, we pay less attention to the pressures around us, and He takes care of our needs (Matthew 6:33). We must also remember that the people around us usually don't know or understand all the factors involved, as in the dramatic case of Joseph and Mary.

A sense of humility is also important. Humble people like Joseph quietly take care of their responsibilities with little concern for fanfare, the limelight, or the approval of others. Joseph's example also teaches that there is no room for wavering as we focus on prompt obedience to God's leading. Three times in the book of Matthew Joseph is shown obeying God's call without a hint of delay (1:24; 2:14, 21).

5. Joseph's role in the unfolding plan of God's redemption was quiet and unassuming, but vitally important. In what ways can God use our "small" acts of obedience in the larger plan of the kingdom of God?

Often as we live faithfully in our daily lives we forget how our seemingly mundane activities can have a huge impact on other people. By building a strong family heritage we may encourage a struggling young couple or even lay the groundwork for our own children or grandchildren to serve the kingdom of God in a significant way.

Our influence as Bible teachers or youth leaders can also mold and shape lives for all eternity. Our prayers offered in secret can open doors and influence circumstances across the globe. Your learners undoubtedly can think of other ways!

Called to Hope in Christ

DEVOTIONAL READING: Psalm 71:1-8.

BACKGROUND SCRIPTURE: Luke 2:22-38.

PRINTED TEXT: Luke 2:22-38.

Luke 2:22-38

22 And when the days of her purification according to the law of Moses were accomplished, they brought him to Jerusalem, to present him to the Lord;

23 (As it is written in the law of the Lord, Every male that openeth the womb shall be called holy to the Lord;)

24 And to offer a sacrifice according to that which is said in the law of the Lord, A pair of turtledoves, or two young pigeons.

25 And, behold, there was a man in Jerusalem, whose name was Simeon; and the same man was just and devout, waiting for the consolation of Israel: and the Holy Ghost was upon him.

26 And it was revealed unto him by the Holy Ghost, that he should not see death, before he had seen the Lord's Christ.

27 And he came by the Spirit into the temple: and when the parents brought in the child Jesus, to do for him after the custom of the law,

28 Then took he him up in his arms, and blessed God, and said,

29 Lord, now lettest thou thy servant depart in peace, according to thy word:

30 For mine eyes have seen thy salvation,

31 Which thou hast prepared before the face of all people;

32 A light to lighten the Gentiles, and the glory of thy people Israel.

33 And Joseph and his mother marveled at those things which were spoken of him.

34 And Simeon blessed them, and said unto Mary his mother, Behold, this child is set for the fall and rising again of many in Israel; and for a sign which shall be spoken against;

35 (Yea, a sword shall pierce through thy own soul also;) that the thoughts of many hearts may be revealed.

36 And there was one Anna, a prophetess, the daughter of Phanuel, of the tribe of Asher: she was of a great age, and had lived with a husband seven years from her virginity;

37 And she was a widow of about fourscore and four years, which departed not from the temple, but served God with fastings and prayers night and day.

38 And she coming in that instant gave thanks likewise unto the Lord, and spake of him to all them that looked for redemption in Jerusalem.

GOLDEN TEXT: Mine eyes have seen thy salvation, which thou hast prepared before the face of all people.—Luke 2:30, 31.

Called to Be God's People
Unit 1: God Calls a People
(Lessons 1-4)

Lesson Aims

After participating in this lesson, each student will be able to:

1. Summarize the encounter between Joseph and Mary and the two prophetic persons in the temple.

2. Explain how Jesus' birth gives hope to the world today.

3. Identify a practical way to follow the example of Simeon and Anna in proclaiming the hope found in Jesus.

Lesson Outline

INTRODUCTION
    A. Brief Encounters, Important Encounters
    B. Lesson Background
  I. OBEDIENCE TO THE LAW (Luke 2:22-24)
    A. Parents' Actions (v. 22)
    B. Law's Requirements (vv. 23, 24)
 II. ENCOUNTER WITH SIMEON (Luke 2:25-35)
    A. Simeon's Background (vv. 25, 26)
    B. Simeon's Song (vv. 27-32)
      Let There Be Light
    C. Simeon's Prophecy (vv. 33-35)
III. ENCOUNTER WITH ANNA (Luke 2:36-38)
    A. Anna's Background (vv. 36, 37)
      Serving God with Prayer
    B. Anna's Remarks (v. 38)
CONCLUSION
    A. Hope in the Heart
    B. Singing Our Hope to the World
    C. Prayer
    D. Thought to Remember

Introduction

A. Brief Encounters, Important Encounters

Can you think of a person whom you met only briefly but who had an impact on your life? I remember a few years ago when I was staying in a hotel while attending a convention. I had no car, so I went down at suppertime to see if I could share a cab to a restaurant. I did find a couple of willing people who shared my situation and we ended up at an Outback Steakhouse.

I realized in the taxi ride that these men were not Christians. They were a fascinating pair, however, both scientists for the National Ocean-ographic and Atmospheric Administration (NOAA). We spent the evening discussing the problems facing the world's oceans, and I learned a lot. I learned that the average depth of the ocean is five miles. This gave me new understanding of the promise in Habakkuk 2:14: "For the earth shall be filled with the knowledge of the glory of the Lord, as the waters cover the sea." What I managed to learn and appreciate from such a brief encounter!

Today's lesson tells the story of the encounter of Jesus and His parents with two special people. We meet these two only briefly in the pages of Scripture, but their witness has the power to have a lasting impact on our lives. They are Simeon and Anna, and they have waited their entire lifetimes to see the promised Messiah. Their personal experience, however, served to do more than allow them to glimpse God's promised Messiah with their own eyes. Both Simeon and Anna have a prophetic ministry to fulfill.

B. Lesson Background

From one perspective the birth of Jesus was a spectacular event. It was heralded by a sky full of angels. A supernatural star marked the occasion. The infant was sought out by wealthy magi from foreign lands. An evil king feared for his throne.

From another perspective, Jesus' birth was remarkably mundane. This is seen in today's lesson as Jesus' parents follow the traditional rituals required of the Jews in regard to a firstborn son. The incident reveals both the faithfulness and the poverty of Joseph and Mary. While this trip to the temple may have been exciting for this rural couple, it was a common exercise among their people.

Yet in the midst of the routine, God had a few more surprises for them. They met Simeon and Anna, people with divine insight beyond the visible circumstances. These two had an understanding of God's master plan for redemption and the central role of Jesus in that plan.

Sometimes we have been taught that the office of prophet ceased with the completion of the Old Testament and that Malachi was the last of the line. Reading the New Testament, however, reveals a lively interest in prophets and prophecy at the time of Jesus. Prophets were not necessarily those who foretold the future, although that may be an aspect of their ministry. Prophets were inspired by the Holy Spirit to preach God's message: a call for justice and repentance among the people and a proclamation of Israel's hope for a Messiah. Several people serve a prophetic role in the Gospel of Luke, including Elisabeth (1:41-45), Zechariah (1:67), John the Baptist (7:26; 20:6), and even Jesus Himself (7:16).

In this lesson, Simeon and Anna are prophetic people. Anna is specifically called a prophetess (Luke 2:36), while Simeon speaks prophetically under the influence of the Holy Spirit (2:25-35).

I. Obedience to the Law
(Luke 2:22-24)

A. Parents' Actions (v. 22)

22. And when the days of her purification according to the law of Moses were accomplished, they brought him to Jerusalem, to present him to the Lord.

The Jews of Jesus' day have strict rituals associated with the birth of a son. In keeping with *the law of Moses* (which Jesus kept all His life), Jesus was circumcised and named on the eighth day (Leviticus 12:3; Luke 2:21).

The *purification* being referred to in this verse is that of the mother. After the birth of a son, the mother is ceremonially unclean for seven days until the circumcision. Although considered "clean" at this point, the mother is required to remain at home another thirty-three days (see Leviticus 12:1-4). At the end of this forty-day period, she goes to the temple in *Jerusalem* (if she can) and offers a sacrifice.

B. Law's Requirements (vv. 23, 24)

23. (As it is written in the law of the Lord, Every male that openeth the womb shall be called holy to the Lord;)

Associated with the purification rites of the mother are the dedication rites for the son. God's instruction to the Jews was that all firstborn males belong to Him (see Exodus 13:2, 12). Therefore, this son must be "bought back" or redeemed from the Lord. A formula for redeeming firstborn sons is given in Numbers 18:15, 16.

24. And to offer a sacrifice according to that which is said in the law of the Lord, A pair of turtledoves, or two young pigeons.

Luke includes a detail here that reveals the financial status of Joseph and Mary. *The law* requires an offering of a yearling lamb and a small pigeon or dove. However, the law allows poor women to bring two birds and no lamb (Leviticus 12:6-8). One of these birds would be burned as a sacrifice while the other was killed and retained as an offering for the temple.

The exotic name *turtledove* may conjure up images of half-bird, half-reptile creatures. This bird name is well known in Europe, but confusing for North Americans. The "turtle" part of the name has nothing to do with actual turtles. It comes from the *turtur* sound of these birds, similar to our word *murmur*. "Turtledove" is a somewhat generic term for small birds or doves used

---

How to Say It

ASHER. *Ash*-er.
BENEDICTUS. *Ben*-eh-*dik*-tus (strong accent on *dik*).
BETHLEHEM. *Beth*-lih-hem.
GENTILES. *Jen*-tiles.
HABAKKUK. Huh-*back*-kuk.
HANNAH. *Han*-uh.
JERUSALEM. Juh-*roo*-suh-lem.
LEVITICUS. Leh-*vit*-ih-kus.
MAGNIFICAT. Mag-*nif*-ih-cot.
MALACHI. *Mal*-uh-kye.
MESSIAH. Meh-*sigh*-uh.
NUNC DIMITTIS (Latin). Nunk Dih-*mit*-us.
PHANUEL. Fuh-*nyoo*-el.
SIMEON. *Sim*-ee-un.
ZECHARIAH. *Zek*-uh-*rye*-uh (strong accent on *rye*).

---

as sacrificial animals (cf. Numbers 6:10). [See question #1, page 152.]

II. Encounter with Simeon
(Luke 2:25-35)

A. Simeon's Background (vv. 25, 26)

25. And, behold, there was a man in Jerusalem, whose name was Simeon; and the same man was just and devout, waiting for the consolation of Israel: and the Holy Ghost was upon him.

Simeon is the name borne by a man who encounters Jesus' family in the temple. This is a famous name, the name of the second son of Jacob by Leah, and therefore the name of one of the twelve tribes of Israel.

Beyond his name we are told three things about Simeon. First, Luke gives a description of his character: he is *just and devout*. Being *just* means that he is a righteous man, a good man. Being *devout* means that he is a man of worship and faith. These two attributes probably make Simeon a regular fixture in the Jerusalem temple.

Second, Luke tells us that Simeon is *waiting for the consolation of Israel*. This means he is waiting for God's Messiah, but the expression gives us insight into what type of Messiah that Simeon expects. The rabbis of Jesus' day sometimes refer to the Messiah as the "consoler" or the "comforter."

This is based on Scriptures such as Isaiah 40:1, 2, where Israel looks forward to God's comfort, meaning His forgiveness and national restoration. Jews like Simeon believe that the Roman occupation of Israel and Jerusalem is a punishment from God that can be lifted only by God's forgiveness and miraculous intervention to rid the land of Romans. As we will see, however, the vision of Simeon is much bigger that mere military victory.

Third, Luke relates that Simeon is a man filled with *the Holy Ghost*. This shows that he is a deeply spiritual man, in tune with God in an extraordinary way.

26. And it was revealed unto him by the Holy Ghost, that he should not see death, before he had seen the Lord's Christ.

While Simeon is never called a prophet, Luke describes him in prophet-like terms. Simeon has received a direct message from God, a revelation. This is a prophecy of a personal nature. Simeon has been told that his life will extend past the birth of the Messiah and that he will lay eyes on this promised *Christ* (which means "anointed one"). We do not know how old Simeon is, but Luke portrays him as one who has waited quite a long time, so he is probably a very old man.

B. Simeon's Song (vv. 27-32)

27. And he came by the Spirit into the temple: and when the parents brought in the child Jesus, to do for him after the custom of the law.

This is a "divine appointment," a meeting arranged by the Holy *Spirit*. Such meetings are rarely understood through foresight, but rather through hindsight. For the author Luke and for the participants, this is not a chance meeting. Many Christians experience the work of God in their lives in such a way. God arranges circumstances according to His will, but rarely reveals this to us ahead of time.

28. Then took he him up in his arms, and blessed God, and said.

There must be something both commanding and reassuring in the presence of Simeon for the young mother to allow a stranger to hold her baby! Notice that Simeon does not presume to bless the child, for that is not his role. He sees and knows that this is the Messiah and gives a blessing of praise to *God* for His faithfulness.

29-32. Lord, now lettest thou thy servant depart in peace, according to thy word: for mine eyes have seen thy salvation, which thou hast prepared before the face of all people; a light to lighten the Gentiles, and the glory of thy people Israel.

Luke now records his third great canticle, the Song of Simeon. This canticle is known as the "Nunc Dimittis," its Latin title, and it has often been set to music in the history of the church. (The other two are the Song of Zechariah, also called the "Benedictus," and the Song of Mary, also called the "Magnificat.")

There is a simple lesson in this song that still applies today. When we have *seen* Jesus (believed

in Him), we may face death with *peace*. This assurance is not for Simeon alone, but should guide every believer as he or she prepares for death. This is a promise that we should all claim!

There are also some important doctrinal teachings in this song. First, Simeon understands God's Messiah to be more than a military leader. He is *salvation*, a Savior. This is in keeping with Matthew's own understanding of Jesus' mission from last week's lesson (Matthew 1:21).

Second, while the Messiah is certainly the fulfillment of Israel's hopes *(the glory of thy people Israel)*, He has a ministry to all people, Jews and *Gentiles*. Simeon has been given an understanding of Jesus' mission to be a Savior for all humanity. This is certainly crucial for those of us who have no Jewish blood in our veins. [See question #2, page 152.]

Third, we gain insight into God's plan for redemption. He did not choose the best candidate among available men or women (like He did with King Saul). Rather, He prepared someone from birth for this unique and essential role. Thus Simeon can look at a helpless baby and know what the future holds.

LET THERE BE LIGHT

Many travelers who suffer from jet lag have tried using the supplement *melatonin*. This supplement is said to help regulate the body's "clock" so that one adjusts more quickly to a different time zone. Recently, researchers claimed that melatonin, which the body produces naturally, is a defense against cancer. The report said that melatonin builds in the darkness. Too much light works against the production of melatonin. The report concluded that we are not getting enough darkness!

That may be true physically, but we certainly have enough darkness spiritually. Many live in spiritual darkness for years. Some live all their lives in this kind of darkness, never seeing the true Light of life! And that is exactly what Simeon was talking about—spiritual light.

One of the first acts of creation was, "Let there be light," and it is interesting that the Bible should use the term *light* to describe the knowledge of God. Eventually, Jesus came as the Light of the world (John 1:4-9). What Simeon foresaw the apostle John experienced. And so have we. There is no life spiritually without Jesus, the Light of the world.   —R. C. S.

C. Simeon's Prophecy (vv. 33-35)

33. And Joseph and his mother marveled at those things which were spoken of him.

Who could blame them! These simple, faithful people are being bombarded by the supernatural elements surrounding the birth of their son. Yet this "marveling" does not lead to disbelief. While *Joseph* and Mary may not understand everything, they act with faith.

34. And Simeon blessed them, and said unto Mary his mother, Behold, this child is set for the fall and rising again of many in Israel; and for a sign which shall be spoken against.

Simeon has a private message for *Mary*. This may indicate his prophetic foresight of Joseph's death before Jesus' adult ministry. Simeon's reference to *the fall and rising again of many* brings to mind the image of Jesus as both a cornerstone and a stumbling stone. Some build upon Him, others are offended by Him (see Romans 9:33; 1 Peter 2:4-8). The word for *rising again* is the word for "resurrecting." This may indicate that Simeon foresees Jesus' later victory over death and His role as the firstfruits of the resurrection of all believers (1 Corinthians 15:20).

Simeon also prophesies that Jesus will be *a sign . . . spoken against.* The word *sign* is used here in the sense of "miracle" (cf. Luke 11:16; 23:8). Jesus will do more than perform miraculous signs. He *is* a miracle! His life is a sign of God's presence and activity (see Luke 11:20). This wondrous life will not be well received by all, however. Some will see Jesus as a threat and oppose Him, even to His death.

35. (Yea, a sword shall pierce through thy own soul also;) that the thoughts of many hearts may be revealed.

The word translated *thoughts* also can be translated as "motives." The ministry of Jesus will bring many hidden thoughts and motives to the surface. Many who give an outward appearance of holiness and righteousness will be revealed as impostors as they oppose Jesus. Simeon gives Mary a hard promise that these attacks on her good and righteous Son will tear her *soul* apart as well. [See question #3, page 152.]

III. Encounter with Anna (Luke 2:36-38)

A. Anna's Background (vv. 36, 37)

36, 37. And there was one Anna, a prophetess, the daughter of Phanuel, of the tribe of Asher: she was of a great age, and had lived with a husband seven years from her virginity; and she was a widow of about fourscore and four years, which departed not from the temple, but served God with fastings and prayers night and day.

One of the most intriguing women in the Bible is a *prophetess* by the name of *Anna* (the Hebrew equivalent is Hannah). Luke seems to know quite a lot about her. Her father's name is *Phanuel,* which means "face of God." She is from *the tribe*

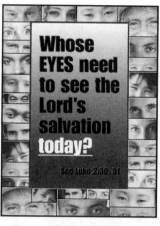

Visual for lesson 4

This visual reminds us that the eyes of all people need to see the Lord's salvation. Who will show them?

of *Asher,* one of the northern ten tribes deported by the Assyrians in the eighth century B.C.

Anna's age may be understood two ways. Luke may be giving us her actual age (i.e., eighty-four years old), or he may be stating how long she has been a widow. If the second option is correct, then Anna could be over one hundred years old.

At any rate Anna is *of a great age.* Any age we can compute means that she has been alive long enough to remember when the Romans conquered the Jewish homeland in 63 B.C.

Most interesting, though, are her spiritual qualifications. She is a prophetess, one blessed with divine insight and messages. Being a prophet is a vocal occupation. We can imagine that Anna speaks words of encouragement and exhortation to the temple pilgrims she encounters. This prophetic vocation consumes her to the point that she lives at the temple and participates constantly in the ongoing *prayers* and religious fasts that take place there. [See question #4, page 152.]

SERVING GOD WITH PRAYER

A minister had been called to serve as the interim preacher in a small church. He was standing at the front door one Sunday morning when an elderly lady came in. She asked for two bulletins. That seemed puzzling.

Then she explained that every week she sent a church bulletin to the man who had been their minister years before. He was now in a nursing home, but every week he received in the mail a bulletin from the church he had served faithfully for many years.

But why not just send him the one she herself used in the worship service? Then he realized that she needed two because she kept the other to pray that week for everyone on the prayer list. He thought, "There is no one I'd rather have praying for me than this aging, thoughtful Christian sister."

Anna, in our text, was like that. At her advanced age her strength and energy must have been limited. There were many things she could not do, but she saw prayer as something she could do. Luke saw it as a way of serving God! Perhaps we think of prayer and service as two very different things, but Luke saw them as the same thing.

Work and worship are not opposites. Sometimes the hardest work we do is worship. And sometimes the most productive work we do is worship. So we should never take it lightly when someone says, "I am praying for you." And we should never take it lightly when someone says, "Pray for me." That could well be the most important service you can offer.   —R. C. S.

B. Anna's Remarks (v. 38)

38. And she coming in that instant gave thanks likewise unto the Lord, and spake of him to all them that looked for redemption in Jerusalem.

Luke indicates that God has arranged another divine appointment. Anna's reaction differs from Simeon's, however. Rather than speak to Jesus' parents, Anna does her usual thing: she talks with anyone who will listen. The time for *redemption* has come!

Conclusion

A. Hope in the Heart

What a difference hope makes! I am reminded of the little boy who had been promised a fishing trip with his father for the next day. As he went to bed he joyfully hugged his father and said, "Thanks, Daddy, for tomorrow." That's hope! Is-

rael had hoped for a Redeemer for centuries before Jesus came. Jesus is hope realized. Paul dedicated himself to preaching this "hope of Israel" (see Acts 28:20).

Hope makes life livable. How can we possibly endure tragedy if we have no hope? How can we face death without the hope of the resurrection? Hope is faith's view of the future. We believe that no matter how bad things may get, God loves us and will never desert us. As John promises, "perfect love casteth out fear" (1 John 4:18).

Dread of the future is the opposite of hope. Fear of the future leads to worry, anxiety, even depression. Hope for the future gives us the strength to face what life throws at us. For decades Simeon and Anna hoped, and God did not disappoint them. He will do no less for us.

B. Singing Our Hope to the World

How can we share hope with our fearful, terrified world? Here are some practical suggestions. First, let your joy out. Don't hoard your joy, share it! Share it with both your believing and nonbelieving friends. A remarkable thing will happen. You won't run out of joy, because God will replenish your supply endlessly. [See question #5, page 152.]

Second, anticipate good things for the future. Anna endured decades of loneliness as a widow for the moment of pure joy she experienced when she saw Jesus. Not everything in the future will be pleasant. But God loves you and will bless you immeasurably if you trust Him. Ultimately God will receive you into His presence and say, "Well done, thou good and faithful servant."

Third, be sure you focus your hope on Jesus, not yourself. If all you have to show a terrified world is your own life, you will not bring hope. We probably all have known people who have been betrayed so many times that they trust no one. They depend only on themselves. What miserable, futile lives they lead! How much better to trust Jesus, the Son of God, the conqueror of death. How much better to live and serve in a community of believers that has the common hope of abundant life because of Jesus Christ! When your life sings hope, it must sing Jesus.

C. Prayer

Dear God, may we be people of hope. May we live as if we know our future is secure. May our lives sing of our hope to a world living desperately without hope. We pray in the name of the One who brings hope to all, Jesus the Christ, amen.

D. Thought to Remember

Live without fear of the future because of the hope Jesus brings.

Home Daily Bible Readings

Monday, Dec. 20—You, O Lord, Are My Hope (Psalm 71:1-8)

Tuesday, Dec. 21—New Things I Now Declare (Isaiah 42:1-9)

Wednesday, Dec. 22—Jesus Is Born (Luke 2:1-7)

Thursday, Dec. 23—Angels Appear to the Shepherds (Luke 2:8-14)

Friday, Dec. 24—The Shepherds See Jesus (Luke 2:15-20)

Saturday, Dec. 25—Jesus Is Taken to the Temple (Luke 2:22-26)

Sunday, Dec. 26—Simeon and Anna Praise God (Luke 2:27-38)

Learning by Doing

This page contains an alternative lesson plan emphasizing learning activities.
Classes desiring such student involvement will find these suggestions helpful.

Learning Goals

After participating in this lesson, each student will be able to:

1. Summarize the encounter between Joseph and Mary and the two prophetic persons in the temple.

2. Explain how Jesus' birth gives hope to the world today.

3. Identify a practical way to follow the example of Simeon and Anna in proclaiming the hope found in Jesus.

Into the Lesson

Before class begins, write on the board, "I'd be happy if only . . . " As your learners arrive, they should naturally begin thinking and talking about how to complete the statement.

As class begins, ask your learners to think not only of their own answers, but answers they have heard from other sources. Allow time for several to give both their own answers and answers that they have heard elsewhere. If you hear the answer "more money," challenge your class to be specific regarding exactly *how* it is that more money would make them happy.

Then say, "Today's lesson is about two people who also had a driving desire. Once that desire was met, they were happy and content."

Into the Word

To set the background for Simeon's hymn, summarize Luke 2:22-28 using the lesson commentary. Then discuss Simeon's hymn itself (vv. 29-32), phrase by phrase. Ask students the significance of each line. Below is the hymn, with some possible answers interspersed.

"Lord, now lettest thou thy servant depart in peace, *[his life is fulfilled; nothing else is needed, so he can die without regret]* according to thy word: *[God apparently had promised Simeon that he would see the Messiah before he died]* For mine eyes have seen thy salvation, *[Jesus' name means 'the Lord saves']* which thou hast prepared before the face of all people; *[God's Messiah was publicly displayed, for all to see]* a light to lighten the Gentiles, *[non-Jews share in the salvation that this Jewish baby brings; see God's promise to Abram in Genesis 12:3]* and the glory of thy people Israel *[the Messiah is the hope of the Jewish nation, the fulfillment of prophecy].*"

Comment on the remaining verses, which cover Simeon's prophecy to Mary, and Anna's encounter with the baby Jesus.

Into Life

State that Simeon and Anna are great examples for us. Their lives were focused on one great hope, and that hope kept them going—even through old age and possible poverty. When that goal was reached, they considered their lives to be complete.

Ask: "What gives you hope during the hard times? What keeps you going when life is tough? What do you consider to be the ultimate purpose of your life?"

These are difficult and sometimes disturbing questions. Stress to the class that you are not expecting audible responses. In fact it might be best to have students simply think about the questions rather than give glib answers that sound spiritual. If time is up, you can close the class at this point with your learners still in a reflective mood.

As an optional activity, write on the board, "My Testimony of Trust." Then ask someone to give a dramatic reading of Habakkuk 3:17, 18. Point out to your learners that they may not be facing the exact situations described in verse 17, which was written for people in an agricultural situation. To make this verse more personal, allow your learners time to substitute mentally certain words that apply to their own situation. (For example they could say, "Even if my company goes bankrupt and I get laid off . . . " or "Even if I do not recover from my arthritis . . . ")

After students have had a few minutes to create their own versions of verse 17, ask for volunteers to share their work. You may have several learners who normally are very quiet and never speak up. They may be the ones who have the most thoughtful answers! Seek out some responses from them.

After several have read their "personal verses," ask the whole class to read verse 18 in unison.

Close in prayer, thanking God for the hope that He provides—hope that can sustain us in every situation we may face. Ask that your learners be given the satisfaction of knowing, when they reach the end of their lives, that they have accomplished what God gave them to do. Pray that each would hear from God, "Well done!"

Let's Talk It Over

The questions on this page are designed to promote discussion of the lesson by the class and to encourage application of the lesson Scriptures. The answers provided are only discussion starters. Let your class talk it over from there.

1. What inspiration can we gain from the fact that Joseph and Mary faithfully fulfilled their obligations under the Old Testament law, despite having been shown special, miraculous attention by God?

People who feel that God has shown them special favor sometimes think that it is not that important for them to serve in some basic and ordinary ways in the church. The earthly parents of Jesus seem to have been just as anxious to fulfill humbly their responsibilities as they were before. They believed they now had far more reason to praise and honor God because of the ways He had worked in their lives.

The same should be true for us. The more we are blessed, the greater should be our desire to serve God and fulfill our responsibilities to Him.

2. Simeon received a special personal blessing, but focused even more on the blessing Jesus would be to others (verses 29-32). How can we each develop that kind of missionary mind-set?

Simeon was apparently aware from his knowledge of the Old Testament that God had often spoken of His love and plan for the people of all nations. Our own study of God's plan for the nations will impress on us that the good news of Jesus is for the whole world, a fact made even clearer in the New Testament. Watching news from around the world, paying attention to the work of missionaries supported by our church, meeting the practical needs of others, and praying for a selfless spirit can help us develop an outward focus.

3. In what ways can Simeon's predictions about Jesus in verses 34 and 35 also come true in our lives?

Once someone comes in contact with the person and work of Jesus Christ, he or she cannot remain neutral. Some choose to trust Him and build their lives on Him. Others become offended or threatened by His claims or demands, becoming His enemies.

We can rise to a new life in Christ and eagerly anticipate a future resurrection through Jesus' victory over death. The ministry of Jesus can also reveal the thoughts and motives of our hearts today as we compare our own lives with His example and teachings. Over time others can determine where our heart really is by seeing the evidence in our lives.

4. It is obvious that both Simeon and Anna enjoyed an extraordinary relationship with God. What can we learn from that to strengthen our own walk with the Lord?

One thing we learn is that people who are constantly in tune with God sometimes get to see and experience things that others miss. In this account it seems that God is honoring two people whose hearts were fully seeking after His own.

Simeon lived for the day he could see God's Messiah. Anna's life was devoted to prayer and worship at the temple. Time with God in prayer, Bible reading, meditation, fasting, corporate worship, and group Bible study increase our understanding of God's heart. In turn, all this will increase our desire to know Him even more.

5. How can we allow true hope to develop and grow in our hearts? Why is it easier to live with hope when we share it with others?

In a world that offers many false and empty hopes, we must determine from the Bible where true hope is found. Simeon and Anna were shown that ultimate hope is found in a Person, God's Messiah, and not in any other person or thing.

Sharing our hope with other believers allows us to celebrate forgiveness and new life with joy. When one of us is facing a heavy burden that threatens to remove our joy, another can point to the God who is bigger than the problems of life. When we feel drawn back to things that offer empty hopes, others can redirect our vision through a loving word or a timely Scriptural reminder. We can remind each other of the big picture of eternity so that we don't allow Satan to bury us in the troubles of the moment (see 2 Corinthians 4:16-18).

Sharing our hope with unbelievers also strengthens and renews hope in our own hearts. As we point them to Jesus and the hope He offers, we are reminded of the wonder and beauty of God's great plan for forgiveness. Their excitement at finding hope helps us rekindle the fire in our own lives that sometimes dies down from lack of attention. Hope shared is hope celebrated!

Jesus Begins His Ministry

DEVOTIONAL READING: Matthew 4:18-25.

BACKGROUND SCRIPTURE: Mark 1:14-28.

PRINTED TEXT: Mark 1:14-28.

Mark 1:14-28

14 Now after that John was put in prison, Jesus came into Galilee, preaching the gospel of the kingdom of God,

15 And saying, The time is fulfilled, and the kingdom of God is at hand: repent ye, and believe the gospel.

16 Now as he walked by the sea of Galilee, he saw Simon and Andrew his brother casting a net into the sea: for they were fishers.

17 And Jesus said unto them, Come ye after me, and I will make you to become fishers of men.

18 And straightway they forsook their nets, and followed him.

19 And when he had gone a little further thence, he saw James the son of Zebedee, and John his brother, who also were in the ship mending their nets.

20 And straightway he called them: and they left their father Zebedee in the ship with the hired servants, and went after him.

21 And they went into Capernaum; and straightway on the sabbath day he entered into the synagogue, and taught.

22 And they were astonished at his doctrine: for he taught them as one that had authority, and not as the scribes.

23 And there was in their synagogue a man with an unclean spirit; and he cried out,

24 Saying, Let us alone; what have we to do with thee, thou Jesus of Nazareth? art thou come to destroy us? I know thee who thou art, the Holy One of God.

25 And Jesus rebuked him, saying, Hold thy peace, and come out of him.

26 And when the unclean spirit had torn him, and cried with a loud voice, he came out of him.

27 And they were all amazed, insomuch that they questioned among themselves, saying, What thing is this? what new doctrine is this? for with authority commandeth he even the unclean spirits, and they do obey him.

28 And immediately his fame spread abroad throughout all the region round about Galilee.

GOLDEN TEXT: Jesus said unto them, Come ye after me, and I will make you to become fishers of men.—Mark 1:17.

Called to Be God's People

Unit 2: Jesus Calls His Followers

(Lessons 5-9)

Lesson Aims

After participating in this lesson, each student will be able to:

1. Describe the activities of Jesus' early ministry and the effect He had on people.

2. Explain how Jesus demonstrated His authority.

3. State one specific way that he or she will submit to Jesus' authority.

Lesson Outline

INTRODUCTION

    A. The Cost of Discipleship

    B. Lesson Background

  I. MESSAGE JESUS PREACHES (Mark 1:14, 15)

    A. Kingdom of God (v. 14)

    B. Repentance and Faith (v. 15)

  II. CHALLENGE JESUS ISSUES (Mark 1:16-20)

    A. Call of Simon and Andrew (vv. 16-18)

       Fishing for People

    B. Call of James and John (vv. 19, 20)

 III. AUTHORITY JESUS DEMONSTRATES (Mark 1: 21, 22)

    A. Location of His Teaching (v. 21)

    B. Effect of His Teaching (v. 22)

 IV. DEMON JESUS TERRIFIES (Mark 1:23-26)

    A. Demon Described (v. 23a)

    B. Demon Rebuked (vv. 23b-25)

    C. Demon Expelled (v. 26)

  V. FAME JESUS EARNS (Mark 1:27, 28)

    A. People's Amazement Grows (v. 27)

    B. Jesus' Fame Spreads (v. 28)

       Fame

CONCLUSION

    A. The Call of God

    B. Prayer

    C. Thought to Remember

Introduction

A. The Cost of Discipleship

A teenage friend of mine recently volunteered for a mission to the children in an inner-city area. She and her teammates spent several days teaching Vacation Bible School lessons to children who otherwise might not have had the opportunity to learn about Jesus.

A few weeks after returning home, she began to suffer with itch, and her mother took her to their family doctor. He examined her, asked her about recent activities, and correctly diagnosed that she was suffering from scabies.

Scabies, in case you've forgotten, is a disease that's supposed to affect the unclean poor of the world, not an American girl from an immaculately clean family. That's how mother and daughter felt, but it didn't alter the diagnosis. Both, but especially the daughter, felt humiliated, embarrassed, and, for no reason, ashamed. As any teenage girl might do, that young lady burst into tears right there in the doctor's office.

The Christian doctor, who correctly diagnosed the ailment, also correctly evaluated the situation. Calling the girl by name, he said, "Don't let this keep you from going on future mission trips. Remember that Jesus Himself had to take risks when He came to earth."

He surely did; and, on a lesser scale, so did Peter, Andrew, James, John, and the other apostles. So have many of His other disciples down through the ages.

When Jesus calls, take up whatever cross comes your way and follow Him. There may be some rough times, some uncomfortable situations, but in the end you'll be glad you answered His call.

B. Lesson Background

Our previous lesson ended in Jerusalem, the city to which Mary and Joseph had taken the baby Jesus "to present him to the Lord, . . . and to offer a sacrifice" (Luke 2:22, 24). Our present lesson begins more than thirty years later, and we switch from Luke's Gospel to Mark's.

With the exception of one brief glimpse of Jesus as a twelve-year-old (Luke 2:41-52), we know nothing of His life from His birth until He was about thirty years old (Luke 3:23). That was when He went to the Jordan to be baptized of John (Luke 3:21, 22).

After His baptism Jesus was led into the wilderness where He fasted and was tempted for forty days. He then returned to the scene of John's baptizing, enlisted His first disciples, and journeyed to Cana in Galilee where He performed His first miracle. At this time He relocated His base of operations from His hometown of Nazareth to Capernaum, which is spoken thereafter as "his own city" (Matthew 9:1).

Having changed His residence to Capernaum, Jesus set out on a journey to Jerusalem to attend the first of the four Passovers of His ministry (John 2:23). During this visit to the Holy City, He cleansed the temple (the first of two times) and had His famous nighttime conversation with Nicodemus (John 2:12–3:21). On His return trip to Galilee, He passed through Samaria, where He had His conversation with the woman at the well. At this time John the Baptist was arrested (Luke 3:19, 20), which sets the scene for our present lesson.

I. Message Jesus Preaches
(Mark 1:14, 15)

A. Kingdom of God (v. 14)

14. Now after that John was put in prison, Jesus came into Galilee, preaching the gospel of the kingdom of God.

Matthew and Luke begin their Gospels with the birth of Jesus. John begins his Gospel by discussing the pre-existence of the Christ. Mark, however, begins his Gospel with the ministry of *John* the Baptist (1:2-8). John the Baptist is remembered as a fearless preacher who never hesitated to condemn sin wherever he found it. At one point he singled out Herod Antipas, the tetrarch of Galilee, and condemned him for living adulterously with his brother Philip's wife. Herod responded by imprisoning John (6:17-29).

As well as can be determined, *John was put in prison* about a year after Jesus launched His own ministry. We are in the second year of Jesus' three-year ministry—it is the so-called "year of popularity." The people in the region of Galilee are about to hear preaching and teaching concerning the long-awaited *kingdom of God.*

B. Repentance and Faith (v. 15)

15. And saying, The time is fulfilled, and the kingdom of God is at hand: repent ye, and believe the gospel.

The gospel that Jesus preaches is that *the kingdom of God is at hand.* That is the good news that the ancient Jews have been anticipating for hundreds of years. This is the culmination of the dreams that the Old Testament prophets had instilled in the hearts of God's people. [See question #1, page 160.]

It will be some time before those who first hear this good news fully comprehend the true nature of this kingdom. It is not to be, as they think, a political or military force that will exalt a newly formed Jewish nation above all the other nations of the earth. Instead, it is to be a spiritual kingdom. It will include all individuals who respond with repentance and belief in the gospel. Jesus' message is similar to that which John had been preaching (see Matthew 3:1, 2).

In preaching to nonbelievers today, the logical and Biblical procedure calls for submission to the entire plan of salvation. This includes, among other things, placing faith and belief in Christ, to be followed by repentance of sins. In Jesus' message to the Jews, however, the order is reversed. The Jews, who are already believers in the one true God, are first commanded to repent of their wicked resistance to God's will. That seems to be a prerequisite to believing the gospel message that the kingdom of God is near.

II. Challenge Jesus Issues
(Mark 1:16-20)

A. Call of Simon and Andrew (vv. 16-18)

16-18. Now as he walked by the sea of Galilee, he saw Simon and Andrew his brother casting a net into the sea: for they were fishers. And Jesus said unto them, Come ye after me, and I will make you to become fishers of men. And straightway they forsook their nets, and followed him.

If we had only Mark's Gospel, we would assume that Jesus' call to these four disciples is extended and accepted at their first meeting. This, of course, is not the case, as the first chapter of John makes clear. From that text we learn that *Simon* (Peter) and *Andrew* already are acquainted with Jesus and have some level of attachment to Him. Perhaps this can be thought of as a loose, informal relationship between Jesus and these men. Now, an official call is extended and accepted. [See question #2, page 160.]

We do well to remember that when we first expose our friends to Jesus, it can be premature to expect them to "forsake *their nets*" and follow Him immediately. Jesus allows time for His words to sink in and be accepted, and so should we. [See question #3, page 160.]

FISHING FOR PEOPLE

We always should be careful not to press an illustration that Jesus uses in ways that He would not intend. For instance, there are many things about fishing that do not fit evangelism.

How to Say It

BABYLONIAN. Bab-ih-*low*-nee-un.
CAPERNAUM. Kuh-*per*-nay-um.
GALILEE. *Gal*-uh-lee.
HEROD ANTIPAS. *Hair*-ud *An*-tih-pus.
JERUSALEM. Juh-*roo*-suh-lem.
MESSIAH. Meh-*sigh*-uh.
NAZARETH. *Naz*-uh-reth.
NICODEMUS. *Nick*-uh-*dee*-mus (strong accent on *dee*).
PHARISEES. *Fair*-ih-seez.
SATAN. *Say*-tun.
SYNAGOGUE. *sin*-uh-gog.
TETRARCH. *teh*-trark or *tee*-trark.
ZEBEDEE. *Zeb*-eh-dee.

A fisherman will often use artificial lures, and that is certainly not an example for evangelism. We are not to win people by deceiving them, nor by promising them something that we cannot deliver.

Perhaps we may use "bait" in the sense that we address "felt needs" in order to get a chance to show people their deepest need, which is Jesus. There is no harm in churches offering recreational, social, or entertainment programs to unbelievers as long as they don't win people "to" what they're winning them "with." Ultimately, we must offer them Christ and eternal life.

In the days of our text, fishing was done with a cast net. Perhaps that idea fits evangelism best of all. As fishermen threw the net around the fish, so we throw arms of love and care around people. Our nets of compassion may include programs for people in prison, for the needy, for the aged, for the sick and dying, for unwed mothers, and for parents with troubled children. When we cast a net of love about them, we will certainly win some of them.

Of course, we will never win all of them. Jesus Himself didn't. But we must be like the persistent fisherman, determined to keep on trying and never give up. Someday conditions will be right, people will respond, and our patience and persistence will pay off. Remaining faithful is the key. God will grant the victory.   —R. C. S.

B. Call of James and John (vv. 19, 20)

19, 20. And when he had gone a little further thence, he saw James the son of Zebedee, and John his brother, who also were in the ship mending their nets. And straightway he called them: and they left their father Zebedee in the ship with the hired servants, and went after him.

After His call to Simon Peter and Andrew, Jesus goes a little farther along the shore to where the sons *of Zebedee, James* and *John,* are *mending their nets.* Jesus calls them into a close discipleship as well.

Luke gives us some information that Mark omits. He says that James and John "were partners with Simon" (Luke 5:10). Mark adds his own tidbit when he relates that Zebedee has *hired servants.* This seems to indicate that he is a man of some means.

III. Authority Jesus Demonstrates (Mark 1:21, 22)

A. Location of His Teaching (v. 21)

21. And they went into Capernaum; and straightway on the sabbath day he entered into the synagogue, and taught.

Capernaum is commonly thought of as Jesus' "headquarters" during His Galilean ministry (Matthew 4:13; Mark 2:1). It is situated on the northwest shore of the Sea of Galilee, and must be a town of considerable size in Jesus' day.

Although this town is repeatedly mentioned in the Gospels (and only there in the New Testament), it is never mentioned in the Old Testament. This has led some students to conclude that it wasn't founded until after the Babylonian captivity. The apostle Paul will later use the same "freedom of the *synagogue"* that we see here in his own preaching and teaching (see Acts 13:15).

Bible students know that Capernaum becomes the scene of some of Jesus' miracles as well as some of His teaching. Because its citizens refuse to repent, however, Jesus predicts a horrible future for them (see Matthew 11:23, 24). Today, the exact location of Capernaum is subject to debate, perhaps testifying to the completeness of its destruction.

B. Effect of His Teaching (v. 22)

22. And they were astonished at his doctrine: for he taught them as one that had authority, and not as the scribes.

By definition, a scribe is a person employed to handle correspondence and to keep records. In the New Testament, *scribes* are learned men who study, interpret, and expound the law. Many references to them can be found in the Gospels, where they are usually associated in a bad light with the Pharisees.

Their teaching is here contrasted with that of Jesus' teaching. His teaching is fresh, open, straightforward, and spontaneous. The scribes' teaching, on the other hand, is little more than a repetition of the sentiments and traditions of the great rabbis of the past. Such teaching lacks both freshness and practicality, often consisting of debates and disputes. When Jesus teaches *as one that had authority,* it is little wonder that He thrills His audiences and creates in them a thirst for more of such teaching.

IV. Demon Jesus Terrifies (Mark 1:23-26)

A. Demon Described (v. 23a)

23a. And there was in their synagogue a man with an unclean spirit.

Some in the Greco-Roman world of Jesus' day believe that demons are the spirits or ghosts of dead men that have taken possession of the living and are controlling them. Greeks also believe that some demons are beneficial, doing good for people.

The Bible, however, doesn't share these views. The demons of the New Testament are always described as *unclean*—that is, wicked agents of the devil, laboring to carry out his unholy will. Although the precise expression "demon possession" is not a Biblical term, it is a convenient phrase to use to describe people who have *an unclean spirit* or demon.

Today many believe that demon possession is restricted to the period surrounding the life of Jesus on earth and is the result of the devil's bold attempt to meet and defeat Jesus in battle. Others, especially missionaries to third-world countries, feel that people are still demonized in the remote areas of the world that have not been penetrated successfully by the light of the gospel. The Bible isn't clear as to which viewpoint is correct.

B. Demon Rebuked (vv. 23b-25)

23b-25. And he cried out, saying, Let us alone; what have we to do with thee, thou Jesus of Nazareth? art thou come to destroy us? I know thee who thou art, the Holy One of God. And Jesus rebuked him, saying, Hold thy peace, and come out of him.

The demon's message is expressed through the voice of the man. The demon not only recognizes that *Jesus* is from *Nazareth,* he also knows Him to be *the Holy One of God.* This is a phrase used to describe the Messiah (Psalm 16:10; Acts 2:27). The demon is also aware that Jesus possesses the power to destroy him and other demons (note the use of the plural *us*).

Skeptics today may claim that what the ancient people thought of as "demon possession" actually was an illness such as schizophrenia or epilepsy. But the ancient people certainly knew the difference between demon possession and other problems; Matthew 4:24 shows this distinction very well. Since children could have evil spirits, the cause of demon possession is not always moral (see Mark 9:14-29).

Jesus' two commands to *Hold thy peace* and *come out of him* are quite forceful. Note that this encounter occurs in what seems to be an unlikely place—a synagogue. All sorts of people come to church!

C. Demon Expelled (v. 26)

26. And when the unclean spirit had torn him, and cried with a loud voice, he came out of him.

The expulsion of this demon is not without pain as the man is *torn* by the departing *spirit.* Later in his Gospel, Mark relates the account of the expelling of a dumb spirit from a child (9:17-27). In that instance, as here, pain is involved.

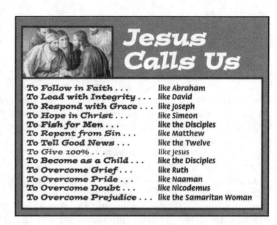

Visual for lessons 5, 13. *This chart provides a summary of the lessons for this quarter. Leave it on display for the next several weeks.*

The New Testament makes it clear that Satan does not want to lose control or influence over a person. Nor does Satan wish to surrender one of his earthly children to the Lord today. Quitting sin is a difficult business that seldom happens without some pain being involved. [See question #4, page 160.]

V. Fame Jesus Earns
(Mark 1:27, 28)

A. People's Amazement Grows (v. 27)

27. And they were all amazed, insomuch that they questioned among themselves, saying, What thing is this? what new doctrine is this? for with authority commandeth he even the unclean spirits, and they do obey him.

From the end of the Old Testament until the time of Jesus—more than four hundred years—the world has been without miracles. Not even John the Baptist is empowered to perform them (John 10:41). This lengthy period, void of the miraculous, contributes to the effect produced by Jesus as He performs "miracles and wonders and signs" (Acts 2:22). That He has the ability to command *unclean spirits* naturally causes amazement. [See question #5, page 160.]

B. Jesus' Fame Spreads (v. 28)

28. And immediately his fame spread abroad throughout all the region round about Galilee.

Jesus permits a limited testimony of this unclean spirit that Jesus is the Holy One of God or Messiah (v. 24, above). But it is not Jesus' desire that demons should testify on His behalf. Such testimony may well have an adverse effect on Jesus' ministry (cf. Acts 16:16-18). On this occasion, however, the testimony of the demon and his expulsion contribute toward the growth of Jesus' fame *throughout all the region round about Galilee.*

FAME

The fame of Jesus has continued to spread. Today there is no name better known on the face of the earth. Jesus is better known than Buddha, better known than Mohammed, and better known than any figure of history or fiction. But that does not mean that everybody knows Him.

There are more than six billion people on planet Earth. A large percentage call themselves Christians. But there are at least one billion people who live in lands where there is no access even to knowledge about Jesus Christ. At the same time that we are comforted in the knowledge that so many have heard of Him, we also are disturbed by the fact that so many have not!

Think about how many one billion is: it is nearly four times the population of the United States! That many people have never had a chance to accept Jesus Christ. We have a lot of work to do to fulfill the Great Commission.

Although the task of world evangelism is far from finished, today we have better tools than ever to accomplish it. With television, the Internet, the ease of printing, and the ease of world travel, we have the best opportunity that Christians have ever had to really finish what Jesus commanded. Imagine yourself among the one billion who have never heard of Him. Wouldn't you want someone to come and tell you?   —R. C. S.

Conclusion

A. The Call of God

Peter, Andrew, James, and John were called by Jesus to become His disciples. In the case of the first two, the nature of their future work is told them—they were to be fishers of men. Probably a similar explanation is given to James and John (the sons of Zebedee), but it is not recorded in any of the Gospel accounts of the event.

More than fifty years ago, I received a similar call from the Lord to become a preacher. Note that I said "similar," not "same." It is similar in that it came from the Lord and was a definite call.

But it was not the same. No, Jesus didn't appear to me in bodily form. He did not come to me in a dream, point His finger at me like Uncle Sam in a famous World War II poster, and say, "I want you." I would have been happy had it been that way, especially had He told me the specific kind of ministry He had in mind for me. That would have made my life much simpler!

Since "my call" didn't include a specific assignment, I have had to use my intelligence to

Home Daily Bible Readings

Monday, Dec. 27—John Proclaims That Jesus Is Coming (Mark 1:1-8)
Tuesday, Dec. 28—Jesus Prepares for His Ministry (Mark 1:9-13)
Wednesday, Dec. 29—Jesus Preaches and Calls Disciples (Mark 1:14-20)
Thursday, Dec. 30—Jesus Teaches and Performs a Miracle (Mark 1:21-28)
Friday, Dec. 31—Jesus Heals Many People (Mark 1:29-34)
Saturday, Jan. 1—Jesus Preaches in Galilee (Mark 1:35-39)
Sunday, Jan. 2—Jesus Proclaims Good News (Matthew 4:16-25)

determine where I could best serve. I'm not sure that my judgments have always been the best, but at the time of making each choice I felt it was the thing the Lord wanted me to do. I have served as a preacher, a missionary, a professor, and an editor. I have pursued all of these ministries because I felt led by God to do so.

I know there are those who contend that their calls were of a supernatural nature. I also know that many who have made such claims have been miserable failures, their efforts resulting in much harm to the kingdom of God.

My call came to me from the Lord, but it came through the Bible. As a young man I read Jesus' command, "Go ye into all the world, and preach the gospel to every creature" (Mark 16:15). I assumed that Jesus was speaking to me and to every other Christian. I had the two essentials that I think constitute a call: a desire to preach and the talent to do so. I put the two together along with the command of Christ, so I went! It was as simple as that.

Jesus is calling you to His service. It may be to become a preacher, a teacher, an elder, or a deacon. Add your desire to serve to your talent and spiritual giftedness to do so. To these also add the need that exists, and you have a call "similar" to that given to Peter, Andrew, James, and John. When you answer that call, you submit to Jesus' authority.

B. Prayer

Dear Lord, may we, like the four fishermen, gladly accept the invitation of Jesus to follow Him and become fishers of men. In Jesus' name we pray, amen.

C. Thought to Remember

May we never cease to hear the call of Jesus.

Learning by Doing

This page contains an alternative lesson plan emphasizing learning activities.
Classes desiring such student involvement will find these suggestions helpful.

Learning Goals

After participating in this lesson, each student will be able to:

1. Describe the activities of Jesus' early ministry and the effect He had on people.

2. Explain how Jesus demonstrated His authority.

3. State one specific way that he or she will submit to Jesus' authority.

Into the Lesson

Before class write "Symbols of Authority" on the board. Ask the students to think of things in our society that symbolize some kind of authority. As an example you might cite the label on the gasoline pumps indicating that a government official has inspected the pumps and certified their accuracy. The consumer can trust the authority of the county government that he or she is getting gasoline that is accurately measured.

Allow a few minutes for the class to think about this, perhaps discussing it informally among themselves. If your class enjoys coffee and pastries during a "fellowship time" before the class starts, ask the students to put this time to good use by talking about these symbols of authority as they visit with one another.

Call the class to order and ask for suggestions. Some of the following may be voiced: a badge (worn by police or fire department personnel or even by convention officials or state-fair judges), the state or county seal (found on government buildings, vehicles, and letterhead), the black robe and gavel of a judge, and a crown.

When the class seems to have exhausted its list of ideas, ask, "Do you know any person who seems to be a symbol of authority—someone whose actions or speech convey authority without any tangible symbol like a badge?" Allow time for responses. Then say, "Jesus was such a person. Again and again, the people who heard Him marveled at His authority. Today's lesson includes one such event."

Into the Word

Ask a volunteer to read Mark 1:14-28 aloud. Then divide the class into five groups and ask each one to take part of the text and to list evidence of Jesus' authority as found in the assigned verses. Assign the text according to the five major subdivisions of the outline on page 154. Provide posters, markers, and other helps for the groups to work and compile their results. Allow six to eight minutes for the groups to work; then call for reports. Some possible answers are:

    I. Mark 1:14, 15—preaching implies a certain authority, especially the call to repent.

    II. Mark 1:16-20—in calling disciples, Jesus requires a submission to His authority. The four fishermen acknowledge that He is worthy of it by following.

    III. Mark 1:21, 22—Jesus' teaching is unique. The people can sense His authority.

    IV. Mark 1:23-26—in commanding that the demon leave the man, Jesus demonstrates an authority that goes beyond the physical and earthly. He has spiritual authority of a kind that does not expire; this is divine authority.

    V. Mark 1:27, 28—the discussion by the people is still focused on the authority that Jesus has over the demon. As His fame spreads, it surely includes this awe-inspiring authority.

Into Life

Say, "To acknowledge that Jesus demonstrated authority two thousand years ago is well and good, but it's not enough. Jesus still has authority today." Ask someone to read Matthew 28:18. Note that Jesus' claim to have "all power" has not been rescinded.

Then ask, "How, then, do we demonstrate our submission to His authority?" Have learners return to their five groups. Each group is to come up with an idea for demonstrating submission to Jesus' authority based on the example they found earlier. Call for reports after a few minutes.

Groups 1 and 2 should come up with something on the order of following as Jesus' disciples today. Group 3 should acknowledge that Jesus' teaching, as well as that of His inspired representatives (apostles and other writers of the New Testament), is authoritative and worthy of our complete acceptance. Groups 4 and 5 should focus on the spiritual and eternal nature of Jesus' authority.

Next, ask your learners to consider one specific way each of them will acknowledge Jesus' authority. Say, "Consider your week ahead. What's on your agenda? How will Jesus' authority make a difference in the decisions that you make and the activities in which you participate?" Close with a prayer of submission to His authority.

Let's Talk It Over

*The questions on this page are designed to promote discussion of the lesson
by the class and to encourage application of the lesson Scriptures. The answers
provided are only discussion starters. Let your class talk it over from there.*

1. Jesus stated in verse 15 that the time was fulfilled and the kingdom of God was at hand. What can this teach us about determining the right timing for something?

Jesus' statement at that particular time helps us realize that God gives His people opportune moments and situations, but not perfect ones. God has been awe-inspiring in His timeliness throughout history. He has always done the right thing at the right time.

Yet not even God was acting within a perfect setting. When Jesus began His ministry, as recorded in our lesson text, John the Baptist was in prison (verse 14), Jesus' own half-brothers did not believe in Him, and Satan already had tried to derail Jesus from His mission. The time was right, but the situation was not perfect. The same will be true in our lives today.

2. In what sense does Jesus call people today to be "fishers of men"?

Like other fishermen of their day, the two sets of brothers in our lesson were committed to hauling in as many fish as possible. Jesus called them to demonstrate the same passion and commitment in bringing as many people as possible to Him for forgiveness and new life.

Today God calls all Christians to participate in this fishing expedition. But some He calls to serve in paid, specialized ministries so they can devote their full energies to that mission. It has been said that the glorious difference between catching fish and catching people is that you catch fish that are alive and they die, but you catch people who are dead and they are brought to life.

3. How does Jesus' call to the fishermen help us understand the difference between being a committed disciple and simply being a follower?

As the lesson writer notes, all four men apparently knew Jesus from previous encounters. But now He calls them to walk away from their way of life, source of income, and place of familiarity to serve with Him on a full-time basis. They knew Jesus before, but there was not a committed relationship.

It is one thing for us to know a little about Jesus and the Bible, but quite another to enjoy a deep, committed relationship in which we follow Him wherever He leads. People followed Jesus in the first century for a variety of reasons: curiosity, fascination, self-interest, etc. Only a few turned out to be true disciples. Jesus' disciples trusted Him enough to follow Him into hostile territories, leper colonies, pushy crowds, and eventual martyrdom. As a result, they changed the world and received eternal life! Jesus can still change the world today through committed disciples.

4. Jesus rescued many who were harassed and hindered by unclean spirits. How can we limit the devil's influence in our own lives?

The most obvious way is to surrender heart and will to the lordship and authority of Jesus Christ, fully renouncing any claim that the devil may have on us. At the time of our conversion, the Holy Spirit comes to live within us (Acts 2:38). The Spirit is more powerful than the evil one (1 John 4:4), but allowing the Spirit to lead fully and to cleanse us is an ongoing process (Galatians 5:16-26).

We also protect ourselves from the devil's lies and temptations by filling ourselves with the Bible's truth. In a practical sense, we must be realistic about the danger of Satan's influence, even in a religious setting like the synagogue that we see in today's text. We should take Satan and his demons seriously, but not live in fear. Jesus is still Lord.

5. In what ways can we also teach with authority like Jesus did?

Only Jesus has all authority "in heaven and in earth" (Matthew 28:18), but we can speak and teach with authority as we accurately convey the authoritative words that God has given to us in the Bible. After Jesus' ascension, the Holy Spirit guided the apostles into all truth and reminded them of things Jesus had taught them (John 14:26; 16:13). We now enjoy the written result of that blessing in the New Testament.

Our world desperately needs an authoritative word from the Lord. Many claim that there is no such thing as absolute truth, and therefore believe that any worldview is just as valid as any other. The tragic result is moral chaos and uncertainty. When we convey the truth from Jesus with the heart of love that Jesus demonstrated, many today will also find it refreshing to hear a clear, authoritative teaching.

Jesus Calls Levi (Matthew)

DEVOTIONAL READING: Ephesians 4:25-32.

BACKGROUND SCRIPTURE: Mark 2:13-17.

PRINTED TEXT: Mark 2:13-17.

Mark 2:13-17

13 And he went forth again by the sea side; and all the multitude resorted unto him, and he taught them.

14 And as he passed by, he saw Levi the son of Alpheus sitting at the receipt of custom, and said unto him, Follow me. And he arose and followed him.

15 And it came to pass, that, as Jesus sat at meat in his house, many publicans and sinners sat also together with Jesus and his disciples; for there were many, and they followed him.

16 And when the scribes and Pharisees saw him eat with publicans and sinners, they said unto his disciples, How is it that he eateth and drinketh with publicans and sinners?

17 When Jesus heard it, he saith unto them, They that are whole have no need of the physician, but they that are sick: I came not to call the righteous, but sinners to repentance.

GOLDEN TEXT: Jesus . . . saith unto them, They that are whole have no need of the physician, but they that are sick: I came not to call the righteous, but sinners to repentance.
—Mark 2:17.

Called to Be God's People
Unit 2: Jesus Calls His Followers
(Lessons 5-9)

Lesson Aims

After participating in this lesson, each student will be able to:

1. Tell how the call of Levi (Matthew) illustrates Jesus' purpose in coming to seek and to save the lost.

2. Identify individuals or groups in the local community who need to hear Jesus' call.

3. Suggest some method by which to bring the lost to Christ.

Lesson Outline

INTRODUCTION
    A. Jesus and Sinners
    B. Lesson Background
  I. SEEKERS AND SOUGHT (Mark 2:13, 14)
    A. Taxing Crowd (v. 13)
    B. Tax Collector (v. 14)
 II. DINNER AND SINNERS (Mark 2:15-17)
    A. Followers (v. 15)
      "Follow Me"
    B. Pharisees (v. 16)
    C. Physician (v. 17)
      A Call to Repentance
CONCLUSION
    A. The Freshly Won
    B. Prayer
    C. Thought to Remember

Introduction

A. Jesus and Sinners

Luke tells of an occasion when a Pharisee named Simon invited Jesus to dine with him. While Jesus was reclining at the table in the style of eating in that day, a sinful woman of the city somehow managed to gain access to the house. As she began to weep profusely, her tears fell on Jesus' feet. She used her hair to wipe His feet and then she poured on them the perfume that she had brought for the purpose.

Well! It was all just too much for Simon to endure. Luke 7:39 records that he said to himself, "This man, if he were a prophet, would have known who and what manner of woman this is that toucheth him; for she is a sinner."

Simon was only partially correct in what he thought. A prophet of God would not necessarily know the moral state of a person. Having such discernment is not a requirement of the office of prophet. But applied to Jesus, the statement is true. As the omniscient Son of God, He should have known everything about the woman. And He did.

That's the beauty of the story. The perfect, sinless Son of God happily accepted the ministrations of sinful people when they came to Him in genuine faith and repentance. "Her sins, which are many, are forgiven," He said, "for she loved [Me] much" (Luke 7:47).

Today's lesson offers us a similar case—that of Levi. To the Pharisees, Levi, a tax collector, was as repulsive as the woman who anointed Jesus' body, perhaps even more so. Yet Jesus was willing to accept an invitation to eat with him and others of his profession.

What the Pharisees failed to recognize is that people can change. Anyone can become a child of the King!

B. Lesson Background

The call of Levi occurred during Jesus' great Galilean campaign. It was perhaps a year or fifteen months after His baptism that Jesus began this preaching and teaching tour. In the Gospel of Mark, this campaign of ministry extends from 1:14 to 9:50.

Not all of this time was spent in Galilee, however. There was an excursion to Jerusalem to attend a Passover feast (John 5:1-47), another to Phoenicia (Matthew 15:21-28; Mark 7:24-30), and four recorded visits to the eastern side of the Sea of Galilee. After each such visit, Jesus returned to Galilee to carry on His ministry there. Levi was called in the early part of this campaign, perhaps sometime in late A.D. 27 or early A.D. 28.

I. Seekers and Sought
(Mark 2:13, 14)

A. Taxing Crowd (v. 13)

13a. And he went forth again by the sea side.

Much of Jesus' ministry occurs in Galilee, the northernmost province of Palestine. Jesus seems to spend a lot of His time near the sea that carries the area's name. In last week's lesson we learned that it was by this sea that He called four disciples, all of whom were later to become apostles. In today's lesson Jesus goes *forth again by the sea side*, where he attracts the usual crowd of people.

The Sea of Galilee is fed by the Jordan River, which passes through it from north to south. The sea (better thought of as a lake because of its size) is thirteen miles in length and eight miles in width at its widest spot. Its greatest depth is about one hundred and fifty feet.

John 21:1 refers to this body of water as "the sea of Tiberias," so designated because of the city of that name on its western shore. John evidently chooses to use this Roman name since his Gospel is to circulate in the Roman world. Elsewhere in the Bible it is called "the lake of Gennesaret" (Luke 5:1), and "the sea of Chinnereth" (Numbers 34:11).

In Jesus' day the area around the lake teems with people. Several cities of fifteen thousand or more ring its shores. Today, only two of them remain, and these are small and insignificant.

13b. And all the multitude resorted unto him.

Everywhere Jesus goes there seems to be a *multitude* or crowd. Most of the inquisitive people come to Him with good motives. But there are exceptions, as some people show up to see what they can manipulate Jesus into doing for them (Luke 12:13; John 6:26). Crowds certainly can be fickle! The crowd that proclaims "Hosanna!" one day (Matthew 21:9) can shout "Let him be crucified!" a short time later (Matthew 27:22).

13c. And he taught them.

Jesus is both teacher and preacher (see Matthew 4:23), and He uses whichever method best suits the occasion. Notice from Matthew 5:2 that the so-called "Sermon on the Mount" is not a preached sermon, but a lesson He taught. Concerning the occasion at hand, teaching seems to predominate.

If digital video recorders had been in existence in Jesus' day, and if one had been in the hand of a disciple who faithfully captured every lesson Jesus taught and every sermon He delivered, how would we feel about those lessons and messages? Would we find His illustrations too simple? His pronouncements too dogmatic? His requirements too demanding? His concepts too "Victorian" or "prudish"?

Jesus is, of course, the greatest teacher of all time. His every word is the Word of God. Even so, we must not assume that people in any particular era will all be pleased with what He says or how He says it.

We're probably correct in assuming that DVDs of His lessons and sermons would be kept on shelves just like His printed words are now. After all, wouldn't it be more enjoyable to watch a science fiction presentation, a romantic movie, or a gangster thriller than to listen to a controversial Rabbi who lived two thousand years ago? Human motives do not change, despite advances in technology. In short, the crowds of today are just as "taxing" in their motives and expectations as those of the first century!

B. Tax Collector (v. 14)

14a. And as he passed by, he saw Levi the son of Alpheus sitting at the receipt of custom.

When Matthew tells of his call in the Gospel that he writes, he refers to himself by that name rather than *Levi*. That he has two names isn't unusual in his day. We know of Silas/Silvanus, John/Mark, Joseph/Barnabas, Saul/Paul, and Nathanael/Bartholomew. Perhaps Jesus renames Levi to be Matthew, as in the case of Simon Peter (Cephas in John 1:42); or Levi may have changed his own name. The name Matthew means "gift of Yahweh" and is still a popular name among Christians.

The name *Alpheus* is also noted in connection with a disciple named James in Matthew 10:3; Mark 3:18; Luke 6:15; and Acts 1:13. Consequently, some believe that Matthew is a brother to that particular James. Against this view is the fact that they are never called as such in the New Testament, nor are their names ever grouped together in the way that is true of other brothers.

The phrase *sitting at the receipt of custom* tells us that Matthew is a tax collector. To his fellow Jews, this occupation brands Matthew as being a collaborator with the hated Romans. Matthew thus would seem to be an unlikely choice for a disciple and eventual apostle! But Jesus obviously sees in him qualities of greatness that only need to be developed. [See question #1, page 168.] As a tax collector, Matthew has skills such as writing and record-keeping that will serve him well when it comes time for him to write his own Gospel about Jesus.

Matthew is mentioned here and in the lists of the Twelve in Matthew 10, Mark 3, Luke 6, and Acts 1 but nowhere else in the New Testament. Tradition has it that he stayed for fifteen years in

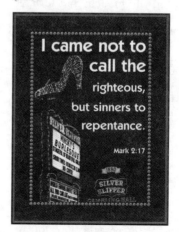

Visual for lesson 6

The Lord came to call even the notorious sinners. Discuss, "Are we ready to receive them?"

his homeland, after which he went to several foreign nations and preached. He may have died a natural death in either Macedonia or Ethiopia, but some legends have it that he died as a martyr.

14b. And said unto him, Follow me.

It seems unreasonable that Matthew should respond instantly to such a simple call as Jesus extends to him here if they are total strangers. Probably, as with the fishermen whom we saw called in last week's lesson, Matthew is already acquainted with Jesus—His mission, message, and methods—prior to receiving this call.

Various levels of relationship to Jesus are evident in the New Testament. Many (such as those mentioned in John 1) are attracted to Him, intrigued no doubt by His teaching. From this larger group, a few are more dedicated (such as the ones who constitute the hundred and twenty of Acts 1:15). The twelve chosen to be apostles are men whom He desires to be with Him constantly during His ministry (Mark 3:14-19).

Before we move on, notice that Jesus doesn't issue some kind of general appeal to the crowd in Mark 2:13 to call forth volunteers to be His very closest disciples. Jesus doesn't say to the crowd, "I'm looking for twelve apostles. If anyone is interested, please step forward for an interview." Instead, He zeroes in on the one He wants, and invites him personally. This may say something about the best way to choose church leaders today.

14c. And he arose and followed him.

Matthew answers the call to enter into a deeper relationship with Jesus. In Mark 3:13-19, Matthew and eleven others are called into a relationship with the Lord that is deeper and more meaningful still. In that passage Jesus "ordained" them "that they should be with him, and that he might send them forth to preach, and to have power to heal sicknesses, and to cast out devils."

Luke 5:28 tells us that Matthew "left all, rose up, and followed him." Perhaps Matthew's humility keeps him from making the "left all" claim for himself in Matthew 9:9.

II. Dinner and Sinners
(Mark 2:15-17)

A. Followers (v. 15)

15. And it came to pass, that, as Jesus sat at meat in his house, many publicans and sinners sat also together with Jesus and his disciples; for there were many, and they followed him.

This feast appears to be something of a farewell party given by Matthew as he makes ready to travel *with Jesus*. It serves as a threshold in Matthew's life, an event that he can later look back upon as a major fork in his earthly journey.

To this feast Matthew has invited his friends and former associates. No doubt he presents Jesus to them, hoping that He will change their lives as He has changed Matthew's own. [See question #2, page 168.]

The expression *for there were many* probably refers to the number of *publicans and sinners* who are present rather than to Jesus' disciples in general. The phrase *and they followed him* would be redundant if it refers to people who are already disciples before the meal begins. If it's correct that the *many* who are present refers to Matthew's friends and associates, then the result of this occasion is that Jesus gains several new disciples.

There are many ways to open the doors of people's hearts so that they will be receptive to the gospel. One oft-used method is "evangelism of the table." Most people will accept an invitation to your home if the invitation includes a meal. Sitting around a table at a meal provides a relaxed atmosphere for guests to converse about your faith. [See question #3, page 168.]

"FOLLOW ME"

Road repairs often involve closing a lane of traffic for a certain distance. When this happens on a two-lane road, the repair crew has to figure out a way to keep a flow of traffic alternating in each direction on the single usable lane.

Sometimes the road repair crew will use a little pickup truck with a big sign on the back that says, "FOLLOW ME." That truck leads traffic to the point where the single lane again becomes

---

How to Say It

AUGUSTINE. *Aw*-gus-teen (strong accent on *Aw*) or Aw-*gus*-tin.
ALPHEUS. Al-*fee*-us.
BARNABAS. *Bar*-nuh-bus.
BARTHOLOMEW. Bar-*thahl*-uh-mew.
CHINNERETH. *Kin*-e-reth or *Chin*-ne-reth.
GALILEAN. Gal-uh-*lee*-un.
GALILEE. *Gal*-uh-lee.
GENNESARET. Geh-*ness*-uh-ret (G as in get).
JERUSALEM. Juh-*roo*-suh-lem.
JORDAN. *Jor*-dun.
JOSEPHUS. Jo-*see*-fus.
LEVI. *Lee*-vye.
MACCABEES. *Mack*-uh-bees.
MACEDONIA. Mass-eh-*doe*-nee-uh.
NATHANAEL. Nuh-*than*-yull (*th* as in *thin*).
PHARISEES. *Fair*-ih-seez.
PHOENICIA. Fuh-*nish*-uh.
SILAS. *Sigh*-luss.
SILVANUS. Sil-*vay*-nus.
TIBERIAS. Tie-*beer*-ee-us.

two. The various drivers in the cars being "led" do not know the name of the person driving the truck, nor have they ever met. Yet they follow him or her with every confidence that the driver of that little truck will safely lead everyone. The pickup truck driver has credibility!

When Jesus said to those first disciples "Follow me," they had no doubt that Jesus would lead them the right way. They knew He would not lead them into sin. They knew He would not lead them to a useless and purposeless life. They did not know exactly where He would lead them—to what cities or towns they would go. But faith grounded in Christ's credibility made them follow.

For us, too, faith demands that we follow Him. We do not always know the exact direction He will lead us. But we know He will not lead us astray. We know He will lead us to the places where life can really count for something. If we follow Him, we will have no regrets. The important thing to remember, however, is that it is we who are following Jesus, and not the reverse.

Humility, faith, and commitment will ensure that we follow our Guide. Even those who would be leaders in the home, the church, or the community must first of all be followers. Jesus still says to people, as He did so long ago, "Follow me." —R. C. S.

B. Pharisees (v. 16)

16a. And when the scribes and Pharisees saw him eat with publicans and sinners, they said unto his disciples.

As stated earlier, *the scribes* are almost always shown in connection with the Pharisees in the Gospels. The *Pharisees,* meaning "separated ones," compose the most prominent religious party of the Jews in Jesus' day.

The first-century Jewish historian Josephus indicates that there were only about six thousand Pharisees at the height of their power. Considering this against a population of perhaps a quarter of a million or more, the Pharisees exercise influence that is out of proportion with their numbers. Their origin is somewhat uncertain, but they apparently date to the time of the Maccabees, about one hundred and sixty years before Christ.

The Pharisees are noted for their strictness (Acts 26:5) and for adherence to such doctrines as special divine providence, immortality of the soul, and future reward for the righteous and punishment for the wicked. They strongly believe in the coming of the Messiah, but most refuse to accept Jesus as being "the One." Pharisees are repeatedly mentioned in the Gospels, where, like a pack of wild dogs, they constantly snarl and snap at Jesus. But Jesus can snap back at times, as we see in Matthew 23:13-36.

16b. How is it that he eateth and drinketh with publicans and sinners?

To the Jews in general and to the Pharisees in particular, no group of men is more detestable than the tax collectors *(publicans)*. The animosity stems in part from the fact that tax collectors are servants of Rome, the pagan power that occupies the land.

Another factor is that the Jews know the character of the tax collectors all too well—most are unjust, noted for their extortion and oppression. The accusation that Jesus eats and drinks with such people is true! See Luke 7:34. Jesus' motive in doing so, of course, is to change them. [See question #4, page 168.]

C. Physician (v. 17)

17. When Jesus heard it, he saith unto them, They that are whole have no need of the physician, but they that are sick: I came not to call the righteous, but sinners to repentance.

Notice that the scribes and Pharisees do not register their objection directly with *Jesus,* but with His disciples (v. 16a). Perhaps they are reluctant to lock horns with Him at this time and in this place. Although the criticism is made to the disciples, it is Jesus who responds.

The application of Jesus' statement is apparent, and the logic underlying it is such that none can question it. We shouldn't conclude from Jesus' statement that He is affirming that the scribes and Pharisees are indeed *whole* or *righteous*—only that they considered themselves to be so. In reality, they are quite ill spiritually.

Whether speaking of the physically, mentally, or spiritually ill, the first step toward recovery is always the admission that a problem exists. Examples abound of sick people whose condition continues to deteriorate because of their refusal to go to a *physician*. At one time or another, most of us have heard a friend or acquaintance who was obviously sick or injured say, "Who needs a doctor? I can take care of myself." We have watched the person's health worsen until it took its toll, and have then found ourselves expressing sympathy to the next of kin at a visitation. "If only she had admitted her problem," we've said to ourselves.

And what about friends and neighbors whose problem isn't physical but spiritual? Think of people whose children are on drugs, who have a pregnant, unmarried daughter, who think that getting drunk each weekend is what life is all about, whose loud arguments keep the entire neighborhood upset. I'm talking about people, who, when approached about the healing of the great physician, respond, "Hey, we're all right. There's not a thing wrong with us. Just leave us alone, okay?" Those who do not admit to having a problem are not motivated to get it fixed.

Jesus' mission to the world is seen in His name, "Yahweh is salvation." It was explained to Joseph by "the angel of the Lord," who told him concerning Mary, "And she shall bring forth a son, and thou shalt call his name Jesus: for he shall save his people from their sins" (Matthew 1:20, 21).

Nowhere is Jesus' mission made clearer than in Luke 19:10 where He said of Himself, "For the Son of man is come to seek and to save that which was lost." Our text expresses the same truth: *I came not to call the righteous, but sinners to repentance.* [See question #5, page 168.]

A CALL TO REPENTANCE

Few people have influenced the course of Christianity more than Augustine of Hippo (A.D. 354–430). But before his conversion he was, by his own account, a great sinner.

When Augustine came to repentance, he reportedly described it like this: "I carried inside me a cut and bleeding soul. How to get rid of it I just didn't know. . . . My soul floundered in the void and came back upon me. Where could my heart flee from my heart? Where could I escape from myself?" That is repentance—genuine, deep repentance!

Properly understood, repentance involves the mind, the emotions, and the will. It means that we turn around and walk a different path. But emotionally, it means we have a sense of sin that sears the soul. If we take our sins lightly, we will take our forgiveness lightly. But if we are truly moved by the awfulness of our sins, then we will truly rejoice at the magnitude of our forgiveness.

Home Daily Bible Readings

Monday, Jan. 3—Jesus Heals a Leper (Mark 1:40-45)
Tuesday, Jan. 4—Jesus Forgives a Paralytic (Mark 2:1-5)
Wednesday, Jan. 5—The Paralytic Stands Up and Walks (Mark 2:6-12)
Thursday, Jan. 6—I Have Come to Call Sinners (Mark 2:13-17)
Friday, Jan. 7—Love and Live in the Light (1 John 2:9-17)
Saturday, Jan. 8—Love One Another (1 John 4:7-21)
Sunday, Jan. 9—We Are Members of One Another (Ephesians 4:25-32)

John Newton (1725–1807) had himself been a great sinner. One of his greatest sins had been to be involved in the slave trade of his day. Yet this one who had tasted the dregs of sinful disobedience could also greatly revel in the joy of forgiveness. He expressed both the realization of his sin and the joy of God's forgiveness when he wrote what is perhaps the most famous of all hymns, "Amazing Grace."

Like King David, the apostle Paul, Augustine, and Newton, we must repent at the deepest level of our being, and then rejoice in our salvation. Only then will we truly know God.   —R. C. S.

Conclusion

A. The Freshly Won

Matthew was excited. His life was being changed for the better and he wanted his old friends to know why. So he prepared a feast and invited them to attend so that he might introduce them to Jesus.

Such an exact situation is rare. The reason? Just after Matthew became a disciple of Jesus, Matthew's circle of friends included his old buddies who were not disciples. But as time moves on Matthew naturally would have less and less contact with his old friends who reject Christ (and reject Matthew as well). Thus Matthew eventually will not be able to witness in the same way that we see in today's lesson.

So it is with present-day disciples. Soon after conversion, a Christian may number many lost individuals as friends and associates. But the longer he or she remains a Christian, the smaller that old circle becomes. This is why it is imperative that the freshly won, while still remembering what it's like to be "sick," testify to those still suffering from the disease of sin. Such testimony, accompanied by a lifestyle that shows godly changes, can have a tremendous impact on the lives of the lost.

B. Prayer

Father, our world is filled with people like Matthew who are spending their time in worldly pursuits, unaware of the happiness that could be theirs as your servants. Help us to befriend them, discover things we have in common with them, and invite them to our homes.

May we do what it takes to bring them to Your Son, the great physician, that they may have eternal life. We can do no less for the One who died for us. In Jesus' name, amen.

C. Thought to Remember

All Christians, like physicians,
should be concerned with the sick.

Learning by Doing

This page contains an alternative lesson plan emphasizing learning activities. Classes desiring such student involvement will find these suggestions helpful.

Learning Goals

After participating in this lesson, each student will be able to:

1. Tell how the call of Levi (Matthew) illustrates Jesus' purpose in coming to seek and to save the lost.

2. Identify individuals or groups in the local community who need to hear Jesus' call.

3. Suggest some method by which to bring the lost to Christ.

Into the Lesson

As students arrive, give each a copy of the following list: an inexpensive watch, a pair of eyeglasses, a twenty-dollar bill, a car title, a picture drawn by a preschooler, a button that fell off a shirt or blouse, last year's tax return, and a shopping list. Ask each to tell how long he or she would look for each item if it were lost.

After a few minutes, ask for volunteers to tell what items they would search longest for. What items would they not look for much at all? Why?

Obviously, we search longest and hardest for those things we value most. Sometimes what we value is not valued by others. Such is the case in today's lesson. Jesus said He came to seek that which was lost. When He came seeking Levi (Matthew), there were some who thought He was wasting His time. But Jesus saw the value of every human. Today's lesson is intended to help us see that value as well.

Into the Word

Distribute a handout that you have prepared in advance. Across the top should appear the following four headings: The Multitude; Levi; Publicans and Sinners; Scribes and Pharisees.

Ask a volunteer to read Mark 2:13-17 aloud. Tell the students to use their handouts to note how the different individuals or groups responded to Jesus. Have them mark these as the text is read. *(1) The multitude was enamored of Jesus (v. 13); they were more curious than committed. (2) Levi became a disciple, leaving his tax collector's booth to follow Jesus (v. 14). (3) The publicans and sinners, apparently at Levi's invitation, also received Jesus' message and became followers (v. 15). (4) The scribes and Pharisees were critical.*

Discuss how the same attitudes are present today. Some people are enamored with Jesus as a celebrity. They like to talk about His teachings or His "revolutionary" behavior, but they are not disciples. Others, of course, are true disciples. They want to follow Jesus. Some of these come from what we may consider to be unlikely sources, but the gospel is for all. And there are some who are openly hostile to the Lord. Sum up with the commentary's description of the various levels of relationship to Jesus under the discussion of verse 14c.

Call attention back to the individuals or groups on the students' charts. Ask, "Why were these people coming to Jesus?" Contrast these purposes with Jesus' purpose. Discuss how Jesus' purpose, "to call . . . sinners to repentance," is seen in His interaction with each.

Into Life

Ask, "What is our purpose today?" Easily your learners might repeat Jesus' own purpose: to call sinners to repentance. Challenge them to defend that statement with evidence. Do our behavior and church programming support the claim? Are we deliberate about calling sinners to repentance?

Divide the class into four groups. Each group will have two assignments. First, group members will suggest potential church programs to reach people in the assigned category. Second, they are to suggest some things individuals can do to reach them.

The four categories, one for each group, correspond with the categories on the chart used earlier. Ask group one to suggest some ways to reach those who are merely curious about Jesus, like the multitude. Group two will suggest ways to minister to new believers, like Levi. Ask group three to suggest ways to reach those who are seeking, like the publicans and "sinners." Finally, ask group four to suggest methods to reach those who are hostile to the gospel, like the scribes and Pharisees.

Allow time for discussion; then call for brief reports. Have the class choose one of the group-effort suggestions and decide how to implement it. Ask each learner to adopt one of the personal methods suggested and implement it to reach out to someone he or she knows who needs the Lord. Close with a prayer that everyone in the class will adopt Jesus' purpose to reach out to those who need Him.

Let's Talk It Over

The questions on this page are designed to promote discussion of the lesson by the class and to encourage application of the lesson Scriptures. The answers provided are only discussion starters. Let your class talk it over from there.

1. How can the church become more of an inclusive community where all unbelievers find hope?

Through teaching and example, the church must work to become a "grace place" where people hear the concept of grace being taught and preached, and where they see it practiced in relationships. Those whose lives are filled with sin, despair, and confusion will then see the church as a place where they can feel loved and find answers for their lives.

Churches must train and organize their members to welcome, assist, and guide guests who attend a class, program, or worship assembly. Wise congregations also plan certain outreach events throughout the year to which the members can invite their friends, co-workers, or other unbelievers.

2. Levi asked his "sinner" friends to a banquet so Jesus could also influence them. How much contact should we as Christians maintain with unbelievers today? At what point do we make ourselves too vulnerable to dangerous influences?

This is a difficult balancing act. On the one hand, we can not be the salt and light of the world if we never make contact with unbelievers. Yet many have allowed themselves to be pulled into the devil's grasp by carelessly befriending the world (see James 4:4). The answer seems to lie in the perfect example of Jesus. He compassionately reached out to the sinners of His day while firmly opposing the sin in their lives.

Levi's example is helpful. He seemed so intent on following Jesus that his only motivation for "partying" with his sinful friends and former co-workers was to introduce them to Jesus, who had called him to eternal life. For our part, we must prayerfully approach such situations. We can allow other Christians to hold us accountable and help us analyze who is exerting the most influence: we or our unbelieving friends.

3. Why is hospitality such an effective method of reaching out to other people in the name of Jesus?

Hospitality demonstrates the kind of love and acceptance God has shown us. The recipients of our warm hospitality will see a reflection of God in us and thus will be much more ready to believe or accept something we tell them about God.

When we invite someone to eat in our home, we are indicating that we accept and trust him or her. Hospitality breaks down barriers, opens up conversation, and allows Christ to reach out through us. It is something any of us can offer as long as we do not let busyness, insecurity, or selfishness interfere.

Hospitality is one of the "one another" commandments of the New Testament (1 Peter 4:9). It is connected to many of the others: it shows love, helping us live in harmony; it can help us express forgiveness; it is an example of service; it is a great way to honor, encourage, or comfort someone; and it can even lead to mutual prayer and confession.

4. How can we as Jesus' disciples avoid the tendency of the Pharisees to focus only on "people as they are now"? What steps would help us show mercy toward others without condoning sinful actions or lifestyles?

The beginning point should always be a constant awareness of our own sin and God's gracious forgiveness. The apostle Paul never forgot how God had rescued him from his sincere but sinful ways (1 Timothy 1:12-16). He had such a deep appreciation for the grace of God that he seemed to be able to speak "the truth in love" effectively (Ephesians 4:15).

Other suggestions: Try to understand a person's particular situation, and why they may live as they live. Focus on what God's grace and power can make a person, rather than what they presently are like. Try to look and listen closely enough to see the heart instead of just the outside. Set a positive example personally. Prayer, of course, always comes first.

5. What do we learn about how God views people from the way that Jesus reacted to the people in this lesson? How can we apply this knowledge?

We quickly notice that Jesus was able to discern the thoughts and intents of people's hearts beyond what was obvious on the surface. Jesus, of course, had a miraculous ability to be able to do so. Even so, our lesson clearly calls us to imitate the love, grace, and acceptance shown by God, instead of the critical, self-righteous attitude of the Pharisees.

Jesus Sends Out the Twelve

DEVOTIONAL READING: Luke 9:1-6.

BACKGROUND SCRIPTURE: Mark 3:13-19; 6:6b-13.

PRINTED TEXT: Mark 3:13-19; 6:6b-13.

Mark 3:13-19

13 And he goeth up into a mountain, and calleth unto him whom he would: and they came unto him.

14 And he ordained twelve, that they should be with him, and that he might send them forth to preach,

15 And to have power to heal sicknesses, and to cast out devils:

16 And Simon he surnamed Peter;

17 And James the son of Zebedee, and John the brother of James; and he surnamed them Boanerges, which is, The sons of thunder:

18 And Andrew, and Philip, and Bartholomew, and Matthew, and Thomas, and James the son of Alpheus, and Thaddeus, and Simon the Canaanite,

19 And Judas Iscariot, which also betrayed him. And they went into a house.

Mark 6:6b-13

6b And he went round about the villages, teaching.

7 And he called unto him the twelve, and began to send them forth by two and two; and gave them power over unclean spirits;

8 And commanded them that they should take nothing for their journey, save a staff only; no scrip, no bread, no money in their purse:

9 But be shod with sandals; and not put on two coats.

10 And he said unto them, In what place soever ye enter into a house, there abide till ye depart from that place.

11 And whosoever shall not receive you, nor hear you, when ye depart thence, shake off the dust under your feet for a testimony against them. Verily I say unto you, It shall be more tolerable for Sodom and Gomorrah in the day of judgment, than for that city.

12 And they went out, and preached that men should repent.

13 And they cast out many devils, and anointed with oil many that were sick, and healed them.

GOLDEN TEXT: [Jesus] ordained twelve, that they should be with him, and that he might send them forth to preach.—Mark 3:14.

Called to Be God's People
Unit 2: Jesus Calls His Followers
(Lessons 5-9)

Lesson Aims

After participating in this lesson, each student will be able to:

1. Tell how Jesus called and commissioned the twelve apostles.

2. Compare and contrast the ministry of the Twelve with the ministry of today's church.

3. Identify his or her own ministry role in the church.

Lesson Outline

INTRODUCTION
    A. Simultaneous Revivals
    B. Lesson Background
  I. THE TWELVE—THEIR CALL (Mark 3:13-19)
    A. Place of the Call (v. 13)
       Unquestioning Response
    B. Purpose of the Call (vv. 14, 15)
    C. People of the Call (vv. 16-19)
 II. THE TWELVE—THEIR MISSION (Mark 6:6b-11)
    A. Example Set (v. 6b)
    B. Apostles Sent (v. 7)
    C. Equipment Limited (vv. 8, 9)
    D. Strategy Outlined (vv. 10, 11)
       Making It Work
III. THE TWELVE—THEIR TRIUMPHS (Mark 6:12, 13)
    A. Their Message (v. 12)
    B. Their Success (v. 13)
CONCLUSION
    A. Christ's Messengers
    B. Prayer
    C. Thought to Remember

Introduction

A. Simultaneous Revivals

When revivals were in vogue some years ago, it was not uncommon for churches in a given area to participate in simultaneous meetings. Usually it was the preachers who led out in the endeavor, choosing an acceptable time and, perhaps, even suggesting a theme. The meetings stirred a lot of interest and often resulted in the conversion of many of the lost.

I remember most pleasantly working in a simultaneous campaign held in the entire country of Australia. Reggie Thomas, an international evangelist, along with his team of workers had contacted many churches in Australia and secured their cooperation. My assignment was to go to a participating church and preach and evangelize for a week. My wife and I have never forgotten the experience, nor have the other preachers who shared in the simultaneous campaign.

Of course, the best part of the entire venture was that lost souls were won to the Lord. It would be too much to claim that the entire country was stirred, but I'm certain that numerous areas were. Many Australians will never be the same again because of those meetings.

Simultaneous undertakings didn't originate with contemporary preachers. Jesus sent out the Twelve on such a campaign, as we will see in today's lesson. The impact of their labors must have been tremendous throughout all of Galilee. As was true of my experience in Australia, I'm sure the apostles never forgot those happy days when two by two they went about preaching that people should repent.

B. Lesson Background

According to Luke, the calling of the twelve apostles was followed (apparently on the same day) by the teaching of the lesson we've come to call the Sermon on the Mount. This has led one writer to refer to it as "The Ordination Address to the Twelve." These events were of tremendous importance to the ministry of Jesus. As part of His preparation before choosing the Twelve, He "went out into a mountain to pray, and continued all night in prayer to God" (Luke 6:12).

It was probably sometime in A.D. 28 when Jesus "ordained" the twelve apostles. Several months would pass before the Master would send forth those Twelve on their mission.

I. The Twelve—Their Call
(Mark 3:13-19)
A. Place of the Call (v. 13)

13. And he goeth up into a mountain, and calleth unto him whom he would: and they came unto him.

As stated in the Lesson Background, the calling of the Twelve is followed by the teaching of the Sermon on the Mount. Since both events occur on *a mountain,* the logical assumption is that the two locations are actually one and the same.

But exactly which mountain this is has been a matter of some controversy. The Sea of Galilee has numerous ridges that rise up from its shores, several of which would be suitable for the two events. From the days of the Crusades, Karn Hattin (the Horns of Hattin) has been suggested by many; this location is four or five miles southwest of Tiberias, on the road to Nazareth. Perhaps the best solution is to understand *into a mountain* as a general reference to "hill country."

No explanation is given as to how Jesus calls *unto him whom he would.* Apparently some signal is given, or a runner sent, to inform certain of His disciples that He wishes them to join Him. Pleased no doubt by the invitation, they are more than happy to obey.

Jesus continues to call people unto Himself today. Although the call is not the same as that heard by these early disciples, it is an equally thrilling call to which the spiritually alert gladly respond. [See question #1, page 176.]

UNQUESTIONING RESPONSE

There was a mission recruiter who received a request from a young woman wanting to be considered for a mission assignment. The recruiter wrote back, "Your interview is scheduled for 4:00 A.M. in the station boiler room."

She was troubled, but at 4:00 A.M. on the appointed day she appeared. The recruiter was late. When he came in, he sat across from her and said, "State your name." She did, but he didn't even write it down. Instead he promptly got up and left, saying merely, "We'll be in touch."

Surely this had to be a joke. But two days later the young woman was called to meet with the board. When the recruiter was asked if he would recommend her, he replied, "Absolutely. Her credentials are good, but most importantly, she followed directions, as unusual as they were. She did not question or rant at the bizarre request. I believe she will be a great servant."

Often the disciples must have had the natural inclination to wonder "why?" when they received their calls. In service to God there always is a "why?" but we should not expect an immediate answer. Even so, that should not hinder the call to duty. What God commands, first and foremost, is to be followed. —J. D. R.

B. Purpose of the Call (vv. 14, 15)

14, 15. And he ordained twelve, that they should be with him, and that he might send them forth to preach, and to have power to heal sicknesses, and to cast out devils.

Mark expresses a double purpose for the ordination of these *twelve.* First, they are to *be with him.* This may reveal to us a "change of allegiance" in their hearts (see Mark 10:28).

But to *be with him* doesn't mean that these twelve will just "hang out" with Jesus. He calls them so that they will be available to be sent *forth* as His official emissaries *to preach, and to have power to heal sicknesses, and to cast out devils.*

In formally setting these men apart, Jesus has yet a third purpose in mind for them, one not

---

HOW TO SAY IT

ACHAIA. Uh-*kay*-uh.
ALPHEUS. Al-*fee*-us.
BARNABAS. *Bar*-nuh-bus.
BAR-THOLAMI. Bar *Thal*-uh-me.
BARTHOLOMEW. Bar-*thahl*-uh-mew.
CEPHAS. *See*-fus.
DIDYMUS. *Did*-uh-mus.
EPHESUS. *Ef*-uh-sus.
EUSEBIUS. You-*see*-be-us.
GALILEE. *Gal*-uh-lee.
GENTILES. *Jen*-tiles.
GOMORRAH. Guh-*more*-uh.
HEROD AGRIPPA. *Hair*-ud Uh-*grip*-puh.
JUDAS ISCARIOT. *Joo*-dus Iss-*care*-e-ut.
KERIOTH. *Kee*-rih-oath.
LEBBEUS. Leh-*bee*-us.
LEVI. *Lee*-vye.
NATHANAEL. Nuh-*than*-yull (*th* as in *thin*).
NAZARETH. *Naz*-uh-reth.
PISIDIAN ANTIOCH. Puh-*sid*-ee-un *An*-tee-ock.
SODOM. *Sod*-um.
SYNAGOGUE. *sin*-uh-gog.
THADDEUS. Tha-*dee*-us.
TIBERIAS. Tie-*beer*-ee-us.
ZELOTES. Zeh-*low*-teez.

---

mentioned by Mark: they are to become the foundation stones upon which Jesus' church is to be built (see Ephesians 2:20). This concept is far more extensive than the other two, and certainly has an importance beyond what any of the Twelve can comprehend at the time.

C. People of the Call (vv. 16-19)

16, 17. And Simon he surnamed Peter; And James the son of Zebedee, and John the brother of James; and he surnamed them Boanerges, which is, The sons of thunder.

Luke 6:13, a parallel account of this event, says that Jesus called the twelve men "apostles." That word refers to what we would think of as ambassadors or envoys. It does not refer to an ordinary messenger, but to a fully authorized and commissioned representative of the sender.

Jesus renames *Simon* to be *Peter* (Greek meaning "rock"), or, as John 1:42 has it, "Cephas" (Aramaic word for "rock"). Peter is the most prominent of the Twelve and one of the great leaders of the early church. He will go on to author the two epistles in the New Testament that bear his name.

James, John, and Peter make up Jesus' inner-circle of disciples (cf. Mark 5:37; 9:2). Like Peter, James and John are fishermen. There are four or five different men bearing the name of James in the New Testament, so we should take care not to get them confused. This particular James will be martyred by Herod Agrippa I in about A.D. 44 (see Acts 12:2).

John, who authors five books of the New Testament, will live to a ripe old age. Tradition says that he spent much of his "golden years" in the city of Ephesus.

We are not told why Jesus gives to James and John the nickname *Boanerges*, meaning *sons of thunder*. The most popular view is that it results from Jesus' recognition of their aggressive personalities as we see in Mark 10:35-37 and Luke 9:54. At no other time in the New Testament is this name used of these two.

18, 19. And Andrew, and Philip, and Bartholomew, and Matthew, and Thomas, and James the son of Alpheus, and Thaddeus, and Simon the Canaanite, and Judas Iscariot, which also betrayed him: and they went into an house.

Andrew, whose name means "manly," is Peter's brother (John 1:40; 6:8). The only reference to Andrew outside the Gospels (as is true of other apostles) is in Acts 1:13. Tradition holds that he was martyred in Achaia (part of Greece) on an X-shaped cross, now called an Andrew's cross.

Andrew is associated on two occasions in the Gospels with *Philip*, a fellow townsman. These two occasions are the feeding of the five thousand (John 6:5-9) and the Greeks' request to see Jesus (John 12:22).

Philip's name means "lover of horses." From the few references to him, he is believed to be a timid man, but not so timid that he won't witness concerning his convictions (see John 1:45). He is last mentioned in Acts 1:13. Tradition says he evangelized in Asia Minor. As a result, the historian Eusebius refers to him as "a great light of Asia."

The man called *Bartholomew* by Matthew, Mark, and Luke is frequently identified with the Nathanael of John 1:45. In favor of this view is the possibility that the word "Bartholomew" could be spelled "Bar-Tholami," meaning "son of Tholami"; this means that "Bar-Tholami" would actually be a surname. Thus the man's full name would be "Nathanael Bar-Tholami." Nothing is known about his life after his being mentioned in Acts 1:13. Even traditions concerning him are subject to question.

We discussed *Matthew* (Levi) in last week's lesson, so we need not repeat that information here.

John informs us that *Thomas* is also called "Didymus," a word meaning "twin" (John 11:16; 20:24; 21:2). If this means that he is a twin as we use that term, we know nothing about his sib-

ling. In the Gospel of John, Thomas is shown to play an important role in Jesus' ministry (see John 11:16; 14:1-6; 20:24-29; 21:1-8).

Unfortunately, Thomas is best remembered for his expression of doubt about Jesus' resurrection. The incident in question has earned him and his kind the title, "Doubting Thomas." But why not call him, "Thomas, Man of Conviction"? After seeing the resurrected Jesus, Thomas certainly became that. Thomas also showed great conviction when he challenged the rest of the disciples to accompany Jesus to death (again, John 11:16). A tradition holds that Thomas labored as far east as India.

Almost nothing is known of *James the son of Alpheus, and Thaddeus, and Simon the Canaanite*. The first of these three may also be "James the less" of Mark 15:40. The man whom Mark calls "Thaddeus" and Matthew 10:3 calls "Lebbeus" must be the "Judas" who is a relative of James in Luke 6:16 and Acts 1:13. Luke 6:15 and Acts 1:13 also clarify the meaning of Simon's surname as "Zelotes" (or Zealot). It is a common practice for a man to have more than a single designation in this era. [See question #2, page 176.]

The man whose name occupies the last position in the list is the traitor, *Judas Iscariot*. He is the son of a certain man named Simon (see John 6:71; 13:2, 26). The word "Iscariot" suggests that the men were from Kerioth, a town in Judah (Joshua 15:25). Judas seems to be highly regarded by the other apostles to the point of being made the treasurer of the group (John 12:6). None of the other apostles will suspect him of his forthcoming treachery.

Before moving on, we can pause to note that there are four listings of the apostles in the New Testament (see Matthew 10:2-4; Mark 3:16-19; Luke 6:13-16; Acts 1:13). In those lists Peter always appears first, Philip is always fifth, and James the son of Alpheus is always ninth. Furthermore, the first four names of the Twelve always remain the first four (although the order of the names changes). The same is true of the second and third groups of four. It's possible that Peter, Philip, and James the son of Alpheus are something like "captains," each in charge of the three others in his group, thus helping expedite various tasks.

II. The Twelve—Their Mission (Mark 6:6b-11)

A. Example Set (v. 6b)

6b. And he went round about the villages, teaching.

Time has now moved forward several months. Jesus has been in his old hometown, Nazareth, where He taught in the synagogue on a Sabbath day. Although many of the people had been astonished at His teaching, they were nevertheless "offended at him" (Mark 6:3). No reason for the offense is stated, but it probably has to do with the people's disbelief that a hometown boy could amount to much.

When Jesus left Nazareth, *he went round about the villages, teaching.* He thus sets an example for His apostles, who are soon to be sent on a mission of their own.

B. Apostles Sent (v. 7)

7. And he called unto him the twelve, and began to send them forth by two and two; and gave them power over unclean spirits.

Since the time that Jesus ordained *the twelve* apostles, He has taught them by word and example of the kind of ministry they are to perform. Now He sends them out to be extensions of His own work. As stated in verses 4, 5 above, when He calls them He specifies three things they are to do. One of these is to cast out devils, or to have *power over unclean spirits.* The fuller account in Matthew 10:8 adds two other things: they are to cleanse lepers and raise the dead.

There are definite advantages to going *forth by two and two.* These include a pooling of wisdom, fellowship, and encouragement. It also results in a more-powerful testimony. Modern-day church calling programs also follow this procedure, with significant results.

C. Equipment Limited (vv. 8, 9)

8, 9. And commanded them that they should take nothing for their journey, save a staff only; no scrip, no bread, no money in their purse: but be shod with sandals; and not put on two coats.

Only essential items are to be taken on the *journey.* No reason is given for the limitations, but perhaps Jesus doesn't want His emissaries to appear affluent. Such an appearance can give the wrong impression of discipleship. No one, then or now, should be induced to become a follower of Jesus for the material things that he or she can get out of following Him. [See question #3, page 176.]

Interestingly, Jesus specifies in this passage that they are to take *a staff* while Matthew 10:10 and Luke 9:3 prohibit them from taking such an item. D. A. Carson suggests that, "It may be that Mark's account clarifies what the disciples are permitted to bring, whereas Matthew's assumes that the disciples already have certain things . . . and forbids them from 'procuring' anything more."

Jesus also places restrictions on taking *scrip* (a kind of knapsack; see 1 Samuel 17:40), *bread,*

Visual for lesson 7

Use today's visual to launch a discussion of how the Lord calls people to His service today.

and *money in their purse.* Their needs apparently are to be met by those among whom they labor (cf. 1 Corinthians 9:14; 1 Timothy 5:17, 18).

Further, they are to wear *sandals* (often made of hard leather, better for rough wear than shoes), but not *two coats.* The picture is that of taking the barest of necessities and traveling light. These limitations, however, are temporary (see Luke 22:35, 36).

D. Strategy Outlined (vv. 10, 11)

10. And he said unto them, In what place soever ye enter into a house, there abide till ye depart from that place.

This verse makes clear that the disciples are not to be *"house* jumpers," always moving about in the hope of getting better accommodations (see also Matthew 10:11 and Luke 9:4). Such action could turn the townspeople against them and make void their testimony.

11. And whosoever shall not receive you, nor hear you, when ye depart thence, shake off the dust under your feet for a testimony against them. Verily I say unto you, It shall be more tolerable for Sodom and Gomorrah in the day of judgment, than for that city.

The Jews believe that even *the dust* of Gentiles is impure and is to be shaken *off* when leaving Gentile territory. By Jesus' instruction, those who reject His messengers are to be treated like profane, pagan Gentiles. Paul and Barnabas apply this teaching toward the people of Pisidian Antioch in Acts 13:51.

Jesus' saying about *Sodom and Gomorrah* does not occur in the most ancient manuscripts of this particular text. However, this warning does appear in Matthew 10:15, so the idea expressed here is indeed part of Jesus' thought.

MAKING IT WORK

Jesus' allowance for His disciples' turning their backs on others were those cases where people don't "receive you" or "hear you." That can be determined only by first trying, instead of (as Jonah) just believing that "this won't do any good."

Frankly, we may wish that the Lord would give a bit more latitude here, because there are some people in our lives with whom cooperation seems next to impossible. We all have our MIPs—our "Most Irritating Personalities." For you it might be the perfectionist or the inflexible person with whom you work. (One lady said, "When I wanted to marry 'Mr. Right,' I didn't know his first name would be 'Always'!") Maybe for others it is the phony, or the obnoxious braggart, or the gushy-touchy-feely-huggy person. But we seldom see ourselves as irritants to others, do we?

If we are going to be effective "point people" for Christ, we must overcome our tendency to avoid the MIPs. This will mean moving beyond mere tolerance. The second greatest commandment, "Thou shalt love thy neighbor as thyself" (Mark 12:31), requires much more than superficial, outward civility.   —J. D. R.

III. The Twelve—Their Triumphs (Mark 6:12, 13)

A. Their Message (v. 12)

12. And they went out, and preached that men should repent.

John the Baptist's message had been one of repentance (Mark 1:4). When Jesus began preaching, He echoed the same theme (Mark 1:15). It is logical, then, that the apostles should preach a message of repentance.

This is a message that never becomes irrelevant. Certainly our times call for it. We need to repent of our practice of abortion, our immoral movies and TV programs, our drunkenness and drug use, our immodest dress that we flaunt before people and God, our indifference to suffering, our disregard of law, and our greed that grows more excessive with each passing year.

Our preachers today, like the apostles of old, need to preach that people *should repent.* When was the last time that you heard such a message from your church's pulpit? [See question #4, page 176.]

B. Their Success (v. 13)

13. And they cast out many devils, and anointed with oil many that were sick, and healed them.

The results of the apostles' efforts are outstanding! *Many devils* are exorcised, and many *sick* are made well. Nothing is said concerning how many repent, but undoubtedly we are correct in assuming that many hearts are softened while many others are hardened. The message of Jesus tends to have those two effects on people! Those who refuse to repent face a dismal future (Revelation 16:8-11).

The anointing *with oil* may have been for medicinal reasons, added to the miraculous healings performed by the apostles. God desires that we use the natural means at our disposal in addition to relying on God's ability to heal as the result of prayer (cf. James 5:14).

Conclusion

A. Christ's Messengers

An old poem says, "Christ has no hands but our hands to do His work today; He has no feet but our feet to lead men in His way." The poem is true. There is no other way for the work of Christ to be done except through people who respond when they hear His call to service. That is God's plan on how He chooses to accomplish the work of His kingdom.

Our service will certainly be different in significant ways from that of the Twelve. But God still expects us to respond. [See question #5, page 176.]

B. Prayer

Dear God and Father, we know there are still many sick and sinful people in this world. Help us to bind up the wounds of the physically ill and preach to the lost a message of repentance unto salvation. In Jesus' name, amen.

C. Thought to Remember

Jesus still calls people to be with Him and to go forth.

Home Daily Bible Readings

Monday, Jan. 10—Jesus Appoints the Twelve (Mark 3:13-19a)

Tuesday, Jan. 11—Jesus Sends the Twelve with Instructions (Mark 6:6b-13)

Wednesday, Jan. 12—The Twelve Have a Mission (Matthew 10:5-15)

Thursday, Jan. 13—The Twelve Have Power and Authority (Luke 9:1-6)

Friday, Jan. 14—Have the Mind of Christ (Philippians 2:1-11)

Saturday, Jan. 15—Press on Toward the Goal (Philippians 3:12–4:1)

Sunday, Jan. 16—Rejoice in the Lord Always (Philippians 4:4-9)

Learning by Doing

This page contains an alternative lesson plan emphasizing learning activities.
Classes desiring such student involvement will find these suggestions helpful.

Learning Goals

After participating in this lesson, each student will be able to:

1. Tell how Jesus called and commissioned the twelve apostles.

2. Compare and contrast the ministry of the Twelve with the ministry of today's church.

3. Identify his or her own ministry role in the church.

Into the Lesson

Prepare a handout that has the heading "Help Wanted." Have students work individually or in small groups to make a list of personal qualities they would look for if they were putting together a team to evangelize your community or a mission field where your church supports a missionary. After few minutes, ask for reports of ideas.

Make a list of the ideas as they are presented. Some ideas may include a history of evangelistic zeal and efforts, compatible personalities, a certain level of education, and a personal reputation for being patient and compassionate.

After a bit of discussion ask, "From what you know of the twelve apostles—before the resurrection—how many of them do you think you would want on your team?" You probably will note that these characteristics are not typical of the apostles. Jesus took an unlikely group of men and molded them into a dynamic force that "turned the world upside down."

Into the Word

Have a volunteer read aloud Mark 3:13-19. Provide some research resources such as Bible encyclopedias, Bible dictionaries, etc., that provide information about the apostles. Divide the class into three or four groups and ask each group to research three or four apostles. You may wish to use the groupings suggested in the lesson commentary.

Have each group give as much detail about their assigned disciples as possible: occupation before joining Jesus' ministry, family connections, etc. Ask them also to suggest what may have made it difficult for each to follow Jesus: What did they have to leave? How hard was it to partner with some of the other disciples? etc. Allow a few minutes for research; then give a reporter from each group two or three minutes to summarize the group's findings.

Now ask another good reader to read Mark 6:6b-13 aloud. Have your learners return to their groups and consider the same disciples they researched earlier. Have them answer the following questions:

1. If you were pairing the disciples, whom would you have selected for each of the disciples you researched earlier? Why?

2. Whom do you think each disciple would least want paired with him? Why?

3. What do you think the disciples you researched thought about the restrictions Jesus put on them for the journey? Why? What could they have learned from the experience?

Once again, allow a few minutes for research and also for each group to report. Add to the reports the information from the verse-by-verse commentary regarding what Jesus intended in giving these instructions. Ask how each disciple may have responded.

Into Life

Note that Jesus called the Twelve "that they should be with him, and that he might send them forth" to spread the good news and to minister to physical needs. Ask, "What is the relationship between being with Jesus and going forth to serve?" Discuss how to keep the two roles in balance in your church and in individual lives. Many believers today want to be with Jesus—in worship, in Bible studies, in fellowship with other believers, etc.—but they do not share the gospel or minister to other needs. How can we help such believers move to full obedience?

Ask, "What if you had been one of the Twelve? Which apostle would you have wanted to pair up with for this mission? Why? Which would you have least wanted to pair with? Why?" Use the students' answers to launch a discussion about what we today need to learn about working together to serve the Lord. How would a mission tour like that of the disciples be received today? What principles—if not the actual practice—of what Jesus told the disciples are most important for evangelism today? Why? Of these, in which does our church excel? Where do we need some improvement?

Then ask each learner to think of his or her own role in this ministry. What does each add to the church's effort to win the lost? In the closing time of prayer, ask God to expand their outreach.

Let's Talk It Over

The questions on this page are designed to promote discussion of the lesson by the class and to encourage application of the lesson Scriptures. The answers provided are only discussion starters. Let your class talk it over from there.

1. How much training and teaching are necessary before a person can serve in Christ's church effectively?

Very little training is needed, if he or she is not given too much responsibility too early. It is important to involve every new disciple in some way. As they serve, they can then be further trained by more mature believers and guided into larger responsibilities that are suited to their personal gifts and abilities.

We should guide new believers in much the same way we give our children increasing levels of responsibility within the home. That, of course, includes regular encouragement and offers of assistance, guidance, and resources. Most of all, we must educate the entire congregation to see that every Christian serves in some type of ministry, and that every ministry is vitally important to the church's overall ministry. (See Ephesians 4:11-13; 1 Peter 4:10, 11).

2. What can we learn about today's church from the diversity seen in Jesus' first disciples?

Matthew had worked for the Roman government, while Simon the Zealot probably believed in the armed overthrow of those occupiers. What difference! We are each uniquely created by God. God never intended for all His disciples to have the same appearance, abilities, interests, roles, or even political viewpoints.

Our differences help strengthen the body of Christ (see 1 Corinthians 12). Jesus knew that His church needed Peters who are bold, forceful, and not afraid of a challenge. Andrews are needed to minister humbly and quietly among people, without regard to who gets credit. We need people like Thomas who will ask questions and refuse to take everything for granted. God can powerfully use people like Simon the Zealot, who will get involved and change society with zeal.

The church must never underestimate the importance of unassuming disciples like Thaddeus and James, who were known simply as the "son of" someone. Most of all, God needs every disciple to serve in his or her uniquely gifted way, while still growing in each area of Christian life.

3. How can we make sure to remember that we are working for God and others, and not for personal gain?

The concept of servanthood implies selflessness. Jesus was the ultimate example of this, as He explained to His squabbling disciples (Matthew 20:26-28). We must not forget that we are continuing Jesus' mission to bring people back to God.

We can also remember the pattern set by Jesus when He sent out the groups of disciples with only essential items for the journey. By developing a simpler lifestyle, the message that we share about Jesus is not as likely to be obstructed or hindered by material things. In the process we will gain credibility and show that we have a healthy perspective on the difference between things that are temporary and things that are eternal.

4. Why is the message of repentance that was preached by the apostles so important, and why is it so often neglected today?

Repentance is one of the prominent teachings in the Bible. It was a central aspect of the preaching of the Old Testament prophets. It was the heart of John the Baptist's ministry, vital in Jesus' preaching (Mark 1:15; Luke 13:1-5), and is a central part of becoming a Christian (Acts 2:38; 3:19).

Unfortunately, the concept of repentance has grown quite unpopular in modern culture that promotes an extreme view of "tolerance." Such a view suggests it is improper or even cruel ever to call into question another person's beliefs or lifestyle. Only when repentance maintains its vital role in Christian life and teaching will the life-changing power of the gospel be seen. Ultimately, failure to repent means eternal destruction.

5. What factors were involved in Jesus' process of preparing some of His disciples to become the "apostles" who later established His church? Why is this important today?

We could state Jesus' process as seeking, exposure, challenge, and learning by doing. Jesus *sought* those willing to assist Him in His ministry. Next, He *exposed* them to the type of work they would do. This gave the apostles the opportunity to see His goals and His methods as well as the joys and heartaches of such a ministry.

Eventually, Jesus issued a *challenge* in terms of a specific call to follow and serve Him. The apostles *learn by doing* as Jesus sends them out in teams of two to experience His mission on their own without Jesus helping or watching.

Jesus Calls for Total Commitment †

DEVOTIONAL READING: Matthew 16:24-28.

BACKGROUND SCRIPTURE: Mark 8:27-38.

PRINTED TEXT: Mark 8:27-38.

Mark 8:27-38

27 And Jesus went out, and his disciples, into the towns of Caesarea Philippi: and by the way he asked his disciples, saying unto them, Whom do men say that I am?

28 And they answered, John the Baptist: but some say, Elijah; and others, One of the prophets.

29 And he saith unto them, But whom say ye that I am? And Peter answereth and saith unto him, Thou art the Christ.

30 And he charged them that they should tell no man of him.

31 And he began to teach them, that the Son of man must suffer many things, and be rejected of the elders, and of the chief priests, and scribes, and be killed, and after three days rise again.

32 And he spake that saying openly. And Peter took him, and began to rebuke him.

33 But when he had turned about and looked on his disciples, he rebuked Peter, saying, Get thee behind me, Satan: for thou savorest not the things that be of God, but the things that be of men.

34 And when he had called the people unto him with his disciples also, he said unto them, Whosoever will come after me, let him deny himself, and take up his cross, and follow me.

35 For whosoever will save his life shall lose it; but whosoever shall lose his life for my sake and the gospel's, the same shall save it.

36 For what shall it profit a man, if he shall gain the whole world, and lose his own soul?

37 Or what shall a man give in exchange for his soul?

38 Whosoever therefore shall be ashamed of me and of my words, in this adulterous and sinful generation, of him also shall the Son of man be ashamed, when he cometh in the glory of his Father with the holy angels.

Jan 23

GOLDEN TEXT: [Jesus] said unto them, Whosoever will come after me, let him deny himself, and take up his cross, and follow me.
—Mark 8:34.

Called to Be God's People
Unit 2: Jesus Calls His Followers
(Lessons 5-9)

Lesson Aims

After participating in this lesson, each student will be able to:

1. Tell what Peter did and did not understand about who Jesus was and what He had come to do.

2. Express the level of commitment that Jesus expects from His followers.

3. Evaluate his or her own level of commitment in following Jesus, and state one specific means of deepening that commitment.

Lesson Outline

INTRODUCTION
  A. Commitment?
  B. Lesson Background
 I. TRUE IDENTITY (Mark 8:27-30)
  A. Jesus' Question (v. 27)
  B. Various Opinions (v. 28)
  C. Correct Understanding (v. 29)
  D. Jesus' Prohibition (v. 30)
 II. COMING DEATH (Mark 8:31-33)
  A. Revelation by Jesus (v. 31)
  B. Rebuke by Peter (v. 32)
  C. Response by Jesus (v. 33)
III. TRUE DISCIPLESHIP (Mark 8:34-38)
  A. Its Requirements (vv. 34, 35)
    Accepting the Pain
  B. Its Wisdom (vv. 36, 37)
  C. Its Alternative (v. 38)
    The Wimp Factor
CONCLUSION
  A. Ordinary Folks
  B. Prayer
  C. Thought to Remember

Introduction

A. Commitment?

Imagine crossing paths with an old friend whom you haven't seen for a half-dozen years. After the usual greetings that include a handshake and a pat on the back, you hold your friend at arm's length and evaluate her. She doesn't appear to have aged much, and you tell her so. She looks to be in great shape and you compliment that. Similar remarks are returned about you and your appearance.

Then you notice that she has about her neck a gold chain to which something that looks like a miniature chair is attached. She sees that you notice, so she volunteers an explanation.

"It's not just an ordinary chair," she says, "but a replica of an electric chair—you know, one used to electrocute people."

While you stand there startled and speechless, she continues. "It's a miniature of the electric chair in which [and she cites the name of a notorious revolutionary] was put to death."

Your astonishment is magnified, but somehow you manage to stammer, "You must really be committed to that man and his philosophies."

Your friend laughs dismissively. "Not really," she says. "I don't even know a whole lot about what he stood for. I just wear the chair because I think it's pretty. Don't you like it?"

After you've said your good-byes, you shake your head in disbelief and mutter under your breath, "She's weird; she's still weird."

The application is pretty obvious. There are many people who wear a cross, the emblem of another revolutionary—a peace-loving, sinless One who proved Himself to be the Son of God. Unfortunately, many of these folks know little about the One the cross represents. And some of those who do know show little commitment to Him. Let it be understood that Jesus never asked anyone to *wear* a cross, but He did insist that those who truly follow Him must *bear* one. That's what today's lesson is about.

B. Lesson Background

Our previous lesson concluded with the successful ministry campaign of the apostles. That endeavor apparently began as the third year of Jesus' ministry—His "year of opposition"—got under way.

Between last week's lesson and today's, one of Jesus' miracles was to feed the five thousand (Mark 6:30-44). The people were of a mind to "take [Jesus] by force, to make him a king" (John 6:15) as a result of that great miracle. When Jesus refused to accept such an earthly crown, His Galilean campaign began to collapse (John 6:66).

Jesus was on the move over the next several months. He went westward to Phoenicia (Mark 7:24-30), and then to the southeast through Galilee to the eastern side of the Sea of Galilee and into the Decapolis. Jesus healed many people in that place (Matthew 15:30), including a deaf man with a speech impediment (Mark 7:31-37). Next, Jesus miraculously fed a multitude of four thousand men, in addition to women and children (Mark 8:1-8).

Then Jesus and His disciples crossed the lake to Dalmanutha, where they were challenged by some Pharisees (Mark 8:10-12). Following this encounter, Jesus returned to the other side of the lake (8:13).

Jesus restored sight to a blind man upon arrival at Bethsaida Julias (8:22-26). From that place Jesus and His apostles traveled approximately twenty-five miles northward into the vicinity of Caesarea Philippi. This is where today's lesson commences.

I. True Identity
(Mark 8:27-30)

A. Jesus' Question (v. 27)

27. And Jesus went out, and his disciples, into the towns of Caesarea Philippi: and by the way he asked his disciples, saying unto them, Whom do men say that I am?

The city of *Caesarea Philippi* (now called Banias) is located about thirty miles east of the seaport of Tyre and some fifty miles southwest of Damascus. While in this region, Jesus and His disciples are at the far northern end of what is considered Israelite territory.

The city of Caesarea Philippi must not be confused with the Caesarea that is on the seacoast (e.g., Acts 10). It is while Jesus and His disciples are near (not in) Caesarea Philippi that Jesus inquires as to what people *say* concerning His identity.

Jesus' question is worded in a slightly different form in each of the three records. Luke 9:18 has it, "Whom say the people that I am?" Matthew 16:13 gives the fullest form, "Whom do men say that I, the Son of man, am?" The existence of these three forms may indicate that Jesus intentionally words His question in more than one way, a device often used by teachers to seek clarity. Each Gospel writer chooses the best way to present the question to a specific audience.

B. Various Opinions (v. 28)

28. And they answered, John the Baptist: but some say, Elijah; and others, One of the prophets.

Some people, influenced no doubt by Herod Antipas (Herod the Tetrarch), confuse Jesus with *John the Baptist*, whom they think has been raised from the dead (Matthew 14:1, 2). The great Gospels professor R. C. Foster suggested that Herod made this false identification because he suffered from a guilty conscience for having beheaded John.

Others identify Jesus with the prophet *Elijah*, whose coming had been predicted in Malachi 4:5, 6. We, of course, know that it was John the Baptist, not Jesus, who fulfilled Malachi's prediction (see Matthew 17:10-13.)

After mentioning John the Baptist and Elijah, Matthew adds the name of Jeremiah before concluding with the generalization *one of the prophets*, as Mark does. People are letting their speculations run wild!

The disciples mention no rumor that Jesus could be the promised Messiah. Even so, there seems to be some thinking in that direction, according to Matthew 9:27; 15:22; and John 4:29. We should note that Jesus doesn't first inquire of His disciples what they think of Him. Perhaps His motive is to have a backdrop of rumors and then paint upon it the truth. Against such a background, truth always shines more gloriously.

C. Correct Understanding (v. 29)

29. And he saith unto them, But whom say ye that I am? And Peter answereth and saith unto him, Thou art the Christ.

After the apostles cite various rumors that are circulating about Jesus' identity—answers that Jesus requests for their sake, not His—the Master then inquires about their own understanding. Bold *Peter*, recognized leader of the Twelve, responds with *Thou art the Christ.* [See question #1, page 184.]

The word *Christ* comes from a Greek word that means "anointed one." The word *Messiah*, derived from a Hebrew word, means the same thing. Three classes of people received sacred anointing in the Old Testament: prophets (e.g., 1 Kings 19:16), priests (e.g., Leviticus 8:12, 30), and kings (e.g., 1 Samuel 10:1). The anointing of Jesus came from the Holy Spirit at the time of Jesus' baptism (Mark 1:9-11).

D. Jesus' Prohibition (v. 30)

30. And he charged them that they should tell no man of him.

Jesus' prohibition to the apostles is in keeping with similar restrictions given to those blessed by His healing power in Mark 1:43, 44; 5:43; and 7:36. The prohibition may have to do with the Twelve's understanding (or misunderstanding) of the nature of Jesus' messiahship. The Jews of the first century are expecting a political Messiah (cf. Acts 1:6). Great harm thus can follow from the apostles' public pronouncement that Jesus is the Christ.

Jesus' entire mission leads to the cross. No action or proclamation from the Twelve can be allowed to derail this plan. This problem has come up among the people at least once already, and Jesus had to fight it off (John 6:14, 15). But even though He commanded the people not to tell anyone, "the more he charged them so much the more a great deal they published it" (Mark 7:36).

How to Say It

BETHSAIDA JULIAS. Beth-*say*-uh-duh *Joo*-lee-ahs.

CAESAREA PHILIPPI. Sess-uh-*ree*-uh Fih-*lip*-pie or *Fil*-ih-pie.

DALMANUTHA. Dal-muh-*new*-thuh.

DAMASCUS. Duh-*mass*-kus.

DECAPOLIS. Dee-*cap*-uh-lis.

ELIJAH. Ee-*lye*-juh.

GALILEAN. Gal-uh-*lee*-un.

GALILEE. *Gal*-uh-lee.

HEROD ANTIPAS. *Hair*-ud *An*-tih-pus.

ISAIAH. Eye-*zay*-uh.

JEREMIAH. Jair-uh-*my*-uh.

LEVITICUS. Leh-*vit*-ih-kus.

MESSIAH. Meh-*sigh*-uh.

PHOENICIA. Fuh-*nish*-uh.

TETRARCH. *Teh*-trark or *Tee*-trark.

TYRE. Tire.

The apostles probably struggle to keep from saying to people, "Come, see the Christ!" How easy it would be for them to brag on their Teacher. Later they will gain the true concept of His messiahship. When that happens and the prohibition is lifted, they will proclaim joyfully, "Therefore let all the house of Israel know assuredly, that God hath made that same Jesus, whom ye have crucified, both Lord and Christ" (Acts 2:36).

II. Coming Death
(Mark 8:31-33)

A. Revelation by Jesus (v. 31)

31. And he began to teach them, that the Son of man must suffer many things, and be rejected of the elders, and of the chief priests, and scribes, and be killed, and after three days rise again.

Jesus already has hinted of His death in Mark 2:20. Now the prediction is much clearer. Other predictions that follow are found in Mark 9:9, 30-32; and 10:32-34.

It is not by accident that Jesus makes this prediction at the time of Peter's great confession. As stated above, Jesus is very likely concerned that the apostles may give the wrong impression of what is involved in His messiahship. So He warns them to keep this fact a secret. By explaining that He is going to *suffer many things . . . and be killed,* He is making an effort to help them understand that He is the One to suffer as predicted in Isaiah 53. At His first coming, Jesus is not some political or military leader who will oust the Romans and establish a world power.

After Jesus is raised from the dead, the apostles will remember this prediction. They will understand that Jesus had been aware of His approaching death. They will then comprehend His words, "I lay down my life, that I might take it again. No man taketh it from me, but I lay it down of myself. I have power to lay it down, and I have power to take it again. This commandment have I received of my Father" (John 10:17, 18).

B. Rebuke by Peter (v. 32)

32. And he spake that saying openly. And Peter took him, and began to rebuke him.

Jesus' open prediction is very forthright. He uses neither parable nor other figure of speech. Although Jesus is completely candid about His coming death and resurrection, the apostles struggle with both concepts right up to the point when Jesus' resurrection becomes an established fact. See Luke 18:31-34.

Peter certainly seems to grasp the first part of Jesus' statement concerning Jesus' death. But the promise of His resurrection—the most wonderful of all promises—Peter seems to miss totally. Unhappy that Jesus could even talk about dying, Peter speaks in order *to rebuke him.*

Matthew 16:22 states the content of Peter's rebuke: "Be it far from thee, Lord: this shall not be unto thee." As D. A. Carson sums it up, "Peter's strong will and warm heart linked to his ignorance produce a shocking bit of arrogance. He confesses that Jesus is the Messiah and then speaks in a way implying that he knows more of God's will than the Messiah himself." [See question #2, page 184.]

C. Response by Jesus (v. 33)

33. But when he had turned about and looked on his disciples, he rebuked Peter, saying, Get thee behind me, Satan: for thou savorest not the things that be of God, but the things that be of men.

Peter's shallow proposal recalls the devil's temptation of Jesus in the wilderness. There *Satan* proposed that Jesus should become a spectacular Messiah rather than a suffering servant (Matthew 4:1-11). At that time Jesus had commanded Satan to depart. Now, addressing Peter with that same name—so that Peter would know whose agent he is—Jesus commands Peter, *Get thee behind me.*

Satan had offered Jesus a shortcut to kingship, and Peter is following the same path. Although Peter is not "literally" Satan, Peter's idea certainly is in line with that demonic source. In Matthew 16:23, Jesus further says to Peter that he is an offense, that is, a stumbling block. This is because Peter's idea will only serve to pull Jesus away from His true mission to accomplish the Father's will. After the resurrection the tables will be turned as Jesus and His crucifixion become a stumbling block to others (1 Corinthians 1:23).

III. True Discipleship
(Mark 8:34-38)

A. Its Requirements (vv. 34, 35)

34, 35. And when he had called the people unto him with his disciples also, he said unto them, Whosoever will come after me, let him deny himself, and take up his cross, and follow me. For whosoever will save his life shall lose it; but whosoever shall lose his life for my sake and the gospel's, the same shall save it.

The crossbearing of which Jesus speaks is not merely the same as having a few bad breaks or enduring the normal hardships of life. Rather, it is the enduring by a Christian of whatever afflictions come upon him or her in laboring for the Master.

The crossbearing of which Jesus speaks involves a denial of self (Romans 14:7-9; 15:2, 3). [See question #3, page 184.] A Christian certainly should not seek after trouble or delight in opposition. [See question #4, page 184.] But when these things come, he or she must accept them in the spirit of Him who bore His cross for all.

Notice that this statement isn't made just to the Twelve, who through their future afflictions will come to understand the high cost of discipleship. It is also made to *the people* (the multitude), some of whom may be considering becoming Jesus' disciples. Better for would-be disciples—both then and now—to be shown the whole picture. They must be made aware of what is entailed in following Jesus before they make a commitment to follow Him. (See Luke 14:25-33.) [See question #5, page 184.]

ACCEPTING THE PAIN

There are many stories and legends that surround Patrick, the great missionary to Ireland who lived about A.D. 389–461. One of the stories that comes from his ministry concerns a time when he was baptizing converts in a river.

Patrick, it seems, had waded out into waist-deep water and had called for the new believers to come to him, one by one, to be baptized. He was holding a staff, called a crosier, in his hands as the people made their way into the water. One who came forth to be baptized was a certain mountain chieftain. While lowering the chief down under the water, Patrick also pressed his staff down into the river bottom.

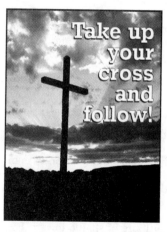

Visual for lesson 8

On the cross Jesus gave His life—100%. Discuss how modern disciples give 100%. Or do they?

People on the riverbank noticed that the chief was limping as he came out of the water. Someone explained to Patrick that he must have bruised the foot of the chief in pressing the wooden staff into the riverbed. Patrick went to the chief at once and asked, "Why didn't you cry out when I struck your foot?" Surprised, the chief answered, "I remembered you telling us about the nails on the cross and I thought my pain was part of my baptism."

How do you handle the pain that Christianity brings?
—J. D. R.

B. Its Wisdom (vv. 36, 37)

36, 37. For what shall it profit a man, if he shall gain the whole world, and lose his own soul? Or what shall a man give in exchange for his soul?

Here Jesus employs an illustration from the world of commerce. Profit and loss are the concern of all people who engage in buying, selling, and investing. In the business world, it doesn't make sense to gain a thousand dollars today if that gain will result in a million-dollar loss tomorrow. How much more foolish it is to trade anything, even *the whole world*, for one's *own soul!*

Jesus believed in Hell and unashamedly taught about it. Jesus said that Hell is a place of "everlasting punishment" (Matthew 25:46), of "everlasting fire" (Matthew 18:8), a place of "eternal damnation" (Mark 3:29), and a place of "outer darkness" where there is "weeping and gnashing of teeth" (Matthew 8:12). "The wrath of God" will abide upon those who lose their souls in Hell (John 3:36).

Unfortunately, this fact does not square with modern ideas of "enlightenment" and "tolerance," where various viewpoints and "alternate life-styles" are not to be judged. This is obviously at odds with the clear teaching of Scripture that a judgment day is coming. On that day some will be given eternal life, while others will be sent away into everlasting punishment (again, Matthew 25:46).

C. Its Alternative (v. 38)

38. Whosoever therefore shall be ashamed of me and of my words, in this adulterous and sinful generation, of him also shall the Son of man be ashamed, when he cometh in the glory of his Father with the holy angels.

The alternative to true cross-bearing discipleship is an attitude of shame toward *the Son of man*. It is also an attitude of shame toward His *words*. Those who possess such an outlook while they live in this world will endure extreme humiliation when the Son of Man—Jesus Himself—returns to claim His own. On that day those disobedient, miserable souls will hear Jesus say, "I never knew you: depart from me, ye that work iniquity" (Matthew 7:23). [See question #6, page 184.]

THE WIMP FACTOR

Pepper Rodgers was the football coach of the UCLA Bruins from 1971 to 1973. Alumni and fans made his life miserable during a season when his Bruins got off to a horrible start. No one would hang out with him. "My dog was my only true friend," Rodgers said. "I told my wife that every man needs at least two good friends. She bought me another dog."

Pepper Rodgers could be rigid in the face of adversity, however. When his players were having difficulty adapting to the wishbone offense he had installed—and the school's alumni de-manded that he adopt another system—Rodgers didn't budge. The wishbone, he reasoned, "is like Christianity. If you believe in it only until something goes wrong, you didn't believe in it in the first place" (*Washington City Paper*, October 26, 2001). During his final year at UCLA, Rodgers's team had a record of nine wins and two losses, putting it ninth in the nationwide United Press International rankings.

A disturbing trend that we witness in Christianity is what we may label (although very untheologically) as "the wimp factor." Modern Christians have too little staying power. Their convictions and dedication last only as long as their circumstances remain ideal (see Matthew 13:5, 20, 21).

Satan must marvel at how often some Christians crumble when just a little heat is applied. Can our faith take some attacks, even "friendly fire," and still hold? Or is there too much "wimp" in our walk?　　　　　　　　　　—J. D. R.

Conclusion

A. Ordinary Folks

Various people from my past come to mind when I think of the word "commitment." Having been a missionary, I naturally focus on those who served on foreign fields. I think of Mac Coffey, Eleanor Brown, Art Morris, Max Randall, and Cyril Simkins—all great soldiers of the cross. They served in Europe, Africa, and Asia. They struggled with new languages, strange customs, debilitating diseases. They were deprived of the advantages of America, not only for themselves, but for their children as well. One of them, Eleanor Brown, was martyred during an African uprising.

As I recall these friends and acquaintances of my youth—all of them now dead—I ask myself what sort of people they were. And I answer, "ordinary folks." They were all just ordinary people who had an extraordinary commitment to Jesus Christ. That's how it was with them; that's how it was with the apostles; and that's how it always seems to be. It's amazing what God can do with ordinary folks who are willing to lose their lives for Him.

B. Prayer

Dear Father, because we know that Jesus is the Messiah, may we heed the call to follow Him. May we lose our lives that we may find the everlasting life that only He offers. In His name we pray, amen.

C. Thought to Remember

The way of a cross leads home.

Home Daily Bible Readings

Monday, Jan. 17—Whoever Believes Has Eternal Life (John 6:41-51)
Tuesday, Jan. 18—Eat My Flesh, Drink My Blood (John 6:52-59)
Wednesday, Jan. 19—This Teaching Is Difficult (John 6:60-69)
Thursday, Jan. 20—Who Do You Say I Am? (Matthew 16:13-20)
Friday, Jan. 21—Let Them Deny Themselves (Matthew 16:24-28)
Saturday, Jan. 22—You Are the Messiah (Mark 8:27-30)
Sunday, Jan. 23—Take Up Your Cross, Follow Me (Mark 8:31-38)

Learning by Doing

This page contains an alternative lesson plan emphasizing learning activities.
Classes desiring such student involvement will find these suggestions helpful.

Learning Goals

After participating in this lesson, each student will be able to:

1. Tell what Peter did and did not understand about who Jesus was and what He had come to do.

2. Express the level of commitment that Jesus expects from His followers.

3. Evaluate his or her own level of commitment in following Jesus, and state one specific means of deepening that commitment.

Into the Lesson

Before the class arrives, write "R H I P" on the board. Below that list the following positions: CEO of a company; head of a prestigious hospital; president (or prime minister) of your country; head of a respected brokerage firm; principal of the local high school; and head of the bank branch office located in a suburban grocery store.

As students arrive, say: "Imagine that you have been selected to fill one of the positions listed. Sure, there will be a lot of responsibility and hard work; but think of the perks that go with each position. If you were selected for one of these positions, what kind of recognition and fame would you expect to receive?" (Remind them that RHIP stands for "rank has its privileges.")

Allow time for discussion, perhaps while your learners are getting coffee and doughnuts. Then ask volunteers to tell which position they would most like to have—at least, if only the benefits had to be considered—and why.

Then point out that today's lesson is about the One who held the highest position imaginable. Yet, instead of seeking the fame and accolades one might have expected, He ordered those closest to Him to keep His high rank private. We have much to learn from this One!

Into the Word

Invite a man who is not a member of your class to come and portray the apostle Peter. Provide him with information from today's lesson commentary and the student handout described below. Encourage him to "get into the part," putting drama and passion into his presentation.

Tell the class, "We have a real treat today. We have present with us someone who was there when the Person of rank we mentioned told His followers to keep things quiet. You can imagine his surprise! I'd like him to tell you about it, and

about his Leader, in his own way. Then you'll have a chance to ask questions. Our guest is Simon Peter!"

Bring "Peter" into the room and ask him to tell his story. He should begin by paraphrasing Mark 8:27-33, told from Peter's perspective. Allow a little embellishment, particularly to add remarks about Peter's thinking and emotions along the way.

When "Peter" finishes, invite questions. Refer your learners to Mark 8:27-33 as a source for questions. Also, note that you have prepared a few sample questions to get them started. Distribute a handout, which includes these questions:

1. Where were the wrong ideas of Jesus' identity coming from? Who was saying those things?

2. How quickly did you respond when Jesus asked who you believed Him to be? Did you blurt it out, or was there a silent pause?

3. What did you think when Jesus charged you not to tell anyone? Did that seem strange to you?

4. You were surprised when Jesus spoke of His death. What was the reaction of the others?

5. How could you have been so bold as to rebuke Jesus?

6. How long did it take for you to really understand what Jesus meant when He said that you "savorest not the things that be of God"?

Ask Peter to go on with the story as he paraphrases Mark 8:34-38. Have "Peter" tell a little of his personal struggle as he came to grips with the concepts of self-denial and servant leadership. He should close with a challenge for modern disciples to take up their crosses and follow.

Into Life

Ask your learners to think about Peter's level of commitment to Jesus on different occasions, ranking them 1 (low) to 5 (high). Where would they rate him at Caesarea Philippi? Where would they rate him at Gethsemane? How about in Acts 4?

Next, challenge the learners to think privately of their own level of commitment. (No discussion is needed.) Are they like Peter at Caesarea Philippi—confessing Jesus with their lips but also contradicting Him? Are they sleeping when they should be praying and fighting when they should be passive as in Gethsemane? Or are they bold to speak even when it may be costly? Are they taking up their crosses? Close with a moment of silent prayer for students to make commitments to grow in their discipleship.

Let's Talk It Over

*The questions on this page are designed to promote discussion of the lesson
by the class and to encourage application of the lesson Scriptures. The answers
provided are only discussion starters. Let your class talk it over from there.*

1. Why is confessing Jesus as the Christ so important for the church, for the individual, and for society?

The confession that Jesus is the Christ stands at the heart of the Christian faith. Jesus Himself said that only through Him could we be restored to a right relationship with God the Father (John 14:6), a truth later emphasized by Jesus' apostles (Acts 4:12).

We may believe in Jesus in our hearts, but only by confessing with our mouths can others be assured of our personal faith (Romans 10:8-10). In a postmodern, pluralistic culture where many believe there is no such thing as absolute truth, it is crucial for us to present boldly Jesus Christ as the Messiah who is the only hope of the world.

2. In what ways might we attempt to correct or rebuke God as Peter did?

We "correct" God by selectively listening to, accepting, or teaching certain parts of what God has said in the Bible. At times we may get caught up in a particular Bible statement to the exclusion of others that provide balance, further instruction, and context.

Another problem is that we can be more focused on the things that are of this world rather than the things that are of God; in such cases we tend not to hear or understand God's words as He desires. Likewise, we may have a tendency to accept, follow, or teach only the parts of the Bible that make us comfortable, or seem to be consistent with prevailing opinions. In such cases we are acting as if we need to correct God or twist His Word to fit the culture.

3. Why is self-denial such a difficult thing for most people?

Self-denial contradicts our very basic tendency toward self-preservation. It also contradicts the prevailing emphasis in Western civilization on pursuing pleasure, materialism, and comfort. As long as we allow our culture to convince us that we deserve more and better of everything then we will never know the godly joy of self-sacrifice. On the other hand, if we focus on Jesus' teaching and personal example of self-denial, we will be more willing to give of ourselves to a cause that is much bigger than our own life.

4. The lesson writer said that taking up our cross does not mean that we deliberately seek after trouble (which could include persecution or martyrdom). What are some questions we could ask ourselves to help us determine the amount of risk we should take in serving Christ?

As we consider various types of service that could bring more opposition or suffering, we need to ask questions that help us see possible scenarios in light of the big picture. Where does God seem to be leading me? How can God best use me? What are my motives in doing this? For whom am I really taking this risk—others or myself? How will this affect my family?

We may also ask if our suffering will open doors for the gospel (Philippians 1:12, 13), or will inspire others (1:14). Can I save many other people in the process of giving myself? What will bring God the greater glory? When we ask ourselves these questions and consult wise Christian friends, God can lead us to serve Him in the ways that will most benefit His mission.

5. Why is it good to explain the cost of Christian discipleship as clearly as possible to a potential disciple?

Simple honesty requires that we tell people about the clear demands that Jesus makes for us. We would think it dishonest if military recruiters told potential recruits only about the prospects for world travel, specialized training, and a good education, but not about the intense conditioning, frightening battles, and possible death. We must tell the world about the blessing of forgiveness, hope, and eternal life, but also that Jesus Himself taught and showed that the road to glory involves a cross.

6. How can we prepare ourselves to stand up boldly for Jesus so that we will not disgrace Him through our fear and shame?

If we obey what Jesus said were the two greatest commandments—loving God above all else and loving others—then we will be anxious to tell others about Him. That will be especially true if we maintain a constant awareness of how much Jesus willingly sacrificed so that we could be forgiven. The result will be that we will take seriously the commission He gave us to offer the good news about salvation to the whole world.

Jesus Defines Greatness

January 30
Lesson 9

DEVOTIONAL READING: Matthew 20:20-28.

BACKGROUND SCRIPTURE: Mark 10:13-45.

PRINTED TEXT: Mark 10:32-45.

Mark 10:32-45

32 And they were in the way going up to Jerusalem; and Jesus went before them: and they were amazed; and as they followed, they were afraid. And he took again the twelve, and began to tell them what things should happen unto him,

33 Saying, Behold, we go up to Jerusalem; and the Son of man shall be delivered unto the chief priests, and unto the scribes; and they shall condemn him to death, and shall deliver him to the Gentiles:

34 And they shall mock him, and shall scourge him, and shall spit upon him, and shall kill him; and the third day he shall rise again.

35 And James and John, the sons of Zebedee, come unto him, saying, Master, we would that thou shouldest do for us whatsoever we shall desire.

36 And he said unto them, What would ye that I should do for you?

37 They said unto him, Grant unto us that we may sit, one on thy right hand, and the other on thy left hand, in thy glory.

38 But Jesus said unto them, Ye know not what ye ask: can ye drink of the cup that I drink of? and be baptized with the baptism that I am baptized with?

39 And they said unto him, We can. And Jesus said unto them, Ye shall indeed drink of the cup that I drink of; and with the baptism that I am baptized withal shall ye be baptized:

40 But to sit on my right hand and on my left hand is not mine to give; but it shall be given to them for whom it is prepared.

41 And when the ten heard it, they began to be much displeased with James and John.

42 But Jesus called them to him, and saith unto them, Ye know that they which are accounted to rule over the Gentiles exercise lordship over them; and their great ones exercise authority upon them.

43 But so shall it not be among you: but whosoever will be great among you, shall be your minister:

44 And whosoever of you will be the chiefest, shall be servant of all.

45 For even the Son of man came not to be ministered unto, but to minister, and to give his life a ransom for many.

Jan 30

GOLDEN TEXT: Whosoever will be great among you, shall be your minister: and whosoever of you will be the chiefest, shall be servant of all.
—Mark 10:43, 44.

Lesson Aims

After participating in this lesson, each student will be able to:

1. Summarize Jesus' prediction of His death and the account of James and John's quest for chief seats in the kingdom.

2. Contrast Jesus' plan with that of James and John.

3. Explain how he or she plans to help someone who is in need.

Lesson Outline

Introduction
    A. Greatness?
    B. Lesson Background
  I. Condition of the Twelve (Mark 10:32a-c)
    A. Their Amazement (vv. 32a, b)
    B. Their Fear (v. 32c)
  II. Prediction of Jesus (Mark 10:32d-34)
    A. To Be Delivered to Enemies (vv. 32d, 33)
    B. To Be Abused and Killed (v. 34a)
    C. To Be Raised (v. 34b)
  III. Request of Zebedee's Sons (Mark 10:35-41)
    A. Request Made (vv. 35-37)
      Me First
    B. Dialogue Intensifies (vv. 38, 39)
      Walking the Walk
    C. Explanation Offered (v. 40)
    D. Displeasure Expressed (v. 41)
  IV. Nature of Discipleship (Mark 10:42-45)
    A. Unlike That of the Gentiles (v. 42)
    B. Like the Pattern Set by Jesus (vv. 43-45)
      Just Like Jesus
Conclusion
    A. So Shall It Not Be Among You
    B. Prayer
    C. Thought to Remember

Introduction

A. Greatness?

Alfred (A.D. 848–899) was the fifth and youngest son of Ethelwulf, King of the West Saxons. At the death of Alfred's brother Ethelred in 871, Alfred ascended to the throne. It was not an ideal time to be crowned king—a Danish invasion of England was under way. Eventually, Alfred managed to assemble an army and defeat the Danes. By 886 he had captured London and soon afterward was recognized as king of all England.

Alfred is the only king the English have ever designated "the Great." And what did he do to merit the title? Among other things he laid the foundation for the unification of England, was a patron of learning, and established trial by jury.

From an earthly point of view, Alfred surely deserves to be labeled "the Great." But the standards by which people judge greatness are not, and never have been, God's standards. Today we'll examine the words of Jesus on this topic. We will see that exercising lordship and authority over people does not fit into His definition of greatness. We will also see that for Jesus and His followers the key words are ministry and service.

B. Lesson Background

Our present lesson takes us into early A.D. 30, several months after Peter's great confession (studied in last week's lesson). It's now probably less than a month before Jesus' crucifixion.

During the months between the events of last week's lesson and today's, Jesus continued His ministry of healing and teaching. His labors covered more than two hundred miles, from Caesarea Philippi in the north to Jerusalem in the south.

Along the way Jesus had passed quietly through Samaria where He rebuked James and John for wanting to call down fire from Heaven upon a Samaritan village (Luke 9:51-56). For a period of time He labored on the eastern side of the Jordan River in Perea.

We also know that Jesus was in Jerusalem to attend the Feast of Tabernacles (John 7:11-52), and back there later to share in the Feast of Dedication (John 10:22-39). Much of the material for this period of Jesus' life is found in either Luke or John, but not in Matthew or Mark.

Just prior to the events of today's lesson, Jesus had His famous encounter with the rich young ruler (Mark 10:17-22) and had spoken to His disciples concerning the peril of riches (Mark 10:23-31). Having just heard Jesus' lecture on the dangers of wealth, it is strange that James and John should request places of leadership in Jesus' kingdom, as we will see them doing today. It's true that they specifically asked for high honor rather money, but it's also true that those two concepts have a way of "finding each other."

I. Condition of the Twelve (Mark 10:32a-c)

A. Their Amazement (vv. 32a, b)

32a, b. And they were in the way going up to Jerusalem; and Jesus went before them: and they were amazed.

Jesus and His entourage are moving toward *Jerusalem* when the event described here occurs. On this journey they will pass through Jericho where Jesus restores sight to blind Bartimeus (Mark 10:46-52) and has His encounter with Zaccheus (Luke 19:1-10). Jesus will arrive in Bethany shortly (John 12:1). Following that, He will enter Jerusalem in triumph (Mark 11:1-10). Jesus' earthly life is about to come to an end.

Jesus recently has been in the Jerusalem area, at Bethany, to raise His friend Lazarus from the dead. That event has stirred more opposition, and a council meeting is called to deal with Jesus. John 11:53 says, "Then from that day forth they [His enemies] took counsel together for to put him to death."

Now Jesus is on His way back to Jerusalem, and His apostles are *amazed* that He should so soon return there after having encountered such harsh opposition. They undoubtedly must possess a vague sense of foreboding that some awful event is about to unfold. This feeling probably has been with them for a while now (cf. John 11:8).

B. Their Fear (v. 32c)

32c. And as they followed, they were afraid.

The apostles' amazement is for their Leader; their fear is for themselves. It is easy for us to imagine that the apostles are such spiritual giants that they never experience the emotions common to the rest of us, but the Gospel records do not so portray them. Even after seeing so many miracles, they have their doubts as well as their fears, their pride as well as their arrogance. At times they are quarrelsome, at other times vengeful (see below).

Jesus already has taught the apostles concerning fear. When He sent them forth on their evan-

---

How to Say It

BARTIMEUS. *Bar*-tih-*me*-us (strong accent on *me*).
CAESAREA PHILIPPI. Sess-uh-*ree*-uh Fih-*lip*-pie or *Fil*-ih-pie.
CAIAPHAS. *Kay*-uh-fus or *Kye*-uh-fus.
CORINTHIANS. Kor-*in*-thee-unz (*th* as in *thin*).
GENTILES. *Jen*-tiles.
JERUSALEM. Juh-*roo*-suh-lem.
LAZARUS. *Laz*-uh-rus.
PEREA. Peh-*ree*-uh.
SALOME. Suh-*lo*-me.
SAMARIA. Suh-*mare*-ee-uh.
SAMARITAN. Suh-*mare*-uh-tun.
ZACCHEUS. Zack-*key*-us.
ZEBEDEE. *Zeb*-eh-dee.

---

gelistic campaign (two lessons ago), He told them, "Fear not them which kill the body, but are not able to kill the soul: but rather fear him which is able to destroy both soul and body in hell" (Matthew 10:28). But even though they had been taught not to fear, still they yield to their natural inclination under the circumstances.

There is a measure of comfort here for all of us. Though we know and love the Master and desire above all else to obey His words, sometimes, like the Twelve, we fail to do so. The spirit is often willing but the flesh proves to be weak. [See question #1, page 192.]

II. Prediction of Jesus (Mark 10:32d-34)

A. To Be Delivered to Enemies (vv. 32d, 33)

32d, 33. And he took again the twelve, and began to tell them what things should happen unto him, saying, Behold, we go up to Jerusalem; and the Son of man shall be delivered unto the chief priests, and unto the scribes; and they shall condemn him to death, and shall deliver him to the Gentiles.

Jesus predicts His death several times in the Gospels (see Matthew 26:2; Mark 8:31; 9:9, 30-32). [See question #2, page 192.] When the Twelve learn that He is to be delivered into the hands of *the Gentiles*, we might think that this will increase their bitterness and multiply their resolve to oppose such an atrocity. But just how much of what Jesus says at this time do they really comprehend? Luke 18:34 states that, "They understood none of these things" and gives as an explanation that the reality of Jesus' pending death was "hid from them."

This fact raises a question: Who is bringing about the hiding? Does God in some miraculous way do it? Isn't it possible that the mind-set of the apostles won't allow themselves to believe it, and in this sense it is hidden from them?

We've all had experiences with things too horrible to believe, things rejected on that basis. For many people—citizens of the United States and their friends, especially—the 9/11 experience fits into this category.

B. To Be Abused and Killed (v. 34a)

34a. And they shall mock him, and shall scourge him, and shall spit upon him, and shall kill him.

In none of His other predictions of death is Jesus so graphic in describing His suffering as here. Not only is He to be killed, but prior to His death He is to be tortured and abused in various ways. Luke 18:32 offers the general idea that Jesus is to be "spitefully entreated."

Mark 14:65 later describes the accuracy of Jesus' predictions. At the conclusion of His trial before Caiaphas, "some began to spit on him, and to cover his face, and to buffet him, and to say unto him, Prophesy: and the servants did strike him with the palms of their hands."

Still later, after Pilate has abdicated his responsibility and turned Jesus over to his soldiers, "they clothed him with purple, and platted a crown of thorns, and put it about his head, and began to salute him, Hail, King of the Jews! And they smote him on the head with a reed, and did spit upon him, and bowing their knees worshipped him" (Mark 15:17-19). Such abuse of the Messiah had been predicted long before. See Isaiah 53.

C. To Be Raised (v. 34b)

34b. And the third day he shall rise again.

As the apostles don't grasp that Jesus is to die, neither do they understand that He will *rise again*. Like the sad news of His death, the glorious revelation of His resurrection is hidden from them. And it stays hidden until after that event.

Immediately after the resurrection, two angels will remind the women at the tomb of Jesus' prediction, and "they remembered his words" (Luke 24:8). His apostles and other disciples similarly became convinced.

III. Request of Zebedee's Sons (Mark 10:35-41)

A. Request Made (vv. 35-37)

35-37. And James and John, the sons of Zebedee, come unto him, saying, Master, we would that thou shouldest do for us whatsoever we shall desire. And he said unto them, What would ye that I should do for you? They said unto him, Grant unto us that we may sit, one on thy right hand, and the other on thy left hand, in thy glory.

Matthew 20:20 notes that the mother of *James and John* comes "to him . . . with her sons." Obviously, all three are heavily involved in making this misguided request. If we combine Matthew 27:56 with Mark 15:40, we discover that the mother's name is Salome. She is neither the first nor last mother to have ambitions for her children. See Genesis 27:5-10.

Shortly before the time of this request, Jesus spoke of the twelve thrones upon which the apostles are to "sit . . . judging the twelve tribes of Israel" (Matthew 19:28). It may be this promise that inspires James and John to make their request for the most important of the twelve seats. To sit on the *right hand* and *left hand* of a sovereign indicates special favor and hence additional authority. [See question #3, page 192.]

Since these two men, along with Peter, comprise an "inner circle" among the apostles, it's understandable that they will assume that they will continue to be singled out for special honor. As for the reason for making this request at this time, we are indebted to Luke. Shortly after this incident, that Gospel writer explains that the apostles "thought that the kingdom of God should immediately appear" (Luke 19:11).

ME FIRST

Eric Ritz tells of a certain executive who was traveling. While waiting at an airport, he learned his flight had been canceled. This forced him to go to another airline to rebook his journey. His patience was gone, so he shoved his way to the front of the ticket line and angrily demanded a first-class ticket on the next available flight. The agent explained that he'd be happy to help, but the man would just have to wait in line like everyone else.

That was too much for the man's ego. He leaned over the counter and said, "Young man, do you have any idea who I am?" Whereupon the ticket agent picked up the microphone and said, "Attention, please. There is a gentleman at the ticket counter who doesn't know who he is. If anyone can identify him, please come to the counter."

That man was really "asking for it"! An inflated view of self indicates a shallow spirit. But when there is genuine communion with God, there is humility; there is the absence of seeing oneself as greater than others. See Romans 12:3.

—J. D. R.

B. Dialogue Intensifies (vv. 38, 39)

38, 39. But Jesus said unto them, Ye know not what ye ask: can ye drink of the cup that I drink of? and be baptized with the baptism that I am baptized with? And they said unto him, We can. And Jesus said unto them, Ye shall indeed drink of the cup that I drink of; and with the baptism that I am baptized withal shall ye be baptized.

Jesus responds to the two in particular and the Twelve in general that they don't understand the full import of the request (cf. Romans 8:17; 2 Timothy 2:12; Revelation 3:21). He illustrates with two figures to teach that the leaders in His kingdom can expect suffering and death rather than greatness and power in their earthly lives. The use of *cup* represents sorrow, judgment, or retribution (see Psalm 75:8; Isaiah 51:17, 18; Jeremiah 25:15-26; 49:12). Jesus previously used the figure of *baptism* in Luke 12:50 to represent immersion in sorrow.

James will experience his cup and baptism of suffering in becoming the first apostle to be martyred (Acts 12:2). John will live a long life, but will be cast into exile (Revelation 1:9).

WALKING THE WALK

Several years ago, *USA Today* reported from an extensive survey that 48 percent of American workers admitted to taking unethical or illegal actions on the job in the year past. Insurance companies state that 20 percent of car write-offs represent deliberate acts by the owners.

Worker's compensation cases are inflated by bogus claims. Female absenteeism for claimed sickness and injury peaks four times a year, just prior to school holidays. Retail stores are paying high prices for more sophisticated electronic equipment in an attempt to capture shoplifters— a multi-billion-dollar annual loss. Such equipment detects one out of every fifty-two customers carrying away at least one item that is not paid for. Throw in cheating on exams, spouses, and tax returns and you have a cloudy picture of modern-day honesty and integrity.

It's easy to get swept up in so much dishonesty, isn't it? After all, "everyone else is doing it." Yet part of the cup that Christ had to drink involved going against the grain of cultural expectations that were opposed to God's will. His disciples are to do so as well. When we do, will we be surprised by the fiery baptism and bitter-tasting cup that can result?   —J. D. R.

C. Explanation Offered (v. 40)

40. But to sit on my right hand and on my left hand is not mine to give; but it shall be given to them for whom it is prepared.

Notice that Jesus does not deny that there will be chief places in the kingdom, only that they *shall be given to them for whom* they're *prepared.* Matthew 20:23 further explains that it is the Father who has assigned the positions for which James and John ask.

Matthew 25:31-40 and John 5:22-30 show that Jesus will indeed have a key role in dispensing reward and punishment. But the authority of Jesus is derived from the Father (Matthew 11:27; 28:18; John 14:28), and the Father evidently reserves some functions for Himself.

D. Displeasure Expressed (v. 41)

41. And when the ten heard it, they began to be much displeased with James and John.

Nothing is stated to show that *the ten* are equally anxious to have the chief places in the kingdom. But from Jesus' reprimand of all twelve, we may fairly surmise that the ten are of a similar mind as the other two. *James and John* have shown themselves to be spiritually immature by attempting to grab the chief spots. The

Visual for lesson 9. *Workers with International Disaster and Emergency Services display true servants' hearts in India and Brazil.*

other ten now show their own spiritual immaturity as they express displeasure out of jealousy. This is not the first time that these twelve have squabbled among themselves (see Mark 9:33-37).

IV. Nature of Discipleship (Mark 10:42-45)

A. Unlike That of the Gentiles (v. 42)

42. But Jesus called them to him, and saith unto them, Ye know that they which are accounted to rule over the Gentiles exercise lordship over them; and their great ones exercise authority upon them.

Jesus defuses this potentially explosive situation by suggesting that the apostles' conduct is similar to what would be found among *Gentiles.* The authority and power of the Roman Empire undoubtedly comes to everyone's mind. In effect, Jesus says that the actions of the apostles are not only unworthy of them, but they are not even Jewish-like. Such a statement should certainly grab the apostles' attention!

B. Like the Pattern Set by Jesus (vv. 43-45)

43-45. But so shall it not be among you: but whosoever will be great among you, shall be your minister: and whosoever of you will be the chiefest, shall be servant of all. For even the Son of man came not to be ministered unto, but to minister, and to give his life a ransom for many.

In verse 40 Jesus indicated that there will be places of honor in His kingdom; He now indicates that these positions will not be based upon earthly standards such as Gentiles employ (v. 42, above). He explains the basis of true leadership in the kingdom. In so doing He switches from discussing the kingdom of God in an "end times" sense (v. 40) to speak of it in a "here and now" sense—that is, the church age. True greatness, Jesus explains, comes from ministering and serving, not from craving and grasping.

The Greek word translated *minister* is the word for the office of deacon in 1 Timothy 3:12, but it does not have that sense here. This word is used of any sort of servant, especially of one who serves at the table. All Christians—whether they hold an official church office or not—are to be ministering servants.

The word for *servant* has the sense of "slave," as it does in 1 Corinthians 9:19 and 2 Corinthians 4:5. What a concept: a "slave" and a "servant" who will be *great* and *chiefest*! The apostles are not to follow the pattern seen in worldly Gentile kingdoms. Rather, they are to imitate the example that Jesus is living out before them. [See question #4, page 192.]

The concept of Jesus' giving *his life a ransom for many* is a rare explanation in the Gospels regarding the reason for Jesus' death. (The apostle Paul will offer a much more extensive explanation of this idea in the book of Romans.) What a life of humility and service! [See question #5, page 192.]

JUST LIKE JESUS

In his book *Reach Out for New Life*, Robert Schuller tells about Dr. Henry Poppen, who served for many years as a missionary to China. Poppen related going to a remote village where, presumably, missionaries had never been. He told the people about Jesus, stressing His kind and gentle manner and His great servanthood. He also stated that Jesus was able to forgive and love those who were unlovable.

When Dr. Poppen finished telling them about Christ, a few of the men came up to him and said, "We know Jesus! He has been here." "No," Dr. Poppen corrected. "He lived and died in a country far from here years ago." "No, no," they insisted. "He died here. Come, we will show you His grave."

They led him outside the village to a cemetery. On one tombstone was the name of a Christian medical doctor, who, on his own, had felt called by Christ to go, live, and die in China. The people had so admired him that they thought he was Jesus, the One Poppen had revealed.

Would anyone confuse your life with that of the Lord? Servanthood is the key to godly greatness.

—J. D. R.

Conclusion

A. So Shall It Not Be Among You

The little church had a real problem. One of its elders—perhaps the most capable man in the congregation—had passed away. His death had left a real void. Because the church was so small, there was no one with the necessary qualifications to take the place of the deceased elder. At least that's how many in the church saw it.

But not everyone agreed. One man in particular had other ideas. He was sure he was ideally qualified to be an elder. So he began a campaign to get "elected."

The trouble is that the man was an alcoholic, and a foul-mouthed one at that. In spite of his character faults, he somehow managed to get his name on the ballot for "election day." But that's as far as he got. The Christian people of the little church, knowing him for what he was, denied him the office that he so diligently sought.

The man reminds us of Simon the sorcerer from Acts 8. Both the would-be elder and the sorcerer thought too highly of themselves; both craved power in the church for the wrong reason; both were kept from sharing in the ministry of the kingdom because of their wrong attitudes.

In effect Jesus said, "You twelve know all too well what the Gentiles are like. My definition of greatness is not the same as theirs. Beware!" Which model of greatness will we choose to follow today?

B. Prayer

Dear God, help us to develop servants' hearts. May our goal ever be to minister to You by serving those who have been created in Your image. Make us realize that when we minister to them we minister to Jesus. In His name, amen.

C. Thought to Remember

Every church has fewer servant-leaders than it really needs.

Home Daily Bible Readings

Monday, Jan. 24—Servant of All (Mark 9:33-37)

Tuesday, Jan. 25—Jesus Surprises His Hearers (Mark 10:13-22)

Wednesday, Jan. 26—Jesus Perplexes the Disciples (Mark 10:23-27)

Thursday, Jan. 27—First Will Be Last, Last First (Mark 10:28-31)

Friday, Jan. 28—Whoever Is Great Shall Be Servant (Mark 10:35-45)

Saturday, Jan. 29—I Came to Serve (Matthew 20:20-28)

Sunday, Jan. 30—The Exalted Will Be Humbled (Matthew 23:1-12)

Learning by Doing

This page contains an alternative lesson plan emphasizing learning activities. Classes desiring such student involvement will find these suggestions helpful.

Learning Goals

After participating in this lesson, each student will be able to:

1. Summarize Jesus' prediction of His death and the account of James and John's quest for chief seats in the kingdom.

2. Contrast Jesus' plan with that of James and John.

3. Explain how he or she plans to help someone who is in need.

Into the Lesson

Provide a handout with the heading, "Opposites." In a column on the left side of the page list several words that have obvious opposites. Provide the opposite for the first as an example, like "light" and "dark." Some suggested words include high, sweet, positive, age, off, truth, strength, arrogance, righteousness, and selfishness.

As students arrive, distribute the handouts. Ask the learners to complete the handouts as they visit with other class members, get coffee, etc., in the moments before class begins.

After the class comes to order, quickly review the list of opposites. Note that the presence of an opposite tends to emphasize the power of an item. For example, the sour taste of grapefruit is more pronounced if it follows something sweet.

Point out that today's lesson puts some opposites into an interesting juxtaposition. Jesus, the epitome of humility and self-denial, is seen in stark contrast to some of His followers, who hope to thrust themselves into positions of leadership ahead of others. What makes the contrast even more striking is that their request comes on the heels of Jesus' predictions of His death.

Into the Word

Ask one or more volunteers to read Mark 10:32-45 aloud. Divide the class into three groups for the following assignments.

Group 1. Review the text and compile a report on the emotions expressed by different persons or groups of people. Explain the reason for each emotion expressed and comment on whether the emotion was warranted or if some other emotion would have been more appropriate. In the latter case, explain how the person(s) could have been expected to display a different emotion.

Group 2. Review the text and compile a report on the dangers or potential dangers cited. Comment on the response to each danger (whether or not those involved responded properly).

Group 3. Review the text and compile a report on the contrasts seen in this passage. Point out the strengths and weaknesses of each side of the contrasts.

Allow about ten minutes for the groups to work; then ask for reports. Expect the following details to emerge from the reports; use the comments in the verse-by-verse exposition to note the significance of these details.

Group 1. The disciples displayed both amazement and fear (v. 32). James and John displayed an attitude of pride or selfishness (vv. 35-37). The ten were displeased with James and John (v. 41).

Group 2. Moving back to Judea put Jesus and the disciples in danger from the Jewish leaders (v. 32). Jesus elaborated on the danger to Himself and how it would turn from potential to actual (vv. 32-34). Jesus told James and John—and also the other ten—of danger they would face in His name (vv. 38, 39).

Group 3. The disciples displayed a contrast in their emotions—amazement and fear (v. 32). The stark contrast here is between Jesus' attitude of self-sacrifice (vv. 33, 34) and James and John's attitude of self-promotion (vv. 35-37). Jesus then pointed out the contrast between the worldly attitude of leadership (v. 42) with the attitude He expects (vv. 43-45). Even within Jesus' remarks is contrast in that "whosoever will be great among you, shall be your minister: and whosoever of you will be the chiefest, shall be servant of all."

Into Life

Distribute a handout for students to note their own response to Jesus' call. The handout should include the following questions:

1. Is your attitude about service more like that of the world (Gentiles) or that of Jesus? How is it demonstrated?

2. Who is someone in need of some service or ministry that you can provide? (This may be a person either inside or outside the church.) How can service on behalf of this person demonstrate Christlike leadership?

3. What will you do this week to follow Jesus' pattern of servant leadership?

Close the session with a prayer for each student to behave more like Jesus and less like James and John.

Let's Talk It Over

The questions on this page are designed to promote discussion of the lesson by the class and to encourage application of the lesson Scriptures. The answers provided are only discussion starters. Let your class talk it over from there.

1. Fear sometimes can keep us from serving God. What are some ways God can teach us and use us despite our fears?

Fear is a God-given emotion to help protect us. Yet sometimes we must act in spite of our fear. Notice that the disciples continued following Jesus toward Jerusalem despite their fears (v. 32). When we do the same thing, it gives God the opportunity to prove to us that He is worthy of our trust and teaches us where to turn when we are afraid.

In the process we learn to focus on Him instead of our problems or fears. This puts things in perspective. As we encounter obstacles or fears while following Jesus, we quit asking ourselves in desperation, "What am I going to do?" and begin asking, "What is God able to do?"

2. What can we learn from the fact that Jesus predicted His own death so many times?

Most of all, Jesus was focusing on His main purpose for coming to this earth. He was born to die for the sins of the world. In a practical sense, Jesus was also trying to prepare His disciples for what was coming. His trials and brutal death would be shocking and unnerving enough for His close friends, but would have been even more difficult with no warning.

Jesus also knew that His followers, then or now, would benefit from repetition. Often we aren't paying attention, or we forget, or our minds are closed by preconceived notions. Jesus' multiple predictions of His pending death were also intended to counter the popular notion of that day that the Messiah would be a military or political hero instead of a spiritual savior.

3. How can we sometimes show spiritual immaturity like James, John, and the other disciples did in today's lesson?

Spiritual immaturity can become evident in a number of ways in the church. Sometimes it can take the form of self-centeredness, pettiness, or pride. It shows itself when we insist on having things our way or insist on being the center of attention. At other times it is seen in divisiveness, power struggles, or threatening to withhold offerings until things are done a certain way.

Some more subtle signs of spiritual immaturity can be selfish or inappropriate requests in our prayers, ignoring things that the Bible makes obvious, or twisting certain Bible teachings to say what we want them to say. Turning issues of expediency (such as the color of the carpet) into matters of doctrine to get our way is spiritually immature and manipulative.

4. How can we encourage Christian service within the church without glorifying people and fostering an unhealthy pride?

We begin by stressing that Christian service is a vital part of Christian living. Our teaching can emphasize examples of humble service recorded in Scripture. Then we must offer ample opportunities for people to use their abilities, personal experiences, and resources to serve others.

As we train others to serve, we must be careful also to instill in them the importance of selflessness and warn of the dangers of pride. When people do offer their willing service, we should recognize their service with thank-you cards and notes. Sometimes we may recognize their service in church publications. The wording that is used in public recognition is important. It may be helpful to talk about how "God has used the willing efforts" of certain people to bless the church and others. Then recognition is given, but the emphasis is more focused on God.

5. What are some guidelines for selecting the kind of selfless church leaders Jesus described in verses 43-45?

When servanthood becomes a natural part of the mind-set of a congregation, leaders will begin to emerge who exemplify that quality. It is helpful to remind the congregation how important a servant's heart is in a godly leader as potential leaders are being discussed. Future leaders can also be discovered simply by looking at the people who have been most involved in serving both in visible and less obvious ways.

As specific people are considered for leadership, it is beneficial to ask questions about them that are related to servanthood. How do they treat other people? Are they overly competitive or critical? Do they demonstrate gentleness, love, and humility? Are they respected? Are they hospitable? Do they seem overly desirous of public recognition? The answers to these questions will show us the way in how the church can best use certain people and personalities in various roles.

Overcoming Grief

DEVOTIONAL READING: Psalm 31:9-16.

BACKGROUND SCRIPTURE: Ruth 1.

PRINTED TEXT: Ruth 1:3-9, 14-18.

Ruth 1:3-9, 14-18

3 And Elimelech Naomi's husband died; and she was left, and her two sons.

4 And they took them wives of the women of Moab; the name of the one was Orpah, and the name of the other Ruth: and they dwelt there about ten years.

5 And Mahlon and Chilion died also both of them; and the woman was left of her two sons and her husband.

6 Then she arose with her daughters-in-law, that she might return from the country of Moab: for she had heard in the country of Moab how that the LORD had visited his people in giving them bread.

7 Wherefore she went forth out of the place where she was, and her two daughters-in-law with her; and they went on the way to return unto the land of Judah.

8 And Naomi said unto her two daughters-in-law, Go, return each to her mother's house: the LORD deal kindly with you, as ye have dealt with the dead, and with me.

9 The LORD grant you that ye may find rest, each of you in the house of her husband. Then she kissed them; and they lifted up their voice, and wept.

. . . .

14 And they lifted up their voice, and wept again: and Orpah kissed her mother-in-law; but Ruth clave unto her.

15 And she said, Behold, thy sister-in-law is gone back unto her people, and unto her gods: return thou after thy sister-in-law.

16 And Ruth said, Entreat me not to leave thee, or to return from following after thee: for whither thou goest, I will go; and where thou lodgest, I will lodge: thy people shall be my people, and thy God my God:

17 Where thou diest, will I die, and there will I be buried: the LORD do so to me, and more also, if aught but death part thee and me.

18 When she saw that she was steadfastly minded to go with her, then she left speaking unto her.

Feb 6

GOLDEN TEXT: Ruth said, Entreat me not to leave thee, or to return from following after thee: for whither thou goest, I will go; and where thou lodgest, I will lodge: thy people shall be my people, and thy God my God.—Ruth 1:16.

Called to Be God's People
Unit 3: Whosoever Will—Come!
(Lessons 10-13)

Lesson Aims

After participating in this lesson, each student will be able to:

1. Relate the series of events that led to Ruth's expression of devotion and loyalty to Naomi.

2. Explain how faith in God makes a difference in dealing with grief.

3. Think of a situation where he or she may be able to help someone in overcoming grief, and pray for wisdom in carrying out such a ministry.

Lesson Outline

INTRODUCTION
    A. Surrounded by Friends
    B. Lesson Background
  I. FAMILY'S DISASTERS (Ruth 1:3-5)
    A. Death of Naomi's Husband (v. 3)
    B. Death of Naomi's Sons (vv. 4, 5)
    The Shadow of Death
  II. NAOMI'S DECISION (Ruth 1:6-9)
    A. Concerning Her Dwelling (vv. 6, 7)
    B. Concerning Her Daughters-in-law (vv. 8, 9)
  III. RUTH'S DECISION (Ruth 1:14-18)
    A. Naomi's Plea (vv. 14, 15)
    B. Ruth's Pledge (vv. 16-18)
    Stand by Me
CONCLUSION
    A. Two Other Women
    B. Prayer
    C. Thought to Remember

Introduction

A. Surrounded by Friends

A reporter from the *Cincinnati Enquirer* went to New York City following the terrorist attacks of September 11, 2001. Her assignment was to observe the rescue operations and to report on the efforts of police and firefighters to find survivors amidst the staggering devastation. One of the firemen at "the hole," which was another name for "Ground Zero," told the reporter that whenever one of the workers found a firefighter they could identify, they immediately sent for that man's company to come down. They would carry him out so that he could be surrounded by his friends.

Later that same day the reporter watched, tears filling her eyes, as a fire truck with sirens

blaring raced through an intersection and stopped in front of the firehouse. Out came all the firefighters in full attire. Upon boarding the truck, the group headed toward "the hole," apparently to pick up the body of another friend.

In some funeral services, pallbearers surround the deceased and carry the body in a casket to the place of burial. Others, however, are needed who will surround the bereaved, offering to support and "carry" them when the burden of their loss seems too great to bear. Ultimately, God is the great carrier in this regard, as described by the prophet Isaiah: "Even to your old age I am he; and even to hoar hairs [meaning gray hair] will I carry you: I have made, and I will bear; even I will carry, and will deliver you" (Isaiah 46:4).

Today's lesson draws our attention to Ruth and Naomi, each of whom had experienced the death of a husband. For Naomi the loss was especially severe, since Ruth's husband was one of Naomi's sons. Through their experiences, we learn that our God is indeed "the God of all comfort; who comforteth us in all our tribulation" (2 Corinthians 1:3, 4).

B. Lesson Background

The book of Ruth has been compared to a beautiful, delicate flower that emerges from the ground and survives amidst an abundance of worthless, unsightly weeds. Or one could think of it as a breath of fresh air, providing some relief from a smog-filled, polluted atmosphere. The first verse of the book gives us the setting: "in the days when the judges ruled." These days were not part of Israel's "golden age"; rather, they were the time characterized by the far from flattering assessment that appears at the conclusion of the book of Judges: "In those days there was no king in Israel: every man did that which was right in his own eyes" (Judges 21:25).

In contrast, the book of Ruth highlights the exemplary faith and devotion of a Moabite woman —an individual outside the "chosen nation" of Israel. Yet she demonstrated the kind of loyalty to the Lord that was sadly missing from God's own people at this time in their history. What Jesus said of a certain centurion could also be spoken of Ruth: "I have not found so great faith, no, not in Israel" (Matthew 8:10). [See question #1, page 200.]

I. Family's Disasters (Ruth 1:3-5)

While the book of Ruth provides a welcome exception to the generally depressing tone of the book of Judges, it does not begin that way. The opening verse mentions a famine that had struck the land, a famine that became so severe as to necessitate a family move from Bethlehem of Judah to Moab, a mountainous region east of the Dead Sea. This would have been a journey of fifty or sixty miles.

A. Death of Naomi's Husband (v. 3)

3. And Elimelech Naomi's husband died; and she was left, and her two sons.

Sometime after the move (the exact time is not given in the text), a tragedy far worse than famine occurs: *Elimelech Naomi's husband* dies. The text gives no details as to the cause. All we are given is the consequence of his passing: Naomi is *left, and her two sons.* One can only imagine how devastated these three individuals feel. Perhaps they question the wisdom of their move and wish they had remained in Judah.

B. Death of Naomi's Sons (vv. 4, 5)

4. And they took them wives of the women of Moab; the name of the one was Orpah, and the name of the other Ruth: and they dwelt there about ten years.

Whether the family discusses returning to Judah after Elimelech's death is not known. Mahlon and Chilion, the two sons (v. 2), take *wives* from *the women of Moab.* Chilion marries a woman named *Orpah*, while Mahlon marries a woman named *Ruth* (Ruth 4:10).

That these two Israelite men marry Moabite women may seem questionable in light of earlier restrictions given in the law of Moses regarding the marriage of foreigners (see Deuteronomy 7:1-4). But marriage with Moabites is not specifically forbidden in the law. The only restriction involving Moabites is found in Deuteronomy 23:3: "An

---

How to Say It

AMMONITE. *Am*-un-ite.
BETHLEHEM. *Beth*-lih-hem.
CENTURION. sen-*ture*-ee-un.
CHEMOSH. *Kee*-mosh.
CHILION. *Kil*-ee-on.
CORINTHIANS. Kor-*in*-thee-unz (*th* as in *thin*).
ELIMELECH. Ee-*lim*-eh-leck.
ELOHIM (Hebrew). el-o-*heem*.
ISAAC. *Eye*-zuk.
JUDAH. *Joo*-duh.
MAHLON. *Mah*-lon.
MOAB. *Mo*-ab.
MOABITES. *Mo*-ub-ites.
NAOMI. Nay-*oh*-me.
ORPAH. *Or*-pah.
REBEKAH. Reh-*bek*-uh.

Ammonite or Moabite shall not enter into the congregation of the Lord; even to their tenth generation shall they not enter into the congregation of the Lord for ever."

Certainly there is a kind of stigma attached to the Moabites, part of it perhaps stemming from the rather sordid account of their origin (Genesis 19:30-38). Apparently there is not yet any relief from the famine in Judah, so Mahlon, Chilion, and their wives, along with Naomi, dwell in Moab *about ten years.*

5. And Mahlon and Chilion died also both of them; and the woman was left of her two sons and her husband.

After the ten-year period mentioned in verse 4 passes, *Mahlon and Chilion* die. While Ruth and Orpah no doubt grieve over their respective losses, the deaths of these two men constitute an especially crushing blow to Naomi. Again, she is *left* (as in v. 3)—only now she is *left of her two sons and her husband.*

Naomi is thus both widowed and childless, a doubly disastrous condition in the ancient world. The first situation leaves her vulnerable to being taken advantage of—a problem that had not improved by Jesus' day (Luke 20:46, 47) and is still evident at times in today's society. The second situation leaves Naomi in a position that carries with it a sense of dishonor or disgrace: she has no sons and thus no means of continuing the family line of her husband Elimelech.

In a sense, Naomi had lost her identity—a condition perhaps reflected in the verse before us by the fact that she is not called by name at this point. She is called only *the woman.*

THE SHADOW OF DEATH

Leadership magazine relates a story about Donald Grey Barnhouse, a great preacher of the past, who lost his wife. In his great grief, he was faced with the daunting task of rearing children alone. On the way to the funeral, the well-dressed youngsters sat quietly in the car. Barnhouse knew their pain was as intense as his. He also knew that their fear was coupled with an uncertainty even greater than his own.

The car stopped at a railroad crossing. Everyone stared ahead as the freight train passed swiftly by, casting an eerie sequence of shadow, sunlight, shadow, sunlight across the car. It was then that the father turned to his oldest child, who was seated in the front.

"Son," he asked, "would you rather be hit by that train or its shadow?" The puzzled boy asked his father to repeat the question. So again the father asked, "Would you rather be hit by that freight train or by its shadow?" Softly came the answer, "The shadow—it can't hurt."

"Kids," the father continued, "because your mom loved Jesus and let Him be her Lord, He made sure death was just a shadow, it couldn't hurt her, only take her from our sight for a while. We'll see her again, in Jesus. That's what's going to help us through."

Historical hindsight reveals God's guiding hand on the lives of Ruth and Naomi as they worked through their grief, although it may not have seemed like it in the pain of the moment. Now that we have the firm and clear hope of the resurrection, how much more are we able to know of God's hand as it guides us through our own pain of loss!   —J. D. R.

II. Naomi's Decision (Ruth 1:6-9)

Once more one can only surmise the barrage of questions and doubts that flood Naomi's mind following the deaths of her sons. Why did her family leave Judah to begin with? Is all of this a punishment from God for leaving the promised land and residing with foreigners? Is it only a matter of time until Naomi herself dies?

A. Concerning Her Dwelling (vv. 6, 7)

6. Then she arose with her daughters-in-law, that she might return from the country of Moab: for she had heard in the country of Moab how that the LORD had visited his people in giving them bread.

Eventually news arrives from back home— good news, for a change. For the first time in the book of Ruth, *the Lord* is mentioned, perhaps an indication that Naomi's plight will begin to improve (though slowly at first). Specifically, the Lord has *visited his people in giving them bread.* The famine is over.

The word *visited* is a significant one in the Bible. In some instances, it describes God's activity on behalf of an individual or a group. Sometimes the visitation is a favorable one, as here in the book of Ruth. On other occasions, the visiting is done for the purposes of punishment and discipline (Exodus 20:5). The New Testament uses similar language when it speaks of the "day of visitation" (1 Peter 2:12), perhaps a reference to the return of Jesus.

7. Wherefore she went forth out of the place where she was, and her two daughters-in-law with her; and they went on the way to return unto the land of Judah.

The picture set forth in this verse is a touching one. Here are three women united by the common bond of tragedy. All three have lost their husbands. Perhaps they determine, at first, that they will try to survive together in Naomi's

homeland of *Judah.* Certainly there is something to be said for such companionship; people who have gone through a similar tragedy or crisis can often lend encouragement to one another by forming a kind of "support group."

B. Concerning Her Daughters-in-law (vv. 8, 9)

8. And Naomi said unto her two daughters-in-law, Go, return each to her mother's house: the LORD deal kindly with you, as ye have dealt with the dead, and with me.

At some point Naomi seems to realize that it is really not in the best interest of her *daughters-in-law* for them to travel to Judah with her. They will be much more apt to find husbands (and therefore security) in their homeland of Moab.

So Naomi urges them to *return each to her mother's house.* In some instances in the ancient Near East, the mother's house seems to serve as a kind of bridal chamber. Genesis 24:67 tells how Isaac brought Rebekah to the tent of his mother, Sarah.

Naomi concludes her plea to her daughters-in-law with a blessing: *the Lord deal kindly with you, as ye have dealt with the dead, and with me.* Naomi thus commits these two women, though they are Moabites, to the Lord's care. Her words reflect her desire that the Lord would reward them for being so kind to her during the tragedies that have befallen them all. She knows that they already have made a genuine sacrifice by being willing to come with her this far.

9. The LORD grant you that ye may find rest, each of you in the house of her husband. Then she kissed them; and they lifted up their voice, and wept.

Again, Naomi expresses her wish that *the Lord* provide each of her daughters-in-law with *rest* by allowing each to settle down in Moab with a *husband.* The concept of rest includes the sense of security and well-being that will be missing from their lives if they remain widows.

From a practical standpoint, Naomi's advice is sound. Actually carrying it out is another matter entirely. The bonds that have been forged from the tears of grief and sorrow are not easy to break. Now come new tears as the three women prepare to part company.

III. Ruth's Decision (Ruth 1:14-18)

In verses 10-13, not included in our printed text, both Ruth and Orpah voice their loyalty to Naomi and state their desire to accompany her to Judah. Naomi then tries to persuade the two of them to look at their situation realistically. She herself has nothing to offer Ruth and Orpah in

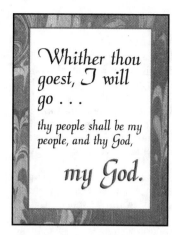

Whither thou goest, I will go . . . thy people shall be my people, and thy God, my God.

Visual for lesson 10

Discuss how Ruth's kind of devotion to God and to one's family can be demonstrated today.

the way of providing the "rest" mentioned in verse 9. Naomi's advanced age makes childbearing an impossibility for her. Even if through some means she is able to become pregnant and bear sons, it does not make sense for Ruth and Orpah to wait until these sons became old enough to marry. It is far better for both of the younger women to resettle in Moab.

Naomi concludes her appeal by declaring, "The hand of the Lord is gone out against me" (v. 13). From her viewpoint, her current situation appears hopeless. She has resigned herself to the fact that the Lord has determined to bring disaster upon her.

Yet it is out of such seemingly hopeless scenarios that the Lord often does His greatest work. In His time His hand will provide abundant blessings to Naomi. However, that thought probably gives little comfort to her at this particular moment.

A. Naomi's Plea (vv. 14, 15)

14. And they lifted up their voice, and wept again: and Orpah kissed her mother-in-law; but Ruth clave unto her.

Naomi's counsel to the daughters-in-law makes perfect sense, but that does not make it any easier to obey. More weeping follows. Finally, *Orpah* decides to bid farewell and kisses *her mother-in-law* one last time. *Ruth*, however, refuses to do so. She clings to Naomi. [See question #2, page 200.]

15. And she said, Behold, thy sister-in-law is gone back unto her people, and unto her gods: return thou after thy sister-in-law.

At this point, Naomi is able to add another reason why Ruth should return to Moab: *thy sister-in-law is gone back.* By mentioning that Orpah is returning to both *her people* and *her gods*, Naomi

highlights two crucial marks of a person's identity in the ancient world. Is Ruth really willing to sever ties with these?

The Hebrew word translated *gods* is *elohim*. Though it is actually a plural form in Hebrew, it is also one of the primary names for the one true God in the Old Testament. While the Moabites worship many gods, they recognize a chief god, who is known as Chemosh. In 1 Kings 11:7 this god is called "the abomination of Moab." Second Kings 3:26, 27 tells how the king of Moab sacrificed his firstborn son (apparently to Chemosh) in an effort to turn the tide of a battle with the Israelites in his favor.

Perhaps Naomi's plea reflects her earlier lament in verse 13: "The hand of the Lord is gone out against me." Is she expressing her own frustration with the Lord by encouraging Ruth to go back to the chief god of her homeland?

B. Ruth's Pledge (vv. 16-18)

16. And Ruth said, Entreat me not to leave thee, or to return from following after thee: for whither thou goest, I will go; and where thou lodgest, I will lodge: thy people shall be my people, and thy God my God.

If Naomi is determined that her daughters-in-law return to Moab, *Ruth* is even more determined to travel on to Judah with Naomi. Naomi may as well "save her breath," because Ruth has her mind made up. For her, there is no turning back. [See question #3, page 200.]

Ruth's statement of devotion in this verse may be considered a kind of "Good Confession" from the Old Testament point of view. She is expressing a firm decision to break ties with the two primary sources of her identity: her *people* and her god. No longer will she see herself as a Moabite; she will be an Israelite. No longer will she honor Chemosh, whose worship includes the sacrifice of children; she will worship the *God* of Israel through the "sacrifice" of her heart and mind. Note that in spite of Naomi's claim that the hand of her God has gone out against her (v. 13), Ruth is still willing to acknowledge Him as her God!

17. Where thou diest, will I die, and there will I be buried: the LORD do so to me, and more also, if aught but death part thee and me.

The words *Where thou diest, will I die, and there will I be buried* reflect the uncompromising commitment that Ruth is making. One's place of burial testifies to one's sense of identity and belonging. Thus Joseph, just before he died in Egypt, requested that his bones be carried from Egypt to Canaan when the Lord delivered His people from bondage there (Genesis 50:24, 25).

Although Ruth has been unquestionably clear in her statement of loyalty, she concludes her words with an oath, using the name of Naomi's God: *the Lord do so to me, and more also, if aught but death part thee and me.* Her pledge can be considered the equivalent of the phrase "till death do us part" in modern marriage vows.

Ruth is making herself accountable to the Lord Himself. If she should in any way break the promise of loyalty she is voicing to Naomi, she is willing to pay whatever consequences the Lord will determine. [See question #4, page 200.]

18. When she saw that she was steadfastly minded to go with her, then she left speaking unto her.

What can Naomi say in rebuttal to such a thorough declaration of devotion? Similar to Jesus, who "steadfastly set his face to go to Jerusalem" (Luke 9:51), Ruth is *steadfastly minded to go with* Naomi. Naomi knows that there is nothing she can do to dissuade Ruth from her intentions, so *she left speaking unto her.* [See question #5, page 200.]

STAND BY ME

In his work *A Grief Observed*, the great C. S. Lewis discussed the personal and aching loss of his wife. He stated that there was "an invisible blanket between the world and me. I find it hard to take in what anyone says. It is so uninteresting."

But he continued, "Yet, I want others to be about me. For I dread the moments when the house is empty. I want them, only if they can be there to talk to one another and not to me. I want them there."

In times of grief, we need each other! This is how God designed us. One of the most powerful ministries (and evangelistic opportunities) that the church can have involves grief recovery. And this isn't just "the preacher's job." It's a job for us all.   —J. D. R.

Home Daily Bible Readings

Monday, Jan. 31—I Am Weary with Weeping (Psalm 6:1-7)

Tuesday, Feb. 1—My Life Is Spent with Sorrow (Psalm 31:9-15)

Wednesday, Feb. 2—My Soul Refuses to Be Comforted (Psalm 77:1-10)

Thursday, Feb. 3—Naomi Loses Her Husband and Sons (Ruth 1:1-5)

Friday, Feb. 4—Go Back to Your Home (Ruth 1:6-11)

Saturday, Feb. 5—Orpah Goes, Ruth Stays (Ruth 1:12-17)

Sunday, Feb. 6—Naomi and Ruth Travel to Bethlehem (Ruth 1:18-22)

Conclusion

A. Two Other Women

In considering the topic of grief, it is also instructive to consider the example of Mary and Martha in their grieving over the death of their brother Lazarus. John 11:20 records the initial reactions of both women when Jesus came to Bethany, the town where the sisters lived. The contrast is striking: "Then Martha, as soon as she heard that Jesus was coming, went and met him: but Mary sat still in the house."

Two points are of special note. The first is that this description echoes what we are told of the sisters in other passages in the Gospels, particularly Luke 10:38-42. There Martha is the aggressive initiative-taker, concerned that everything be "just right" for her guests (Jesus and His disciples). Mary, on the other hand, is the quiet, meditative individual, satisfied to sit at Jesus' feet and take in whatever He has to say. Observe that in John 11:20, it is Martha who immediately goes out to meet Jesus when He arrives. Mary, the more reflective of the two, prefers to remain in the house.

The two sisters' different responses illustrate an important truth: people express grief in different ways. Some are very open and verbal about how they feel; others are more withdrawn and introspective. Some need the company of other people; others prefer to be alone. For some, tears come easily and frequently; others carry the look of those who are grief-stricken, but there are no tears.

To both sisters Jesus offers His presence and, even more significantly, His power. He raised Lazarus from the dead with only a command. Death submitted to the Master just as quickly as the winds and waves of a raging storm had done earlier. Jesus remains, by virtue of His own resurrection, the great overcomer. He empowers us to be overcomers as well (Romans 8:37-39).

B. Prayer

Father in Heaven, thank You that in Your Son Jesus we can be "more than conquerors." Whenever circumstances such as death tear us away from those we love, may we remember that nothing can separate us from Your love. Grant us remembrance as well that there will be a day when tears are no more. In Jesus' name, amen.

C. Thought to Remember

His oath, His covenant, His blood,
Support me in the whelming flood;
When all around my soul gives way,
He then is all my hope and stay.
     —Edward Mote (1797–1874)

Learning by Doing

This page contains an alternative lesson plan emphasizing learning activities.
Classes desiring such student involvement will find these suggestions helpful.

Learning Goals

After participating in this lesson, each student will be able to:

1. Relate the series of events that led to Ruth's expression of devotion and loyalty to Naomi.

2. Explain how faith in God makes a difference in dealing with grief.

3. Think of a situation where he or she may be able to help someone in overcoming grief, and pray for wisdom in carrying out such a ministry.

Into the Lesson

Before class make copies of the word search puzzle below. Give each student a copy when he or she arrives. Your learners should naturally start working on the puzzle during the informal time of visiting before class starts. If needed, allow a few minutes to complete the puzzle after class begins.

```
H N B U O E T E O C A N N P B
I U O U H O U S E H M D T C E
C T S R R E N O N I J O O M H
F L M B P I E T U L D T A A O
V E A A A A E L E I R E Y B L
O E V V H N H D H O N L A O D
I E I S E L D T D N T C Y T I
C L S H M O O E T S H R D M H
E I I V B T S N A A T R D M B
R M T C A S R F D N O Y H D R
U E E U I P D U U L N B E O E
T L D K E A J O K I N D L Y A
H E E F E D C M N I N A E W D
W C H T N A O M I I H R E S T
E H S O D E A D M P E O P L E
```

Inform your learners that there are twenty-six words from today's lesson text in the puzzle grid. See how many they can find before you reveal the following list of the hidden words: behold, bread, buried, Chilion, clave, country, dead, death, Elimelech, house, husband, Judah, kindly, kissed, Lord, Mahlon, minded, Moab, Naomi, Orpah, people, rest, Ruth, steadfastly, visited, voice.

Into the Word

Ask a volunteer to read Ruth 1:3-9, 14-18 aloud. Briefly review the story, pointing out locations on a map. Then ask your learners to imagine what Naomi might have written to a friend or relative in Judah while she was in Moab. Ask students either to write these imaginary "letters" or to discuss in small groups what she could have included. Challenge your learners to consider the following occasions for writing: the death of Elimelech (v. 3), the marriages of Chilion and Mahlon (v. 4), the deaths of Chilion and Mahlon (v. 5), the decision to return to Judah (vv. 6, 7), the anticipation of arriving in Judah with Ruth (vv. 8, 9, 14-18).

Encourage the learners to write their letters with feeling consistent with the facts being related. The earlier letters should be filled with the grief of bereavement in a foreign land. That grief should be apparent even in the second letter, which concerns the sons' marriages as Naomi comes to terms with the idea of her Hebrew sons marrying Moabite women. (Refer the learners to Deuteronomy 23:3-6 for a little insight on the significance of this.)

The final letter should indicate Naomi's grief as it is tempered by the compassionate love of Ruth, who is accompanying Naomi to Judah. Your best letter writers may even include a note of anticipation for the future.

Into Life

Ask the learners to suggest situations that produce grief today. Write these on the board or overhead transparency. Ideas include death of a loved one, rejection by a prodigal son or daughter, loss of a job, relocation to a new city, an incident that divides a family or church, and divorce. Ask, "How does one's faith in God help make these events easier to bear?"

Try to get learners to avoid "glittering generalities" in their responses. Challenge them to be specific about ways that their faith encourages them in times of grief. Two situations should become clear in this discussion. First, one's personal faith helps him or her to bear up under trial better than one without faith. Second, the presence of others who share that faith is comforting to the believer. Ruth provided this benefit to Naomi.

Ask your students to consider the people they know in their neighborhoods, families, or other "circles of influence." Are some of these suffering through grief? Encourage your learners to look for ways to minister to those who grieve. Close with prayer, asking for God's guidance.

Let's Talk It Over

The questions on this page are designed to promote discussion of the lesson by the class and to encourage application of the lesson Scriptures. The answers provided are only discussion starters. Let your class talk it over from there.

1. Christians are sometimes guilty of condemning those who are not like them in all matters of church life. From the story of Ruth, what do we learn about those who are outside of "our" group and how we are to relate to them?

Ruth was a Moabitess, a citizen of a pagan nation. Although her heritage was not of the true faith of Israel, she did express and exercise faith in the God of Israel.

Within Christianity today, there are many who may not be of our own heritage but who still love and loyally serve the God of the Bible and the Christ of the New Testament. For any person who expresses true faith in Christ we should find and build upon our common ground. We are often quick to build walls between us and those who differ from us because walls are much easier to build than bridges. Walls seem "safe," while bridges seem "risky."

But Christ calls us to be bridge-builders. There was no greater gulf to bridge than the "sin chasm" between God and humans. But Christ bridged that gap. He will help us as we strive together toward Christian unity.

2. Why is it important to "be there" for those going through times of grief? How can we do a better job at this?

Scripture teaches that we are to "weep with them that weep" (Romans 12:15). God has created us with the desire for fellowship. He established the home and the church to provide this fellowship. God declared that it was not good for man to be alone (Genesis 2:18).

People who are "on their own" during times of grief have no one to help them work through the pain. They have no one to remind them that they are still loved. People in grief need someone to reassure them that certain feelings and thoughts that they have (denial, anger, etc.) are natural parts of the grieving process.

It is a mistake simply to tell a grieving person, "If you need anything, just let me know." It's rare that they will respond to that offer. Much better is to see exactly how the person needs to be helped, and then just do it.

3. Family loyalty is a lost concept in many cases today. How can we demonstrate loyalty to family? Or is this really that important?

In the modern world there are many things that attack the very fabric of the family unit. Family members are separated by distance and divorce. Internally, family structures fall apart from bitterness, apathy, etc. It is imperative for Christians to realize that the foundational societal structure given by God is the family (see Exodus 20:12).

The old concept of "quality time" is inadequate. Families need to set aside *quantity* time to be together. It is not the giving of gifts or the buying of things that are needed to build strong homes; it is instead the investment of time and energy in each other's lives that is required.

4. We often struggle with the right thing to do in certain circumstances. What do we learn about the right thing from Ruth and Orpah?

Christians may hold the false belief that there is just one right answer and one proper thing to do in any given situation. They worry and fret over this, seeking some sign from God before they act.

But consider Ruth and Orpah, who were both in the same circumstance. Orpah left Naomi, while Ruth stayed. Was one right and one wrong? Not necessarily. God leaves many choices up to His people. As long as we are not violating general principles or specific commandments found in His Word, there may be two or more viable options. Each option may be acceptable to God, depending on the circumstances, individual needs, and personalities involved.

5. Sometimes we can be fickle! We are hot and cold, up and down. In spiritual matters this is a dangerous way to live. How can we steadfastly focus on the way of God? How have you been able to do this?

To stay on track spiritually, we must set our gaze forward. With heart and mind, there must be a resolute decision not to turn aside. Staying focused is a matter for each individual. Whether it be Joshua saying, "As for me and my house, we will serve the Lord" (Joshua 24:15) or Paul's "forgetting those things which are behind, and reaching forth unto those things which are before" (Philippians 3:13), a conscious decision has to be made to be "steadfast, unmovable, always abounding in the work of the Lord" (1 Corinthians 15:58).

Overcoming Pride

DEVOTIONAL READING: **Mark 7:1-5, 14-23.**

BACKGROUND SCRIPTURE: **2 Kings 5.**

PRINTED TEXT: **2 Kings 5:1-15a.**

2 Kings 5:1-15a

1 Now Naaman, captain of the host of the king of Syria, was a great man with his master, and honorable, because by him the LORD had given deliverance unto Syria: he was also a mighty man in valor, but he was a leper.

2 And the Syrians had gone out by companies, and had brought away captive out of the land of Israel a little maid; and she waited on Naaman's wife.

3 And she said unto her mistress, Would God my lord were with the prophet that is in Samaria! for he would recover him of his leprosy.

4 And one went in, and told his lord, saying, Thus and thus said the maid that is of the land of Israel.

5 And the king of Syria said, Go to, go, and I will send a letter unto the king of Israel. And he departed, and took with him ten talents of silver, and six thousand pieces of gold, and ten changes of raiment.

6 And he brought the letter to the king of Israel, saying, Now when this letter is come unto thee, behold, I have therewith sent Naaman my servant to thee, that thou mayest recover him of his leprosy.

7 And it came to pass, when the king of Israel had read the letter, that he rent his clothes, and said, Am I God, to kill and to make alive, that this man doth send unto me to recover a man of his leprosy? Wherefore consider, I pray you, and see how he seeketh a quarrel against me.

8 And it was so, when Elisha the man of God had heard that the king of Israel had rent his clothes, that he sent to the king, saying, Wherefore hast thou rent thy clothes? let him come now to me, and he shall know that there is a prophet in Israel.

9 So Naaman came with his horses and with his chariot, and stood at the door of the house of Elisha.

10 And Elisha sent a messenger unto him, saying, Go and wash in Jordan seven times, and thy flesh shall come again to thee, and thou shalt be clean.

11 But Naaman was wroth, and went away, and said, Behold, I thought, He will surely come out to me, and stand, and call on the name of the LORD his God, and strike his hand over the place, and recover the leper.

12 Are not Abana and Pharpar, rivers of Damascus, better than all the waters of Israel? may I not wash in them, and be clean? So he turned and went away in a rage.

13 And his servants came near, and spake unto him, and said, My father, if the prophet had bid thee do some great thing, wouldest thou not have done it? how much rather then, when he saith to thee, Wash, and be clean?

14 Then went he down, and dipped himself seven times in Jordan, according to the saying of the man of God: and his flesh came again like unto the flesh of a little child, and he was clean.

15a And he returned to the man of God, he and all his company, and came, and stood before him: and he said, Behold, now I know that there is no God in all the earth, but in Israel.

**Feb
13**

Lesson Aims

After participating in this lesson, each student will be able to:

1. Relate how Naaman overcame his pride in order to receive the divine cure from his leprosy.

2. Explain how pride keeps people today from enjoying divine favor.

3. Identify an area in his or her own life where pride needs to be defeated and express a commitment to release that pride.

Lesson Outline

INTRODUCTION
  A. It's All About *Me*
  B. Lesson Background
  I. SYRIAN'S PLIGHT (2 Kings 5:1-4)
    A. Naaman's Situation (v. 1)
    B. Possible Solution (vv. 2-4)
 II. KING'S PANIC (2 Kings 5:5-7)
    A. Letter Sent (v. 5)
    B. Letter Read (vv. 6, 7)
III. PROPHET'S PROPOSAL (2 Kings 5:8-15a)
    A. Elisha's Command (vv. 8-10)
    B. Naaman's Pride (vv. 11, 12)
      Pride Before a Fall
    C. Servants' Counsel (v. 13)
      "I Really Mean It!"
    D. Naaman's Compliance (v. 14)
    E. Naaman's Confession (v. 15a)
CONCLUSION
  A. A Prayer for Our Time
  B. Prayer
  C. Thought to Remember

Introduction

A. It's All About *Me*

During a National Football League game in October 2002, a player caught a pass and scored a touchdown for his team. Following his dash into the end zone, the player reached down to his shoes, pulled out a felt-tip marker, autographed the football, and handed it as a souvenir to a friend sitting in the front row.

While some harshly criticized the player for his actions, others saw the incident as just another example of the self-promotion that characterizes so much of the sports world today. As one columnist noted, the motto in sports these days seems to be, "Wake up and smell the *me*."

People often have referred to the 1960s as the "Me Generation." But that label could be attached to every generation of humanity, for pride knows no limits or restrictions of time or geographical boundaries. In our lesson today, we will see pride manifest itself in the thinking of Naaman, a Syrian military commander afflicted with leprosy. His pride almost resulted in his rejection of the only remedy for his condition.

Some of Naaman's servants, however, had the courage to speak up and call attention to the folly of his behavior. To Naaman's credit, he was willing to swallow his pride and obey the Lord's word as conveyed through His prophet.

If only God's own people had demonstrated such humility, how different their history would have been!

B. Lesson Background

The story of Naaman occurred during the ministry of the prophet Elisha. At this point in the history of God's people, the twelve tribes had been divided into two separate nations for a little less than a hundred years. Elisha's ministry was primarily to the northern kingdom (usually referred to as Israel), where Baal worship had made serious inroads because of the influence of King Ahab and his pagan wife Jezebel.

The text for today from 2 Kings refers to the king of Israel and the king of Syria, though it does not mention either by name. Most likely the king of Israel was Joram or Jehoram (but usually spelled as Joram in most English Bibles to distinguish him from the Jehoram who was king of Judah at about the same time). The king of Syria (sometimes called Aram) was probably Ben-Hadad II.

I. Syrian's Plight
(2 Kings 5:1-4)

A. Naaman's Situation (v. 1)

1. Now Naaman, captain of the host of the king of Syria, was a great man with his master, and honorable, because by him the LORD had given deliverance unto Syria: he was also a mighty man in valor, but he was a leper.

Naaman is introduced to us as *captain of the host of the king of Syria*. This means that he is a high-ranking officer in the army of that country. He has distinguished himself in this capacity, as indicated by the descriptions that he is *a great man, honorable,* and *a mighty man in valor.*

But while Naaman is unquestionably a capable leader, he is in truth an instrument in the greater, more honorable, and mightier hands of the Lord. It is through Naaman that *the Lord had given deliverance unto Syria.*

When we study Old Testament history, we usually think of God's activity in delivering His people from their oppressors (as in the exodus or in the days of the judges). But God is the Lord of all nations (Isaiah 14:26, 27). He is as capable of aiding them as He is of aiding the Israelites. In this case His deliverance of Syria may refer to a victory that that nation achieved over the Assyrians around the middle of the ninth century B.C., the time in which the events in today's lesson take place.

One might think that the fact that Naaman is *a leper* would prevent him from carrying out any kind of military activity. However, the Hebrew word often translated *leprosy* in our Bible does not always indicate the severe, debilitating affliction ("Hansen's Disease") that we often associate with that term. It can also describe less serious skin conditions, such as psoriasis or eczema.

Naaman's condition, whatever it may be, is most likely in its earliest stages. Note Naaman's reference to "the place" in verse 11, as if there is a specific spot on his skin that is particularly troublesome.

B. Possible Solution (vv. 2-4)

2, 3. And the Syrians had gone out by companies, and had brought away captive out of the land of Israel a little maid; and she waited on Naaman's wife. And she said unto her mistress, Would God my lord were with the prophet that is in Samaria! for he would recover him of his leprosy.

The strategy of the *Syrians* against Israel at this particular time involves dispatching a series of *companies,* or smaller bands of troops, that engage the Israelites in brief skirmishes at certain key locations. Often both captives and goods are seized in the process.

During one such excursion, the Syrians had taken *captive . . . a little maid,* or young girl. Many of the captives exhibit bitterness or hatred toward their captors. This Israelite girl, however, apparently develops a great respect for Naaman, whose *wife* she serves. (This may say something about how Naaman and his wife treat this girl.)

One day the girl voices her concern for her *lord* (Naaman) to Naaman's wife. The girl is con-

vinced that if only Naaman could consult *the prophet* (Elisha) *that is in Samaria, he would recover* (cure) *him of his leprosy.* [See question #1, page 208.]

4. And one went in, and told his lord, saying, Thus and thus said the maid that is of the land of Israel.

The *one* in this verse is most likely Naaman, who tells *his lord* (here the word *lord* refers to the king of Syria) about the Israelite girl's suggestion. This explains why the king of Syria responds in the next verse of our text.

II. King's Panic
(2 Kings 5:5-7)
A. Letter Sent (v. 5)

5. And the king of Syria said, Go to, go, and I will send a letter unto the king of Israel. And he departed, and took with him ten talents of silver, and six thousand pieces of gold, and ten changes of raiment.

The phrase *Go to, go* conveys a sense of urgency, as if to say, "Indeed, or by all means, go!" In speaking these words, *the king of Syria* indicates his concern for Naaman's health. The king, too, respects this "mighty man in valor" (v. 1) and values his skill on the battlefield.

The fact that the king of Syria could send a letter to *the king of Israel* may reflect more cordial relations than could be indicated by the skirmishes mentioned earlier. However, a treaty was agreed to by the Israelites and the Syrians during the reign of King Ahab (1 Kings 20:34). The existence of this treaty seems to be recognized during King Joram's reign as well, in spite of the occasional Syrian raids into Israel.

In the ancient Near East, it is common to provide some kind of payment whenever certain services are requested of a prophet. This is characteristic of pagan prophets more than it is of the Lord's prophets, as illustrated by Elisha's later refusal to accept any such offer from Naaman (2 Kings 5:15, 16). But Naaman, coming from a pagan background, believes that such a payment is part of the "protocol" when dealing with a prophet.

The Syrian's gift is impressive indeed: *ten talents of silver, and six thousand pieces of gold, and ten changes of raiment.* The word *pieces* is

GOLDEN TEXT: His servants came near, and spake unto him, and said, My father, if the prophet had bid thee do some great thing, wouldest thou not have done it? how much rather then, when he saith to thee, Wash, and be clean? Then went he down, and dipped himself seven times in Jordan, . . . and he was clean.—2 Kings 5:13, 14.

italicized in the King James translation, indicating that it does not appear in the original Hebrew text. Most commentators suggest that the standard of measurement is probably the shekel, which weighs just a bit over four-tenths of an ounce. At three hundred dollars per ounce today, this amount of gold equates to over seven hundred thousand U.S. dollars!

To get an idea of the value of ten talents of silver, consider that King Omri of Israel bought the hill on which he built the city of Samaria for just two talents of silver (1 Kings 16:24). *Ten changes of raiment*, or clothing, would be quite an addition to anyone's wardrobe, even today.

B. Letter Read (vv. 6, 7)

6. And he brought the letter to the king of Israel, saying, Now when this letter is come unto thee, behold, I have therewith sent Naaman my servant to thee, that thou mayest recover him of his leprosy.

The contents of this *letter* may provide another illustration of the pagan mind-set of the Syrians. Apparently the king of Syria assumes that the prophet in Samaria is under the control of the king (as prophets usually are in pagan countries). So the Syrian king directs his request for Naaman's healing directly to Joram, *the king of Israel.* Another possibility is that the king of Syria assumes that Joram knows of Elisha and will convey the message of the letter to him.

7. And it came to pass, when the king of Israel had read the letter, that he rent his clothes, and said, Am I God, to kill and to make alive, that this man doth send unto me to recover a man of his leprosy? Wherefore consider, I pray you, and see how he seeketh a quarrel against me.

The king of Syria probably is not aware of the tension that exists between the prophet Elisha and the spiritually weak King Joram (see 2 Kings

---

How to Say It

ABANA. *Ab*-uh-nuh or Uh-*ban*-uh.
AHAB. *Ay*-hab.
BAAL. *Bay*-ul.
BEN-HADAD. Ben-*hay*-dad.
DAMASCUS. Duh-*mass*-kus.
ECZEMA. *ek*-zuh-muh.
ELISHA. E-*lye*-shuh.
JEZEBEL. *Jez*-uh-bel.
NAAMAN. *Nay*-uh-mun.
OMRI. *Ahm*-rye.
PHARPAR. *Far*-par.
PSORIASIS. suh-*ri*-uh-sis *(ri* as in *rye).*
SAMARIA. Suh-*mare*-ee-uh.
SYRIA. *Sear*-ee-uh.

6:30-32, where Joram is most likely the king described in the text). When Joram reads *the letter,* he does not think of Elisha at all. He views the letter as nothing more than a political ploy devised by the king of Syria to start a conflict with *Israel.*

III. Prophet's Proposal (2 Kings 5:8-15a)

A. Elisha's Command (vv. 8-10)

8. And it was so, when Elisha the man of God had heard that the king of Israel had rent his clothes, that he sent to the king, saying, Wherefore hast thou rent thy clothes? let him come now to me, and he shall know that there is a prophet in Israel.

When the prophet *Elisha* hears of the king's alarmed reaction, he chides the king for such a faithless response. This issue is nothing to tear one's *clothes* over. *Let him come now to me, and he shall know that there is a prophet in Israel* (even if King Joram doesn't).

Joram has asked the question, "Am I God?" (v. 7). Certainly, he is not, nor is Elisha; but Elisha is a *man of God* who will address the concerns expressed by the king of Syria. The real King in *Israel* is still the Lord.

9. So Naaman came with his horses and with his chariot, and stood at the door of the house of Elisha.

Elisha's message is passed on to Naaman, who proceeds to the prophet's *house.* The text mentions Naaman's *horses* and *chariot,* perhaps to highlight the fact that Naaman has brought his typical military entourage.

Naaman probably hopes to impress *Elisha* with just how worthy he is of the prophet's attention. So he stands *at the door of the house,* waiting (perhaps somewhat impatiently) for the prophet to come out.

10. And Elisha sent a messenger unto him, saying, Go and wash in Jordan seven times, and thy flesh shall come again to thee, and thou shalt be clean.

In most pagan environments, a prophet shows great respect for the king and for other important leaders (such as someone of Naaman's reputation). Perhaps Naaman expects *Elisha* to emerge from his house and express his admiration that such a renowned individual would come all the way from Syria for his assistance. If so, how surprised and offended Naaman must be that Elisha himself does not even bother to appear!

Instead, the prophet merely sends a *messenger,* whose word is simple: Naaman must *wash* in the *Jordan* River *seven times;* then his leprosy will be cured.

B. Naaman's Pride (vv. 11, 12)

11. But Naaman was wroth, and went away, and said, Behold, I thought, He will surely come out to me, and stand, and call on the name of the LORD his God, and strike his hand over the place, and recover the leper.

Naaman is *wroth*, or furious, both at the prophet's refusal to *come out* to see him and even more by such a seemingly ridiculous "prescription" for his leprosy. Again, perhaps Naaman's more pagan-oriented thinking contributes to his reaction. He expects a much more elaborate, flamboyant display of power—something appropriate for a man of his standing. To be told he must go to the Jordan River, probably about twenty miles away, is an insult. [See question #2, page 208.]

12. Are not Abana and Pharpar, rivers of Damascus, better than all the waters of Israel? may I not wash in them, and be clean? So he turned and went away in a rage.

From the standpoint of sheer logic, Naaman's response to the prophet's suggested cure seems to make sense. If a river is part of the remedy for his leprosy, why does it have to be the Jordan, which is often sluggish and muddy? There are rivers in Syria and its capital *Damascus* that are just as good, if not better.

Clearly, Naaman's ego has taken a beating. He has come to Elisha with a certain set of expectations, and none of them has been met. So he turns and leaves *in a rage.* [See question #3, page 208.]

PRIDE BEFORE A FALL

Sometimes pride encourages people to get into deep trouble. Pride manifests itself in various ways, one of which is known as "résumé padding." Perhaps one of the saddest such cases came to an ominous close on May 16, 1996, when Admiral Jeremy M. "Mike" Boorda, U.S. Navy Chief of Naval Operations, committed suicide.

U.S. President Bill Clinton had appointed Admiral Boorda to his prestigious post in early 1994. Subsequently, word got out that one or more of the combat decorations that the admiral claimed may not have been officially awarded. Rather than "face the music," Admiral Boorda ended his life with a gunshot through the chest.

After expressing deep regret over the incident, one Navy officer said, "No officer should ever be in a position where he or she fears the truth. But integrity is like virginity—once you've lost it, it's gone for good." That analogy may be a bit overstated, but the danger of pride is still shockingly clear. After leading us into wrong paths, pride can yield horrible consequences if we don't take steps to reverse it. —J. D. R.

Visual for lesson 11. *The Jordan river, where Naaman exchanged his pride for God's grace. Discuss how people today need to release pride to find grace.*

C. Servants' Counsel (v. 13)

13. And his servants came near, and spake unto him, and said, My father, if the prophet had bid thee do some great thing, wouldest thou not have done it? how much rather then, when he saith to thee, Wash, and be clean?

Naaman is blessed to have some very discerning (not to mention courageous!) *servants,* who take it upon themselves to approach the frustrated Syrian. They bring their own brand of logic to the situation. They begin by addressing Naaman as *father,* another indication of the high respect in which Naaman is held by all who know him.

They then point out that if Elisha had told Naaman to perform some feat of strength or endurance *(some great thing)* to prove his worth, Naaman would have accepted the challenge. He ought therefore to accept the very simple request of the prophet, even though it seems absurd. The issue comes down to this: how badly does Naaman want to rid himself of his leprosy?

"I REALLY MEAN IT!"

Picture this: you hire a reputable company to paint the exterior of your house. You are going on vacation, so you anticipate that the job will be finished when you return. You choose the colors and negotiate the price. You want it basic white with green trim. The contract is signed and you depart.

When you come back, your contractor has painted your house yellow with blue trim. He says to you, "I know what you asked for, but I think this will be a more appealing combination and will really stand out in this community. So I took the liberty of changing your color scheme."

Perhaps your painter will think that your complaints sound unreasonable and restrictive. But you don't think so, and neither will a judge!

Why is it, then, that when the Almighty gives a specific command, His subjects have the audacity to declare that something else—something less or more—is what they'll do? How can we expect Him to be pleased and accept us with this kind of an attitude?

God was clear in Old Testament times that His commands were not negotiable or optional. In the New Testament era, we may be tempted to pay less attention to God's commands and laws because we live under grace. But it is vital to remember that "this is the love of God, that we keep his commandments" (1 John 5:3). —J. D. R.

D. Naaman's Compliance (v. 14)

14. Then went he down, and dipped himself seven times in Jordan, according to the saying of the man of God: and his flesh came again like unto the flesh of a little child, and he was clean.

It is never easy to confront and try to reason with an angry person. Naaman's servants are to be commended for their willingness to do so. Their gentle but persuasive and firm logic convinces Naaman that his immediate reaction was wrong.

So he proceeds to go to the *Jordan* River and dip *himself seven times*. And as the *man of God* had promised, Naaman's *flesh* becomes *like unto the flesh of a little child*. It should be noted that Naaman's heart has become as that of a little child as well, for he has humbled himself before the Lord and His messenger Elisha. [See question #4, page 208.]

E. Naaman's Confession (v. 15a)

15a. And he returned to the man of God, he and all his company, and came, and stood before him: and he said, Behold, now I know that there is no God in all the earth, but in Israel.

Home Daily Bible Readings

Monday, Feb. 7—These Evil Things Defile a Person (Mark 7:17-23)

Tuesday, Feb. 8—Trap My Enemies in Their Pride (Psalm 59:10-17)

Wednesday, Feb. 9—God Will End Arrogant People's Pride (Isaiah 13:9-13)

Thursday, Feb. 10—Naaman Hopes for a Cure (2 Kings 5:1-5a)

Friday, Feb. 11—Elisha Tells Naaman What to Do (2 Kings 5:5b-10)

Saturday, Feb. 12—Naaman Is Cured (2 Kings 5:11-14)

Sunday, Feb. 13—Naaman Accepts the God of Israel (2 Kings 5:15-19)

Naaman's attitude is radically different from what it had been previously. He is a different man—both on the outside and on the inside.

The inward change in Naaman is reflected in his words to *the man of God*, Elisha: *Now I know that there is no God in all the earth, but in Israel.* We noted in last week's lesson that Ruth made a kind of "Good Confession" in her declaration of commitment to Naomi's God (Ruth 1:16). Naaman now makes a similar statement.

Notice that Naaman is not merely adding the God of Israel to the list of gods that he already worships. Rather, he is acknowledging that *there is no God in all the earth, but in Israel.* Earlier, Naaman had referred to the Lord as Elisha's God (v. 11). Now he is affirming, like Ruth, that "your God is my God." [See question #5, page 208.]

Conclusion

A. A Prayer for Our Time

For a number of years, Richard Halverson served as chaplain of the United States Senate. One of his duties in this position was to offer a prayer at the beginning of each session of the Senate. On May 2, 1984, Halverson gave the following prayer. As you read it, consider its relevance to our lesson and our lives.

"Almighty God, we have come a long way since our birth as a republic, but we have wandered somehow. Our Founding Fathers held freedom of religion as fundamental. We have translated their deep conviction into freedom from religion.

"We have become technological giants, and spiritual and moral dwarfs. We are sophisticated in scientific progress and primitive in spiritual development.

"We are knowledgeable in the ways of the world and ignorant in the ways of God. We live as though man is the center of the universe and God a peripheral invention of pious enthusiasts.

"We are abundantly rich in material resources and abysmally poor in spiritual and moral capital.

"Dear God, help us get our act together before it is too late. In the name of Him who is the Way, the Truth, and the Life. Amen."

B. Prayer

Father, we confess how often pride has kept us from a closer walk with You. Break down our self-made walls this day in Jesus' name, amen.

C. Thought to Remember

"A proud man is always looking down on things and people: and, of course, as long as you are looking down, you cannot see something that is above you."—C. S. Lewis (1898–1963)

Learning by Doing

This page contains an alternative lesson plan emphasizing learning activities.
Classes desiring such student involvement will find these suggestions helpful.

Learning Goals

After participating in this lesson, each student will be able to:

1. Relate how Naaman overcame his pride in order to receive the divine cure from his leprosy.

2. Explain how pride keeps people today from enjoying divine favor.

3. Identify an area in his or her own life where pride needs to be defeated and express a commitment to release that pride.

Into the Lesson

Begin the session by telling the students you'd like their help in proposing to the major TV networks a new reality show. The program will bring famous people onto the set to determine who is the most arrogant! You need their help in coming up with a list of athletes, performers, politicians, and others who have a chance at the title, "World's Most Arrogant Human." (No local people allowed! All suggestions must be famous people not personally acquainted with anyone in the class.)

Let the students enjoy this exercise without allowing it to get out of hand. Poking a little good-natured fun at athletes who dance or gyrate after they score or at politicians who promise the sun, moon, and stars to get elected should be harmless. But don't let the talk turn political or into personal attacks at certain celebrities based on your learners' opinions or positions.

After a few minutes, ask, "Who would want this title? Anyone?" After the class acknowledges that this would not be a coveted position, ask, "Why is arrogance (or pride) looked on so negatively?" Discuss the irony of pride's being universally recognized as bad, but just about as universally practiced.

Observe that today's lesson looks at an example of one who could have earned the title, "World's Most Arrogant." But when he released his pride, he became one of the world's most blessed.

Into the Word

Today's lesson comes from a text that is a favorite source of Bible drama for children. If possible, recruit some children from grades 5 and 6 who enjoy acting to act out the events of 2 Kings 5:1-15. (You'll need to recruit and work with the children in advance.) Otherwise, have a good reader read the text aloud.

Provide a handout to guide students through the Bible study. Students may work individually or in small groups to complete the table described below. At the top of the handout should be the title, "The Problem of Pride." Below that should be a table or grid with the following headings: *Potential Reasons for Pride; Evidence or Demonstrations of Pride; Reasons Pride Was Inappropriate.* Down the left side should be the following: Naaman, Servant girl, King of Israel, Elisha.

When you call for reports, fill in a copy of the chart with your learners' answers, supplementing as necessary. Naaman may have been proud because of his high position and success. His pride is evidenced by his hurt feelings and his initial refusal to submit. He had no reason for pride because he himself was powerless to do anything about his condition; he was dependent on God. Had he continued in pride, he would have forfeited his opportunity for healing.

The servant girl could have been proud because she knew the God who could heal Naaman. She showed no evidence of pride, however. She was God's servant first.

The king of Israel was likely proud of his position. He shows pride in that he thought the request for Naaman's healing was "all about him"; he failed to recognize the opportunity to point Naaman to God. He should have been humbled, knowing God to be the true king.

Elisha could have shown pride because he was specially blessed by God to do miracles and foretell future events. But he shows none of that. He recognized his power was from God, not himself.

Into Life

Point out the potential result of Naaman's pride: forfeiture of healing. Ask, "How does pride keep people today from enjoying divine favor?" Potential answers include the failure to find salvation, as those who take pride in their own efforts are unable to appreciate salvation by grace. Be sure to explore potential results of pride among Christians—what blessings do we who are saved also miss out on because of pride? Also, think of fractured relationships that are not mended because of pride.

Wrap up the class with a challenge for each student to examine his or her life for signs of pride. Close with prayer for greater humility.

Let's Talk It Over

The questions on this page are designed to promote discussion of the lesson
by the class and to encourage application of the lesson Scriptures. The answers
provided are only discussion starters. Let your class talk it over from there.

1. People face many needs in life. The ultimate answer to life's most pressing needs are found in God. How can you be used to point people to the God who gives help?

The little girl in this story is a prime example of sharing one's faith. She could not provide the healing Naaman needed, but she could point him to the one who could.

Often in the church we are told to "go and tell" the message of salvation through Jesus Christ. Sometimes we may not be able to teach someone who is searching or to provide all the answers to a lost neighbor or friend. But we can point them in the right direction. Instead of "go and tell," evangelism sometimes is summed up in the words "come and see" (cf. John 1:46). All of us can invite someone to come to church where they can meet the One who can cleanse, heal, and forgive.

2. The directives of God, though straightforward, sometimes seem strange to us. Why does God choose to work in this way?

Naaman could not believe that simply going and washing in a dirty river could somehow cleanse him of his leprosy. Either he considered it too simple a request, too strange a request, or beneath his dignity.

On the Day of Pentecost when the people asked what they must do to be saved, Peter responded, "Repent, and be baptized" (Acts 2:38). Some who hear that today think that plan is simplistic; they would rather try to earn their salvation through good works. Others consider baptism to be a strange thing that is beneath their personal dignity. But God has chosen to do things in His own way, perhaps to test our willingness to submit. In doing so He says that He makes foolish the wisdom of this world (1 Corinthians 1:20).

3. Pride apparently caused Naaman to balk at the suggestion of dipping in the Jordan River. How does pride keep us from following God's will today?

Satan is a master at using pride to thwart the purpose of God in the lives of Christians. Pride in possessions causes some to think they should automatically be in positions of authority and control in the church. Pride in a good knowledge of the Bible can cause a Christian to look down on and question the faith of a fellow Christian who has not reached that same level of knowledge.

Pride in position can cause a church leader to "lord it over" others in the church and become authoritarian and even abusive. Pride keeps Christians from serving in some of the so-called "menial" tasks such as assisting in work projects, going into the inner city, or taking part in a short-term mission trip. In each case, pride has caused one to look out for self first.

4. Simply doing things God's way is the best way. What foundational areas of obedience concerning God's will are you lacking in?

Naaman finally was convinced to obey and go dip in the Jordan River. God has called us to some foundational areas of obedience as well. Whether it be simply to offer a cup of cold water in the name of Jesus (Matthew 10:42) or to visit the fatherless and widows in their time of need (James 1:27), these are essential ministries with which any Christian can be involved.

Simple acts of obedience you may need to perform could be to offer forgiveness to someone who has wronged you or a word of encouragement to someone who is discouraged. Obedience instead of questioning and adherence to the way of God instead of complaining about the Word of God are vital for a proper relationship with our Heavenly Father.

5. It was after he was cleansed that Naaman finally confessed his belief in the one true God. How are we even more blessed in our acknowledgment of God?

A popular adage tells us that "seeing is believing." Thomas the apostle subscribed to this notion (see John 20:25).

But Jesus tells us that those who have not seen and yet have believed are blessed (John 20:29). Today many still look for a sign before they will believe and accept the will of God. But "an evil and adulterous generation seeketh after a sign" (Matthew 12:39). We may not have walked with Jesus and seen His miracles personally, but we believe the written testimony about those wondrous signs (John 20:30, 31). A prayer we pray may not be answered as we desire, but still we believe God is good and is yet in control. This makes us truly blessed.

Overcoming Uncertainty

DEVOTIONAL READING: John 3:18-21.

BACKGROUND SCRIPTURE: John 3:1-21.

PRINTED TEXT: John 3:1-17.

John 3:1-17

1 There was a man of the Pharisees, named Nicodemus, a ruler of the Jews:

2 The same came to Jesus by night, and said unto him, Rabbi, we know that thou art a teacher come from God: for no man can do these miracles that thou doest, except God be with him.

3 Jesus answered and said unto him, Verily, verily, I say unto thee, Except a man be born again, he cannot see the kingdom of God.

4 Nicodemus saith unto him, How can a man be born when he is old? can he enter the second time into his mother's womb, and be born?

5 Jesus answered, Verily, verily, I say unto thee, Except a man be born of water and of the Spirit, he cannot enter into the kingdom of God.

6 That which is born of the flesh is flesh; and that which is born of the Spirit is spirit.

7 Marvel not that I said unto thee, Ye must be born again.

8 The wind bloweth where it listeth, and thou hearest the sound thereof, but canst not tell whence it cometh, and whither it goeth: so is every one that is born of the Spirit.

9 Nicodemus answered and said unto him, How can these things be?

10 Jesus answered and said unto him, Art thou a master of Israel, and knowest not these things?

11 Verily, verily, I say unto thee, We speak that we do know, and testify that we have seen; and ye receive not our witness.

12 If I have told you earthly things, and ye believe not, how shall ye believe, if I tell you of heavenly things?

13 And no man hath ascended up to heaven, but he that came down from heaven, even the Son of man which is in heaven.

14 And as Moses lifted up the serpent in the wilderness, even so must the Son of man be lifted up:

15 That whosoever believeth in him should not perish, but have eternal life.

16 For God so loved the world, that he gave his only begotten Son, that whosoever believeth in him should not perish, but have everlasting life.

17 For God sent not his Son into the world to condemn the world; but that the world through him might be saved.

GOLDEN TEXT: Jesus answered, Verily, verily, I say unto thee, Except a man be born of water and of the Spirit, he cannot enter into the kingdom of God. That which is born of the flesh is flesh; and that which is born of the Spirit is spirit.—John 3:5, 6.

**Feb
20**

Called to Be God's People
Unit 3: Whosoever Will—Come!
(Lessons 10-13)

Lesson Aims

After participating in this lesson, each student will be able to:

1. Recount what Jesus told Nicodemus about the new birth.

2. Compare and contrast the lifestyles of those who have been born again with the lifestyles of unbelievers.

3. Give thanks to God for sending Jesus and giving us new birth.

Lesson Outline

INTRODUCTION

  A. How to Find God

  B. Lesson Background

 I. NEED FOR A NEW BIRTH (John 3:1-3)

  A. Inquiry (vv. 1, 2)

    On Target?

  B. Confrontation (v. 3)

 II. RECEIVING THE NEW BIRTH (John 3:4-11)

  A. Water and Spirit (vv. 4-7)

  B. Wind and Spirit (v. 8)

  C. Question and Answer (vv. 9-11)

III. UNDERSTANDING THE NEW BIRTH (John 3:12-17)

  A. Life, Not Death (vv. 12-15)

    Doing Right, Wrong, and Nothing

  B. Salvation, Not Condemnation (vv. 16, 17)

CONCLUSION

  A. New Birth Produces New Life

  B. Prayer

  C. Thought to Remember

Introduction

A. How to Find God

The topic "how to find God" is not new. People have been attempting to make a connection with God (or "the gods," as the case may be) throughout history. The early twenty-first century is no exception.

There seems to be no consensus, however, on how God may be found. For example, a 2001 Barna Research survey reported that 51 percent of American adults believe that it is possible to earn a place in Heaven by being "generally good" or by "doing good things." A 1994 Barna survey revealed that only 39 percent of Americans believe that a failure to accept Jesus as Savior will result in being "condemned to Hell." A 2002 Barna survey showed that 37 percent of U.S. adults consider themselves to be "Christians," while they also declare that they have not been born again.

The existence of so many religious beliefs with contradictory ideas certainly presents us with a mess! Yet in the midst of such confusion, Jesus says without hesitation that people will not see the kingdom of God unless they are born again.

B. Lesson Background

John writes his Gospel to convince his readers that Jesus is "the Christ, the Son of God" (John 20:31). John does this by recording important miracles and teachings.

One of the earliest recorded teachings of Jesus focuses on a private conversation with a certain Nicodemus, a very religious Jew who was a teacher himself. When Nicodemus sought out Jesus to learn more about Him, Jesus confronted that learned man with the most important challenge of his life. This challenge made him step beyond his beliefs to examine his relationship with God in a new and powerful way.

I. Need for a New Birth (John 3:1-3)

Jesus' days are busy. So on occasion He looks forward to quiet time (e.g., Luke 4:42). But this particular evening is interrupted by a visitor. In spite of Jesus' weariness, He finds time to teach.

A. Inquiry (vv. 1, 2)

1. There was a man of the Pharisees, named Nicodemus, a ruler of the Jews.

The Pharisees consider themselves to be the guardians of God's laws. They have counted more than six hundred commands in the Old Testament, which they then interpreted and supplemented. Ultimately, they ended up making their interpretations into a protective hedge around God's laws. Most Pharisees reject Jesus because they believe He broke the law (e.g., Matthew 12:1-14).

Not only is *Nicodemus* a Pharisee, but he is also *a ruler of the Jews*. This means that he is part of the Jewish Supreme Court known as the Sanhedrin, which also opposes Jesus.

ON TARGET?

Tony Evans tells about a man who visited a farm and noticed that on the barn were several bull's-eye targets. On closer inspection he discovered that in the middle of each of those targets was a single shot, dead center.

The man complimented the farmer upon learning that he was the one who had handled the rifle. "You must be an expert marksman—smack in the middle every time." The farmer replied, "Well, to be truthful, I just fired away and painted all those bull's-eyes after I shot."

Evans concludes: "I've run across a lot of thoughtless and aimless people. Are you clear and purposeful, aiming at a legitimate target, or are you just trying to learn how to paint well?"

Right here was where the Pharisees had a problem. The Scripture interpretations they came up with were justified by painting bull's-eyes around them. But unlike the farmer in the story above, the Pharisees were unwilling to recognize the illegitimacy of what they were doing. What about us?   —J. D. R.

2. The same came to Jesus by night, and said unto him, Rabbi, we know that thou art a teacher come from God: for no man can do these miracles that thou doest, except God be with him.

Many Pharisees believe that *Jesus* performs miracles by satanic power (e.g., Matthew 12:24). Nicodemus proves that he is not one of them when he addresses Jesus as *Rabbi* (teacher). Nicodemus risks much by holding this opinion in opposition to his fellow Pharisees.

Even so, many today criticize Nicodemus for coming *by night.* Is Nicodemus using the cover of darkness out of fear of his fellow Pharisees? (See John 9:22.) Perhaps Nicodemus purposely hides his beliefs because he thinks that this is the only way to retain his seat on the council.

We should not overlook the fact that John uses the word "night" in his Gospel figuratively to include moral and spiritual darkness (see John 9:4; 11:10; and 13:30). This may be John's subtle way of telling us that Nicodemus's spiritual darkness is worse than he realizes, despite his confession "Rabbi." We see this darkness lift as Nicodemus later speaks in Jesus' defense (John 7:50-53) and helps Joseph of Arimathea prepare Jesus' body for burial (John 19:38, 39). [See question #1, page 216.]

B. Confrontation (v. 3)

3. Jesus answered and said unto him, Verily, verily, I say unto thee, Except a man be born again, he cannot see the kingdom of God.

Jesus often begins discussions by saying something so bold that He immediately grabs people's attention. Nicodemus wants to learn more from Jesus, but does not expect Him to teach a radical transformation. The implication is that the scholarly and distinguished Nicodemus still lacks this transformation.

Jesus begins with *verily, verily.* This is the translation of the Greek word *amen,* which means "let this truly be." So Jesus is stating a truth of utmost importance: only those who undergo a new birth will see God's *kingdom.* The Greek word translated *again* can also mean "from above," and Jesus may be using both meanings at once. Thus this new birth is not only a rebirth but it is also "from above" as it is accomplished by the power of God.

No one is exempt, not even Nicodemus. Certainly he is very religious. As a Pharisee he keeps himself from everything that breaks God's law. He does not dream of lying, stealing, or killing. But Jesus makes it clear that even Nicodemus must *be born again.* No matter how "religious" he is, he will not *see* God's *kingdom* without a new birth.

Jesus' kingdom is not of this world (John 18:36). Most of the Jews in Jesus' day expect God's kingdom to be a political realm where Jews will be militarily, politically, and materially greater than all Gentile nations. But God's kingdom is within, where God rules in the heart (Luke 17:21).

II. Receiving the New Birth (John 3:4-11)

Jesus certainly has the attention of Nicodemus. Nicodemus is full of questions and Jesus now answers them—and more!

A. Water and Spirit (vv. 4-7)

4. Nicodemus saith unto him, How can a man be born when he is old? can he enter the second time into his mother's womb, and be born?

Nicodemus is incredulous, even scornful, in his reply. He wants an explanation. "A *man* cannot reenter *his mother's womb* and be reborn, can he? Exactly what do you mean, Jesus, by saying that a man must be 'born again'?"

5. Jesus answered, Verily, verily, I say unto thee, Except a man be born of water and of the Spirit, he cannot enter into the kingdom of God.

Jesus' response is very similar to what He has just declared in verse 3. The main difference is that He substitutes *born of water and of the Spirit* for "born again."

Very few Christians doubt that the Holy Spirit plays a vital part in being born again (see Romans 2:29; 2 Corinthians 3:6). After we are born again, we are "led by the Spirit of God" (Romans 8:14) and we walk in His ways (Romans 8:4; Galatians 5:16, 25).

On the other hand, there is a great deal of disagreement over the meaning of *water* in this context, and there are numerous ideas. One idea is that the reference is to the amniotic fluid that

How to Say It

ARIMATHEA. *Air*-uh-muh-*thee*-uh (*th* as in *thin*; strong accent on *thee*).
CARPE DIEM (Latin). kar-pay *dee*-um.
EZEKIEL. Ee-*zeek*-ee-ul or Ee-*zeek*-yul.
GENTILE. *Jen*-tile.
ISAIAH. Eye-*zay*-uh.
NICODEMUS. *Nick*-uh-*dee*-mus (strong accent on *dee*).
PHARISEES. *Fair*-ih-seez.
RABBI. *Rab*-eye.
SANHEDRIN. *San*-huh-drun or San-*heed*-run.

surrounds a baby in the womb before physical birth occurs. Another idea is that Jesus is talking about John's baptism as practiced, for example, in Matthew 3:6. Still another idea is that Jesus is thinking about Christian baptism such as we see Peter proclaim in Acts 2:38. A fourth idea is that Jesus is drawing upon Old Testament images of water and Spirit. These four theories do not exhaust the list of proposals!

Since Jesus seems to want "born again" in verse 3 to mean the same thing as *born of water and of the Spirit*, then the reference cannot be to amniotic fluid. What Jesus has in mind is one spiritual rebirth, not a physical birth plus a spiritual rebirth. The idea that *water* refers to John's baptism is not strong, because that baptism is designed to be temporary (Acts 19:1-5).

The idea that *water* may refer to Christian baptism has a great appeal when we consider the importance that this concept receives in the New Testament (e.g., Colossians 2:12). However, the problem with this idea is that Christian baptism does not come into being until the Day of Pentecost (Acts 2:38). If Jesus is referring to Christian baptism here, then it means that He is scolding Nicodemus in verse 10 (below) for failing to understand something that has not yet even come into practice.

A good case can be made for a reference to the Old Testament ideas of water and Spirit. See especially Ezekiel 36:25-27. There, *water* stands for cleansing from impurity while *Spirit* points to transformed hearts. Nicodemus, the Old Testament scholar, should understand these things. In passing we may note that as the Old Testament Passover celebration foreshadows the Lord's Supper of the New Testament era, so also do certain Old Testament images of water point toward the New Testament practice of baptism (1 Peter 3:18-22).

6. That which is born of the flesh is flesh; and that which is born of the Spirit is spirit.

God's *Spirit* produces the new birth. "Not by works of righteousness which we have done, but according to his mercy he saved us, by the washing of regeneration, and renewing of the Holy Ghost" (Titus 3:5). This rebirth, then, is a renewal. It is accomplished as the Spirit of God brings new life to our dead spirits.

We come into this world by *flesh.* But our rebirth is by the Spirit! This rebirth produces spiritual fruit—"love, joy, peace, long-suffering, gentleness, goodness, faith, meekness, temperance" (Galatians 5:22, 23). Those who are *born of the Spirit* mind the things of the Spirit, while those born only from the flesh mind the things of the flesh (Romans 8:5). [See question #2, page 216.]

7. Marvel not that I said unto thee, Ye must be born again.

Jesus has said that people *must be born again.* Now He changes to the pronoun *ye* (which is plural in the Greek) to make the idea even stronger. The word *must* tells us that being born again is not optional. All of this apparently causes Nicodemus to *marvel,* but it shouldn't! An Old Testament scholar such as he should realize the importance of the need for a new nature.

B. Wind and Spirit (v. 8)

8. The wind bloweth where it listeth, and thou hearest the sound thereof, but canst not tell whence it cometh, and whither it goeth: so is every one that is born of the Spirit.

Jesus refers to *the wind* to illustrate the unseen work of *the Spirit.* When the wind blows, it blows where it wishes, so to speak. We hear *the sound,* but we do not know where that gust of wind has come from or where it will go after it passes. The wind itself is unseen, but the effect that it has on us is quite noticeable. We see the branches of the trees bending. We feel a cool breeze.

Similarly, no one can see the movements of the Holy Spirit Himself. No one can see the gift of the Spirit or the Spirit's indwelling (Acts 2:38). Physically, the renewed person looks the same, but the fruit of the Spirit will show the Spirit's effects (see v. 6, above).

In Ezekiel 37, God's breath or Spirit brings life from death in the valley of dry bones. So it is with all genuine Christians. (The ancient word for *wind* is the same as the word for *Spirit,* making the comparison even more interesting.)

C. Question and Answer (vv. 9-11)

9, 10. Nicodemus answered and said unto him, How can these things be? Jesus answered and said unto him, Art thou a master of Israel, and knowest not these things?

Nicodemus is still struggling to understand, so Jesus reminds him that a *master* (that is, teacher) *of Israel* should not be mystified at these concepts. The original language has the word *the* before *master*, which has caused some to speculate that Nicodemus is a teacher with an official position.

Nicodemus, who is very familiar with what we call the Old Testament, should know about God's power to renew. He should also know of his own need for renewal. Further, Nicodemus should know that people are not justified by their own righteousness (Isaiah 64:6) and that people need God's mercy to be cleansed from sin (Psalm 51:1, 2).

It is God's Spirit who can breathe new life into the heart of someone who is dead in sins. And it is only the Spirit who can do so. The Pharisees are blind to these facts, however (Luke 18:9-14). [See question #3, page 216.]

11. Verily, verily, I say unto thee, We speak that we do know, and testify that we have seen; and ye receive not our witness.

This is the third time Jesus uses *Verily, verily*. As before, these words create an air of authority and seriousness regarding the discussion at hand. By using the plural *we*, Jesus may be mocking the "we know" that Nicodemus uses in verse 2, above. The plural *ye* can be understood as a disdainful "you people." These are the people who have rejected John the Baptist's testimony, and now they are rejecting Jesus as well (Luke 7:29, 30).

III. Understanding the New Birth (John 3:12-17)

People must be born again. Yet no one would have that opportunity were it not for the fact that God chooses to love lost humanity. "Herein is love, not that we loved God, but that he loved us, and sent his Son to be the propitiation for our sins" (1 John 4:10).

A. Life, Not Death (vv. 12-15)

12. If I have told you earthly things, and ye believe not, how shall ye believe, if I tell you of heavenly things?

Jesus informs this teacher of Israel that the things thus far spoken of are relatively easy compared with other topics. Although the new birth is from above, it is *earthly* in the sense that it takes place here on earth. If Nicodemus cannot understand this, then how can he possibly comprehend the grandeur of *heavenly things?*

13. And no man hath ascended up to heaven, but he that came down from heaven, even the Son of man which is in heaven.

Visual for lesson 12

Today's visual illustrates the climax of Jesus' conversation with Nicodemus.

No one has ever gone *up to heaven* to learn about that place (Proverbs 30:4). But Jesus knows about Heaven because He came from there. [See question #4, page 216.] Thus Jesus has the authority to speak about things that only He has seen. Jesus is no average person! (The most ancient manuscripts do not include the last four words *which is in heaven.*)

14, 15. And as Moses lifted up the serpent in the wilderness, even so must the Son of man be lifted up: That whosoever believeth in him should not perish, but have eternal life.

The Israelites sinned, so God sent poisonous snakes. But to save those who wanted to be spared, God commanded Moses to construct a brass serpent on a pole. People were invited to look up at the serpent. If they looked in faith, God saved them from the snakes' venom (Numbers 21:4-9).

It can be said that humanity has been "bitten" by the old serpent, Satan (Genesis 3; Revelation 12:9). In a way somewhat similar to the brass snake, Jesus is lifted up on a cross (John 8:28; 12:32, 34). People who look to Him in faith will be saved. A worse fate awaits those who are lost—the lake that burns with fire and brimstone (Revelation 21:8). But those who look in faith to Jesus will not perish but will have eternal life. See the next verse.

DOING RIGHT, WRONG, AND NOTHING

A certain life insurance agent had a unique way of encouraging potential clients to make timely decisions. The agent would make his presentation and lead right to the moment of closing the sale. If the potential client said, "That's such a big decision, I'd really like to think on it," the agent had a ready response.

"Of course, I can see that," the agent would say. "Tell you what: you sleep on it. And *if* you wake up in the morning, we'll talk some more." What a powerful point!

The Latin phrase *carpe diem* is also powerful. This phrase, popularized in the 1989 movie *Dead Poet's Society,* means "seize the day." Jesus said something similar when, in talking about His own ministry, He stressed that "the night cometh, when no man can work" (John 9:4). Time is running out!

Theodore Roosevelt (1858–1919) once said, "In any moment of decision the best thing you can do is the right thing, the next best thing is the wrong thing, and the worst thing you can do is nothing." There is a lot of truth in this observation. However, when it comes to accepting Christ as Savior, "doing the wrong thing" and "doing nothing" really amount to the same thing.

Each of us is just a heartbeat away from eternity. Can we risk deciding *anything* but the right thing as we seize this day? —J. D. R.

B. Salvation, Not Condemnation (vv. 16, 17)

16. For God so loved the world, that he gave his only begotten Son, that whosoever believeth in him should not perish, but have everlasting life.

This single verse contains the gospel in a nutshell. God's love is self-sacrificing and embraces the entire *world* (not just Israel). People are lost in sin and will *perish* if something is not done. Jesus is God's *Son,* a gift to the world. Eternal rewards and punishment await. People either perish or they have eternal *life,* depending upon how they respond to Jesus.

17. For God sent not his Son into the world to condemn the world; but that the world through him might be saved.

Jewish teachers believed that Messiah came *to condemn* Gentile nations, setting Israel over the nations. But Jesus here says that He came to save *the world.* Jesus has indeed come to judge the world (John 9:39), but that is not the same as condemning the world. Eventually He will return to both judge and condemn those who reject the gospel. But when He first comes to earth, His purpose is to be their Savior. [See question #5, page 216.]

Conclusion

A. New Birth Produces New Life

Jesus has made it clear: everyone must be born again. This new birth results in a complete transformation. It is made possible by the power of God's Holy Spirit.

However, many today want to hold back part of their lives for themselves. They want to straddle the fence. They don't want to truly change, because that would mean giving up some favorite vices. But Jesus demands complete transformation. "Therefore if any man be in Christ, he is a new creature: old things are passed away; behold, all things are become new" (2 Corinthians 5:17).

When writing later, the apostle John will list tests by which people can judge whether or not they have been born again. Consider the following, all from the letter we call 1 John:

"Ye know that every one that doeth righteousness is born of him" (2:29).

"Whosoever is born of God doth not commit sin" (3:9).

"Every one that loveth is born of God" (4:7).

"Whosoever believeth that Jesus is the Christ is born of God" (5:1).

"For whatsoever is born of God overcometh the world" (5:4).

So the new birth that Jesus demands is not merely some theological term to be studied by Bible scholars. It is a radical change of heart and lifestyle. Do you meet these tests?

B. Prayer

Father, thank You for Your great love that sent Jesus to die for our sins. Thank you that we can experience a new birth so that no matter how bad our sins have been we can find forgiveness and new life through the power of Your Holy Spirit. But Father, our thankfulness is not enough. Help us to take the message of transformed hearts to others! In Jesus name, amen.

C. Thought to Remember

"Whosoever believeth that Jesus is the Christ is born of God" (1 John 5:1).

Home Daily Bible Readings

Monday, Feb. 14—You Have Been Born Anew (1 Peter 1:18-23)

Tuesday, Feb. 15—Born of God, Children of God (1 John 2:29–3:5)

Wednesday, Feb. 16—Born of God, Conquer the World (1 John 5:1-5)

Thursday, Feb. 17—How Can I Be Born Again? (John 3:1-5)

Friday, Feb. 18—How Can These Things Be? (John 3:6-10)

Saturday, Feb. 19—God So Loved the World (John 3:11-16)

Sunday, Feb. 20—Jesus Came to Save the World (John 3:17-21)

Learning by Doing

This page contains an alternative lesson plan emphasizing learning activities. Classes desiring such student involvement will find these suggestions helpful.

Learning Goals

After participating in this lesson, each student will be able to:

1. Recount what Jesus told Nicodemus about the new birth.

2. Compare and contrast the lifestyles of those who have been born again with the lifestyles of unbelievers.

3. Give thanks to God for sending Jesus and giving us new birth.

Into the Lesson

Begin the session by asking learners to take the following quiz. (Answers in parentheses are the results of a 1999 Gallup poll in the U.S., which may be somewhat different from the Barna Research surveys noted in the Introduction.)

1. In the U.S., what percentage of people believe in God? *(86 percent)*

2. What percentage believe that good people go to Heaven, whether or not they believe in God? *(44 percent)*

3. What percentage believe that religions other than their own offer true paths to God? *(75 percent)*

4. What percentage believe that they earn a place in Heaven by being good and doing good things? *(60 percent)*

Briefly discuss how the students' expectations compare with the Gallup survey. Which statistic surprises them most? Why? Observe that there is obviously much confusion about the issue of salvation. This confusion is not new. A similar confusion was evident from the earliest days of Jesus' ministry—even from a learned teacher who ought to have known better. His name was Nicodemus, and what Jesus told him is as important for us today as it was for him.

Into the Word

Prepare in advance to have three good readers to read John 3:1-17. One should read the words of Nicodemus, another the words of Jesus. The third will narrate, reading all the words that are not quotes from Jesus or Nicodemus. Have the one who reads the words of Nicodemus also prepare a brief report about the Pharisees.

After the text has been read, ask "Nicodemus" to tell about the Pharisees. What was their purpose? *(They wanted to maintain the observance of God's law in society.)* What was wrong with them? *(They became legalistic, keeping a rigid form of the law but not its spirit.)* Why did they oppose Jesus? *(He did not cater to their interpretations or their expectations of who they thought the Messiah ought to be.)* Note that all this made Nicodemus's interview with Jesus quite remarkable.

Point out that the Pharisees had the wrong idea about salvation—as many today do as well. Jesus attempted to set him straight. His words will help set people today straight as well.

Ask, "How does this text answer some of the misconceptions about salvation that we discussed earlier?" Give a few minutes for the class to make some comparisons, working individually or in small groups. Then ask for reports. The following points should be noted:

1. Only 86 percent of the people surveyed even believe in God. Salvation depends on believing in God in order to believe in His Son (vv. 14-17).

2. Forty-four percent believe that good people go to Heaven, whether or not they believe in God. However, see Romans 3:10-18; Hebrews 11:6.

3. Three-fourths believe religions other than their own offer true paths to God. Jesus said that only He, the One "that came down from heaven," is capable of granting salvation (John 3:13).

4. Sixty percent believe that they earn a place in Heaven by being good and doing good things. However, see John 3:3-8; Ephesians 2:8, 9.

Say, "Our actions reflect our beliefs. How does one who believes in God's Son differ in behavior from one who does not?" Take a few minutes to field answers. This is a "what?" question, but push deeper by asking, "why?"

Into Life

Ask class members, "Do you ever find yourself slipping into the same behaviors as those we have noted that characterize unbelievers? What do you do to reaffirm your faith and redirect your behavior?" Discuss this issue briefly, encouraging your learners to take seriously the matter of acting on faith.

Point out that God's gracious plan of salvation is a wonderful gift. The fact that salvation is not a matter of works should give each of us great joy. Salvation could only have come about as it did—by Jesus' paying the price for our sins Himself. Ask each student to write a brief prayer, poem, or song of thanks to God for sending Jesus and giving us new birth.

Let's Talk It Over

The questions on this page are designed to promote discussion of the lesson by the class and to encourage application of the lesson Scriptures. The answers provided are only discussion starters. Let your class talk it over from there.

1. Nicodemus serves as an example of a (somewhat) humble person coming to a spiritual awakening. In what ways were you like Nicodemus in coming to Christ in the beginning? How can you follow the example of Nicodemus as you draw closer to the Savior?

Answers to the first question will be highly individual, so expect a free-flowing (and perhaps emotional) discussion. Concerning the second question, a vital step in coming into a closer relationship with Christ is to believe that He exists and that He rewards those who diligently seek after Him (Hebrews 11:6).

For some of your learners, drawing near to Christ today will not be a first-time experience, but something that they need to do because they have drifted away. It is said that no matter how far you have drifted from Christ, He is only one step away when you turn back to Him. Remember: when the gap between a person and God widens, it is not God who is doing the moving!

2. Birth is followed by life. This is a straightforward thought, but one that often is neglected spiritually. How do we demonstrate our life in the Spirit?

Living in the Spirit means walking in the Spirit and working in and by the power of the Spirit. One thing that God desires of His followers is that they grow and develop in the use of their spiritual gifts, as noted in Romans 12, 1 Corinthians 12, and Ephesians 4.

The spiritual gifts, such as teaching, administration, and mercy, are things we practice as we are led in life by the Spirit of God. Spiritual gifts are service gifts or ministry gifts given to help the body of Christ accomplish its purpose. To fail to recognize how God has gifted you is a sign that the Spirit is not an active, life-giving influence in your life. To realize how God *has* gifted you and then fail to use those gifts is even worse!

3. Like Nicodemus, we sometimes fail to know or understand foundational things. Why do we fail in this regard?

Because of personality differences, people will fail in their understanding for various reasons. Pride and arrogance definitely can be factors. Generally speaking, however, James 4:2 teaches that "ye have not, because ye ask not."

But even as we ask for godly wisdom, we must guard against wrong or selfish motives. Improper motives sometimes lead us to use wisdom in ways that result in an attempt to straddle the line between friendship with this world and friendship with God. If we fall into this trap, we will not receive.

It takes a humble spirit to receive the things of God. Receiving from God also demands submission to the will of God (see James 4:3-7).

4. What principles for living do we learn from Jesus' descent into this world? How do we emulate Him in this regard?

Philippians 2:1-11 calls the Christian to humble service. Jesus, in coming down to earth, serves as the model for this. His descent from Heaven included becoming a man—not just a man, but also a model of servanthood.

In His role as a servant, Jesus was obedient to death. From this we learn that a Christlike attitude involves giving up things that we may feel are ours by right. It means that we are willing to suffer in our own lives so that the needs of others are met. It is only after we descend into a life of servanthood that we can expect to be raised to the highest place. Jesus himself said, "he that humbleth himself shall be exalted" (Luke 14:11; 18:14).

5. Jesus came into the world for the sake of saving this world, not condemning it. How should this guide us as we live out our lives of Christlikeness?

Sometimes Christians are quick to condemn those both within and outside of the church. But if anyone had the power and right to condemn, it was Jesus. He seemed to offer condemnation reluctantly, in extreme cases (e.g., Matthew 23). We, too, should be reluctant to condemn.

A more productive approach is to be salt in the world, providing a proper flavor and preservative in which Christ is exalted (Matthew 5:13). It is our task to be lights for Christ, showing the proper lifestyle (Matthew 5:14-16). When we do, we will convict this world through the power of the Spirit working within us. Instead of putting the world down, our task is to pull it up. Encourage your learners to give some very specific ways of doing this.

Overcoming Prejudice

DEVOTIONAL READING: John 4:35-42.

BACKGROUND SCRIPTURE: John 4:1-42.

PRINTED TEXT: John 4:7-10, 19-26.

John 4:7-10, 19-26

7 There cometh a woman of Samaria to draw water: Jesus saith unto her, Give me to drink.

8 (For his disciples were gone away unto the city to buy meat.)

9 Then saith the woman of Samaria unto him, How is it that thou, being a Jew, askest drink of me, which am a woman of Samaria? for the Jews have no dealings with the Samaritans.

10 Jesus answered and said unto her, If thou knewest the gift of God, and who it is that saith to thee, Give me to drink; thou wouldest have asked of him, and he would have given thee living water.

. . . .

19 The woman saith unto him, Sir, I perceive that thou art a prophet.

20 Our fathers worshipped in this mountain; and ye say, that in Jerusalem is the place where men ought to worship.

21 Jesus saith unto her, Woman, believe me, the hour cometh, when ye shall neither in this mountain, nor yet at Jerusalem, worship the Father.

22 Ye worship ye know not what: we know what we worship; for salvation is of the Jews.

23 But the hour cometh, and now is, when the true worshippers shall worship the Father in spirit and in truth: for the Father seeketh such to worship him.

24 God is a Spirit: and they that worship him must worship him in spirit and in truth.

25 The woman saith unto him, I know that Messiah cometh, which is called Christ: when he is come, he will tell us all things.

26 Jesus saith unto her, I that speak unto thee am he.

GOLDEN TEXT: There is neither Jew nor Greek, there is neither bond nor free, there is neither male nor female: for ye are all one in Christ Jesus.—Galatians 3:28.

Feb
27

Called to Be God's People
Unit 3: Whosoever Will—Come!
(Lessons 10-13)

Lesson Aims

After participating in this lesson, each student will be able to:

1. Tell how Jesus' love defeated prejudice in the case of the woman from Samaria.

2. Explain how acceptance of people from different backgrounds can present opportunities to lead others to Christ.

3. Identify a personal prejudice and suggest a specific action that he or she can take to replace it with Christ's love.

Lesson Outline

INTRODUCTION
    A. Centuries of Prejudice
    B. Lesson Background
  I. UNEXPECTED CONVERSATION (John 4:7-9)
    A. Startling Request (vv. 7, 8)
    B. Ancient Animosity (v. 9)
      Categories
  II. UNEXPECTED SOLUTION (John 4:10, 19-26)
    A. Deepest Thirsts (v. 10)
    B. Profound Truth (vv. 19-22)
      Intolerance at Its Worst and Best
    C. True Worshipers (vv. 23, 24)
    D. Divine Savior (vv. 25, 26)
CONCLUSION
    A. Jesus the Solution
    B. Prayer
    C. Thought to Remember

Introduction

A. Centuries of Prejudice

Gene Brown tells of two apples that were looking down upon the world. One said, "Look at all those people fighting, robbing, rioting—no one seems willing to get along with his fellow human being. Someday we apples will be the only ones left. Then we'll rule the world." The second apple replied, "Which of us—the reds or the greens?"

Today's lesson will help us to understand that even though the power of prejudice wrecks society and brings misery to everyone in some way, Jesus Christ has the power to transform our lives and break down barriers of prejudice. *The American Heritage Dictionary* defines prejudice as an

"irrational suspicion or hatred of a particular group, race, or religion." People have been long divided by these very things. India's caste system divides one billion people by profession, wealth, religion, and family heritage. Many religious groups fight over power, territory, and sacred sites.

Prejudice is learned. Children of many races may be playing happily together until one parent says, "Stay away from those people." Such preconceived notions fail to treat people individually, are not based on all the facts, and forget God's love for the entire world.

Prejudice is sin and has its roots in selfishness, pride, anger, and hatred. It ignores compassion, mercy, love, and forgiveness. The power to overcome prejudice comes from God. In today's lesson Jesus will brush aside the prejudices of His day and help a social outcast find new hope.

B. Lesson Background

While in Judea, Jesus decided to travel north to preach in Galilee (John 4:3). To get there He had to go through Samaria (4:4) if He wanted to take the shortest route. At midday Jesus and His disciples arrived at a well about a half-mile from the village of Sychar (4:5). Jesus was weary, so He sent His disciples for food (4:8) while He stayed at the well (4:6).

History was all around Him as He sat there. Tradition holds that Jacob himself had dug that well nearly two thousand years earlier. This is "near to the parcel of ground that Jacob gave to his son Joseph" (John 4:5; see also Genesis 48:22). A short distance away were Mounts Gerizim and Ebal, where people had recited God's blessing and curses at the command of Moses (Deuteronomy 27:4-26). Some fourteen centuries earlier, Joshua stood on Mount Ebal and encouraged all Israel to keep God's law (Joshua 8:30-35). Also nearby was Joseph's tomb.

But Jesus did not have time to dwell on history. A woman had appeared, carrying a water jar. The woman who approached the well had no idea that she was about to come face to face with the long-awaited Messiah. She had no idea that she was about to have a conversation that would change her life.

A story is told about U.S. President Thomas Jefferson and a group trying to cross a raging river. The bridge was washed away, so each rider crossed the river on horseback, fighting the deadly current. A stranger who had no horse asked the President to take him across the river. He agreed.

So the man climbed on, and the two of them made it safely to the other side. As the stranger came down from the horse, someone asked him why he had asked the President for help. The man was shocked because he had no idea that he had been talking with the President! The woman in today's lesson who has come to draw water was about to talk with Someone greater than any president or earthly king.

I. Unexpected Conversation
(John 4:7-9)

A. Startling Request (vv. 7, 8)

7, 8. There cometh a woman of Samaria to draw water: Jesus saith unto her, Give me to drink. (For his disciples were gone away unto the city to buy meat.)

Jesus is thirsty, but He cannot just turn on the tap. A water vessel will need to be lowered on ropes into the well and hauled back up again. If Jesus' disciples had been there, they would have brought Him *water*. But they are in nearby Sychar finding food (John 4:5). Having no container for drawing water, Jesus asks this *woman of Samaria* for help.

Jewish men of this period usually do not address women in public. The first-century Jewish historian Josephus says that women are inferior to men in all things. A certain Jewish prayer for men includes thanks for not being made a woman! In about 180 B.C., a Jewish writer penned the following: "Better is the wickedness of a man than a woman who does good; it is a woman who brings shame and disgrace" (Sirach 42:14). When Jesus' disciples return, even they will be amazed that He is talking with a woman (John 4:27).

Jesus does not condone this demeaning attitude. Several women follow Him and supply material help to His ministry (Luke 8:1-3). Also, Paul mentions many women who were his fellow laborers in the gospel. He publicly praises them for their hard work and valuable contribution for Christ's church (Romans 16:1-16). [See question #1, page 224.]

We should not overlook the fact that the woman in today's lesson is a person of loose morals (see John 4:17, not in our text for today). Married five times, she now lives with a man who is not her husband. This may explain why she is alone at the well at noon. Women usually come to the well when it is cooler (morning or evening) and chat with their friends. Perhaps they shun this woman for her lack of morals, forcing her *to draw water* in the heat of the day, alone.

B. Ancient Animosity (v. 9)

9. Then saith the woman of Samaria unto him, How is it that thou, being a Jew, askest drink of me, which am a woman of Samaria? for the Jews have no dealings with the Samaritans.

The designation *Samaria* comes from 1 Kings 16:24. The reason that *Jews have no dealings with the Samaritans* is an interesting and sad story.

When King Solomon died in about 930 B.C., the nation of Israel split into two parts. Some tribes appointed their own king, and that king established idolatrous worship sites involving two golden calves (1 Kings 12:28-30). God's prophets warned them, but their continued idolatry brought judgment.

As a result, many people in these tribes were scattered into various countries by their Assyrian captors in 722 B.C. Other captive peoples were brought into Israel, where they intermarried with those Israelites who were left in the land (2 Kings 17).

The descendants of those intermarriages became the Samaritans of Jesus' day. The "pure-blood" Jews had come to view them, to put it crudely, as "half-breeds." This taint resulted in antagonism between the Jews who returned from the Babylonian exile after 539 B.C. and the Samaritans. When the Samaritans offered to help rebuild the temple, the Jews refused (Ezra 4:1-5). This angered the Samaritans, and we see some of this anger come out when Nehemiah begins to rebuild the city walls (Nehemiah 4:1, 2).

In Jesus' day the Jews still look with suspicion upon this group of people. Jews are afraid of being corrupted by people who are not pure Israelites. So by the time that Jesus is born, Jews have few dealings with Samaritans (although the disciples apparently think it is okay to buy food from them; see John 4:8).

Jesus' enemies will try to discredit Him by calling Him a Samaritan (John 8:48). Perhaps we can compare the Samaritans' experience with that of African-Americans, who once were not allowed to use the same drinking fountains or dining facilities as whites.

Thus it is no wonder that the woman is amazed that this Jew not only talks with her, but also actually asks for a drink from her vessel! The woman probably recognizes Jesus as *a Jew* either by His clothing or by His accent (cf. Matthew 26:73). Certainly after she experiences His attitude of openness she will be more ready to hear what He has to say.

Christians must still overcome prejudice. How do people perceive our attitudes toward those of a different race, social background, religion, or culture? Even when it comes to religion, Christians can love and show respect to others without compromising Christian truth. Jesus broke social and religious taboos, and so must we. [See question #2, page 224.]

Categories

Years ago, the magazine *Psychology Today* reported on a survey taken of eleven major symphony orchestras to learn what players in one section of instruments thought of the musicians in other sections. The survey revealed that those playing stringed instruments were thought of as effeminate wimps and prima donnas. Brass players were seen to be loud, beer-drinking jocks. Percussionists were categorized as insensitive, unintelligent, and hard-of-hearing, yet humorous and fun at parties. Those who played woodwinds were held in the highest esteem—described as quiet, meticulous, and intelligent, though quite egotistical.

Can you believe that professional musicians could hold such critical and stereotypical views of each other? Before we gasp too much, however, perhaps we should stop and take a look at our own biases.

We often are guilty of generalizations, aren't we? We practice "lumping" when we note someone from another part of the country, or from another school or community, and have some experience with them. We destroy those biases when we remember that "there is neither Jew nor Greek, there is neither bond nor free, there is neither male nor female: for ye are all one in Christ Jesus" (Galatians 3:28).   —J. D. R.

II. Unexpected Solution
(John 4:10, 19-26)
A. Deepest Thirsts (v. 10)

10. Jesus answered and said unto her, If thou knewest the gift of God, and who it is that saith to thee, Give me to drink; thou wouldest have asked of him, and he would have given thee living water.

A stranger is asking the woman for a *drink* and yet claiming to have a supply of *water* that is somehow greater than the water in Jacob's well. This woman has no idea what a privilege it is to be there at that moment in history! God has a *gift* for all of humanity—Jews, Samaritans, and Gentiles alike. This gift, freely given, is greater than any earthly thing that the woman can possibly imagine.

Hundreds of years earlier, the Israelites had forsaken God, "the fountain of living waters" (Jeremiah 2:13). Even so, God had predicted through a prophet that a day would come when "living waters shall go out from Jerusalem" (Zechariah 14:8). Jesus is the One who has that *living water!*

B. Profound Truth (vv. 19-22)

19. The woman saith unto him, Sir, I perceive that thou art a prophet.

The dialogue of verses 11-18 (not in today's text) leads up to this point. The woman considers Jesus to be *a prophet* because He has told her things about herself (in vv. 16-18) that a stranger could not know without having divine knowledge. He knows about her five previous marriages and how she is now living with a man who is not her husband.

20. Our fathers worshipped in this mountain; and ye say, that in Jerusalem is the place where men ought to worship.

With this statement the woman zeroes in on the major point of theological dispute between Jews and Samaritans. Jacob had built an altar near this very spot (Genesis 33:20). Later, Moses warned the people that they were to worship at one altar only, the one chosen by God (Deuteronomy 12:1-14). The tabernacle served as the one sacred site until it was replaced by the more permanent temple structure (1 Kings 6).

When King Solomon died, the northern tribes established sacred sites in Bethel and Dan (1 Kings 12:25-33). The Jews rebuilt the temple in *Jerusalem* after the exile (Ezra 6:13-15), while the Samaritans worshiped on Mount Gerizim, a bit to the southwest of Mount Ebal. These rival places of worship perpetuate the differences between these two peoples. But the woman assumes that *a prophet* from God can settle the matter.

21. Jesus saith unto her, Woman, believe me, the hour cometh, when ye shall neither in this mountain, nor yet at Jerusalem, worship the Father.

How to Say It

Assyrian. Uh-*sear*-e-un.
Bethel. *Beth*-ul.
Deuteronomy. Due-ter-*ahn*-uh-me.
Ebal. *Ee*-bull.
Ezra. *Ez*-ruh.
Galilee. *Gal*-uh-lee.
Gerizim. *Gair*-ih-zeem or Guh-*rye*-zim.
Jacob. *Jay*-kub.
Jeremiah. Jair-uh-*my*-uh.
Jerusalem. Juh-*roo*-suh-lem.
Josephus. Jo-*see*-fus.
Judea. Joo-*dee*-uh.
Nehemiah. *Nee*-huh-*my*-uh (strong accent on *my*).
Samaria. Suh-*mare*-ee-uh.
Samaritans. Suh-*mare*-uh-tunz.
Sirach. *Sigh*-rak.
Solomon. *Sol*-o-mun.
Sychar. *Sigh*-kar.
Zechariah. *Zek*-uh-*rye*-uh (strong accent on *rye*).

This is "part one" of a three-part response by Jesus. With the coming of the Christian age, sacred sites lose their meaning except for historical purposes. As beautiful as the Jewish temple is, it is only made out of gold, stones, and cedar; it is subject to destruction (Matthew 24:1, 2).

The church, however, is made of living stones. It is not limited by geographical boundaries. Believers everywhere are the living stones that comprise it (Ephesians 2:19-22; 1 Peter 2:5, 6). This temple is not made with human hands and cannot be destroyed. Christians must not argue over sacred sites as people of other religions do. Instead, Christians must encourage others to become stones in Christ's living temple. [See question #3, page 224.]

22. Ye worship ye know not what: we know what we worship; for salvation is of the Jews.

Although Jesus treats the woman with respect and compassion, He does not support her false ideas. Some people think that to be free from prejudice means to accept all points of view as valid. Christians can treat Jews and Muslims with respect and demonstrate Christ's love without compromising Christian truth that Jesus alone is the way, the truth, and the life.

Jesus tells the woman that the Samaritans are wrong about their *worship*, and that God offers *salvation* through *the Jews* (cf. Romans 1:16). Jesus, after all, is a Jew from the line of David as the Scriptures promise for the Messiah (Jeremiah 33:15). Salvation is to be offered first to the Jews. After that, the gospel is to be taken to Samaria and then to the Gentiles (Acts 1:8).

INTOLERANCE AT ITS WORST AND BEST

As I write this, it is April 29, 2003, a date designated as "Holocaust Remembrance Day." The beginning of the Holocaust can be dated to 1933, the year that Adolf Hitler became Reichs Chancellor (or Prime Minister) of Germany. His reign of terror came to an end in 1945 with the fall of his Third Reich.

In the intervening years, Hitler and his cronies conducted a campaign that resulted in the state-sponsored murder of six million Jews. The Nazis had deemed this group of innocent people to be "life unworthy of life." This was intolerance at its worst!

The mind-set that resulted in this tragedy is still with us today. Television images from around the world remind us of this nightly. In order to stem this tide of hatred, we see a greater emphasis on teaching "tolerance" at all levels of society. People are encouraged to accept and respect differences of race, culture, and religion.

Somewhere along the way, however, we seem to have lost the distinction between "tolerance

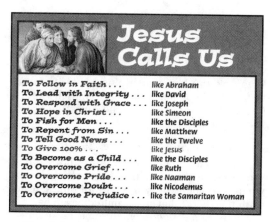

To Follow in Faith . . .	like Abraham
To Lead with Integrity . . .	like David
To Respond with Grace . . .	like Joseph
To Hope in Christ . . .	like Simeon
To Fish for Men . . .	like the Disciples
To Repent from Sin . . .	like Matthew
To Tell Good News . . .	like the Twelve
To Give 100% . . .	like Jesus
To Become as a Child . . .	like the Disciples
To Overcome Grief . . .	like Ruth
To Overcome Pride . . .	like Naaman
To Overcome Doubt . . .	like Nicodemus
To Overcome Prejudice . . .	like the Samaritan Woman

Visual for lessons 5, 13. *Display the same visual as was used for lesson 5. use it to review the lessons of the past quarter.*

for all people" and "tolerance for all ideas." As Christians we must embrace the former while we reject the latter.

Our model for this distinction is Jesus as He speaks to the Samaritan woman at the well. Jesus sets an example for us as He crosses social and religious barriers to reach out in respect to someone who needs salvation. But at the same time His compassion and love require Him to confront her about her false religious viewpoint. This is intolerance at its best!
—R. L. N.

C. True Worshipers (vv. 23, 24)

23, 24. But the hour cometh, and now is, when the true worshippers shall worship the Father in spirit and in truth: for the Father seeketh such to worship him. God is a Spirit: and they that worship him must worship him in spirit and in truth.

At the most foundational level, *worship* means to ascribe worth to God. We can do this properly only when our worship is *in spirit* (is centered on nothing but God) *and in truth* (is faithful to God's Word).

God is interested in what happens in our hearts. The first and greatest commandment is to love God with the entire heart, soul, and mind (Matthew 22:37, 38). We must worship with the feelings of the heart, the fervency of the soul, and the power of the will. We must worship with sorrow over sins and joy over God's mercy and grace. We must worship with gratitude for God's blessings of creation and redemption through Jesus. Only this kind of worship changes the heart and life of the worshiper.

Worship that is concerned only with outward form and ritual lacks the key elements of love, gratitude, and repentance. [See question #4, page 224.] When those things are missing, God is not truly worshiped. He rejects all such attempts.

Passages such as Amos 5:21-23; 6:5, 6; Malachi 1:6-8; and James 2:1-4 show us that God is well aware of improper motives in worship. When we think of worshiping in spirit and in truth, let us remember that Jesus Himself is truth (John 14:6), and it is He who gives the Spirit without limit (John 3:34).

D. Divine Savior (vv. 25, 26)

25, 26. The woman saith unto him, I know that Messiah cometh, which is called Christ: when he is come, he will tell us all things. Jesus saith unto her, I that speak unto thee am he.

The word *Messiah* refers to someone anointed or selected by God for a special mission. The woman knows something of this promised One. She may be thinking of Moses' promise of a prophet "like unto" him (Deuteronomy 18:15) as he instructed the people to listen to this prophet.

So the woman knows that the Messiah will have the answers. *Jesus* tells her plainly that He is that promised Messiah.

Conclusion

A. Jesus the Solution

As the Messiah, Jesus brings salvation to the lost—Jew, Samaritan, and Gentile alike. He came to bring all together as part of one family in His church. In fact that is what happened. The gospel was first offered to Jews in Jerusalem (Acts 2:17-41). These Jewish Christians then took the gospel to Samaritans (Acts 8:4-8, 14-17). Then Jewish Christians took the gospel to Gentiles (Acts 13 and following).

As a result, old barriers of hostility and prejudice were broken down (Ephesians 2:11-22).

Home Daily Bible Readings

Monday, Feb. 21—Christ Is All and in All (Colossians 3:11-17)
Tuesday, Feb. 22—Jesus Travels to a Samaritan City (John 4:1-6)
Wednesday, Feb. 23—Jesus Speaks About Living Water (John 4:7-12)
Thursday, Feb. 24—The Samaritan Woman Wants Living Water (John 4:13-18)
Friday, Feb. 25—I Am the Messiah (John 4:19-26)
Saturday, Feb. 26—Come and See the Man (John 4:27-34)
Sunday, Feb. 27—Many Samaritans Believed Jesus' Word (John 4:35-42)

Jews, Samaritans, and Gentiles can forget old divisions; they can enjoy oneness in the church (Galatians 3:28; Ephesians 4:4-6). [See question #5, page 224.]

General Robert E. Lee (1807–1870) is said to have been a devout follower of Jesus Christ. Soon after the end of the American Civil War, he visited a church. During the Communion service, so the story goes, he knelt beside a black man. An onlooker said, "How could you do that?" Lee is said to have replied, "My friend, all ground is level beneath the cross." When Christians have that attitude, prejudice will end.

But smashing such barriers is not really the ultimate goal. Instead, the ultimate goal is eternal life. The woman in today's lesson responded by bringing others to Jesus. She left her water jar and returned to town saying, "Come, see a man, which told me all things that ever I did: is not this the Christ?" (John 4:29).

Many Samaritans of Sychar believed on Him because of the testimony of the woman. They even begged Him to stay with them (4:40) and they believed Jesus' teachings (4:39-41). This shows that the woman was able to make an impact on her community, in spite of her past, because of the power of Jesus' words.

Today we see religious groups continue to squabble over sacred sites around the world, especially in Jerusalem. Yet while all this fussing goes on and on, Jesus still offers a message that goes beyond geographical and ethnic barriers. Jesus can still break down racial barriers so that all peoples can belong to the greatest family in the world.

As we think about our part in proclaiming this message, we as Christians must do several things. First, ask God to forgive our past prejudices. Second, ask God to substitute love, compassion, and mercy for hatred, suspicion, and pride in our hearts. Third, follow Jesus' example in how He treated the woman in today's lesson. Fourth, offer Jesus as the Savior to all members of the human race. What a privilege it is to spread that message by our actions, attitudes, and words!

B. Prayer

Father, thank You for Jesus who offers salvation to all. Help us to show others by our words and actions that Jesus can solve our deepest needs, even the need for eternal life. In Jesus' name, amen.

C. Thought to Remember

"Now therefore ye are no more strangers and foreigners, but fellow citizens with the saints, and of the household of God" (Ephesians 2:19).

Learning by Doing

This page contains an alternative lesson plan emphasizing learning activities.
Classes desiring such student involvement will find these suggestions helpful.

Learning Goals

After participating in this lesson, each student will be able to:

1. Tell how Jesus' love defeated prejudice in the case of the woman from Samaria.

2. Explain how acceptance of people from different backgrounds can present opportunities to lead others to Christ.

3. Identify a personal prejudice and suggest a specific action that he or she can take to replace it with Christ's love.

Into the Lesson

Before class make arrangements with two students to perform a very brief skit. For their "costumes" find some large pieces of cardboard, such as the shipping carton for a range or refrigerator. Cut out two apple shapes large enough for the students to hold in front of themselves and expose only their heads (and perhaps their feet). Paint one cutout red and one green.

Have the students memorize the dialogue between the apples in the Introduction to today's lesson (page 218). Introduce the skit by saying, "Two apples looked down upon the world." Let the two actors perform. Then say, "Why is it so easy for us to focus on negatives and differences instead of positives and similarities?" In the discussion note how this attitude is the basis for racism and other forms of prejudice. Ask, "What is the solution to this kind of prejudice?" Observe that the love of Jesus breaks down barriers instead of putting them up. Indicate that today's lesson gives us a concrete example of that fact.

Into the Word

Read John 4:7-10, 19-26 aloud. Ask students to make a list of differences between Jesus and the woman, things that might be cause for separation. Provide paper and pencils as needed. Your learners should note the following differences: man/woman; Jew/Samaritan; worship in Jerusalem/worship in "this mountain"; highest morals/loose morals; knowledgeable worship/ignorant worship.

Ask learners for the differences they noted, writing each in a single column on the board or overhead transparency. Also ask, "How did Jesus overcome these distinctives? What did this communicate?" A list like the following should develop: He ignored the social distinctive (gender)

by talking with the woman. This communicated a sense of value; He did not consider the woman inferior or worthless.

Jesus also overcame the religious distinctives with His willingness to address a religious issue in a kind but firm way. This communicated not only truth but personal respect. The woman, with her misguided religious viewpoint, needed to hear both.

Point out that Jesus acted from love. No matter what potential barriers stood between Jesus and this woman, love was the key to breaking them down. It was in the woman's best interest to receive the living water Jesus had to offer. That is love: acting in the best interest of another.

Into Life

Point to your list of distinctives between Jesus and the woman. Ask, "How are these same differences and prejudices seen in society today?" Discuss the problems of social, racial, and religious prejudice. Observe that some prejudices are based in purely externals (gender, race, etc.). Other matters are more internal, based on decisions we make (social issues, morality issues, etc.).

Ask, "How can we take a proper stand on such issues without disrespecting people themselves?" As the class talks about this, note Jesus' method. He told the truth, even pointing out faults in the woman's religion, but He did not accuse. He did not withdraw. He did not treat her unkindly. Try to get the learners to suggest tangible ways of doing that today.

For example, if racial prejudice is a particularly troublesome issue in your community, what can your church do to demonstrate that this issue is not a barrier—or that you do not want it to be? If your church is 99 percent one race, how do you demonstrate that people of other races are welcome? What are you doing to reach out to people of other races? Are you targeting ministry events for people of various races and economic statuses? Are you taking a public stand for issues of justice that will benefit people of other races more than yourself?

Encourage your learners to be as specific as possible. Then close with a prayer that God will help you and your class to practice the love of Christ in ways that will tear down the walls that divide your community.

Let's Talk It Over

The questions on this page are designed to promote discussion of the lesson by the class and to encourage application of the lesson Scriptures. The answers provided are only discussion starters. Let your class talk it over from there.

1. Discrimination toward women is still a reality in modern culture. How can the church demonstrate God's expectations in this area?

Though we like to think we do not have this attitude, it is seen in various ways in the life of the church. Some stereotypes that men consider to be humorous are really putdowns of women.

In our sermons, lessons, and writing, we can use inclusive language. We can do this while still recognizing that there are God-ordained role distinctions between men and women (1 Timothy 2:12). Yet even the way we present these role distinctions can be improved in order to build up rather than demean women.

2. Just as with discrimination toward women, we also like to think that we do not have any racial prejudice and that we do not practice racial discrimination. How can we go beyond talk and really demonstrate this?

A principle of church growth is called the "homogenous unit principle." It states that people do not like to cross racial or cultural lines to identify with a church. Because of this principle, many churches choose not to reach out across racial or ethnic lines.

Refusing to allow this non-biblical principle to guide our outreach is a good place to begin. Sometimes it is a language barrier that exists in addition to racial issues. If so, steps may be taken to plant a church to reach this segment of the population. This can be done by having a service at a different time in the existing facility. We can also cross the racial divide by including examples of people of different races and ethnic backgrounds in positive ways in our illustrations. Another option is to contact a church that ministers to another race and hold a joint worship service.

3. God cannot be contained in a building, yet often we try to do so. What are some dangers of equating worship with a particular place?

Our love of our places of worship can stall the growth of the church. We like our auditoriums! Some do not think of building a larger auditorium and converting the current one into classrooms or a fellowship hall because it has become their "sanctuary."

Also, some will battle against relocation because they, their parents, or grandparents helped to build the current building. We become so committed to the window given in memory of a loved one or to the pew dedicated to the honor of another that we stay in that small and inadequate space. Growth and ministry are then stifled. When this happens, we, in effect, begin to worship a place of worship instead of Christ.

4. Sometimes our worship becomes merely a performance of certain traditions. How can we transform our worship services beyond mere ritual?

Some churches have made a ritual out of the order of worship, the style of music, or how the Lord's Supper is served. To make a change in any of these forms of worship is considered tantamount to changing the Word of God.

One of the first things we must do is teach the difference between Scripture and tradition. Instituting minor changes may go hand in hand with this teaching. Though we don't make changes simply to make changes, we can incorporate some adjustments that may help us to refocus our priorities. A church growth adage states: "If you always do what you've always done, you'll always get what you always got."

5. Two of the more prevalent types of prejudice discussed above involve race and gender. What are some other types of prejudice that the church needs to be aware of and confront?

Age bias is growing in many churches. This happens on both ends of the age continuum. Young people may feel that the older folks are out of touch. As a result, the younger people fail to learn from the wisdom and experience that the more senior saints have to offer. Some older people feel that younger Christians are not as committed to Christ because of a style of music or style of dress that they prefer.

Others discriminate unknowingly along socioeconomic lines. We have special trips for our youth that cost money, but some are not able to attend because they cannot afford to do so. Another form of discrimination takes place when we look at the church background and affiliation of a person and automatically think that this person does not love Christ or the Bible. Vital to the life of the church is to begin to deal with individuals, taking time to learn with and from each other.

Spring Quarter, 2005

God's Project: Effective Christians

Special Features

Lessons

About These Lessons

This quarter's lessons are taken from Paul's letters to the Romans and the Galatians. While all of Paul's writings in the New Testament are important for Christians to study, Romans and Galatians could be considered his "dynamic duo." Their emphasis on such crucial themes as justification by faith, the role of the law of Moses, and the proper use of Christian freedom will contribute significantly to helping you achieve this quarter's goal: producing effective Christians.

Mar 6
Mar 13
Mar 20
Mar 27
Apr 3
Apr 10
Apr 17
Apr 24
May 1
May 8
May 15
May 22
May 29

Quarterly Quiz

The questions on this page may be used in several ways: as a pretest at the beginning of the quarter; as a review at the end of the quarter; or as a review after each lesson. The questions are based on the Scripture text of each lesson (King James Version). **The answers are on page 228.**

Lesson 1

1. What is "revealed from heaven against all ungodliness and unrighteousness of men"? *Romans 1:18*

2. Paul says regarding sinful human beings that their throat is like an open _____ and that the poison of _____ is under their lips. *Romans 3:13*

Lesson 2

1. Paul tells us that the goodness of God leads us to _____. *Romans 2:4*

2. On the day of God's righteous judgment, He will render to every man according to his _____. *Romans 2:6*

Lesson 3

1. According to Paul, what quality do tribulations produce? *Romans 5:3*

2. What is "shed abroad in our hearts" by the Holy Spirit? *Romans 5:5*

3. Complete this verse: "But God commendeth his love toward us, in that, while we were yet sinners, ..." *Romans 5:8*

Lesson 4

1. Who told Peter and the "other disciple," "They have taken away the Lord out of the sepulchre, and we know not where they have laid him"? *John 20:1, 2*

2. When Peter and the "other disciple" ran to the tomb of Jesus, Peter reached the tomb first. T/F *John 20:4*

3. Paul says that we are buried with Christ by _____ into death. *Romans 6:4*

Lesson 5

1. Paul writes that to be carnally minded is _____. *Romans 8:6*

2. What does the "Spirit of adoption" cause us to cry? *Romans 8:15*

Lesson 6

1. Paul quotes a Scripture that describes the beautiful (feet, hands, or lips?) of those who preach the gospel of peace. *Romans 10:15*

2. Which prophet asked the question, "Lord, who hath believed our report?" *Romans 10:16*

3. Complete this verse: "Faith cometh by hearing, and hearing by the ____ ____ ____. *Romans 10:17*

Lesson 7

1. Paul tells Christians to present their bodies a _____ _____. *Romans 12:1*

2. By giving food and drink to an enemy, what are we heaping on his head? *Romans 12:20*

Lesson 8

1. Christians should "judge this rather," that no one puts a _____ or an occasion to fall in a brother's way. *Romans 14:13*

2. Paul desired that the Roman Christians glorify God with one _____ and one _____. *Romans 15:6*

Lesson 9

1. Paul was not at all surprised that the Galatian Christians had departed so quickly from the true gospel. T/F *Galatians 1:6*

2. According to Paul, what penalty should someone who preaches another gospel suffer? *Galatians 1:8, 9*

Lesson 10

1. Paul says that "by the works of the _____ shall no flesh be _____." *Galatians 2:16*

2. Paul called the Galatians "foolish" because of their failure to obey the truth they had been taught. T/F *Galatians 3:1, 3*

Lesson 11

1. Paul writes that the law was "ordained by" (angels, Moses, or priests?) in the hand of a mediator. *Galatians 3:19*

2. If we are Christ's, then whose seed are we? *Galatians 3:29*

Lesson 12

1. Paul warns the Galatians that if they are _____, then Christ will be of no profit to them. *Galatians 5:2*

2. In what commandment is all the law fulfilled? *Galatians 5:14*

Lesson 13

1. What quality is listed first among the fruit of the Spirit? What quality is listed last? *Galatians 5:22, 23*

2. In what spirit should we seek to restore someone who has been "overtaken in a fault"? *Galatians 6:1*

Participants in God's Project

by Marshall Hayden

THE GOSPEL ACCORDING TO PAUL." That's what many students of the Bible have called the book of Romans, and that is the section of the Word of God that draws our attention for the first eight lessons of this quarter. The shorter, possibly earlier, letter to the Galatians will be the focus of our study for the remaining Sundays. The lessons from Galatians will be a splendid supplement to the faithful doctrine/faithful life studies from Romans. Like Romans, Galatians discusses what it means to be justified by faith in Jesus Christ, not by the works of the law of Moses (or of any works-oriented system). Both books also discuss the proper and godly use of our freedom in Christ and our need to appreciate the freedom that other Christians have. We should be stronger, surer, and more clearly characterized by joy after we have finished this study together.

Have you ever heard someone open a series of remarks with the words, "I have bad news and good news"? In Romans the apostle Paul first presents the bad news that sets the stage for the good news. In Romans 3:23 (a verse many have memorized) he writes, "For all have sinned, and come short of the glory of God." That's the bad news. We have missed the mark; we have failed to honor the image of God in which He created us (Genesis 1:26, 27). The prodigal son in Jesus' well-known parable speaks for every human being when he declares, "I have sinned against heaven, and in thy sight, and am no more worthy to be called thy son" (Luke 15:21). The first three chapters of Romans make that truth very clear. Jews have sinned. Gentiles have sinned. No one is exempt from this disheartening news: we *all* have sinned.

But then comes the good news! God Himself has made a way to cure our terminal condition of sin-sickness.

Unit 1: March
Saved by God

Lesson 1: All Have Sinned. As we read the first three chapters of Romans, some may recall a statement that became associated with a former President of the United States: "Let me make one thing perfectly clear." That's what Paul is doing. And what he says is clearly distressing! By the time we have completed reading our Scripture text for the first lesson, his point cannot be missed: *we have sinned.* Yet even as Paul admits that grim truth, he cannot restrain himself from mentioning the good news. Part of the text for this lesson removes our self-made excuses, but the other part presents a God-made answer: the gospel of Christ that remains "the power of God unto salvation to every one that believeth" (Romans 1:16).

Lesson 2: God's Judgment Is Just. This lesson leaves us ready to approach the judgment seat of God and confess, "Guilty, Your Honor." We know it's true. Paul helps us see that. He encourages us to avoid all pretense of superiority. He reminds us that judging is God's business, that He is very good at it, and that He does not need our help! Like the first lesson, this one is not silent about the good news. We will learn about repentance and about Christ, the Way.

Lesson 3: Justified by Faith. Here the good news becomes especially clear. We will be reminded of what faith means, what it does, how it begins, and what it produces. The theme of this lesson makes it abundantly clear that only in Christ does justification occur.

Lesson 4: Victory in Christ. This is the Easter Sunday lesson—always a time to celebrate what sets Christian faith apart from anything the world has to offer. The key word for this study is *life*. The thrilling message that we will study from the Gospel of John (in addition to our continued study from Romans) calls to mind the story of a little boy who was standing outside the window of a small-town hardware store where he had been permitted to paint an Easter scene. A man came by and asked him about the hillside, the crosses, and the people he had painted. "That's Jesus," he said, pointing to the center cross. "Them's the soldiers. They killed Him." Then he was silent. But as the man began to walk away the boy shouted, "Hey, Mister, there's more—He rose again!"

Thank God there's more.

Unit 2: April
The Christian Life

Lesson 5: Live by the Spirit. This lesson introduces Unit Two in our study of Romans. In Unit One we lay a foundation of Biblical doctrine, which is essential for living the Christian life. Here we will see how Paul discusses some of the practical applications of doctrinal truth. Romans 8:12 is a key verse in this lesson: "Therefore, brethren, we are debtors, not to the flesh, to live after the flesh." The fleshly part of each person exerts a powerful pull, but a Christian's spiritual part, empowered by God's Holy Spirit, makes him a champion in the "tug of war."

Lesson 6: Find Salvation in Christ. In this lesson we will talk about lives that call on the name of the Lord. What does it mean to "confess the Lord Jesus"? This is something that we do before other people—not just once, as part of accepting Christ as Savior—but regularly before others whose reaction may be less than encouraging. In response to this study, we should also think about appealing to others to call on the name of Jesus. We should consider our responsibility as Christians to support other Christians willing to travel to both faraway and nearby places—individuals who have feet ready to go and tongues ready to speak "glad tidings of good things."

Lesson 7: Display the Marks of a Christian. Romans 12 is a clear and helpful description of several of the characteristics that should mark our lives as we live out our Christian walk. With this study we shall see how the book of Romans demonstrates a pattern often seen in Paul's letters—moving from foundational doctrine to practical personal conduct. This will be a good week for making a list, checking it twice, and examining what God thinks about our daily living and what alterations we need to make.

Lesson 8: Accept One Another. In the previous lesson, Paul led us to examine whether we handle our personal lives faithfully. This week we study a passage that challenges us to handle our Christian fellowship faithfully. There are reminders about personal value to God, freedom,

and responsibility. And there is a call to unity in Christ, something not always easy to achieve. But it is immeasurably important for us to practice it—for ourselves, for seekers who may be watching, and for the Lord.

Unit 3: May
Set Free

Lesson 9: Believe No Other Gospel. Our studies in Galatians will remind us not to drift into any concept of a "works" salvation. God is the author of grace, Jesus Christ is the deliverer of grace, and we are the recipients of grace. We shall see that first-century Christians were tempted to look for a counterfeit "salvation" that was more complicated than Christ and less dependent on Christ. It is a temptation from which twenty-first-century Christians are not exempt, and one we must be prepared to resist.

Lesson 10: Know Salvation by Faith. Some of the Galatians, it seems, had come to think that the gospel of grace was just too good to be true. Surely we need some "additional" revelation, they thought. Surely there must be other good works that we need to do. Not so! This study will offer some significant insights into what it means for Christ to live in us (Galatians 2:20).

Lesson 11: Understand the Purpose of the Law. This week's lesson begins to make the transition in Galatians that we saw in Romans—moving from essential doctrinal truth to essential practical application. The Old Testament law prepared people to meet Jesus. It defined sin; now Jesus has been offered to remove sin. He removes old burdens, and He removes old barriers.

Lesson 12: Live in Christian Freedom. Jesus Christ sets us free—free from sin and death, and free from continuing in sin. We will be reminded this week that we are not free to do whatever we want, but we are gloriously free to do what Christ wants. We are also free to serve others.

Lesson 13: Participate in the Community of Faith. This is a great concluding lesson for the quarter—practical and terrifically important! Paul describes what life is like when the Holy Spirit of God is in charge. The class will be challenged to take a long, hard look at the implications and applications of the fruit of the Spirit in the Christian's life and within the community of Christians. We will see the importance of personal accountability (carrying our own loads), and with that the importance of helping and being helped with loads when they are just too much for one person to handle.

Thirteen lessons about being effective Christians! What better topic could we study?

Answers to Quarterly Quiz
on page 226

Lesson 1—1. the wrath of God. 2. sepulchre, asps. **Lesson 2**—1. repentance. 2. deeds. **Lesson 3**—1. patience. 2. the love of God. 3. Christ died for us. **Lesson 4**—1. Mary Magdalene. 2. false. 3. baptism. **Lesson 5**—1. death. 2. Abba, Father. **Lesson 6**—1. feet. 2. Isaiah. 3. the word of God. **Lesson 7**—1. living sacrifice. 2. coals of fire. **Lesson 8**—1. stumblingblock. 2. mind, mouth. **Lesson 9**—1. false. 2. Let him be accursed. **Lesson 10**—1. law, justified. 2. true. **Lesson 11**—1. angels. 2. Abraham's. **Lesson 12**—1. circumcised. 2. Thou shalt love thy neighbor as thyself. **Lesson 13**—1. love, temperance. 2. the spirit of meekness.

Churches in Macedonia and Galatia

The Gospel of Grace

Romans and Galatians share themes. Written at about the same time, these two letters contain some of Paul's most explicit explanations of the difference between the gospel of grace and the law of works. We will explore some of those themes in the coming quarter. Note some of the similarities on the chart below.

Romans	Galatians
"The gospel . . . is the power of God unto salvation" (Romans 1:16) **Lesson 1**	"The gospel . . . is not after man. . . . but by the revelation of Jesus Christ" (Galatians 1:11, 12) **Lesson 9**
"Justified by faith" (Romans 5:1) **Lesson 3**	"Not justified by the works of the law, but by . . . faith" (Galatians 2:16) **Lesson 10**
The law was weak and ineffectual (Romans 8:3) **Lesson 5**	The law was temporary, until faith came (Galatians 3:23-25) **Lesson 11**
Serve one another (Romans 12) **Lesson 7**	Use the fruit of the Spirit, not provoking or envying one another (Galatians 5:22-26) **Lesson 13**
Work together, not judging one another, but glorifying God "with one mind and one mouth" (Romans 14; 15:5, 6) **Lesson 8**	Exercise Christian liberty to "serve one another" (Galatians 5:13) **Lesson 12**

Effective Christians

Doctrine = Practice

by Ronald G. Davis

Iғ Goᴅ's ᴘʀᴏᴊᴇᴄᴛ ɪs ᴇꜰꜰᴇᴄᴛɪᴠᴇ Cʜʀɪsᴛɪᴀɴs, what exactly is it that makes a Christian effective? What is needed is the very same thing anyone with any responsibility needs: ability to make the responses necessary to accomplish the task! That is, a person can do what is needed to fulfill his or her purpose. What, then, is it that the Christian needs to do? To be built up (along with fellow Christians) in strength of faith; to worship and praise the Lord; to announce the good news of salvation to all who will listen. He or she has the same purposes as does the church: edification, fellowship, worship, and evangelism. The epistles Paul wrote to the Roman and Galatian Christians of the first century carry the same Spirit-filled power and necessity to us twenty-first-century Christians.

The Core of Effectiveness

At the core of Christian effectiveness is a working knowledge of the Word of God. And few books of the Bible offer the practical power of Romans and Galatians. Certainly in the study of these epistles in this quarter, the teacher will want to encourage and facilitate a deep, usable knowledge of the grand truths studied. Bible memorization must be at the forefront of strategies used.

The Golden Text highlighted each week reveals some of those grand truths. Consider having a learner with an effective voice record all thirteen Golden Texts and references and get cassettes duplicated or CDs burned for distribution to all class members. (Note: The *King James Version* is free of copyright restrictions.) When these are distributed, announce the intention and suggest that learners fill their opportune times—driving, cooking, washing dishes, resting —listening to these verses repeatedly.

In these texts there are other significant, most-worthy-to-be-memorized verses. Consider handing out a one-a-day worksheet for a selected verse (other than the Golden Text) of each week with seven different activities to be used one a day. For example, in the first lesson Romans 1:16 is a theme verse. The worksheet might resemble the following, with the direction to tear off each day as it is completed:

Sunday—"For I am not ＿＿ of the ＿＿ of Christ: for it is the ＿＿ of God unto ＿＿ to every one that ＿＿." Monday—"Rof I am ton aadehms of the eglops of Christ rof it is the eoprw of God unto aailonstv to eervy one that beeehiltv." Tuesday—am ashamed believeth Christ every for for God gospel I is it not of of of one power salvation that the the to unto. Wednesday—Gps J bn opu btibnfe pg uif hptqfm pg Disjtu gps ju jt uif qpxfs pg Hpe voup tbmwbujpo up fwfsz pof uibu cfmjfwfui. Thursday*—IRU J CO QRW HZO-HTLK QH WKH MUYVKR QH INXOYZ IRU KV KU WKH UTBJW QH JRG YRXS BJUEJCRXW VQ MDMZ GVM XLEX KNURNDNCQ. Friday—"For

＿ ＿＿ ＿＿＿＿＿＿ ＿＿ ＿＿＿＿
＿: for ＿＿ ＿＿＿＿＿＿＿ ＿＿ ＿＿＿＿＿
＿ ＿＿＿ unto ＿＿＿＿＿＿＿＿＿＿ to ＿

＿＿＿＿＿." Saturday—Quote Romans 1:16.

Many learners find that memorization and melody go hand in hand. Who can resist a snappy jingle? (In fact, who can get one out of his or her head?) Probably in your group of learners there are some who would find joy in developing a singable tune for selected verses from this quarter's study. Early in the quarter (or previous to its start) seek volunteers to compose a simple tune for verses you identify as important. For example, from lesson two, "There is no respect of persons with God," Romans 2:11; from lesson three, "Justified by faith, we have peace with God through our Lord Jesus Christ," Romans 5:1; from lesson 10, "If righteousness come by the law, then Christ is dead in vain," Galatians 2:21b. As a sample, Romans 5:1 lends itself to a five-syllable, five-syllable, six-syllable rhythm. Of course, the writer could add or alter words slightly to develop a singable chorus; for example, Romans 2:11 could be effective as:

There is no respect of persons with God;
There is no respect of persons with God;
There is no respect of persons with God,
So why is there prejudice in us?

*[*Solution for Thursday: move up in the alphabet by the number of letters in any given word.]*

The Fabric of the Gospel

After the first four lesson titles emphasizing grand doctrinal truths, the last nine lesson titles are all imperatives to do something. Though we tend to separate doctrinal and practical elements of the gospel, someone has rightly said, "There is nothing more practical than solid doctrine, and there is nothing more doctrinal than sound practice." Paul's "woven" version of the gospel, with doctrine as the foundation and practice as the structure, is a marvel of design—God's design.

For a session and text of your choice develop a front-and-back sheet of Doctrine and Practical Application pairs. Print the sheet so that the related practice is on the reverse of the doctrinal truth. Put about ten pairs on the sheet, cut them apart for the activity described below. As a sample, consider the lesson and text for May 1: Galatians 1:1-12. Here are possible doctrine and practice "pairs": (1) Our Lord Jesus Christ will deliver us from this present evil world (v. 4), and "As I read the bad news in the newspaper or watch it on television, I can praise the Lord that He will take me away from all the wickedness." (2) God the Father raised Jesus from the dead (v. 1), and "I can remain joyful when I attend the funeral of a godly friend or family member." (3) Perverted forms of the gospel have existed since the first century (v. 7), and "I must examine every presentation of the gospel—from religious television to popular media—for accuracy to the Word of Christ." (4) Even angels have no authority to change the gospel, to make it more demanding or less demanding (v. 8), and "Watching such TV shows such as 'Touched by an Angel' must not dilute my understanding of God's love and His expectation of repentance and obedience to Christ as Lord." (5) The pure gospel is that preached by Paul and the apostles in the first century (vv. 8, 9), and "My study of the Gospels and the book of Acts and the epistles is the safest way to learn the gospel." (6) Being a servant of Christ, I will not necessarily please many (v. 10), and "I must be willing to 'hate . . . father, and mother, and wife, and children, and brethren, and sisters' to be Jesus' disciple, if it comes to a choice" (see Luke 14:26). (7) The good news of the gospel is not man-made truth, but revelation from God (vv. 11, 12), and "I must reject all explanations of truth that are of purely human origin and speculation." (8) There is a curse on the one who distorts or rejects the gospel of Christ (vv. 8, 9), and "I must work to correct and edify anyone whom I find distorting the gospel, to save that person from God's curse." (9) The office of apostle is by the authority and declaration of God (v. 1), and "Anyone who makes a claim for 'apostolic succession' and purports to be one must be challenged by the Word." (10) The heart of the gospel is the grace of Christ (v. 6), and "I have no anxiety about being good enough for God, for by grace I am saved."

When class members arrive, hand each a rectangular piece carrying one of the doctrinal truth/practical application pairs. (Duplicate the sheet if you have more than ten class members.) Direct them to look at only one side. When you come to the "Into the Word" segment of your class time, say to them, "Your task is to decide what 'should' be on the other side of your sheet—if you see a doctrine (with verse reference), what could be the practical application? If you see a practical application, what doctrine (and verse[s]) is relevant?" Let group members share some of their statements and their decisions for the reverse, and then let them read both sides. Of course, their speculative decisions need not match the statements and references given. Discuss the differences when they are seen.

Into Life

The epistles were designed by God and the Spirit to challenge Christians to be true to the doctrine they have been taught. Doctrine is true whether individuals apply it to life or not, but the only personal value that doctrine has is seen in daily application. There is the "What's So" of the gospel, but there is also the "So What?"

With every lesson, the wise teacher realizes his study and plan is incomplete until he asks, "So what? What is there about today's truths that can make a difference in the life of my learners this week?"

Teach your students to read the epistles with a "So What?" attitude—that is, to ponder the personal consequences of each truth revealed. Consider dividing your class into two groups for reading the texts antiphonally one or more weeks of the quarter: one group to read a verse, and the second group to exclaim, "So What!" after each.

For example, for Lesson 8 first group would read Romans 14:1, "Him that is weak in the faith receive ye, but not to doubtful disputations"; the second group would say, "So What!" and so on through the entire text, verse by verse. Be certain to explain that this is in no way questioning the validity of the text, but is a simple challenge to consider the text personally and behaviorally.

If you typically end your class in prayer, suggest that the class—rather than adding a loud "Amen!" at the end—add a loud "Amen! So What!" as an indication they not only affirm the truth but intend to apply it.

All Have Sinned

DEVOTIONAL READING: Psalm 59:1-5.

BACKGROUND SCRIPTURE: Romans 1:16-20;
3:9-20.

PRINTED TEXT: Romans 1:16-20; 3:9-20.

Romans 1:16-20

16 For I am not ashamed of the gospel of Christ: for it is the power of God unto salvation to every one that believeth; to the Jew first, and also to the Greek.

17 For therein is the righteousness of God revealed from faith to faith: as it is written, The just shall live by faith.

18 For the wrath of God is revealed from heaven against all ungodliness and unrighteousness of men, who hold the truth in unrighteousness;

19 Because that which may be known of God is manifest in them; for God hath showed it unto them.

20 For the invisible things of him from the creation of the world are clearly seen, being understood by the things that are made, even his eternal power and Godhead; so that they are without excuse.

Romans 3:9-20

9 What then? are we better than they? No, in no wise: for we have before proved both Jews and Gentiles, that they are all under sin;

10 As it is written, There is none righteous, no, not one:

11 There is none that understandeth, there is none that seeketh after God.

12 They are all gone out of the way, they are together become unprofitable; there is none that doeth good, no, not one.

13 Their throat is an open sepulchre; with their tongues they have used deceit; the poison of asps is under their lips:

14 Whose mouth is full of cursing and bitterness:

15 Their feet are swift to shed blood:

16 Destruction and misery are in their ways:

17 And the way of peace have they not known:

18 There is no fear of God before their eyes.

19 Now we know that what things soever the law saith, it saith to them who are under the law: that every mouth may be stopped, and all the world may become guilty before God.

20 Therefore by the deeds of the law there shall no flesh be justified in his sight: for by the law is the knowledge of sin.

GOLDEN TEXT: As it is written, There is none righteous, no, not one.—Romans 3:10.

God's Project: Effective Christians
Unit 1: Saved by God
(Lessons 1-4)

Lesson Aims

After this lesson, a student should be able to:

1. Summarize what Paul says about people's need for a solution to their sin problem and the helplessness of the law to provide it.

2. Compare the problems Paul cites with the problems we see in our own culture.

3. Memorize Romans 1:16, 17.

Lesson Outline

INTRODUCTION
    A. No Singular Saints
    B. Lesson Background
  I. ANSWER TO SIN (Romans 1:16, 17)
    A. Gospel of Christ (v. 16a)
    B. Power of God (v. 16b)
    C. Righteousness by Faith (v. 17)
 II. RESPONSIBILITY FOR SIN (Romans 1:18-20)
    A. Ungodliness Revealed (v. 18)
    B. Ungodliness Inexcusable (vv. 19, 20)
      Invisible but Abundantly Evident
III. EXPERIENCE OF SIN (Romans 3:9-12)
    A. Same Failure in Everyone (v. 9)
    B. Same Failure to Seek God (vv. 10, 11)
    C. Same Failure to Do Good (v. 12)
IV. CHARACTER OF SIN (Romans 3:13-18)
    A. Affects Our Tongues (vv. 13, 14)
      The Power of Speech
    B. Affects Our Feet (vv. 15-17)
    C. Affects Our Eyes (v. 18)
 V. DEFINER OF SIN—THE LAW (Romans 3:19, 20)
    A. Confirms Our Guilt (v. 19)
    B. Fails to Address Guilt (v. 20)
CONCLUSION
    A. No Superiority in Sinners
    B. Every Glory in Salvation
    C. Prayer
    D. Thought to Remember

Introduction

A. No Singular Saints

The headings on the Gospels and epistles that we find in our modern Bibles were not in the original text. Someone added the word *saint* to names such as Matthew and John (for example), resulting in "The Gospel According to Saint Matthew" or "Saint John." Interestingly, the word for *saint* (meaning "holy one," or someone "set apart," thus describing any Christian) never occurs in the singular form in the New Testament. It is always plural. Songs in Heaven are not going to be solos. They are going to be sung by "a great multitude, which no man could number" (Revelation 7:9). The Christian life was never intended to be a solo. It is designed to be lived with and for *others*.

It is true also that we are not plagued by the curse of sin alone. Each of us has fallen short of the glory of God, just as the first human beings, Adam and Eve, did. The seductive summons from our fleshly side has pressured all of us, has been most enticing, and cannot be successfully resisted in our own strength.

"Misery loves company," an old saying tells us. We have abundant company in the misery caused by sin, but in Christ we have company in the victory that He provides (company that we can really love!). Throughout this quarter, we are going to talk a good deal about both kinds of "company." [See question #1, page 240.]

B. Lesson Background

Paul, formerly Saul the persecutor of Christians, is the author of the letter to the Romans. He is sending it to the congregation of believers in Rome, with the hope that he would follow the letter personally before very long (Romans 1:10, 11). Some of the men and women whom he had loved and taught and led to Christ seem to have traveled to Rome ahead of him for one reason or another (persecution, employment, or other factors). That is clear from the list of personal greetings that Paul includes at the end of the letter in chapter 16.

A church was growing in Rome—made up of individuals who were likely present in Jerusalem on Pentecost (Acts 2:10) and of newly converted believers. It seemed most important to Paul that they grow in the right direction. They needed a strong doctrinal base, and they needed some practical spiritual direction. In this letter they received both.

Paul wrote Romans about the year A.D. 56 or 57, which would have been approximately twenty years after his own conversion. Apparently the letter was written from Corinth during Paul's third missionary journey. He refers to the hospitality of a man named Gaius in Romans 16:23; Gaius was a convert of Paul's in Corinth (1 Corinthians 1:14).

The contents of Romans reflect Paul's experience in presenting a gospel that is both thorough and orderly, as well as one that deals with some of the normal daily issues and relational matters faced by growing Christians. He is in the prime years of his ministry, and he is able to present the fruit of his personal familiarity with bringing people to Christ and providing an atmosphere for their growth. He is prepared to send a letter that covers many important issues, counters some spiritual errors, and emphasizes core truths of the Christian faith.

The maturity of the church in Rome was already well known. "Your faith is spoken of throughout the whole world," Paul writes in Romans 1:8. He wanted to meet the Christians there and share in their growth. His desire was to help them, while also benefiting from their gifts (Romans 1:12).

I. Answer to Sin
(Romans 1:16, 17)

A. Gospel of Christ (v. 16a)

16a. For I am not ashamed of the gospel of Christ.

In this verse we read one of the most familiar statements in all of the letters written by Paul—a statement that is important for us to affirm to ourselves, to our family in *Christ*, and to our neighbors who are in need of good news. Paul indicates in the previous verses (13-15) that he is eager to preach Christ to the faithful in Rome and to work with them in reaching others for Christ in that great city.

B. Power of God (v. 16b)

16b. For it is the power of God unto salvation to every one that believeth; to the Jew first, and also to the Greek.

It is difficult to determine whether the church in Rome consisted of mostly Jews or Gentiles. Clearly there were some of both present. As noted earlier, some of the Jewish believers in the church in Rome were likely present in Jerusalem to observe Pentecost. They heard the gospel from Peter, who presented Jesus as the Messiah and Savior. Those Jews were among the *first* to hear the good news; but back in Rome were Greeks, who also needed to know this *power of God unto salvation*.

The Greek word translated *power* is the source of such English words as *dynamite*, *dynamo*, and *dynamic*. Not only did the gospel possess the power to save *every one that believeth*, it also had the power to break down the walls separating Jews and Gentiles—a point discussed further by Paul in Ephesians 2:11-22.

C. Righteousness by Faith (v. 17)

17. For therein is the righteousness of God revealed from faith to faith: as it is written, The just shall live by faith.

Why is the gospel such a crucial message? Because *therein is the righteousness of God revealed*. The gospel tells sinful people how to become right with God. That is something that we can never earn or achieve through our own efforts; Isaiah 64:6 says that "all our righteousnesses are as filthy rags" before God. Our only hope is to accept by faith the gift of God's righteousness provided by Him through the death of Jesus. As Paul wrote to the Corinthians, "For he hath made him to be sin for us, who knew no sin; that we might be made the righteousness of God in him" (2 Corinthians 5:21).

What does the phrase *from faith to faith* mean? It is difficult to know exactly what Paul had in mind. Perhaps he is indicating that faith must govern our approach to God throughout our walk with Him. We never outgrow our need for faith. And God never changes that requirement. [See question #2, page 240.]

II. Responsibility for Sin
(Romans 1:18-20)

A. Ungodliness Revealed (v. 18)

18. For the wrath of God is revealed from heaven against all ungodliness and unrighteousness of men, who hold the truth in unrighteousness.

Sin can never be taken lightly. *The wrath of God* is the reaction of a holy, righteous God to something that blatantly violates that holiness and righteousness. That wrath, says Paul, *is revealed from heaven against all ungodliness and unrighteousness of men*. Paul's use of the present tense is noteworthy. God's wrath is not associated with only the final Judgment Day. His wrath is manifested in this life. Paul describes how this takes place in verses 21-32 of this chapter.

Paul also describes how sinful humans *hold the truth in unrighteousness*. Note that there is a good way to "hold the truth"; for example, an elder is to be "holding fast the faithful word as he hath been taught" (Titus 1:9). Here in Romans 1, however, Paul is concerned with how those in rebellion against the Creator suppress His truth and hinder its progress by their sinfulness. Human beings have always been experts at

---

How to Say It

CORINTH. *Cor*-inth.
CORINTHIANS. Ko-*rin*-thee-unz.
ECCLESIASTES. Ih-klees-ee-*az*-tees.
GAIUS. *Gay*-us.
SEPULCHRE. *sep*-ul-kur.

drowning divine truth in an ocean of excuses and evil behavior. It goes without saying that the present day is no exception.

B. Ungodliness Inexcusable (vv. 19, 20)

19, 20. Because that which may be known of God is manifest in them; for God hath showed it unto them. For the invisible things of him from the creation of the world are clearly seen, being understood by the things that are made, even his eternal power and Godhead; so that they are without excuse.

God's creative *power* shouts through all He has made, and it echoes throughout the universe. David observed, "The heavens declare the glory of God; and the firmament showeth his handiwork" (Psalm 19:1). This marvelous world, our amazing bodies, the atmosphere, the cycle of life involving plants and animals—all of this communicates one clear message: "Creator." *By the things that are made*, we can see the Maker. The term *Godhead* means "divine nature"—those attributes that make God who He alone is.

We can also understand that along with God's designs in nature are His designs for those made in His image. And it is not difficult to understand that we have violated them. We are indeed *without excuse*. [See question #3, page 240.]

In Romans 1:21–2:29, Paul continues to provide support for the "bad news"—every human being is a sinner. This includes Gentiles, who do not have the benefit of what may be termed the "special revelation" of God's law, and Jews, who do. In the remainder of our printed text, Paul reaches the conclusion of his argument and paves the way for his discussion of the grace of God.

INVISIBLE BUT ABUNDANTLY EVIDENT

On May 24, 1844, Samuel Morse opened the telegraph age when he sent a message by his special "code" from the United States Capitol to his partner in Baltimore, Maryland. The message he sent was brief but stirring: "What hath God wrought?" The telegraph enabled people to communicate with each other over great distances by means of wire and a pair of telegraph keys (and,

---

VISUALS FOR THESE LESSONS

The small visual pictured in each lesson (e. g., page 238) is a reproduction of a large, full-color poster included in the *Adult Visuals* packet for the Spring Quarter. The packet is available from your supplier. Order No. 392.

---

of course, a knowledge of Morse code). Technology changed again on March 10, 1876, when Alexander Graham Bell demonstrated his new invention, the telephone.

However, on January 18, 1903, a totally new era dawned in the field of communications when Guglielmo Marconi (Goog-lee-*el*-mo Mar-*coe*-nee) stood on Cape Cod and sent through the airwaves a fifty-four-word greeting from President Theodore Roosevelt across the Atlantic Ocean to King Edward VII of England. King Edward responded with a message to President Roosevelt. Today, we take for granted the fact that even our telephones are wireless and are beginning to rival computers in their many functions.

Before electricity was discovered and before the telegraph, telephone, radio, and television were invented, the average person had no sense of the unseen forces that would allow modern communications. On the other hand, the evidence of God's invisible power has *always* been all around us. According to Paul, there's no excuse for missing it.   —C. R. B.

III. Experience of Sin
(Romans 3:9-12)

A. Same Failure in Everyone (v. 9)

9. What then? are we better than they? No, in no wise: for we have before proved both Jews and Gentiles, that they are all under sin.

In Romans 3:1, 2, Paul cites the spiritual benefits associated with being one of the *Jews*. Do those benefits automatically make them *better than* the *Gentiles? No, in no wise.* (Absolutely not!) Both groups have "missed the mark" in God's eyes, and such failure is called *sin*.

B. Same Failure to Seek God (vv. 10, 11)

10, 11. As it is written, There is none righteous, no, not one: there is none that understandeth, there is none that seeketh after God.

At this point, Paul begins to marshal an impressive array of evidence from the Old Testament to strengthen his argument for the sinfulness of humanity. The quotations begin with the authoritative phrase *as it is written.* *There is none righteous, no, not one* is taken from Ecclesiastes 7:20. The remainder of the verse is found in Psalms 14:2, 3 and 53:2, 3. These bold, uncompromising statements (note the repetition of *none*) strike hard at the proud, self-confident, God-defying attitude of many in our society.

C. Same Failure to Do Good (v. 12)

12. They are all gone out of the way, they are together become unprofitable; there is none that doeth good, no, not one.

These statements continue Paul's use of Psalms 14:3 and 53:3 as cited under the previous verse. Note once again Paul's all-inclusive language, letting no one off the hook. *All* are guilty; *there is none that doeth good, no, not one.*

That people have *gone out of the way* means that we have departed from God's way and "have turned every one to his own way" (Isaiah 53:6). One might also consider how so many go "out of their way" to become *unprofitable.* Some of the profitless living that people pursue requires a great deal of creativity, energy, and deception, when a profitable, godly life would give greater immediate return as well as the glorious long-term return on their investment.

"Going out of the way to become unprofitable" has a very familiar ring to it. It's quite a contemporary perversion, and it's also quite foolish.

IV. Character of Sin
(Romans 3:13-18)

A. Affects Our Tongues (vv. 13, 14)

13. Their throat is an open sepulchre; with their tongues they have used deceit; the poison of asps is under their lips.

Here Paul uses the words of Psalms 5:9 and 140:3 to continue his indictment of humanity. The word pictures that Paul employs are instructive. Both an *open sepulchre* and *the poison of asps* convey the image of death. *Deceit* is often necessary to cover one's tracks after unkind or bitter words have been uttered. Colossians 4:6 offers a more positive word picture: "Let your speech be always with grace, seasoned with salt."

14. Whose mouth is full of cursing and bitterness.

Cursing is often thought of in terms of blasphemy against God. But cursing can also be aimed at human beings. That is what the context of Psalm 10:7, cited by Paul in this verse, is describing. [See question #4, page 240.]

THE POWER OF SPEECH

An old joke tells of a "space saucer" that landed at 3:00 A.M. in the driveway of a deserted gas station. The space aliens got out of their ship, examined the pumps, looked around a bit, then reboarded their ship and flew off into space. The pilot radioed back home and said, "The Earthlings look very much like us, but they refused to talk to us. All they do is stand around with their tails in their ears." Watching people today walk around with their heads tilted sideways and with one arm holding a tiny cell phone to an ear may cause one to think the old joke has come true! Everyone seems to be talking on the phone most of the time—in restaurants, theaters, church services, and even funerals!

The number of minutes per year that Americans spent talking on cell phones skyrocketed from 20 billion in 1993 to 580 billion in 2002—an increase of almost 30 times! The number of cell phone users has increased at a similar rate. The number of auto accidents caused by cell phone usage has also climbed so much that many cities and states have outlawed the use of such phones while driving.

It cannot be denied that "talk" has changed the way we live and act—and that is exactly the point Paul makes in Romans 3 as he describes humanity's sinfulness. Evil speech can produce evil actions. If we wish to live righteously, we must pay attention to the way we talk. —C. R. B.

B. Affects Our Feet (vv. 15-17)

15. Their feet are swift to shed blood.

The way we talk affects the way we walk. Bitter action follows bitter words. Violence (the shedding of *blood*) is the fruit of unchecked anger.

Verses 15-17 include a reference to the words of Isaiah 59:7, 8, as Paul's unflattering picture of humanity without God continues.

16, 17. Destruction and misery are in their ways: and the way of peace have they not known.

Picture a tornado that leaves a path of *destruction and misery* in its wake. Such are the consequences of sinful ways—both in the sinner's life and in those affected by his or her wayward words and deeds.

In the twenty-first-century Western world, one finds numerous living illustrations of the apostle's insights into human sinfulness drawn from the Old Testament. "We can get along just fine without God," say the secular humanists. But even just a cursory survey of the past forty years demonstrates the emptiness of their claim. Our knowledge has increased significantly in many fields during that time, but *the way of peace* is *known* less and less as people depart further and further from the Prince of peace.

C. Affects Our Eyes (v. 18)

18. There is no fear of God before their eyes.

Here we see the root of all the trouble described in the previous eight verses. *There is no fear of God before their eyes* (Psalm 36:1). God is not treated with reverence. He is not the reference point for the discussion of issues involving human conduct. He is viewed by many as a hindrance to their desire to be their own god. It is the same lie whispered by the serpent in the Garden of Eden (Genesis 3:4, 5).

V. Definer of Sin—the Law
(Romans 3:19, 20)

A. Confirms Our Guilt (v. 19)

19. Now we know that what things soever the law saith, it saith to them who are under the law: that every mouth may be stopped, and all the world may become guilty before God.

The *law* in this verse may refer to more than just the law of Moses. Since Paul has just finished a series of quotations from different portions of the Old Testament, he may be using *law* as a designation for the entire Old Testament. Those quotations have not described Jews only; they have been clear in their emphasis that "there is none righteous, no, not one" (v. 10). The effect is to reinforce what Paul stated in verse 9: that "both Jews and Gentiles . . . are all under sin." Or, as he states in the verse before us, *all the world* stands *guilty before God. Every mouth* must be *stopped*, or silenced, before the Creator.

With the precision of a skilled prosecutor, Paul has presented an airtight case for humanity's guilt. The evidence is irrefutable; we have no choice but to agree with it. We are indeed guilty as charged. [See question #5, page 240.]

B. Fails to Address Guilt (v. 20)

20. Therefore by the deeds of the law there shall no flesh be justified in his sight: for by the law is the knowledge of sin.

The *law* plays a pivotal role in the plan of God. The law points out our need, our spiritual nakedness as it were. That's its job—to highlight the bad news: *by the deeds of the law shall no flesh be justified.* If that were the end of the story, what a dismal picture! But it isn't; now we are ready to receive the good news, to which Paul turns in the next portion of Romans.

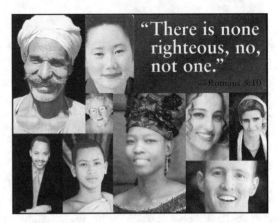

"There is none righteous, no, not one." —Romans 3:10

Visual for lesson 1. *This visual of people from around the world helps emphasize the fact that no nation or people-group is unaffected by sin.*

Conclusion

A. No Superiority in Sinners

As we noted at the beginning of our study, there are no singular saints. None of us should try to go solo in faith's pilgrimage or toward faith's destination. [See question #6, page 240.]

In addition, there are no singular sinners. We have all fallen short of God's glory. And there is no superiority in sinners—big ones and little ones, favored ones and disdained ones. Both Jews and Gentiles are guilty. Both need a Savior. And both have a Savior.

B. Every Glory in Salvation

Consider the words of the Bible's Golden Text: "For God so loved the world, that he gave his only begotten Son, that whosoever believeth in him should not perish, but have everlasting life" (John 3:16). To Paul's words, "There is none that doeth good, no, not one" (Romans 3:12), we can answer, "There is 'no, not one' for whom Jesus did not die." *Whosoever!*

C. Prayer

Help us, dear Father, to see our sin and the consequence of it. How thankful we are that we can rest in Jesus, Your Son, our Savior. How thankful that we do not rest there alone, but in fellowship with others who name the Name. Thank You for providing the good news, for no one else could have provided an answer for our sin. Through Christ, our perfect Redeemer, we pray. Amen.

D. Thought to Remember

Instead of trying to cover up our sin on our own, let us allow Jesus' blood to cover it.

Home Daily Bible Readings

Monday, Feb. 28—No One Does Good (Psalm 14:1-6)

Tuesday, Mar. 1—The Wicked Won't Turn to God (Psalm 10:1-6)

Wednesday, Mar. 2—Sinners Can't Accuse Others (John 8:1-9)

Thursday, Mar. 3—The Gospel Has Saving Power (Romans 1:16-20)

Friday, Mar. 4—We Are All Sinful (Romans 8:9-14)

Saturday, Mar. 5—We Are All Guilty (Romans 3:15-20)

Sunday, Mar. 6—We Have All Sinned (1 John 1:5-10)

Learning by Doing

This page contains an alternative lesson plan emphasizing learning activities.
Classes desiring such student involvement will find these suggestions helpful.

Learning Goals

After this lesson, a student should be able to:

1. Summarize what Paul says about people's need for a solution to their sin problem and the helplessness of the law to provide it.

2. Compare the problems Paul cites with the problems we see in our own culture.

3. Memorize Romans 1:16, 17.

Into the Lesson

On three cards measuring at least six by eight inches, write the letters L-A-W on one side and the letters S-I-N on the other side. Tape the cards as lift flaps to the wall or chalkboard, with the letters L-A-W showing. As class begins, say, "Under each of these letters is the letter of a related word. What letters would you expect to find?" As soon as someone guesses an S, an I, or an N and you show the underside of the flap, someone will probably identify the hidden word. Once a learner does, ask, "How are these two words related?" Expect such responses as, "The law reveals sin" and "The law is the target; sin is the miss."

Next, distribute to the class a copy of two lists from an exhaustive concordance of the Bible. One list will contain occurrences of the word *law* and the other list occurrences of the word *sin* in the Epistle to the Romans. Note that the two words *sin* and *law* are very common in this letter: *law* occurs more than sixty times; *sin* occurs more than forty times. Have someone quickly read the reference list for law, asking all others to follow the sin reference list with the direction to yell "Stop!" whenever the lists coincide. Have those verses read to show the relationships between the two concepts as Paul describes them.

Into the Word

Give learners a copy of Romans 3:20 in this format: "Therefore, _____ _____ there shall no flesh be justified _____: for _____ is the knowledge _____." In addition, give them this list of prepositional phrases deleted from the verse and printed here alphabetically: "by the deeds," "by the law," "in his sight," "of sin," "of the law." Tell them this is the "Prepositional Proposition" that is the key truth of today's study. Give them time to put the prepositional phrases into the appropriate spaces. Emphasize the key truth: the law makes

sin clear, but it does not justify anyone of his or her sins.

Recruit two of your best oral readers to read Hebrews 8:6–9:15, alternating verses. Though this will take three to four minutes, it will provide an excellent explanation of the relationship between the law and the gospel. The Holy Spirit, through the writer of that text (and surrounding contexts), develops the full contrast between the righteousness that comes by the law and the righteousness that comes by faith in Christ.

Direct attention to verses 12-18 of Romans 3, in which Paul notes the sins common in his culture. Say, "Paul highlights some of the sins common in his first-century Roman world. Those of you whose age is an even number, make a list of those sins. Those of you whose age is an odd number, make a list of the common sins of our twenty-first-century world." Give three or four minutes, then ask for the "Roman" list of sins. After each is mentioned, ask those with the "our time" list if they have included the same or a corresponding sin. Deceit, cursing, violence, no fear of God—all are as common today as in Paul's lifetime. Conclude with a clause from today's text (Romans 1:20): "The Romans of Paul's time —'they are without excuse.' Those of our time— 'they are without excuse.'"

Into Life

Remind the group: "Romans 1:16 must be the motto for the Christian's daily experience. Find that verse and put your finger on it." Ask for volunteers to stand and affirm that truth, personalizing it in whatever way each one finds appropriate. For example (and you as the teacher may need to be the first to do so): "For I, *(insert your name)* am not ashamed of the gospel of Christ; for it is the power of God for salvation to everyone who believes, including me!" After several have volunteered, ask the class to read this verse in unison. Make sure everyone has the same version of the passage. (This activity is included in the student book.)

Point out that having no shame in the gospel implies that one will stand up for and promote its truths at every opportunity. Suggest that class members keep a mental "log" this coming week of occasions when they show no shame in the gospel and occasions when they are more hesitant to stand up for it.

Let's Talk It Over

The questions on this page are designed to promote discussion of the lesson by the class and to encourage application of the lesson Scriptures. The answers provided are only discussion starters. Let your class talk it over from there.

1. How has your own life been influenced by the community of saints or the community of sinners? In what ways have others influenced you to some specific act, either good or evil?

Although "peer pressure" is often considered a teenager's problem, adults can also find themselves influenced by friends, family, media, and culture to do things they would otherwise not have done. Positive examples may include giving up smoking because you have children, changing your vocabulary because you became a Christian, or volunteering in your church or community because a friend is doing it. Negative examples may include viewing a movie or television show that is very popular but that promotes sinful behavior, or drinking at a company party because "everyone is doing it."

2. What is the difference in these two statements: "the just shall live by faith," and "living by faith will make a person just"? What is the significance of God's choosing the first statement rather than the second one?

It is helpful to distinguish between the faith that saves and the faith that serves. Being declared "just" or "justified" before God is not a matter of our achievement (of "living by faith"), but of trust in God's provision. God has declared that Christians are just because of their trust in Jesus' death for them. Because we are just, we are to live by faith. We do not become just because of our living by faith. Rather, we live by faith because we have become just.

3.What are some of the "invisible things" (attributes of God) that you have "clearly seen" in creation? How does seeing God's character and power in creation remove the excuses that we and others might make for our sin?

Anytime we admire a sunset, marvel at the intricacy of a spider web, look with wonder at the sky, or gaze in fascination at an animal, we are seeing the fingerprints of the Creator's hand. Although the revelation we see in creation is not as specific as the revelation in God's Word, we can see from the creation that God exists, that He is intimately involved in every aspect of our being, that He cares for us, that we are unique among His creatures, and that we live in a world perfectly designed for us.

4. In his description of the effect of sin in Romans 3:12-18, Paul seems to focus particularly on our speech (note his references to "throat," "tongues," "lips," and "mouth"). In what ways does sin affect our speech?

Certainly the impact of sin on human speech involves much more than just "cussing." Paul also mentions "deceit" and "bitterness" in this passage and uses the phrase "the poison of asps" in association with one's speech. Angry words that are uttered hastily and without thinking can have devastating consequences in a family or in a church. Such words take only seconds to speak, but their impact can affect relationships for years in some cases! The lesson writer cites Paul's words in Colossians 4:6 about one's speech being "always with grace, seasoned with salt." That is a much more encouraging metaphor than "the poison of asps"!

5. If we are saved by grace, what role does God's law play in our lives?

The law still points us to God's plan for moral living. Obeying that moral law brings glory to God, serves as a testimony to His power and His wisdom, and shows our love for Him. The law reveals our guilt before God and removes our excuses for sin; thus does it show our need for a Savior and prepares us to receive His grace.

6. Can we truly express the fullness of Christianity without identifying with and participating in a community of believers (a church)? What do you think of the statement, "I can worship God just as well on my own as I can in a church"?

Consider the comparison of the church with a human body—a metaphor developed most fully in Romans 12:1-8 and 1 Corinthians 12:12-27. It is clear from this comparison that no one is meant to "solo" as a Christian. "The body is not one member, but many" (1 Corinthians 12:14). In addition, one may observe that it is impossible to claim a relationship with the Head of the church (Jesus) while refusing to have any ties with His body. Also worth consideration are the various "one another" commands in the New Testament, such as the exhortation in Hebrews 10:24, 25. Again, these make it clear that God does not intend for any Christian to be "quarantined."

God's Judgment Is Just

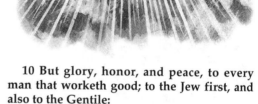

DEVOTIONAL READING: **Psalm 50:1-15.**

BACKGROUND SCRIPTURE: **Romans 2:1-16.**

PRINTED TEXT: **Romans 2:1-16.**

Romans 2:1-16

1 Therefore thou art inexcusable, O man, whosoever thou art that judgest: for wherein thou judgest another, thou condemnest thyself; for thou that judgest doest the same things.

2 But we are sure that the judgment of God is according to truth against them which commit such things.

3 And thinkest thou this, O man, that judgest them which do such things, and doest the same, that thou shalt escape the judgment of God?

4 Or despisest thou the riches of his goodness and forbearance and long-suffering; not knowing that the goodness of God leadeth thee to repentance?

5 But, after thy hardness and impenitent heart, treasurest up unto thyself wrath against the day of wrath and revelation of the righteous judgment of God;

6 Who will render to every man according to his deeds:

7 To them who by patient continuance in well doing seek for glory and honor and immortality, eternal life:

8 But unto them that are contentious, and do not obey the truth, but obey unrighteousness, indignation and wrath,

9 Tribulation and anguish, upon every soul of man that doeth evil; of the Jew first, and also of the Gentile;

10 But glory, honor, and peace, to every man that worketh good; to the Jew first, and also to the Gentile:

11 For there is no respect of persons with God.

12 For as many as have sinned without law shall also perish without law; and as many as have sinned in the law shall be judged by the law;

13 (For not the hearers of the law are just before God, but the doers of the law shall be justified.

14 For when the Gentiles, which have not the law, do by nature the things contained in the law, these, having not the law, are a law unto themselves:

15 Which show the work of the law written in their hearts, their conscience also bearing witness, and their thoughts the mean while accusing or else excusing one another;)

16 In the day when God shall judge the secrets of men by Jesus Christ according to my gospel.

GOLDEN TEXT: God shall judge the secrets of men by Jesus Christ according to my gospel.
—Romans 2:16.

God's Project: Effective Christians
Unit 1: Saved by God
(Lessons 1-4)

Lesson Aims

After this lesson, a student should be able to:

1. Contrast the perfect judgment of God with the faulty judgment of people.

2. Explain why something better than "justice" is needed.

3. Express a commitment to live with a non-judgmental attitude toward others, keeping in mind the coming judgment of God.

Lesson Outline

INTRODUCTION
    A. Judge Without Limits
    B. Judges with Limits
    C. Lesson Background
I. UNQUALIFIED JUDGE (Romans 2:1-4)
    A. Condemns What He Does (v. 1)
    B. Expects an Exemption (vv. 2, 3)
    C. Declines Repentance (v. 4)
      Firefighters or Firebugs?
II. QUALIFIED JUDGE (Romans 2:5-16)
    A. Renders Righteous Verdicts (vv. 5-8)
      Choices
    B. Exhibits No Favoritism (vv. 9-11)
    C. Upholds the Law (vv. 12-15)
    D. Judges Through Jesus (v. 16)
CONCLUSION
    A. Caution
    B. Prayer
    C. Thought to Remember

Introduction

A. Judge Without Limits

Several times in the Scriptures we read strong cautions about our all-too-human tendency to make ourselves seem better by depicting others as somehow worse. As we study the Scripture for today, we will talk more about that. One aspect of this matter should never be ignored. There is One who has every right to judge and whose judgment is administered with true justice. His nature requires it. The patriarch Abraham asked this poignant question found in Genesis 18:25: "Shall not the Judge of all the earth do right?" The implied answer is yes, He will. God is the Judge without biases or limits of any kind. His judgment is flawless.

Within today's generation are those who insist that no authoritative standard of right and wrong exists. Each person has the power to decide what is right for himself or herself. Everything is relative. As much as some may think that this is a new position, it is, of course, not new at all. (See Judges 21:25 for an example of how Old Testament Israel embraced this same philosophy.) [See question #1, page 248.]

God has established His laws, and they are to be obeyed. He is the ultimate Supreme Court before whom all are accountable (Romans 14:10).

B. Judges with Limits

How different is the subject of judging when human beings are doing it! Our Scripture today, along with others, carries strong warnings against judging. It is addressed to Christians, who are not immune to imperfect attitudes or behavior in this area. We are not to exhibit superiority over others, or suggest that we are without flaws, or claim that we "would never be caught dead" doing what has ensnared another (especially if we have engaged in the same behavior).

Beside the many prohibitions against improper judging are other Scriptures that encourage judging of the proper kind. That is not the focus of today's lesson, but it is a teaching that we must keep in mind. Jesus told those skeptical of Him to "judge righteous judgment" (John 7:24). Paul reminded the Corinthian church that "the saints shall judge the world" (1 Corinthians 6:2). And they are to use God's clear teaching (such as that cited in 1 Corinthians 5 and 6 involving sexual immorality) to call each other to purity and to separate themselves from the impure who claim to be Christians.

Christians must not try to judge unbelievers for their wrongdoing; that is the job of civil authorities (Romans 13:1-5). But they must apply Christian standards to those who profess faith in Christ, and they must address failure with an eye toward repentance and recovery. And they are to settle disputes among themselves by themselves, rather than bringing other Christians before a pagan court. [See question #2, page 248.]

There are no limits to God's judgment. There are limits to ours. That's why the Scripture for today is so important!

C. Lesson Background

In today's text from Romans 2, Paul is taking an approach with the Christians in Rome that is similar to the disarming, yet effective, approach taken by Amos, the prophet to Israel (the northern kingdom), in the middle of the eighth century B.C. Plagued by ungodly leadership and inward spiritual apathy, Israel was falling apart.

The people needed to understand that God's judgment was imminent. But how would this sheep farmer and fig picker from the south (Judah) get their attention?

First, Amos brought up the topic of judgment in such a way as to gain the attention and the approval (maybe even cheers) of his listeners. He told them how God was going to rain down judgment on other peoples with whom the northern kingdom was often at odds. "Yes!" they shouted. "They deserve to be destroyed!" He even capped his introduction with a word of judgment against Judah, Israel's spiritual sibling and archrival. Then, before the residents of the north could stop cheering, Amos unloaded God's word of judgment against *them*. So they got the message through a very clever, "back door" method.

Paul takes a very similar approach in the book of Romans. The Jews knew (and Paul confirmed this) that the Gentiles around them were vile and sinful. And they were without excuse for being so. As Paul states in Romans 1:18-32, they could see the evidence for God all around them—an orderly, powerful Creator, who had not hidden himself at all. And within them was created the capacity for responding to Him in faith. They simply chose to ignore the evidence and thus the source of the evidence.

With the beginning of Romans 2, Paul will begin to make the case that the Jews have sinned as well. Thus they have the very same need for salvation that the Gentiles possess.

I. Unqualified Judge (Romans 2:1-4)

A. Condemns What He Does (v. 1)

1. Therefore thou art inexcusable, O man, whosoever thou art that judgest: for wherein thou judgest another, thou condemnest thyself; for thou that judgest doest the same things.

We know this pattern within ourselves all too well. We tend to raise our voices loudest against those sins in others that are no temptation at all for us (so we can feel quite superior), or against those that have been the greatest problem for us (so we can divert attention away from our own flaws). Any Christian who commits a sin against which he or she has spoken passionately has ruined his or her witness—possibly beyond repair.

This is what upsets Paul the most—the double standard. "Don't do as I do—do as I say." One set of rules for you and another for me!

B. Expects an Exemption (vv. 2, 3)

2. But we are sure that the judgment of God is according to truth against them which commit such things.

Most certainly *the judgment of God* will be carried out *against* anyone who dares to commit the sins that he himself would condemn in another. Do we really believe that God will let us get by with that?

We can also be certain that God judges *according to truth*. His judgment is not tarnished by any of the biases, prejudices, or limited insight that affect our perspective. His judgment is truly just. [See question #3, page 248.]

3. And thinkest thou this, O man, that judgest them which do such things, and doest the same, that thou shalt escape the judgment of God?

We are familiar with how modern society has attempted to "repackage" certain sins so as to mask their true identity and lessen their offensiveness. Homosexuality is an "alternative lifestyle"; abortion is just another means of "birth control." Christians are not immune from this same practice. Stealing is never acceptable, but my inaccurate accounting to the Internal Revenue Service is justified because of how the government wastes money. Other people gossip; I "pass along helpful information."

Get serious! We know better! And we had better live according to what we know.

Keep in mind that the phrase *O man* is not addressed just to male human beings. It is a generic term and speaks to both men and women.

C. Declines Repentance (v. 4)

4. Or despisest thou the riches of his goodness and forbearance and long-suffering; not knowing that the goodness of God leadeth thee to repentance?

If we are so arrogant as to judge others while ignoring our own sin, we may be too blind to see the need for our *repentance* and to avail ourselves of the *riches* of God's *goodness*. That condition will never change unless we are honest with ourselves and with God and repent. Surely we can see how patient God has been—with people such as Old Testament Israel, the first disciples of Jesus, and us. We should not deceive ourselves by thinking that such patience reflects God's indifference to our sinfulness. It does not!

FIREFIGHTERS OR FIREBUGS?

In 1991, within a span of just a few weeks, three firefighters were arrested in Southern California. One was a fire captain, who was also a

---

How to Say It

AMOS. *Ay*-mus.
CORINTHIANS. Ko-*rin*-thee-unz.
PHARAOH. *Fair*-o.

highly respected arson investigator. He was charged with setting three fires and implicated in several others. A second firefighter was charged with setting nine fires, and a third with starting twenty-two fires.

Among the nineteen thousand arsonists arrested each year in the United States, only a small percentage are firefighters. One study indicates that only four percent of firefighters are also arsonists, but some experts think the problem is much more extensive.

Why would someone who makes a living fighting fires *start* them? The evidence indicates some common factors in this phenomenon. The guilty person is usually a volunteer or someone who gets paid for each fire he fights. Often he is new at the job and wants to be accepted into the firefighting fraternity. What better way to gain acceptance than to fight a fire—even if you have to start it yourself? Often the firefighter/arsonist will be the first to arrive at the scene of the fire—"a hero on the front lines," so to speak.

In a sense, all of us have the potential to wear the "hat" of either firefighter or "firebug." Perhaps we try to put out "moral fires" by calling attention to the sins of others, in hopes of gaining acceptance from the morally upright. Paul says we have no excuse for such judging, if at the same time we are guilty of starting similar moral conflagrations ourselves. There is no room in the kingdom for such a double standard.   —C. R. B.

II. Qualified Judge
(Romans 2:5-16)

A. Renders Righteous Verdicts (vv. 5-8)

5. But, after thy hardness and impenitent heart, treasurest up unto thyself wrath against the day of wrath and revelation of the righteous judgment of God.

Notice that in verses 5-11, Paul's focus is on two groups (and only two!). Just as there are only two ways (Matthew 7:13, 14), there will be only two groups assembled at the final judgment—as Jesus noted in describing the judgment (Matthew 25:31, 32). Some individuals will come with hard hearts and will reap condemnation. Some will approach the Judge with repentant hearts and righteous lives; they will reap glory. And that will be true for both Jews and Gentiles.

The phrase *hardness and impenitent heart* brings to mind the Pharaoh of Egypt, who initially hardened his heart against God and whose heart God eventually hardened. God's action with the Pharaoh seems similar to the process described in Romans 1, where God "gave [sinners] up" or "over" to the consequences of the actions they chose to do (vv. 24, 26, 28). Each

resistance moves one's heart further from repentance. It is worth noting that the Greek word translated *treasurest up* is the same word used by Jesus in Matthew 6:19, 20 to describe laying up treasures in Heaven. What are we "treasuring up"—wealth or wrath?

6. Who will render to every man according to his deeds.

One day God's judgment will be administered, in the form of both punishment and reward. This final rendering will not be determined arbitrarily. *Every man* (once again, a generic term for every human being) will face the consequence of his or her choices and of the *deeds* based on those choices. God has made this clear repeatedly in Scripture. [See question #4, page 248.]

7. To them who by patient continuance in well doing seek for glory and honor and immortality, eternal life.

Back and forth Paul goes, from one side of the truth to the other. His point is very, very hard to miss. Our deeds matter. Our deeds show on whose side we are. They demonstrate whose message we have accepted and under whose authority we live. We can be our own conductor and follow our own "road map" (which is ultimately Satan's). That means that we will experience God's wrath. Or we can accept God as our conductor, follow His directions, and find *glory*, *honor*, *immortality*, and *eternal life*.

In this verse are some good words for Christians: *patient continuance*, *well doing*, and *seek*. Don't give up!

8. But unto them that are contentious, and do not obey the truth, but obey unrighteousness, indignation and wrath.

Here once more is the other side, the other choice. Some will be *contentious* and resist God's authority. Like stubborn children they will refuse to *obey*. They see no need for God (perhaps they see faith in Him as a "crutch" for the weak); they will pursue *unrighteousness* (bad judgment blended with a bad attitude) instead.

If that is the path I choose to follow, I can count on God's *indignation and wrath*. The two choices are pretty clear, aren't they?

CHOICES

Mary Hutto was a very frugal woman, but few knew her motivation for it. This 1927 graduate of Western Kentucky University in Bowling Green, Kentucky, married and became an English teacher. She and her husband had no children. After he died in an auto accident in 1953, she never remarried.

When Mary's father died in 1957, she began operating the family-owned boarding house near the university campus. Her great appreciation for her alma mater moved her to do all she could for the students of the school. To make as much space as possible available for university students, she lived in a makeshift cubicle, separated from the rest of the hallway by a sheet she hung there.

Mary Hutto saved her money and invested it carefully, in part because she was afraid she might not have enough for her old age. It turned out that she did. When she died in 2001 at the age of 95, she left her estate to her alma mater in the form of an endowment for scholarships. The gift totaled three and a half million dollars! Mary Hutto chose to live carefully, thus enabling her to bless the lives of others.

Paul tells us that God's judgment will evaluate each of us according to the choices we make in our lives. Wise choices will bring rich rewards; foolish choices will be appropriately punished. Which kind of choices are we making? Are others being blessed by them?   —C. R. B.

We are not to judge— God will judge.

Visual for lesson 2. *The visual for today's lesson can be used to highlight the truth that God is our ultimate judge.*

B. Exhibits No Favoritism (vv. 9-11)

9. Tribulation and anguish, upon every soul of man that doeth evil; of the Jew first, and also of the Gentile.

The warning continues. The *tribulation and anguish* of final judgment will be the lot of all those who are outside Christ—those who have made *evil* their trademark and who have refused to surrender their valued self-rule. But it is also true that a great deal of spiritual tribulation and anguish is the plight of unbelievers and evildoers in this life, as Romans 1:18-32 indicates.

Here Paul highlights another truth that he is passionate about conveying: an evildoing, Christ-rejecting *Jew* will be treated the same as an evil-doing, Christ-rejecting *Gentile*. There is no difference!

10, 11. But glory, honor, and peace, to every man that worketh good; to the Jew first, and also to the Gentile: for there is no respect of persons with God.

The phrase *to the Jew first, and also to the Gentile* is reminiscent of what Paul stated in Romans 1:16 about the recipients of the gospel's powerful salvation message. Since the Jews were the first to hear such a message, they are to be judged first. However, the standard of judgment is to be the same for both Jews and Gentiles. *Glory, honor, and peace* will be the precious possession of everyone *that worketh good*. Keep in mind, though, that generous levels of glory, honor, and peace are already the possession of Christians who live each day exercising the kind of goodness that only one in Christ is equipped to practice.

There is no respect of persons with God means that God does not operate arbitrarily or selec-

tively. Anyone outside of Christ will receive the judgment that a sinner deserves.

C. Upholds the Law (vv. 12-15)

12. For as many as have sinned without law shall also perish without law; and as many as have sinned in the law shall be judged by the law.

This verse summarizes Paul's comments in chapter 1 that disarm any Gentiles who may plead ignorance regarding the reality and the will of God. They are "without excuse," because the visible world provides adequate instruction on these matters (Romans 1:18-20). They have not lived up to the knowledge of God that they were given. Therefore, without a Savior they will *perish*. [See question #5, page 248.]

Moreover, those who have had *the law* (Jews) are reminded that they have not kept it. They have not lived up to the knowledge of God they possessed (an even brighter light than the Gentiles had). They *shall be judged by the* (written) *law*, and without a Savior they too will be lost.

13. (For not the hearers of the law are just before God, but the doers of the law shall be justified.

Here is an additional truth to consider: just to hear God's *law* (from teachers or parents) will not save anyone either. Were either Jews or Gentiles to have kept faithfully the law of which they were aware, that law would have been their salvation. Keep in mind that Paul is speaking hypothetically in this verse; neither he, nor any other Jew, nor any Gentile, had been able to do that.

14. For when the Gentiles, which have not the law, do by nature the things contained in the law, these, having not the law, are a law unto themselves.

What could be termed a "godly instinct" was available to *the Gentiles*, even though they did not have the opportunity to study or know the law that was revealed to the Jews. When the Gentiles obeyed God's law, even though they possessed it through instinct rather than revelation, they were acknowledging that there is a law, that it comes from God, and that they are accountable for their obedience to this law.

This needs to be kept in mind in understanding the phrase *a law unto themselves*. This language does not mean that the Gentiles are free to make up their own standard of conduct and to do as they please. Within themselves, they have been given a moral awareness of God's standards of right and wrong. They demonstrate that awareness in the manner described in the following verse.

15. Which show the work of the law written in their hearts, their conscience also bearing witness, and their thoughts the mean while accusing or else excusing one another.)

Gentiles have the capacity for distinguishing between right and wrong. *Conscience*, which compares our deeds with a certain standard of judgment and convicts us of wrongdoing when we violate that standard, is part of that capacity. The Gentiles are capable of knowing *in their hearts* what God's requirements are. They can understand their obligation to and their accountability to their Creator. When they do right, they are excused from any feeling of wrongdoing. When they do wrong, they are accused and feel a sense of guilt.

D. Judges Through Jesus (v. 16)

16. In the day when God shall judge the secrets of men by Jesus Christ according to my gospel.

Home Daily Bible Readings

Monday, Mar. 7—God Is a Righteous Judge (Psalm 7:6-17)

Tuesday, Mar. 8—God Himself Is Judge (Psalm 50:1-15)

Wednesday, Mar. 9—Do Not Judge Others (Romans 2:1-5)

Thursday, Mar. 10—God Will Judge All (Romans 2:6-11)

Friday, Mar. 11—Doers of the Law Are Justified (Romans 2:12-16)

Saturday, Mar. 12—Do Jews Follow the Law? (Romans 2:17-24)

Sunday, Mar. 13—Real Jews Obey the Law (Romans 2:25-29)

Verses 13-15 are treated as a parenthesis, providing added commentary on the theme of judgment raised in verse 12. With the verse before us, Paul concludes his comments on judgment by calling attention to *the day* when *the secrets of men* will be judged. Yes, the doers of the law will be justified rather than the hearers (v. 13), but God's judgment will also examine the inner thoughts and motives. Such a universal failure and a universal need serve to introduce the universal solution.

That solution is highlighted by the reference to *Jesus Christ* as the One by whom God will carry out His judgment. How can this be part of the *gospel*, or good news? The good news is that our judge is also our advocate (1 John 2:1)—the One who, as one illustrative image has described it, removed His royal robes, came down from the judicial bench, and offered to take the punishment that we, though guilty, should have received. Those who refuse to accept that solution of grace will face condemnation.

Note Paul's reference to *my gospel*. That term reflects no selfishness on the apostle's part. Today the gospel is ours—not to be hoarded but to be shared with the world. We are stewards of that blessing, even as we are stewards of everything we have (1 Corinthians 4:7).

Conclusion

A. Caution

Our own failures put us in no position to judge someone else's failures. Whatever our heritage or our history, we are all in the same boat (and the boat is sinking!). We need help. We need to be rescued. And in order for that to happen, there must be a confession on our part. We must acknowledge that we are to blame for our condition. Even though we may be inclined to confess our neighbor's sin or compare ourselves with someone far worse in our eyes, we must end such self-deceit. We must confess our personal sin and our personal need for Jesus as our Savior. That will change our perspective on our neighbor, too, as we realize that judging is not our job—it's God's. [See question #6, page 248.]

B. Prayer

Our Father, most of us studying today have gratefully confessed Christ and accepted Your good news. Now we present for Your use our lives, willing to confess Jesus before those who do not know Him. To You be the glory forever for all You have done. In Jesus' name. Amen.

C. Thought to Remember

Don't take God's grace for granted.

Learning by Doing

This page contains an alternative lesson plan emphasizing learning activities.
Classes desiring such student involvement will find these suggestions helpful.

Learning Goals

After completing this lesson, a student should be able to:

1. Contrast the perfect judgment of God with the faulty judgment of people.

2. Explain why something better than "justice" is needed.

3. Express a commitment to live with a nonjudgmental attitude toward others, keeping in mind the coming judgment of God.

Into the Lesson

Recruit a class member to introduce you as follows: "All rise! Court is now in session; the honorable (your name) presiding." Walk in (or simply stand). If possible, wear a black robe and carry a gavel. As an alternate introduction, ask if anyone in the class has ever served as a spokesperson for a jury. If so, have the person describe what the experience was like. If not, ask class members, "How would you feel if you were asked to serve in such a capacity?"

Into the Word

Say, "Paul's strategy as he writes to the Roman Christians (and to us) is to ask questions and then give the Spirit's answer to the question. I have a series of questions for which the answers are found in the verses of today's text from Romans 2:1-16." Assign a verse of today's text to each learner. (If you have more than sixteen learners, assign some verses to pairs of learners; if you have fewer, give more than one verse to several.)

Ask the following questions—best done in random order—and ask learners to cite their verses as answers. Give them an opportunity to explain their connections as well. (It is possible that a learner will be able to justify a match other than that suggested as follows.) Each question's answer can be found in the verse with the same number as the question.

Questions: (1) Can a judge preside over a case dealing with a crime (sin) of which he is guilty? (2) How will God judge those who accuse others of a sin of which the accuser is guilty? (3) Will an accuser get away with judging others for sins of which he is guilty? (4) What should a guilty accuser/judge remember about the character of God? (5) What characteristic in a person will result in having to face God's wrath and righteous

judgment? (6) On what basis will God judge every person? (7) What attitude is necessary in one who seeks eternal life? (8) In the matter of obedience, what is our choice? (9) What will be the ultimate end of the one who does evil, whether Jew or Gentile? (10) What will be the ultimate reward for everyone who (through faith) does good? (11) As a judge, what is God's most outstanding attribute? (12) Is this statement true: "Ignorance of the law will be no excuse"? (13) Is awareness of the law's teaching sufficient to provide justification? (14) Is it possible for a person who does not possess the written law of God to know how God wants him or her to live? (15) What role does one's conscience play in holding him or her accountable to the law of God? (16) Through whom will God carry out His final judgment? Allow discussion and comments with each issue introduced.

Into Life

Tell your class, "A critical, condemning attitude is learned behavior. To unlearn it, one must replace critical, condemning statements with praising, edifying statements." Divide the group into two sides. Ask one side to suggest common negative statements that may be said (or at least thought) in each of the following situations. Ask the other side to suggest an alternative positive remark.

Situation 1: a person comes to a church service wearing what many would consider to be inappropriate clothing. *Situation 2:* a family habitually positions itself to be first in line at a church fellowship dinner. *Situation 3:* a preacher occasionally makes grammatical errors in his oral presentations. *Situation 4:* an older lady with diminished hearing talks out loud in a worship service. *Situation 5:* a youth minister allows elementary children to run noisily before the adult worship is concluded. *Situation 6:* a driver regularly parks in a drop-off area at church and leaves his car there for a period of time. If time allows, suggest other situations at church or from everyday life.

As learners leave today, hand each of them a toothpick with a small "flag" attached that has the Scripture reference *Matthew 7:1-3* printed on it. Tell the learners that the toothpick and the reference are to encourage them to think about the "toothpick/two-by-four" principle of Christian living.

Let's Talk It Over

The questions on this page are designed to promote discussion of the lesson by the class and to encourage application of the lesson Scriptures. The answers provided are only discussion starters. Let your class talk it over from there.

1. What would the world look like if there were no such concept as judgment? Would it be better or worse? Why?

Some may think that living without judgment would result in greater freedom to do as one pleases. But without an awareness of and a respect for the consequences of certain actions, a society can quickly devolve into the kind of anarchy described in Judges 21:25: "In those days there was no king in Israel: every man did that which was right in his own eyes."

Some may claim that they would prefer a world without judgment, but would they really want to live in a society without laws or police or courts? What about a world that did not expect medications to meet scientific criteria, or buildings to adhere to codes, or contracts to be binding? In places where these expectations do not exist, we see rampant abuses of power, the belief that "might makes right," and innocents killed and injured by the action (or inaction) of others.

2. How should the knowledge of God's ultimate judgment influence our judgment of others? Does this mean that we should never exercise judgment of others' morality, wisdom, or interpretation of Scripture?

Certainly the knowledge of God's judgment should give us pause when we are tempted to judge others. We must not forget that the grounds for all judgment come from God Himself. God judges all according to the truth. However, if we completely separate ourselves from exercising any degree of discernment, we would ourselves be in violation of God's truth. It is a delicate balance—weighing God's Word, our own flawed practice of that Word, the expectation of our own judgment by God, and the need to confront lovingly those who are not adhering to God's Word. All of us must pray for wisdom to keep these factors in proper balance.

3. What is the difference between our judgments and God's judgments?

The stark differences between the kind of judgment that we can offer and that which only God can administer reveals why He must judge and we must not. God knows what is in a person's heart. We do not and cannot. God is the one personally offended by sin. We may only be indirectly affected by someone's sin or not personally affected at all. Moreover, God offers grace and justification through the death of His Son. We cannot. Since we do not know a person's motives, are not the ones sinned against directly, and cannot offer grace and justification, we are in no position to judge. God is.

4. If we are under God's grace, why does Paul emphasize that God "will render to every man according to his deeds"? Is Paul advocating a works salvation? Explain.

Although salvation is by grace, our works are not unimportant. The actions we take (and those we avoid) reveal the depth and the seriousness of our commitment and our faith. Just as important as our actions are the motives behind them. If our motivation for good deeds is to seek God and please Him, if our deeds flow from the grace we have received, then His blessing will follow. If our motivation is selfish, then our "good works" will earn the contempt they deserve.

5. What should we conclude about those who have never heard the gospel? Can they be saved? What about those who live by the Old Testament law but do not believe in Christ?

Paul (along with other New Testament writers) makes it quite clear that no one can be saved apart from faith in Jesus. Those who had the written law of God could not keep it. Those who did not have the written law still had what may be termed a "godly instinct," which they violated. None of us has an excuse, "for there is none other name under heaven given among men, whereby we must be saved" (Acts 4:12).

6. How can our judgment of our neighbors affect our evangelism of them? Isn't witnessing itself a form of judgment?

If we hold our neighbors in contempt rather than seeing them with compassion, we certainly cannot effectively share God's grace. Refusing to witness is a greater judgment than witnessing. The first attitude says, "You are irredeemable." The second says, "I am a fellow sinner, but I have found a better way." Remember that Jesus came to seek and to save the lost. We dare not allow our churches or our testimonies to exist only for the sake of the saved!

Justified by Faith

DEVOTIONAL READING: **2 Corinthians 3:4-11.**

BACKGROUND SCRIPTURE: **Romans 5:1-21.**

PRINTED TEXT: **Romans 5:1-11, 18-21.**

Romans 5:1-11, 18-21

1 Therefore being justified by faith, we have peace with God through our Lord Jesus Christ:

2 By whom also we have access by faith into this grace wherein we stand, and rejoice in hope of the glory of God.

3 And not only so, but we glory in tribulations also; knowing that tribulation worketh patience;

4 And patience, experience; and experience, hope:

5 And hope maketh not ashamed; because the love of God is shed abroad in our hearts by the Holy Ghost which is given unto us.

6 For when we were yet without strength, in due time Christ died for the ungodly.

7 For scarcely for a righteous man will one die: yet peradventure for a good man some would even dare to die.

8 But God commendeth his love toward us, in that, while we were yet sinners, Christ died for us.

9 Much more then, being now justified by his blood, we shall be saved from wrath through him.

10 For if, when we were enemies, we were reconciled to God by the death of his Son; much more, being reconciled, we shall be saved by his life.

11 And not only so, but we also joy in God through our Lord Jesus Christ, by whom we have now received the atonement.

· · · · · · · · · · · ·

18 Therefore, as by the offense of one judgment came upon all men to condemnation; even so by the righteousness of one the free gift came upon all men unto justification of life.

19 For as by one man's disobedience many were made sinners, so by the obedience of one shall many be made righteous.

20 Moreover the law entered, that the offense might abound. But where sin abounded, grace did much more abound:

21 That as sin hath reigned unto death, even so might grace reign through righteousness unto eternal life by Jesus Christ our Lord.

GOLDEN TEXT: Therefore being justified by faith, we have peace with God through our Lord Jesus Christ.—Romans 5:1.

> *God's Project: Effective Christians*
> Unit 1: Saved by God
> (Lessons 1-4)

Lesson Aims

After this lesson a student should be able to:

1. Tell about our need for peace with God, the source of that peace, and the attending result of that peace.

2. Compare what Christ did for us as "sinners" with the "much more" that He does for those who have been reconciled.

3. Resolve to face with joy, patience, and hope a situation that currently causes tribulation.

Lesson Outline

INTRODUCTION
    A. One Way to Peace
    B. Lesson Background
I. FAITH'S PROVISIONS (Romans 5:1, 2)
    A. Brings Peace (v. 1)
    B. Accesses Grace (v. 2a)
    C. Presents Hope (v. 2b)
II. FAITH'S PROGRESS (Romans 5:3-5)
    A. From Tribulation to Patience (v. 3)
    B. From Patience to Experience (v. 4a)
    C. From Experience to Hope (vv. 4b, 5)
    Triumphing Over Troubles
III. CHRIST'S ATONEMENT (Romans 5:6-11)
    A. Death for Sinners (vv. 6-8)
    B. Blessings for the Reconciled (vv. 9-11)
IV. CHRIST'S ACHIEVEMENTS (Romans 5:18-21)
    A. Righteousness (v. 18)
    B. Obedience (v. 19)
    C. Grace (vv. 20, 21)
    Still Reigning
CONCLUSION
    A. Yes—One Way to Perfect Peace
    B. Prayer
    C. Thought to Remember

Introduction

A. One Way to Peace

Peace! What a wonderful word! Think for a moment about the Christmas cards that you received just a few months ago. Wasn't that word the focus of many of them? If you had asked individuals during that season what gift they wanted, wouldn't many have mentioned peace?

Today, Palm Sunday, begins what many refer to as "Passion Week" in the life of Christ. The events of this week reveal the climax of God's plan to bring His kind of peace—real peace—to the world. While that plan involved the agony and brutality of the cross, the week itself started with a celebration. As Jesus rode into Jerusalem on a donkey, the people rejoiced and expressed their welcome by placing palm branches and garments in His path. [See question #1, page 256.]

As the week progressed, the opposition to Jesus from His enemies intensified. The climax was the crucifixion, when God's peace was achieved through man's terror. Isaiah described this as vividly as any prophet: "But he was wounded for our transgressions, he was bruised for our iniquities: the chastisement of our peace was upon him; and with his stripes we are healed" (Isaiah 53:5). Three days later came resurrection morning. And today He lives!

This is the way to real peace. God planned it. Jesus provided it. And we can accept it. Peace talks are often held in today's world to suggest ways to reach the ever-elusive goal of peace. Consider today's lesson on this "Triumphal Entry" Sunday a genuine "peace talk."

B. Lesson Background

The first two lessons of this quarter came from the opening chapters of Romans, drawing a clear picture of the need of sinners, both Jewish and Gentile. "For all have sinned, and come short of the glory of God" (Romans 3:23). Having spelled out this need, Paul then begins to explain the remedy. In chapter 4 he introduces an example, Abraham, who through faith was justified by God. "Abraham believed God, and it was counted unto him for righteousness" (Romans 4:3). Not by works! God's grace was required— even for this Old Testament saint. Abraham was a good man, but he could not have done enough to earn God's favor. He trusted God, and that trust was the reason for his being considered "righteous" in God's sight. [See question #2, page 256.]

Like Abraham, we are called to travel the same route—the way of faith.

I. Faith's Provisions
(Romans 5:1, 2)

A. Brings Peace (v. 1)

1. Therefore being justified by faith, we have peace with God through our Lord Jesus Christ.

Any occurrence of the word *therefore* should encourage the Bible student to ask what it is "there for." In this case, it points back to Paul's use of Abraham as an illustration of grace and *faith* in the previous chapter. That example may have been cited by Paul in an effort to appeal to the Jews to accept the concept of salvation by grace and faith. If the man considered the "father of the Jewish people" was a recipient of grace and was counted righteous by faith, then his descendants should not try to create some other means of coming to God.

Also worth noting is what Paul has already said about the desperate human condition. All have sinned—Jews and Gentiles; no one is excluded. The finger of God has been pointed at every human being, and our sins have been painted in the dark colors they deserve.

Then the sun breaks through (or perhaps we should say, "Son"). Jesus "was delivered for our offenses" and was "raised again for our justification" (Romans 4:25). How does justification take place? We are *justified* by God's actions, not ours. He simply asks for our trust—our faith—which is exactly what He asked from Abraham.

Perhaps we have heard various definitions of justification, one being an appropriate play on the English word: being justified means being treated "just as if I'd" never sinned. God Himself has provided the means for bridging the rift between us, for making *peace*. That means is Jesus.

B. Accesses Grace (v. 2a)

2a. By whom also we have access by faith into this grace wherein we stand.

By using the word *grace*, the apostle reinforces his central point. There are no "works" that gain our justification. Salvation has been provided by God. It is a gift that we must receive. *Faith* in Jesus gives us *access* to grace.

Think of it this way. To gain an audience with a world leader, the chief executive of a large organization, or someone with a very full calendar, we must not only make an appointment, we also need to be ushered in by someone close to the important person. Jesus (through our trust in Him) ushers us into the presence of the God of grace. And Jesus continues to give us access to God and His grace (Hebrews 7:25).

C. Presents Hope (v. 2b)

2b. And rejoice in hope of the glory of God.

Hope is a frequently misunderstood word. Often people use it to talk about something they would love to have or see happen, but they don't know whether they will get it and see it or not. "One can only hope," they reply rather passively as to whether what they desire will really occur.

But the Bible uses the word *hope* quite differently. In Christ we *rejoice in hope*. What He has promised, He will do. For one in Christ there is no doubt. The quality of hope hinges on the character of the one in whom hope is placed. What more needs to be said? We acquire true

hope when we abandon the futile practice of trusting in ourselves to shape the future and put our future in the hands of *God*. [See question #3, page 256.]

When we are in Christ we have peace, grace, and hope. And there is more!

II. Faith's Progress
(Romans 5:3-5)

A. From Tribulation to Patience (v. 3)

3. And not only so, but we glory in tribulations also; knowing that tribulation worketh patience.

In Christ we have resources for handling the circumstances that come our way, such as *tribulation*. When faith is our guiding principle, what appear to be very bad situations can yield good results. (Read Paul's later affirmation in Romans 8:28.) Those results are not always immediately seen. (Think of what happened to Joseph in the Old Testament and his declaration concerning God's purpose in Genesis 45:4-8.) Thus there is often a need for *patience*. This is not a passive resignation, but rather an active perseverance. Trouble teaches us to wait, and it teaches us to cope by use of the resources that God provides.

B. From Patience to Experience (v. 4a)

4a. And patience, experience.

Lessons in *patience* come from several directions and at various stages of life. When tribulation comes in different forms and at different times, patience is necessary. Yet through the patient handling of circumstances, the discovery of solutions, and the discipline of waiting, a wealth of *experience* is gained. And that experience can often provide encouragement to someone who needs advice from an individual who's "been there" (2 Corinthians 1:3, 4).

C. From Experience to Hope (vv. 4b, 5)

4b. And experience, hope.

At this point, Paul may appear to be going in circles. As Christians we possess a faith-based *hope*. In living out that hope, we will encounter tribulation. The tribulation will teach us patience. The patience will provide vital *experience*. And that experience, in turn, will reinforce our hope. However, let us not think of this as a circle as much as an advancing spiral. With each round of faith-guided living (which blends trouble and joy

---

How to Say It

ABRAHAM. *Ay*-bruh-ham.
ISAIAH. Eye-*zay*-uh.

and lessons learned), we gain strength, we are able to stretch our spiritual muscles, and we become more valuable to the Master.

5. And hope maketh not ashamed; because the love of God is shed abroad in our hearts by the Holy Ghost which is given unto us.

When we place our *hope* in God, we will not be disappointed. Paul emphasizes that all of the attributes he has described in this passage come from God and that God guides the entire process by which they are acquired. He even provides the means for maintaining what He has *given*, namely, *the Holy Ghost*, who gives us *love* and helps us grow in love. When love is clearly visible in the church, it is a sure sign of the Holy Spirit's presence. [See question #4, page 256.]

TRIUMPHING OVER TROUBLES

The headline read, "'Runner' Wins the Inspiration Prize, Hands Down." The "runner" was Bob Wieland, a Vietnam veteran who lost both legs in that war. The "inspiration prize" was simply finishing the 26.2 miles of the 2003 Los Angeles Marathon, using his hands to swing his torso along the course. Wieland has been doing marathons and triathlons for twenty years. He has even done a "walk" across America! He wears padded trousers that allow him to rock backward and forward as he uses his hands like legs. His "hand shoes"—as he calls them—are gelpads with handles. The 57-year-old Wieland crossed the finish line of the Los Angeles Marathon in a total time of 173 hours and 45 minutes—more than seven days!

Some of us who are able-bodied and younger than Wieland may well question our own physical, emotional, and spiritual stamina when compared with his. He gives God the credit for his feat and says, "It was done only by the grace of God."

Wieland's efforts illustrate what Paul says in our text today about "tribulations." Overwhelming difficulties can produce patience, experience, and hope—if we place our trust in God. At first, this hope may simply be that we will find a "normal" life again, but ultimately it becomes the hope—the assurance—that God will someday make all things right. —C. R. B.

III. Christ's Atonement
(Romans 5:6-11)

A. Death for Sinners (vv. 6-8)

6. For when we were yet without strength, in due time Christ died for the ungodly.

Due time is God's time! Paul calls it "the fulness of the time" in Galatians 4:4. It is remarkable to study the various prophecies fulfilled by Jesus, especially those surrounding His death. But the most remarkable aspect of the death of *Christ* is that He *died for the ungodly*—the weak, the undeserving, those *without strength* to save themselves. That includes all of us.

7. For scarcely for a righteous man will one die: yet peradventure for a good man some would even dare to die.

What is the difference between a *righteous man* and a *good man*? Some would say that the righteous man describes an especially pious individual who possesses a "holier-than-thou" attitude. He may be highly respected, but he is not the kind of person for whom someone else would be willing *to die*. The good man would be someone whose good deeds make him a much more likable individual, and thus someone for whom others would be more apt to die.

Others believe that there is basically no difference between the righteous man and the good man and that Paul is making the same claim in two different ways. The first part of the verse states Paul's claim in a negative way; the second states it in a more positive manner. Either way, the gist of Paul's thought is this: people are not likely to give their lives on behalf of even the best of human beings.

8. But God commendeth his love toward us, in that, while we were yet sinners, Christ died for us.

Here is the dramatic difference between *God* and human beings. He has extended *his love toward us*, in the form of His crucified Son. And He has done this for *sinners*—not righteous men, not good men, but those who were anything but righteous and good! This is real love—the kind of love that can come only from God.

Not only does God commend, or show, such love, but He also commands that Christians demonstrate that love to others (John 13:34, 35; 1 John 4:11), even to our enemies (Matthew 5:44). [See question #5, page 256.]

B. Blessings for the Reconciled (vv. 9-11)

9. Much more then, being now justified by his blood, we shall be saved from wrath through him.

Justification is the present possession of the Christian. We can be at peace with God. The work of Christ has been done. We are new creatures (2 Corinthians 5:17), we wear a new name, and we have a new destiny that will not be realized until this time in our present world is finished and our time in Heaven has begun. We will be *saved from wrath*, from Hell, from the place prepared for those who have trusted in their way rather than God's way. Thus our past, present, and future are all in God's hands.

10. For if, when we were enemies, we were reconciled to God by the death of his Son; much more, being reconciled, we shall be saved by his life.

Here is a reminder of the change in our status, thanks to Jesus. The ungodly, the sinners, are *enemies* of *God*. Sin severed the relationship between sinner and Creator. God provided the way by which those who are separated from Him can come back and be *reconciled* to the One who bore no responsibility for the breach. Only He could take care of this, and He has.

Next comes the consequence of that reconciliation through Jesus' *death*. Now that Jesus is alive and reigning as Lord, how *much more* will He help those who have accepted His gift of salvation! We can have no doubt that Jesus will return someday and complete God's plan of redemption. [See question #6, page 256.]

11. And not only so, but we also joy in God through our Lord Jesus Christ, by whom we have now received the atonement.

From our study of verse 3, we can see that Paul's phrase *and not only so* is simply an expression that he uses to say, "There is more." We have been reconciled (reunited) to *God*. We have been saved from sin and death by means of His grace. As a result, we can have *joy*. Like hope, joy is more than just a fleeting emotion; it is a constant sense of gratitude and praise for all that God has done and will do.

Paul notes that all of what he has just described comes *through our Lord Jesus Christ*. This includes the *atonement*, which is often defined as being made "at one" with God. The Greek word used here is a form of the same word that is translated "reconciled" in verse 10.

IV. Christ's Achievements (Romans 5:18-21)

A. Righteousness (v. 18)

18. Therefore, as by the offense of one judgment came upon all men to condemnation; even so by the righteousness of one the free gift came upon all men unto justification of life.

In the verses of chapter 5 not included in our printed text (vv. 12-17), Paul raises the issue of Adam's sin and its impact versus Christ's death and its impact. The primary emphasis of Paul's teaching is that Jesus' death has reversed the effects of Adam's sin. Life, not death, reigns for the followers of Jesus.

In the verse before us, Paul states that Adam's *offense*, or sin, cost him, and it has cost *all* of humanity. In a sense, Adam acted as a representative for the entire human race (some use the term "federal head"), just as Jesus represented all hu-

"Therefore being justified by faith, we have peace with God through our Lord Jesus Christ."
—Romans 5:1

Visual for lesson 3

The dove is considered a symbol of peace. Use this visual as you study Romans 5:1.

manity when He died for all on the cross (2 Corinthians 5:14). Specifically what God's *judgment . . . upon all* as a result of Adam's sin involved is not defined by Paul. What is important to understand is that the impact of Christ's death *(justification)* countered the impact of Adam's sin *(condemnation)*. The phrase *the righteousness of one* most likely describes one act (Jesus' death) rather than one man (Jesus). Jesus' perfect life of righteousness qualified Him to be the perfect sacrifice who died in the place of sinners so that the *free gift* of *life* could be made available to them (2 Corinthians 5:21).

B. Obedience (v. 19)

19. For as by one man's disobedience many were made sinners, so by the obedience of one shall many be made righteous.

This reinforces the teaching of the last verse. Adam disobeyed God, and he has been our model. Because of his *disobedience*, sin intruded and scarred the atmosphere of peace and harmony that God created, and it has been doing so ever since. And we have been good students of our "model." We have disobeyed God as well; "death passed upon all men, for that all have sinned" (Romans 5:12).

Jesus provided a different kind of "model." We can be *made righteous* by His redeeming act, His *obedience* to God through His death on the cross (Philippians 2:8). (*The obedience of one* highlights one act, Jesus' death, as did "the righteousness of one" in the previous verse.)

C. Grace (vv. 20, 21)

20. Moreover the law entered, that the offense might abound. But where sin abounded, grace did much more abound.

As we noted in the previous lesson, *the law* has spelled out right and wrong very well. Its revelation of God's standards makes it painfully clear that that we have violated them. But there is more power in *grace* than there is in *sin*.

21. That as sin hath reigned unto death, even so might grace reign through righteousness unto eternal life by Jesus Christ our Lord.

Sin's rule has an expiration date, and that will be whenever Christ returns (Matthew 13:40-42). However, the reign of sin in an individual's life can be overthrown when he or she accepts *Jesus Christ* as *Lord*. At that point, the *reign* of *grace* replaces the reign of *sin*. In addition, *eternal life* becomes one's possession through a knowledge of Christ (John 17:3).

But don't misunderstand or become too complacent: sin will keep picking at the Christian. Sin will be relentless in attempting to trap him or her. It may even win some skirmishes. In Christ, however, the war has been won; sin's reign is at best shaky. And when the Christian dies and goes to be with Christ (Philippians 1:23), sin's influence in that person's life is finished. The experience of eternal life moves to a higher, greater level. The reign of grace and the overthrow of sin will be complete.

STILL REIGNING

Sin is everywhere. We have grown used to (and in some cases even inoculated against) the reality of auto theft, embezzlement, drunk driving, and even murder and war—except, of course, when we ourselves or those we love are victims. But doesn't it seem as if people are constantly finding new ways to sin? For example, the Internet has created many opportunities for such twisted "creativity."

Home Daily Bible Readings

Monday, Mar. 14—We Are Justified and Become Heirs (Titus 3:1-7)

Tuesday, Mar. 15—Ministry of Justification Abounds in Glory (2 Corinthians 3:4-11)

Wednesday, Mar. 16—Like Abraham, We Have Faith (Romans 4:13-25)

Thursday, Mar. 17—We Are Justified by Faith (Romans 5:1-5)

Friday, Mar. 18—Christ Died for Us Sinners (Romans 5:6-11)

Saturday, Mar. 19—Christ Brings a Free Gift (Romans 5:12-17)

Sunday, Mar. 20—Grace Abounds All the More (Romans 5:18-21)

An example of this is the too-good-to-be-true opportunities to cash in on someone else's apparent difficulties that often come in the form of Internet scams. Sexual predators in America search "chat rooms" for unsuspecting young people.

One troublesome example of this new-way-to-sin phenomenon occurred recently when a twenty-one-year-old committed suicide in front of his computer videocam. While he was online "chatting" with a large number of strangers, he was overdosing on drugs. Many of those with whom he was chatting were indifferent to what they saw happening on their computer monitors. Some were even arguing about who would get his drug paraphernalia after he died!

As Paul tells us, sin has "abounded" and "hath reigned unto death" (Romans 5:20, 21). We're seeing more of this as time goes on. The only answer for this world and all its hurting people is the "abounding" grace of God through Jesus.

How good a job of communicating that grace is our church doing?   —C. R. B.

Conclusion

A. Yes—One Way to Perfect Peace

You may have heard the advice often given to a prospective husband and wife who are Christians. If each of them will maintain an honest and strong relationship with Jesus and will join hands and hearts with Him, they will strengthen their union with one another. The same principle is true for friendships in general. If two people are close friends with Jesus, that common bond with Him will make them close friends with each other.

That's the primary reason that peace is not happening in hundreds of places around our world. There is no common bond with Jesus. Why should we expect peace in these places? The presence of such situations reinforces the missionary mandate, doesn't it? "Go ye therefore, and teach all nations, baptizing them in the name of the Father, and of the Son, and of the Holy Ghost" (Matthew 28:19).

There is only one way to peace—the Prince of peace!

B. Prayer

Father, we marvel at the depth of Your love and the breadth of Your grace. We are humbled to be the beneficiaries of such blessings. As we rejoice in the hope of life through Your Son, we commit ourselves to sharing that hope and growing in Your grace. In Jesus' name. Amen.

C. Thought to Remember

No God—no peace; know God—know peace.

Learning by Doing

This page contains an alternative lesson plan emphasizing learning activities.
Classes desiring such student involvement will find these suggestions helpful.

Learning Goals

After this lesson a student should be able to:

1. Tell about our need for peace with God, the source of that peace, and the attending result of that peace.

2. Compare what Christ did for us as "sinners" with the "much more" that He does for those who have been reconciled.

3. Resolve to face with joy, patience, and hope a situation that currently causes tribulation.

Into the Lesson

Display the word *tribulation* twice on the board with letters top to bottom to form two acrostics. Divide the class into two halves for responding to the following exercise. Ask one half to suggest negative words that are synonymous with or related to tribulation. Ask the other half to suggest only positive words, essentially the opposite of what people would normally associate with tribulation. Here are two possibilities; first, for the negative side: T—troubles, R—ridicule, I—insults, B—bitterness, U—unfairness, L—libel, A—anguish, T—travails, I—injuries, O—oppression, N—need; for the positive side, here are some suggestions: T—thanksgiving, R—rejoicing, I—inspiration, B—blessings, U—understanding, L—long-suffering, A—anticipation, T—treasured, I—invigorating, O—opportunity, N—nurturing.

If the groups have difficulty getting started, write in a sample word or two for each. Alternate between the two sides until most letters are accounted for. Say, "Though this first column represents what we most often associate with tribulation and suffering, the right column represents what tribulations and suffering can be to the Christian. The positive side of tribulation is what Paul stresses in today's study."

Into the Word

Establish groups small enough for discussion, and give each group one of the following case studies. Tell the groups, "Decide what you would say or write to these Christians upon hearing of their difficulties, based on Romans 5:1-11."

Situation 1: The Dooley family has just been told that Mrs. Dooley, age 47, has stage two breast cancer. The family was already struggling with the marital difficulties of one of their children and the college academic problems of another. What do you say to them?

Situation 2: Cliff Davis, age 60, has just lost his job of thirty-five years to "downsizing." His wife does not work. The Davises had recently made a commitment to support a young couple planning to go as missionaries to the Czech Republic and had also made a down payment on a small retirement property at a nearby lake. What do you say to them?

Situation 3: Effin Hubersch has recently become a Christian in a predominantly Muslim nation. Animosities abound from his family, at his job, and in his community. He faces social shunning, job loss, harassment, vandalism of his property, and possible violence. What do you say to him?

Situation 4: Kathy Rogers has recently canceled her marriage engagement. She has friends who blame her for what happened. Some friends of the prospective groom have cut off all contacts with her and will not return telephone calls. She has gifts to return. Her own family lives about a thousand miles away and can offer little support. What do you say to her?

After a short time of discussion, let each group report its decision. Though you should allow each group the freedom of thought, you can anticipate remarks about the peace (v. 1), hope (vv. 2, 4, 5), love (vv. 5, 8), salvation (vv. 9, 10), and joy (v. 11) that Paul emphasizes.

At this point, ask learners to look at verses 18-21 of the text. Ask, "What is there in these verses that speaks of the calamities and anxieties that beset us in this life?" Also ask, "What other words of comfort and grace do these truths suggest for occasions of tribulation and suffering?" Once again, allow for the freedom of insights, but expect comments on the awful consequences of sin in the world and the fact that by God's grace there is a life coming that will be free of such struggles and tribulations.

Into Life

Ask the class to suggest godly commitment statements based on the pattern "Even when . . . I will . . ." based upon truths in today's text. For example, "Even when death stares me in the face, I will anticipate eternal life in Christ"; and "Even when another's self-centeredness has harmed my relationships, I will forgive that person as God forgave me in Christ." (A similar activity is included in the student book.)

Let's Talk It Over

The questions on this page are designed to promote discussion of the lesson by the class and to encourage application of the lesson Scriptures. The answers provided are only discussion starters. Let your class talk it over from there.

1. Today we observe Palm Sunday—the day on which Jesus entered Jerusalem on a donkey. Why did some people find Jesus' entry into Jerusalem objectionable? Why do people today find Jesus objectionable?

Jesus is always an agent for change. For those in the first-century religious power structure of Jerusalem, that change threatened their positions of authority and much of their doctrine. Today the changes Jesus brings still threaten people. Some people share the first-century concerns of power and doctrine. For others, Jesus threatens their sinful lifestyle, their sense of fairness ("I am the way"), or their spirit of self-sufficiency. We should never underestimate the enduring offense of the cross. (See 1 Corinthians 1:18, 23-25.)

2. Is there a conflict between faith and works? What is their relationship to each other? How does the example of Abraham illustrate this relationship?

We are justified by faith, but it is a faith that works. James 2:14-26 discusses what it means to be justified by works, but in no way does James contradict what Paul is saying in Romans. Quite the contrary—both Paul and James would agree that faith has a tangible quality to it. If you cannot see a person's faith, you can legitimately question whether it is actually present. Abraham was justified by faith, but his faith led him to abandon his country, travel to an unknown destination, and ultimately to prepare his son Isaac as a sacrifice (replaced by God at the last minute with a ram). Abraham's faith worked.

3. How do we determine whether we really "hope" for something or only "wish" for it? Do we merely "wish" for Heaven? What is the difference?

Hebrews 6:19 speaks of Christian hope in this manner: "which hope we have as an anchor of the soul, both sure and steadfast." Our commentary writer notes, "The quality of hope hinges on the character of the one in whom hope is placed" (page 251). A wish is an expression of a longing, without any confidence that it will be fulfilled. The emphasis of the wish is on the desire itself. Hope expresses a longing with confidence that it will be fulfilled. The emphasis is not on the desire, but on the One who can fulfill that desire.

4. What has your experience taught you about hope? How has God's work in your life given you hope for His work in the future?

Every person's experiences will differ, but God uses each of those experiences to teach each of us about His faithfulness. The Israelites were often told to remember what they had experienced as a nation (in other words, their history) so that they would never forget God's faithfulness to them. (Read Psalm 106 for an example of such an account.) Each of us would do well to keep a journal or diary of events in our lives that testify to God's faithfulness to His Word. And we should remind ourselves of the promise in Philippians 1:6: "He which hath begun a good work in you will perform it until the day of Jesus Christ."

5. If Jesus died for sinners, why do so many churches exist primarily for the benefit of the saints? How can our churches do a better job of sharing the love Christ has for the ungodly?

It is so easy to forget that the church is probably the only group that exists primarily for the sake of "nonmembers"! Many churches fall into a "maintenance" mode, content to "stay the course." In so doing, they lose their passion for the task that Jesus gave us to do just before His ascension: the Great Commission. Churches need to provide continual training in the area of evangelism—not just in the area of "door-to-door" work but also in what can be termed "lifestyle evangelism" or "servant evangelism." We dare not forget that at one time we were counted among God's enemies; without Jesus' death for our sins, we would be hopeless and helpless.

6. Why does Paul emphasize that we were God's "enemies"? How can such language help to clarify our spiritual focus?

Although we might prefer to believe that we were innocent bystanders to the war between God and Satan, that is not the case. We had indeed chosen a side. Until we chose to follow Christ, we were soldiers in Satan's army, working for his cause and doing his bidding. The question of choosing sides in this battle is still relevant. If your earthly life ended today, whose leadership would claim your eternity?

Victory in Christ

DEVOTIONAL READING: **Romans 6:15-23.**

BACKGROUND SCRIPTURE: **John 20:1-10;
Romans 6:1-14.**

PRINTED TEXT: **John 20:1-10; Romans 6:1-14.**

John 20:1-10

1 The first day of the week cometh Mary Magdalene early, when it was yet dark, unto the sepulchre, and seeth the stone taken away from the sepulchre.

2 Then she runneth, and cometh to Simon Peter, and to the other disciple, whom Jesus loved, and saith unto them, They have taken away the Lord out of the sepulchre, and we know not where they have laid him.

3 Peter therefore went forth, and that other disciple, and came to the sepulchre.

4 So they ran both together: and the other disciple did outrun Peter, and came first to the sepulchre.

5 And he stooping down, and looking in, saw the linen clothes lying; yet went he not in.

6 Then cometh Simon Peter following him, and went into the sepulchre, and seeth the linen clothes lie,

7 And the napkin, that was about his head, not lying with the linen clothes, but wrapped together in a place by itself.

8 Then went in also that other disciple, which came first to the sepulchre, and he saw, and believed.

9 For as yet they knew not the Scripture, that he must rise again from the dead.

10 Then the disciples went away again unto their own home.

Romans 6:1-14

1 What shall we say then? Shall we continue in sin, that grace may abound?

2 God forbid. How shall we, that are dead to sin, live any longer therein?

3 Know ye not, that so many of us as were baptized into Jesus Christ were baptized into his death?

4 Therefore we are buried with him by baptism into death: that like as Christ was raised up from the dead by the glory of the Father, even so we also should walk in newness of life.

5 For if we have been planted together in the likeness of his death, we shall be also in the likeness of his resurrection:

6 Knowing this, that our old man is crucified with him, that the body of sin might be destroyed, that henceforth we should not serve sin.

7 For he that is dead is freed from sin.

8 Now if we be dead with Christ, we believe that we shall also live with him:

9 Knowing that Christ being raised from the dead dieth no more; death hath no more dominion over him.

10 For in that he died, he died unto sin once: but in that he liveth, he liveth unto God.

11 Likewise reckon ye also yourselves to be dead indeed unto sin, but alive unto God through Jesus Christ our Lord.

12 Let not sin therefore reign in your mortal body, that ye should obey it in the lusts thereof.

13 Neither yield ye your members as instruments of unrighteousness unto sin: but yield yourselves unto God, as those that are alive from the dead, and your members as instruments of righteousness unto God.

14 For sin shall not have dominion over you: for ye are not under the law, but under grace.

GOLDEN TEXT: Knowing that Christ being raised from the dead dieth no more; death hath no more dominion over him.—Romans 6:9.

Lesson Aims

After completing this lesson, a student should be able to:

1. Recount the events of resurrection morning, and tell how that event is "replayed" every time a believer is baptized.

2. Contrast the life of sin with the "resurrected" life of the believer raised to "walk in newness of life."

3. Use poetry, art, or music to celebrate the victory over death that we have because of Jesus.

Lesson Outline

INTRODUCTION
  A. Take Heart—Jesus Lives!
  B. Lesson Background
I. JESUS' RESURRECTION (John 20:1-10)
  A. Mary's Distress (vv. 1, 2)
  B. Peter and John's Discovery (vv. 3-10)
      Fact and Artifact
II. THE CHRISTIAN'S RESURRECTION (Romans 6: 1-14)
  A. Dead to Sin (vv. 1-3)
  B. Raised with Christ (vv. 4, 5)
  C. Freed from Sin (vv. 6-11)
      "Free" but Still a Prisoner
  D. Called to Righteousness (vv. 12-14)
CONCLUSION
  A. Why Sunday?
  B. Prayer
  C. Thought to Remember

Introduction

A. Take Heart—Jesus Lives!

As Christians around the world celebrate Easter Sunday today, many will read from 1 Corinthians 15—the "resurrection chapter" of the Bible. In verses 19 and 20 of this chapter, Paul offers a striking contrast between life without and with the hope of resurrection: "If in this life only we have hope in Christ, we are of all men most miserable. But now is Christ risen from the dead, and become the firstfruits of them that slept." He concludes the chapter on this triumphant and encouraging note: "Therefore, my beloved brethren, be ye steadfast, unmovable, always abounding in the work of the Lord, foras-much as ye know that your labor is not in vain in the Lord."

The apostle's words ring just as true in the twenty-first century as they did in the first. To those who at times may envy the prosperity and self-assurance of the godless or who become discouraged at the lack of fruit in their labors for Christ, take heart! Today provides a wonderful opportunity to remind ourselves of what distinguishes Christian faith from other "faiths." The difference is like night and day—or, to use today's emphasis, death and life.

B. Lesson Background

Following the crucifixion and burial of Jesus, those who felt the deepest disappointment were most likely the eleven faithful disciples of Jesus. These men had left their families and jobs; they had spent most every day since then listening to His teaching and assisting Him as He carried out His ministry.

There were also several godly women who had invested their time, care, and resources in the ministry of Jesus. They had traveled with Jesus and His disciples and had "ministered unto him of their substance" (Luke 8:3). Perhaps they had provided assistance with food and clothing, and had offered spiritual nourishment through their prayers and encouragement. Perhaps they, along with the disciples, held expectations that Jesus would establish His kingdom (political in nature) and overthrow the Romans. Now He was disgraced and dead.

Some of Jesus' followers realized that the least they could do was to be sure that Jesus was buried with proper dignity. So Joseph of Arimathea and Nicodemus prepared His body (John 19:38-42). Some of the women watched as He was placed in Joseph's new tomb (Matthew 27:61). Then early on the first day of the week, the women went back to the site, eager to add their skillful and sensitive touch to the burial preparation. They were concerned about how the stone could be rolled back from the tomb in order to give them access to Jesus' body.

Today's printed text includes John's account of resurrection morning. Although he focuses especially on Mary Magdalene, it is clear from the other three accounts that other women came to the tomb early that day (Matthew 28:1; Mark 16:1; Luke 23:55–24:1). Mary serves as a model of devotion to Jesus—present at the cross, the burial site, and the empty tomb.

The other part of the lesson text continues our study of Romans by including a section of chapter 6. There we will consider the kind of resurrection that we are to experience in response to Christ's resurrection.

I. Jesus' Resurrection
(John 20:1-10)

A. Mary's Distress (vv. 1, 2)

1. The first day of the week cometh Mary Magdalene early, when it was yet dark, unto the sepulchre, and seeth the stone taken away from the sepulchre.

It is *early* (perhaps as early at 4:00 A.M.) on *the first day of the week* when *Mary Magdalene* approaches the *sepulchre*. She is eager to carry out her act of devotion to Jesus. Like the other women, she wonders about the *stone* being rolled back so that His body can be respectfully attended to; but she is dismayed to find the tomb is open. Has someone stolen or mistreated the body? Why has it not been protected?

2. Then she runneth, and cometh to Simon Peter, and to the other disciple, whom Jesus loved, and saith unto them, They have taken away the Lord out of the sepulchre, and we know not where they have laid him.

Mary leaves the scene in a panic. She hurries to report to *Peter* and *the other disciple*. Apparently this *other disciple* is John, who keeps himself in the background through use of this phrase in his Gospel, along with the phrase, the disciple *whom Jesus loved* (also John 19:26; 21:7, 20).

Notice that Mary's words to Peter and John reflect her belief at this point that the body of Jesus has been *taken away*. For now, she is not thinking in terms of a resurrection. She also uses the term *we*, referring to the other women who had accompanied her to the tomb.

B. Peter and John's Discovery (vv. 3-10)

3-5. Peter therefore went forth, and that other disciple, and came to the sepulchre. So they ran both together: and the other disciple did outrun Peter, and came first to the sepulchre. And he stooping down, and looking in, saw the linen clothes lying; yet went he not in.

Both disciples hurry to the tomb. Most commentators propose that John was somewhat younger than *Peter* and therefore more athletic. Perhaps Peter is stouter and stronger, but not as fast afoot as John. John arrives at the tomb *first*, but he is not as inquisitive as Peter. He sees *the linen clothes* used for burial *lying* inside the tomb, but he does not go in.

6, 7. Then cometh Simon Peter following him, and went into the sepulchre, and seeth the linen clothes lie, and the napkin, that was about his head, not lying with the linen clothes, but wrapped together in a place by itself.

Bible students are accustomed to Peter's bold, daring words and actions (although sometimes ill-advised!) as recorded in the Gospels. Here he goes *into the sepulchre* and notes the *linen clothes* and the *napkin,* or cloth, that had been wrapped around Jesus' *head*. This cloth is now *wrapped . . . in a place by itself.* Such neatness does not support the view, touted by some skeptics, that thieves had stolen Jesus' body (Mary's first thought). Robbers are not concerned with good manners!

Notice the hurrying and running that has already taken place in response to the empty tomb. The good news of the resurrected Christ should put some urgency in our steps—not only on Easter Sunday but every day. [See question #1, page 264.]

8. Then went in also that other disciple, which came first to the sepulchre, and he saw, and believed.

Drawing on Peter's courage, John also enters the tomb. He sees the items noted in the previous verse. Remember that John is the one writing this report, especially when it is noted that he not only sees, but also believes at this time. Exactly what John believes is not stated, but he must believe that Jesus is indeed alive. That John's belief in Jesus is not fully informed is clear from the next verse.

9. For as yet they knew not the Scripture, that he must rise again from the dead.

As yet, none of the disciples understand the messianic expectation of the *Scripture* (in this case the Old Testament) correctly. Like many, they expect a triumphant, earthly ruler, who will restore Israel's greatness by overthrowing the hated Romans—not a man who will be executed as a common criminal and then *rise again from the dead*. [See question #2, page 264.]

10. Then the disciples went away again unto their own home.

Uncertain about what else to do or think, these *disciples* take the only course of action available at this point: they go *home*. Later in this chapter, John records Jesus' appearances to Mary Magdalene (vv. 11-18), the disciples minus Thomas (vv. 19-23), and the disciples with Thomas (vv. 24-29). Another appearance to

---

How to Say It

ARIMATHEA. *Air*-uh-muh-*thee*-uh (strong accent on *thee* as in *thin*).

ELIJAH. Ee-*lye*-juh.

LAZARUS. *Laz*-uh-russ.

MAGDALENE. *Mag*-duh-leen or Mag-duh-*lee*-nee.

NICODEMUS. *Nick*-uh-*dee*-muss (strong accent on *dee*).

SEPULCHRE. *sep*-ul-kur.

seven of the disciples, recorded in John 21, concludes with a focus on the future service of Peter and John (vv. 15-23).

FACT AND ARTIFACT

The "most studied artifact" in history is said to be the Shroud of Turin. Many believe it to be the actual burial cloth of Jesus referred to in today's text from John's Gospel. It is a linen cloth, fourteen and a half feet long and three and a half feet wide, bearing the image of a man who was beaten and crucified. Reliable records of the shroud go back to about A.D. 1350 when it was owned by Geoffrey de Charny, a French knight.

Since 1578, the shroud has been kept in a special repository in a cathedral built in Turin, Italy, specifically for housing the relic (thus the name, "Shroud of Turin"). It has been inspected and investigated innumerable times and is the subject of considerable speculation. In 1988, the shroud was subjected to radiocarbon dating by three different laboratories. The researchers concluded that it dates to approximately A.D. 1325, plus or minus about sixty years.

All of this may be interesting to contemplate; but when all is said and done, the matter of the shroud is irrelevant to our faith. The basis of the Christian faith lies in the risen Lord, who appeared over a forty-day period to numerous individuals and to more than five hundred at one time (Acts 1:3; 1 Corinthians 15:6). We believe, not because of a "most studied artifact," but because of an indisputable fact of history: Christ is risen! [See question #3, page 264.]   —C. R. B.

II. The Christian's Resurrection (Romans 6:1-14)

A. Dead to Sin (vv. 1-3)

1. What shall we say then? Shall we continue in sin, that grace may abound?

Last week's lesson was taken from Romans 5. There we noted Paul's concluding contrast between the reign of *sin* (leading to death) and the reign of *grace* (leading to eternal life) that is meant to overthrow sin's power. At the beginning of chapter 6, Paul anticipates a question that some may raise concerning grace. If it is indeed true that "where sin abounded, grace did much more abound" (Romans 5:20), isn't the next "logical" step to say, "Let's sin all we want, then we'll really give God's grace a chance to work"? (Perhaps some in the church in Rome were actually proposing such a concept, so it was an idea that needed to be addressed quickly and decisively.)

True, God is a God of grace. He is able and willing to forgive the most terrible sins. But God wants us to grow toward righteousness, as Paul will emphasize in this chapter. As someone has put it, "God loves us as we are, but He loves us too much to let us stay that way."

2. God forbid. How shall we, that are dead to sin, live any longer therein?

Paul's answer to the question raised in verse 1 is unmistakably clear: *God forbid* ("Of course not!"). A vital part of the acceptance of Jesus Christ as Savior and Lord is becoming dead to sin through repentance. The Christian is "under new management." [See question #4, page 264.]

3. Know ye not, that so many of us as were baptized into Jesus Christ were baptized into his death?

Baptism is designed to be a defining moment in our relationship with God. Just as *Jesus* was buried in a tomb, the one who accepts Jesus is buried in the "watery grave" of Christian baptism. We are *baptized into his death*; that is, baptism represents our acceptance of Jesus' death as our own. It is a burial of the old self. The penalty for our sin is removed in accepting Jesus' death as the substitute for ours. And sin, as the controlling force in our lives, is dead. Its mastery over us has been broken.

B. Raised with Christ (vv. 4, 5)

4. Therefore we are buried with him by baptism into death: that like as Christ was raised up from the dead by the glory of the Father, even so we also should walk in newness of life.

Paul continues his explanation of the dynamic image of Christian *baptism*. A candidate is *buried* in water and raised from that water in an act that identifies him or her with the Son of God, who was buried and *raised* for us. God's power and love raised Jesus, and in baptism His power is also at work in those who have chosen to follow Jesus. Paul notes this in Colossians 2:12: "buried with him [Christ] in baptism, wherein also ye are risen with him through the faith of the operation of God, who hath raised him from the dead."

Paul also calls attention to what is to take place following the act of baptism. This is clear from the phrase *walk in newness of life*. The term *walk* is often used by Paul to describe a person's lifestyle, whether good or bad. Baptism is a spiritual turning point in one's life; a baptized individual must never live the same as he or she did prior to baptism.

Clearly baptism is much more than just a ritual or ceremony. It marks a transformation from death to life; it is, spiritually, a matter of life and death.

5. For if we have been planted together in the likeness of his death, we shall be also in the likeness of his resurrection.

Jesus was buried and raised for us. And when we have surrendered to Jesus' lordship, after our *death* and burial in baptism, we will be raised with Him. Christian baptism is a *likeness of*, or a demonstration or reenactment of, the central facts of the gospel message as defined by Paul in 1 Corinthians 15:1-4 (the death, burial, and *resurrection* of Jesus). Baptism provides a wonderful opportunity to be like Jesus!

C. Freed from Sin (vv. 6-11)

6, 7. Knowing this, that our old man is crucified with him, that the body of sin might be destroyed, that henceforth we should not serve sin. For he that is dead is freed from sin.

In the remainder of this chapter and in chapters 7 and 8, Paul will continue to describe the ongoing battle in which Christians are engaged—a battle of which we are all keenly aware. As long as we live in this world, the fleshly part of us (the body) will be calling for attention; and that will be the part of us through which Satan will work the hardest to capture our allegiance and erode our faith.

Here the apostle insists that we do not take orders from *sin* anymore or from its headquarters. He uses the term *our old man* to describe the individual under sin's rule. But now that we are new creatures in Christ Jesus (2 Corinthians 5:17), we live under a new master, or by the "new man" (Ephesians 4:24). We do *not serve sin.* We serve a new master—Christ. We are not freed from temptation, but we are *freed from sin* as the controlling factor in our lives. God has also given us His Holy Spirit to equip us for the battle, and the Spirit is stronger than Satan (1 John 4:4). Sin will continue to entice, but now it has "met its match." The will to resist temptation operates only in the person in whom the Holy Spirit is at work.

8. Now if we be dead with Christ, we believe that we shall also live with him.

Our symbolic death and burial in baptism illustrates our death to the old way of life—the time when we were living under the power of sin. Now we are *dead* to that; now we truly *live*, with *Christ* at the helm. That eternal life begins with our relationship with Christ (John 17:3), and it extends into eternity.

9. Knowing that Christ being raised from the dead dieth no more; death hath no more dominion over him.

Prior to Jesus, other individuals had been raised from the dead, such as the widow's son in the time of Elijah (1 Kings 17:17-24) and Lazarus (John 11:38-44). But these all eventually died again. *Christ* was *raised from the dead* to die *no more*. The Christian faces death knowing that it

Visual for lesson 4. *The visual for today's lesson can help reinforce the message of victory over death through Jesus' resurrection.*

is a beaten enemy because of Jesus' resurrection. Thus what is true of Jesus is true of the Christian: *death hath no more dominion over him.*

10. For in that he died, he died unto sin once: but in that he liveth, he liveth unto God.

When Jesus died, it appeared that *sin* had won. The enemies of truth rejoiced. But their celebration was short-lived. Christ's victory over the power of sin was decisive. Jesus' death does not need to be repeated; it happened *once* for all (Hebrews 9:24-28). Jesus now lives *unto God*, dwelling with the Father as He did before laying aside His glory to come to earth.

11. Likewise reckon ye also yourselves to be dead indeed unto sin, but alive unto God through Jesus Christ our Lord.

As Christians we are *dead indeed unto sin.* Paul has already made that clear. But that is more than just a point of doctrine; we are to live like that—*alive unto God*, alive in the presence of God, alive for God and His eternal purposes. [See question #5, page 264.]

"FREE" BUT STILL A PRISONER

J. C. Fuller declined his girlfriend's request that he go to church with her one Sunday morning in 1952. Instead, he went out drinking. Later that day his girlfriend saw him talking to another girl. They argued, and in his drunken state Fuller fired the shotgun he was carrying. He was arrested and convicted of attempted murder.

While in the middle of his four-year prison sentence, Fuller was on a work crew building a bridge. He saw poisonous cottonmouth snakes swimming in the stream where the crew was required to work. He was deathly afraid of snakes, so he complained to the guard, who shrugged and said with no sympathy, "There's the road."

The next morning Fuller took to the road and disappeared for forty-seven years. Early in 2000, a prison fugitive squad was reviewing old cases and tracked Fuller down. Because by then he was seventy-six years old, he was allowed to serve out the rest of his sentence with no penalty for his escape.

J. C. Fuller was never actually free from his wrongdoing, although he lived all those years without being confined in any prison. Nearly five decades were spent in a captivity of the spirit, knowing that the debt for his crime had never been paid. How different it is with us who know Christ! We are dead to sin—no longer under its control. We are alive to God, living under His dominion by the miracle of the grace He showed to us at the cross of Christ! —C. R. B.

D. Called to Righteousness (vv. 12-14)

12. Let not sin therefore reign in your mortal body, that ye should obey it in the lusts thereof.

"Live according to who (and whose) you are," the apostle writes. You have been set free, so live as a free individual. You have become a child of God. You have an alternative to the path of *sin*. Sin no longer has to *reign* over you; through Christ you can reign over it.

13. Neither yield ye your members as instruments of unrighteousness unto sin: but yield yourselves unto God, as those that are alive from the dead, and your members as instruments of righteousness unto God.

Christians live in the era between the moment that *God* dealt *sin* a deathblow through Jesus' death and resurrection and the final victory that will occur at Jesus' return. During this interval, we are to live under God's authority, reflecting the *righteousness* that He requires of His people (Ephesians 4:24). [See question #6, page 264.]

Home Daily Bible Readings

Monday, Mar. 21—Walk in Newness of Life (Romans 6:1-5)

Tuesday, Mar. 22—Not Under Law, But Under Grace (Romans 6:6-14)

Wednesday, Mar. 23—Be Slaves of Righteousness (Romans 6:15-23)

Thursday, Mar. 24—Jesus Rises to New Life (Luke 24:1-9)

Friday, Mar. 25—The Resurrection of Jesus (John 20:1-10)

Saturday, Mar. 26—Jesus Appears to Mary (John 20:11-18)

Sunday, Mar. 27—Jesus Appears to the Disciples (John 20:19-23)

Here Paul tells us that our bodily *members* are not Satan's possession now; they are God's *instruments*. We are to use our eyes, our hands, our feet, our minds, and our mouths in a way that shows we are people who are *alive from the dead*. That does not simply mean avoiding wicked uses of those features; it also means putting them to work to serve, to bless, and to draw others to the righteous God.

14. For sin shall not have dominion over you: for ye are not under the law, but under grace.

This may be considered a summary of Paul's answer to the question raised in verse 1. We must not keep sinning, because *sin* is our former master. Although Paul has not mentioned *the law* yet in this section, the law is part of the reason for sin's mastery; it points out our sin. The problem is that the law cannot provide an answer to that mastery. It cannot free us from the guilt it produces. Only God's *grace* can supply what we need and solve our dilemma. By grace, death has been destroyed, sin's hold has been broken, and the law has been fulfilled through the perfect obedience of Jesus.

Conclusion

A. Why Sunday?

One of God's commandments to Old Testament Israel was to remember the Sabbath and keep it holy—the seventh day, the day He rested from creation. It was to be a day for worship and for rest. God knew that both were essential for an effective, obedient life. The Sabbath principle is still vital to observe. Our bodies, minds, and spirits still need worship and rest.

So why do we Christians worship on Sunday instead of Saturday? Because it is the resurrection day! Through Jesus' death and resurrection, a New Covenant with God has been established. He was raised for us, and we shall be raised with Him. The empty tomb has opened up the fullness of Heaven. The church is a place of *life*, and that life is in Christ.

B. Prayer

To the truths that we celebrate on this glorious day, our Father, we commit our lives. That You would permit Your only begotten Son to be crucified for us is beyond our comprehension, but it is the reason for our profound gratitude. That You brought Him back to life is the cause for our celebration. And that we shall live as children of life rather than as slaves of death is our commitment. In Jesus' name. Amen.

C. Thought to Remember

"Because I live, ye shall live also" (John 14:19).

Learning by Doing

This page contains an alternative lesson plan emphasizing learning activities.
Classes desiring such student involvement will find these suggestions helpful.

Learning Goals

After this lesson a student should be able to:

1. Recount the events of resurrection morning, and tell how that event is "replayed" every time a believer is baptized.

2. Contrast the life of sin with the "resurrected" life of the believer raised to "walk in newness of life."

3. Use poetry, art, or music to celebrate the victory over death that we have because of Jesus.

Into the Lesson

Display this caption: "Nothing There—Good or Bad?" Bring several empty containers, such as an opaque two-liter bottle, a cereal box, a shoebox, and a paper bag. Say, "Empty objects like these seem to promise something, but do not deliver. Ask the group to make two lists: one, of items whose emptiness is associated with something bad, and the second, of items whose emptiness suggests something good. For the former list, such items as a car's fuel tank, a depleted bank account, a burglarized home, or a computer's hard drive may be suggested. The latter list may be a bit more difficult to compile, but such items as a completed regimen of oral medication, garbage cans at the end of pick-up day, and a dry basement after heavy rains may be suggested. (Consider prompting class members for this second list by asking, "When are the times that you are happy to find nothing when something bad could be there?") As the discussion ensues, someone may suggest Christ's empty tomb. That is the item you should add to the list, if no one does.

Into the Word

As learners look at John 20:1-10, designate three sections of the class to be the Mary group, the Peter group, and the John group. As you read the following "clues," ask the appropriate group to stand after each. (1) "I stood at the empty tomb . . . and ran away." (2) "I stood at the empty tomb . . . and looked in but did not enter right away." (3) "I stood at the empty tomb . . . and rushed right in." (4) "I stood at the empty tomb . . . first of all the followers of Jesus to do so." (5) "I stood at the empty tomb . . . and thought the body of Jesus had been stolen." (6) "I stood at the empty tomb . . . ahead of a slower disciple." (7) "I stood at the empty tomb . . . and saw Jesus' empty bur-

ial clothes." (8) "I stood at the empty tomb . . . and was the second to go in." (9) "I stood at the empty tomb . . . and immediately understood the Scripture that Jesus had to rise from the dead." Groups that should stand are as follows: 1—Mary; 2—John; 3—Peter; 4—Mary; 5—Mary; 6—John; 7—John, Peter; 8—John; 9—no one stands; see verse 9. (A similar activity is included in the student book.)

Say, "Most of us have seen the old frontier 'Wanted' posters that read 'Dead or Alive.' Paul's words in Romans 6:1-14 are directed to Christians and may be summarized: 'Wanted: Dead *and* Alive!'" Ask your learners to scan that text quickly and make a count of the number of times *dead* (and derivatives) and *live* (and derivatives) appear. (They should find more than ten for *dead* and about eight for *live*.) Once several indicate their count, ask, "How is it that we as Christians are both dead and alive?"

After a discussion that includes references to the text, have two class members pantomime a baptismal scene of one lowering the other into and out of the water. Afterward, ask, "How is the early church's practice of baptism (immersion) a perfect picture of the Christian's dying to sin and being resurrected to new life?" Such elements as submission and humility, stopping one's breathing, being washed/cleansed, beginning one's breathing again, and others may be suggested.

Into Life

Give each student a sheet of paper onto which you have drawn or copied the simple outline of a tombstone. Add a small decorative drawing of the garden tomb of Jesus with the stone rolled away. Direct attention once again to the text from Romans 6, and assign the learners to compose an appropriate epitaph for their tombstones. Give an example or two, such as, "Raised up from the dead; By Jesus I'm led" and "Buried with Christ _____(date)_____; Made Alive with Him _____(date)_____."

Choose a familiar hymn or gospel song dealing with our new life in Christ, and have a musical class member lead in singing it. Such songs as "Because He Lives" by the Gaithers, "Christ the Lord Is Risen Today" (especially the stanza beginning, "Soar we now, where Christ has led"), "Buried With Christ" by Ryder and Kirkpatrick, or another your class enjoys may be used.

Let's Talk It Over

The questions on this page are designed to promote discussion of the lesson by the class and to encourage application of the lesson Scriptures. The answers provided are only discussion starters. Let your class talk it over from there.

1. Why does the resurrection matter? Some believe that the only important thing about Christianity is the positive example of Jesus' life—are they correct? Why, or why not?

It is safe to say that without Christ there can be no Christianity. Equally true is the statement that without Christ's death *and* resurrection there is no Christianity. No other faith puts so much emphasis on the reality of historical events. No other faith is utterly dependent on the reality of a single miracle. Christianity is not simply the efforts of people to try to live like Christ and follow His teachings the best they can. Christianity instead requires people to admit that they *cannot* live like Christ and that they *cannot* consistently follow His teachings. Christianity teaches that because of Christ's death and resurrection, there is forgiveness and hope for those who have sinned and power to live as God intended man to live.

2. Why was it so hard for Jesus' disciples to understand and believe in the resurrection? Do you think it is easier or harder to believe today?

Jesus' disciples had seen people die before, and they had seen Jesus raise certain individuals from the dead. However, it must have been devastating for them to watch the one who had given life to others allowing Himself to be crucified—apparently powerless to save His own life. Then to realize that He had been buried in a tomb must have finalized the sad series of events in their minds. Sometimes we like to think that if we had lived in Bible times, believing in Jesus would have been so easy. That is simply not true. The disciples were human beings just like us; they struggled with the same doubts, worries, and questions that plague people today.

3. What convinced you of the reality of Jesus' resurrection? What is the best way to convince someone else of that reality?

Each person should reflect on his or her own "faith journey." Some, like Thomas, tend to be skeptical by nature. Such individuals may have questions that they need to work through carefully before they will profess faith in Jesus. Ultimately the most important testimony to the reality of Jesus' resurrection is the Scripture. In Luke 16:19-31 we read Jesus' story of Lazarus and the rich man. He described what happened after both men died. From his place of torment, the rich man pleaded with Abraham to send Lazarus back to his five brothers to warn them of that place. Abraham told him, "They have Moses and the prophets; let them hear them" (v. 29). Jesus was saying that all of the evidence one needs for faith is in God's Word.

4. If we are "dead to sin," why do so many of us struggle with temptation?

Paul's exhortations concerning a Christian's armor (Ephesians 6:10-18) tell us that we must always be on guard against our enemy, Satan. Satan is an expert at picking the specific areas of weakness in our characters. For one person the weakness may be greed, for another it may be lust, and for another it may be pride. However strong those temptations may be, in Christ we have been given the power to resist the enemy and to say "No." Remember the words of 1 John 4:4: "Greater is he that is in you, than he that is in the world."

5. Whom do you know who exemplifies the phrase, "alive unto God"? What can you learn from him or her about living for God?

God is so good about bringing role models into our lives to provide the counsel and encouragement that we need. Most of us will find such people in our churches or, if we are especially blessed, in our families. If they are missing from our lives, we can certainly look to the pages of Scripture and to the biographies of noteworthy Christians for our inspiration and guidance.

6. What does it mean to have victory in Christ? What difference does this victory make in our lives—both now and in the future?

Unfortunately, far too many of us sometimes feel anything but victorious. We need to remember that sanctification is a process. Although we do have victory in Christ because of His death and resurrection, there are times when we need to keep the "big picture" in mind and realize that ultimate victory is indeed promised in God's Word to those who are faithful. Let us remember that we are all a work in progress, but we can make progress because of Christ's work in us through the Holy Spirit.

Live by the Spirit ✳

DEVOTIONAL READING: Romans 7:1-6.

BACKGROUND SCRIPTURE: Romans 8:1-17.

PRINTED TEXT: Romans 8:1-17.

Romans 8:1-17

1 There is therefore now no condemnation to them which are in Christ Jesus, who walk not after the flesh, but after the Spirit.

2 For the law of the Spirit of life in Christ Jesus hath made me free from the law of sin and death.

3 For what the law could not do, in that it was weak through the flesh, God sending his own Son in the likeness of sinful flesh, and for sin, condemned sin in the flesh:

4 That the righteousness of the law might be fulfilled in us, who walk not after the flesh, but after the Spirit.

5 For they that are after the flesh do mind the things of the flesh; but they that are after the Spirit, the things of the Spirit.

6 For to be carnally minded is death; but to be spiritually minded is life and peace.

7 Because the carnal mind is enmity against God: for it is not subject to the law of God, neither indeed can be.

8 So then they that are in the flesh cannot please God.

9 But ye are not in the flesh, but in the Spirit, if so be that the Spirit of God dwell in you. Now if any man have not the Spirit of Christ, he is none of his.

10 And if Christ be in you, the body is dead because of sin; but the Spirit is life because of righteousness.

11 But if the Spirit of him that raised up Jesus from the dead dwell in you, he that raised up Christ from the dead shall also quicken your mortal bodies by his Spirit that dwelleth in you.

12 Therefore, brethren, we are debtors, not to the flesh, to live after the flesh.

13 For if ye live after the flesh, ye shall die: but if ye through the Spirit do mortify the deeds of the body, ye shall live.

14 For as many as are led by the Spirit of God, they are the sons of God.

15 For ye have not received the spirit of bondage again to fear; but ye have received the Spirit of adoption, whereby we cry, Abba, Father.

16 The Spirit itself beareth witness with our spirit, that we are the children of God:

17 And if children, then heirs; heirs of God, and joint-heirs with Christ, if so be that we suffer with him, that we may be also glorified together.

GOLDEN TEXT: For as many as are led by the Spirit of God, they are the sons of God.
—Romans 8:14.

God's Project: Effective Christians
Unit 2: The Christian Life
(Lessons 5-8)

Lesson Aims

After participating in this lesson, a student should be able to:

1. Tell how Paul contrasts the life lived in the flesh with one lived in the Spirit.

2. Cite contemporary evidence of living in the flesh and living in the Spirit.

3. Identify a compulsive or addictive behavior that interferes with his or her life in the Spirit, and commit to greater submission to the Spirit in that area of life.

Lesson Outline

INTRODUCTION
    A. It's No Cartoon
    B. Lesson Background
 I. WAY TO FREEDOM AND LIFE (Romans 8:1-8)
    A. In Christ Jesus (vv. 1, 2)
    B. Not in Law and Flesh (vv. 3-8)
      The Price of Living in the Flesh
 II. WALK OF FREEDOM AND LIFE (Romans 8:9-14)
    A. In Debt to the Spirit (vv. 9-11)
    B. No Debt to the Flesh (vv. 12-14)
III. PROMISE OF FREEDOM AND LIFE (Romans 8:15-17)
    A. Adoption as Sons (vv. 15, 16)
      Wanted! (In the Best Sense of the Word)
    B. Joint-heirs with Christ (v. 17)
CONCLUSION
    A. Letting the Winner Win
    B. Prayer
    C. Thought to Remember

Introduction

A. It's No Cartoon

Those of us who read the comic pages in the newspaper every morning have developed our favorites over the years. One of the great favorites from yesteryear for this writer was "Priscilla's Pop." The lingering image that comes to mind is young Priscilla (who is eight to ten years old) listening to a little angel on one shoulder debate with a little devil on the other shoulder. Most of us can readily relate to such an image. For Christians, it should bring to mind Paul's words about the tug-of-war that we experience between the flesh and the Spirit. In this case, it's no cartoon and nothing to laugh about.

How can we learn to listen to the right message and stand on the right side? That's what today's lesson will help us understand.

B. Lesson Background

Last week we read a portion of John's record of resurrection morning. The dawning of a new day brought the dawning of a new era of life and hope by virtue of Jesus' resurrection. Such news should put a spring in our step, as it did for Mary Magdalene, Peter, and John, all of whom started running when confronted with the astonishing (but true!) news of an empty tomb. Then we read Paul's words in Romans 6, challenging all Christians to live as resurrected people. We don't live under sin's control anymore. Being alive unto God and to righteous living is now the order of the day. Christian baptism is the landmark event that dramatizes the change from death to life by the picture of being buried in and then emerging from water.

As we proceed in our study of Romans, we see Paul continuing to contrast the old life under sin and the law with the new life in Christ. In particular, he focuses on the ongoing tension between those two paths experienced by himself (and all of us). This leads to the frank and challenging comments in our text from Romans 8.

A brief word is in order concerning Paul's teaching in Romans 7, especially verses 7-25. Is Paul relating his experience before or after becoming a Christian? It is probably best to see these verses as a description of Paul's (and the Christian's) continual struggle with the sin factor following conversion. That struggle—the issue of whether sin or righteousness should "reign" in our lives—is introduced in Romans 6:12. At the end of chapter 7, Paul expresses the intensity of the struggle in these words: "O wretched man that I am! who shall deliver me from the body of this death? I thank God through Jesus Christ our Lord. So then with the mind I myself serve the law of God; but with the flesh the law of sin" (Romans 7:24, 25). In Romans 8 Paul elaborates on the deliverance offered to us in Christ.

I. Way to Freedom and Life
(Romans 8:1-8)

A. In Christ Jesus (vv. 1, 2)

1. There is therefore now no condemnation to them which are in Christ Jesus, who walk not after the flesh, but after the Spirit.

God has solved what we cannot solve. God has paid a price that we cannot and could never pay. His Son took the *condemnation* that we deserved because of our sin. Even though our past is shot through with inconsistencies and failures, even though our present practice is imperfect, and even though we can count on facing Satan's "fiery darts" in the future, *there is . . . now no condemnation*—because we *are in Christ Jesus.*

To be in Christ, however, involves more than just a position or standing. To accept Christ as Savior marks the beginning of a process of growth. The word *walk* implies a way of living— a commitment to growing in the will of God. Because we are now Christ's, we are to take orders from *the Spirit*, not from *the flesh*. The term *flesh* most likely refers to the physical body, which is the source of sinful desires and "fleshly lusts, which war against the soul" (1 Peter 2:11). We are not guided by these desires; because we are in Christ, we are guided by the Spirit's desires.

2. For the law of the Spirit of life in Christ Jesus hath made me free from the law of sin and death.

A new *law* is at work in the Christian. This law is not loaded with restrictions, prescriptions, accusations, or condemnations. It offers *life*, not death—including possibilities, opportunities, freedom from *sin and death*, and help through God's *Spirit*. [See question #1, page 272.]

B. Not in Law and Flesh (vv. 3-8)

3. For what the law could not do, in that it was weak through the flesh, God sending his own Son in the likeness of sinful flesh, and for sin, condemned sin in the flesh.

The law called people to obedience. It pointed out failures, but it provided no forgiveness for those failures and no power to do better. The law itself was good; in fact, Paul calls it "holy" in Romans 7:12. But it was *weak through the flesh.* Humanity has not been able to keep the standards set forth in the law. And the flesh always pulls us in the opposite direction from that established by God's law.

God addressed the law's failure by *sending his own Son in the likeness of sinful flesh.* "The Word was made flesh" (John 1:14) but came only in the *likeness* of sinful flesh. Jesus had a human body, but Jesus controlled that body and did not allow the flesh to become the starting point for sin (as we have done). His perfection qualified Him to become the sacrifice at the cross for those who had sinned (all humanity). Thus God *condemned* our *sin in the flesh* of Jesus. Then God brought Jesus back to life. Sin, death, and the flesh were defeated. [See question #2, page 272.]

4. That the righteousness of the law might be fulfilled in us, who walk not after the flesh, but after the Spirit.

On our own, we could never fulfill *the righteousness of the law.* Jesus did so—first, by keeping the law perfectly, and, second, by suffering

the punishment of death that the law required of lawbreakers (again, describing all human beings). Those who accept Christ as Savior accept His death on their behalf and are thereby viewed as righteous by God. "For he hath made him to be sin for us, who knew no sin; that we might be made the righteousness of God in him" (2 Corinthians 5:21). But as noted earlier, to be in Christ is more than a position. Here Paul encourages those in Christ to *walk* (live) *not after the flesh, but after the Spirit.* Thus the law is *fulfilled in us* who live under the control of the Holy Spirit.

5. For they that are after the flesh do mind the things of the flesh; but they that are after the Spirit, the things of the Spirit.

So many people in our world today invest their lives in the immediate. They live for the moment. They take orders from their impulses and their appetites. Consequences mean little or nothing to them. To *mind the things of the flesh* is to follow the standard of conduct described so clearly by the apostle John: "For all that is in the world, the lust of the flesh, and the lust of the eyes, and the pride of life, is not of the Father, but is of the world" (1 John 2:16). The flesh conveys a signal, and if we are committed only to this world and to the moment, we rush to obey that signal. But when the *Spirit* of God is actively working in us, we are receiving input from another "signal." And we must listen to that which is higher and permanent, not that which is lower and temporary. [See question #3, page 272.]

6. For to be carnally minded is death; but to be spiritually minded is life and peace.

The word *carnal* means "fleshly," as in the word *incarnation*, which describes how Jesus "came in flesh" when He came to our world. It is important that we know the consequences of being *carnally minded.* If we take orders from the flesh, *death* will be the unavoidable result. Death is primarily separation from God; therefore it includes not only physical death but also spiritual death in sin. But if we take orders from God's Spirit, we will share the quality and quantity of *life* in the Spirit. Which will it be—death or life, torment or *peace?* Whose orders will we follow? Which signal will we heed?

7. Because the carnal mind is enmity against God: for it is not subject to the law of God, neither indeed can be.

How to Say It

ABBA. *Ab*-uh.
ARAMAIC. Air-uh-*may*-ick.

All we have to do is read again the Ten Commandments that God gave His people through Moses to see the contrast between *the carnal mind* and *the law of God*. When one is *subject* to the flesh, he or she is not subject to God but is God's enemy. [See question #4, page 272.]

The warning against being driven by the flesh does not mean that all of our physical requirements or interests are evil. God created us. And He made life to be enjoyed. But it is clear that some appetites are in opposition to the will of God and that even the good appetites or desires can be abused by someone who does not honor God and His law.

8. So then they that are in the flesh cannot please God.

Later in this letter, Paul writes the following: "I beseech you therefore, brethren, by the mercies of God, that ye present your bodies a living sacrifice, holy, acceptable unto God, which is your reasonable service" (Romans 12:1). We *please God* when we present our bodies for His use, not when we let fleshly desires control how we use our bodies. [See question #5, page 272.]

THE PRICE OF LIVING IN THE FLESH

A complaint Muslims have directed at those of us in the Western world in recent years is that we are exporting a fleshly, materialistic message through the television programs that all too many love to watch. (It seems there are two extremes involved here: one culture has few restrictions on what it allows people to do to express themselves; the other is highly repressive of any kind of individual expression.) Nevertheless, it's no secret that Westerners live in a worldly, sensuous culture.

Advocates of personal freedom sometimes miss the point that freedom calls for responsibility. For example, Erika Harold—Miss America 2003—was roundly criticized for advocating sexual abstinence for young people. The pageant was caught in the bind of hypocrisy: in previous years one winner had been forced to resign because she had posed for revealing photos in a popular men's magazine; another resigned under pressure after a former boyfriend claimed to have seminude photos of her. This prompted one observer to ask about the 2003 pageant, "Who would have thought a virtuous winner would be censured for her virtue?"

Western culture seems to be schizophrenic on moral matters. While wanting freedom to do as they please, most people don't want to pay the price that living for the flesh always exacts. The ultimate price is death, because the flesh sets itself against God, who is the only source of life.

—C. R. B.

II. Walk of Freedom and Life (Romans 8:9-14)

A. In Debt to the Spirit (vv. 9-11)

9. But ye are not in the flesh, but in the Spirit, if so be that the Spirit of God dwell in you. Now if any man have not the Spirit of Christ, he is none of his.

Again, Paul highlights the contrast between being *in the flesh* and *in the Spirit*. Christians, by virtue of their alignment with *Christ* and the "newness of life" that they have been given (Romans 6:4), are not flesh-guided people. "You have the *Spirit of God* in you," says Paul. So we must take our cues from the Spirit, not from the flesh. If we are controlled by the flesh, we are not of Christ. If we are guided by the Spirit, we show that we are His; and we witness to others of the difference our faith makes.

"Are you for me or against me?" God would ask. We can't sit on the fence, and we can't have it both ways. Flesh or Spirit?

Let us also notice the word *ye*. This word is a second person plural in the Greek text. The business of the Christian walk, of living with Christ in us, is carried out in a fellowship of believers. In fact, in the first Corinthian letter Paul writes, "Know ye not that ye are the temple of God, and that the Spirit of God dwelleth in you?" (1 Corinthians 3:16). There too the words *ye* and *you* are in the plural. The Spirit of God energizes the individual believer, and the Spirit of God energizes the church.

Have you noticed in this passage how Paul refers to the Holy Spirit as the Spirit of life, the Spirit of God, the Spirit of Christ, and later as the Spirit of adoption (v. 15)? Don't be stymied by these different names. With each one Paul refers to the holy presence whom God gives to each Christian. The same divine person is described each time.

10. And if Christ be in you, the body is dead because of sin; but the Spirit is life because of righteousness.

Here the apostle makes the same point in a slightly different way. The Christian's *body* will die *because of sin*. But because of God's grace, because the *righteousness* of Christ has covered our sins, He has presented us with the offer of *life* through His Son and with the power for living that life through His *Spirit*.

It should be noted that some have suggested that the word *Spirit* does not refer to the Holy Spirit but to the human spirit, as contrasted with the body. (The Greek word translated *Spirit* is not capitalized, even when it refers to the Holy Spirit.) The body is going to experience death, but our spirits have been given new life in Christ because of the Holy Spirit's presence. This is certainly another possible way to interpret Paul's words.

11. But if the Spirit of him that raised up Jesus from the dead dwell in you, he that raised up Christ from the dead shall also quicken your mortal bodies by his Spirit that dwelleth in you.

The death of the body, mentioned in the previous verse, is not the last word on the subject. The same Holy *Spirit* who lives in us and empowers us spiritually will also *quicken*, or give life to, our *bodies*. The Spirit's presence in us now is considered an "earnest" or "down payment" of greater blessings to come (2 Corinthians 1:21, 22; Ephesians 1:13, 14).

B. No Debt to the Flesh (vv. 12-14)

12. Therefore, brethren, we are debtors, not to the flesh, to live after the flesh.

We don't owe our *flesh* anything. When our fleshly appetites scream for our attention, they don't have to be fed. They must be evaluated in light of our higher, spiritual citizenship. Satisfying them may be acceptable, or it may be improper to do so. The Holy Spirit provides the Christian the power to say no to those cries of the body that it would be sinful for us to satisfy. We are *debtors* to God who has provided us with such power.

13, 14. For if ye live after the flesh, ye shall die: but if ye through the Spirit do mortify the deeds of the body, ye shall live. For as many as are led by the Spirit of God, they are the sons of God.

To *live after the flesh* is a path to certain death—spiritually, physically, and eternally. What we must do is *mortify*, or kill, *the deeds of the body*, meaning those deeds that reflect the influence of the flesh. Accepting the Spirit's guidance indicates our status as *sons of God*.

It should be clear that at some point all of us must face the harsh reality of death. The key question is when we shall do this. Through Jesus we can address it now, by dying to sin and putting to death the deeds of the flesh, so that we can receive abundant and eternal life. If we fail to address it now, we will remain spiritually dead in our sins and we will face physical death without the hope available in Christ. [See question #6, page 272.]

III. Promise of Freedom and Life (Romans 8:15-17)

A. Adoption as Sons (vv. 15, 16)

15. For ye have not received the spirit of bondage again to fear; but ye have received the Spirit of adoption, whereby we cry, Abba, Father.

Visual for lessons 5, 11

Use today's visual when focusing on the freedom Jesus gives us from sin and death.

The Aramaic word *Abba* is rather close to our very familiar, warm, and intimate nickname "Daddy." Jesus addressed His *Father* in this manner (Mark 14:36). Through Jesus we are made heirs to a magnificent inheritance, for we have been adopted into the Father's family. In a sense we are slaves, or servants, as Paul says in Romans 6:16-22. But that servanthood is offered willingly on our part as Christians, in gratitude to the Lord for all He has done for us in Christ. The motivation is love, not *fear*.

WANTED! (IN THE BEST SENSE OF THE WORD)

Key in the word *adoption* in an Internet search engine and about a tenth of a second later you are likely to get nearly eight million Web sites! There are sites for "adopting" such creatures as fairies, centaurs, mermaids, pegacorns—a combination of the mythical unicorn and the winged-horse Pegasus—and other imaginary creatures. Many other sites give information about subjects of more worthwhile adoptions such as abandoned animals.

One of the ironies of contemporary culture is the vocal group of people who show more concern for mythical creatures and abandoned animals than they do for unwanted children! During the "abortion wars" of the last few decades, those involved in the debate have sometimes acted as if the only issue were whether a baby (or "product of conception," depending on one's position on the subject) is killed or carried to full term. Even though many thoughtful people have advocated adoption as an alternative to abortion, the heated rhetoric on both sides has occasionally obscured the quiet voice of reason.

The fact is, a multitude of potential parents would love to adopt someone else's unwanted child. Such people are demonstrating God's kind of love: we may be lost, fearful of the future, unwanted, or unloved by family or friends who should care for us, but God will graciously adopt us into the wonderful warmth of His spiritual family.   —C. R. B.

16. The Spirit itself beareth witness with our spirit, that we are the children of God.

When we cry "Abba, Father," we testify that we recognize God as our Father and ourselves as *children of God*. God's Spirit confirms this, bearing *witness with our spirit*. Two possible interpretations of this verse have been suggested. Some believe we are to allow the Holy Spirit to be in clear and constant communication with our spirits, as we eagerly submit to His shaping of our attitudes, our words, and our walk. Others see the Spirit's witness as directed toward the Father, similar to the intercession that He makes for us before God, according to Romans 8:26, 27.

B. Joint-heirs with Christ (v. 17)

17. And if children, then heirs; heirs of God, and joint-heirs with Christ, if so be that we suffer with him, that we may be also glorified together.

Here Paul raises the possibility that we may *suffer* for Christ's sake. Certainly that was true for some of the Christians in Rome. It was true for Paul. It is true for many Christians today—in the Western world as well as in other countries. Paul encourages us to keep the "big picture" in mind: we are *heirs of God, and joint-heirs with Christ*. The path of suffering ends with being *glorified together* with Christ and with all who have traveled the same path.

In his commentary on the book of Romans in the *Standard Bible Studies* series, Bruce Shields

has a keen insight into this promise that as heirs we shall be glorified:

"*Glory* refers to the image of God in which Adam was created, the glory Adam lost as a result of the fall, the glory of God, which each sinner lacks (Romans 3:23), the glory of the life that Jesus led, and the glory for which we may hope (Romans 5:2). Thus Paul, with this promise of glorification, reaches back to original creation, deals with the reality of new creation, and looks forward to the restoration of God's purpose in creation—a restoration that awaits the final judgment" (Bruce Shields, *Romans*, Standard Publishing, 1988, p. 99).

Conclusion

A. Letting the Winner Win

Our role in this business of life is not to take the "lead" part. That is the role the devil wants us to think we are taking, when in reality he is calling the shots. The devil is stronger than we are. He seeks to set up headquarters in our flesh. He desires to take our God-given appetites and twist them to accomplish his evil ends. He's like the little demon on the shoulder of the cartoon character Priscilla (mentioned in the Introduction), using persuasive words and attractive images to turn her head his way.

God, however, is far stronger than the devil. And He has put in place a plan for our redemption. He has done all of the grace-founded work to make it possible. The devil still harasses us, but the "angel" on the shoulder of the Christian is the Holy Spirit. This means that as a Christian, I am the weakest party in this situation, yet the exercise of my will determines the outcome. God is already the winner, by virtue of the death and resurrection of Jesus. But He has so limited himself, through a free will that He has given me, that I must decide to let the winner win. It may sound strange, but the pathway to victory lies in surrender.

B. Prayer

Forgive us, Father, when we boast of anything except the cross of our Lord Jesus Christ. Accept our joyful gratitude that comes from knowing that He has paid the debt we owed. Help us understand what it means to live as debtors to the Spirit, not the flesh. May we do away with any "interference" that keeps the Spirit's signal from being heard. In Jesus' name. Amen.

C. Thought to Remember

Jesus gave up His glory and put on flesh so that we could conquer the flesh and share in His glory.

Home Daily Bible Readings

Monday, Mar. 28—New Life of the Spirit (Romans 7:1-6)

Tuesday, Mar. 29—Sin Brings Death (Romans 7:7-13)

Wednesday, Mar. 30—The Struggle with Sin (Romans 7:14-19)

Thursday, Mar. 31—Captive to the Law of Sin (Romans 7:20-25)

Friday, Apr. 1—Live According to the Spirit (Romans 8:1-5)

Saturday, Apr. 2—You Are in the Spirit (Romans 8:6-11)

Sunday, Apr. 3—Led by the Spirit (Romans 8:12-17)

Learning by Doing

This page contains an alternative lesson plan emphasizing learning activities.
Classes desiring such student involvement will find these suggestions helpful.

Learning Goals

After completing this lesson, a student should be able to:

1. Tell how Paul contrasts the life lived in the flesh with one lived in the Spirit.

2. Cite contemporary evidence of living in the flesh and living in the Spirit.

3. Identify a compulsive or addictive behavior that interferes with his or her life in the Spirit, and commit to greater submission to the Spirit in that area of life.

Into the Lesson

Buy and bring enough of the following stickers to class to allow you to give one of each to each learner: one, a sticker of an angel; two, a sticker of a small imp or devil. Have an angel sticker stuck to one of your own shoulders; have a devil sticker stuck to the other. Direct everyone to follow your example with the stickers they have received. Recruit a good reader to read aloud the following short poem: "Got the devil on your shoulder?/ Hear him whisper in your ear?/ Can you tell he is a-lying?/ Do you know it's right to fear?/ He says, 's'Better, child, it's better,/ Than the burden God will lay/ On your shoulder: heavy, hurting;/ Better, better, child, I s-s-s-say!'/ Got the devil on your shoulder?/ Hear him shouting in your ear?/ Can you tell he is a-lying?/ Do you know it's right to fear?"

Use the lesson commentator's introductory paragraph, "It's No Cartoon," to lead to the study of today's text from Romans 8.

Into the Word

Recruit a person to don Roman-style clothing and a prisoner's shackles to play the role of Paul for a monologue, using Romans 7:14-25. This text, preceding today's printed text, is Paul's very personal statement of the deep spiritual tension that all Christians experience. If your actor can memorize the passage and deliver it passionately, so much the better.

Once that text has been presented, introduce the following activity that you will entitle, "Split Personality." Divide a letter-size sheet of paper into two vertical halves and six left and six right sections. Write the following words randomly into the twelve resulting rectangles, one word per area: *alive, carnal, child, condemned, debtor, enemy, freed, friend, heir, slave, spirit, weak.*

Make a copy of this sheet for each learner and distribute the copies. Then give this direction: "Fold and tear apart the sections of this sheet. In the hand on the side where you have the devil/imp sticker stuck to your shoulder, hold the six terms the devil is 'whispering in your ear.' In the other hand, hold the ones your 'angel' is encouraging you to be." (If you are not using the stickers, simply specify left and right.)

Once the learners have had the opportunity to tear their paper and decide where to place the pieces, tell them you are going to read today's text and that as you do they should pull out appropriate words from their stacks. For example, after reading verses one and two, the appropriate words to be drawn are *condemned* and *freed.* Say something to this effect: "The devil's side keeps reminding us that we are sinners through and through and don't stand a chance, but the Spirit's side affirms that we are free!" Using the labels will help the class members focus as you deal with the basic principles of the text, employing notes from the commentary.

Into Life

Many adults include walking in their daily exercise regimen. Give learners a copy of this list of seven "daily walking mottoes" to quote to themselves—one per day for the next week. (These can be used by learners even if they do not engage in any kind of walking activity.) (1) Though I have sin in my life, today I walk without the condemnation of sin; (2) Though I have aches and pains, today I walk free from the law of sin and death; (3) Though my mind keeps drifting to the needs of my physical body, I walk thinking of the things of the Spirit; (4) Though death is sure and true, I walk alive in the Spirit of righteousness; (5) Though fears and fearful things surround me, I walk as a child of God, not a slave of fear; (6) Though I may share in the sufferings of my Lord, I walk also in His glory; (7) Though others I pass may walk with the burden of sin, I walk free in Christ Jesus.

When each learner has a copy, read the list antiphonally; that is, you read the "Though" clause of each, and ask the class to read the "I walk" clause in unison. Suggest that the learners modify the wording to make a rhythm as they walk, possibly creating a simple tune for each grand truth.

Let's Talk It Over

The questions on this page are designed to promote discussion of the lesson by the class and to encourage application of the lesson Scriptures. The answers provided are only discussion starters. Let your class talk it over from there.

1. How does a law of life differ from a law of death? What difference does the awareness of this make in your own life?

A law of death focuses on the "do nots" and the penalties that accompany disobedience. A law of life focuses on the rewards for those who obey. A law of death emphasizes consequences; a law of life emphasizes benefits. The implications of such a law of life for our own lives are profound: fear is replaced by hope, dread is replaced by anticipation, and condemnation is replaced by salvation. We should be grateful that in Christ we have been made "free from the law of sin and death" (Romans 8:2).

2. Since the law came from God, why was it not sufficient to save us? Why did Jesus have to die? What does that death mean for us?

The failure of the law lay not in the giver of the law, but in the receivers. Paul tells us in Romans 8:3 that the law "was weak through the flesh." So God sent "his own Son in the likeness of sinful flesh" and "condemned sin in the flesh." Jesus had to die because of the law's requirement of a perfect sacrifice. Only Jesus could provide such a sacrifice because of the universality of humanity's sin (Romans 3:23). But His resurrection ushered in a new "law"—one of grace and faith and life.

3. What are some "things of the flesh"? What are some "things of the Spirit"? How can we tell the difference?

Galatians 5:19-21 is instructive, for it details the "works of the flesh." Every item in this list reflects our commentator's words: "They [who live by the flesh] live for the moment. They take orders from their impulses and their appetites. Consequences mean little or nothing to them" (page 267). In contrast to the works of the flesh is the "fruit of the Spirit," listed in Galatians 5:22, 23. The difference may be summarized as follows: those who live by the flesh live to please themselves; those who live by the Spirit live to please God and others.

4. What is a good life? Can you live a truly good life without God's Spirit?

It is instructive to consider Jesus' encounter with the rich young ruler. Responding to the young man's words, "Good Master," Jesus said, "Why callest thou me good? none is good, save one, that is, God" (Luke 18:18, 19). If the "good life" refers only to material possessions, exemplary moral behavior, or a quality family life, then a good life is attainable for many. However, for those without the Spirit of God, a good life as measured by the law of God is impossible to experience. A decent quality of life can be had without the Spirit, but ultimately decency—eternal decency—comes only through a relationship with Jesus Christ and the sanctifying power of God's Spirit.

5. Why is it impossible to please God "in the flesh"? What about those who believe they are "good enough" or that God will not punish people who live a moral life?

The simple reason that we cannot please God in the flesh is that God and the flesh are diametrically opposed to each other. We must come to God, not on our terms, but on His, such as those stated in Hebrews 11:6: "He that cometh to God must believe that he is, and that he is a rewarder of them that diligently seek him." Those who do not believe in God or those who refuse to accept His authority in their lives should not have any expectation that God will accept them. God will not force himself upon someone who chooses to ignore or oppose Him (the case of Saul/Paul is a very rare exception).

6. How does one "mortify" the flesh? Is the practice of certain individuals in church history who beat themselves to remove impure thoughts an appropriate example for us?

As has been noted in previous questions, "flesh" as used in this study is primarily a spiritual concept. It refers not so much to the physical body as to those desires that arise from seeking to satisfy the body apart from God's will. To "mortify" the flesh means bringing all desires under the control of God's Spirit. It is true that some individuals and groups throughout church history have taken such words as "mortify" literally. But that is not the intent of this command, any more than we are to be literally "crucified" to fulfill Galatians 2:20. Such a literal action will never address the real problem, which is in the heart, as Jesus taught (Matthew 15:18-20).

Find Salvation in Christ

DEVOTIONAL READING: Hebrews 5:5-10.

BACKGROUND SCRIPTURE: Romans 10:5-21.

PRINTED TEXT: Romans 10:5-17.

Romans 10:5-17

5 For Moses describeth the righteousness which is of the law, That the man which doeth those things shall live by them.

6 But the righteousness which is of faith speaketh on this wise, Say not in thine heart, Who shall ascend into heaven? (that is, to bring Christ down from above:)

7 Or, Who shall descend into the deep? (that is, to bring up Christ again from the dead.)

8 But what saith it? The word is nigh thee, even in thy mouth, and in thy heart: that is, the word of faith, which we preach;

9 That if thou shalt confess with thy mouth the Lord Jesus, and shalt believe in thine heart that God hath raised him from the dead, thou shalt be saved.

10 For with the heart man believeth unto righteousness; and with the mouth confession is made unto salvation.

11 For the Scripture saith, Whosoever believeth on him shall not be ashamed.

12 For there is no difference between the Jew and the Greek: for the same Lord over all is rich unto all that call upon him.

13 For whosoever shall call upon the name of the Lord shall be saved.

14 How then shall they call on him in whom they have not believed? and how shall they believe in him of whom they have not heard? and how shall they hear without a preacher?

15 And how shall they preach, except they be sent? as it is written, How beautiful are the feet of them that preach the gospel of peace, and bring glad tidings of good things!

16 But they have not all obeyed the gospel. For Isaiah saith, Lord, who hath believed our report?

17 So then faith cometh by hearing, and hearing by the word of God.

GOLDEN TEXT: If thou shalt confess with thy mouth the Lord Jesus, and shalt believe in thine heart that God hath raised him from the dead, thou shalt be saved.—Romans 10:9.

God's Project: Effective Christians
Unit 2: The Christian Life
(Lessons 5-8)

Lesson Aims

After this lesson a student should be able to:

1. Tell what Paul means when he concludes, "So then faith cometh by hearing, and hearing by the word of God."

2. Explain the importance of confessing faith as it relates to one's own salvation and to the salvation of others.

3. Prepare a personal testimony about what it means to be saved.

Lesson Outline

INTRODUCTION
  A. The Right Question
  B. Lesson Background
 I. KEEPING THE LAW (Romans 10:5-7)
  A. Moses' Words on Law (v. 5)
  B. Moses' Words on Faith (vv. 6, 7)
 II. LIVING BY FAITH (Romans 10:8-13)
  A. An Affirming Faith (vv. 8-10)
   Two Kinds of Confession
  B. An Available Faith (vv. 11-13)
 III. SPREADING THE FAITH (Romans 10:14-17)
  A. Helping People Call (v. 14)
  B. Helping Messengers Go (v. 15)
   Clear Communication
  C. Helping Sinners Listen (vv. 16, 17)
CONCLUSION
  A. Not Trying
  B. But Trusting
  C. Prayer
  D. Thought to Remember

Introduction

A. The Right Question

The jailer in the city of Philippi surely had heard what was being said over the "grapevine" about Paul and Silas and about the impact of their preaching. Then he found himself personally involved with these two men after they had cast the fortune-telling demon from the slave girl, were accused of causing social chaos by the owners of the girl, and were stripped and beaten. After the jailer had done his duty, placing Paul and Silas in an inner cell and fastening their feet in the stocks, he probably figured he was finished with them.

Then came the earthquake at midnight. When the jailer saw that the prison doors all were opened, he thought the prisoners had fled, putting his own life in great jeopardy. Then when he realized that no one had escaped, he seems to have been overwhelmed with a sense that what he was witnessing was not a natural occurrence. There was something or someone divine at work. Perhaps the jailer realized that he needed to know more about the message Paul and Silas had been preaching. "Sirs, what must I do to be saved?" he asked (Acts 16:30). He could not have asked a more important question!

In our text for today from Romans 10, Paul says that the "righteousness which is of faith" does not ask questions such as "Who shall ascend into heaven?" to bring Christ down, or "Who shall descend into the deep?" to bring Christ from the dead (vv. 6, 7). It is not by any mighty deeds of ours that we become right with God. It is only by the "mighty deeds" of Christ's death and resurrection that we are saved. It is not our place to suggest what we should do to be saved; it is our place to follow the plan established by God. The jailer's question revealed a searching mind. Paul and Silas were happy to provide the answer, and later the jailer and his household were baptized (Acts 16:31-34).

B. Lesson Background

In last week's study from Romans 8, we considered the ongoing battle that Christians face between the flesh and the Holy Spirit, who enables us to overcome the flesh. Paul reminded us that the law plays a prominent part in our sin problem, in that the law points out our sins and makes them abundantly clear. The law, however, offers no solution to the guilt it creates. That solution is found only in Christ.

In the rest of chapter 8 (not covered last week), Paul continues to focus on the blessings provided through our relationship with Christ. He especially highlights the assurance of final and complete victory over the fallen sinful world, proclaiming that we are "more than conquerors through him that loved us" (Romans 8:37).

In chapter 9 Paul introduces a new theme in his letter—the place of the Jews in God's redemptive plan. His discussion springs from his personal passion for his people (he calls the Jews his "brethren" and his "kinsmen according to the flesh" in verse 3) and his desire that they know the Christ who has done so much for him (Romans 9:1-5). That concern continues in chapter 10, which begins with Paul writing, "Brethren, my heart's desire and prayer to God for Israel is, that they might be saved" (v. 1). The apostle describes them as zealous, yet lacking knowledge.

Their desire to follow the law of Moses and thus pursue "their own righteousness" (v. 3) is ill-founded, now that "Christ is the end of the law for righteousness to every one that believeth" (v. 4). A new way, the way of salvation by grace through faith, is now open for all to accept, but, sadly, many of Paul's "kinsmen according to the flesh" have rejected it.

Paul proceeds to contrast the righteousness based on keeping the law with the righteousness available through faith. He shows that the way of faith in Christ is the way by which both Jew and Gentile must come to God. He also challenges Christians to accept the responsibility for making that message known so that others may call on the name of the Lord and be saved.

I. Keeping the Law
(Romans 10:5-7)

A. Moses' Words on Law (v. 5)

5. For Moses describeth the righteousness which is of the law, That the man which doeth those things shall live by them.

There are only two potential ways to obtain *righteousness*, or a right standing with God: law-keeping and grace through faith. *Moses* is recognized as Israel's lawgiver. So it is fitting to cite him as an authority on law-keeping.

The passage Paul quotes is from Leviticus 18:5: *the man which doeth those things shall live by them*. In other words, with the principle of righteousness by law-keeping the responsibility is squarely on our shoulders. If one should obey every aspect of the law, then he or she would be right with God. But that *if* is huge! In fact, Paul has shown earlier that no one can be justified through keeping the law (Romans 3:20).

B. Moses' Words on Faith (vv. 6, 7)

6, 7. But the righteousness which is of faith speaketh on this wise, Say not in thine heart, Who shall ascend into heaven? (that is, to bring Christ down from above:) or, Who shall descend into the deep? (that is, to bring up Christ again from the dead.)

Now Paul describes *the righteousness which is of faith*. In so doing he quotes from Deuteronomy 30:12-14 (which is included in verses 6-8 of our text). He pictures someone trying to *ascend into heaven* in order to *bring Christ down from above* or making an attempt to *descend into the deep* in order to *bring up Christ . . . from the dead*. It should be noted that Paul's citation varies somewhat from the words in Deuteronomy, which speak of going "beyond the sea" rather than *into the deep* to bring someone back from the dead. Paul should be seen as giving an inspired inter-pretation of Moses' words and applying them to a New Covenant setting. His desire is to show that the righteousness obtained by faith is not based on our deeds. Even if we could perform heroic deeds such as those described in these verses, that would not be enough to gain right standing with God.

Some Bible commentators have noted the significance of Paul's use of the book of Deuteronomy to make his case for righteousness by faith. Moses spoke the words of Deuteronomy when the Israelites were on the brink of entering the promised land. He wanted to impress upon the people the covenant that God had made with them. Here in Romans, Paul desires to impress upon his Jewish readers the New Covenant that God has established. Just as God brought His word to Israel through Moses (see Deuteronomy 30:11-14), God now has brought His living Word through Jesus Christ, whom Paul has already declared to be "the end of the law" (Romans 10:4).

Thus it is not by human good works or devoted efforts that righteousness with God is obtained. Salvation is not the result of our perfection or hard work. Salvation is the result of Christ's perfection and God's work through Him on our behalf. Indeed, we do not have to bring *Christ down;* He has already come. Nor do we have to bring Him *up* from the grave; God has done that (Romans 8:11).

II. Living by Faith
(Romans 10:8-13)

A. An Affirming Faith (vv. 8-10)

8. But what saith it? The word is nigh thee, even in thy mouth, and in thy heart: that is, the word of faith, which we preach.

Here is the difference between the way of law keeping (works) and the way of *faith*. We do not have to travel to a distant realm and accomplish daring feats in order to impress God. *The word is nigh thee, even in thy mouth, and in thy heart*. The message is close to us and ready to be accepted—if we respond in faith. Salvation is not a matter of trying through our own efforts to reach God; it is accepting God's love that is offered to us. Righteousness is received, not achieved.

How to Say It

ANTIOCH. *An*-tee-ock.
BARNABAS. *Barn*-uh-bus.
DAMASCUS. Duh-*mass*-cuss.
DEUTERONOMY. Due-ter-*ahn*-uh-me.
ISAIAH. Eye-*zay*-uh.
PHILIPPI. Fuh-*lip*-pie or *Fill*-uh-pie.

9. That if thou shalt confess with thy mouth the Lord Jesus, and shalt believe in thine heart that God hath raised him from the dead, thou shalt be saved.

This verse calls to mind what Jesus said about the importance of confessing Him before others (Matthew 10:32, 33). On the basis of this emphasis, many churches ask those who desire to accept Christ to express a "confession" of *Jesus as Lord*. In some cases, a person is asked to repeat a statement of faith in Jesus; in others, people are asked to express their faith in their own words. It should be noted that the declaration "Jesus is Lord" was a pivotal part of Christian confession and belief early in the history of the church.

Notice the requirement of both an external response (confessing the Lord Jesus) and an internal one (believing in one's *heart*). These should not be considered works to earn righteousness, but expressions of faith that accept the righteousness God is eager to give. [See question #1, page 280.]

Consider also that Paul is addressing Christians who are living in a pagan context. It isn't always easy to confess Christ in such a setting, is it? Today we are living in an increasingly pagan environment. The number of opportunities to "confess" our faith in Christ are many; are we using them as we should?

10. For with the heart man believeth unto righteousness; and with the mouth confession is made unto salvation.

A verse such as this one should not be considered to be the entirety of God's plan of *salvation* to receive His *righteousness*. The lesson from two weeks ago examined Paul's teaching about baptism in Romans 6. And just because this verse says nothing about repentance does not mean that Paul considers it insignificant or unnecessary. In the context of Romans 10, Paul has been focusing in particular on the *heart* and the *mouth* (mentioned in verses 6-8 in the reference from Deuteronomy). He wants to show that becoming right with God does not require the kind of efforts described in verses 6 and 7; it requires simple obedient faith.

Both believing and confessing are meant to be more than one-time actions associated with becoming a Christian. Faith in Jesus and confession of Him as Lord must become the hallmarks of a Christ-centered life. [See question #2, page 280.] While living a godly life is crucial, we must also be able to put our faith into words.

TWO KINDS OF CONFESSION

During the aftermath of the corporate financial scandals of the late 1990s, many corporate executives were convicted of their crimes; but few of the guilty actually confessed to having done any wrong. One of the companies that had illegally "cooked" their books was Peregrine Systems, a San Diego software company. Months after the investigations began, the Chief Financial Officer (CFO) of the company finally admitted in court that he had conspired with others in the firm to deceive investors into thinking the company was strong and growing when it actually was doing much worse.

The CFO confessed to having signed nine quarterly reports and two annual reports that he knew to contain "materially false statements and omissions." He also implicated the company's outside accounting firm, saying it had encouraged unethical accounting practices. So while the CFO was selling his stock for four million dollars, the company was collapsing, costing shareholders more than *two billion dollars!* By admitting his guilt, the man was able to decrease significantly his time served in prison.

How different our confession of Christ is! Of course, there must be an admission of guilt for our sins. We can't get around that! But our confession is also meant to be part of a daily lifestyle demonstrating to the world the fact that Christ has rescued us from sin and its eternal consequences.
—C. R. B.

B. An Available Faith (vv. 11-13)

11. For the Scripture saith, Whosoever believeth on him shall not be ashamed.

Paul cites another Old Testament passage—Isaiah 28:16 in this instance. It reinforces the point he made earlier in Romans 10:4, that "Christ is the end of the law for righteousness to every one that *believeth*."

12. For there is no difference between the Jew and the Greek: for the same Lord over all is rich unto all that call upon him.

Jews and Gentiles enter into God's promise on the same basis—through faith in Christ. That is the only way! *There is no difference!* Paul's language is reminiscent of what he stated earlier about the sin problem that Jews and Gentiles have in common. "There is no difference: for all have sinned, and come short of the glory of God" (Romans 3:22, 23). What a refreshing change from bad news to good news! *The same Lord* whose righteous standard we have failed to meet offers His riches to *all that call upon him.*

13. For whosoever shall call upon the name of the Lord shall be saved.

Whosoever! It's the same promise found in the Bible's "Golden Text"—John 3:16. But note the condition: each must *call upon the name of the Lord*—on the name of Jesus. This is another example of Paul's use of the Old Testament; he cites Joel 2:32, as Peter did on the Day of Pentecost when preaching the first gospel sermon (Acts 2:21).

Again, we should mention the importance of taking all that the Scriptures say about what is necessary to be *saved*. "Calling" on the Lord is in line with Paul's emphasis in this passage on the need to "confess with thy mouth the Lord Jesus" in order to be saved (vv. 9, 10).

We should also add that when Jesus returns, everyone will pay homage to Him and call on His name (Philippians 2:10, 11); but those who wait until that time will have waited too long. If we do not call on His name voluntarily now, we will be forced to do so at His return.

III. Spreading the Faith
(Romans 10:14-17)

A. Helping People Call (v. 14)

14. How then shall they call on him in whom they have not believed? and how shall they believe in him of whom they have not heard? and how shall they hear without a preacher?

Paul follows his statement of the responsibility of all people to call on the Lord with a challenge to those who have called on Him and are saved to do all they can so that others will know of that responsibility. *How* will people be made aware of whom they need to call on to be saved? How will they know how to accept God's gracious gift of salvation?

Calling on the name of the Lord and receiving God's salvation only happens when one believes. And one can't *believe* until he or she has *heard*. And one can't hear unless there is someone—a *preacher*—who is willing to tell the story.

God has chosen to use human instruments to convey His message of salvation. Paul himself, although addressed by Jesus on the road to Damascus, did not hear the gospel from Jesus. Instead, Jesus told him to "go into the city, and it shall be told thee what thou must do" (Acts 9:6). Paul was instructed by another human being. And so it is today; we are God's instruments to make known His grace to others.

The Greek word translated *preacher* describes a herald or an announcer who runs ahead of a king and proclaims what the king wishes others to know. Certainly the task of preaching can be done by any Christian who tells the good news to someone else. At the same time, there must be those who will give their lives to preaching and teaching in the setting of the local church. The church always has needed those willing to answer such a calling. And those who are ready to do so need to be supported and sent, as the next verse indicates. [See question #3, page 280.]

Visual for lesson 6

BEAUTIFUL

"How beautiful are the feet of them that preach the gospel of peace, and bring glad tidings of good things!"—Romans 10:15

This visual helps highlight the reference to "beautiful feet" in Romans 10:15.

B. Helping Messengers Go (v. 15)

15. And how shall they preach, except they be sent? as it is written, How beautiful are the feet of them that preach the gospel of peace, and bring glad tidings of good things!

Ultimately, Jesus sends us to go and carry His message to the world; we call His words the "Great Commission." But the church also plays a vital part in sending, as illustrated by Barnabas and Saul, who were "sent" by the church in Antioch on their first missionary journey (Acts 13:1-3). Once again, Paul cites an Old Testament reference (Isaiah 52:7) to make his point. In their original context, Isaiah's words described the *glad tidings* of the deliverance of God's people from captivity in Babylon. Paul uses these words to refer to the glad tidings of deliverance from sin through the *gospel of peace*.

Those who bear such good news are pictured as having *beautiful . . . feet*. Usually the heralds who traveled many miles to convey a message arrived at their destination with dusty, dirty feet. The appearance of their feet was anything but beautiful; the beauty was to be found in the contents of the message delivered. Later Paul will describe the Christian's armor as including "feet shod with the preparation of the gospel of peace" (Ephesians 6:15).

CLEAR COMMUNICATION

Autism is a developmental disorder that is found in every country and region of the world. It affects about one or two people in every thousand. A typical autistic trait is the inability to communicate or interact normally with others. Sometimes the person is a "savant"—a person possessing extraordinary abilities with mathematical calculations, for example. More often autism is characterized by repetitive motions such as rocking the body or flailing the limbs, as if the brain were not in control.

A breakthrough in the study of autism occurred just a few years ago when doctors were introduced to Tito, a fourteen-year-old autistic boy from India. He had trouble speaking, but could express himself eloquently in written form. He has said that his constant random movements are a way for his brain to "prove that he exists," by developing an awareness of his connection with his body. Doctors are excited about having Tito's first-person information on autism. For the first time, they can better understand the condition by communicating with an autistic child who can explain his disorder.

With the spiritual "disorder" of sin, our problem is not that the doctor (God) cannot understand us. Rather, it is that we seem unable or unwilling to hear Him! However, the world's sinfulness can be transformed into spiritual wholeness and "order" if we who possess the gospel will send those who can speak, so that those who need Christ can hear and believe.   —C. R. B.

C. Helping Sinners Listen (vv. 16, 17)

16. But they have not all obeyed the gospel. For Isaiah saith, Lord, who hath believed our report?

Here is a harsh reality that can dampen the enthusiasm of confessing, preaching, and sending. Not *all* to whom we tell *the gospel* will receive it gladly. In the context, Paul is lamenting the fact that so many Jews, his "kinsmen according to the flesh," have neither *believed* nor *obeyed* the gospel. Again, the words of *Isaiah* are cited. This verse, from Isaiah 53:1, comes in the context of one of the most powerful messianic prophecies in the Old Testament. [See question #4, page 280.]

Home Daily Bible Readings

Monday, Apr. 4—Christ, the Source of Eternal Salvation (Hebrews 5:5-10)
Tuesday, Apr. 5—On Your Lips, in Your Heart (Romans 10:1-8)
Wednesday, Apr. 6—Christ Is Lord of All (Romans 10:9-13)
Thursday, Apr. 7—Faith Comes Through Christ's Word (Romans 10:14-21)
Friday, Apr. 8—Israel Is Not Lost to Christ (Romans 11:1-6)
Saturday, Apr. 9—Gentiles Also Receive Salvation (Romans 11:13-18)
Sunday, Apr. 10—All Will Be Grafted Together (Romans 11:19-23)

17. So then faith cometh by hearing, and hearing by the word of God.

It is up to the church, the body of Christ, to see that everyone hears about Jesus. That means missionaries, sent and supported. That means teachers, trained and developed within the body. That means preachers, called, prepared, and supported both prayerfully and financially. There are many "parachurch" organizations that can accomplish these important tasks, but the local church remains God's primary appointed vehicle for making it possible for men and women to hear *the word of God.*

Conclusion

A. Not Trying

Religion is not a bad word. James speaks of "pure religion and undefiled before God and the Father" (James 1:27). But when the issue is how to be right with God, the word *religion* may communicate the wrong message—a message that our works can somehow save us. It is not through our efforts that we are saved. You may know someone who is waiting until he or she is living a "better life" before accepting Christ. That may seem like a noble desire. But we do not need to be "better" to be right with God; we need a Savior *now.* To wait until we are more "presentable" to God misses the point of the gospel. God wants us as we are.

As an old gospel song puts it, "Why do you wait, dear brother?"

B. But Trusting

God offers life, salvation, and peace. He has reached out to us. "The word is nigh"—not in a distant realm. We can do everything outlined by Paul in today's text. We can believe. We can confess. We can call on the name of the Lord. God has not made the way difficult. Sometimes people make the way hard because of their own attitudes, and sometimes, sadly, God's own people make it difficult for others because of their inconsistent witness. [See question #5, page 280.]

C. Prayer

Father, use our feet to carry the gospel around the corner or around the world—wherever You would have us go. Use our hands to enable other feet to go. Use our tongues to confess that Jesus Christ is Lord. Help us to speak and live in His name. We pray in His name. Amen.

D. Thought to Remember

"How beautiful are the feet of them that preach the gospel of peace, and bring glad tidings of good things!" (Romans 10:15).

Learning by Doing

This page contains an alternative lesson plan emphasizing learning activities.
Classes desiring such student involvement will find these suggestions helpful.

Learning Goals

After this lesson a student should be able to:

1. Tell what Paul means when he concludes, "So then faith cometh by hearing, and hearing by the word of God."

2. Explain the importance of confessing faith as it relates to one's own salvation and to the salvation of others.

3. Prepare a personal testimony about what it means to be saved.

Into the Lesson

Have a class member ready to repeat (annoyingly) everything you say as you begin. Announce your intention to read a key definition for today's study, and then read aloud the following definition of the word *confess*: "to admit a weakness or mistake; to affirm a view or opinion; to declare a personal faith in; to acknowledge guilt." Hesitate after each phrase to allow your "echo" to chime in. At the end, note that the Greek word for *confess* is *homologeo* (hom-uh-luh-*geh*-o), essentially meaning, "to say the same thing." Thank your learner for his or her help.

Ask the class, "What are some things that absolutely cannot be done unless the doer has certain vital information?" Though learners may identify others, answers may include opening a combination lock without the combination or accessing a person's e-mail without his password. When these items have been noted, say, "Without certain information about God's character and will, no one can be saved. In today's text from Romans 10, Paul declares some of those truths foundational for salvation."

Into the Word

Give students a copy of the following statements. Ask them to write in the verse number most closely related to each idea, using the numbers 5 through 17 from today's text in Romans 10. Each number is to be used once. (1) Believing is not quite enough. (2) Certain truths never bring shame. (3) Each good deed I do is another rung up the ladder to Heaven. (4) Even the best news is not always well received. (5) Faith is intrinsically tied to facts. (6) Foot models are relatively anonymous, but they show something most people value. (7) My physical heritage means nothing to God. (8) If I could just never do anything wrong, life would be good. (9) It's right

on the tip of my tongue! (10) Knowing where a person goes after death would help me trust God. (11) Rhetorical questions do not make good test questions. (12) Some names have even more value than their etymology implies. (13) When it's in my heart, I will talk about it.

Though learners may be able to justify other choices, here are the choices intended here: 1—v. 9; 2—v. 11; 3—v. 6; 4—v. 16; 5—v. 17; 6—v. 15; 7—v. 12; 8—v. 5; 9—v. 8; 10—v. 7; 11—v. 14; 12—v. 13; 13—v. 10. (This activity is included in the student book.) After learners have time to examine the text and respond, read the text a verse at a time and ask learners to identify what they have chosen for the "matching" idea. When differences occur, ask for an explanation.

Note that in Romans 10:14, 15, Paul uses a series of rhetorical questions ("How shall . . . ?") to show the need for the presentation of the gospel. Put these letters on display: A C E H N T T Y. Ask the group to identify two words that answer Paul's rhetorical questions. (The words are *They can't.*) Say, "Certain truths are obvious, and this is one: 'Unless we act to see that the gospel is preached and taught, no one can be saved!'"

Into Life

Prepare two sets of peel-and-stick lapel labels with the following statements printed on them: *Set one:* "I Confess!"; *Set two:* "I Have Pretty Feet!" Let each learner choose the one he or she wants. Suggest that learners wear their label one day during the coming week as a possible stimulus toward sharing a basic gospel truth with someone who inquires as to the tag's significance. Those who choose to do so will need a short, non-threatening response. As a group, develop such a statement for each label. For example, for the former, "I confess that Jesus is Lord over all, and He is rich to all who call upon Him." For the latter, "Peacemakers always come on beautiful feet. I want mine to carry a word about peace with God in Christ."

To conclude, have a world map displayed where all can see it. Ask learners to identify some of the Christian peacemakers who are taking the gospel to various locations around the world. Write each name on a self-stick note and apply in the approximate location. Then ask for class members to volunteer to pray and thank God for these "beautiful feet" people.

Let's Talk It Over

The questions on this page are designed to promote discussion of the lesson by the class and to encourage application of the lesson Scriptures. The answers provided are only discussion starters. Let your class talk it over from there.

1. If salvation is primarily an issue of a penitent and believing heart, then why even bother with a physical act such as an audible confession? Why not just confess within our hearts "Jesus is Lord" and let it go at that?

Before we downplay the importance of physical acts with regard to salvation, we should remember that the cross itself was a physical act. Surely no Christian thinks that that event was unimportant because it was "physical"! The crucifixion was an event witnessed by many and proclaimed through the centuries. Our own audible confession shows others that we agree with the need for the cross of Christ. With our audible confession we help fulfill the Great Commission (Matthew 28:19, 20).

Don't forget: when Jesus returns, that will be a physical event as well!

2. What are some ways that we can make belief and confession "the hallmarks of a Christ-centered life," as the lesson writer suggests? What will be the result if our belief and confession don't match our lifestyles?

Answers will be highly individual, and it's important to be specific. Don't let your learners get away with "glittering generalities" such as "be more loving."

One conclusion will apply to everyone: if we're talking one way but living another way, people will know! The result will be a ruined witness for Christ. Even if we're able to hide our inconsistencies from other people for a time, God still has perfect and exhaustive knowledge of our hearts. We may well find ourselves under the condemnation that we are "beautiful on the outside" but "full of hypocrisy and wickedness" on the inside (Matthew 23:27).

3. How can we encourage more preachers to come from our churches? What qualifies someone to become a preacher?

Churches who hold their own preachers in high regard tend to send more "Timothys" out than those lacking respect for their preachers. In Romans 10:15, Paul quotes Isaiah 52:7 as a tribute to those who "preach the gospel of peace." We must constantly encourage our young men to consider the call to the ministry through such means as youth groups and Christian service

camps. At the same time, we should also acknowledge that "preaching" (in the sense of proclaiming good news) is not something reserved for a few specially trained individuals. Any Christian has "glad tidings" to convey. In that sense, we are all called to be preachers, and all our congregations have unique opportunities to bear witness of Christ.

4. Why are people so resistant to the gospel? And why are we as Christians so often afraid to share the gospel?

Resistance can arise because of many factors. Some enjoy the "pleasures of sin." Others hold tightly to false doctrines or false religions. Still others regard Christians as hypocrites, or they see the failures of supposedly "faithful" Christians as a testimony against the faith. Too often, though, the resistance to sharing the gospel is at least as great as the resistance to hearing it. In many cases, our resistance to sharing may be traced to fear—fear of rejection, fear of failure, or fear that a question may be raised for which we have no answer. We need to remind ourselves constantly that someone at some point told us the good news about Jesus. Is it right for us to keep that news to ourselves?

5. Is there a distinction between religion and Christianity? If so, what is it? Do we want to be "religious" people? Why, or why not?

Our commentary writer distinguishes between religion and Christianity with the words "trying" and "trusting." Religion is a set of rules that, if we abide by them, compel God to act in a certain way. God then becomes dependent on our behavior, following our lead instead of acting according to His own character and righteousness.

Christianity, however, is a relationship based on faith. We obey, but not because our obedience somehow forces God to accept us. Rather, we obey because we can rely on God's faithfulness to His word and His promise. It is not our obedience that determines God's actions. It is God's faithfulness to Himself first and then to us that prompts our obedience. If we seek to be known as "religious," then our religion should be seen as a response to God's grace in Christ. James 1:27 uses the word *religion* of certain good works that should characterize a Christian.

Display the Marks of a Christian

DEVOTIONAL READING: **Romans 12:3-8.**

BACKGROUND SCRIPTURE: **Romans 12:1-21.**

PRINTED TEXT: **Romans 12:1, 2, 9-21.**

Romans 12:1, 2, 9-21

1 I beseech you therefore, brethren, by the mercies of God, that ye present your bodies a living sacrifice, holy, acceptable unto God, which is your reasonable service.

2 And be not conformed to this world: but be ye transformed by the renewing of your mind, that ye may prove what is that good, and acceptable, and perfect will of God.

· · · · · · · · · · · · · ·

9 Let love be without dissimulation. Abhor that which is evil; cleave to that which is good.

10 Be kindly affectioned one to another with brotherly love; in honor preferring one another;

11 Not slothful in business; fervent in spirit; serving the Lord;

12 Rejoicing in hope; patient in tribulation; continuing instant in prayer;

13 Distributing to the necessity of saints; given to hospitality.

14 Bless them which persecute you: bless, and curse not.

15 Rejoice with them that do rejoice, and weep with them that weep.

16 Be of the same mind one toward another. Mind not high things, but condescend to men of low estate. Be not wise in your own conceits.

17 Recompense to no man evil for evil. Provide things honest in the sight of all men.

18 If it be possible, as much as lieth in you, live peaceably with all men.

19 Dearly beloved, avenge not yourselves, but rather give place unto wrath: for it is written, Vengeance is mine; I will repay, saith the Lord.

20 Therefore if thine enemy hunger, feed him; if he thirst, give him drink: for in so doing thou shalt heap coals of fire on his head.

21 Be not overcome of evil, but overcome evil with good.

GOLDEN TEXT: Let love be without dissimulation. Abhor that which is evil; cleave to that which is good. Be kindly affectioned one to another with brotherly love; in honor preferring one another.—Romans 12:9, 10.

God's Project: Effective Christians
Unit 2: The Christian Life
(Lessons 5-8)

Lesson Aims

After this lesson a student should be able to:

1. List several actions that characterize those who are "living sacrifices."

2. Suggest some ways these behaviors can have a positive impact on the community in which he or she lives.

3. Identify one of these behaviors that is particularly challenging, and express a resolve to make it more typical in his or her life.

Lesson Outline

Introduction

A. Positive Christians in a Negative World

There are two ways of looking at the sin-tainted world around us. The first sees people's hatred and disregard toward others and despairs.

"It's no use. Why try to make any difference? Just look out for yourself and don't bother anyone else." The second sees the same needs and the same failures, but thinks of the possibilities for improvement and the divine resources behind them. "Yes, sin abounds; but grace abounds more. Yes, sin may win some occasional battles, but God's righteousness will win the war."

Too many Christians have bought into the idea that serious faith fosters an outlook of worry, gloom, and doom. One is reminded of the story of two men who met along the street. "Say," said one to the other, "aren't you a minister?" "No," said the other man, "I've just been sick a lot recently."

As Christians we should live out the hope we have found in Christ and do so with a joy that will cause others to crave what they see in us.

B. Lesson Background

Last week's study came from Romans 10, where Paul contrasts a "works" approach to being right with God with a "faith" approach. This teaching is found within a larger portion of Romans (chapters 9-11), where Paul considers the place of the Jews in God's plan of redemption. Paul concludes chapter 11 with a doxology praising God for the "depth of the riches both of [His] wisdom and knowledge" (v. 33).

Today's lesson is taken from Romans 12. This chapter begins a new direction in Paul's train of thought. Chapters 1-11 have been primarily doctrinal in their focus. With chapter 12 the apostle begins to examine some of the practical issues that relate to living for Christ in both the church and the world—among Christians and non-Christians. However, this "new" section is very clearly linked with what has preceded through Paul's use of the word *therefore* in verse 1. Paul's purpose in doing this should be clear: doctrine is practical as well as theological. What we believe must affect how we live. If it doesn't, then the world has every right to question the value of what we believe. For if our faith in Christ is making no real difference in our lives, why should others embrace it?

I. Reason for Goodness
(Romans 12:1, 2)

A. God's Mercy (v. 1)

1. I beseech you therefore, brethren, by the mercies of God, that ye present your bodies a living sacrifice, holy, acceptable unto God, which is your reasonable service.

Apparently some of those in the church in Rome had not fully grasped the necessity of combining Christian faith with godly living. Perhaps their pagan background made it especially challenging to sever ties with the past and die to sin (Romans 6:2). Here Paul encourages Christians to understand that it is our *reasonable service* to live in this manner.

Why is this lifestyle *reasonable?* Paul says *by*, or because of, *the mercies of God*. The word *therefore* links this phrase to what Paul has written previously—not only in the immediately preceding verses, but also in the entire epistle to this point. Everything that Paul has discussed in the letter thus far, particularly concerning God's grace as demonstrated in Jesus Christ, could be summarized by *the mercies of God*. God in mercy gave His only begotten Son to die as a sacrifice to cover our sins. Therefore, it is perfectly reasonable for us to live *holy* lives in service to One who provided such a sacrifice. The concept of a *living sacrifice* contrasts the Christian's sacrifice with the slain sacrifices of the Old Testament system.

It should be noted that the phrase *reasonable service* is subject to other interpretations, because Paul uses certain Greek words that have what may be termed a "double meaning." The word *reasonable* can also mean "spiritual," which may call attention to the true nature of worship (cf. John 4:24). *Service* can also be translated as "worship." The thought of this idea would be to emphasize that worship is not something that is meant to occur on Sundays only but on a daily basis through the holy lives we lead.

To be *holy* means to be "set apart." We are not to do this physically, which would make it impossible for us to have any impact on others, but spiritually. If we set apart our lives to God in this way, our sacrifices will be *acceptable* and enthusiastically received. [See question #1, page 288.]

"GLORY" AT WHAT PRICE?

Steve Fossett was dropping toward the inky South Pacific at thirty-five hundred feet per minute. A violent, nighttime storm had ripped open his balloon's skin, and most of the burners that heated air to keep the ship aloft had blown out. Fossett was certain he would die in his fourth unsuccessful attempt to fly around the world alone; this time he was *really* going to fail!

At one point, something knocked Fossett unconscious. When he came to, the balloon's capsule was upside down in the ocean, more than five hundred miles from land. Fossett managed to get his life raft free and swim with it to the surface where, twenty-one hours later, he was rescued by a sailboat.

Fossett made one more unsuccessful attempt to be the first person to attain his goal, and the five tries cost him six million dollars! But instead of accepting numerous failures, his thinking was renewed by the noble goal ahead of him. Finally, on July 2, 2002, Steve Fossett entered the record books as his *sixth* solo attempt to circumnavigate the globe in a hot-air balloon succeeded!

As Christians, we seek a different kind of glory from what Steve Fossett sought; and we make a different kind of sacrifice to attain it. He almost sacrificed his life to find fame; we are called upon to turn our bodies into *living* sacrifices to find eternal life in the glory of the perfect will of God. Ours is the better way, by far.

—C. R. B.

B. Renewed Mind (v. 2)

2. And be not conformed to this world: but be ye transformed by the renewing of your mind, that ye may prove what is that good, and acceptable, and perfect will of God.

Some are familiar with how the first part of this verse reads in J. B. Phillips' translation: "Don't let the world around you squeeze you into its own mold." Most parents have had to confront a child about some wrongdoing, only to hear the reply, "But everyone is doing it!" (That is usually a better reason *not* to do something!) Yet even adults can wrestle with "peer pressure." [See question #2, page 288.]

Conformed or *transformed?* That is the question Paul challenges us to ask. To be transformed must start from the inside out, or as Paul says, *by the renewing of your mind*. Wicked thoughts precede wicked deeds (Matthew 15:18-20); godly thoughts produce godly deeds. When our minds are renewed, we are ready to practice those *good, and acceptable, and perfect* qualities that Paul will mention later in this chapter.

The renewing Paul describes is part of the "newness of life" that we receive in Christ (Romans 6:4; Colossians 3:10). It cannot occur through our own efforts. "Self-help" is out of the question in this area!

II. Showing Goodness to God's People (Romans 12:9-13)

A. Loving (v. 9)

9. Let love be without dissimulation. Abhor that which is evil; cleave to that which is good.

In the remainder of Romans 12, Paul elaborates on what being a living sacrifice entails. In the portion of the chapter not included in our

---

How to Say It

DISSIMULATION. dis-sim-you-*lay*-shun.
ISAIAH. Eye-*zay*-uh.

printed text (verses 3-8), Paul highlights the importance of using our various gifts in the Lord's service. Verse 9 begins a section of short, specific commands concerning the attitudes and actions that should characterize every Christian.

Love is the starting point. This is in keeping with what Paul writes elsewhere in his epistles, most notably in 1 Corinthians 13. Jesus pointed out that love is the essence of the Old Testament law (Mark 12:28-34). Love is also the central feature of the New Covenant era (John 13:31-35). This kind love can be defined as "wanting the best for another"; and, although feelings are a part of it, it is primarily a matter of the will. Note that when Paul describes the fruit of the Spirit in a Christian's life, he starts with love (Galatians 5:22).

Paul states that love must be *without dissimulation*. This means that love must be genuine, without hypocrisy. [See question #3, page 288.]

In addition, Paul tells us to *abhor*, or hate, what is *evil* and to *cleave to that which is good*. There is room for hatred in the Christian life, but it is not a hatred of people. This describes a loathing of sin and a sense of disgust at the destruction that it causes both in individual lives and in the fabric of society.

B. Honoring (v. 10)

10. Be kindly affectioned one to another with brotherly love; in honor preferring one another.

These words describe a code of conduct that is far removed from the "me first" mentality of the modern world. They include the words *one to another* and *one another*—words found in other New Testament passages that remind us that we do not live the Christian life in a vacuum.

C. Serving (v. 11)

11. Not slothful in business; fervent in spirit; serving the Lord.

The Greek word translated *business* does not refer to a secular job or profession; it describes the zeal one should have for *serving the Lord*. Thus it is similar in meaning to the phrase *fervent in spirit*. Our fire can burn even through difficult times, because it is fed by the presence of the Holy Spirit.

D. Rejoicing (v. 12)

12. Rejoicing in hope; patient in tribulation; continuing instant in prayer.

We noted in Lesson 3 that Biblical *hope* does not have any "maybe" in it. It is confident assurance. It rests in God's promises through Christ. Those who possess it have every reason to rejoice, because they know that in the end, Christ and Christ's people will triumph. So we can be

patient in tribulation, calm in the face of any storm.

The last phrase in this verse describes a key ingredient to developing the attitudes and actions found in this verse and in this passage: think of an open line to the Father! A life that is *continuing instant in prayer*, or that prays without ceasing (1 Thessalonians 5:17)! A mind-set that is ready for prayer at any time! [See question #4, page 288.]

E. Sharing (v. 13)

13. Distributing to the necessity of saints; given to hospitality.

Just as God makes the sun to shine and the rain to fall on the just and the unjust (Matthew 5:45), His children are called to assist many individuals who have needs. But Scripture emphasizes our singular responsibility for our brothers and sisters in Christ. Paul writes, "As we have therefore opportunity, let us do good unto all men, especially unto them who are of the household of faith" (Galatians 6:10).

Hospitality is one of the characteristics of those who serve as elders (also called bishops, 1 Timothy 3:2). But it should also be a trademark of all Christians. Those in God's family should be able to count on one another for food, shelter, security, and friendship in times of need.

YOU MEAN IT'S NOT ABOUT ME?

A California woman was surfing the Internet when she "met" a man in North Carolina. She decided to meet him in person—in hopes of marrying him, she later admitted—so she traveled to North Carolina to do so. Perhaps that would have been nobody else's business, except that she left behind, uncared for and alone, her two children, ages four and seven. She left frozen food in the refrigerator and told them to hide if anyone came to the apartment. After she had been gone for three weeks, a neighbor heard the children crying and notified the police. When the mother returned home, she told authorities that the relationship with her newfound fiancé had foundered. They informed her that she was facing criminal charges of child abandonment.

This woman's story is an illustration of a serious ailment in modern culture: the selfish tendency to think, "It's all about me." We can forgive this in small children, since they haven't developed the mental or emotional maturity to know differently. But as our children grow, a part of the socializing (or we could say civilizing) process that we engage in is to help them mature into adults who care for someone other than themselves. And, as Paul says, true *Christian* maturity is demonstrated when we think of the needs of others ahead of our own. Christians learn from the example of Christ and His selfless spirit that life is about others, and not "all about me." —C. R. B.

III. Showing Goodness to the World (Romans 12:14-19)

A. Acting, Not Reacting (v. 14)

14. Bless them which persecute you: bless, and curse not.

Now we come to the more challenging part of Paul's exhortations—the ones requiring a higher measure of Christian maturity. It's one thing to help the "saints" (v. 13); it's quite another to show kindness to those who are "unsaintly." Yet, as Jesus pointed out in the Sermon on the Mount, if we love only those who love us, how are we any different from the pagans (Matthew 5:46, 47)?

In this area, as in others, the master teacher guides us not only by His words, but also by His example. The prophet Isaiah spoke of His behavior during His so-called "trial": "He was oppressed, and he was afflicted, yet he opened not his mouth: he is brought as a lamb to the slaughter, and as a sheep before her shearers is dumb, so he openeth not his mouth" (Isaiah 53:7). Instead of cursing His accusers and tormentors, He prayed for them: "Father, forgive them; for they know not what they do" (Luke 23:34).

B. Empathizing (v. 15)

15. Rejoice with them that do rejoice, and weep with them that weep.

Notice the word *empathizing* in the heading of this section of the lesson. "Empathy" goes much deeper than sympathy. While sympathy describes a compassion or "suffering with" another, empathy is the ability to experience the feelings and emotions of another. Generally speaking, it is easier to *weep with* those who *weep* than it is to *rejoice with* those who *rejoice*. Most of us can offer examples of weeping with those who have gone through situations such as a critical illness, a death in the family, a job loss, or some other crisis. (Or we can recall times when others have wept with us.) Sometimes sitting and weeping with another Christian, without words, speaks volumes of love.

On the other hand, when someone else receives a promotion that we thought we had earned or is able to purchase a special possession that we had hoped for, it can be a bit harder to rejoice at that person's success. In truth, however, both the hardships and the blessings that others experience can be a gauge of whether we have learned to be Christlike in our attitudes. [See question #5, page 288.]

DISPLAY THE MARKS OF A CHRISTIAN

Be sincere • Hate what is evil • Cling to good • Be devoted to one another • Honor one another above yourself • Keep your spiritual fervor • Be joyful in hope • Be patient in affliction • Be faithful in prayer • Share with God's people who are in need • Practice hospitality • Bless those who persecute you • Rejoice with those who rejoice • Mourn with those who mourn

Live in harmony with one another • Do what is right in the eyes of everybody • Live at peace with everyone • Do not lack in zeal • Do not curse • Do not be proud • Associate with people of low position • Do not be conceited • Do not repay anyone evil for evil • Do not take revenge • Leave room for God's wrath • Do not be overcome by evil, but overcome evil with good

—taken from Romans 12:9-21

Visual for lesson 7. *This visual calls attention to the dos and don'ts that constitute the "marks of a Christian" as found in Romans 12.*

C. Showing No Favoritism (v. 16)

16. Be of the same mind one toward another. Mind not high things, but condescend to men of low estate. Be not wise in your own conceits.

James challenges our tendency, even in the church, to treat the well-to-do with more respect than we treat the "have-nots" who enter our facilities. He pictures saying, "Sit thou here in a good place" to a rich man, and, "Stand thou there, or sit here under my footstool" to a poor man in shabby clothing (James 2:3). That is hardly an example of being *of the same mind one toward another*. To treat others in the body of Christ as equals—despite clothes, checkbooks, education, or heritage—is to treat them the way the head of the church would. One of the most compelling descriptions of Jesus' ministry is this: "The common people heard him gladly" (Mark 12:37).

The word *condescend* sometimes has negative connotations in modern usage. Here it simply means "to be at home among" or "to feel comfortable around" those *of low estate*. We should not be ashamed to be seen with such individuals, nor should we worry about what others will think of us. Jesus' opinion is the only one that matters.

D. Promoting Peace (vv. 17-19)

17. Recompense to no man evil for evil. Provide things honest in the sight of all men.

This reinforces some of Paul's earlier teaching. Revenge and dishonesty are never acceptable for the Christian. Paul's emphasis on *no man* and *all men* show that his words apply to our conduct in the world as well as in the church.

18. If it be possible, as much as lieth in you, live peaceably with all men.

Here, too, is a challenge concerning *all men*—not just fellow Christians. It is important that we wage peace, not war, even among those who are not peaceful themselves. At the same time, Paul realizes that peace does not lie completely with us and that some will resist our well-intentioned efforts. "Do all that you can," he says.

19. Dearly beloved, avenge not yourselves, but rather give place unto wrath: for it is written, Vengeance is mine; I will repay, saith the Lord.

Concerning those individuals who remain stubbornly hostile to our initiatives on behalf of peace, or who oppose us in any way, Paul tells us to *avenge not* ourselves. *Give place unto wrath* literally reads in the Greek text, "Give place to the wrath." The remainder of the verse makes it clear that we should give proper place to the wrath of God, allowing Him to render judgment in His own way and in His own time. Paul is saying, "Don't let your anger lead you to take upon yourself something that is God's prerogative. You are not God. He will take care of administering *vengeance*." The Old Testament reference cited is from Deuteronomy 32:35. [See question #6, page 288.]

IV. Showing Goodness to an Enemy (Romans 12:20, 21)

A. Person (v. 20)

20. Therefore if thine enemy hunger, feed him; if he thirst, give him drink: for in so doing thou shalt heap coals of fire on his head.

It is one thing to offer food and *drink* to brothers and sisters in Christ. Here Paul describes the "second mile" attitude that should characterize those who walk with Jesus. We should be prepared to help even an *enemy*.

Home Daily Bible Readings

Monday, Apr. 11—Instructions for Living (Colossians 4:2-6)

Tuesday, Apr. 12—Live a Life Pleasing to God (1 Thessalonians 4:1-12)

Wednesday, Apr. 13—Hold Fast to What Is Good (1 Thessalonians 5:12-22)

Thursday, Apr. 14—Do What Is Right (2 Thessalonians 3:6-13)

Friday, Apr. 15—Members One of Another (Romans 12:1-5)

Saturday, Apr. 16—Marks of the True Christian (Romans 12:6-13)

Sunday, Apr. 17—Overcome Evil with Good (Romans 12:14-21)

The meaning of heaping coals of fire on someone's head has been subject to much discussion. The reference itself is found in Proverbs 25:21, 22. One suggestion is that it pictures the sense of shame or remorse that "burns" within a person when treated with kindness by someone whom the person deliberately tried to hurt in some way. Possibly such a gesture of kindness will serve as a witness to the person of the difference our faith in Christ has made in our lives.

B. Principle (v. 21)

21. Be not overcome of evil, but overcome evil with good.

Simply put, the world should not be influencing the Christian; the Christian should be influencing the world. As noted in the introductory material to today's lesson, Christians should seek to be a positive force in a negative world. They should take the initiative on behalf of what is *good* and "act, not react."

Conclusion

A. Reasonable and Spiritual

Even the most challenging among Paul's exhortations in today's text (such as the positive treatment of people outside the circle of the church, and even of enemies) are not unreasonable. But we cannot carry them out without looking to Jesus. In many instances, we can read examples in the Gospels of Jesus doing just what Paul tells Christians to do. We must also remember that we experienced Jesus' patience with us when we were acting as His enemies. We continue to experience His patience whenever remnants of our old life disturb our relationship with Him and we need forgiveness.

As Paul tells us in Romans 12:1, to offer our bodies as a living sacrifice, holy and acceptable to God, is our reasonable service. What could be more reasonable than a practical Christianity that touches my hands, my heart, my tongue, my feet, my attitude, and my acts of generosity—even toward enemies?

B. Prayer

To be like Jesus, our blessed Redeemer! That is our earnest prayer, dear Father. We ask that You will guide us in making Jesus' way of living a more consistent and visible part of our lives. Grant us wisdom to take the initiative more in demonstrating Jesus' way to others, and when we do so help us to maintain a servant's heart. In Jesus' name we pray. Amen.

C. Thought to Remember

Don't be conformed; be transformed.

Learning by Doing

This page contains an alternative lesson plan emphasizing learning activities.
Classes desiring such student involvement will find these suggestions helpful.

Learning Goals

After this lesson a student should be able to:

1. List several actions that characterize those who are "living sacrifices."

2. Suggest some ways these behaviors can have a positive impact on the community in which he or she lives.

3. Identify one of these behaviors that is particularly challenging, and express a resolve to make it more typical in his or her life.

Into the Lesson

Near the entrance to your classroom, display a large sheet of paper with a drawing of a large tin can. Beside the can, draw the outline of a human figure. (This "person" should be at least four feet in height.) To the left of the "can," have the word *Ingredients;* under the figure to the right, have the label *A Living Sacrifice.* As members arrive, draw their attention to the figure, provide a marker, and ask each person to add something to the "list of ingredients" that make up a "living sacrifice." If you need to help them get started, put one or two "ingredients" on the list, such as *faithfulness* and *humility.* You will use this drawing and list later during "Into the Word."

Into the Word

Recruit one of your better oral readers to stand beside you as you read today's text from Romans 12 verse by verse. After each verse, have that reader read the corresponding verse from a paraphrase such as J. B. Phillips' *The New Testament in Modern English* or *The Promise (Contemporary English Version).*

Read Romans 12:1, 2 again, with emphasis, then assign each learner one of the verses from Romans 12:9-21. (As an assigning method, cut thirteen strips an inch wide and four inches long, write the number of a verse on each, 9 through 21, and insert the strips into your Bible, with the number placed at the center and one or two inches of the paper sticking out. As learners write on the "can" after entering the room, have each pull out a slip from the Bible.) Later you can say, "Look at the verse assigned to you from Romans 12 by the numbered slip. The Bible lists the ingredients of a living sacrifice, and we want to draw our 'recipe' from there."

Then say, "The challenge is clear: we are to be living sacrifices. Examine the verse assigned to you to find the 'ingredients' of a living sacrifice. Compare what you find with our 'can' we have labeled. If you find in your verse an ingredient we have listed, say, 'It's in there!' and come to the sketch and check the ingredient off. If you find an ingredient we have not included, come to the 'can,' write the new ingredient in, and then say, 'It's in there!'" After each ingredient is confirmed or added, ask the learner to identify and read his or her assigned verse. Though you will allow the learners latitude in the "ingredients" they write in, such elements as the following will be appropriate: love (v. 9), honor (v. 10), zeal (v. 11), joy (v. 12), generosity (v. 13), graciousness (v. 14), sympathy (v. 15), humility (v. 16), honesty (v. 17), peace (v. 18), and submission to God (v. 19).

As a way of reviewing these ideas through the coming week, suggest to your learners that they each set a clean, empty can on a work space near them. The can will spur their thinking concerning our daily need to "stir in" the ingredients of holiness and righteousness.

Into Life

Say, "I want you to take the following 'Report Card' home with you this week to evaluate how 'living' you are as a Christian sacrifice." Make copies of the following and distribute one to each learner with directions to "grade yourself, using a **D** for 'barely breathing' to an **A** for 'fully alive.' When you're done, take the report to your Heavenly Father for His commendation and challenge." (A similar activity is in the student book.)

REPORT CARD for _____(name)_____.

This learner shows the following progress in *Basic Christian Living:*

___ sincere love

___ association with good

___ devotion to the brothers and sisters

___ deferring to the well-being of others

___ zeal and spiritual fervor

___ joy and hope

___ patience in difficulty

___ faithfulness in prayer

___ generosity with the needy

___ hospitality

___ kindness to persecutors

___ rejoicing with achievements of others

___ empathizing with those who hurt

___ harmonious, peaceful living

___ humility

Let's Talk It Over

The questions on this page are designed to promote discussion of the lesson by the class and to encourage application of the lesson Scriptures. The answers provided are only discussion starters. Let your class talk it over from there.

1. What does it mean to "present your bodies a living sacrifice"?

You may have heard the story of the chicken and the pig who were discussing the farmer's breakfast. The pig told the chicken, "Eggs are an offering. Bacon is a sacrifice!" King David understood this concept: "Neither will I offer burnt offerings unto the Lord my God of that which doth cost me nothing" (2 Samuel 24:24). Dying for the Lord is difficult. Living for the Lord is also difficult—some would say even more difficult. Living sacrifices require putting God first, even when it is embarrassing, inconvenient, or unappreciated.

2. Should we be governed by "majority rule" in matters of faith and practice? Why is conforming to the majority opinion in such matters displeasing to God?

Parents realize that "everyone is doing it" is a ridiculous excuse for wrongdoing. Unfortunately, many Christians use a form of this excuse to explain their own beliefs or behavior. God calls us to be transformed into the likeness of His Son, separating ourselves from the whims and fads of the world and focusing our eyes on Jesus. Majorities can be deceived, manipulated, bribed, cajoled, or confused. If God's Word has spoken clearly on a certain issue, it is an insult to His authority to think we can somehow "overturn" His truth by voting whether to accept it or not.

3. How can we show God's love to others? What is the difference between the love God wants us to share and the love we often see demonstrated in worldly relationships?

God's kind of love, as our commentator describes, is wanting "the best for another" and is "primarily a matter of the will." It starts by loving good rather than evil, then loving others more than ourselves. Godly love will never tempt another to sin. Godly love is not selfish. Godly love does not manipulate. Worldly love may be guilty of any or all of these. Often it is not love as much as it is lust, which hardly wants the best for another.

4. How does "rejoicing in hope" relate to being "patient in tribulation"? How does our "continuing instant in prayer" make these other two possible?

Sometimes our present circumstances are far from pleasant. All of us will suffer times of loss, times of sickness, times of discouragement, times of failure, times of bereavement, or times of loneliness. Many Christians around the world could add persecution for their faith to that list. If our joy is based on our circumstances, it will be fleeting at best.

However, in Christ we have the hope that eternity will be better than anything we ever experience in this life. We can patiently endure suffering, knowing that a better reality awaits us. The closer we are to God through "continuing instant in prayer," the easier it is to see by faith the eternal reality that He has promised.

5. Why should we "rejoice with them that do rejoice, and weep with them that weep"? What are some practical ways we can do this?

The mind-set of the world is to ask, "What's in it for me?" God calls us to a different mind-set, one that shares joys and burdens alike. You may have heard the saying that a joy shared is twice the joy, while a burden shared is half the burden. Perhaps you have found this to be true in your own life. We should rejoice in the successes of others and support others in times of pain. Both our joys and our concerns can be expressed through cards, phone calls, e-mails, personal visits, and gestures of kindness appropriate to a person's situation and needs.

6. How can we live at peace with all men? How far should we go to live at peace? How should our view of a righteous God influence our desire to get even with others who have hurt us?

Paul does not say that we must have peace at any price. As one who suffered in a variety of ways (see 2 Corinthians 11:23-27), Paul knew all too well that peace in some cases may not be possible, despite one's best efforts. Being persecuted for the cause of Christ, however, is far different from conflict resulting from one's sin or selfish behavior (1 Peter 3:14, 15). Even when persecuted for Christ's sake, we can have His peace within, knowing that we are in God's will. Ultimately we can count on God righting the wrongs of this life, punishing the guilty, and rewarding the righteous.

Accept One Another

April 24
Lesson 8

DEVOTIONAL READING: **James 4:7-12.**

BACKGROUND SCRIPTURE: **Romans 14:1-13; 15:5, 6.**

PRINTED TEXT: **Romans 14:1-13; 15:5, 6.**

Romans 14:1-13

1 Him that is weak in the faith receive ye, but not to doubtful disputations.

2 For one believeth that he may eat all things: another, who is weak, eateth herbs.

3 Let not him that eateth despise him that eateth not; and let not him which eateth not judge him that eateth: for God hath received him.

4 Who art thou that judgest another man's servant? to his own master he standeth or falleth. Yea, he shall be holden up: for God is able to make him stand.

5 One man esteemeth one day above another: another esteemeth every day alike. Let every man be fully persuaded in his own mind.

6 He that regardeth the day, regardeth it unto the Lord; and he that regardeth not the day, to the Lord he doth not regard it. He that eateth, eateth to the Lord, for he giveth God thanks; and he that eateth not, to the Lord he eateth not, and giveth God thanks.

7 For none of us liveth to himself, and no man dieth to himself.

8 For whether we live, we live unto the Lord; and whether we die, we die unto the Lord: whether we live therefore, or die, we are the Lord's.

9 For to this end Christ both died, and rose, and revived, that he might be Lord both of the dead and living.

10 But why dost thou judge thy brother? or why dost thou set at nought thy brother? for we shall all stand before the judgment seat of Christ.

11 For it is written, As I live, saith the Lord, every knee shall bow to me, and every tongue shall confess to God.

12 So then every one of us shall give account of himself to God.

13 Let us not therefore judge one another any more: but judge this rather, that no man put a stumblingblock or an occasion to fall in his brother's way.

Romans 15:5, 6

5 Now the God of patience and consolation grant you to be likeminded one toward another according to Christ Jesus:

6 That ye may with one mind and one mouth glorify God, even the Father of our Lord Jesus Christ.

Apr 24

GOLDEN TEXT: Now the God of patience and consolation grant you to be likeminded one toward another according to Christ Jesus: that ye may with one mind and one mouth glorify God, even the Father of our Lord Jesus Christ.
—Romans 15:5, 6.

God's Project: Effective Christians
Unit 2: The Christian Life
(Lessons 5-8)

Lesson Aims

After participating in this lesson, a student should be able to:

1. Summarize Paul's teaching about the need for Christians not to judge each other.

2. Discuss the importance of Christians being united by their relationship with Jesus Christ, even when they hold differing opinions on some issues.

3. Suggest a specific issue that divides believers in his or her church, and suggest a means of coming to unity.

Lesson Outline

Introduction

A. To Judge or Not to Judge

When it comes to judging, criticism, rebuke, or discipline, a Christian must carefully consider what he or she says and does in the light of three key principles. The first principle is found in Romans 2: one must not judge using a "double standard." It is wrong for me to censure a brother or sister in Christ for a particular action if I am engaging in the same kind of behavior myself (Romans 2:1). The second principle is that anything that is spoken to a wayward brother or sister must be done in the interest of restoring that person to fruitful service (Galatians 6:1). And the third principle is that our opposition to a particular action must be grounded in the teaching of Scripture (2 Timothy 3:16, 17).

Parents face similar issues with their children all the time. If we who are parents desired to correct every childish mistake, we would have to be full-time shadows. We would end up robbing a child of the opportunity to learn through experience. And we would risk bringing up a child who becomes a duplicate of us, not his or her own person, and not necessarily what God created him or her to be. Generally speaking, with children we have to "choose our battles." We must stand firm on the issues that are truly important—those that relate primarily to what God has clearly defined as right and wrong.

When it comes to confrontation within the body of Christ, we must also, in a sense, "choose our battles." Or, to be more accurate, we must let God choose them. Sin cannot be glossed over and ignored. It hurts the sinner and the body of Christ as a whole too much to let that happen. In 1 Corinthians 5 Paul describes a situation that the church in Corinth had to address. A man was treating his father's wife as though she were *his* wife, which clearly broke God's law. In such a case discipline had to be applied.

On the other hand, matters of opinion are not in the same category as the precepts that God has set; matters of opinion are issues of individual conscience. We must not allow such as these to become causes of division in the body of Christ. Each of us must be sparing with judgments and unsparing with love.

B. Lesson Background

In this quarter's second lesson, taken from Romans 2, we discussed God's judgment and some issues concerning our judging of others. Today's lesson continues our study of the concluding portion of Romans where Paul examines the practical side of our walk with Christ. It is a continuation of what it means to "present your bodies a living sacrifice" (Romans 12:1). We spent last week examining some of what Paul says in Romans 12 about those attitudes and actions that strengthen the fellowship in the church and the church's witness in the world.

In Romans 13 Paul considers the topic of a Christian's duty to civil authorities. He refers to the "higher powers" as "ordained of God" (v. 1) and to the person in civil authority as a "minister of God" (vv. 4, 6). Living by the principles of Christian conduct outlined in chapter 12 constitutes a witness to those in authority: "Do that which is good, and thou shalt have praise of the same" (Romans 13:3). The chapter concludes with exhortations such as "cast off the works of darkness" (v. 12), "put on the armor of light" (v. 12), "walk honestly" (v. 13), and "put ye on the Lord Jesus Christ" (v. 14). In today's lesson, which is primarily from Romans 14, we consider another aspect of life in the church. The topic is disagreements among Christians over what may be termed "nonessential" matters.

I. Eating Different Foods (Romans 14:1-4)

A. Respect the Weak (vv. 1-3)

1. Him that is weak in the faith receive ye, but not to doubtful disputations.

The meaning of *weak in the faith* must be determined by the context of this passage and by the specific issues Paul raises. Judging from the following verses, Paul is not dealing with faith in relationship to salvation (as in a phrase such as "justified by faith"). He is concerned mainly with the practical side of Christian faith. Those who are weak in the faith are those Christians who do not seem to understand fully what their faith in Christ allows and does not allow them to do. Perhaps they had not yet been able to break away from former scruples they had strongly held.

Although Paul does not specifically mention the "strong" Christians until Romans 15:1, he suggests in the verse before us how the strong are to treat the weak. The strong must *receive* the weak, welcoming them without creating *doubtful disputations*. In other words, the issues that have the potential to create such disputations should not be raised so as to make the weak Christian uncomfortable or put him or her on the defensive. These are matters of opinion (which will become clear in the following verses) and should not be allowed to cause tensions or rifts in the body of Christ. [See question #1, page 296.]

2. For one believeth that he may eat all things: another, who is weak, eateth herbs.

In Rome and in other first-century churches where there were both Jews and Gentiles who had accepted Christ as Lord, some of the "disputations" mentioned in verse 1 included questions related to which foods were acceptable to *eat*. For many Gentile Christians, the Old Testament laws regarding food were of no concern. They accepted what Paul would later tell Timothy: "For every creature of God is good, and nothing to be refused, if it be received with thanksgiving" (1 Timothy 4:4). But many Jewish Christians

were not able to go that far. When the meat served to them did not come from an acceptable animal (according to what they had been taught from the law of Moses), they would simply eat *herbs*, a term more properly understood as describing vegetables.

In other settings, the Gentile Christians would have been considered *weak*. During their pre-Christian days, the meat they ate was often used in presenting sacrifices to pagan idols. For some who had become Christians, it was difficult for them to eat such meat when they were aware of its pagan connections. To the "strong," however, their freedom in Christ eliminated all of these old scruples. They could eat such meat, recognizing that since an idol was nothing, there was no way that good meat could be "contaminated" by a superstitious ceremony. Paul deals with these issues more specifically in 1 Corinthians 8, but they also would have been prominent in Rome as well. [See question #2, page 296.]

3. Let not him that eateth despise him that eateth not; and let not him which eateth not judge him that eateth: for God hath received him.

Here's the guideline. The key issue is not what is eaten; it is the attitude of the eaters. The "anything goes" eater must not *despise*, or be critical of, the one who eats only vegetables. And the one who cannot bring himself to eat the meat in question is not to put down the one who enjoys it. If each one has surrendered to the lordship of Jesus Christ, then *God* has *received him*. And if God has accepted him, he is my brother. If she belongs to the Lord, she is my sister. Who am I to exclude someone whom God has adopted into His family?

B. Do Not Judge (v. 4)

4. Who art thou that judgest another man's servant? to his own master he standeth or falleth. Yea, he shall be holden up: for God is able to make him stand.

We are all servants of one *master*—the Lord. No individual is the master of another. The master makes the rules, and we help each other keep the master's rules. But we don't make the rules for each other, particularly where matters of opinion are concerned. *God* alone determines whether someone stands or falls—that is, whether someone's conduct is acceptable or not.

How to Say It

CORINTHIANS. Co-*rin*-thee-unz.
DISPUTATIONS. dis-pyoo-*tay*-shunz.
ISAIAH. Eye-*zay*-uh.

We must constantly bear in mind that God's grace is the only hope that any of us has to *stand* before Him. I must recognize that, in spite of my numerous flaws and my imperfect service, God is ready and willing to help me stand. Shouldn't I treat others with the same measure of grace with which I want God to treat me?

II. Observing Different Days (Romans 14:5, 6)

A. One's Choice (v. 5)

5. One man esteemeth one day above another: another esteemeth every day alike. Let every man be fully persuaded in his own mind.

Here is another subject where Christians will hold differing opinions: the observance of special days. Most likely the issue for Paul's readers involved the observance of various Jewish holy days by those who came to Christ from a Jewish background. We know that Paul himself continued such observances after he became a Christian (Acts 20:16). But he did not try to force his opinion on others, nor did he condemn those who chose not to observe the days that he honored. This perspective is reflected in his advice to the Roman Christians: *Let every man be fully persuaded in his own mind.*

This issue probably gives us a more contemporary illustration than the discussion over food. Some thoroughly enjoy the celebration of various holidays such as Christmas and Easter. Others do not believe in observing those days at all because they are troubled by possible links to paganism. Those who try to include a Christian emphasis in their observance of these days reason that the world's attention is already drawn somewhat to Jesus' birthday and to His resurrection. Why not take advantage of that attention to get a word in for the truth? [See question #3, page 296.]

Whatever our convictions on this matter, Paul would tell us to be loyal to them, to put energy into whatever God-honoring activity we believe in, and to realize the right of another to see such a matter as this differently from us.

B. One's Creator (v. 6)

6. He that regardeth the day, regardeth it unto the Lord; and he that regardeth not the day, to the Lord he doth not regard it. He that eateth, eateth to the Lord, for he giveth God thanks; and he that eateth not, to the Lord he eateth not, and giveth God thanks.

This is a review of the principle Paul has stated, as applied to both the observance of certain days and the eating of certain foods. If I celebrate special days, I should celebrate them to the glory of *the Lord*. If I treat every *day* the same, I must make sure that today, and the next day, and the next honor God. If I feel free to eat anything, I should enjoy it, giving *thanks* to the Provider of everything. If I choose to eat with more discretion, I should do that to honor God as well. In other words, the lordship of Christ should affect all I do.

WHAT WERE THEY THINKING?

Ted VanCleave is an inventor. One of his "bright ideas" was the creation of an inflatable greeting card, but he couldn't get a patent for it. However, in the process he discovered patents for a number of other interesting inventions. Here are some examples:

• a helium-filled bed that floats to the ceiling during the day to provide more room in small apartments.

• three-legged panty hose (so when one leg is ruined, you don't have to throw them away).

• an alarm that beeps and flashes a light when the baby wets his diapers.

• a fork for dieters (when you take a bite a red light comes on, encouraging you to wait for another bite until the light turns green).

• a watch that counts "dog time" (it multiplies seconds, minutes, and hours by seven so you can see how "Fido" keeps time).

Your reaction may be much like mine: What were they thinking? We may have the same question about the religious scruples of other people, similar to those that surfaced in Paul's day about eating (or not eating) certain foods, or keeping certain days as holy days. Today it could be some other matter of opinion related to Christian conduct. Here is Paul's instruction: each person should be fully persuaded about the issue in his or her own mind, and no one should judge others regarding matters where God has not given specific directions.
—C. R. B.

III. Recognizing a Common Bond (Romans 14:7-9)

A. We Need Others (v. 7)

7. For none of us liveth to himself, and no man dieth to himself.

Each Christian is a child of God; thus, we are all brothers and sisters in Christ. We are far more interdependent than we are independent. Our primary dependence is upon the Lord, as Paul points out in the next verse.

B. We Are the Lord's (vv. 8, 9)

8. For whether we live, we live unto the Lord; and whether we die, we die unto the Lord: whether we live therefore, or die, we are the Lord's.

In this context, Paul is emphasizing that every Christian is responsible to the Lord, even in matters of opinion such as observing special days and eating certain foods. The lordship of Christ should influence every aspect of life, not just what may be considered "major" decisions.

To *die unto the Lord* should provide a most comforting thought. Whatever the circumstances of one's death may be, whether quiet, peaceful, violent, or catastrophic, whether at home or in a hospital bed, the Lord will never abandon one of His own.

9. For to this end Christ both died, and rose, and revived, that he might be Lord both of the dead and living.

Here Paul reinforces his teaching on "doubtful disputations" by reminding us of that concerning which there can be no doubt whatsoever: the central facts of the gospel (cf. 1 Corinthians 15:1-4). Let us never lose sight of what really matters in all of this! Christ's death spells death for death. And His resurrection spells life for those who belong to Him. The Calvary/burial/resurrection events seal Jesus' lordship. Any matters of opinion must pale in comparison with this glorious message. [See question #4, page 296.]

IV. Recognizing a Common Duty (Romans 14:10-13; 15:5, 6)

A. Withholding Present Judgment (v. 10)

10. But why dost thou judge thy brother? or why dost thou set at nought thy brother? for we shall all stand before the judgment seat of Christ.

Because of what Jesus has done (as described in the previous verse), only He has the right to serve as Judge. No one else has the right to *judge* a *brother*. We must remember that Paul has not been writing about immoral behavior or heresies that are practiced or endorsed by individuals or groups within the church. He has been talking about matters of opinion. To judge our brothers and sisters on such issues and to treat them as *nought*, or nothing, because their perspective is different from ours is out of line. We are all accountable to *Christ*, and we must allow Him to be the pattern for all our attitudes and actions toward others. [See question #5, page 296.]

B. Awaiting Future Judgment (vv. 11, 12)

11. For it is written, As I live, saith the Lord, every knee shall bow to me, and every tongue shall confess to God.

In our study of Romans, we have witnessed Paul's frequent use of the Old Testament Scriptures to support his teaching on various topics. Here he quotes from Isaiah 45:23 to reinforce

"As I live, saith the Lord, every knee shall bow to me, and every tongue shall confess to God."
—Romans 14:11

Visual for lesson 8

Today's visual encourages us to bow the knee before God now—while we have the opportunity.

what he has stated previously concerning final judgment. Someday *every knee shall bow* and *every tongue shall confess to God*. The question is whether we will do that gladly and willingly (because we chose to do it during our earthly lives) or fearfully (because we refused to make spiritual matters a priority). [See question #6, page 296.]

12. So then every one of us shall give account of himself to God.

We owe an accounting, but not to another person. We owe it to *God*. Together *every one of us* will stand before God's judgment seat. No one will be exempt!

C. Maintaining Brotherhood (v. 13)

13. Let us not therefore judge one another any more: but judge this rather, that no man put a stumblingblock or an occasion to fall in his brother's way.

Here Paul provides a positive alternative to the kind of negative judging that has been his primary concern thus far. Whenever we find ourselves dwelling on our differences with others and becoming frustrated and impatient with them, it may be a good time to stop and consider how we can be a help to them—to enable them to obey Christ and serve Him more fully.

Instead of dwelling on the occasions when an individual has stumbled, let us determine what we can do to keep that person from stumbling again. Staying in touch, becoming a prayer partner, providing words of encouragement, and offering good options to potentially harmful choices can help someone stand rather than *fall*. And possibly someday that brother or sister whom we help may be the person who helps us stand strong and avoid a fall of our own.

LOOKING OUT FOR OTHERS

SAD—Seasonal Affective Disorder—seems to affect especially those people who live in the far north, where winter brings on what may be described as a "darkness of the spirit." Alcoholism is a frequent side effect of SAD, as people try to anesthetize themselves against the gloom of shortened days and long winter nights. Of course, since alcohol is itself a depressant, the problem is compounded.

Alaska rates at or near the top in America in incidents of drunken driving, vehicle fatalities, and other deaths related to alcohol. Alaska also has high rates of suicide and abusive home situations. To combat this problem, more than a hundred native Alaskan villages control the use and/or sale of alcohol.

A few years ago, two Alaskan villages experimented by relaxing their laws on alcohol use. After six months of winter had passed, they decided to reinstate the restrictions. Families were starving, teenagers were becoming drunk in public, sexual assaults increased, and public officials were drinking on the job. In essence, the two villages decided that they needed to look out for the "weaker brothers" by removing a "stumblingblock" from their paths.

Whatever we think secular society's role should be in such matters, Christians who seek to practice Biblical principles are obligated to ensure that their behavior does not lead other believers into sin. It's not only a case of following the "golden rule"; it's a matter of helping one another "with one mind" to glorify Christ. —C. R. B.

D. Being Likeminded (15:5, 6)

5. Now the God of patience and consolation grant you to be likeminded one toward another according to Christ Jesus.

Home Daily Bible Readings

Monday, Apr. 18—Speak No Evil Against One Another (James 4:7-12)

Tuesday, Apr. 19—Do Not Grumble Against One Another (James 5:7-12)

Wednesday, Apr. 20—Do Not Judge One Another (Romans 14:1-6)

Thursday, Apr. 21—Each Will Be Accountable to God (Romans 14:7-13)

Friday, Apr. 22—Do Not Ruin Another Through Food (Romans 14:14-18)

Saturday, Apr. 23—Do Not Make Another Stumble (Romans 14:19-23)

Sunday, Apr. 24—Live in Harmony with One Another (Romans 15:1-6)

God has shown extraordinary *patience* with us. Should we not try to exhibit patience with one another—for example, concerning the kind of issues Paul has addressed in this section of Romans? We would do well to reread Jesus' parable of the unforgiving servant—a man who all too quickly forgot the grace with which his master had treated him (Matthew 18:21-35).

Being *likeminded* does not mean that we agree on every issue that surfaces. Paul has already stated in Romans 14 that there will be disagreements among Christians on certain subjects. To be likeminded means that we all determine to have the same attitude toward one another—an attitude that is patterned *according to Christ Jesus.*

6. That ye may with one mind and one mouth glorify God, even the Father of our Lord Jesus Christ.

Here is a picture of what Heaven will be like—speaking with united attitudes and singing with united voices as we praise the *Father* and the *Christ.* Shouldn't we be "rehearsing" now? We will not always sing the same notes, but we will be in harmony because our minds are focused on the same goal—seeking to *glorify God.*

Conclusion

A. The Power of Positive Judging

Don't you like the way Paul points us in the direction of positive judging? "But judge this rather, that no man put a stumblingblock or an occasion to fall in his brother's way" (Romans 14:13). Do I apply myself to figuring out how I can help my brother or sister to stand, and not fall?

The writer of Hebrews encourages Christians to get together and to exhort each other, to help each other hold fast to the profession of their faith. "Let us consider one another to provoke unto love and to good works" (Hebrews 10:24). That's the kind of positive judging that will make Almighty God smile, will draw His family closer together, and will give the world a taste of what they're missing when they remain outside of God's family.

B. Prayer

Our Father, the God of patience and consolation, help us to be patient with one another. Help us to be judges in a positive way, not a negative one. Help us to leave ultimate judgment to You alone and to trust Your perfect righteousness, wisdom, mercy, and love. In Jesus' name. Amen.

C. Thought to Remember

We should not allow our differences over nonessential matters to cloud our view of the Son.

Learning by Doing

This page contains an alternative lesson plan emphasizing learning activities. Classes desiring such student involvement will find these suggestions helpful.

Learning Goals

After this lesson a student should be able to:

1. Summarize Paul's teaching about the need for Christians not to judge each other.

2. Discuss the importance of Christians being united by their relationship with Jesus Christ, even when they hold differing opinions on some issues.

3. Suggest a specific issue that divides believers in his or her church, and suggest a means of coming to unity.

Into the Lesson

Prepare the following handout. (This activity is included in the student book.) Put the word *WEAK* at the top of a piece of paper and *STRONG* at the bottom. Leave enough space in between for eight lines of writing. Tell the class, "It takes some real work to go from being WEAK to being STRONG, especially when applied to Christian growth. Listen to the following clues and fill in this 'ladder' by changing or adding one letter at each 'rung' in order to go from WEAK to STRONG." (Note that at the clues with a plus sign, a letter will be added.)

W E A K

–top of a mountain	_ _ _ _ (PEAK)
–a type of moss	_ _ _ _ (PEAT)
–holding one's anger, with "up"	
	_ _ _ _ (PENT)
–a small liquid measure	_ _ _ _ (PINT)
–to put words into visible form (+)	
	_ _ _ _ _ (PRINT)
–a quick, short race (+)	
	_ _ _ _ _ _ (SPRINT)
–a season of the year	
	_ _ _ _ _ _ (SPRING)
–what impels and restricts a yo-yo	
	_ _ _ _ _ _ (STRING)

S T R O N G

Option: Ask two or three class members to sit before the group for a "Likes and Dislikes" survey. Allow each to respond to the following (or similar) statements: (1) My favorite food is . . . ; (2) One thing I will not eat is . . . ; (3) My favorite sports team is . . . ; (4) My favorite singer is . . . ; (5) My ideal vacation site is . . . ; (6) My attitude toward going to the movies is . . . ; (7) My favorite color is . . . ; (8) The TV newscast I am most likely to listen to and watch is . . . .

After the variety of responses, say, "It is clear that we do not agree on many matters. Some differences may have consequences as to our relationships with others. Most do not." (Be sure to limit the discussion of each statement.)

Into the Word

Give learners paper and pen to use in responding with AGREE or DISAGREE to the following statements related to points made in today's lesson. You can either copy the statements onto the papers or simply read them aloud for learner response. (1) We must not allow matters of opinion or matters of individual conscience to become tests of fellowship. (2) For "strong" Christians, freedom in Christ eliminates all of the old scruples of behavior from their concern. (3) The "weak"—with more sensitive consciences—are the ones with stronger principles and stronger feelings. (4) I must not exclude or look down on someone who is part of the family of God, even if his or her eating habits are questionable. (5) We help each other keep the Master's rules, but we don't make the rules for each other. (6) Each of us is related to God, so we cannot help being related to each other. (7) Christ's death spells death for death. (8) When we are tempted to evaluate another person's conduct, we should remember that our time is better spent evaluating how we can encourage that person. (9) We can still be of one mind, even though we disagree concerning certain issues. As you listen to the responses, ask learners to identify verse numbers from the printed text that support their comments.

Into Life

Have class members divide into small discussion groups, and give the following directions to each group: "What are some matters with which you find yourself disagreeing with fellow church members, or even church leaders? List them. Establish a 'Consequence Sequence'; that is, number your entries from most serious to least serious. Decide which of the principles from today's study apply to dealing with each matter. Decide what these principles tell you about how to relate to your 'disagreeable' brothers and sisters." Give the groups enough time to work on this assignment, then call them together for reports from each. (A similar activity is included in the student book.)

Let's Talk It Over

The questions on this page are designed to promote discussion of the lesson by the class and to encourage application of the lesson Scriptures. The answers provided are only discussion starters. Let your class talk it over from there.

1. What are "doubtful disputations"? How can we determine what items are essential (where there is no room for compromise) and what items are not essential (where there is room for compromise)?

The "essential vs. nonessential" items will likely be viewed differently from one church to another and from one Christian to another. Some churches rely upon written creeds to sort out these differences, while others take a more "hands-off" approach and allow individual believers to decide these matters. The best approach to these issues is to use the plain meaning of the Bible as the arbiter in any discussion about Christian essentials. Few who take Scripture seriously would disagree that the Bible's teaching is clear in key areas of doctrine and morality.

2. How can we tell if we are the "strong" Christian or the "weak" one? How do our responsibilities toward each other differ depending on which type of Christian we are?

When Paul uses "strong" and "weak" in some of his letters, he pictures the weak Christian as one who is more vulnerable to sin in a particular situation. The strong Christian is not guided by some of the scruples and restrictions that are still important in the thinking of the weak Christian. We may think that "strength" and "weakness" would be determined by how long an individual has been a Christian. But that may not necessarily be the case. In fact, a Christian could be considered "strong" in one area of conduct and "weak" in another. Christlike attitudes must be allowed to govern each situation. As Paul says, let no one "put a stumblingblock or an occasion to fall in his brother's way" (Romans 14:13).

3. Should Christians celebrate Christmas and Easter? In what manner should Christians observe national holidays (such as a country's Independence Day)?

Paul's point in today's Scripture is not to argue for or against any position one may take on such questions as these. Rather, he is telling us essentially to "live and let live" on such issues. Questions about holidays are not in the realm of essentials and not worth dividing over. Whether we celebrate or not—let us remain true to our own convictions. If we violate those convictions, or if we lead someone else to violate his or her convictions, then we have sinned. Whether we celebrate or not is an individual decision.

4. How does our modern sense of independence and self-centeredness compare to the Bible's sense of interdependence and self-sacrifice? How would you evaluate contemporary culture after reading Romans 14:7-9?

Jesus was (and is) the ultimate example of self-sacrifice. He did not regard His life as His own, but lived in submission to God. He did not seek His own good, but the good of others. He did not demand His own rights, but forgave His enemies. Philippians 2:5-11 powerfully describes the degree of Jesus' sacrifice. Society today seems obsessed with self-promotion and self-gratification. Whereas Paul would say, "We are the Lord's," the modern mind-set would declare, "My life is my own, and I'll live it as I please."

5. When we judge others, what role are we usurping? What do we have in common with those whom we judge?

"We shall all stand before the judgment seat of Christ," as Paul states in Romans 14:10. God is the ultimate judge, and He is the only one who can justly judge. Judgment is an act that appropriately happens between unequals: a boss judges the work of an employee, a general judges the readiness of his soldiers, a teacher judges the work of her pupils. When it comes to spiritual matters, we will all be equally subordinate to the final judgment of God.

6. When Paul (quoting Isaiah) says "every knee shall bow . . . and every tongue shall confess," is he teaching a universal salvation?

This is not a promise of universal salvation. Paul is using the passage from Isaiah to reinforce his teaching that all must face the judgment seat of Christ (Romans 14:10). Everyone will be accountable to Him; not even the most defiant, blasphemous sinner will be exempt. We must bow the knee and confess Jesus as Lord now in this life while we have the opportunity to do so. If we do not, we will be forced to do so at Christ's return; and that will make His return a day of terror, not triumph.

Believe No Other Gospel

DEVOTIONAL READING: Acts 13:26-33.

BACKGROUND SCRIPTURE: Galatians 1.

PRINTED TEXT: Galatians 1:1-12.

Galatians 1:1-12

1 Paul, an apostle, (not of men, neither by man, but by Jesus Christ, and God the Father, who raised him from the dead;)

2 And all the brethren which are with me, Unto the churches of Galatia:

3 Grace be to you, and peace, from God the Father, and from our Lord Jesus Christ,

4 Who gave himself for our sins, that he might deliver us from this present evil world, according to the will of God and our Father:

5 To whom be glory for ever and ever. Amen.

6 I marvel that ye are so soon removed from him that called you into the grace of Christ unto another gospel:

7 Which is not another; but there be some that trouble you, and would pervert the gospel of Christ.

8 But though we, or an angel from heaven, preach any other gospel unto you than that which we have preached unto you, let him be accursed.

9 As we said before, so say I now again, If any man preach any other gospel unto you than that ye have received, let him be accursed.

10 For do I now persuade men, or God? or do I seek to please men? for if I yet pleased men, I should not be the servant of Christ.

11 But I certify you, brethren, that the gospel which was preached of me is not after man.

12 For I neither received it of man, neither was I taught it, but by the revelation of Jesus Christ.

May 1

GOLDEN TEXT: I certify you, brethren, that the gospel which was preached of me is not after man.—Galatians 1:11.

God's Project: Effective Christians
Unit 3: Set Free
(Lessons 9-13)

Lesson Aims

After this lesson a student should be able to:

1. Give reasons why there is only one gospel revealed by God.

2. Identify ancient and modern false gospels.

3. Make a commitment to remain faithful to the gospel of Jesus Christ.

Lesson Outline

INTRODUCTION
    A. Is It Really Good News?
    B. Lesson Background
  I. PAUL'S AUTHORITY (Galatians 1:1-5)
    A. His Calling (vv. 1, 2)
    B. His Message (vv. 3-5)
 II. PAUL'S CONCERN (Galatians 1:6-9)
    A. Some Are Deserting the Gospel (v. 6)
    B. Some Are Perverting the Gospel (v. 7)
    C. A Stern Warning (vv. 8, 9)
      Deserting and Perverting
III. PAUL'S GOSPEL (Galatians 1:10-12)
    A. Not Intended to Please Men (v. 10)
      Would Paul "Go for Ratings"?
    B. Not Revealed by Men (vv. 11, 12)
CONCLUSION
    A. Benedict Arnold
    B. Prayer
    C. Thought to Remember

Introduction

A. Is It Really Good News?

In our Scripture text today, Paul expresses his concern over a school of thought that referred to itself as *gospel* but wasn't. It called on people to depend on their own righteousness, particularly as expressed in Old Testament law-keeping, to get into Heaven. This message that Christians must fulfill all the Jewish laws was being specifically imposed upon the Gentile converts to Christianity. Paul could not call this good news, because it went back to a system that could not save people in the first place.

Let's say you and a companion are stranded on a desert island. Your companion says, "Guess what, there is a ship willing to pick us up. It is only one hundred miles away. The problem is we have to swim to meet it." That would not be good news. But if the ship has promised to come and pick you up, *that* would be good news. Certain teachers had been telling the Christians in Galatia that they had to, in effect, "swim" for their salvation. That can hardly be good news.

Paul was the ideal person to address this issue for at least three reasons. First, he himself had tried the system of salvation through keeping the law of Moses. If there was anyone who knew the fruitlessness of trying to get to Heaven by rigorous law-keeping, it was Paul. He described himself as "blameless" concerning "the righteousness which is in the law." Yet he came to realize that only "the righteousness which is of God by faith" is worth possessing (Philippians 3:6, 9).

Second, Paul was the right person to convey this message to Gentile Christians since, although he was an exemplary Jew, he had grown up in the Gentile world. In fact, when Jesus appeared to Paul (then Saul) on the road to Damascus, He told him that he was being sent to the Gentiles (Acts 26:17).

Third, Paul was equipped to deal with this matter because he was acquainted with the Galatians by reason of his first missionary journey. During that time, he had introduced them to the gospel of grace. They were more likely to listen to Paul because his earlier conduct among them had testified to his concern for their spiritual welfare.

B. Lesson Background

As we begin this series of lessons from Galatians, it is important to look at some general information about the history of both the territory and the church.

While Romans is considered Paul's greatest work, many would rank Galatians a close second. Some have called this book Paul's "Magna Carta." Others have called it the "Christian Declaration of Independence." The sixteenth-century reformer Martin Luther, whose wife's name was Katherine, referred to Galatians as his "Katherine" because of the high esteem in which he held it.

Unlike the majority of Paul's letters, Galatians was not written to a specific church in a city. For example, Romans was sent to Rome, and Philippians was sent to the city of Philippi. But Galatians was written to a group of churches in a province called Galatia. This province received its name from the Gauls who settled there in 279 B.C. The Gauls were originally a warlike Celtic people living in what is today northern France. A colony of them settled in what is now northern Turkey, but they were defeated by the Romans in 189 B.C. Later, in 25 B.C., the Romans captured that area, joined it with another area to the south, and named the province Galatia.

Bible scholars debate whether Paul is writing Galatians to the earlier and more northern area where the Gauls first lived, or whether he has the southern and newer part of the Roman province in mind. Most scholars have settled on the southern area as the most likely option. This would fit very well with events recorded in Acts, and it would date Galatians as one of Paul's first letters, or perhaps the very first. (Suggested dates would range from A.D. 48 to A.D. 52.) The area of southern Galatia would have included the cities of Iconium, Lystra, Derbe, and Pisidian Antioch. These were all churches that Paul founded during his first missionary journey with Barnabas, recorded in Acts 13 and 14.

Two primary issues underlie today's lesson and the entire book of Galatians. The first is that Paul himself is under attack. Some of his opponents claim he is not a real apostle and therefore has no real authority. Paul spends a great deal of time, particularly in the opening chapter of the letter, defending his apostleship; for if his authority is undermined, so is his message. Thus it is not just Paul himself under attack, but also the gospel. [See question #1, page 304.]

This leads us to the second problem the book addresses. The Galatians had accepted the gospel Paul preached, but were now being seduced into thinking that they had to embrace all the law of Moses to be saved. The uniqueness of the gospel of grace was being compromised.

I. Paul's Authority (Galatians 1:1-5)

A. His Calling (vv. 1, 2)

1. Paul, an apostle, (not of men, neither by man, but by Jesus Christ, and God the Father, who raised him from the dead.)

Paul immediately identifies himself by the title *apostle*. This claim serves to counter one of the problems noted under the Lesson Background—namely, that there are people doubting the legitimacy of Paul's apostleship.

Admittedly, Paul is not one of the original twelve apostles. He himself points out in this opening chapter that he has no close association with any of the Twelve (Galatians 1:15-19). Since an apostle was to have witnessed the resurrection (Acts 1:21, 22; 22:12-15), Jesus' appearance to Paul on the road to Damascus enables him to carry the title *apostle* legitimately, though Paul recognizes that he is "one born out of due time" (1 Corinthians 15:8).

The word *apostle* describes an envoy or ambassador. Paul is an apostle with a special assignment to the Gentiles (Acts 9:15; 22:21; 26:17), and Jesus gave him that assignment. No group of *men* or individual *man* is the source of his ministry; he is called *by Jesus Christ* and ultimately *God the Father*. [See question #2, page 304.]

2. And all the brethren which are with me, Unto the churches of Galatia.

At the beginning of his letters, Paul normally identifies by name those who are traveling with him. Here he refers to them by the general term of *brethren*. Paul never considers his ministry a private matter. Others share with him in the preaching of the gospel and are often mentored by him (Timothy is probably the best example).

As stated earlier, the recipients of this letter are a group of *churches* in the region of *Galatia*. The work of the church is carried out primarily through local congregations. Paul intends for all the churches in Galatia to receive this message.

B. His Message (vv. 3-5)

3. Grace be to you, and peace, from God the Father, and from our Lord Jesus Christ.

Paul continues with his characteristic greeting of *grace . . . and peace*. The words *grace* and *peace* are typical greetings of the day; *grace* is the typical Greek greeting, while *peace* is directed to those from a Jewish background. To any Christian, those two words possess a fuller meaning and significance.

4. Who gave himself for our sins, that he might deliver us from this present evil world, according to the will of God and our Father.

Paul now describes the ministry of Jesus using three phrases. First, he says that Jesus *gave himself for our sins*. Jesus' death on the cross was not an accident. It was for that reason that He came to earth. To view His death as simply a heroic act or as the death of a martyr is to miss its divinely intended purpose. Paul writes in 1 Corinthians 15:3 that part of the gospel is the fact that "Christ died for our sins."

How to Say It

ANATHEMA. uh-*nath*-uh-muh.
ANTIOCH. *An*-tee-ock.
ARABIA. Uh-*ray*-bee-uh.
BARNABAS. *Barn*-uh-bus.
DAMASCUS. Duh-*mass*-cuss.
DERBE. *Der*-bee.
GALATIANS. Guh-*lay*-shuns.
GAULS. Gawlz.
ICONIUM. Eye-*coe*-nee-um.
JUDAIZERS. *Joo*-day-eye-zers.
LYSTRA. *Liss*-truh.
PHILIPPI. Fuh-*lip*-eye or *Fill*-uh-pie.
PISIDIAN. Puh-*sid*-ee-un.

Second, Jesus is described as the One who came to *deliver us from this present evil world.* The Greek word translated *world* is rendered more accurately by the word *age.* Thus Paul is not describing how Jesus will one day take us away from this planet (though He certainly will do that). His primary focus is on Jesus' deliverance of us from the evil system that pervades this planet. When we discuss the "world of politics" or the "world of sports," we don't mean there is a separate planet for these activities; we are speaking of a system. The "world of evil" is one under the control of the "evil one," or Satan. A person who becomes a Christian becomes part of a different realm—one that is "not of this world" (John 18:36).

Third, Jesus acted *according to the will of God and our Father.* On one occasion Jesus stated, "My meat is to do the will of him that sent me, and to finish his work" (John 4:34). As noted earlier, Jesus' death was part of the Father's plan— "the determinate counsel and foreknowledge of God" (Acts 2:23). [See question #3, page 304.]

5. To whom be glory for ever and ever. Amen.

At this point Paul breaks forth into a note of praise. This happens from time to time in his writings, but not in a salutation. Paul may include his praise here because he knows he has to say some difficult things right away to the Galatians.

II. Paul's Concern
(Galatians 1:6-9)

A. Some Are Deserting the Gospel (v. 6)

6. I marvel that ye are so soon removed from him that called you into the grace of Christ unto another gospel.

Usually, following the salutation, Paul continues his letters with a word of encouragement, a prayer, or some personal reminiscences. These items are absent in the letter to the Galatians. The problem threatening the Galatians is too serious to postpone.

Paul is astonished that some among the Galatians are *so soon removed from him that called you.* We could say that they were acting like traitors, deserting the gospel that Paul had so faithfully taught them. In the Greek language, the word Paul uses for *removed* indicates that this desertion was ongoing and in the process of occurring even as Paul was writing his letter. It is not something completed or in the past.

Within this verse are two phrases that can be interpreted in more than one way. When Paul marvels at how *soon* the Galatians have removed themselves, he may be talking about how this occurred so soon after he presented the gospel to

them or how soon they deserted after hearing the "other gospel." The other question concerns the words *him that called you.* The *him* may refer to God or it may refer to Paul. In the latter case, Paul would be expressing his personal hurt at seeing his message rejected in this way.

What was the other *gospel* that the Galatians were embracing? It was most likely that of a group known as the "Judaizers." These were first-century Jewish Christians who believed in Jesus, but also believed that everyone needed to keep all the Old Testament laws as well. This would particularly include the rite of circumcision. At the gathering in Jerusalem often called the "Jerusalem Conference," the position of the Judaizers was rejected by the leaders of the church in Jerusalem (Acts 15:1-29). They declared that Gentiles could come to Christ alone, without the added requirement of keeping the Old Testament law.

Paul describes this gospel as *another gospel.* There were two words Paul could have used for *another.* One would mean "another of the same kind." His other choice would be to speak of "another of a different kind." Paul uses the latter word. Thus, this other gospel is so heinous in Paul's eyes that he sees it as totally different from the genuine gospel. [See question #4, page 304.]

B. Some Are Perverting the Gospel (v. 7)

7. Which is not another; but there be some that trouble you, and would pervert the gospel of Christ.

Paul is so opposed to this "other gospel" that he goes on to declare it is not really a gospel at all. What makes this situation especially dangerous is that this other gospel resembles the *gospel of Christ* in some ways, but is, in fact, a perversion of it. We could also describe it as a "counterfeit" gospel.

Paul characterizes those promoting this false message as *some that trouble you.* Those individuals who started the controversy resulting in the Jerusalem Conference are described as those who "have troubled you with words, subverting your souls, saying, Ye must be circumcised, and keep the law" (Acts 15:24). Jewish traditions were meaningful to people of a Jewish background, but those traditions meant little to Gentiles.

Note how firmly Paul expresses himself in this section of Galatians. We must remember that Paul had started these churches, so he had the authority to speak to them in this manner. To Paul, this is not just an attack on him personally, but an attack on the gospel itself. Someone attacking the gospel has the potential to shake the faith of those Christians who may not be strong enough to withstand such an attack.

C. A Stern Warning (vv. 8, 9)

8. But though we, or an angel from heaven, preach any other gospel unto you than that which we have preached unto you, let him be accursed.

The main point of this verse is simple: the message is more important than the messenger. Paul regarded this *other gospel* that the Galatians had heard as so dangerous that he declared that those who propagate it should be *accursed*. The Greek word translated *accursed* is *anathema*, which describes being under a curse or under the wrath of God. In other words, Paul would have any such false teacher be eternally condemned. Paul applies the word to himself in Romans 9:3 where he writes of his concern for Jews who are lost: "I could wish that myself were accursed from Christ for my brethren."

Paul reinforces his statement by adding that even if *an angel from heaven* should *preach* another gospel, he should be sentenced to this same judgment. It does not matter how attractive, appealing, or eloquent a teacher may be; if the content of the message contradicts the true gospel, then both the messenger and the false message come under condemnation.

9. As we said before, so say I now again, If any man preach any other gospel unto you than that ye have received, let him be accursed.

Paul states the curse *again*. He reminds the Galatians that they already know the true gospel. It has already been preached to them and they have accepted it. Anyone who preaches *any other gospel* is to *be accursed*.

DESERTING AND PERVERTING

You, too, can be a "ghostbuster" (with apologies to the comedy film by that name from several years ago). You can get a college degree from a California-based online institution after taking courses in alchemy, herbology, and both basic and advanced witchcraft. You can buy a book entitled, *Complete Idiot's Guide to Ghosts and Hauntings;* or, for only $150, you can get a home-study course that will declare you a Certified Ghost Hunter™. You will learn such important "facts" (please note the quotation marks!) as these: most ghosts have names; they are harmless; they haunt us because they are trapped outside our world; they miss their loved ones or are trying to avenge some evil done to them in this life; they don't realize they are dead; the really bad ones were never human.

Throughout history, people have been tempted to turn away just a bit (sometimes quite a bit!) from the simple truths found in God's Word. Ghost-hunting and witchcraft are only two examples. In Paul's time, there were Chris-

Churches in Macedonia and Galatia

Visual for lesson 9. *Today's visual includes a map of the region of Galatia. Use it as you introduce students to the book of Galatians.*

tians who could not believe the simple truth of the gospel: that salvation comes not through our own works or knowledge, but through the grace of God found in Jesus Christ. When we desert the truth, we usually end up perverting it as well!

—C. R. B.

III. Paul's Gospel (Galatians 1:10-12)

A. Not Intended to Please Men (v. 10)

10. For do I now persuade men, or God? or do I seek to please men? for if I yet pleased men, I should not be the servant of Christ.

Paul raises the questions found in this verse because it is quite likely that his accusers suggested he was preaching grace to *please* his audience. We can see how some could make this erroneous assumption. To some, the message of God's grace looked like it was letting people "off the hook" by relieving them of having to be concerned about their sin. (Paul deals with this issue more directly in Romans 6.)

Is Paul simply currying favor with his listeners by telling them what they want to hear? Paul strenuously denies that he is trying to please people. The reactions of people to what he has to say is not (and never was) a determining factor in Paul's ministry. If he tailors his message to fit what the audience wants to hear, then he will be an unfaithful messenger. Paul's primary concern is to be a *servant of Christ* by speaking the truth. [See question #5, page 304.]

WOULD PAUL "GO FOR RATINGS"?

The quest for audience ratings (and thus advertising income) brings us a variety of television programs, including soap operas, late-night talk and comedy shows, crime-solving dramas, and game shows. In recent years the so-called "reality" shows became some of the most highly rated programs. These shows placed ordinary people in settings that supposedly tested their skills at surviving difficult situations or handling relationships with other people. Most of us haven't figured out how the term *reality* was supposed to fit. Putting strangers in contrived circumstances that bring out their character faults in front of millions of viewers, while TV cameras and crews create the illusion of danger, doesn't seem very "real," does it?

But here's a surprise: the top-rated TV show in New York City on Christmas morning in recent years has been nothing more than a picture of a yule log burning in a fireplace while Christmas carols play in the background! Television station WPIX has found that people are more pleased with tradition than with newness or "pizzazz"—at least on that one day of the year.

If the apostle Paul had been a TV programmer, it's not likely he would have "gone for ratings." He was interested in pleasing God, not men. In a day when most people seem interested only in what is "new," we must also make sure we hold on to what is *true!*   —C. R. B.

B. Not Revealed by Men (vv. 11, 12)

11. But I certify you, brethren, that the gospel which was preached of me is not after man.

Paul goes on to *certify*, or state confidently, that not only is his *gospel* not designed to please men, but also its source is not to be found in men. He did not invent it, nor did he receive it from any other *man.*

12. For I neither received it of man, neither was I taught it, but by the revelation of Jesus Christ.

Home Daily Bible Readings

Monday, Apr. 25—Do Not Be Led Astray (2 Corinthians 11:1-15)
Tuesday, Apr. 26—In Christ All Things Hold Together (Colossians 1:15-23)
Wednesday, Apr. 27—We Bring You the Good News (Acts 13:26-33)
Thursday, Apr. 28—Everyone Who Believes Is Set Free (Acts 13:34-41)
Friday, Apr. 29—Bring Salvation to All (Acts 13:44-49)
Saturday, Apr. 30—Do Not Turn to Another Gospel (Galatians 1:1-7)
Sunday, May 1—Only One Gospel Directly from God (Galatians 1:8-12)

Paul affirms that his message came from divine *revelation*. It did not come by way of tradition or by rabbinical instruction, both of which are important sources of truth to the Jews (and to the Judaizers whom Paul seeks to refute). It came *by the revelation of Jesus Christ*. This revelation includes not only Jesus' appearance to Paul on the road to Damascus, but also later instruction that may have occurred during the time Paul spent in Arabia (Galatians 1:17).

Like the rest of Scripture, the gospel that Paul teaches is no mere human invention. A way revealed by God was necessary, for left to our own devices and investigations we never would find the way to Heaven.

Conclusion

A. Benedict Arnold

Every nation or culture has stories of both heroes and traitors. Communities often raise statues to those individuals who are considered heroes. They do no such thing for those regarded as traitors.

Consider an example from one famous traitor story. What do you think of when you hear the name of Benedict Arnold? If you know American history, chances are it is not good. Benedict Arnold started out as one of George Washington's most trusted generals. Perhaps due to disappointment or jealousy, he offered to join the British side. As a result, neither side respected him. The fact is, you can't be on two sides at once, or as Jesus put it, "No man can serve two masters" (Matthew 6:24).

Paul saw the desertion of the Christians in Galatia in similar strong terms. He could not understand how anyone would embrace a position that endangered one's soul and placed one on the losing side. Paul's message to the Galatians and to us is to stay loyal to the gospel. If we fail to do so, this is the equivalent of being a traitor to the cause. If we do stay true to the gospel, we will be numbered among the heroes of faith.

B. Prayer

Gracious Father, we thank You that we do not have to depend on our righteousness to enter into Heaven. If we did, there would be no good news for us. Your gospel is the best news we have ever received. We thank You for Jesus, the author and bearer of this good news, and we pray in His name. Amen.

C. Thought to Remember

"[Jesus] gave himself for our sins, that he might deliver us from this present evil world" (Galatians 1:4).

Learning by Doing

This page contains an alternative lesson plan emphasizing learning activities. Classes desiring such student involvement will find these suggestions helpful.

Learning Goals

After this lesson a student should be able to:

1. Give reasons why there is only one gospel revealed by God.

2. Identify ancient and modern false gospels.

3. Make a commitment to remain faithful to the gospel of Jesus Christ.

Into the Lesson

Write on a poster or on the chalkboard: "Why is truth important? What are the consequences of falsehood?" Then write the following circumstances under the above heading:

• From your auto mechanic
• From your doctor
• From your child's schoolteacher
• From your spiritual mentor

As you write each circumstance, allow the class members to share answers about why truth is important in that situation and why falsehood is dangerous.

Make the transition to today's Bible study by pointing out that if we demand nothing but the truth in areas such as these just mentioned, why should we settle for anything less in matters with eternal ramifications? We must be certain that we have the truth when learning about such issues. If we do not, our eternal destiny is at risk. The experience of the Galatian churches will help us keep our eyes on the true gospel.

Into the Word

Activity #1. Begin the Bible study with a brief lecture on the background of the book of Galatians. Use the notes in the Lesson Introduction, the Lesson Background, and the comments on Galatians 1:1, 2 to complete this lecture. Prepare and display the outline below as you speak.

I. GALATIANS
   A. Paul's Magna Carta
   B. Christian Declaration of Independence
   C. Esteemed by Martin Luther
II. PAUL'S AUDIENCE
III. PAUL'S RESPONSE TO ATTACKS
   A. On Paul Himself
   B. On the Gospel
IV. PAUL, AN APOSTLE

Activity #2. The following tasks may be done by small groups or by the entire class, depending upon time available and class preference. If using small groups, give each group a marker

and poster board and the following instructions. Also give Group 2 a photocopy of the lesson commentary on Galatians 1:6-9.

Task #1. Read Galatians 1:3, 4. These verses summarize what Jesus did on our behalf. Discuss and list the significance of the following phrases about Jesus' work drawn from this text. Be ready to share your notes with the class.

• Gave himself
• For our sins
• Delivered us from this present evil world
• According to the will of God

Task #2. Read Galatians 1:6-9 and the lesson commentary on these verses. Your task is to discuss and summarize Paul's concerns for the Galatians and their spiritual welfare.

Task #3. Read Galatians 1:10-12. You have two tasks. First, list and comment on the key phrases that give authority to the gospel of which Paul speaks. Second, Paul's opponents were suggesting that he was preaching grace simply to please his audience. How might preaching grace (versus the Old Testament law) be misunderstood as letting people "off the hook"? Why would Paul's critics have viewed this as an easy gospel?

If using groups for the above exercise, allow each group to report its conclusions.

Into Life

To apply this Scripture to everyday life, ask people to cite ways to be sure we stay connected with the true gospel of Jesus Christ. List their answers on a piece of poster board. Ideas may include study or know God's Word, maintain a daily Bible study time, attend Sunday school, invite a guest teacher or speaker on apologetics (a defense of basic Christian beliefs), always test teachings against God's Word, pray for wisdom, and other suggestions.

After compiling the list, ask groups of three or four people to discuss and select what they think are the two most important or helpful ideas on the list. Most groups will likely select an answer indicating the need for an intimate knowledge of the Bible.

Conclude the lesson by asking these same groups to pray together. Each person is to pray for himself and for one other person or group in the church, focusing on praying for faithfulness to the true gospel.

Let's Talk It Over

The questions on this page are designed to promote discussion of the lesson by the class and to encourage application of the lesson Scriptures. The answers provided are only discussion starters. Let your class talk it over from there.

1. What are some occasions when we may need to remind someone of our authority or position? Have you ever had your position or authority challenged? What was the result?

Unfortunately, when we need to remind others of our position or authority, they are usually challenging that authority in some way. Probably the most common example occurs when children defy parental authority. A parent cannot allow his or her authority to be undermined. Although the resulting confrontation can be difficult, it is far better in the long run to maintain one's authority than to allow rebellion to go unchecked. In Paul's case, people were directly questioning his authority as an apostle. Indirectly they were challenging God himself, since He had chosen Paul as His messenger. That kind of rebellion could not go unanswered.

2. How can we identify a "calling"? How can we tell if God has actually called a certain preacher, or if he is speaking on his own authority?

A calling from God is personal and is sometimes difficult to explain or understand. Certainly a measure of giftedness plays into it; for example, someone who cannot carry a tune is not likely called to lead worship. Temperament and desire also indicate the presence of a calling. In addition, the counsel of trusted Christian friends can be used to assist in evaluating the validity of what one believes is a call. To determine whether God has indeed called an individual, keep in mind Paul's counsel to Timothy about the importance of both life and doctrine (1 Timothy 4:16). Is the individual in question consistent in demonstrating Christian character? And if someone is preaching a false gospel or a watered-down version of the true gospel, then his calling did not come from God.

3. What sets Jesus apart from other spiritual leaders? How can we distinguish Jesus' claims from others in the religious world?

Our commentator notes three phrases from Galatians 1:4 that describe the ministry of Jesus. Most noteworthy among these is the first one: He "gave himself for our sins." No other religious leader claimed to be a personal sacrifice for our sins. Some may have tried to set an example of holy living or taught others a holy way, but none of them claimed to have personally taken our sins and wiped them away. In addition, in 1 Corinthians 15:4, Paul cites the resurrection of Jesus as part of the gospel. This too distinguishes Jesus and His message from other religions or supposed ways to God. There are many resources available today in the field of apologetics that can aid Christians in providing a defense of their faith in Jesus.

4. Why do some people abandon the gospel? What makes competing religions and worldviews attractive?

There is no one answer to these questions. Some people are attracted to other faiths because of confusion about true Christianity. Some are attracted because they are personally drawn to an adherent of a competing gospel, or, unfortunately, because they are driven from the faith by someone who claims to be a Christian but exhibits little of God's grace in his or her own life. Keep in mind that Satan is a master at making falsehood attractive; in fact, he masquerades as "an angel of light" (2 Corinthians 11:14).

5. Are we ever tempted to soften the gospel message so we do not offend others? Do churches sometimes focus too much on grace and not enough on personal responsibility or moral absolutes?

Today's world often accuses Christianity of being intolerant because of the message that Jesus is the only way to Heaven (John 14:6). In the face of such hostility, it can be easy for Christians to become intimidated into silence.

We must remember and emphasize, however, that this is not *our* position; it is Jesus' position—and He has the credentials to back it up. It is true that some churches overemphasize one part of the gospel message over another, but this is by no means limited to churches that seem to preach an "easy grace." A "doctrinally pure" church that never emphasizes God's love for the lost or that focuses only on moral issues every week is also altering the gospel. The church must strive for a proper balance in presenting its message. Perhaps the following five-word phrase from Ephesians 4:15 will keep our focus where it should be: "speaking the truth in love."

Know Salvation by Faith

DEVOTIONAL READING: Galatians 3:6-14.

BACKGROUND SCRIPTURE: Galatians 2:15–3:5.

PRINTED TEXT: Galatians 2:15–3:5.

Galatians 2:15-21

15 We who are Jews by nature, and not sinners of the Gentiles,

16 Knowing that a man is not justified by the works of the law, but by the faith of Jesus Christ, even we have believed in Jesus Christ, that we might be justified by the faith of Christ, and not by the works of the law: for by the works of the law shall no flesh be justified.

17 But if, while we seek to be justified by Christ, we ourselves also are found sinners, is therefore Christ the minister of sin? God forbid.

18 For if I build again the things which I destroyed, I make myself a transgressor.

19 For I through the law am dead to the law, that I might live unto God.

20 I am crucified with Christ: nevertheless I live; yet not I, but Christ liveth in me: and the life which I now live in the flesh I live by the faith of the Son of God, who loved me, and gave himself for me.

21 I do not frustrate the grace of God: for if righteousness come by the law, then Christ is dead in vain.

Galatians 3:1-5

1 O foolish Galatians, who hath bewitched you, that ye should not obey the truth, before whose eyes Jesus Christ hath been evidently set forth, crucified among you?

2 This only would I learn of you, Received ye the Spirit by the works of the law, or by the hearing of faith?

3 Are ye so foolish? having begun in the Spirit, are ye now made perfect by the flesh?

4 Have ye suffered so many things in vain? if it be yet in vain.

5 He therefore that ministereth to you the Spirit, and worketh miracles among you, doeth he it by the works of the law, or by the hearing of faith?

GOLDEN TEXT: I am crucified with Christ: nevertheless I live; yet not I, but Christ liveth in me: and the life which I now live in the flesh I live by the faith of the Son of God, who loved me, and gave himself for me.—Galatians 2:20.

Lesson Aims

After participating in this lesson, students should be able to:

1. Define and explain the doctrine of justification by faith.

2. Compare their own awareness of God's grace to that experienced by the early Christians.

3. Prepare a testimony of God's grace to be used in everyday life.

Lesson Outline

INTRODUCTION
   A. Send Me Back to Jail
   B. Lesson Background
I. JUSTIFICATION BY FAITH DEFENDED (Galatians 2:15-21)
   A. Provides Man's Only Hope (vv. 15, 16)
      The Failure of Law
   B. Does Not Promote Sin (vv. 17-19)
   C. Honors the Death of Christ (vv. 20, 21)
II. JUSTIFICATION BY FAITH TESTED (Galatians 3:1-5)
   A. How Did You Receive the Holy Spirit? (vv. 1, 2)
   B. How Did You Begin to Grow? (vv. 3, 4)
   C. How Did God Reveal His Power? (v. 5)
      Spiritual Progeria
CONCLUSION
   A. God's Plus Sign
   B. Prayer
   C. Thought to Remember

Introduction

A. Send Me Back to Jail

Let's suppose you had spent much of your life in prison. At some point the appropriate government official gives you a pardon. You are set free! What would people think if you immediately turned around and walked back into the prison and said, "I don't want to go. I want to stay here." People would think you had lost your mind. And they would probably be right.

A similar kind of decision on the part of the Galatians troubled Paul. These believers had heard Paul's preaching and had learned the glory of God's grace. They had heard the message that liberated Peter and Paul and the rest of the early Christians from a law-oriented means of being right with God. Paul could not understand why anyone would want to go back to a system that was oppressive, frustrating, and did not accomplish what it was intended to do.

Today's lesson shows Paul pleading with the Galatians, both on a logical and an emotional level. It is clear from the apostle's impassioned words that he is greatly concerned that those whom he had worked so hard to bring to Christ remain free in Christ.

B. Lesson Background

Before studying these verses, we must keep in mind that the Jews in Paul's time had a very different understanding of the word *law* than we do. We tend to think of *law* as including civil rules and regulations—prescriptions that govern our conduct with each other. While there was an element of that within Old Testament laws, that system was primarily a way to get right with God. To the Jew in Paul's time, these laws consisted of not only regulations concerning one's relationships with others, but also ceremonial regulations covering such matters as worship and diet. Moral and ethical living was only a part of what the Jews thought of when they used the word *law*.

There is another important factor in the background of this text, and Paul alludes to it in the verses immediately preceding the first part of our text. It concerns Paul's report of a serious disagreement between him and Peter (Galatians 2:11-14). The conflict arose over how Peter treated certain Gentiles at Antioch where Paul and Barnabas were ministering. Antioch was the first church to evangelize large numbers of Gentile converts. Peter had previously spoken eloquently on two occasions about accepting the Gentiles. The first followed the conversion of Cornelius and his household (Acts 11:1-18); the second came at the Jerusalem Conference (Acts 15:6-11).

However, during the incident cited by Paul in Galatians, Peter shunned Gentile believers in order to spend time with Jewish Christians. Paul notes that Peter did this, "fearing them which were of the circumcision" (Galatians 2:12). Peter seems to have yielded to a measure of "peer pressure" and had demonstrated some of the qualities associated with the "old" Peter (unreliable, quick to falter under pressure). No doubt Peter's actions hurt many of the newer Gentile Christians. Peter's behavior had even affected Barnabas (v. 13), who was known for his generous spirit. Paul confronted Peter and told him that what he was doing was wrong. That surely took some courage!

This confrontation between Paul and Peter, along with the material we are covering in today's lesson, show how controversial the question of Jew/Gentile relations was in the early church. When one reads the book of Acts, he cannot help but see that God is nudging and pushing the church to reach out to Gentiles with the gospel message. The gospel first comes to Jews, then to Samaritans, then to an Ethiopian Jewish proselyte, and finally to Cornelius, a Gentile. As noted earlier, it was Peter, not Paul, who welcomed the first Gentile convert. This may be another reason why Paul was so disturbed about Peter's conduct in Antioch.

Following the report of this difficult confrontation, Paul elaborates on the importance of justification by faith. Perhaps this teaching was some of what he shared with Peter.

I. Justification by Faith Defended (Galatians 2:15-21)

A. Provides Man's Only Hope (vv. 15, 16)

15. We who are Jews by nature, and not sinners of the Gentiles.

The word *we* may refer to Peter and Paul, to all the apostles, or to the early Jewish Christians in general. All of these were *Jews by nature*; that is, they were born Jewish. Certainly there were some advantages to being Jewish. The Jews had a long experience with understanding God's law, celebrating God's redemption, and listening to God's prophets tell of a coming Messiah. This was all part of their history as God's chosen people. (See Romans 9:4, 5.)

By referring to the *Gentiles* as *sinners*, Paul is sarcastically using language that was being used against the Gentiles. According to Jewish tradition, it was not that Gentiles were incapable of doing any moral good. They may do some good deeds, but since they do not have the law, they cannot please God. From the law's point of view, they were sinners. [See question #1, page 312.]

The argument Paul is getting ready to make is essentially the same as his argument in Romans 2:17-29. Physical descent has nothing to do with one's salvation. Christ has come to save all people. As Paul teaches in both Romans and Galatians, the true "sons of Abraham" are those individuals who exercise faith as he did and are thus counted righteous in God's eyes (Romans 4:11, 12, 20-25; Galatians 3:7-9, 29).

16. Knowing that a man is not justified by the works of the law, but by the faith of Jesus Christ, even we have believed in Jesus Christ, that we might be justified by the faith of Christ, and not by the works of the law: for by the works of the law shall no flesh be justified.

When Paul says, *Knowing that a man is not justified by the works of the law*, he is not speaking of any person in particular but of all humanity in general. He is confident of this claim, as one who had at one time sought righteousness by means of the law (Philippians 3:6). (Note that he affirms three times in this single verse that *the works of the law* cannot provide justification.) By using the word *we*, he maintains that Peter knows this, too. And Peter should have been just as confident of this truth, given his experiences with the household of Cornelius and at the Jerusalem Conference.

There is only one way to be justified, states Paul, and that is *by the faith of* (or in) *Jesus Christ*. The word translated as *justified* comes from the language of the courtroom. It literally means "to declare innocent." The law of Moses could never produce such an outcome. For one thing, no one can ever keep the law perfectly. Second, it is possible for someone to keep the law outwardly, yet without any inner love, faith, or commitment to God. On one occasion, Jesus noted the Pharisees' failure to observe the "weightier matters of the law" while paying close attention to certain external details (Matthew 23:23).

This does not mean that works are unimportant. Good works are meant to be a sign of our love for Christ and evidence of a living faith. Paul tells us in Ephesians 2:10 that Christians are "created in Christ Jesus unto good works, which God hath before ordained that we should walk in them." What Paul is specifically dealing with in Galatians is depending on the Old Testament law as a means of salvation. He asserts that keeping the law can never make anyone good enough to enter Heaven. His teaching on this point is the same as that found in the early chapters of Romans. [See question #2, page 312.]

THE FAILURE OF LAW

Some people who live east of the Rocky Mountains refer to the West Coast of America as "the left coast" (for more reasons than just the fact that it appears on the left side of the map of

---

How to Say It

ANTIOCH. *An*-tee-ock.
BARNABAS. *Barn*-uh-bus.
CORNELIUS. Cor-*neel*-yus.
ETHIOPIAN. Ee-thee-*o*-pea-un.
GALATIANS. Guh-*lay*-shuns.
GENTILES. *Jen*-tiles.
JUDAISM. *Joo*-day-iz-um.
PHARISEES. *Fair*-uh-sees.
PROSELYTE. *prahss*-uh-light.
SAMARITANS. Suh-*mare*-uh-tuns.

the United States). The San Francisco Bay area, in particular, has long been known for its left-ward-leaning politics and more recently for being a bastion of "political correctness."

An example of the kind of thinking that brings derision on some Californians came about in the spring of 2003. In the San Francisco peninsula city of Palo Alto, the city council passed a resolution that forbade city officials from making facial expressions that showed "disagreement or disgust" during council meetings, including rolling the eyes, sticking out the tongue, sneering, and frowning. The council quickly became the butt of jokes by comedians and everyday folks alike, so after a month, they backed down and simply called for "respectful silence and decorum."

These council members finally learned what Paul knew about law. You cannot make a person "good" or "just" simply by passing laws. You can enforce "good" behavior; but unless the heart is in it, there is no moral content to those actions. In urging the Galatians not to revert to the law of Moses, Paul is saying that moral regeneration comes through faith in Christ. That alone can justify us; laws, no matter how well intentioned, cannot.   —C. R. B.

B. Does Not Promote Sin (vv. 17-19)

17. But if, while we seek to be justified by Christ, we ourselves also are found sinners, is therefore Christ the minister of sin? God forbid.

In this verse, Paul attempts to anticipate some objections that might be raised against his position. He seems to be addressing those who think his emphasis on grace will promote *sin*. Some might argue with Paul that all of his talk of grace and justification by faith will lead to moral laxity. People will think they can do anything they want with impunity, then simply ask to be forgiven. Paul strongly denies that this is the outcome of the gospel of grace. He declares that *Christ* would never do anything that would make us sin more and thus make Christ to be *the minister of sin*. The whole idea leads Paul to respond with *God forbid*. [See question #3, page 312.]

Once again, we can see a similarity between this teaching and what Paul outlines in his letter to the Romans. In this case the similarity is found in Romans 6, where Paul says, "Shall we continue in sin, that grace may abound? *God forbid*" (Romans 6:1, 2).

18. For if I build again the things which I destroyed, I make myself a transgressor.

In the previous verse, Paul considered the possible objection of some that the doctrine of justification could actually be promoting sin. In this verse, he maintains that what would consti-

tute sin would be a return to embracing the law as a means of salvation. This is most likely what he means by his reference to building *again the things which I destroyed*. Even though Paul believed that the law is good and has a purpose (Romans 7:7-12), he recognized that he had, in a sense, *destroyed* the system of law by preaching grace, not law, as the way to be right with God.

In its simplest terms, Paul is describing a situation where a person would come to Christ but later try to go back to keeping the law of Moses as a means of salvation. Anyone who does so would be a *transgressor*.

Again, it is helpful to compare Paul's teaching here with what he says in Romans: "Christ is the end of the law for righteousness to every one that believeth" (Romans 10:4). It is also similar to the theme of the book of Hebrews, which seeks to encourage Jewish Christians not to abandon their faith and return to Judaism. The key word in Hebrews is *better*, because the writer wants to show that the New Covenant under Christ is superior to the Old Covenant (Hebrews 8:8-13).

19. For I through the law am dead to the law, that I might live unto God.

The law has fulfilled its function when it has led a person to see his need for grace. There is no reason to go back to it, once one has experienced grace. The law taught Paul that he was a sinner and that his sins could be dealt with only by becoming *dead to* (forsaking) *the law*. The law shows us our need for a Savior, thus preparing us for the good news of the gospel. Once one accepts Christ as Savior, there can be no turning back to the law.

Indirectly, Paul is saying that the law demands death for sin and that there has been a death. It is Jesus' death that satisfies the law's demands. To accept His death as the substitute for ours is the only way for us to *live unto God*. [See question #4, page 312.]

C. Honors the Death of Christ (vv. 20, 21)

20. I am crucified with Christ: nevertheless I live; yet not I, but Christ liveth in me: and the life which I now live in the flesh I live by the faith of the Son of God, who loved me, and gave himself for me.

This is one of the most well-known verses in the book of Galatians. How are we *crucified with Christ*? He bore our sins on the cross. We are united with Him when we accept His death as the substitute for ours. How do we *live*? Once more, it is helpful to consider Paul's teaching on this matter in Romans, particularly in Romans 6. There he says that just as Jesus arose from the dead to live a new life, through baptism we rise from our death to sin to "walk in newness of life" (Romans 6:4). That new life is lived under a new master; as Paul puts it, *Christ liveth in me.* He empowers us to keep the law as well as forgiving us of our failures to keep it. Thus our lives are not ours anymore; they belong to Christ. If we accept this, says Paul, why would we want to continue to serve sin? Why should we return to the law? [See question #5, page 312.]

21. I do not frustrate the grace of God: for if righteousness come by the law, then Christ is dead in vain.

Paul brings his argument to a compelling conclusion. He has answered his critics and now claims that if they are right, then the death of Christ means nothing. If *the law* were sufficient as a means of making us right with God, Jesus would not have had to die.

II. Justification by Faith Tested (Galatians 3:1-5)

A. How Did You Receive the Holy Spirit?

(vv. 1, 2)

1. O foolish Galatians, who hath bewitched you, that ye should not obey the truth, before whose eyes Jesus Christ hath been evidently set forth, crucified among you?

The Greek word translated *foolish* means literally "to have no mind." It does not mean uninformed or ignorant. The word implies that the *Galatians* know the *truth* but have not acted on it. They provide an excellent illustration of why Scripture so often warns God's people against being deceived. The Phillips' translation renders *foolish Galatians* as "dear idiots." Perhaps such a phrase captures both Paul's deep love for the Galatians and his disappointment at how quickly they have forsaken the truth of the gospel.

Paul sees the Galatians' rejection of the gospel as so absurd that surely someone must have *bewitched* them. The Greek term carries with it the idea of casting a spell by "the evil eye." This does not mean that Paul actually believes someone can be bewitched. He is simply using a figure of speech to make his point. Today we might say something like, "Who has hypnotized you?" but we would not mean for that to be taken in a literal sense.

Paul goes on to describe Jesus' crucifixion as being *evidently set forth* before the Galatians' *eyes.* The word translated *set forth* was normally used to refer to a placard that was set up in a public place. Jesus' crucifixion was clearly, unmistakably set before the Galatians through the preaching of the gospel. How could they reject such a message and act as if they never heard it? Other commentators believe that this verse sim-

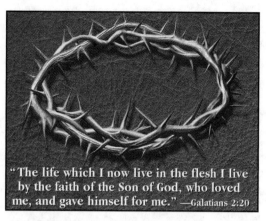

"The life which I now live in the flesh I live by the faith of the Son of God, who loved me, and gave himself for me." —Galatians 2:20

Visual for lesson 10. *Use this visual as you discuss what Paul's words, "I am crucified with Christ," mean for Christians today.*

ply describes how Jesus himself was put on public display when He was *crucified.*

2. This only would I learn of you, Received ye the Spirit by the works of the law, or by the hearing of faith?

Paul then asks the Galatians how they *received* the Holy *Spirit.* Did that happen *by the works of the law*? Absolutely not; the Spirit was received *by the hearing of faith.* Most likely this expression conveys the idea of "believing the message you heard." The thought is similar to that found in Romans 10:17: "So then faith cometh by hearing, and hearing by the word of God." [See question #6, page 312.]

B. How Did You Begin to Grow? (vv. 3, 4)

3. Are ye so foolish? having begun in the Spirit, are ye now made perfect by the flesh?

Paul asks *Are ye so foolish?* using the same word for *foolish* that he used in verse 1. Then, building on his argument in the preceding verse, Paul argues that if the Galatians' Christian lives began by receiving *the Spirit* through faith, how could growth be maintained by striving to live Christ's life *in the flesh*? The fact is that this is an impossibility. Moving from life under the control of the Spirit to life under the control of the flesh would be going backward, not forward. The longer a Christian lives, the more he or she should be less tied to the flesh and more attuned to the Holy Spirit. Paul will call further attention to this in Galatians 5:16-26. We will be studying a portion of this passage in Lesson 13.

4. Have ye suffered so many things in vain? if it be yet in vain.

What have the Galatian Christians *suffered*? We do not know for sure about the *many things* to which Paul is referring. He may be describing the kind of physical suffering common to all human beings. He may be citing the persecution experienced by the Galatians.

Another possibility is that Paul is using "suffer" in an older and more general sense to simply describe the events that have happened to the Galatians—in other words, their experiences since obeying the gospel. Paul would then be asking, "Does all that you have received since coming to Christ mean nothing to you?"

C. How Did God Reveal His Power? (v. 5)

5. He therefore that ministereth to you the Spirit, and worketh miracles among you, doeth he it by the works of the law, or by the hearing of faith?

Paul's final question in this section of Scripture asks the Galatians to think back to when they saw the power of God at work in various *miracles*. When miracles happened, asks Paul, did they come as a consequence of keeping the old law? The answer is no. Paul uses once more the phrase *the hearing of faith*. Again, he emphasizes that whatever spiritual blessings the Galatians have experienced have come in response to the message of God's truth rather than through legalistic observances.

SPIRITUAL PROGERIA

Situations are not always as they appear on the outside. A tragic example of this can be seen in the victims of what is known as Hutchinson-Gilford progeria (pro-*jair*-ee-uh) syndrome. This syndrome develops because a single DNA molecule (out of three billion DNA units in the human genetic structure) is misplaced. Children born with progeria seem to be normal at birth, but within eighteen months they begin a process of accelerated aging. They become three-foot-tall,

thirty-five-pound "old people." Their skin becomes wrinkled and their bones become fragile and subject to fractures—traits we expect in people of advanced years. Most victims of progeria lose their hair by the time they are four years old, and they usually die of heart disease or stroke by the time they are thirteen.

Some among the Galatian Christians apparently thought they could become mature spiritually by going back to the law. However, Paul tells them that situations are not as they seem: legalism is a deadly syndrome that produces only the *appearance* of spiritual health. But legalism quenches the power of the Holy Spirit—God's power to give us life. All too soon it becomes clear that there is no energizing spirit working in those who trust in the works of legalism. They may grow "old," but will never grow to real maturity in Christ.   —C. R. B.

Conclusion

A. God's Plus Sign

One Sunday morning a small boy entered the sanctuary of a church building for the very first time. He was completely unfamiliar with the Christian faith and with many of the characteristics of a church building that most Christians take for granted. Among the first items he noticed was the large cross attached to the wall at the front of the sanctuary. Turning to the adult who had brought him that morning, he asked, "Say, why is that plus sign on the wall up there?"

That young man spoke far more truth than he realized. The cross is indeed God's "plus sign." It speaks to us of all the blessings God wants to add to our lives. He wants to add all that was subtracted when man sinned in the Garden of Eden.

Some believe that being a Christian is a losing proposition—that one does not get back as much as he gives up. That is the very opposite of what Jesus taught: "Whosoever will lose his life for my sake shall find it" (Matthew 16:25). So the little boy was right. In a world where so much that confronts us is negative, the cross remains God's plus sign.

B. Prayer

Dear Father, thank You for setting me free. Having left the prison of sin, help me not to live like a prisoner. Help me to give my life to You, in gratitude for all You have given me. Through Christ, whose death and resurrection made the difference. Amen.

C. Thought to Remember

We are not saved because of how good we are. We are saved because of how good God is.

Home Daily Bible Readings

Monday, May 2—Righteousness Through Faith (Romans 3:21-26)

Tuesday, May 3—Grace Given to You in Christ (1 Corinthians 1:3-9)

Wednesday, May 4—Fullness of Life in Christ (Colossians 2:6-14)

Thursday, May 5—Good News for Gentiles and Jews (Galatians 2:5-10)

Friday, May 6—We Are All Saved by Faith (Galatians 2:15-21)

Saturday, May 7—Law or Faith (Galatians 3:1-5)

Sunday, May 8—All Receive the Spirit's Promise (Galatians 3:6-14)

Learning by Doing

*This page contains an alternative lesson plan emphasizing learning activities.
Classes desiring such student involvement will find these suggestions helpful.*

Learning Goals

After this lesson students should be able to:

1. Define and explain justification by faith.

2. Compare their own awareness of God's grace to that experienced by the early Christians.

3. Prepare a testimony of God's grace to be used in everyday life.

Into the Lesson

Begin this lesson with a brief skit that you should give to three people during the week. Ask them to meet about thirty minutes before class for a brief rehearsal. Encourage them to be creative and to "ham it up." Use simple props to represent a jail cell. A sign on the wall can read "County Jail." Include two chairs with a small table or crate between them. Two prisoners will be playing cards or checkers on the table or crate. Their small talk could include why they are incarcerated, family background, etc. It should be clear that one prisoner has spent most of his adult life in prison. The third character will be the jailer who arrives and announces to the prisoner who has been in jail most of his life that the state governor has given him a pardon. As this prisoner walks out of the cell, he suddenly hesitates and says, "I don't want to go," and goes back into the cell. The jailer asks if he has lost his mind.

Make the transition to Bible study by stating that if something like this actually happened, people would think such a prisoner had lost his mind. Yet this is how many Christians live today. They continue to struggle with a legalism that keeps them from enjoying the freedom of God's grace.

How do we overcome such a mind-set? Paul's letter to the Galatians can help us discover the joy of living in God's grace.

Into the Word

Use three class members to prepare a series of brief presentations to be used as part of your Bible study time. Select and meet with these people early in the week to explain their tasks. Each person is allowed a maximum of five minutes for his or her presentation. Give each presenter a photocopy of the entire commentary on today's text.

Presentation #1: Begin with a brief lecture based on the Lesson Background on pages 306

and 307 of the lesson commentary. Put the following outline on a piece of poster board or on the chalkboard.

    I. Old Testament Law

    II. The Gentile Controversy: Paul and Peter

    III. Justification by Faith

Teacher: Make the transition to the next presentation by emphasizing that we need to understand the difference between justification by faith and justification by the law. Read Galatians 2:15-21 before the next presentation.

Presentation #2: This presentation will focus on Galatians 2:16. Use the lesson commentary and a Bible dictionary to define justification, and explain the difference between justification by faith and justification by the law. Also address the question, "Does this mean that works are unimportant?"

Presentation #3: Using Galatians 3:1-5, explain and list on a poster board or on the chalkboard reasons why justification by faith is a better system than justification by the law. After completing this presentation, ask class members if they have other ideas to add to the list.

Make the transition to applying this lesson by reminding the class of the opening skit. It appears that the Galatian Christians, although freed from the law of Moses, wanted to go back to it.

Into Life

Use all the following activities if time permits.

Activity #1: Brainstorming. Ask the class, "What might be symptoms or examples of a Christian who is living with a 'justification by the law' mentality? What kinds of behavior or thoughts might be handicapping this person's sense of freedom?" List these symptoms or examples on the chalkboard.

Activity #2: Helping a Friend. Ask the class to imagine a Christian friend who is handicapped by some of the symptoms or examples cited during the previous activity. Ask class members how they would explain the joy of "justification by faith" to such a person.

Activity #3: Creative Praise. Celebrate God's grace and justification by faith by compiling a list of songs and lines from songs that highlight faith and grace. Conclude by singing one of those songs (such as "Amazing Grace," "Faith is the Victory," or "I Will Sing of the Mercies of the Lord Forever").

Let's Talk It Over

The questions on this page are designed to promote discussion of the lesson by the class and to encourage application of the lesson Scriptures. The answers provided are only discussion starters. Let your class talk it over from there.

1. Do we ever feel superior to those who do not know Christ? Why is this an easy trap to fall into? What are some ways we can avoid looking down on those who have yet to hear the gospel?

We can become like the Pharisees in Jesus' day, who "trusted in themselves that they were righteous, and despised others" (Luke 18:9). We too can consider non-Christians in disparaging terms. The trap of thinking "we're better than they are" can affect our ability to evangelize and can destroy any witness we may have in the community. It is important to remember that whether we grew up in the church or came to Christ later in life, we are no better than anyone else is. We are all sinners, saved by grace and not by any merit of our own. Far from being about us, salvation is all about God and His grace.

2. Have you ever felt that you were not "good enough" for God? How can we address these issues in ourselves and in others?

The reality is that none of us is "good enough" for God. That is really the whole point of the doctrine of grace. God knew that we could never earn our own salvation. For many people, it is easier to believe that God can forgive them than it is for them to forgive themselves. As Christians we must continually remind people that salvation is through God's grace, not through their own efforts. This message is not an invitation to sin. Rather, it is a message that offers forgiveness and empowers us to live for God in freedom rather than in fear.

3. In what ways do our sins reflect upon the Savior? How do non-Christians tend to react when learning of a Christian's sin?

One may suggest two responses to the first question. First, the sins of Christians do not diminish or tarnish the work of Christ. Our sins are our own and are in no way a consequence of anything Jesus has done. However (and second), we should be honest and acknowledge that people will have a hard time seeing the light of Jesus if the vessels carrying that light are dirty. Non-Christians are often quick to point out the hypocrites and failures in the church, particularly if they are prominent people in the Christian world. Perhaps we can point out that Jesus, the Head of the church, knew that that His church would not be perfect. He often spoke of false teachers and of those who would be wolves dressed in sheep's clothing (Matthew 7:15).

4. Is Jesus the only way to salvation? If we claim that Jesus is the only way, are we being judgmental and arrogant?

This cuts to the heart of Christianity. The central tenet of Christianity is that Jesus' death and resurrection were essential for the salvation of all people, Jew and Gentile alike. Jesus himself said, "I am the way, the truth, and the life: no man cometh unto the Father, but by me" (John 14:6). Claiming that Jesus is the only way is simply being true to the Bible. Is it judgmental to believe that Jesus is the only way to Heaven? Yes. But it is also judgmental not to believe it, and in such a case we are placing our judgment above God's.

5. How are we "crucified with Christ"? How can we be crucified and yet live? In what ways can we identify with Christ's death?

Some people take this passage far too literally and actually hang from crosses as a form of physical identification with Christ's crucifixion. Although Jesus' crucifixion was very real and led to His death, Paul is referring in Galatians 2:20 to a spiritual crucifixion where we nail our sins, our old way of living, and our dependence on the law to the cross. Perhaps the most profound way to identify with Christ's death is the act of baptism by immersion, as described in Romans 6:1-4. Symbolically, the immersed person dies to his old life, is buried in the water, and then rises to begin a new life.

6. How did you come to faith in Christ? What experiences led you to do so? What is your testimony of your own faith journey?

In Romans 10:14, 15, Paul asks several rhetorical questions to emphasize that ultimately we come to faith through someone sharing the gospel with us. That person may have been a preacher speaking from a pulpit, a teacher using a lectern, a small group leader sharing from her notes, or a parent praying by a child's bedside. Regardless, at some point you heard the message and responded to it. Hearing the testimonies of other Christians as to how they came to Christ can be very uplifting.

Understand the Purpose of the Law

DEVOTIONAL READING: **Romans 3:27-31.**

BACKGROUND SCRIPTURE: **Galatians 3:19–4:7.**

PRINTED TEXT: **Galatians 3:19-29; 4:4-7.**

Galatians 3:19-29

19 Wherefore then serveth the law? It was added because of transgressions, till the seed should come to whom the promise was made; and it was ordained by angels in the hand of a mediator.

20 Now a mediator is not a mediator of one, but God is one.

21 Is the law then against the promises of God? God forbid: for if there had been a law given which could have given life, verily righteousness should have been by the law.

22 But the Scripture hath concluded all under sin, that the promise by faith of Jesus Christ might be given to them that believe.

23 But before faith came, we were kept under the law, shut up unto the faith which should afterward be revealed.

24 Wherefore the law was our schoolmaster to bring us unto Christ, that we might be justified by faith.

25 But after that faith is come, we are no longer under a schoolmaster.

26 For ye are all the children of God by faith in Christ Jesus.

27 For as many of you as have been baptized into Christ have put on Christ.

28 There is neither Jew nor Greek, there is neither bond nor free, there is neither male nor female: for ye are all one in Christ Jesus.

29 And if ye be Christ's, then are ye Abraham's seed, and heirs according to the promise.

Galatians 4:4-7

4 But when the fulness of the time was come, God sent forth his Son, made of a woman, made under the law,

5 To redeem them that were under the law, that we might receive the adoption of sons.

6 And because ye are sons, God hath sent forth the Spirit of his Son into your hearts, crying, Abba, Father.

7 Wherefore thou art no more a servant, but a son; and if a son, then an heir of God through Christ.

GOLDEN TEXT: When the fulness of the time was come, God sent forth his Son, made of a woman, made under the law, to redeem them that were under the law, that we might receive the adoption of sons. And because ye are sons, God hath sent forth the Spirit of his Son into your hearts, crying, Abba, Father.—Galatians 4:4-6.

Lesson Aims

After completing this lesson, students should be able to:

1. Explain the word pictures of law and grace that Paul chose to use in this passage.

2. Identify blessings and responsibilities that come with God's adoption of each of us.

3. Express to God a sense of joy in knowing that they have been adopted by Him.

Lesson Outline

INTRODUCTION

    A. Temporary, But Necessary

    B. Lesson Background

I. THE FAILURES OF THE LAW (Galatians 3:19-22)

    A. Temporary (vv. 19, 20)

    B. Unable to Save (vv. 21, 22)

    Only a Temporary Thing

II. THE FUNCTION OF THE LAW (Galatians 3:23-26)

    A. A Prison Guard (v. 23)

    B. A Tutor (vv. 24-26)

    Needed: A Guide

III. THE FULFILLMENT OF THE LAW (Galatians 3:27-29; 4:4-7)

    A. By Grace We Put on Christ (v. 27)

    B. By Grace We Are United (v. 28)

    C. By Grace We Are Adopted (v. 29; 4:4-7)

CONCLUSION

    A. A Rich Relative

    B. Prayer

    C. Thought to Remember

Introduction

A. Temporary, But Necessary

There are many items in life that have a purpose, but are only temporary. Training wheels have a significant part to play in learning to ride a bicycle, but no one would argue that it is superior to riding without them. Braces have a purpose, but no one would argue that wearing braces is superior to unadorned, straight teeth. That something is temporary does not negate its importance or, in some cases, its necessity.

To Paul, the law of Moses was temporary, but necessary. It is fascinating to think that someone like Paul became the one to convey such a message as this. He had, at one time, given his entire life to the law and claimed that he was "blameless" concerning "the righteousness which is in the law" (Philippians 3:6). Then came the dramatic encounter with Christ on the road to Damascus, after which Paul gave his life to Christ and to the cause he had once tried to eliminate from the face of the earth. This Christ declared on one occasion that He had not come to destroy the law and the prophets, but to fulfill them (Matthew 5:17). Paul accepted this new perspective on the law; however, as we have noted during our studies from Galatians, not all first-century Christians were as willing to do so. Clarifying the purpose of the law was one of the reasons for Paul's letter to the Galatians.

B. Lesson Background

In today's printed text, Paul continues his efforts to instruct the Galatian Christians about the correct relationship between law and grace. Because of Paul's preaching of the gospel of grace, some opponents accused Paul of having no use for the Old Testament law at all. While Paul presented the new message of grace without apology, he also readily acknowledged that there was a purpose for the old law of Moses. He strenuously maintained that the new is superior, but that the old had a purpose in God's plan.

The verses that precede our printed text from Galatians 3 deal with God's covenant with Abraham. Paul raises this issue in order to show that God dealt with people on the basis of grace before the law of Moses was given. He shows that God's covenant with Abraham was based on grace and that Abraham had to respond to God by faith. He "believed God, and it was accounted to him for righteousness" (Galatians 3:6). Paul then notes that in one sense, God "preached . . . the gospel unto Abraham, saying, In thee shall all nations be blessed" (v. 8). We will see in our lesson today how Paul develops this thought and concludes by describing Christians as "Abraham's seed."

I. The Failures of the Law (Galatians 3:19-22)

A. Temporary (vv. 19, 20)

19. Wherefore then serveth the law? It was added because of transgressions, till the seed should come to whom the promise was made; and it was ordained by angels in the hand of a mediator.

Paul set forth such a strong case for grace and faith that his opponents sometimes accused him of being anti-law. In this verse and the verses to follow, Paul asks and answers the question, *Wherefore then serveth the law?* He maintains that the law was quite necessary; it had a definite purpose in God's plan.

That purpose is then stated as follows: the law *was added because of transgressions*. One of the purposes of the law of Moses was to expose sin and identify specific sins. This function was only temporary, however. The law was in effect *till the seed*, or the offspring, *should come to whom the promise was made*. The word *seed* in the Bible often refers to a person's progeny or descendants. In this case it is referring to one individual—Jesus Christ. Paul had made this point earlier in verses 16 and 17 of this chapter. Those verses make it clear that the *promise* mentioned in verse 19 is the promise God gave to Abraham. Verse 19 thus links Jesus to the promise made to Abraham that his seed would bless the entire world. [See question #1, page 320.]

In illustrating the superiority of the way of grace to the old law, Paul points out that the law was *ordained*, or put into effect, *by angels in the hand of a mediator*. That angels played a part in the giving of the law at Mount Sinai may be drawn from Deuteronomy 33:2. Stephen mentions angels and the giving of the law in his speech before the Sanhedrin (Acts 7:53). Hebrews 2:2 describes "the word spoken by angels" in a context that is referring to the law of Moses. Perhaps this is one reason why Paul mentions the possibility of an "angel from heaven" being the source of another gospel (Galatians 1:8). The *mediator* Paul mentions is Moses.

While all of this is a testimony to the importance of the law, it also helps to highlight how differently the New Covenant was delivered. This will become a bit clearer as we proceed further in our study.

20. Now a mediator is not a mediator of one, but God is one.

Paul's argument in this verse seems to be as follows: *a mediator* represents both sides of a covenant, but a promise depends on only *one* side. In this way, Paul makes a case for the superiority of the New Covenant. Why is it superior? *God* himself came to us in the person of Jesus Christ. It is true that there are places in Scripture where Jesus is referred to as a mediator (as in 1 Timothy 2:5), but Paul is forming a different kind of argument when he uses the word here. Since Jesus is divine, He can offer the promise of God's grace to us without any outside help.

B. Unable to Save (vv. 21, 22)

21. Is the law then against the promises of God? God forbid: for if there had been a law given which could have given life, verily righteousness should have been by the law.

Here Paul affirms that *the law* must never be considered an enemy to *the promises of God*. Paul does not want his teaching to be misunderstood to say that. Elsewhere Paul maintains that "the law is holy, and the commandment holy, and just, and good" (Romans 7:12). Both the law and the promises are from God, but each serves a distinct purpose. When we learn that we have broken the law and that the law provides no remedy for our inability to keep it, then it leads us to Christ and to the ability of His grace to provide what the law cannot. In God's plan, law and grace are meant to complement, not contradict, one another. The law diagnoses our illness, and Jesus, the Great Physician, provides the cure.

22. But the Scripture hath concluded all under sin, that the promise by faith of Jesus Christ might be given to them that believe.

If our hope lies in our ability to keep the law, then we are in serious trouble. Since no one can keep the law perfectly, all we can do is to throw ourselves on the mercy of the court. And there is mercy! We must *believe* in and accept the *promise* of God given through *Jesus Christ*. Paul's teaching here is quite similar to that found in Romans 3:19-26.

ONLY A TEMPORARY THING

More than seventy-five years ago, bubble gum "popped" onto the scene. The popular gooey pink stuff was invented by Walter Diemer, an accountant who was working for a chewing gum company. Diemer wanted to make the gum colorful, and he had no food coloring except pink; so pink it was—and has been since (with some additional colors featured to offer some variety). The first five pounds of the stuff were sold in a Philadelphia grocery store for a penny a piece. It was gone within a few hours.

How about some more statistics to "chew on"? Bubble gum is comprised of sixty to seventy percent sugar. The biggest bubble on record is twenty-two inches in diameter. And, contrary to what your mother may have told you, if you swallow your bubble gum, it won't stay in your stomach for seven years.

How to Say It

ABBA. *Ab*-uh.
ABRAHAM. *Ay*-bruh-ham.
DAMASCUS. Duh-*mass*-cus.
DEUTERONOMY. Due-ter-*ahn*-uh-me.
GALATIANS. Guh-*lay*-shuns.
GETHSEMANE. Geth-*sem*-uh-nee.
SANHEDRIN. *San*-huh-drun or San-*heed*-run.
SINAI. *Sigh*-nye or *Sigh*-nay-eye.

Why bring up the subject of bubble gum when today's lesson is about the Old Testament law? (I thought you'd never ask!) Many a mother has responded to the disheartening sight of her child's face covered by a popped bubble by asking, "Won't you *ever* grow up?" By the time most people get through high school—or at least college—they outgrow the need they once felt to have nearly their entire face enclosed in bubble gum. And, at some point in the process of gaining spiritual maturity, most serious seekers after God's will will outgrow the illusory and temporary satisfaction that comes from living by law. Eventually the successful quest for spiritual maturity brings one to the joy of living by faith in the grace of God. —C. R. B.

II. The Function of the Law (Galatians 3:23-26)

A. A Prison Guard (v. 23)

23. But before faith came, we were kept under the law, shut up unto the faith which should afterward be revealed.

Here Paul describes us as *kept under the law.* The meaning of the Greek word used here carries the idea of being imprisoned. We are in such a condition because we are in fact guilty of sin. Every human being has been confined to a place on "death row." But the situation is not hopeless. A pardon has been provided through the death of Jesus. By *faith* in Him, we can be released from our prison. [See question #2, page 320.]

B. A Tutor (vv. 24-26)

24. Wherefore the law was our schoolmaster to bring us unto Christ, that we might be justified by faith.

We are bound no more by sin.
—*Romans 8:1, 2*

We are bound no more by law.
—*Galatians 3:23*

Visual for lessons 5 and 11

Use this visual when discussing Galatians 3:23 and Paul's description of the law as a prison.

This verse presents a very meaningful word picture. It refers to *the law* as *our schoolmaster.* The Greek word for *schoolmaster* describes someone who had a significant role to play in a child's upbringing. Another word for this person might be "guardian" or "tutor." This person was given the responsibility of monitoring and disciplining a child from about six years of age until sixteen. He was not the child's actual teacher; the tutor often supervised the child as he went to and from school each day. He would then be in charge of monitoring the child's behavior after school—checking on the company he kept and the activities in which he participated. He was also in charge of making sure that the child's homework was done. In addition, the tutor supervised any household chores or other activities for which the child was responsible. Usually such a monumental task was given to a trusted slave.

In Paul's day the tutor could sometimes be considered harsh and cruel. After all, he was given full authority to discipline a child. Most any child longed for the day when he would be rid of his tutor, for that day marked his freedom!

It should not be difficult to understand why Paul uses this word picture of a tutor to describe the function of the law. The law's purpose is *to bring us unto Christ, that we might be justified by faith.* The law's purpose was never to save anyone; it was to show the need for the one who can save everyone.

25. But after that faith is come, we are no longer under a schoolmaster.

Completing his illustration, Paul says that now that faith has *come, we are no longer under a schoolmaster* or tutor. The law's job as a tutor is only temporary. It is "out of work" once we come to Christ and discover the freedom that He alone can provide. At that point, we have "matured" to where we are part of God's family. The tutor is no longer necessary.

NEEDED: A GUIDE

Most people in the over-60 generation can remember when Edmund Hillary (now Sir Hillary) and Tenzing Norgay (*Ten*-sing *Nor*-gay) became the first men to successfully reach the peak of Mt. Everest and live to tell about it. (Some believe that others may have reached the summit, but lost their lives on the way back down.) The Hillary-Norgay team accomplished their feat in 1953.

Fifty years later, in 2003, a Hillary-Norgay team was on the mountain again. This time it was the sons of those heroes, filming a TV special about the fascination the mountain still has for adventurers. Although people from all over the world have tried to climb the mountain, they always go with an experienced guide, usually a Sherpa—a member of the Tibetan tribe that lives in the vicinity of the mountain. For the kind of danger the mountain holds, a trustworthy guide is an absolute necessity.

The role of a guide is the role the law of God has played in the spiritual history of the human race. It has taught us about the dangers of the towering cliffs and treacherous crevasses of sin that can bring disaster for the unwary and inexperienced. The law has prepared us for the next guide—Jesus Christ—who can take us to the next spiritual "level." As Paul notes in today's text, eventually we outgrow our need for the law as a "schoolmaster"; but we will always need Jesus to take us the rest of the way to the Father.

—C. R. B.

26. For ye are all the children of God by faith in Christ Jesus.

Previously Paul described us as prisoners and as youths under the authority of a tutor. How our status has changed! Now we are *children of God by faith in Christ Jesus.*

III. The Fulfillment of the Law (Galatians 3:27-29; 4:4-7)

A. By Grace We Put on Christ (v. 27)

27. For as many of you as have been baptized into Christ have put on Christ.

Here Paul calls upon the Galatians to reflect upon the time of their conversion. His words are reminiscent of his teaching from Romans 6, noted in Lesson 4, concerning baptism as the time when someone who has died to sin is raised to "walk in newness of life" (Romans 6:1-4).

Paul adds that those who *have been baptized into Christ have put on Christ.* The expression "put on" signifies putting on clothes or in this case being "clothed with Christ." Paul is probably referring to the fact that the righteousness of Christ is now our righteousness. His "robe of righteousness" (Isaiah 61:10) has replaced our "filthy rags" (Isaiah 64:6). As we grow in the Christian life, we should become more and more like Christ and more comfortable wearing His "wardrobe." Note Paul's instructions to the Roman Christians: "Put ye on the Lord Jesus Christ, and make not provision for the flesh, to fulfil the lusts thereof" (Romans 13:14). [See question #3, page 320.]

B. By Grace We Are United (v. 28)

28. There is neither Jew nor Greek, there is neither bond nor free, there is neither male nor female: for ye are all one in Christ Jesus.

Paul goes on to describe the special unity that belongs to Christian believers. When Paul says *there is neither Jew nor Greek, . . . bond nor free, . . . male nor female,* he is not suggesting that all these distinctions are completely eliminated. That would be nonsense. There are still differences of nationality, gender, and status in the Christian community. What Paul is declaring is that these distinctions do not make one better than another in God's eyes. God does not love one race over another. He does not love someone in a higher social class more than someone in a lower social class. He does not love men more than women. Keep in mind that all of these statements would have been considered quite radical and controversial in Paul's day.

It is interesting that Jewish men in New Testament times often prayed a prayer in which they thanked God that they were not born a Gentile, a slave, or a woman. Note that Paul uses this same order of Gentile, slave, and woman when he declares that *all* of these are *one in Christ Jesus.* We will always have our differences in the body of Christ, but our commitment to Christ transcends such barriers. [See question #4, page 320.]

C. By Grace We Are Adopted (v. 29, 4:4-7)

29. And if ye be Christ's, then are ye Abraham's seed, and heirs according to the promise.

Jews saw themselves exclusively as children of Abraham and took great pride in such a status (Matthew 3:9; John 8:39). Paul maintains that all Christians are *Abraham's seed.* This concludes Paul's consideration of Abraham, which began in Galatians 3:6. Abraham lived before the law of Moses was given, and his faith was "accounted to him for righteousness." Christians who have responded to Christ by faith are thus Abraham's offspring and *heirs* of the *promise* God made to him: "In thee shall all nations be blessed" (Genesis 12:3; Galatians 3:8).

4:4. But when the fulness of the time was come, God sent forth his Son, made of a woman, made under the law.

God's *law* was the standard *under* which people lived for some time, *but when the fulness of the time was come,* or at just the right time, *God sent forth his Son.* This suggests that the coming of Christ was planned by God to happen according to His timetable. Scholars have noted that the political, social, economic, and geographical conditions were just right for a Messiah when Jesus entered the world. [See question #5, page 320.]

By saying that Jesus was *made of a woman,* Paul was simply reminding the Galatians that Jesus was both divine and human. God "gave his only begotten Son" (John 3:16), but He entered our world as all human beings do—through the process of birth. Jesus was not merely sent to humanity; He became humanity (Philippians 2:5-8). Paul describes Jesus in a similar manner in Romans 1:3, 4: "made of the seed of David according to the flesh; and declared to be the Son of God with power, according to the Spirit of holiness, by the resurrection from the dead."

When Paul points out that Jesus was *under the law*, he is saying that Jesus was born into the Jewish system, as a citizen of the Jewish nation. It is worth noting that the one who made us free from the law and opened up the way of grace to us was the only one who ever lived that law perfectly. Admittedly, there were times when the Pharisees tried to suggest that Jesus had broken some minor aspect of the ceremonial laws (such as when He healed people on the Sabbath, as in Luke 13:10-17), but this was according to their legalistic interpretation of the law.

5. To redeem them that were under the law, that we might receive the adoption of sons.

Jesus lived under the law (as the previous verse tells us), but He came to earth *to redeem them that were under the law*. The term *redeem* means "to buy back." Jesus' ministry was twofold; first, He rescued us from the tyranny of the law. But He did not do that merely to send us out on our own. He has also adopted us into His family as His *sons*. The use of the word *sons* is not meant to exclude women from the family of God, for Paul has previously stated that male and female are one in Christ (3:28). Here he is reinforcing that concept by saying that all can enjoy a "son-like" status in Christ.

6. And because ye are sons, God hath sent forth the Spirit of his Son into your hearts, crying, Abba, Father.

Not only has God "sent forth" *his Son* (v. 4), but He has also *sent forth* His *Spirit*. With the sensitivity to God that the Spirit gives us, we are moved to cry out to Him, *Abba, Father*. We noted in Lesson 5, taken from Romans 8, that *Abba* signifies intimacy, being roughly equivalent to the word *Daddy*. This is the word Jesus used when He prayed in Gethsemane (Mark 14:36).

Paul also notes that we have received the Spirit *into* our *hearts*. To Paul and other Biblical writers, the heart represents where our will resides as well as our emotions. We know that neither of these originates from the organ that pumps blood, but we still use the word *heart* in similar ways today. When Paul states that the Holy Spirit is in our hearts, it means that we have embraced the Spirit with our entire being.

7. Wherefore thou art no more a servant, but a son; and if a son, then an heir of God through Christ.

This verse summarizes our transformation. A Christian is no *more a servant, but a son*. And as a son he is an *heir* to all the riches that our Father intends for us to have. [See question #6, page 320.]

Conclusion

A. A Rich Relative

Imagine what it would be like to discover that you have a rich, long-lost relative. One day you are going about your business at home and a lawyer knocks on your door. He asks you to identify yourself, and you do. He then tells you that a wealthy, long-lost relative has died and named you an heir to his wealth. You become an instant millionaire. At least that's how the story might unfold. But it seldom happens that way.

Well, something even better *has* happened. As Christians, we have been given full rights as sons of God and are now heirs of the great spiritual blessings that our Father wants to give. We are destined to receive "an inheritance incorruptible, and undefiled, and that fadeth not away, reserved in heaven" (1 Peter 1:4). That's even better than the fantasy, don't you think?

B. Prayer

Father, I thank You for the law, even though I no longer depend on it. I needed to know I was a sinner, so I could come to Your Son to save me from my sins. As much as I appreciate Your law, I rejoice in the gift of grace. Through Jesus, the grace giver. Amen.

C. Thought to Remember

The law diagnoses our illness, and Jesus provides the cure.

Home Daily Bible Readings

Monday, May 9—God's Law Is Perfect (Psalm 19:7-14)

Tuesday, May 10—Understanding the Law (1 Timothy 1:3-11)

Wednesday, May 11—Jesus Fulfills the Law (Matthew 5:17-22)

Thursday, May 12—We Uphold the Law Through Faith (Romans 3:27-31)

Friday, May 13—Why the Law? (Galatians 3:19-23)

Saturday, May 14—The Law Was Our Disciplinarian (Galatians 3:24-29)

Sunday, May 15—No Longer Slave But Heir (Galatians 4:1-7)

Learning by Doing

This page contains an alternative lesson plan emphasizing learning activities.
Classes desiring such student involvement will find these suggestions helpful.

Learning Goals

After completing this lesson, students should be able to:

1. Explain the word pictures of law and grace that Paul chose to use in this passage.

2. Identify blessings and responsibilities that come with God's adoption of each of us.

3. Express to God a sense of joy in knowing that they have been adopted by Him.

Into the Lesson

Option #1: Invite a parent of an adopted child (or a teen or adult who has been adopted) to give a brief testimony about why adoption is special to both parent and child. If available, both persons may speak to this issue. Try to limit this introduction to around ten minutes.

Make the transition to Bible study by telling the class that these testimonies help us understand the Christian's special relationship with God as He adopts us into His family.

Option #2: Write the words "Children of God" on the chalkboard. Tell the class that one of the warmest pictures of our relationship with God is the word *Father*. Our hymns, songs, and choruses often speak of this Father/child relationship. Ask the class to work in groups of three or four (or whatever size is most appropriate for your class size) and make a list of lines from Christian music that speak of this Father/child relationship with God. Provide each group with two hymnbooks or songbooks. After listing these lines on the chalkboard, use the same transition to Bible study suggested under *Option #1*.

Into the Word

Summarize the lesson Introduction and Background from the lesson commentary for today's study, found on page 314. Then divide the class into four study teams. Give each team a written copy of its task, a photocopy of the lesson commentary, and a piece of paper for compiling notes.

Team #1: Answer the following questions about the Old Testament law. Use them to explain to the rest of the class God's purpose in giving the law to His chosen people.

1. What is the purpose of the law as implied in Galatians 3:19?

2. What limitations of the law are revealed in Galatians 3:21, 22?

3. Galatians 3:21 reveals that the law should not be considered bad or viewed as God's enemy. What do you think are some of the good features of the Old Testament law?

Team #2: Paul uses two word pictures of the law in Galatians 3:23-26. Read the text and the lesson commentary. Prepare a brief presentation to the rest of the class, explaining what Paul was trying to teach in each word picture about the role of the law.

Word Picture #1: A Prison Guard (Galatians 3:23)

Word Picture #2: A Tutor (Galatians 3:24-26)

Team #3: In Galatians 3:27, Paul offers two snapshots of the purpose of Christian baptism. Read this text and the lesson commentary. Prepare a brief presentation to the rest of the class about what Paul is communicating in these word pictures.

Word Picture #1: Baptized into Christ

Word Picture #2: Putting on Christ

Team #4: Read Galatians 3:29–4:7 and the lesson commentary on these verses. Discuss the following questions and share your findings with the rest of the class.

1. Why would Paul emphasize to the Galatians that believers are Abraham's seed?

2. What is the significance of the word *redeem* in Galatians 4:5? Define *redeem*.

3. Why should the phrase *Abba, Father* be special to adopted children of God?

4. What are some of the other blessings that come with being an adopted child of God?

After the groups share their findings, provide a brief summary of the lesson comments on Galatians 3:28.

Into Life

In closing, focus on the phrase *Abba, Father.* Review the meaning of the word *Abba.* Tell the class that God wants an intimate relationship with us as His children. Write the words *emotional*, *social*, and *material* beside each other on the chalkboard, creating three columns. Ask the class to share blessings that may come to us as God's children in these areas. Then ask them to share responsibilities that also come to us as God's children in these areas.

Ask the teams formed earlier to pray together, focusing on expressing the joy and security that come from knowing God as Father.

Let's Talk It Over

The questions on this page are designed to promote discussion of the lesson by the class and to encourage application of the lesson Scriptures. The answers provided are only discussion starters. Let your class talk it over from there.

1. How should we understand the law of Moses from a Christian perspective? What purpose did (or does) the law serve?

As our commentator says, "One of the purposes of the law of Moses was to expose sin and identify specific sins" (p. 315). None of us can look at ourselves through the lens of the law and honestly say that we are without sin. As Romans 3:23 tells us, "All have sinned, and come short of the glory of God." Although we are not under the civil or ceremonial restrictions of the law (avoiding unclean foods, observing specific feasts, etc.), the moral principles woven through its pages come from the same God and Father of our Lord Jesus Christ. Thus, Christians should have a profound respect for and understanding of the law, for it is the very Word of God.

2. In what ways does law imprison us? Why are these experiences necessary?

First, consider civil law. Obviously many people are literally imprisoned by the law because of some offense: drug use, theft, murder, etc. All of us, however, find our freedom "imprisoned" or restricted by laws. I do not have the freedom to drive recklessly through a residential neighborhood. I do not have the freedom to dig up my neighbor's flowers if I don't like the color. I do not have the freedom to write a check for more money than I have in my account. At the same time, I should be grateful to live in a society of laws that apply to all persons. Thus, I would not want my neighbors to drive recklessly in my neighborhood, take my flowers, or write bad checks to me. Paul speaks of the law of Moses as a kind of prison in Galatians 3:23. It shows us our guilt, but it provides no solution; we could say that the law locks us up and throws away the key. Only Christ has the key to set us free.

3. What does it mean to "put on Christ"? What were we wearing before that? How does "wearing" Christ change us?

Isaiah 64:6 says, "We are all as an unclean thing, and all our righteousnesses are as filthy rags." If the best we could do (righteous acts) are considered filthy rags, then wearing Christ should completely transform us. Indeed, to carry the metaphor further, Jesus tells Christians in Revelation 3:18, "I counsel thee to buy of me gold tried in the fire, that thou mayest be rich; and white raiment, that thou mayest be clothed." Later, in Revelation 7:9, 10, John writes of seeing a great multitude gathered, wearing white robes. These white-robed individuals are those who have remained faithful to Jesus and are in His presence.

4. How does God view our racial, ethnic, social, and gender differences? How should we view them?

If clothes make the person, then putting on Christ should definitely change the way we look at each other. Those who are clothed with Christ, regardless of race, social class, or gender, are part of one family. Just as a parent wishes to see all of his or her children get along with each other, so God wishes us to see our brothers and sisters as He does—children clothed in the same garments, dependent on the same grace.

5. In what ways was Jesus sent in "the fulness of the time"? What have we done to prepare for His return?

Our commentator reminds us that "the political, social, economic, and geographical conditions were just right for a Messiah when Jesus entered the world" (page 317). God had established a stable Roman government to foster a peaceful environment, and had led that government to build roads and enforce the rule of law. A previous conqueror had spread a unifying language (Greek) throughout the Mediterranean world. Moreover, a "forerunner," John the Baptist, had come to prepare the way for the Lord. We do not know when Jesus will return, but we too need to be preparing the way (in our own lives and the lives of others) for His return.

6. What does it mean to be "adopted" by God?

Upon being adopted by God, we have the full rights of heirs. More than that, we experience the love of the heavenly Father, welcoming us into His family. We do not have to worry about our Father ever abandoning or deserting us, for "he is faithful that promised" (Hebrews 10:23). We can have faith, we can have hope, and we can have the assurance of eternal life; for we have been adopted as sons of the heavenly Father.

Live in Christian Freedom

DEVOTIONAL READING: 1 Peter 2:11-17.

BACKGROUND SCRIPTURE: Galatians 5:1-15.

PRINTED TEXT: Galatians 5:1-15.

Galatians 5:1-15

1 Stand fast therefore in the liberty wherewith Christ hath made us free, and be not entangled again with the yoke of bondage.

2 Behold, I Paul say unto you, that if ye be circumcised, Christ shall profit you nothing.

3 For I testify again to every man that is circumcised, that he is a debtor to do the whole law.

4 Christ is become of no effect unto you, whosoever of you are justified by the law; ye are fallen from grace.

5 For we through the Spirit wait for the hope of righteousness by faith.

6 For in Jesus Christ neither circumcision availeth any thing, nor uncircumcision; but faith which worketh by love.

7 Ye did run well; who did hinder you that ye should not obey the truth?

8 This persuasion cometh not of him that calleth you.

9 A little leaven leaveneth the whole lump.

10 I have confidence in you through the Lord, that ye will be none otherwise minded: but he that troubleth you shall bear his judgment, whosoever he be.

11 And I, brethren, if I yet preach circumcision, why do I yet suffer persecution? then is the offense of the cross ceased.

12 I would they were even cut off which trouble you.

13 For, brethren, ye have been called unto liberty; only use not liberty for an occasion to the flesh, but by love serve one another.

14 For all the law is fulfilled in one word, even in this; Thou shalt love thy neighbor as thyself.

15 But if ye bite and devour one another, take heed that ye be not consumed one of another.

GOLDEN TEXT: For, brethren, ye have been called unto liberty; only use not liberty for an occasion to the flesh, but by love serve one another.—Galatians 5:13.

God's Project: Effective Christians
Unit 3: Set Free
(Lessons 9-13)

Lesson Aims

After participating in this lesson, students should be able to:

1. Explain how God's grace sets us free from bondage to the law.

2. Make the connection between their freedom from the law and their responsibility to love.

3. Identify one way to show love to a Christian brother or sister during the coming week.

Lesson Outline

INTRODUCTION
    A. Freedom—Now What?
    B. Lesson Background
  I. MAINTAINING FREEDOM (Galatians 5:1-6)
    A. Stand Fast (v. 1)
    B. Choose Grace over Law (vv. 2-4)
      Spiritual Recidivism
    C. Express Faith Through Love (vv. 5, 6)
 II. THREAT OF FALSE TEACHERS (Galatians 5:7-12)
    A. Hindering Believers (vv. 7, 8)
    B. Exerting Great Influence (v. 9)
    C. Confusing the Church (vv. 10-12)
III. DEMONSTRATING FREEDOM (Galatians 5:13-15)
    A. Serving One Another (v. 13)
      The Right Kind of Service
    B. Fulfilling the Law (v. 14)
    C. Avoiding Destructive Conduct (v. 15)
CONCLUSION
    A. Get Out of the Pit
    B. Prayer
    C. Thought to Remember

Introduction

A. Freedom—Now What?

Freedom is a word almost universally treasured. We desire freedom, not only for the society where we live, but also for our personal lives. To many, freedom is not a concept readily associated with the church and the Christian life. Often unbelievers see freedom as incompatible with any kind of Christian experience. They view Christian faith as a kind of "ball and chain" that limits one's freedom, or as a "crutch" that one uses only in time of great need.

However, we have seen quite clearly in our studies this quarter that Paul regards the Chris-

tian life as a life of wonderful *freedom*—from sin, from law-keeping as a way of salvation, and from death. Paul has spent a major portion of his letter to the Galatians trying to help the Galatians understand their freedom in Christ and avoid returning to the slavery of the law. With today's lesson we come to another series of issues relating to Christian freedom: What does our freedom in Christ allow us to do? How do we best exercise this freedom?

Many countries in our world have desired freedom for a long time. Often they have failed to learn from the examples of other countries that gained freedom, yet didn't quite know what to do with it. These countries were not prepared for what living in freedom is like. They did not anticipate the many adjustments in thinking and acting that accompany possessing freedom. The same thing can happen to Christians; they must never forget that freedom in Christ carries with it certain responsibilities.

Even though a Christian living in the age of grace does not look to the law for salvation, this does not mean that a person is under no authority at all. He or she has changed masters, is now under the authority of Jesus, and seeks to please Him. Love for God and love for others is meant to be the natural (or perhaps more accurately, *supernatural*) outgrowth of being saved and possessing the Holy Spirit. One commentator has observed that in Christ we are not free to sin, but we have become free to not sin.

B. Lesson Background

Today's lesson (and next week's as well) will focus on how the free Christian should live. Our study last week concluded with Paul's statement of our special status in Christ. We are no longer servants, but sons and heirs (Galatians 4:7). In the remaining verses of chapter 4, Paul addresses some personal issues concerning his relationship with the Galatians. His words deal with how warmly they accepted him when he came and worked among them. Paul also includes some allusions to a physical problem, possibly involving his eyes, with which he apparently struggled (verses 13-15). Paul expresses his fervent love for the Galatians (he calls them "my little children" in verse 19) and his concern for their spiritual welfare. Later in the chapter, Paul uses an extended allegory concerning Hagar and Sarah to reinforce his teaching concerning the superiority of the New Covenant.

With chapter 5, Paul moves from the theological to the practical (as he usually does in his letters to churches). This section includes several personal exhortations to the Galatians to remain faithful to Christ.

I. Maintaining Freedom
(Galatians 5:1-6)

A. Stand Fast (v. 1)

1. Stand fast therefore in the liberty wherewith Christ hath made us free, and be not entangled again with the yoke of bondage.

Paul exhorts the Galatians (and us) to *stand fast . . . in the liberty wherewith Christ hath made us free.* We should adamantly refuse to go back to a life characterized by slavery to sin. Paul's words offer a special challenge to avoid the kind of slavery promoted by the Judaizers, who insist that obedience to the law is a condition of salvation.

Notice Paul's reference to a *yoke of bondage.* A yoke is a heavy piece of equipment used on an animal to keep it under control, especially to do farm work. It is a fitting way to illustrate the burdensome demands of the law of Moses. Even Peter used this same word picture when he addressed the Jerusalem Conference concerning the issue of Gentile Christians and the law. He referred to the law as a yoke "which neither our fathers nor we were able to bear" (Acts 15:10). Jesus also used a yoke as a figure of speech, but in a much different way. He assures us that His yoke is "easy" and His burden is "light" (Matthew 11:28-30).

The Greek word translated *entangled* is a word often used by hunters. It describes a snare that would be placed to trap an animal. Paul earnestly desires that the Galatians and all Christians enjoy their freedom in Christ. [See question #1, page 328.]

B. Choose Grace over Law (vv. 2-4)

2. Behold, I Paul say unto you, that if ye be circumcised, Christ shall profit you nothing.

Paul begins this verse with emphatic words that capture one's attention immediately. He says *behold* or "look" (perhaps we could render it "please listen"), and he adds the emphatic *I Paul say unto you.* He means for his readers to pay close attention to what he is about to say: *if ye be circumcised, Christ shall profit you nothing.*

Paul's words appear to condemn circumcision completely. Yet it was not Paul's intent to eliminate the practice of circumcision altogether. He had his "son in the faith," Timothy, circumcised. Timothy's mother was Jewish, but his father was a Gentile. In this case, Paul knew that neither Jew nor Gentile would accept Timothy, for both sides would see him as belonging to the other. To avoid such a controversy and to aid Timothy's ministry among the Jews, Paul circumcised him (Acts 16:1-3). Note that this was a choice made by the parties involved; no outside group

was putting pressure on them to do this act or making it a test of salvation.

On the other hand, as Paul relates earlier in Galatians, Titus was *not* circumcised because certain "false brethren" (apparently belonging to the Judaizers) were trying to force the matter. As Paul notes, "Our liberty which we have in Christ Jesus" was at stake (Galatians 2:3-5). This is the view of circumcision that Paul is confronting in the verse before us. To believe that something else besides Jesus is necessary for salvation is the same as saying that Jesus is inadequate. This is why Paul's attitude is so uncompromising. Jesus cannot be a person's Savior unless He is that person's *only* Savior. [See question #2, page 328.]

3. For I testify again to every man that is circumcised, that he is a debtor to do the whole law.

One commentator observes that Paul is not condemning the act of circumcision as much as the theology of circumcision that the Galatians are in danger of embracing. When Paul warns them against letting themselves be *circumcised,* it is because of the reason they are considering circumcision. He explains the devastating consequences of such a decision. If the Galatians accept the Judaizers' position that circumcision is necessary for salvation, they then accept a works-oriented view of salvation. This means that they must also commit themselves to keeping all the other laws and regulations of the Old Covenant. From what Paul states elsewhere in Galatians, this is already happening (Galatians 4:10).

4. Christ is become of no effect unto you, whosoever of you are justified by the law; ye are fallen from grace.

In this verse, Paul cites two consequences of attempting to be *justified by the law.* First, he makes essentially the same point he made in verse 2: *Christ is become of no effect unto you.* Do the Galatians really want to accept a teaching that leads to such a result as this? Do those who have accepted Jesus' sacrifice on the cross for their sins really want to embrace something that will make that sacrifice of no effect? Surely their

---

How to Say It

CORINTHIANS. Ko-*rin*-thee-unz (*th* as in *thin*).
GALATIANS. Guh-*lay*-shuns
HAGAR. *Hay*-gar.
JUDAIZERS. *Joo*-day-eye-zers.
PHILIPPIANS. Fih-*lip*-ee-unz.
TIMOTHY. *Tim*-o-thee (*th* as in *thin*).

goal must be to draw closer to Christ, not to become His enemy.

The second consequence is that those who seek to be justified by the law have *fallen from grace*. Justification by the law and justification by grace are two completely different paths. Those going back to the law are choosing the wrong course, and there will be no grace available to them if they continue on that course. [See question #3, page 328.]

SPIRITUAL RECIDIVISM

The word *recidivism* (re-*sid*-uh-viz-um) refers to the process of reverting to a previous state of being, and is often used with regard to various addictive behaviors and criminal lifestyles. Sometimes these behaviors work in conjunction with each other. For example, some statistics indicate that more than 30 percent of the people arrested for DUI (driving under the influence of alcohol) are repeat offenders. Most recidivists deny that they either have an addiction to alcohol or are a danger to themselves and others when they drive while drunk. Obviously, the human mind has a tremendous capacity to deceive itself!

When Paul talks about returning to the bondage of the Old Testament law, he is describing a form of addictive behavior. The legalist keeps saying, in effect, "I just know that if I try harder this next time, I can do it right and make myself right with God." But like the alcoholic or drug addict or compulsive gambler, spiritual recidivism is the result.

The real solution to this problem is to admit our failures and trust in Christ's forgiveness and the power of the Spirit of God to bring hope to a hopeless situation. We can never be good enough to deserve God's love. Instead, God offers His love to all who, through faith in Christ, accept His redeeming, renewing power.   —C. R. B.

C. Express Faith Through Love (vv. 5, 6)

5. For we through the Spirit wait for the hope of righteousness by faith.

At any point in our growth in Christ, we realize that we still fall short of all He wants us to be. We know that complete righteousness in Christ cannot be ours until we leave this world and go to be with Him for eternity. So we *wait for the hope of righteousness by faith*. Where do we get the stamina to wait? The Holy *Spirit* keeps us strong and focused.

This is a very different perspective from the works-oriented or law-oriented approach to salvation. Rather than seeing the Galatians fall from grace by depending on their own works, Paul would have them live by faith and wait for God's

completion of His work in them. Consider Paul's words to the Philippian Christians and his confidence "that he which hath begun a good work in you will perform it until the day of Jesus Christ" (Philippians 1:6).

6. For in Jesus Christ neither circumcision availeth any thing, nor uncircumcision; but faith which worketh by love.

Neither circumcision . . . nor uncircumcision has any value for those who are *in Jesus Christ*. Paul has already made it quite clear that circumcision is worthless as a supposed "supplement" to the gospel of grace. It is hard to miss that message in Galatians. But notice that Paul also says that uncircumcision means nothing. He probably does not want the Gentile Christians among the Galatians to view themselves as superior to the Jewish believers for seeing the latter as having participated in a now-obsolete ritual.

Paul is then quick to address the possible suggestion that a Christian living under grace can do anything he chooses to do; since, after all, Paul has just spoken in rather negative terms of law-keeping. His response is that Christian *faith* must express itself through *love*. Faith that saves is a faith that works. This is essentially the same point James makes in his epistle when he affirms that faith without works is dead (James 2:26).

II. Threat of False Teachers (Galatians 5:7-12)

A. Hindering Believers (vv. 7, 8)

7. Ye did run well; who did hinder you that ye should not obey the truth?

Paul frequently uses athletic metaphors, referring especially to running and boxing (Acts 20:24; 1 Corinthians 9:24-27; Galatians 2:2; 2 Timothy 4:7). Here he says that the Galatians had started their race *well*, but something has impeded their progress.

The picture Paul seems to be describing is one in which a runner jumps in and cuts off another runner or in some way impedes the progress of another runner. Notice also that here, as in the previous verse, Paul emphasizes that saving faith must be an active faith. We must do more than simply believe the truth; we must *obey the truth*. The Galatian Christians had been hampered from doing that.

8. This persuasion cometh not of him that calleth you.

The word *persuasion* in this verse describes the change of conviction on the part of the Galatians, caused by the influence of the Judaizers. That change did not originate from *him that calleth you*—that is, God. God would not call people to two radically different kinds of approaches to

Him. He would never call people to law and grace at the same time.

B. Exerting Great Influence (v. 9)

9. A little leaven leaveneth the whole lump.

This statement may be a proverb that was in current use in Paul's time. Whether this is the case or not, it certainly reflects the teaching of Jesus, who used the illustration of *leaven* or yeast on more than one occasion. In one of His parables, He used leaven in a positive way (Matthew 13:33); other times He used it to describe the influence of false teaching (as in Matthew 16:12).

In the verse before us, Paul uses leaven to picture the influence of the Judaizers and their false doctrine. Leaven works silently, but is very effective at permeating every part of the bread dough. Such is the effect of false teaching in the church, whether in an ancient or modern setting.

C. Confusing the Church (vv. 10-12)

10. I have confidence in you through the Lord, that ye will be none otherwise minded: but he that troubleth you shall bear his judgment, whosoever he be.

Paul has full *confidence . . . through the Lord* (literally, "in the Lord") that the Galatians will not be swayed by the Judaizers' teaching and that they will not embrace "another gospel" (Galatians 1:6). Note that Paul speaks of *he that troubleth you.* Is he speaking of an actual person, or is he using this word in a more general sense? We do not know. Perhaps he is referring to the leading proponent and preacher of the law-based system promoted by the Judaizers. What is quite clear is that there is a *judgment* awaiting such individuals who are obstructing people from the way to Heaven.

11. And I, brethren, if I yet preach circumcision, why do I yet suffer persecution? then is the offense of the cross ceased.

This verse indicates that some of Paul's opponents suggest that he still believes in, practices, and preaches *circumcision* in the same manner that they do. But Paul maintains in the verse before us that this is not true at all. His opponents may cite Timothy's situation as proof that Paul still advocates circumcision. Perhaps some use what happened to Titus (Galatians 2:3) to claim that Paul is inconsistent in his teaching.

In his response, Paul raises a valid point: if these critics claim that I agree with them in the matter of circumcision, then *why* do they still persecute me? If this is the reason for his *persecution*, the *offense of the cross* has *ceased*. This is another way of saying that Paul cannot serve two masters or preach two "gospels." The Judaizers

Visual for lesson 12. *Use this visual to encourage students to think of creative ways to "serve one another."*

would be glad to accept a gospel that includes the requirement of circumcision. Paul's insistence on the crucified Christ as the heart of his gospel is a stumblingblock to them, as it is to many Jews of the day (1 Corinthians 1:23). [See question #4, page 328.]

12. I would they were even cut off which trouble you.

This is about as strong a statement as Paul can make in his opposition to the Judaizers. He wishes that these false teachers *were even cut off.* It appears that Paul is saying that those who advocate the "cutting off" that occurs at circumcision should continue their action and castrate themselves. If circumcision is really that important, and if it makes someone right before God, then why stop with circumcision itself? Why not go all the way to castration? (Some of the pagan religions of the time practice this act as a sign of devotion to their deities.) The apostle's tone may be sarcastic, but no one can deny his determined opposition to the Judaizers and their message.

Others take a different view of what Paul is saying. They believe that the words *cut off* refer to cutting oneself off from communion with other Christians. In this case, Paul would be saying that the false teachers are so dangerous that he does not want them to have any fellowship with the Galatian Christians.

III. Demonstrating Freedom (Galatians 5:13-15)

A. Serving One Another (v. 13)

13. For, brethren, ye have been called unto liberty; only use not liberty for an occasion to the flesh, but by love serve one another.

Christian *liberty* must not become license (see Jude 4). The freedom we have in Christ should not be used to satisfy *the flesh*. Instead, we should use our freedom as an opportunity to *serve one another*—to care for others rather than satisfy our base desires. The flesh desires to use people; the Holy Spirit within us desires to serve people. Christian freedom means the freedom to live as our Creator intended us to live.

THE RIGHT KIND OF SERVICE

Does "Horn & Hardart" mean anything to anyone? How about "Automat"? Those two names were attached to what was once the world's largest restaurant chain. It was also America's first fast-food chain, and its first site opened in Philadelphia in 1902. What set the company apart was a precise business plan that dictated exact uniformity of quality, service, and price. There were no waiters. Food was dispensed from coin-operated machines—similar in principle to what one finds in some hospital waiting rooms these days. You could see the food, make your selection, insert your coins, open a sliding glass window, and take the item from the case. The food is said to have always been of high quality and low cost. The last Automat closed in 1991, but while they lasted, their system was very efficient and automated—and all very impersonal.

When Paul talks about serving one another, efficiency seems not to have been the key factor on his mind. Instead, love is the key. True Christian service is not automatic (or even necessarily efficient). It is not based on a law or an organization handbook that tells us how to do it "the right way." It is not "doing as we please," but "pleasing to do what love calls us to do." It means loving those we serve, not serving only those we love.

—C. R. B.

Home Daily Bible Readings

Monday, May 16—The Truth Will Make You Free (John 8:31-38)
Tuesday, May 17—Live As Free People (1 Peter 2:11-17)
Wednesday, May 18—Free in Christ (1 Corinthians 7:17-24)
Thursday, May 19—Freed from Slavery by Christ (Hebrews 2:14-18)
Friday, May 20—Christ Has Set Us Free (Galatians 5:1-5)
Saturday, May 21—Faith Working Through Love (Galatians 5:6-10)
Sunday, May 22—Love Your Neighbor as Yourself (Galatians 5:11-15)

B. Fulfilling the Law (v. 14)

14. For all the law is fulfilled in one word, even in this; Thou shalt love thy neighbor as thyself.

Why would Paul talk about fulfilling *the law*, when he has spoken against a system of law? The reason is that the ultimate fulfillment of the law is something God still desires. Only Jesus and the system of grace can accomplish that ultimate fulfillment. To *love thy neighbor as thyself* means demonstrating the attitudes and actions that fulfill the requirements of the law of Moses. Paul elaborates on this in Romans 13:8-10. Verse 10 says, "Love worketh no ill to his neighbor: therefore love is the fulfilling of the law."

C. Avoiding Destructive Behavior (v. 15)

15. But if ye bite and devour one another, take heed that ye be not consumed one of another.

This describes what happens when there is an absence of love and the desire to "serve one another" (v. 13). What a tragedy that alleged Christians should act this way—biting and devouring *one another* through petty squabbles, unkind words, and selfish attitudes! What a sad witness to an unsaved world! [See question #5, page 328.]

Conclusion

A. Get Out of the Pit

Several times in our studies from Galatians thus far, we have noted that there is something wrong with being set free and then going back into bondage. Today's lesson has emphasized that the new life of freedom in Christ carries responsibility, but it is a joyous responsibility.

Suppose that you risked life and limb to free someone from a deep pit. Would you feel gratified if the person jumped back into the pit? No, you would be outraged! All that effort and sacrifice for nothing! You would want the person you rescued to enjoy his freedom and use it wisely.

God has not freed us to return to a life of bondage or to waste the new life He has provided. Today's Scripture challenges us to "stand fast" in the freedom we have been given. That's the best way to honor the One who set us free.

B. Prayer

Dear Father, help me to see my freedom in Christ not as an entitlement but as a gift. In appreciation, help me to use my gift wisely for my sake, for others' sake, but most of all for Your sake. Through Christ our Lord. Amen.

C. Thought to Remember

We are not free to sin, but we have become free to not sin.

Learning by Doing

This page contains an alternative lesson plan emphasizing learning activities.
Classes desiring such student involvement will find these suggestions helpful.

Learning Goals

After this lesson students should be able to:

1. Explain how God's grace sets us free from bondage to the law.

2. Make the connection between our freedom from the law and our responsibility to love.

3. Identify one way to show love to a Christian brother or sister during the coming week.

Into the Lesson

Write these words at the top of two poster boards, creating one column on each poster: *National Freedoms* and *Christian Freedoms*. Ask the class to work in teams of two and complete the first column. They should list national freedoms guaranteed in the Constitution of the United States (or a similar document, if other nationalities are present) and practical applications or illustrations of each of those freedoms. Cite an example for the class such as the freedom of religion and the freedom to worship as one desires. Ask the teams to share their findings as you list them on the poster board.

After completing the first exercise, ask the entire class to work together to do the same exercise for *Christian Freedoms*. Tell the class that Paul says, "Christ hath made us free" (Galatians 5:1). Class members are to give examples of freedom in Christ. Do not provide examples for this column unless the class has a hard time getting started. List answers on the second poster board. Leave these posters taped to the wall. (This exercise is also in the student activity book.)

Make the transition to today's Bible study by telling the class that people treasure freedom. The opposite of freedom is slavery or bondage. Interestingly, however, we find people in the New Testament who found freedom in Christ, but seemed to want to revert back to a system of bondage. Would Christians today ever consider doing such an absurd thing? We may be surprised as we study today's Scripture.

Into the Word

Activity #1. Early in the week, recruit a class member to prepare a brief report on circumcision according to Jewish law. He or she should speak of its role and importance in Jewish life. Even the circumcision ceremony, as practiced by Jews, may be of interest to the class. Give this person a Bible dictionary to assist with preparations.

Begin the Bible study by reading through the printed text from Galatians 5. Then tell the class that circumcision is an important part of Paul's focus in this text. Introduce the class member who is to give a brief introduction of this practice as a background for this study.

Activity #2: Begin this activity by giving a brief lecture or statement about the purpose of today's passage. See the Introduction in the commentary for assistance with this part of the presentation. Hand out photocopies of the lesson commentary to the teams used during the "Into the Lesson" segment. Explain that you are going to assign one phrase from this passage to each team. Their task is to read the entire text, read the lesson commentary on the phrase or sentence assigned, and prepare a presentation about how that phrase or sentence fits into today's lesson theme. The phrases to assign are as follows:

v. 1: *Yoke of bondage*

v. 6: *Circumcision . . . nor uncircumcision*

v. 7: *Ye did run well; who did hinder you?*

v. 9: *A little leaven leaveneth the whole lump*

v. 11: *Then is the offense of the cross ceased*

v. 12: *I would they were even cut off*

v. 13: *Called unto liberty*

v. 14: *Love thy neighbor as thyself*

Allow each team to report its conclusions.

Into Life

Remind the class that part of Paul's teaching in Galatians 5 is that the privileges of freedom also bring responsibility. Prepare another poster board headed *National Responsibilities*. Ask the class for examples of responsibilities that come with our national freedoms and list them on the poster board. Mount another poster board with the heading *Christian Responsibilities* and ask the class for items to list under this heading.

To conclude, give each student an inexpensive, light-colored pen. Have available several fine-tip markers to write on these pens. Tell the class that Paul makes it clear that our Christian freedom brings with it an obligation to "serve one another" (v. 13). Ask class members to use the list of responsibilities just created to identify one "service project" he or she will do for another person this week. They are to write a one- or two-word reminder of that commitment on the pen. They also should carry and use the pen all week as a reminder of their commitment.

Let's Talk It Over

The questions on this page are designed to promote discussion of the lesson by the class and to encourage application of the lesson Scriptures. The answers provided are only discussion starters. Let your class talk it over from there.

1. Why would someone choose to go back into slavery? Do we ever choose slavery over freedom in our own lives?

Although slavery can be oppressive, freedom can be terrifying. There is a kind of comfort in knowing what my boundaries are, what I am expected to do, and who is in charge of my life. After seeing God's hand move in a miraculous way by witnessing the plagues strike the Egyptians, and then after leaving Egypt, the Israelites grumbled almost incessantly, wanting to return to the familiarity and security of oppression. We may also be tempted to retrace the familiar paths of sin in preference to the unfamiliar paths of freedom.

2. Why did Paul place so much emphasis on the issue of circumcision ("if ye be circumcised, Christ shall profit you nothing")? What was at stake in this matter?

Paul was not so much against the practice of circumcision as he was against what circumcision represented. One of his primary reasons for writing Galatians was that adult Gentile Christians who had never been circumcised faced the dilemma of having to undergo the procedure in order to please their Jewish Christian brothers, even though it had nothing to do with God's requirements for salvation. Circumcision for health or hygienic reasons was not the issue. The issue was whether Gentiles could come to Christ and Christ alone, or whether they had to observe the law of Moses in addition.

3. Few Christians today wrestle with the theology of circumcision, but are there areas in our lives today that may have the moral equivalence of circumcision? Are there aspects of the law that draw us despite our acceptance of God's grace?

Many people try to add various moral requirements and even political requirements to one's Christian life. We need to be careful that we do not identify a specific political view as being "the Christian view," or that we confuse an outward morality with an inward spirituality. When we reduce Christianity to a formula such as, "I don't smoke or drink or cuss or chew," we run the risk of robbing God's grace of its power and replacing it with a salvation by works.

4. What is the difference between suffering and persecution? Is persecution a necessary part of the Christian life?

One should distinguish between the suffering that is a part of the impact of sin upon our world and persecution, which is a part of the impact of our faithfulness to Christ. Persecution has been part of the Christian "landscape" from the beginning of the church. It should be noted, however, that persecution did not dampen the spirits of the early Christians. Acts 5:41 tells how the apostles rejoiced because they were found worthy of suffering for the name of Jesus. The stoning of Stephen initiated a persecution that drove many Christians out of Jerusalem; however, "they that were scattered abroad went every where preaching the word" (Acts 8:4).

Paul warned Timothy, "All that will live godly in Christ Jesus shall suffer persecution" (2 Timothy 3:12). Some Christians in the Western world may wonder how "godly" they are since they seem to suffer little persecution, especially when compared with believers elsewhere. However, the degree or the manner of persecution can vary, depending on the society in which one lives. Persecution can be physical (and is in many parts of the world), but it can also be verbal and social.

5. Why is serving one another the antithesis of sinning against one another? How does serving one another relate to loving one another?

It has been noted that the middle letter in the word *sin* is *i*. The point of this is to call attention to the fact that sin is essentially self-centered. Sin involves defying the authority of God and making self the master of our lives. In contrast, the servant's heart seeks to please God and puts the needs of others first. Someone once observed, "You can give without loving, but you cannot love without giving." True Christian love cannot hide itself. It sacrifices for others, it gives to others, it serves others, it encourages others. (Review Paul's definition of love in 1 Corinthians 13.) Instead of reacting to other people and situations, love acts; it reaches out to others and creates situations that bless and encourage them and that show Christ to them. When we sin against one another, we are expressing something quite different from love.

Participate in the Community of Faith

DEVOTIONAL READING: 1 John 3:14-23.

BACKGROUND SCRIPTURE: Galatians 5:22–6:10.

PRINTED TEXT: Galatians 5:22–6:10.

Galatians 5:22-26

22 But the fruit of the Spirit is love, joy, peace, long-suffering, gentleness, goodness, faith,

23 Meekness, temperance: against such there is no law.

24 And they that are Christ's have crucified the flesh with the affections and lusts.

25 If we live in the Spirit, let us also walk in the Spirit.

26 Let us not be desirous of vainglory, provoking one another, envying one another.

Galatians 6:1-10

1 Brethren, if a man be overtaken in a fault, ye which are spiritual, restore such a one in the spirit of meekness; considering thyself, lest thou also be tempted.

2 Bear ye one another's burdens, and so fulfil the law of Christ.

3 For if a man think himself to be something, when he is nothing, he deceiveth himself.

4 But let every man prove his own work, and then shall he have rejoicing in himself alone, and not in another.

5 For every man shall bear his own burden.

6 Let him that is taught in the word communicate unto him that teacheth in all good things.

7 Be not deceived; God is not mocked: for whatsoever a man soweth, that shall he also reap.

8 For he that soweth to his flesh shall of the flesh reap corruption; but he that soweth to the Spirit shall of the Spirit reap life everlasting.

9 And let us not be weary in well doing: for in due season we shall reap, if we faint not.

10 As we have therefore opportunity, let us do good unto all men, especially unto them who are of the household of faith.

GOLDEN TEXT: Bear ye one another's burdens, and so fulfil the law of Christ.
—Galatians 6:2.

God's Project: Effective Christians
Unit 3: Set Free
(Lessons 9-13)

Lesson Aims

After completing this lesson, a student should be able to:

1. Explain the meaning and application of "the fruit of the Spirit."

2. Describe the behaviors Paul associates with the fruit of the Spirit.

3. Identify one or more ways he or she will become more Christlike in daily living.

Lesson Outline

INTRODUCTION
  A. No Hermits Here
  B. Lesson Background
 I. THE SPIRIT AND HIS FRUIT (Galatians 5:22, 23)
  A. God-oriented Virtues (v. 22a)
  B. Others-oriented Virtues (v. 22b)
  C. Self-oriented Virtues (vv. 22c, 23)
    A Wonderful Variety of Fruit
II. THE SPIRIT AND OUR ATTITUDES (Galatians 5: 24-26)
  A. Crucifying the Flesh (v. 24)
  B. Maintaining a Daily Walk (v. 25)
    His Father's Walk
  C. Keeping a Humble Attitude (v. 26)
III. THE SPIRIT AND OTHERS (Galatians 6:1-10)
  A. Helping the Fallen (v. 1)
  B. Bearing Others' Burdens (vv. 2-5)
  C. Showing Generosity (vv. 6-10)
CONCLUSION
  A. How to Create a Wonderful Life
  B. Prayer
  C. Thought to Remember

Introduction

A. No Hermits Here

The Christian life cannot be lived in isolation. God has always intended that His people be part of a community. In the New Testament context, that community is the church. All of us at one time or another have found ourselves disappointed in the behavior of others—even of those we believed were Christians. During such experiences, we may wish that we could become a hermit so that we could have no contact with people at all. Yet if we did that, we would soon find such a life boring and unsatisfying. Besides, the community of believers needs us, and we need the community.

Today's lesson focuses on Paul's sensitivity to the church as a community and how the members are to function in relation to each other. Some may think of life in the Spirit as a totally inner experience or as something between "me and God." But life in the Spirit is intended to be lived out among human beings and in the body of Christ, His church. Perhaps we are sometimes like Linus, in the *Peanuts* comic strip, who declared, "I love mankind. It's people I can't stand!" But as followers of Jesus, we have to do more than tolerate each other. We must work together with our brothers and sisters for the good of the greatest cause there is.

B. Lesson Background

This lesson (the final one in this quarter of studies) begins with a look at a passage of Scripture familiar to many: Paul's description of the fruit of the Spirit. In fact, the Holy Spirit is a very prominent part of our lesson text.

Notice that Paul's discussion of the fruit of the Spirit follows a rather dismal section of Scripture. In that section, Paul lists the "works of the flesh." What an evil list it is! His list of vices includes adultery, fornication, uncleanness, lasciviousness, idolatry, witchcraft, hatred, variance, emulations, wrath, strife, seditions, heresies, envyings, murders, drunkenness, and revelings (Galatians 5:19-21).

Paul then proceeds to describe the changes that the Holy Spirit brings into our lives. His concern is not just what the Holy Spirit does for us personally, but what He does for us in relationship to the community of faith—the church.

Some note that Paul chose to refer to the *fruit* of the Spirit, not the *works* of the Spirit (as he did the *works* of the flesh). Fruit serves as a better analogy, since it is what a tree was created to produce. The fruit is the tree's natural product. We were created by God to live holy lives; such holiness should proceed naturally from our lives.

The metaphor of fruit-bearing is helpful for another reason. Fruit is a positive product. The virtues that make up the fruit of the Spirit are all positive virtues. This is significant, since so many people erroneously define Christianity in terms of negative qualities. In addition, fruit is not just to be seen and admired for its beauty; it is to be used. Fruit may be beautiful to the sight and pleasant to the taste, but most of all it should provide nourishment. That is what a Christian's testimony should offer to those with whom he or she is associated.

Some commentators have called attention to the fact that Paul uses *fruit* (singular) not *fruits* (plural). Is there any significance to this? Perhaps. If the plural form were used, someone might treat these qualities as a kind of checklist ("I'm strong in this area, but weak in this one"). By use of the singular *fruit*, Paul is highlighting the fact that all of these qualities come from one source—the Holy Spirit. Christian growth is not a matter of "self-help" or "self-improvement"; it comes through allowing the Holy Spirit greater control of our lives. [See question #1, page 336.]

As a final note, many commentators have observed that the qualities listed by Paul in this passage can be studied in groups of three. That is how we will approach the passage in this study. However, it is best not to be too dogmatic about such an order or grouping.

I. The Spirit and His Fruit (Galatians 5:22, 23)

A. God-oriented Virtues (v. 22a)

22a. But the fruit of the Spirit is love, joy, peace.

The first three of the *fruit* appear to be primarily inner virtues. They are virtues that are very much a part of the nature of God Himself. It is no surprise that *love* leads the list. Placing love first among the Spirit's fruit is consistent with Paul's teachings elsewhere, particularly in 1 Corinthians 13.

Joy and *peace* are similar inner qualities. A close relationship exists between joy and peace. There is an old saying that peace is joy resting and joy is peace dancing. The word translated *joy* does not describe a pleasant feeling brought on by favorable circumstances, but an inner joy that defies circumstances. It is the kind of joy that filled the apostles after they had been beaten for speaking in the name of Jesus (Acts 5:40, 41). Only God can bestow such joy.

Peace, as used in the Scriptures, means more than just the absence of conflict. It is a sense of calm assurance at knowing that God is in control. Jesus spoke of such peace to His disciples as His crucifixion drew ever closer (John 14:27; 16:33). Paul could speak of such peace, even when writing from a prison in Rome (Philippians 4:6-9).

B. Others-oriented Virtues (v. 22b)

22b. Long-suffering, gentleness, goodness.

The next three virtues deal more with social situations. *Long-suffering*, *gentleness*, and *goodness* are all best expressed in our relationships with others.

Long-suffering is rendered as "patience" in many modern translations. It is indeed that, but it is much more. It is not just the ability to endure problems, but to triumph over them. The variety of circumstances and people that we encounter in our lives helps us develop and use this virtue. Someone has remarked that the incidents in life that we refer to as "interruptions" (and usually do not welcome) are really God's appointments that He brings our way for a purpose. Often our spiritual growth is part of that purpose.

The Greek word translated *gentleness* became very special to the early Christians. This word actually sounds like the title *Christ*. When Jesus says that His yoke is "easy," this is the word He uses (Matthew 11:30). We should seek to treat others as Jesus has treated us.

The word used for *goodness* is very similar to the word for *kindness*. A form of this word is used later in our printed text to describe how Christians should treat all people (Galatians 6:10). Goodness implies personal moral excellence, but it also means looking beyond oneself to meet the needs of others.

C. Self-oriented Virtues (vv. 22c, 23)

22c, 23. Faith, meekness, temperance: against such there is no law.

The last three virtues, *faith*, *meekness*, and *temperance*, are all linked to one's personal discipline. The word translated *faith* can also be translated as faithfulness or loyalty. It probably carries that meaning in this verse.

Meekness is a quality that is often viewed in negative terms. Jesus mentioned this quality in the Beatitudes when He said, "Blessed are the meek" (Matthew 5:5). Perhaps part of our problem is that the word sounds like "weak," though as someone once observed, "If you think meekness is weakness, try being meek for a week!" Meekness is not weakness; it is strength under control. Jesus is described as having this trait (Matthew 11:29, 2 Corinthians 10:1).

Finally, there is *temperance*. This word, like meekness, speaks of self-control. Temperance often has been applied to a person's ability to control the intake of alcoholic beverages, but the original Greek word has many more applications than that. For an interesting study, see Acts 24:25; 1 Corinthians 7:9; 9:25; Titus 1:8; and

---

How to Say It

CORINTHIANS. Ko-*rin*-thee-unz (*th* as in *thin*).

EPHESUS. *Ef*-uh-sus.

GALATIANS. Guh-*lay*-shuns.

LASCIVIOUSNESS. luh-*siv*-ee-us-ness.

TITUS. *Ty*-tus.

2 Peter 1:6, where this same word occurs in both noun and verb forms.

Paul closes this list by telling his readers that *no law* needs to be enforced to restrain or punish those who possess the fruit of the Spirit. Indeed, their actions fulfill the law.

A WONDERFUL VARIETY OF FRUIT

Perhaps you've seen the advertisements in the Sunday newspaper "magazine" section offering a plant that grows potatoes underground and tomatoes on the vine above ground. Or possibly you've noticed a nursery catalog selling a fruit tree that will grow several different varieties of fruit. For example, one company offers trees that combine two, three, and even four different varieties on one tree. Or, as one more example of what is horticulturally possible, the branches of a desired variety of fruit can be grafted onto a hardy rootstock for optimum performance in a given climate or environment. Whatever the combination of fruits you are seeking, the desired results can be achieved through the process of grafting.

Our text in Galatians for today suggests that a similar principle is at work in the realm of what we might describe as "spiritual horticulture." God wants us to become like Him, and the "root stock" of the flesh does not bear the right kind of fruit. So when we become Christians, God "grafts" His Holy Spirit onto our spirits, and the miracle begins: nine varieties of spiritual fruit growing on one "tree"! And these are far lovelier, far more "tasty" than any we can ever produce by ourselves.   —C. R. B.

II. The Spirit and Our Attitudes (Galatians 5:24-26)

A. Crucifying the Flesh (v. 24)

24. And they that are Christ's have crucified the flesh with the affections and lusts.

This statement is similar in meaning to Paul's declaration in Galatians 2:20: "I am crucified with Christ." To say that we *are Christ's* means to repent utterly and completely of our old way of life, which is patterned after *the flesh*. We are to repudiate totally the *affections*, or passions, associated with that lifestyle. The word *crucified* emphasizes how drastic and decisive we must be about breaking ties with sin and determining to serve Christ. [See question #2, page 336.]

B. Maintaining a Daily Walk (v. 25)

25. If we live in the Spirit, let us also walk in the Spirit.

The word *If* in this statement could also be rendered "since." Since *the Spirit* is the source of our new life in Christ (Romans 8:10), then we need to let the Spirit guide our daily *walk*. All of our thoughts, words, and deeds should come under His control.

In this verse Paul uses a very specific word for *walk*. It is a different word from that used in verse 16, where Paul tells us to "walk in the Spirit." The word in the verse before us describes keeping in step or walking together as a military unit would do when marching. To place this verse together with the previous one gives us a useful definition of Christian maturity. We must say no to what is evil by crucifying the flesh, and we must say yes to what is good by walking in step with the Spirit.

HIS FATHER'S WALK

One bright, crisp winter morning in northern Iowa, a young father who stood six feet tall decided to introduce his two-year-old son to the beauty of new-fallen snow. Ten inches had fallen overnight and lay in pristine whiteness on the ground. The toddler only recently had mastered the art of walking, so this was his first real adventure in the snow.

The father started breaking the trail with his son following him, but he forgot how short those little legs were. Soon a plaintive wail came: "Daddy, wait for me!" The boy was trying to put his feet in the footprints of his father, and those footprints were just too far apart for the much smaller legs to match!

Obviously, the moral "steps" that our Heavenly Father can take are much too far apart for us to match in our own power. However, He has given us the Holy Spirit to help us match our steps with His. Through the Spirit's power, we can have our Father's walk.   —C. R. B.

C. Keeping a Humble Attitude (v. 26)

26. Let us not be desirous of vainglory, provoking one another, envying one another.

While this verse appears at the end of Galatians 5, it also serves to introduce the teaching found in the next chapter about relationships within the body of Christ. Paul warns Christians not to be *desirous of vainglory;* that is, we should not become conceited, or so self-centered and self-righteous that we take pleasure in *provoking one another* (to unnecessary and fruitless arguments) and *envying one another.*

Notice that both extremes of our potential responses to people are included in this verse. On the one hand, we may look at our neighbor with pride, thinking that we are better. On the other hand, we may view our neighbor with envy, thinking he or she is better (or more talented, more popular, etc.) than we are. Neither approach is appropriate for someone led by the Spirit.

III. The Spirit and Others
(Galatians 6:1-10)

A. Helping the Fallen (v. 1)

1. Brethren, if a man be overtaken in a fault, ye which are spiritual, restore such a one in the spirit of meekness; considering thyself, lest thou also be tempted.

Here Paul describes a circumstance that provides an excellent test of whether or not we are walking in step with the Spirit. How do we react if someone is *overtaken in a fault?* The idea of being *overtaken* conveys the concept of being caught, or ensnared, in the fault itself rather than being caught by another person. Perhaps it is not an act of blatantly defying God's authority; yet if it is left unchecked, it may lead to more serious actions.

How should we respond? Some would prefer to ignore the situation and assume it is not their responsibility; others would respond by condemning, rejecting, and shunning the guilty party.

Here is Paul's directive: the *spiritual* person will desire to *restore such* an individual. The idea is to make a person whole again. This idea is also found in 1 Peter 5:10, where the same Greek word is used to show God's willingness to make us "perfect."

Notice also that we are to restore the person with *meekness*. Restoration likely will never be accomplished if a fallen person is treated with contempt. With this counsel, Paul includes a warning against self-righteousness: *considering thyself, lest thou also be tempted.* Elsewhere he issues this warning: "Wherefore let him that thinketh he standeth take heed lest he fall" (1 Corinthians 10:12). [See question #3, page 336.]

B. Bearing Others' Burdens (vv. 2-5)

2. Bear ye one another's burdens, and so fulfil the law of Christ.

The responsibility to *bear . . . one another's burdens* is closely related to Paul's teaching in the previous verse. It may appear that this verse contradicts what Paul says a short time later in verse 5: "Every man shall bear his own burden." However, the word for *burdens* in verse 2 and the word for *burden* in verse 5 are different words in the Greek text.

The word for *burden* in verse 2 describes a very heavy burden—one that a person cannot possibly carry alone. It is the duty of a Christian brother or sister to help. The word for *burden* in verse 5, on the other hand, refers to a much smaller load. It is one that need not be shared with anyone else, for it cannot be shared with

Visual for lesson 13. *This visual reminds us of the truth that we reap what we sow—in both the natural world and the spiritual world.*

anyone else; it is each person's accountability before God's judgment seat.

3. For if man think himself to be something, when he is nothing, he deceiveth himself.

Here Paul addresses an attitude that could hinder some from bearing the burdens of others (v. 2). Some may *think* themselves too important or too busy to help another in need. That attitude adds up to *nothing* in God's eyes. We are deceiving ourselves with such thinking; we are certainly not fooling God and probably not too many other people.

4. But let every man prove his own work, and then shall he have rejoicing in himself alone, and not in another.

Rather than trying to judge and critique others, *let* each person simply *prove*, or test, himself. We may think ourselves better than someone else until we compare ourselves with God. *Rejoicing* comes as we grow according to His standard, not our own flawed, self-made standards.

5. For every man shall bear his own burden.

Here is the reason why each person needs to examine himself closely: *every man shall bear his own burden.* The significance of the word *burden* was noted earlier in the comments on verse 2. What Paul is describing here is simply the accountability of each of us to God.

C. Showing Generosity (vv. 6-10)

6. Let him that is taught in the word communicate unto him that teacheth in all good things.

This verse covers a new topic—possibly one that the Galatians needed assistance in addressing. What responsibility does the church have to those who teach *the word?* Paul says that those who receive such instruction should help in the financial remuneration of those who instruct. In other words, the preacher or teacher of a congregation should expect that those who benefit from his teaching will support him financially. The word *communicate* implies sharing—in this case, a sharing of material blessings. [See question #4, page 336.]

7. Be not deceived; God is not mocked: for whatsoever a man soweth, that shall he also reap.

This principle can apply to a variety of areas, including Christian stewardship (2 Corinthians 9:6-8). In this context, Paul's words should be understood in light of what he has stated about living in the flesh and living in the Spirit in chapter 5 (and in the next verse as well).

8. For he that soweth to his flesh shall of the flesh reap corruption; but he that soweth to the Spirit shall of the Spirit reap life everlasting.

We should not sow to please the *flesh*, because if we do that we will surely *reap corruption*. That corruption includes both the physical and spiritual consequences of choosing to live in sin. Many will recall the old expression, "sowing his wild oats." Someone once remarked that it doesn't make sense to sow your wild oats and then pray for a crop failure. The positive application of the principle is this: the one who sows *to the Spirit* will *reap life everlasting*.

9. And let us not be weary in well doing: for in due season we shall reap, if we faint not.

This verse adds a word of encouragement that Christians often need. Paul does not want his Galatian readers (or us) to become *weary in well doing*. *In due season*, or when the time is right, we will *reap* a harvest. Paul is picturing the farmer who gets tired in the process of planting, weeding, and watering his crop, while at the same time having to contend with unfavorable weather conditions. But the farmer is encouraged to know that in due time the harvest will make all his labors worthwhile.

This verse reminds us of a very real truth: sometimes the Christian life can be tiring. It can be discouraging trying to help people. But like the farmer, we also wait for a harvest time, when our faithful efforts will be rewarded.

10. As we have therefore opportunity, let us do good unto all men, especially unto them who are of the household of faith.

Paul challenges us to use every *opportunity* we have to *do good*. We should seek to do good to *all* people, but we have as Christians a special responsibility to help those within *the household of faith*, or the family of believers. It is a sign of spiritual maturity if Christians are willing to do good to all people and surely a sign of immaturity if they will not do good to those with whom they share the common bond of faith and fellowship in Jesus. [See question #5, page 336.]

Conclusion

A. How to Create a Wonderful Life

A well-known motion picture illustrates the kind of life that can be created if we are committed to contributing to the well-being of others around us. That movie is *It's a Wonderful Life*. Perhaps you remember that the main character, George Bailey, reaches the depths of despair at one point. He thinks he has been a miserable failure. Then his guardian angel allows him to see what the world would be like if he had never been born. George sees how he had filled his life with simple acts of kindness done for the sake of simple people. When George saw what his community would have been like if those acts had not been done, he realized how significant his life had been. The world was a meaner, crueler world without the influence of George Bailey.

We Christians do not live in isolation. We come in contact with many people every day. Do we allow God to work through us to bless others? If we do, we will find that we have created for others and ourselves a wonderful life.

B. Prayer

Dear Father, I pray that my fruit is good fruit. I pray that my conduct is winsome. I pray that my service is sweet. I thank You that through Your Spirit You have given me both the graces of Christ and the places to demonstrate them. In the name of our Lord Jesus. Amen.

C. Thought to Remember

"And let us not be weary in well doing: for in due season we shall reap, if we faint not" (Galatians 6:9).

Home Daily Bible Readings

Monday, May 23—A Tree and Its Fruit (Matthew 7:15-20)

Tuesday, May 24—Where Two or Three Are Gathered (Matthew 18:15-20)

Wednesday, May 25—Be Rich in Good Works (1 Timothy 6:11-19)

Thursday, May 26—Let Us Love One Another (1 John 3:18-24)

Friday, May 27—The Fruit of the Spirit (Galatians 5:22-26)

Saturday, May 28—Bear One Another's Burdens (Galatians 6:1-5)

Sunday, May 29—Work for the Good of All (Galatians 6:6-10)

Learning by Doing

This page contains an alternative lesson plan emphasizing learning activities. Classes desiring such student involvement will find these suggestions helpful.

Learning Goals

After this lesson a student should be able to:

1. Explain the meaning and application of "the fruit of the Spirit."

2. Describe the behaviors Paul associates with the fruit of the Spirit.

3. Identify one or more ways he or she will become more Christlike in daily living.

Into the Lesson

Prepare a table of sliced fruit for class members to eat as they enter the room. Have two bowls of each kind of fruit prepared. One bowl will be fruit that is old, wrinkled, or spoiling. (Often this can be prepared by just leaving the fruit out and unprotected for a few days.) The other bowl will contain freshly prepared fruit. Suggested fruits include whole bananas, orange slices, melon slices, strawberries, or pineapple. You may wish to have a fruit dip available. Have disposable bowls, silverware, and napkins at the table. As students enter, invite them to have a snack from the table of fruit you have prepared.

After the class is seated, note that people did not make selections from the bowl containing the old and spoiled fruit. Ask the class what the difference is between good and bad fruit. What makes fruit go bad? Make the transition to today's Bible study by telling the class that Paul uses the analogy of good fruit to teach us about the kind of lives followers of Jesus should live.

Into the Word

Prepare three posters. Each poster should have one of these three headings: "The Spirit and His Fruit" (Galatians 5:22, 23); "The Spirit and Our Attitudes" (Galatians 5:24-26); and "The Spirit and Others" (Galatians 6:1-10). The first poster also should have these statements evenly spaced down the page: "God-oriented Virtues" (that especially reflect God's nature); "Others-oriented Virtues" (expressed in relationships with others); and "Self-oriented Virtues" (that reflect personal disciplines).

Poster #1 (The Spirit's Fruit). Read Galatians 5:22, 23. Tell the class that some Bible commentators divide the fruit of the Spirit into three categories of three qualities each. As you cover each quality, write it in the appropriate space on the outline. Offer brief comments on each, using the material in the lesson commentary. After completing the list, ask the class, "Why do you think Paul used the phrase *fruit of the Spirit* instead of *works of the Spirit* or *fruits of the Spirit?* How is the metaphor of fruit helpful?" (See the Lesson Background on pages 330 and 331.)

Poster #2 (Our Attitudes). Read Galatians 5:24-26. Write the phrase *Crucify the Flesh* on the poster board while asking, "What does it mean to crucify the flesh?" After this discussion, write "Walk in the Spirit" on the poster board while asking, "What does this phrase mean? What criteria would you use to determine if someone were walking in the Spirit?"

Poster #3 (Blessing Others). Ask the class to read Galatians 6:1-10 and then list the ways this text says that we can be a blessing to others. Write these on the poster board. Then ask these discussion questions: "What could make it difficult to restore a person who has been involved in a 'fault' (Galatians 6:1)? How can this be accomplished?" Jot down the class's comments on the poster. (Note also the lesson writer's comments on the meaning of the word "fault.")

In addition, use the commentary to explain the apparent contradiction when Paul says to "bear . . . one another's burdens" (v. 2) and to "bear [our] own burden" (v. 5).

Into Life

(The following activity is included in the student book activity page.) On another poster board, create a chart with two columns with the heading "Fruit in Real Life." In the left column list the nine qualities of the fruit of the Spirit from Galatians 5:22, 23. Then ask the class to think of persons they know or examples with which they are familiar of people living out one of these qualities. As they share their stories or testimonies, jot down a note in the right column about how that quality was demonstrated. (Be prepared to give an example to start the discussion.)

Tell the class that Paul is encouraging Christians to live out these qualities each day. Ask members to consider the models of application just cited and to identify one of the qualities of the Spirit's fruit that they would like to "bear" in their lives this week. They are to write that target "fruit" on a piece of cardboard you distribute that is about the size of a business card.

Close the class by asking class members to pray for each other in groups of three or four.

Let's Talk It Over

The questions on this page are designed to promote discussion of the lesson by the class and to encourage application of the lesson Scriptures. The answers provided are only discussion starters. Let your class talk it over from there.

1. Is the "fruit of the Spirit" something given wholly from God, or is there a personal component we contribute? What part of this list comes from our personal efforts, and what part comes from God's grace?

We should not try to attach a percentage to this (80 percent versus 20 percent or 90 versus 10). Clearly both God's part and our part are necessary, and the Scripture teaches the importance of both. If I cannot get along with my neighbor, I should not use the excuse that I am waiting for the Spirit to give me love. Scripture commands me to love my neighbor as myself; and when I seek to do what the Scripture says and ask for the Spirit's help, the Spirit will give me the power I need. We cannot live in the Spirit's presence and not bear fruit. The closer we are to the Spirit, the more fruit we will bear.

2. How can we crucify the flesh with its lusts? What role does walking in the Spirit play in this matter?

When Paul preached the gospel in certain places, those who heard his message sometimes responded in very dramatic ways. In Ephesus, for example, the new believers publicly burned their sorcery scrolls—an act which cost them a great deal financially (Acts 19:18, 19).

Modern believers have followed this example by discarding or destroying magazines or compact discs that are inappropriate. As we become more acquainted with the Spirit and His desires, we should find ourselves more completely repudiating the sinful desires of our past and longing for the things of God.

3. When we see a Christian brother or sister involved in the kind of "fault" described in Galatians 6:1, how should we respond? What does our response say about God, about the behavior, and about ourselves?

Paul tells us to respond to such a brother or sister with gentleness, humility, and caution. We need to recognize that "there but for the grace of God go I," and remind ourselves that we are sinners saved only by grace. A response of kindness, warning our fellow believer of the potential danger he or she faces yet showing the same grace God has given us, has the potential to restore the fallen. Responding in this way reveals the love of God, the seriousness of sin, and the concern of the church. To respond in a negative, condemning manner risks driving the person away from the church and from Christ entirely.

4. How do we show appreciation to our preachers and teachers? Should a preacher's salary reflect the average salaries in the congregation? Why, or why not?

Appreciation can be expressed through other means than salary. However, salary is important. A preacher's salary communicates to him the worth placed on his work. Part of the reason for the high turnover in pulpits is the lack of respect many preachers receive—some of which is a direct result of congregations failing to remunerate them fairly.

If a church cannot afford to pay the preacher comparably with other professionals having similar education and responsibility (public school teachers and principals are often a good benchmark), then the leadership should be honest with the preacher about this. If the preacher should need to provide his family with an additional source of income, that should be done with the understanding that his time for carrying out ministry responsibilities will be affected. The leadership should communicate this message to the congregation.

5. Why is there a special emphasis by Paul on fellow believers ("the household of faith") as the recipients of our good works?

Often we think of benevolence as being part of a church's outreach to the community. It is indeed that, but we should never forget those in need within our own congregations. We should have a special desire to help our Christian family, just as we would have a special concern for our parents, children, and siblings.

Single mothers, widows, college students, and the working poor are examples of groups within our churches that often can use tangible help. Sometimes an oil change, a meal taken to someone's home, or free babysitting while parents run necessary errands can make a huge difference in people's lives. This is ministry! Such acts also witness to the community as those who receive such kindnesses relate their experiences to others they know.

Summer Quarter, 2005

Jesus' Life, Teachings, and Ministry

(Synoptic Gospels)

Special Features

Lessons

Unit 1: Jesus' Life

Unit 2: Jesus' Ministry of Teaching

Unit 3: Jesus' Ministry of Compassion

About These Lessons

This quarter takes us into first Mark, then Matthew, then Luke to focus on the theme of *Christ*. The Old Testament points toward Him. The letters of Paul point back to Him. The book of Revelation lifts our hearts to consider His return. Could there be anything more important—or could there be any greater privilege—than studying Jesus' life and ministry?

Jun 5
Jun 12
Jun 19
Jun 26
Jul 3
Jul 10
Jul 17
Jul 24
Jul 31
Aug 7
Aug 14
Aug 21
Aug 28

Quarterly Quiz

The questions on this page may be used in several ways: as a pretest at the beginning of the quarter; as a review at the end of the quarter; or as a review after each lesson. The questions are based on the Scripture text of each lesson (King James Version). **The answers are on page 340.**

Lesson 1

1. John preached the baptism of repentance for the remission of sins. T/F *Mark 1:4*

2. What town did Jesus leave to come to John to be baptized? *Mark 1:9*

3. How long was Jesus in the wilderness being tempted by Satan? (three days, ten days, forty days?) *Mark 1:13*

Lesson 2

1. What was the first thing Jesus said to the man who was sick of the palsy? *Mark 2:5*

2. Jesus overheard the scribes' whispered accusations that He was speaking blasphemy. T/F *Mark 2:6-8*

Lesson 3

1. The false witnesses accused Jesus of saying that He would destroy the _____. *Mark 14:57, 58*

2. To whom did the Jewish leaders deliver Jesus for trial? (Herod, Pilate, Annas?) *Mark 15:1*

Lesson 4

1. Very early Sunday morning the women came to the sepulchre to anoint Jesus' body with spices. T/F *Mark 16:1, 2*

2. The first person Jesus appeared to after He arose was (Peter, John, Mary Magdalene). *Mark 16:9*

3. When Jesus appeared to the eleven disciples, what did He tell them to do? *Mark 16:15*

Lesson 5

1. Jesus said we are blessed when we are reviled and persecuted for His sake. T/F *Matthew 5:11*

2. A candle belongs on a candlestick, not under a _____. *Matthew 5:15*

Lesson 6

1. Unlike the hypocrites who pray on street corners, where are Jesus' disciples told to pray? *Matthew 6:6*

2. God knows what we need (before, when, after?) we ask Him. *Matthew 6:8*

Lesson 7

1. Jesus said it was given to the disciples to know the _____ of the kingdom of heaven. *Matthew 13:11*

2. What did the people do with their eyes so they wouldn't have to see? *Matthew 13:15*

Lesson 8

1. How many talents did the servant owe the king? (100, 1,000, 10,000) *Matthew 18:23, 24*

2. How did that servant respond to a fellow servant's request regarding a small debt? *Matthew 18:29, 30*

3. The lesson Jesus was trying to teach is that we are to _____ others. *Matthew 18:35*

Lesson 9

1. The Holy Spirit will be the One who divides the sheep from the goats at the final judgment. T/F *Matthew 25:31, 32*

2. Doing a kindness for one of the least of our brethren is the same as doing it for _____. *Matthew 25:40*

Lesson 10

1. Jesus read from the Scriptures at the synagogue in Nazareth, the town where He grew up. T/F *Luke 4:16, 17*

2. Jesus said the Scripture reading from Isaiah (was, would be?) fulfilled (that day, after His death, in the end times?). *Luke 4:21*

3. When the crowd in the synagogue became angry, what did they try to do to Jesus? *Luke 4: 28, 29*

Lesson 11

1. Whom did Jairus ask Jesus to heal? (his servant, his wife, his only daughter?) *Luke 8:41, 42*

2. The woman who was healed by touching Jesus' garment was sick for _____ years. *Luke 8:43, 44*

3. How did the crowd respond when Jesus said the girl was not dead, but sleeping? *Luke 8:52, 53*

Lesson 12

1. The first question the lawyer asked Jesus was, "Who is my neighbor?" T/F *Luke 10:25*

2. When he left the injured man at the inn, what did the Samaritan do? (slipped quietly away, promised to pay his bill, refused to pay?) *Luke 10:35*

Lesson 13

1. Jesus said that the one who humbles himself will be _____. *Luke 14:11*

2. What was the first excuse given for not attending the great supper? *Luke 14:18*

3. Anyone who does not hate his own life cannot be Jesus' disciple. T/F *Luke 14:26*

The Historical Jesus

by Ronald L. Nickelson

MANY SCHOLARS OF DECADES PAST occupied their time with searches or "quests" for "the historical Jesus." The New Testament, so they thought, presents us merely with "the Christ as preached" by first-century Christians, and the picture of Christ that those early believers painted may or may not square with actual history.

Their questions and their "quests" should cause us to ask an important question: Is it plausible that the apostles and other first-century Christians could get so carried away with what they *wanted* to believe that they embellished and stretched the truth?

There are many ways to approach this question, and there are many ways to examine the evidence. In the limited space we have here, we shall consider only one: the martyrdom of the apostles. Historical records and tradition confirm that most of the apostles suffered this fate. This fact raises a powerful question: Would rational people willingly die for a Christ whom they knew wasn't really who they said He was? To think that the apostles would first create a fiction and then be willing to give up their lives for that fiction is an idea with no credibility.

Jesus is just who the Bible says He is: the Son of God. This quarter's lessons help us explore that fact from various angles.

Jesus' Life, Teaching, and Compassion

The Bible tells us many things about Jesus Christ, but it doesn't tell us *everything* about His time on earth (see John 21:25). The information that the Bible does give us about Jesus' life and work is enough to establish our belief in Him (see John 20:30, 31). This is where our thirteen lessons will take us in the coming quarter.

Unit 1: June
Jesus' Life (Mark)

Have you noticed that people respond best to leaders who have appropriate credentials and qualifications? People are even more responsive when such leaders demonstrate a genuine understanding of their followers. In **Lesson 1** we see Jesus' authority declared, by both divine and human voices, at the time of His baptism. In facing and responding to temptations, Jesus showed us that He understood the human condition.

Lesson 2 looks at miracles as reflections of both Jesus' power and caring. Many people suffer from some condition or circumstance; both they and those who would like to help can feel overwhelmed and powerless. But in Christ we are not helpless. Jesus' miracles establish both the depth of His caring and His power to bring healing.

Lesson 3 shows how the intense opposition to Jesus eventually led to His trial and crucifixion. Those who do what is right are often viewed as a threat to society—and even as threats to the status quo of the religious community. By submitting to arrest, Jesus showed us (among other things) that living in faithfulness to God's plan can indeed lead to rejection and persecution. Ultimately, however, that rejection and persecution fulfill God's plan.

Lesson 4 proclaims God's victory in the resurrection. Have you ever noticed that when things go from bad to worse to worst that people tend to accept the situation as inevitable and hopeless? Yet Jesus' empty grave witnesses to God's ultimate power to exceed all human expectations.

There has never been a life like that of Jesus!

Unit 2: July
Jesus' Ministry of Teaching (Matthew)

Culture and media reinforce one another in equating "the good life" with material wealth, power, and sensual pleasure. Even so, many people feel they never have enough; but in their pursuit for more they do not find true happiness or real living. In **Lesson 5** we will see Jesus teaching that true happiness is found in the spirit in which one gives and lives. It is also found in how one glorifies God. True happiness is not found in possessions and controls.

In **Lesson 6** we are in the Sermon on the Mount. Truly this is one of the greatest teaching events in all of history! Its lessons "cut against the grain" in so many ways. For example, all of us are aware that society tends to recognize and reward people who make visible their charitable activities; thus some people engage in such activities to get earthly recognition. But Jesus instead emphasizes the spiritual disciplines that sustain and strengthen a close personal relationship with God. Public displays designed for earthly recognition mean nothing to Him!

Lesson 7 examines Jesus' use of parables as a teaching tool that both clarifies and conceals. Most discussions about "the meaning of life" can seem abstract, complex, and impractical, right? Jesus bypassed this problem by using imagery from everyday life. When He did, He was able to communicate deep truths.

Lesson 8 focuses on teachings of forgiveness. This can be both our favorite and least favorite topic at the same time! Most people desire forgiveness when they have wronged another, but often find it difficult to forgive others. The parable in today's lesson will move us beyond a limited view of forgiveness. It will, instead, call forth a spirit of forgiveness toward others as God has forgiven us.

Lesson 9, which deals with teachings on "the last days," explores the relationship between God's future and our present-day living. Many people claim that there is a tension between religious devotion and involvement in social concerns (poverty, hunger, etc.). This lesson will show us otherwise in an unmistakable way.

There has never been teaching like that of Jesus!

Unit 3: August
Jesus' Ministry of Compassion (Luke)

People of all ages question their ultimate goals and purpose. What does God expect of me? We see the depth of this hunger when we consider how books such as *The Purpose-Driven Life* and *The Purpose-Driven Church* have become runaway best-sellers. **Lesson 10** shows us how focused Jesus was on knowing and completing His mission. He refused to be distracted. And our mission is an extension of His.

Lesson 11 shows us two instances when Jesus healed others out of compassion. Although surrounded by a crowd that thirsted for His teaching, Jesus took time out to minister directly to individuals. His actions provide us with a window into the relationship between faith and wholeness.

One does not have to look far to find instances of human tragedy that could have been prevented if someone had cared enough to help or intervene. **Lesson 12** challenges us to consider compassion in light of what it means *to be* and *to recognize* a neighbor. Here we will see Jesus teach that love of God and neighbor characterizes lives that are pleasing to God. The Parable of the Good Samaritan is familiar; its lesson is ever new.

Lesson 13 rounds out our quarter by exploring issues of humility and hospitality, including how we view ourselves and how we respond to the hospitality of others. Our natural tendency is to put ourselves first, but this makes it difficult to recognize Jesus as Lord. Jesus teaches us to view things from a new perspective: We are to view ourselves with humility. Seeking honor and being a "glory grabber" will interfere with our ability to be compassionate toward others. Being included in God's kingdom is honor enough.

There has never been compassion like that of Jesus!

The Ring of Truth

In using the word *ring* I am not referring to a circular metal band. Rather, I am referring to a sound that expresses a quality. Can you hear "the ring of truth" in this quarter's lessons?

The concept of truth is in a state of flux in the early twenty-first century. Back in the nineteenth and twentieth centuries, debates were usually about "what" was true. Concerning human origin, for example, a "modernist" would argue that evolution was true, while a "creationist" would argue for the truth that God created humanity in His own image. Despite this disagreement, however, both the modernist and the creationist would agree that the concept of truth required one position or the other to be true, but not both.

But now we're in the era of "postmodernism." This worldview proposes that truth is *personal.* Under this idea, evolution can be true for one person while at the same time creationism can be true for others. But there's a big problem with this view of truth: it ignores God as the giver of all truth. Jesus claimed to be sent from the Father, and Jesus proved His claim through miracle and teaching. As you work through these lessons, will you hear that ring of truth?

Answers to Quarterly Quiz
on page 338

Lesson 1—1. true. 2. Nazareth of Galilee. 3. forty days. **Lesson 2**—1. "Son, thy sins be forgiven thee." 2. false; He perceived what they were thinking. **Lesson 3**—1. temple. 2. Pilate. **Lesson 4**—1. true. 2. Mary Magdalene. 3. go into all the world and preach the gospel. **Lesson 5**—1. true. 2. bushel. **Lesson 6**—1. in their closets. 2. before. **Lesson 7**—1. mysteries. 2. closed them. **Lesson 8**—1. 10,000. 2. cast him into prison. 3. forgive. **Lesson 9**—1. false; the Son of man. 2. Jesus. **Lesson 10**—1. true. 2. that day. 3. cast Him down headlong from the brow of the hill. **Lesson 11**—1. his only daughter. 2. twelve. 3. they laughed Him to scorn. **Lesson 12**—1. false. 2. promised to pay his bill. **Lesson 13**—1. exalted. 2. he had to see a piece of ground that he had bought. 3. true.

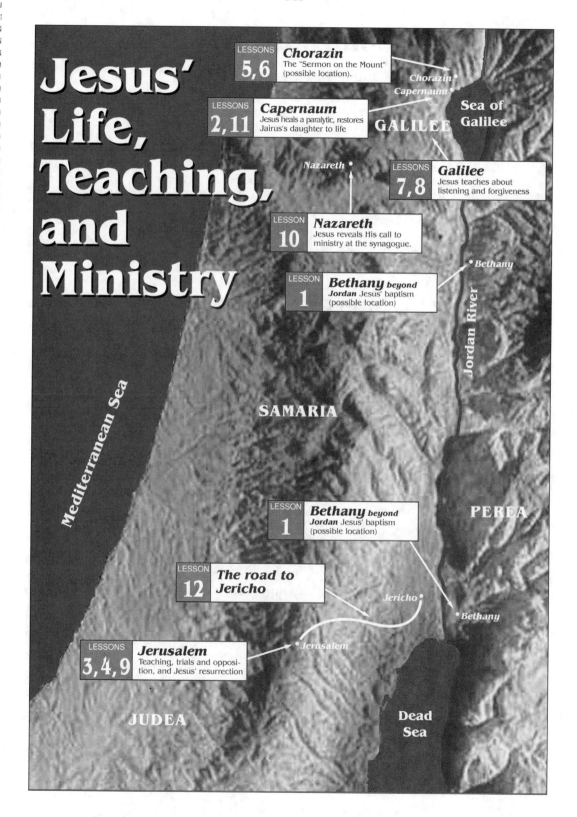

Jesus' Life, Teaching, and Ministry

LESSONS 5,6 — **Chorazin** The "Sermon on the Mount" (possible location).

LESSONS 2,11 — **Capernaum** Jesus heals a paralytic, restores Jairus's daughter to life

LESSONS 7,8 — **Galilee** Jesus teaches about listening and forgiveness

LESSON 10 — **Nazareth** Jesus reveals His call to ministry at the synagogue.

LESSON 1 — **Bethany** *beyond Jordan* Jesus' baptism (possible location)

LESSON 1 — **Bethany** *beyond Jordan* Jesus' baptism (possible location)

LESSON 12 — **The road to Jericho**

LESSONS 3,4,9 — **Jerusalem** Teaching, trials and opposition, and Jesus' resurrection

Mediterranean Sea

Chorazin

Capernaum

Sea of Galilee

GALILEE

Nazareth

Bethany

Jordan River

SAMARIA

PEREA

Bethany

Jericho

Jerusalem

JUDEA

Dead Sea

Jesus Confronts the World

Chronology of the Summer Lessons

Jesus launched His ministry with His baptism "in the fifteenth year of the reign of Tiberius Caesar" (Luke 3:1). This we know was about A.D. 26 or 27. From there we can with reasonable certainty date the rest of His ministry, although the different arrangement of the material in each of the Gospels does present some chronological challenges.

From the beginning of His ministry Jesus' popularity grew and grew, reaching a climax at the feeding of the 5,000, when many wanted to force Him to become king (John 6:15). His challenging teaching on the next day caused many to abandon Him (John 6:66). The opposition, which had been present almost from the start, began to grow stronger and became more threatening during the last year of Jesus' ministry.

Of course, it all worked together to accomplish the Father's plan. In a final week that began with "Palm Sunday" (the triumphal entry), Jesus challenged the religious leaders, taught His disciples, and laid down His life. Early sunday morning He took it up again and appeared to several of His close followers, starting with Mary Magdalene.

Launching the Ministry (A.D. 26-27)

Lesson 1: Baptism and Temptations	Mark 1:4-13
Lesson 10: Called to a Mission	Luke 4:16-24, 28-30

Growing Popularity (A.D. 27-29)

Lesson 2: Miracles	Mark 2:1-12
Lesson 5: Experiencing True Happiness	Matthew 5:1-16
Lesson 6: Practicing Genuine Righteousness	Matthew 6:1-15
Lesson 7: Learning to Listen	Matthew 13:9-17
Lesson 11: Healing the Incurable	Luke 8:40-56

Mounting Opposition (A.D. 29-30)

Lesson 8: Receiving and Giving Forgiveness	Matthew 18:21-35
Lesson 12: Being a Good Neighbor	Luke 10:25-37
Lesson 13: Accepting the Invitation	Luke 14:7-11, 15-27
Lesson 9: Meeting Human Needs	Matthew 25:31-46

Climax: Crucifixion & Resurrection (A.D. 30)

Lesson 3: Trials and Opposition	Mark 14:53-65; 15:1-3
Lesson 4: Triumph	Mark 16:1-16

Baptism and Temptations

June 5
Lesson 1

DEVOTIONAL READING: Matthew 12:15-21.

BACKGROUND SCRIPTURE: Mark 1:4-13.

PRINTED TEXT: Mark 1:4-13.

Mark 1:4-13

4 John did baptize in the wilderness, and preach the baptism of repentance for the remission of sins.

5 And there went out unto him all the land of Judea, and they of Jerusalem, and were all baptized of him in the river of Jordan, confessing their sins.

6 And John was clothed with camel's hair, and with a girdle of a skin about his loins; and he did eat locusts and wild honey;

7 And preached, saying, There cometh one mightier than I after me, the latchet of whose shoes I am not worthy to stoop down and unloose.

8 I indeed have baptized you with water: but he shall baptize you with the Holy Ghost.

9 And it came to pass in those days, that Jesus came from Nazareth of Galilee, and was baptized of John in Jordan.

10 And straightway coming up out of the water, he saw the heavens opened, and the Spirit like a dove descending upon him:

11 And there came a voice from heaven, saying, Thou art my beloved Son, in whom I am well pleased.

12 And immediately the Spirit driveth him into the wilderness.

13 And he was there in the wilderness forty days tempted of Satan; and was with the wild beasts; and the angels ministered unto him.

GOLDEN TEXT: And there came a voice from heaven, saying, Thou art my beloved Son, in whom I am well pleased.—Mark 1:11.

Jesus' Life, Teachings, and Ministry
Unit 1: Jesus' Life
(Lessons 1-4)

Lesson Aims

After participating in this lesson, each student will be able to:

1. Retell Mark's account of Jesus' baptism and temptations.

2. Explain what Jesus' baptism and temptations tell us about His identity and authority.

3. Name one reason why he or she is willing to follow the leadership of Jesus Christ.

Lesson Outline

INTRODUCTION
  A. Great Leaders
  B. Lesson Background
 I. FORERUNNER OF THE GREATEST ONE (Mark 1:4-8)
  A. John's Actions (vv. 4, 5)
    Making a U-Turn
  B. John's Appearance (v. 6)
  C. John's Announcement (vv. 7, 8)
II. ARRIVAL OF THE GREATEST ONE (Mark 1:9-11)
  A. Baptism (v. 9)
  B. Holy Spirit (v. 10)
  C. Voice from Heaven (v. 11)
III. TEMPTATION OF THE GREATEST ONE (Mark 1:12, 13)
  A. Spirit's Action (v. 12)
  B. Elements of Jesus' Temptation (v. 13)
    Our Enemy
CONCLUSION
  A. The Victor
  B. Prayer
  C. Thought to Remember

Introduction

A. Great Leaders

What makes a great leader? What credentials do we look for? Is it dynamism, like that of Alexander the Great? Is it political skill, like that of Abraham Lincoln? Is it integrity, like that of Mohandas Gandhi? Is it determination, like that of General George Patton? Is it a combination?

Christians want to be effective leaders in carrying out their God-given mission. But Christians are concerned with more than the world's standards of leadership. Christians have to ask, "What does God seek in a leader?" Mark's Gospel can help us understand the answer to that ques-

tion. In certain ways, both Jesus and John the Baptist are models of leadership for us.

B. Lesson Background

The original readers of Mark's Gospel were probably preoccupied with a crucial question: How can a crucified man be the promised Messiah, sent from God? For most observers, suffering crucifixion at the hands of the Roman imperial authorities would signal defeat. How could God's Anointed One be defeated?

One aim of Mark's Gospel is to answer this question. It shows us through the actions of Jesus that He is different from all others. There have been great prophets in the past, but none with the authority of Jesus. But what does Jesus do with His authority? He does not use it to serve Himself. Rather, He surrenders Himself to the will of God. God's purpose for Him is that He is to give His life willingly for the sake of sinners. He dies on the cross at Golgotha, but not because He is defeated. In the cross is His greatest victory as He pays sin's penalty on our behalf.

Mark begins presenting Jesus' credentials as the Messiah from his very first verse, where he declares that Jesus is the "Christ" (synonymous with "Messiah," meaning "Anointed One"). Then he launches immediately into a narrative that shows both what accredits Jesus as God's Anointed One and what kind of Anointed One He truly is.

I. Forerunner of the Greatest One (Mark 1:4-8)

We may be surprised, though, that Mark's Gospel first describes not Jesus but John the Baptist. John is a crucial figure in all the Gospels. He stands at the end of the line of God's prophets. He announces that God is about to fulfill His promises by establishing His rule. But John's testimony about Jesus shows Jesus to be an even greater figure. In fact, John declares that his most important role is to point to the greater One who is to come.

A. John's Actions (vv. 4, 5)

4. John did baptize in the wilderness, and preach the baptism of repentance for the remission of sins.

John is known in the New Testament as "the Baptist" (Mark 8:28) because he plunges repentant people in water for the cleansing of their sins. The Mosaic law had established situations in which the Jewish people were required to undergo a ceremonial washing (Exodus 19:10; 30:18-21; Leviticus 14:8, 9; etc.). But in those ceremonies, a person washed oneself. John's action is different. As the prophet of God, he plunges the person under the water.

For people accustomed to washing themselves for ceremonial cleansing, this action clearly represents something different. John's baptism differs from the washings practiced by the Pharisees and the Essenes of the day. John's baptism calls for repentance, and it is for everyone. Only God can wash people so that they are truly cleansed of *sins*. That is what John's baptism declares.

It is significant that John performs his baptisms *in the wilderness*. The Bible uses *wilderness* to refer to places that are unpopulated, usually deserts. The actual place where John baptizes is the wilderness around the Jordan River; this is not to be confused with the wilderness of Sinai, where the Israelites had wandered (Numbers 14:32, 33; Jeremiah 2:6). Even so, the location serves as a potent reminder of that earlier time. This wilderness was the place of preparation for entering the land of promise. [See question #1, page 350.]

So John's message is an announcement that God is freeing His people from captivity for entry into a greater promise. This is the very promise that the Old Testament prophets had given: when God brings His magnificent act of salvation, it will be like the exodus, only greater. God begins by using John the Baptist to prepare "the way of the Lord," meaning Jesus—the One who will bring this promise to fruition (see Isaiah 40:3, quoted in Mark 1:3).

We remember that the generation that witnessed the exodus refused to believe in the power of God, and so they died in the wilderness without entering into the promise. John understands that his own generation, like others, is much the same. That is why God's offer of cleansing requires repentance. To receive this cleansing, people must admit their rebellion against God. Baptism can have no significance apart from the faithful trust in the power of God to forgive on the part of the one baptized. John's actions signal that the promise of God to free and forgive His people is about to be fulfilled. John's act of *baptism* looks forward to the appearance of the One who will bring that salvation.

MAKING A U-TURN

Some comedian once said that the greatest contribution the state of California has made to civilization is the legal U-turn! Of course, the Golden State has made many contributions to civilization, and that is probably the least. But we are happy when we are driving down the street and discover that it both possible and legal to make a U-turn.

We may think of repentance as a "spiritual U-turn." Often the Bible uses the word *turn* for *repentance*. A cynical world says, "Once a thief, always a thief." But both Old and New Testaments assure us that we *can* make a U-turn. The message of the prophets was, "Repent" (Ezekiel 14:6; 18:30-32). That was the message of John the Baptist (Matthew 3:2). Later it would become the message of Jesus (Luke 13:3).

All of us know of people who made drastic and lasting U-turns in life. We ourselves, for that matter, are proof that one can turn *from* sin and *to* Christ. Both those prepositions are used in connection with repentance: we turn from something and we turn to something (Acts 20:21). Yet it is not enough to say that a spiritual U-turn is possible. The Bible makes it plain that the U-turn is mandatory. If we do not make that turn, we will certainly perish (again, Luke 13:3). —R. C. S.

5. And there went out unto him all the land of Judea, and they of Jerusalem, and were all baptized of him in the river of Jordan, confessing their sins.

John's contemporaries are clearly impressed by his actions. Large numbers gladly submit to this offer of being immersed in water for God's cleansing from sin. Submitting to baptism goes hand in hand with *confessing* one's *sins*. Just as there can be no genuine baptism without faithfully turning toward God and away from rebellion, so there can be no genuine baptism without the heartfelt confession that we have rebelled against God.

B. John's Appearance (v. 6)

6. And John was clothed with camel's hair, and with a girdle of a skin about his loins; and he did eat locusts and wild honey.

John's unusual clothing reminds his audience of the great prophet Elijah (2 Kings 1:8). Elijah

---

How to Say It

BEZALEEL. Bih-*zal*-ih-el.

ELIJAH. Ee-*lye*-juh.

ESSENES. *Eh*-seenz.

EZEKIEL. Ee-*zeek*-ee-ul or Ee-*zeek*-yul.

GOLGOTHA. *Gahl*-guh-thuh.

HABAKKUK. Huh-*back*-kuk.

ISAIAH. Eye-*zay*-uh.

JEREMIAH. Jair-uh-*my*-uh.

JERUSALEM. Juh-*roo*-suh-lem.

LEVITICUS. Leh-*vit*-ih-kus.

MESSIAH. Meh-*sigh*-uh.

PHARISEES. *Fair*-ih-seez.

PHILISTINES. Fuh-*liss*-teens or *Fill*-us-teens.

prophesied over eight hundred years earlier, at a time of crisis for Israel when militant paganism threatened to overwhelm the worshipers of the God of Israel. In that crisis the prophet called on the people to turn away from idols and return to the living God (1 Kings 18). John's appearance puts that message in a similar context.

John's diet fits the setting of his ministry. No conventional crops will grow in the arid wilderness, so John eats what is available from foraging. *Locusts* are what we call grasshoppers. Living in the barren desert, John relies on the food that God provides, like Israel receiving manna (Exodus 16) or Elijah receiving food from ravens (1 Kings 17:6). It is the food of one who waits patiently for God to fulfill His promise of blessing.

C. John's Announcement (vv. 7, 8)

7. And preached, saying, There cometh one mightier than I after me, the latchet of whose shoes I am not worthy to stoop down and unloose.

The entire description of John the Baptist underlines his importance in God's plan. But his message focuses on One of greater importance, One with supreme importance. The coming One will be so superior to John that John regards himself as unworthy even to do the stoop labor, characteristic of slaves, of undoing the thongs on that One's sandals.

John's statement is very provocative. Who could this be—this *mightier* Person with whom even God's prophet (John) pales in comparison? Not even angels are worthy of such veneration. Humans, all of them, are the pinnacle of God's creation, second only to God Himself (Genesis 1:26, 27). Only God is worthy of an honor that places Him on a plane far above human beings. So, by speaking of the coming One as fundamentally greater than himself, John opens the door to the central question in Mark's Gospel: Is this One much more than just an ordinary human being? Mark will soon show us that the answer is *yes*. [See question #2, page 350.]

8. I indeed have baptized you with water: but he shall baptize you with the Holy Ghost.

Sometimes Christians imagine that the Holy Spirit does not appear on the scene until New Testament times, but this is not the case. In the Old Testament, the Holy Spirit was present and active in many ways.

For example, God's Spirit enabled Bezaleel to design the tabernacle (Exodus 31:2-5), Samson to overcome the Philistines (Judges 13:25), and especially the prophets to speak the message of God (1 Samuel 10:10). But in the Old Testament the Spirit of God is given to just a few of God's people, not to all.

Even so, the prophets looked forward to the time when God would give His Spirit to all His people. That gift would mean renewed blessing producing real righteousness among His people (Isaiah 32:15; Ezekiel 36:27). It would mean new life (Ezekiel 37:14). It would mean that God's people would speak His message with boldness (Joel 2:28-32).

No one can give God's Spirit but God. John's promise that the coming greater One will *baptize you with the Holy Ghost* says flatly that that One will do what only God can do. Therefore, who can this greater One be but God Himself? [See question #3, page 350.]

John draws a contrast between his own action of baptizing in *water* and the greater One's action in giving the Holy Spirit. Some say that this shows that John's own administration of water baptism is relatively unimportant. But this is not John's implication. John is simply pointing out that as a mere human he does not personally do what only God can do. But as a divinely given aspect of God's plan for humanity, baptism has profound importance.

Is John's practice of baptism the same as Christian baptism in the name of Jesus? The witness of the New Testament shows us that while these are different, they are closely related. Disciples of John who believed in Jesus after His resurrection were rebaptized into the name of Jesus (Acts 19:1-7). John's baptism looked *forward* to the coming greater One who would fulfill God's promises. Baptism in the name of Jesus looks *back* to the actual fulfillment of those promises. As such, baptism should have a powerful effect on our thinking and behavior. To discover the meaning of baptism, study passages such as Acts 2:38; Romans 6:1-7; Galatians 3:27; Colossians 2:12; and 1 Peter 3:21.

II. Arrival of the Greatest One (Mark 1:9-11)

In Mark, Jesus' first appearance is at His own baptism. This scene gives us a glimpse of the role that Jesus will play in God's plan.

A. Baptism (v. 9)

9. And it came to pass in those days, that Jesus came from Nazareth of Galilee, and was baptized of John in Jordan.

Jesus comes to *John* to receive the baptism that John offers. Mark's Gospel does not tell us directly why Jesus does this, but we can infer the reason from the context. First, Jesus does not come, as others do, for cleansing from sin. Soon He will begin to cast out demons, showing His mastery over sin and Satan (Mark 3:23-27) and offering forgiveness of sin on His own authority (Mark 2:5).

In Matthew 3:15, Jesus Himself provides a direct answer regarding the meaning of His baptism when He notes that it is "to fulfil all righteousness." In this act of submission, Jesus identifies Himself with John's message; it is Jesus' ministry that will fulfill that message. Jesus' baptism also identifies Him as the greater One of whom John has spoken. The actions that accompany Jesus' baptism will make that clear.

B. Holy Spirit (v. 10)

10. And straightway coming up out of the water, he saw the heavens opened, and the Spirit like a dove descending upon him.

Following closely on John's promise, the Holy Spirit's appearance identifies Jesus as the One who gives the Holy *Spirit*. Because Mark's Gospel has just related John's promise about the giving of the Spirit, the Spirit's descent from Heaven on Jesus is God's statement that Jesus is the One who will fulfill that promise.

C. Voice from Heaven (v. 11)

11. And there came a voice from heaven, saying, Thou art my beloved Son, in whom I am well pleased.

By itself, the descent of the Spirit on Jesus may not tell us much. But the *voice* that accompanies that action fills out the picture. Mark does not tell us whose voice this is. But because the voice says something very similar to statements of God in the Old Testament, there is no doubt who is speaking.

The words of the voice are very similar to two important Old Testament passages, namely Psalm 2:7 and Isaiah 42:1. The combination of these texts helps us understand who Jesus is and what He will do.

Psalm 2 is a celebration of God's rule over His people through the king whom He appointed. It begins by commenting on the rage and pretensions of the pagan nations. Where is God, since the wicked seem to rule the world? The psalmist answers that God still rules in Heaven and will establish His rule on earth through His ap-

Visual for lesson 1

Display this map throughout the quarter to provide a geographical perspective of the lessons.

pointed King. It looks forward to the Messiah who will defeat God's enemies and bring about God's will "on earth as it is in heaven."

Isaiah 42 speaks of the Servant of the Lord who will make God known to all the nations. His method will not be to conquer with the sword but to serve with gentleness. Thereby He will bring light to the nations.

God's words at Jesus' baptism identify Him with these two Old Testament concepts. Jesus is the promised King, the One appointed by God to establish His rule. He will do that, not by conquest, but by mercy. He will defeat God's enemies, but He will do it by what seems to be His own defeat. By submitting to death on the cross, Jesus will make the mercy of God available to all and will reign as God's King.

As Christians look at the world, they can easily sink into frustration and discouragement. It often seems that wickedness has won the day. [See question #4, page 350.] This outlook is not new (see Judges 6:13; Habakkuk 1:2-4). What God announces here shows us otherwise. God is working out His plan. Yet He does it "not with swords loud clashing, Nor roll of stirring drums," but with the Servant-King who rules by giving Himself for unworthy people.

III. Temptation of the Greatest One (Mark 1:12, 13)

Mark tells us very little about Jesus' temptation after His baptism. Rather, Mark sets a scene and lets us infer the outcome.

A. Spirit's Action (v. 12)

12. And immediately the Spirit driveth him into the wilderness.

Having just descended on Jesus, the Holy *Spirit* sends Jesus *into the wilderness.* Mark uses a strong verb that implies urgency. What Jesus does in the wilderness is important to His mission and God's purpose.

Again, *wilderness* is an important place for Israel. In the wilderness under Moses, Israel failed its test. How will Jesus stand up to His wilderness challenge?

B. Elements of Jesus' Temptation (v. 13)

13. And he was there in the wilderness forty days tempted of Satan; and was with the wild beasts; and the angels ministered unto him.

Mark's spare details show us the main thrust of Jesus' *wilderness* experience. As we observed before, the prophets spoke of God's promised salvation as an event like Israel's exodus from Egypt, only greater. Jesus now goes to the wilderness for *forty days,* like Israel after the exodus for forty years, and confronts temptation. His temptation comes from the chief adversary himself, Satan. Though the situation is dangerous, as suggested by wild beasts, Jesus receives supernatural care from *angels.*

What, then, is the outcome of this confrontation? Mark will show us in what follows. Jesus' first miracle in Mark is the casting out of a demon (Mark 1:23-26). Jesus continues to prevail whenever He encounters Satan's demonic servants (3:11). In fact, He says that His casting out of demons demonstrates that He has bound the "strong man," Satan himself (3:27). Jesus freely offers forgiveness for the sin that Satan has inspired (2:5).

In all, Jesus' ministry brings defeat to Satan and relief to those whom Satan has oppressed. Clearly, Jesus has prevailed from the beginning. [See question #5, page 350.]

Home Daily Bible Readings

Monday, May 30—You Are My Son (Psalm 2:7-12)

Tuesday, May 31—Baptism for Repentance and Forgiveness (Mark 1:4-8)

Wednesday, June 1—John the Baptist's Message (Matthew 3:7-12)

Thursday, June 2—Jesus Is Baptized (Matthew 3:13-17)

Friday, June 3—Jesus Is Baptized and Tested (Mark 1:9-13)

Saturday, June 4—Here Is My Servant (Matthew 12:17-21)

Sunday, June 5—Jesus Is Tempted by the Devil (Matthew 4:1-11)

OUR ENEMY

The (in)famous French philosopher Voltaire (1694–1778) was dying. Someone at his bedside asked him to renounce the devil. Voltaire purportedly replied, "I am in no position to make any enemies."

But the devil already was Voltaire's enemy! The apostle Peter referred to the devil as such (1 Peter 5:8). The very word *Satan* means "adversary." Sometimes when a very good man dies, people say, "He never had an enemy." Not true! We all have an enemy. As surely as God wants the best for us, the devil wants the worst for us. As deeply as God loves us, Satan hates us. His promise to Eve didn't come true, and neither will his promises to us. Yet, strangely enough, we keep on believing them. If you trust God, He will never fail you. If you trust the devil, he will always disappoint you.

We may have a hard time visualizing Satan, and we do not need to. (We have an equally hard time visualizing God!) The important thing is that we realize that there is a great spiritual struggle going on. Good and evil, God and Satan, are locked in combat (with the decisive battle already fought at the cross and the empty tomb). We cannot stay out of the struggle that continues. We enlist on one side or the other. Since we already know the final outcome, how foolish we would be to enlist on Satan's side—the losing side. He will always be our enemy until his final defeat (Revelation 20:10).   —R. C. S.

Conclusion

A. The Victor

At the end of the story, as Jesus goes to His death, we may think that Satan has prevailed. But the resurrection will show us the real outcome. Jesus was not defeated in the cross. Rather, in the cross He was victorious over sin and Satan. When it seems that evil cannot be overcome, we can remember the One who has defeated the evil one for all time. We understand this final outcome all the better when we look at how Jesus began His ministry. It began with the Father's approval.

B. Prayer

Heavenly Father, we seek Your approval this day on our thoughts and actions as we look in humble gratitude back to the approval You pronounced on Your Son. May we live our lives in rejection of the evil that Jesus came to defeat. In Jesus' name, amen.

C. Thought to Remember

When in doubt, continue to follow Christ.

Learning by Doing

This page contains an alternative lesson plan emphasizing learning activities.
Classes desiring such student involvement will find these suggestions helpful.

Learning Goals

After participating in this lesson, each student will be able to:

1. Retell Mark's account of Jesus' baptism and temptations.

2. Explain what Jesus' baptism and temptations tell us about His identity and authority.

3. Name one reason why he or she is willing to follow the leadership of Jesus Christ.

Into the Lesson

On four or five seats in your classroom place a small gift-wrapped (empty) box. On four or five seats, place a small candy bar. On four or five, tape a quarter (25 cents). Ignore any initial comments regarding the items. As class begins, ask, "Were any of you tempted to open or pocket the item on your seat? Did you find the items tempting?" After a few responses, ask, "How do these items represent temptations common to people?" Curiosity can lead to exploratory behavior; appealing smells and tastes can lead to sampling and overindulgence; money can lead to greed—all are common temptations.

As an alternate introduction, display this letter series: S S E U L B F M C I O S N S T I R O O N L. Ask the class to decipher the word puzzle. (It is the word *submission* merged with the word *self-control*—alternating letters.) Once someone suggests the correct intention, note that in today's lesson text Jesus demonstrates how the godly live lives both of submission and of self-control as He yields to John's baptism and as He resists the devil's strongest temptations.

Into the Word

Display a sketch titled "East Gate Wilderness Mall," showing a basic floor plan for a shopping mall with ten to twelve "business spaces" available. Explain that the ford crossing the Jordan near Jericho, the general location of John's preaching and baptizing, was indeed the "East Gate" for northern travelers coming to Jerusalem. Indicate that you are going to write in the names of "shops" and that you want learners to relate each one to a verse in today's text. Use the following sample "shop" names (or others of your own creation) with verse identification and brief explanation: *4J Travel Agency* (vv. 4, 5)—four Js are Judea, Jerusalem, Jordan, and John; the people all traveled to where John was; *Nothing But Sandals* (v. 7)—the reference to unloosing shoes; *Healthy Diet Shoppe* (v. 6)—a reference to the unusual but kosher diet of John; *Birds from Above* (v. 10)—a reference to the Spirit descending from Heaven in the form of a dove; *Wild Kingdom* (v. 13)—only Mark makes reference to the wild animals in the wilderness; *Dry Goods for Men & Women* (v. 5)—after being immersed in the water the believers needed dry clothing; *Big Amps* (v. 11)—the clear and loud voice from Heaven; *Something Better* (v. 8)—John's act was good, but the better baptism would be later with the Spirit; *UnFriendly Advice Counseling Services* (v. 13)—with the *Un* careted above the line as if a correction; the reference is to Satan's evil suggestions to Jesus in the guise of helping Him; *Driven! Taxi Services* (v. 12)—the Spirit drove Jesus to His appointment with the devil.

Rather than suggesting "shop" names yourself, your class may well want to suggest relevant "shop" names, if you explain the sketch and give them an example or two.

Into Life

Provide a sheet of paper for each learner to make a quick sketch of the "East Gate Wilderness Mall" as you have completed it. Suggest that they save this in their Bibles at Mark 2 for review this coming week. Suggest further that they make a mental connection between today's text and the shops that they walk by or drive by. For example, passing a store specializing in sound equipment should remind them of God's voice from Heaven announcing His pleasure with His Son's submission; passing a health foods store can bring to mind John's careful and healthful diet (and the Bible's general expectations for healthy eating).

Recommend a careful reading of the accounts of Matthew and Luke regarding Jesus' wilderness temptations from Satan. Matthew 4:1-11 and Luke 4:1-13 provide important details regarding the ways Jesus responded to the various temptations. Encourage your learners to look around in the coming week and note those images that speak to the reality of the evil one today. They should also be able to quote a verse that is relevant to the image and context. For example, seeing a demonic tattoo on a passerby could recall, "Thou shalt worship the Lord thy God, and him only shalt thou serve" (Matthew 4:10).

Let's Talk It Over

The questions on this page are designed to promote discussion of the lesson by the class and to encourage application of the lesson Scriptures. The answers provided are only discussion starters. Let your class talk it over from there.

1. "This wilderness was the place of preparation for entering the land of promise." Some people find times of trial and hardship to be a "wilderness experience." What kinds of "wilderness experiences" have you endured, and what "promise" came after?

Most adults have encountered some period of difficulty in life. Perhaps the first few years of marriage were lean ones economically. Through that experience the couple may have learned greater dependence on God and greater pleasure in the "little things" of life. Perhaps one in your class did not come to know the Lord until adulthood. That long "wilderness" period may have taught him or her to value salvation in ways that others in your class cannot appreciate.

2. John's behavior was not offensive, but it did command attention! John used that attention to point people to Jesus. How can Christians today draw attention to themselves in such a way as to point people to the Lord? What errors need to be avoided in such an effort?

The most important mistake to avoid is that of drawing attention to ourselves and keeping it there. When we become the focal point, we are not pointing to Jesus. The Pharisees made that mistake. By pointing to Jesus, we say, "Of ourselves, we are not holy, but we know the Holy One, and He can make you holy."

In that spirit, individual Christians and churches can demonstrate Christ's love in very public ways. One church built a playground and publicly said the neighborhood children were welcome. Another church hosted free community cookouts with professional entertainment. These and other methods can be used to open doors of ministry and evangelism later.

3. Twice it is pointed out that John's message of the coming One indicated that this One would be no less that God Himself. How diligent are we in making sure the world knows we follow Jesus because He is more than a mere man— that He is God himself? What more can we do?

The secular culture we live in has no problem with venerating humans as outstanding leaders, teachers, and examples for others to follow. As long as Jesus is seen as one of them, then He is simply one among many. There is no compelling reason to follow Him instead of another. Our task is to point out the uniqueness of Jesus (John 14:6; Acts 4:12). The works of outstanding leaders are remarkable, but they do not lead to eternal salvation. Jesus alone offers saving grace through His work. The facts of history prove this.

4. In what ways does it seem to you that "wickedness has won the day" in our culture? What do you do to resist the feelings of despair or frustration over that? How can we demonstrate that the victory still belongs to the Lord?

Violent crime, racial inequities, anti-Christian bias in the educational system and in the media, abortion, and highway rage are just a few of the examples that can be offered. Some are dramatic and explosive. Others are more stealthy, making them hard to pinpoint and address.

"Speaking the truth in love" remains the answer to these issues. We do ourselves and our cause no favors when we stoop to the level of the wicked and seek violent solutions to these problems. We must share the gospel of Christ, living by the royal law of love and offering hope to those who have no hope. Not all of these problems will be solved in this world, but we know there is a better world to come when these things will not be present. (See 1 Corinthians 15:58.)

5. Jesus' ministry brings defeat to Satan and relief to those whom Satan has oppressed. How does our church imitate Jesus' ministry in these two points? What more can it do? And how about your own individual efforts—how are you demonstrating these ministry emphases? What more can you do?

Many churches have an unbalanced ministry focus. Many focus on relief to the suffering: they render physical help to the poor and homeless, seek political justice, and otherwise promote social issues. Others emphasize evangelism, defeating Satan through the blood of Jesus, and looking forward to Heaven as the solution to social inequities in this life. Jesus' ministry kept both of these in focus. He came to bring eternal life (John 3:16, 36; 5:24; 6:40; 10:28), but He also ministered the earthly needs of people, healing the sick and condemning the injustice of the Jewish leaders. We today need to work at maintaining the same balance.

Miracles

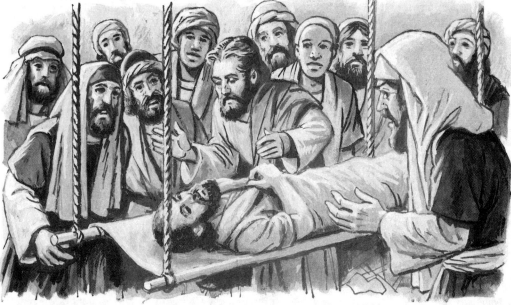

DEVOTIONAL READING: Mark 7:31-37.

BACKGROUND SCRIPTURE: Mark 2:1-12; 3:1-6; 8:1-10.

PRINTED TEXT: Mark 2:1-12.

Mark 2:1-12

1 And again he entered into Capernaum after some days; and it was noised that he was in the house.

2 And straightway many were gathered together, insomuch that there was no room to receive them, no, not so much as about the door: and he preached the word unto them.

3 And they come unto him, bringing one sick of the palsy, which was borne of four.

4 And when they could not come nigh unto him for the press, they uncovered the roof where he was: and when they had broken it up, they let down the bed wherein the sick of the palsy lay.

5 When Jesus saw their faith, he said unto the sick of the palsy, Son, thy sins be forgiven thee.

6 But there were certain of the scribes sitting there, and reasoning in their hearts,

7 Why doth this man thus speak blasphemies? who can forgive sins but God only?

8 And immediately, when Jesus perceived in his spirit that they so reasoned within themselves, he said unto them, Why reason ye these things in your hearts?

9 Whether is it easier to say to the sick of the palsy, Thy sins be forgiven thee; or to say, Arise, and take up thy bed, and walk?

10 But that ye may know that the Son of man hath power on earth to forgive sins, (he saith to the sick of the palsy,)

11 I say unto thee, Arise, and take up thy bed, and go thy way into thine house.

12 And immediately he arose, took up the bed, and went forth before them all; insomuch that they were all amazed, and glorified God, saying, We never saw it on this fashion.

GOLDEN TEXT: That ye may know that the Son of man hath power on earth to forgive sins, (he saith to the sick of the palsy,) I say unto thee, Arise, and take up thy bed, and go thy way into thine house.—Mark 2:10, 11.

Lesson Aims

After participating in this lesson, each student will be able to:

1. Summarize the story of the paralytic who was made whole in body and in spirit.

2. Explain why Jesus' healing ministry was central to His identity as the Son of God.

3. Give praise to God for His power and willingness to make persons whole.

Lesson Outline

INTRODUCTION
 A. The Case of Steve
 B. Lesson Background
 I. PACKED HOUSE (Mark 2:1, 2)
 A. Travels (v. 1)
 B. Preaching (v. 2)
 II. DRAMATIC ENTRANCE (Mark 2:3, 4)
 A. "Plan A" (v. 3)
 B. "Plan B" (v. 4)
 III. DRAMATIC PRONOUNCEMENT (Mark 2:5)
 IV. THREE RESPONSES (Mark 2:6-12)
 A. Offended Hearts (vv. 6-9)
 The Personal Touch
 B. Obedient Heart (vv. 10-12a)
 A Changed Man
 C. "Praise God" Heart (v. 12b)
CONCLUSION
 A. Our Physical Condition
 B. Miracles and Us
 C. Our Reaction to the Miraculous
 D. Prayer
 E. Thought to Remember

Introduction

A. The Case of Steve

I once was leading a Wednesday night Bible study group through 1 Thessalonians. One of the participants was a young man, Steve, afflicted with cerebral palsy. This condition left him nearly helpless from a physical standpoint. Steve had to be rolled into the room in his wheelchair by a helper. He tried diligently to follow our study in his own Bible, but his lack of limb control had caused him to rip many pages while trying to turn them, leaving a badly tattered Bible. Steve's participation in discussion was ponder-

ous, even painful. He either spelled out words by pointing to a signing board or tried to verbalize his comments using a voice that was difficult to understand. Sometimes the other adults in this group were impatient as Steve tried to ask a question, for I usually needed him to repeat it many times before I could understand it.

As we got to 1 Thessalonians 4, we began to talk about the nature of Christ's second coming. Suddenly, Steve motioned that he wanted to ask a question. He was very excited, and this caused the question to be even harder to decipher than usual. He enthusiastically repeated it many times until I finally got it. The question was this, "When Jesus comes, will I get a new body?"

I have always had a relatively healthy body, so it took me a second to appreciate the implications of this question. Steve looked forward to the day when his poor, twisted body would be able to walk and talk just like all the "normal" people he observed around him. What a great day that will be! Steve passed away a few years ago without being healed from cerebral palsy, even though I know he prayed for this healing many times. It thrills my heart to know that he is now praising God with no impediment of his defective earthly body.

Today's lesson is about a "Steve" from the ministry of Jesus. He, too, had a nearly helpless physical condition. Surely he also dreamed of being "normal," of walking without help and talking so that he was easily understood. In today's marvelous story, this man received a new body, a miracle of wholeness from Jesus.

B. Lesson Background

The second and third chapters of Mark's Gospel contain several brief stories, sometimes referred to as "conflict narratives." In these accounts Jesus or His disciples do something that causes people to be upset with them.

In Mark 2:1-12 the healing of the paralytic is accompanied by a pronouncement of forgiveness of sins, causing the Jewish leaders to view Jesus as a blasphemer. In 2:13-17 Jesus attends a celebration at the home of His new disciple, Levi (also known as Matthew). The Jewish religious leaders see this party group as "the wrong crowd," and Jesus is again criticized. As with the paralytic, Jesus draws a connection between physical health and spiritual health, saying, "They that are whole have no need of the physician, but they that are sick: I came not to call the righteous, but sinners to repentance" (2:17).

Mark 2 ends with two more stories in which Jesus and His disciples are criticized over their fasting practices and over a perceived violation of ancient Sabbath-day regulations.

These conflicts reach something of a climax in Mark 3:1-6, the story of the man with the "withered hand." Here Jesus is challenged to make a sobering choice: ignore a suffering man or break the Sabbath. By healing the man verbally, Jesus not only avoids obvious Sabbath work, but also takes advantage of the opportunity to expose publicly the hypocrisy of His opponents. This humiliation infuriates Jesus' opponents to the point that they develop a plot to kill Him (Mark 3:6). This early foreshadowing of the death of Jesus is then worked out in the remaining chapters of Mark.

The spiritual depravity of Jesus' opponents is illustrated in the last conflict narrative in this part of Mark, a story where Jesus is accused of being demon possessed (3:20-30). The intensity of this clash is shown when Jesus pulls out the heaviest of theological artillery and warns His opponents that they are dangerously near to committing an unforgivable sin (3:29).

Today's lesson, the story of the healing of the paralytic, shows some of the terrible tensions that Jesus encountered in His ministry. On the one hand, He found people in desperate need of the forgiveness and healing that He freely offered. Their faith, their gratitude, and their blessings inspire and encourage us. On the other hand, Jesus was dogged by critics who hoped for His failure, were constantly offended by His claims, and resented His refusal to submit to their authority.

I. Packed House
(Mark 2:1, 2)
A. Travels (v. 1)

1. And again he entered into Capernaum after some days; and it was noised that he was in the house.

Jesus makes the small fishing village of Capernaum His headquarters in the early days of His ministry. This is the town of Simon Peter and Andrew, and Jesus may be staying in Peter's house (Mark 1:21, 29). The expression *in the house* means that He resides there on a semipermanent basis. This is the place where Jesus had healed the mother-in-law of Peter (Mark 1:30, 31).

Capernaum is a well-known archaeological site in Israel today. It is located on the north end of the Sea of Galilee, about three miles west of the inlet of the Jordan River.

B. Preaching (v. 2)

2. And straightway many were gathered together, insomuch that there was no room to receive them, no, not so much as about the door: and he preached the word unto them.

If this takes place at the house of Peter, we may have some remarkable information available to help us understand this setting. Modern archaeologists believe they have found the actual house of Peter at the ancient site of Capernaum. The foundations of this house were buried under the remnants of various ancient churches that had been built over it. Inscriptions and other evidence indicate that this place was considered holy by Christians from early times, lending credence to the theory that it was originally the house of Peter.

Such homes usually consisted of a rectangular, one-story building surrounded by a large, walled courtyard. Peter's (apparent) house in Capernaum was approximately twenty-eight feet long and would have been fifteen to eighteen feet deep. The interior is now packed with perhaps fifty to sixty people, causing an overflow into the courtyard. The text notes that Jesus preaches *the word* to this spiritually thirsty crowd. This is His message of faith and repentance, announcing the presence of the kingdom of God (Mark 1:14, 15). [See question #1, page 358.]

II. Dramatic Entrance
(Mark 2:3, 4)
A. "Plan A" (v. 3)

3. And they come unto him, bringing one sick of the palsy, which was borne of four.

What is wrong with this man? His condition is so helpless that he has to be carried on a bed or stretcher with one person at each corner. This probably is not a bed rigged up just for the occasion. The man has to be carried anywhere he goes, for he cannot walk. Perhaps he is carried daily to a begging spot in this portable bed (e.g., Acts 3:2).

What, exactly, is his disease? The text only describes his condition, not the underlying cause of the condition. The word that we see translated *palsy* is the Greek word *paralytikos* from which we get our English word *paralytic*. This means the man has use of neither his arms nor his legs.

How to Say It

BLASPHEMER. *blas*-feem-er.
BLASPHEMY. *blas*-fuh-me.
CAPERNAUM. Kuh-*per*-nay-um.
GALILEE. *Gal*-uh-lee.
ISAIAH. Eye-*zay*-uh.
LEVI. *Lee*-vye.
LEVITICUS. Leh-*vit*-ih-kus.
MESSIANIC. mess-ee-*an*-ick.

This could be a condition from birth, the result of an accident, or the product of a stroke—we simply don't know. What we *do* know is that the *four* friends think that if they can bring the man to Jesus then Jesus can help.

B. "Plan B" (v. 4)

4. And when they could not come nigh unto him for the press, they uncovered the roof where he was: and when they had broken it up, they let down the bed wherein the sick of the palsy lay.

The house is so packed with people that the band of stretcher-bearers has no chance of getting their man close to Jesus. The paralytic's friends are not easily thwarted. "Plan A" didn't work, so now it's on to "Plan B." They carry their disabled friend to *the roof* and proceed to break a hole in it. Then they use the stretcher as a platform to lower their friend to Jesus.

Common houses in Palestine in this time are of one story with a staircase or ladder outside to give access to the roof. The roof area could be used for storage, sometimes having a lightweight shed built on it. The roof itself is made of crossbeams with branches laid across them. This is then covered with mud, hardened by the sun. This is a durable system, hard enough to walk upon.

The drama of this event should not be missed. The digging surely showers the packed people below with dirt. The descending bed doubtlessly clears a space near Jesus for the man to rest, perhaps causing some to flee. We marvel at the audacity of these friends to risk the wrath of the homeowner, at their strong faith that Jesus can heal, and at their great love to do such a crazy thing for the paralytic. One author has described this as a "silent but dramatic plea for healing." [See question #2, page 358.]

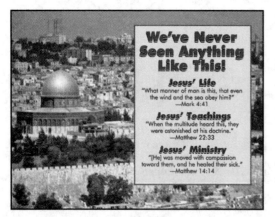

We've Never Seen Anything Like This!

Jesus' Life
"What manner of man is this, that even the wind and the sea obey him?"
—Mark 4:41

Jesus' Teachings
"When the multitude heard this, they were astonished at his doctrine."
—Matthew 22:33

Jesus' Ministry
"[He] was moved with compassion toward them, and he healed their sick."
—Matthew 14:14

Visual for lessons 2 and 11. *You may wish to keep this visual aid posted to set the tone for each of this quarter's three subunits.*

III. Dramatic Pronouncement (Mark 2:5)

5. When Jesus saw their faith, he said unto the sick of the palsy, Son, thy sins be forgiven thee.

Jesus maintains control over this chaotic situation. He immediately recognizes an act of *faith* and a need for physical healing. [See question #3, page 358.] His words, however, are confusing. What is the connection between faith, healing, and the need for forgiveness? Jesus' startling pronouncement *thy sins be forgiven thee* elicits three responses from those who hear it.

IV. Three Responses (Mark 2:6-12)

A. Offended Hearts (vv. 6-9)

6, 7. But there were certain of the scribes sitting there, and reasoning in their hearts, Why doth this man thus speak blasphemies? who can forgive sins but God only?

Mark first tells of the response of *the scribes* in the house. Scribes are respected, authoritative interpreters of the Jewish law. They instantly detect a possible violation. *Sins* are forgiven by *God only,* and only through long-practiced methods of sacrifices and priests. See Exodus 34:7 for God proclaiming the power to forgive sins. See also Psalm 103:2, 3 and Isaiah 43:25. [See question #4, page 358.]

These men already have been portrayed as seeing Jesus as a possible rival teacher, one with extraordinary spiritual authority (Mark 1:27). None of them would presume to be able to pronounce forgiveness. They conclude that Jesus possesses no such rightful authority either, and, therefore, His pronouncement is nothing less than blasphemy. Blasphemy in this context is to infringe upon authority that belongs rightfully to God. Blasphemy is a capital offense under the Jewish law (Leviticus 24:16).

8, 9. And immediately, when Jesus perceived in his spirit that they so reasoned within themselves, he said unto them, Why reason ye these things in your hearts? whether is it easier to say to the sick of the palsy, Thy sins be forgiven thee; or to say, Arise, and take up thy bed, and walk?

Jesus undoubtedly startles the scribes by reading their thoughts. His comment reflects the ancient way of referring to mental processes. The people of Jesus' time see the heart as more than the center of emotions. For them, the heart is also the intellectual center, and in particular it is the source of the human will. So their reasoning is really a spiritual matter, a lack of faith. To make His purpose completely clear, Jesus challenges the scribes to differentiate between forgiving and healing. Both require authority that they do not possess. Both call for the power of God.

It seems uncomfortable to look at this man as a gross sinner. What is his sin problem? How can a paralytic get into sin? To think this way, however is to underestimate the universal, pervasive problem of human sinfulness. Disabled people sin, too! Sin extends beyond our actions. It includes our mental life. The mental life of the paralytic may have been consumed by sexual sin, by bitter rejection of God, or by personal dishonesty. We don't know.

We may not all be physically disabled, but we are all spiritually disabled because of sin. Everyone stands before God as a sinner in need of forgiveness. And just as we have no power to miraculously heal our bodies, we have no power to grant God's forgiveness to ourselves. Both are gracious acts of God that must be received in faith rather than demanded or expected.

THE PERSONAL TOUCH

There is a gallery in England that displays what many call "holy relics." They say that they have a bone from the skull of John the Baptist. They display a lock of hair said to be from the head of Mary, the mother of Jesus. There is even a column that is supposed to be the one against which Jesus leaned when He was scourged! Of course, it is most unlikely that any of the relics are genuine. They may be a source of inspiration, but little more. Some, though, claim that they have been healed by these things.

You will notice that Jesus healed personally. Most of us think that today healing still comes directly and personally from the Lord, not indirectly and impersonally from some object that may or may not have been associated with Him. When we pray for health or healing today, we should not expect that some object over which someone has prayed will accomplish what we desire. Neither should we expect that there are magic words that, if only said properly, will accomplish healing.

We should expect, rather, that a loving Lord hears our prayers and answers them in accordance with His own wisdom, knowledge, and love. This means that we may have to wait until we are in Heaven to receive the healing for which we pray. It also means that we can pray freely, for if we ask for something we should not have, a wise and loving Father will respond in the way that is best. —R. C. S.

B. Obedient Heart (vv. 10-12a)

10, 11. But that ye may know that the Son of man hath power on earth to forgive sins, (he saith to the sick of the palsy,) I say unto thee,

Arise, and take up thy bed, and go thy way into thine house.

Supernatural claims demand supernatural evidence. For example, if I claim the supernatural ability to fly like Superman, no one would believe me unless I demonstrate the fact by soaring into the air unaided. To make the supernatural claim that Jesus is the Son of God requires a demonstration of supernatural evidence.

Jesus deliberately links the healing and the forgiving. Only the power of God can instantly heal a paralytic. Only the authority of God can allow for forgiveness of *sins*. Jesus says, in effect, "I have authority in both areas. Because there is no visible sign of forgiveness, I will show my authority in a tangible way by healing this man. I will make him whole spiritually and physically."

Jesus is making a messianic claim by doing this. The Gospel of Mark is very careful in its presentation of Jesus as the Son of God. Mark 1:1 indicates that this is the core of the book's message. At His baptism, Jesus is identified as God's Son (Mark 1:11). Later, at the transfiguration, God not only reinforces this identification, but also commands that Jesus must be heard (Mark 9:7). To truly hear Jesus is to believe Him and obey Him. This is what the man is being asked to do. If we are to receive forgiveness, this is what we are asked to do.

12a. And immediately he arose, took up the bed, and went forth before them all.

To put it simply, the man believes and obeys. As there can be no certain evidence of the man's forgiveness without the healing, there can be no evidence of his faith without his obedience. By *took up the bed*, we envision a portable device that can be rolled up.

A CHANGED MAN

The advertising slogan for the Louisiana tourist industry is, "Come as you are. Leave different!" That describes the experience of the paralyzed man in today's lesson. It also describes the experience of everyone who receives Jesus as Savior. The man in today's lesson was a changed man in two ways. He was a changed man physically. Four friends carried him in; he walked out carrying his mat. As important as that was to him, there was another change even more important: he was carried in a sinner; he walked out a forgiven man.

Today there are many victims of paralysis, some famous and some unknown. No doubt they pray for the same healing as the man in our text. Some may receive it now and some may have to wait until Heaven. But think for a moment of that other change. When we seek the forgiveness of our sins, we do not go away disappointed. We *are* forgiven, and that change is of far greater magnitude than any physical healing.

Remember that we will have these bodies for only a little while. We will have our souls (and resurrected bodies) for eternity. For the soul to be crippled by sin is the greater tragedy—and to have the inner person forgiven, made whole, is the greater miracle. While we marvel at what this man experienced in his body, we marvel more at what all of Christians have experienced in their souls.   —R. C. S.

C. "Praise God" Heart (v. 12b)

12b. Insomuch that they were all amazed, and glorified God, saying, We never saw it on this fashion.

We should not miss the reaction of the crowd to all of this. They are *amazed*. This language is often used in the Gospels and Acts to describe the realization of a crowd that they had just witnessed a miracle (compare Mark 5:42). The Greek term translated *amazed* is the word from which we get our English words *ecstasy* and *ecstatic*. This powerful reaction is followed by an immediate acknowledgement that *God* is the source of this miracle. [See question #5, page 358.]

Conclusion

A. Our Physical Condition

In the mind of the ancient Jew, illness and disability were thought to be punishment for sin; this is seen clearly in John 9:2. Today, we know this to be true on a limited scale. Behavior defined as sinful by the Bible is often dangerous or even disease-producing. A reckless, pleasure-seeking lifestyle may have consequences for our health. However, we all know of many instances of disease or injury suffered by good and righ-teous people. Where is the power of God in all of this?

B. Miracles and Us

We use the word *miracle* loosely in today's world. We speak of the latest computer triumph as a "technological miracle." We refer to a new advance in medical treatment as a "miracle drug." We call the rapid growth of a company's stock value "miraculous." But none of these things are really miracles. All can be explained through careful study and analysis.

A true miracle is a supernatural event, something beyond rational or scientific explanation. Such wonders may be spiritual or physical, just as the paralytic is healed spiritually and physically in this story. Spiritual transformation is no less miraculous than unexplainable physical change. May we never forget that God's forgiveness is also a miracle.

C. Our Reaction to the Miraculous

When God works miraculously, we don't always understand. Here are three suggestions to help us deal with this issue in our lives.

First, God is in control of His miracles; we aren't. Why do righteous people suffer diseases, injuries, and personal disasters? Why doesn't God always heal when we ask for healing? The bottom line is that God in His wisdom determines the time, place, and circumstance of His miraculous intervention in our lives.

Second, since we sometimes don't understand God's miraculous works, our only reaction is to praise Him as the crowd did in today's lesson. God's work is always a cause for worship. To do this is an act of obedience that should be natural for the believer.

Third, every time we pray we expect the miraculous. If we petition God with prayers of faith, we are asking Him to make "Situation A" into "Situation not-A." Such praying is good and proper; it is an act of both obedience and faith.

D. Prayer

Creator God, You formed the universe out of nothing by the power of Your Word. You continue to work miracles that are beyond our comprehension. While we are in constant need of Your providential power, today we ask that You make us more aware and appreciative of Your wonders in our lives so that we may be brought to Your throne in praise again and again. We pray in the name of Your Son, amen.

E. Thought to Remember

God's miracles should cause us
to give Him glory.

Home Daily Bible Readings

Monday, June 6—Jesus Heals the Demoniac (Mark 5:1-13)

Tuesday, June 7—He Has Done Everything Well (Mark 7:31-37)

Wednesday, June 8—How Many Loaves Do You Have? (Mark 8:1-5)

Thursday, June 9—Four Thousand Are Fed (Mark 8:6-10)

Friday, June 10—Stretch Out Your Hand (Mark 3:1-6)

Saturday, June 11—Son, Your Sins Are Forgiven (Mark 2:1-5)

Sunday, June 12—I Say to You, Stand Up (Mark 2:6-12)

Learning by Doing

This page contains an alternative lesson plan emphasizing learning activities.
Classes desiring such student involvement will find these suggestions helpful.

Learning Goals

After participating in this lesson, each student will be able to:

1. Summarize the story of the paralytic who was made whole in body and in spirit.

2. Explain why Jesus' healing ministry was central to His identity as the Son of God.

3. Give praise to God for His power and willingness to make persons whole.

Into the Lesson

Display a list of six Biblical miracles with the heading "Miracles," and ask the class to number them from "greatest" to "least." Consider these six (or choose your own): Red Sea held back for Israel to cross—Exodus 14:21, 22; Walls of Jericho collapse—Joshua 6:20; Samuel's spirit appears to Saul and his medium—1 Samuel 28: 11-19; Elijah is taken to Heaven in a fiery chariot—2 Kings 2:11; Apostles speak in unlearned languages—Acts 2:4; Paul heals the lame man of Lystra—Acts 14:8-10.

Let the class make their decisions, and then ask, "What is it that makes a miracle a miracle?" Expect to receive responses about their extraordinary nature, their value as evidence, and their divine origin. Also ask, "How can we decide if one miracle is greater than another?" After the group responds, make the points that each miracle was God's intervention into His established "natural law," and that each is equally purposeful in the revelation of His will.

Then say, "In today's text in Mark 2, Jesus equates a healing miracle with another act that only God can do. Look carefully for how these two are connected."

Into the Word

Hand four blank index cards to each learner. Direct everyone to write the following four letters on the cards, one letter per card: *F, P, R, S.* Have one of your better oral readers stand and read the text, Mark 2:1-12, loudly and clearly.

Next, tell the group to conceal the text from their eyes. Then say to them, "I am going to read several questions regarding the facts of today's text. I want you, after each question, to hold up the card bearing the first letter of the word from the text answering my question." Use the following questions to review the content: (1) "How many friends carried the man unable to walk?"

(**F**our); (2) "What did Jesus do once the crowd assembled?" (**P**reached); (3) "What was the condition of the man brought to Jesus?" (**P**alsy); (4) "Of what was it said in this text that there was none?" (**R**oom); (5) "What was it about the men carrying their friend that impressed Jesus?" (**F**aith); (6) "What was said about the position of the scribes in the house?" (**S**itting); (7) "What part of the house was opened to get the lame man to Jesus?" (**R**oof); (8) "What did Jesus say about the lame man's sins?" (**F**orgiven); (9) "How did Jesus address the man brought to Him?" (**S**on); (10) "How did Jesus know the Jewish scholars were accusing Him?" (**S**pirit); (11) "From what Jesus said, what was the lame man's greater problem?" (**S**in); (12) "What did Jesus say the healing was evidence of?" (**P**ower).

Let all reveal their cards after each question. Then let one student give the answer orally.

At the end, give this assignment to the learners: "Use the four letters in your hand—in any order you choose—to compose a 'headline' for the events of the text. Feel free to add articles, prepositions, or other words." Give them a few examples:

> "Rejoice! **P**alsied Man **S**aved and **F**orgiven";
> "**S**cholars **R**eject **P**aralytic's **F**orgiveness";
> "**F**orgiveness **R**iles **P**roud **S**cribes."

Allow enough time and then let several give their "headlines."

Into Life

The miracle in Mark 2:1-12 begins with faith (read v. 5) and ends with praise (read v. 12). Ask the class to answer this question, "What role do the miracles of the Bible play in your faith?" Ask also, "Compare your own response to Jesus' miracles to that of those present during His ministry. How do you fare in the comparison?" If you think your learners need a few texts to examine, suggest they look at records of miracles in other chapters in Mark's Gospel, perhaps Mark 1:25-28 and Mark 4:35-41.

Ask your class to make a commitment to the following practice by signing the statement you give them (also in the student book accompanying this series): "I will—each time I read of one of the miracles of the Bible—stop to glorify God for His power and grace." Close with a prayer appropriate to this promise.

Let's Talk It Over

The questions on this page are designed to promote discussion of the lesson by the class and to encourage application of the lesson Scriptures. The answers provided are only discussion starters. Let your class talk it over from there.

1. When Jesus gathered a crowd, He "preached the word" to them. Why do we so often do something else—like have a concert, a meal, or a dramatic production? How can we follow Jesus' example more closely?

Many churches have used concerts, meals, dramas, and other events as the means of drawing a crowd. There is nothing wrong with that. The church today needs to be creative in the methods it uses to attract people to hear the Word.

The question is, "How much 'preaching' of the Word can we combine with those events?" Some feel much "preaching" will be manipulative in such a setting—sort of a spiritual "bait and switch." They use these events to let the community know of the church's presence, but little of her message is communicated. Others feel that the church needs to take advantage of the opportunity to communicate the gospel to the people while they are there. For a church to communicate a spiritual message is not manipulative, they say, but is what one would expect from a church.

2. The paralytic and his friends were determined to see Jesus—nothing would stop them. Why, then, are some believers so easily discouraged from attending worship services? The air conditioning must be just right, the pews padded, the music according to their preference, etc. To what extent should the church accommodate such people? Won't the truly faithful come even if they are uncomfortable?

Even among those who followed Jesus there were varying levels of commitment. The church today wants to attract people of all levels—from no faith to strong faith. Surely the faithful will gather together to worship even if the building is uncomfortable. (Though even they have many options today and will likely choose comfort and worship when they can!) But the uncommitted have a different value system. They need to be met where they are and led to a greater level of commitment. If that can happen by making them comfortable, then there is nothing wrong with padding the pews and adjusting the thermostat.

3. Mark tells us that Jesus "saw their faith." How can people see our faith today?

"Faith without works is dead" (James 2:20, 26). And Jesus said, "By their fruits ye shall know them" (Matthew 7:20). Thus, people will "see" our faith in the same way Jesus saw these men's faith: by actions. When the crowd blocked the path of the paralytic's friends, their faith would not be dimmed. In the same way, extreme circumstances make the level of our faith apparent. Are we easily discouraged, or does our faith rise to the occasion? Perhaps some in your class can give examples of demonstrations of faith.

4. The scribes were moved by jealousy to oppose Jesus. Paul encountered some of the same rival spirit from Christian preachers (Philippians 1:15). How can we be sure we do not yield to a spirit of jealousy when someone else performs a ministry in a way that results in attention and honor that we do not share?

It is very easy to become jealous. When another gets attention and affirmation that we don't, we can feel hurt. Perhaps Paul provides the best answer: "What then? notwithstanding, every way, whether in pretense, or in truth, Christ is preached; and I therein do rejoice, yea, and will rejoice" (Philippians 1:18).

We, too, need to focus on the ministry that is being performed and whether Christ is being exalted. If He is, even if by less-than-honorable servants, we can take joy in that. As for our own efforts, we can remember Hebrews 6:10: "For God is not unrighteous to forget your work and labor of love."

5. The crowd was "amazed" and they "glorified God" when the man was healed. What can we do to rekindle that same sense of awe in our worship?

We who have been Christians for many years may approach worship with a lack of enthusiasm, expecting nothing new. "Familiarity breeds contempt," the old adage goes. But we dare not allow that to happen! We can concentrate on some of the psalms that praise God for His mighty acts, for His love and mercy, and for His constant faithfulness. We can read again the accounts of the crucifixion and resurrection, remembering the eternal results for us.

Our worship will be only as meaningful as we have prepared ourselves to make it. It is the state of our hearts that make for awe in worship, and not things that others do.

Trials and Opposition

DEVOTIONAL READING: Mark 14:17-21.

BACKGROUND SCRIPTURE: Mark 14:53-65; 15:1-5.

PRINTED TEXT: Mark 14:53-65; 15:1-3.

Mark 14:53-65

53 And they led Jesus away to the high priest: and with him were assembled all the chief priests and the elders and the scribes.

54 And Peter followed him afar off, even into the palace of the high priest: and he sat with the servants, and warmed himself at the fire.

55 And the chief priests and all the council sought for witness against Jesus to put him to death; and found none.

56 For many bare false witness against him, but their witness agreed not together.

57 And there arose certain, and bare false witness against him, saying,

58 We heard him say, I will destroy this temple that is made with hands, and within three days I will build another made without hands.

59 But neither so did their witness agree together.

60 And the high priest stood up in the midst, and asked Jesus, saying, Answerest thou nothing? what is it which these witness against thee?

61 But he held his peace, and answered nothing. Again the high priest asked him, and said unto him, Art thou the Christ, the Son of the Blessed?

62 And Jesus said, I am: and ye shall see the Son of man sitting on the right hand of power, and coming in the clouds of heaven.

63 Then the high priest rent his clothes, and saith, What need we any further witnesses?

64 Ye have heard the blasphemy: what think ye? And they all condemned him to be guilty of death.

65 And some began to spit on him, and to cover his face, and to buffet him, and to say unto him, Prophesy: and the servants did strike him with the palms of their hands.

Mark 15:1-3

1 And straightway in the morning the chief priests held a consultation with the elders and scribes and the whole council, and bound Jesus, and carried him away, and delivered him to Pilate.

2 And Pilate asked him, Art thou the King of the Jews? And he answering said unto him, Thou sayest it.

3 And the chief priests accused him of many things; but he answered nothing.

GOLDEN TEXT: The chief priests and all the council sought for witness against Jesus to put him to death; and found none.—Mark 14:55.

Jesus' Life, Teachings, and Ministry
Unit 1: Jesus' Life
(Lessons 1-4)

Lesson Aims

After participating in this lesson, each student will be able to:

1. Describe the trial process that led to the death of Jesus.

2. Contrast the innocence of the One accused with the guilt of His accusers.

3. Express gratitude to God for the sacrifice of His innocent Son to save them from their sins.

Lesson Outline

INTRODUCTION
   A. Blamed, but Innocent
   B. Lesson Background
 I. TAKEN TO TRIAL (Mark 14:53, 54)
   A. Jesus and His Enemies (v. 53)
   B. Peter and the Servants (v. 54)
 II. PLOT TO ELIMINATE (Mark 14:55-59)
   A. Witnesses Disagree, Part 1 (vv. 55, 56)
     The Verdict Before the Trial
   B. Witnesses Disagree, Part 2 (vv. 57-59)
 III. HEART OF THE MATTER (Mark 14:60-65)
   A. Who Are You, Jesus? (vv. 60-62)
   B. Blasphemy! (vv. 63-65)
 IV. PILATE THE DUPE (Mark 15:1-3)
   A. Accurate Response (vv. 1, 2)
   B. No Response (v. 3)
     When Silence Is Golden
CONCLUSION
   A. Why Did They Kill Jesus?
   B. The Innocence and Sacrifice of Jesus
   C. Prayer
   D. Thought to Remember

Introduction

A. Blamed, but Innocent

An office helper knocked at the door of my seventh-grade classroom with a note for the teacher. I barely noticed. But terror gripped me when the teacher read the note. It said that I was to report to the vice principal's office immediately. It only took me a few seconds to be escorted down the hall to the vice principal, but my heart pounded and my mind raced. The vice principal was in charge of one thing at that school: student discipline. I was in big trouble! What had I done?

Sitting in the office was a member of the janitorial crew. He simply said, "Yes, that's him," and left. The vice principal closed the door and asked, "Why did you do it? Did you think you would get away with it?" Confused and scared, I pleaded with him to explain. He was so angry that it took him a while to give me an answer. I had been identified as having committed a major act of vandalism in one of the rest rooms. The positive identification by the janitor left no room for doubt in the vice principal's mind.

I tried every way I could to convince the man that I was innocent (which I was), but his mind was made up. He had found a guilty party, and he would not rest until proper punishment had been administered. Now, I must admit that I had been in this vice principal's office before under different circumstances where I was not innocent. I was hardly above suspicion. He was thus resistant to all my pleas of blamelessness.

In today's lesson Jesus is accused of a crime in spite of His innocence. Unlike me, He had no earlier unfavorable marks against Him. He had lived a life innocent of any and all sin. Unlike me, too, He did not protest against His accusers. He quietly accepted an unjust sentence of death, and in so doing He changed the world forever.

B. Lesson Background

The celebration of Passover in first-century Jerusalem was one of the greatest festivals of the ancient world. Jerusalem was a city of perhaps fifty thousand in population. (Some estimates put the "normal" population as high as one hundred twenty thousand.) Using information from a Jewish historian named Josephus, scholars estimate that this population swelled manyfold during Passover week.

Not all of these visitors were observant Jews. Herod Antipas, ruler of Galilee, came down from his capital city of Tiberias. Pilate, the Roman governor, came up from beautiful Caesarea, bringing plenty of troops with him to keep the peace. It was a time of great pageantry, celebration, and excitement.

The center of attention was the Jewish temple, a marvel of the ancient world. This enormous, magnificent complex of buildings had acres of open space to accommodate all the visitors. Business was brisk as the temple vendors had their biggest days of the year. Profits were high as Jewish pilgrims paid cash for Passover necessities.

The south end of the temple campus housed a colossal "stoa," or covered porch, approximately three hundred yards long and forty-five to fifty yards wide. At the western end of this stoa was an apse that served as the official meeting site of the Sanhedrin, the Jewish High Council. The

Sanhedrin was closely connected to the temple. It not only convened there normally, but many of the Sanhedrin councilors probably had commercial interests in the temple businesses. (See a panoramic computer reconstruction of Herod's Temple on the Web site of The Jerusalem Archaeological Park at www.archpark.org.il.)

There is some reason to believe that the author, John Mark, may have been an eyewitness to some of the events he describes in chapters 14, 15, and 16. This is based on the theory that the naked runner of Mark 14:51, 52 was Mark himself. This detail is not used in the other Gospels, so some have seen it as Mark's insertion of a personal detail, almost a "cameo" appearance. If this is true, we should expect to read Mark's account all the more eagerly since we are reading the words of a witness to some of these events.

I. Taken to Trial
(Mark 14:53, 54)

A. Jesus and His Enemies (v. 53)

53. And they led Jesus away to the high priest: and with him were assembled all the chief priests and the elders and the scribes.

The high priest is not named here, but the parallel account in Matthew 26:57 indicates it is Caiaphas. John 18:13 notes a trip to the home of Annas, the father-in-law of Caiaphas and former high priest. It is possible that these two have adjoining homes in the same compound.

The assembly is called "the council" in Mark 14:55 (below). The Greek word translated *council* there is *synedrion* from which we get our English word *Sanhedrin*. For the Sanhedrin to meet at the house of Caiaphas rather than at its official temple site is highly unusual. This is necessitated by the very early hour and by the nasty nature of the business at hand.

Mark lists three general categories within the assembly. *Chief priests* are the elite of the Jerusalem priests and are members of the Sadducee party. *Elders* are older, respected members of the Jerusalem ruling community. Some of these may be of the Pharisee party. *Scribes* are needed experts in the Jewish legal code; many of these are likely Pharisees. There are seventy-one members in this body during the time of Jesus.

B. Peter and the Servants (v. 54)

54. And Peter followed him afar off, even into the palace of the high priest: and he sat with the servants, and warmed himself at the fire.

Peter is drawn irresistibly to Jesus, even in this dangerous time. His motives are probably a mixture of loyalty and curiosity, but he is positioned to act out his prophesied denials of Jesus. Many sermons have been preached using this verse to show that following Jesus from *afar off* is a contradiction in terms. True commitment is shown by the desire to be as close to Jesus as possible. Casual Christianity is elsewhere described as "lukewarm" and is rejected by Jesus (Revelation 3:16). [See question #1, page 366.]

II. Plot to Eliminate
(Mark 14:55-59)

A. Witnesses Disagree, Part 1 (vv. 55, 56)

55, 56. And the chief priests and all the council sought for witness against Jesus to put him to death; and found none. For many bare false witness against him, but their witness agreed not together.

There is no intention of giving Jesus a fair trial, for His death is predetermined by God (Mark 8:31; 10:33) and by *the council* itself (14:1). It is obvious that the witnesses are lying, because their testimony is contradictory. It is sad that in this assembly, which serves as the Supreme Court for the Jews of Jesus' day, there is no one with enough conscience to denounce the entire proceedings. The situation echoes Isaiah 59:4, "None calleth for justice." The people of God forget that God's demand for justice has never gone away. [See question #2, page 366.]

THE VERDICT BEFORE THE TRIAL

The following account is true. A minister was conducting a revival meeting in a country church. As was the custom there, every day he was entertained for the noon meal in the home of one of the families of the church. On this particular day the hostess remarked that her daughter-in-law would be absent because of jury duty.

How to Say It

ANNAS. *An*-nus.
CAESAREA. Sess-uh-*ree*-uh.
CAIAPHAS. *Kay*-uh-fus or *Kye*-uh-fus.
GALILEE. *Gal*-uh-lee.
HEROD ANTIPAS. *Hair*-ud *An*-tih-pus.
JERUSALEM. Juh-*roo*-suh-lem.
JOSEPHUS. Jo-*see*-fus.
LEVITICUS. Leh-*vit*-ih-kus.
MESSIANIC. Mess-ee-*an*-ick.
PHARISEES. *Fair*-ih-seez.
PONTIUS PILATE. *Pon*-shus or *Pon*-ti-us *Pie*-lut.
SADDUCEES. *Sad*-you-seez.
SANHEDRIN. *San*-huh-drun or San-*heed*-run.
TIBERIAS. Tie-*beer*-ee-us.

They had barely begun the meal when the daughter-in-law walked in. Of course, everyone asked her what had happened. She replied, "They wouldn't let me sit on the jury. I don't know why. They asked me if I thought the defendant was guilty and I said, 'If he weren't guilty, they wouldn't have arrested him,' and they put me off of the jury."

Something like that happened at the trial of Jesus. Verse 55 makes it plain that the verdict already had been decided before the trial began. The authorities were looking for witnesses who would testify the way they wanted, for they already had decided that Jesus must die.

Since Jesus was guilty of no crime, they had to invent something, twisting His words. In their time as in ours, court testimony is taken very seriously. To testify falsely is both a crime and a sin. To encourage someone to testify falsely also is both a crime and a sin. Many witnesses could have been found to testify in His favor, but none were sought or desired. When people treat us unfairly because we are Christians, will we be surprised?   —R. C. S.

B. Witnesses Disagree, Part 2 (vv. 57-59)

57-59. And there arose certain, and bare false witness against him, saying, We heard him say, I will destroy this temple that is made with hands, and within three days I will build another made without hands. But neither so did their witness agree together.

In the debate that follows, an issue finally emerges: Jesus apparently poses a threat to the *temple* itself. Threats against sacred sites can draw the death penalty in the Greco-Roman world. This was equally true for the Jews of Old Testament times (see Jeremiah 26:1-11).

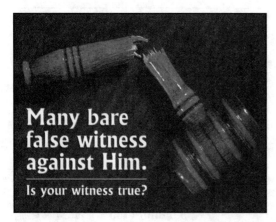

Many bare false witness against Him.

Is your witness true?

Visual for lesson 3. *Many spoke against Jesus falsely in His day. Use this visual to encourage discussion of how people do this yet today.*

Mark does not record Jesus' direct statement concerning destroying and rebuilding *this temple* as is found in John 2:19. However, Jesus' comments there refer to His own body, according to John 2:21. Those who heard Jesus talk of this destruction (including the *false* witnesses here) missed the figurative meaning.

III. Heart of the Matter
(Mark 14:60-65)

A. Who Are You, Jesus? (vv. 60-62)

60. And the high priest stood up in the midst, and asked Jesus, saying, Answerest thou nothing? what is it which these witness against thee?

The plot to kill *Jesus* is in danger of unraveling because of the lack of integrity in the Sanhedrin's process. Caiaphas sees this and tries a new tactic: he attempts to get Jesus to incriminate Himself. A time-tested trial practice is to put the accused on the *witness* stand and hope for a misstatement.

61. But he held his peace, and answered nothing. Again the high priest asked him, and said unto him, Art thou the Christ, the Son of the Blessed?

Jesus refuses to respond. There is an element of truth in the charge that He claimed to be able to destroy and rebuild the "temple" (see previous discussion), but it is no use explaining His meaning or defending Himself (see Isaiah 53:7). The *high priest*, therefore, introduces a new charge: that Jesus claims to be *the Christ*, the Messiah, the long-awaited chosen One. *Son of the Blessed* is equivalent to "Son of God" (see Matthew 26:63).

62. And Jesus said, I am: and ye shall see the Son of man sitting on the right hand of power, and coming in the clouds of heaven.

Jesus now breaks His silence to respond to Caiaphas's question. To sit at *the right hand of power* is an allusion from Psalm 110:1, a messianic psalm. Jesus thus confirms His identity and claims a Scripture. His answer has the effect of saying, "You won't see my power now, but my time is coming." [See question #3, page 366.]

B. Blasphemy! (vv. 63-65)

63, 64. Then the high priest rent his clothes, and saith, What need we any further witnesses? Ye have heard the blasphemy: what think ye? And they all condemned him to be guilty of death.

Blasphemy is deliberate disrespect for God or divine things. For the ancient Jew, any human claiming to be God is both a deceiver and a blasphemer. The penalty is *death* (Leviticus 24:16). Jewish belief in one God does not allow for any type of divine human being. For Jesus to claim to be the Son of God makes Him a usurper of God's authority in the council's eyes. There is only one problem: Jesus' claim is true! Tragically, this possibility is not considered by the Sanhedrin. Both of the charges against Jesus (temple destroyer, messianic pretender) are used as taunts against Him as He is on the cross (Mark 15:29, 32).

Mark records that *the high priest rent his clothes.* While the tearing of clothes is well known in the Bible as a sign of great distress (compare Numbers 14:6; Acts 14:14), this is more than a symbolic act. Mark uses this detail to show the highly charged atmosphere. The vaunted Sanhedrin has degenerated into little more than an angry mob.

65. And some began to spit on him, and to cover his face, and to buffet him, and to say unto him, Prophesy: and the servants did strike him with the palms of their hands.

The uncontrolled fury boils over into physical violence. Mark draws a strong contrast between Jesus' power (14:62) and His brutal humiliation. There is no hint that Jesus protests or even protects Himself. He fulfills the role of the Servant of Isaiah 50:6: "I gave my back to the smiters, and my cheeks to them that plucked off the hair: I hid not my face from shame and spitting." [See question #4, page 366.]

IV. Pilate the Dupe
(Mark 15:1-3)

A. Accurate Response (vv. 1, 2)

1. And straightway in the morning the chief priests held a consultation with the elders and scribes and the whole council, and bound Jesus, and carried him away, and delivered him to Pilate.

This verse introduces Pontius *Pilate,* the Roman governor who will be eternally blamed for his complicity in the death of *Jesus* Christ. Pilate is the most powerful person in Jerusalem that day, a ruthless man with Roman troops available to impose his will. Yet even the mighty Pilate is not in control of this situation.

We are also presented with the complete Sanhedrin in a morning meeting, probably at their appointed place in the southeast corner of the temple. This meeting is designed to get Jesus to Pilate near dawn. Roman officials are known to be early risers, preferring to finish their business by noon and leave the remainder of the day for personal pursuits.

There are a few hours between the initial meeting at the house of Caiaphas and the official meeting of *the whole council* in this instance. These are hours for Jesus to endure the mocking humiliation of His captors.

2. And Pilate asked him, Art thou the King of the Jews? And he answering said unto him, Thou sayest it.

The Sanhedrin and the Roman governor are forced into an uneasy alliance in order to maintain order in Judea. While the Jews of the high council surely resent the foreign occupation of their homeland, they know that riots and rebellion will be crushed by the Roman legions, creating risk to their businesses and fortunes.

This tension is shown here. Pilate asks a clever question designed to cover his concerns and to tweak the nose of the Sanhedrin. He interrogates Jesus as a potential political criminal, an illegal king. At the same time he belittles both Jesus and the Jews by asking if a bound, beaten man is *the King of the Jews.*

Jesus' affirmative response gives pause to wonder at the irony of it all. His answer is as much for the mob as it is for Pilate. He is not only the "true temple," the Son of God and the promised Messiah, He is also their King! His rejection by His own people has the effect of saying, "We don't want our own king anymore. We like having a pagan, uncircumcised Roman Caesar as our king" (see John 19:15).

B. No Response (v. 3)

3. And the chief priests accused him of many things; but he answered nothing.

Our lesson ends with a silent Jesus. Silence in the face of charges does not mean guilt. Jesus' silence allows Him to rise above the unjust nature of the situation and fulfill the mission for which He has been sent: salvation (Luke 19:10). Earlier, Jesus claimed only to say the things that the Father told Him to say (John 12:49). The One who sent Him gives Him no words here. He speaks the silence of God. [See question #5, page 366.]

WHEN SILENCE IS GOLDEN

An old Swiss inscription says, "Silence is golden." Someone else added that sometimes silence is just plain yellow! But it was not cowardice that caused Jesus to be silent before His accusers. Think how much dignity He would have lost if He had shouted back, "Liars! Liars! They are all liars!" Jesus knew the truth of what Solomon said long before: there is "a time to keep silence" (Ecclesiastes 3:7). The Roman writer Plutarch (A.D. 46–120) said, "It is a point of wisdom to be silent when occasion requires."

Jesus was intelligent and eloquent enough to defend Himself. But He had in mind a plan more important than His own safety. That plan was the salvation of humanity! So when He was brought to trial before Herod, He again said nothing. He would not satisfy the curiosity of Herod nor still Herod's fears that Jesus was really John the Baptist come back from the dead. Nor would He entertain Herod with miracles done for show.

We must stand in awe and admiration at the self-control of our Lord—and take it as a model for ourselves. Sometimes we must rise above the situation, rather than being caught up in it. May we always see the bigger picture!   —R. C. S.

Conclusion

A. Why Did They Kill Jesus?

Many have been blamed for the death of Jesus: Judas, Pilate, Caiaphas, Satan, even God. Theologically, we know that Jesus had to die to save us. But what happened historically? Why was the Jewish Sanhedrin so intent on having Jesus killed?

Bible scholars have been debating this question for many years. Some claim that the Jewish leaders sought Jesus' death because He had challenged their authority. Others claim that the Sanhedrin feared Jesus would lead a revolt against the Romans, resulting in the crushing of the Jews in Palestine. Still others see the Jewish authorities as pawns being manipulated by Satan in Satan's attempt to thwart Jesus.

While all of these explanations have merit and Scriptural support, we can find the primary reason on the lips of the Sanhedrin members themselves: "If we let him thus alone, . . . the Romans shall come and take away both our place and nation" (John 11:48). In this passage, *place* can refer to the temple. Many scholars thus theorize that the primary menace posed by Jesus was a threat to the Jerusalem temple. The temple was the engine that drove the economy of Judea. It was still under construction in Jesus' day, so it supplied jobs for construction workers. Thousands worked as priests and attendants. Temple pilgrims needed food and accommodations. Furthermore, the magnificent temple, begun by Herod the Great, was a source of enormous pride for all Jews. It was one of the most beautiful buildings in the ancient world.

Jesus' actions in cleansing the temple and criticizing the gouging business monopolies associated with it were threats that could not be tolerated. If this theory is correct, the misguided Sanhedrin was not trying to protect the religion of Israel. Rather, it was protecting its own economic security. And history has shown repeatedly that money serves well as a motive for murder.

B. The Innocence and Sacrifice of Jesus

Skeptics have wanted to say that Jesus is surely responsible for His own death, that He had done something wrong. Yet the authors of the New Testament are consistent in saying that Jesus was not executed for any crime. Even Pilate, the jaded Roman governor, recognized this when he said, "I find no fault in this man" (Luke 23:4).

While there was no legal reason to execute Jesus, there was a spiritual reason. In 2 Corinthians 5:21 Paul states, "For he hath made him to be sin for us, who knew no sin; that we might be made the righteousness of God in him." People were separated from God because of sin. We had no way to atone for our sins, because that required a perfect, eternal sacrifice. This was Jesus' purpose. His innocence was central to His sacrifice. Without the innocence, His sacrifice was inadequate. Without the sacrifice, His innocence was irrelevant. This is why, at the beginning of Jesus' ministry, John the Baptist cried out, "Behold the Lamb of God, which taketh away the sin of the world!" (John 1:29). This is why, many years later, Peter still wrote of "the precious blood of Christ, as of a lamb without blemish and without spot" (1 Peter 1:19).

C. Prayer

Father, we come before You to thank You for the willing sacrifice of Your Son. How it must have hurt You to see Him condemned as a criminal! The death of Jesus at the hands of sinners was the greatest injustice in all of history. Yet, in Your providence, this injustice served to justify us, changing us from unrighteous to righteous through Jesus' blood payment of our penalty. For this we thank You, Jesus, and we give the Father all praise and glory. In Jesus' name, amen.

D. Thought to Remember

The death of the innocent One was history's greatest injustice, yet humanity's greatest hope.

Home Daily Bible Readings

Monday, June 13—Jesus Predicts Peter's Denial (Mark 14:26-31)
Tuesday, June 14—Jesus Is Betrayed by Judas (Mark 14:43-50)
Wednesday, June 15—False Testimony Is Given About Jesus (Mark 14:53-59)
Thursday, June 16—Jesus Is Condemned (Mark 14:60-65)
Friday, June 17—Peter Denies Jesus (Mark 14:66-72)
Saturday, June 18—Jesus Goes Before Pilate (Mark 15:1-5)
Sunday, June 19—Pilate Hands Jesus Over to Die (Mark 15:6-15)

Learning by Doing

This page contains an alternative lesson plan emphasizing learning activities.
Classes desiring such student involvement will find these suggestions helpful.

Learning Goals

After participating in this lesson, each student will be able to:

1. Describe the trial process that led to the death of Jesus.

2. Contrast the innocence of the One accused with the guilt of His accusers.

3. Express gratitude to God for the sacrifice of His innocent Son to save them from their sins.

Into the Lesson

Recruit a person to present the following monologue as Peter on the evening of Jesus' arrest. Have your "Peter" sitting in front of the class, huddled as if warming himself by an open fire. Monologue: "The fire was doing little good. I was cold to the bone. The air was chilly, but the glances of the others around the fire were even more chilling. First one . . . and then another . . . and then another pointed an accusing finger at me, accusing me with the truth. 'You are one of His disciples, a Galilean!' What could I do? There was a threat with every accusation. I had to deny it: 'I am not!' The silent echo of my denial only added to my shuddering. . . . There! *[pointing, as he sees Jesus being led by]* There my Master is being led away! He sees me! Oh! Mercy for my sin!"

Ask the class how well this portrayed scene represents what the Scriptures say about Peter's traumatic occasion. Suggest they look at the Mark 14:53, 54, 66-72 and the other Gospel accounts (Matthew 26:69-75; Luke 22:54-62; John 18:15-18, 25-27) for an analysis.

Into the Word

Note to your class that the Hebrew and Greek words transliterated *Satan* in the Scriptures means *the accuser*. Point out that in the scenes described in today's text "the chief priests accused him [Jesus] of many things" (Mark 15:3). Have a dictionary definition of *accuse* ready to be read aloud. The definition will typically include such elements as blaming, faultfinding, and bringing legal charges. Ask the class to identify the nature of the accusations made against Jesus. Ask them to characterize the accusers.

Give your learners the following two-word sentences to put in the correct chronological order, per the text. (This activity is included in the student book.) The sentences are given here in alphabetical order, per first words. Numbers in parentheses indicate the correct chronological order. *Jesus affirms* (9); *Jesus captured* (1); *Jesus condemned* (11); *Jesus mistreated* (12); *Jesus reaffirms* (14); *Jesus silent* (7); *Jesus silent* (16); *Leader dismayed* (10); *Leaders accuse* (15); *Leaders assemble* (2); *Peter follows* (3); *Pilate questions* (13); *Priests question* (6); *Priests question again* (8); *Witness sought* (4); *Witnesses lied* (5). After a few minutes, work your way through the list and compare events to the printed text.

The Golden Text for today's lesson (Mark 14:55) is an excellent summary of the story. Help your class memorize it in the following way. Divide the class as it is seated into four groups and ask the groups to repeat a phrase after you. Group one gets "The chief priests and all the council"; group two: "sought for witness against Jesus"; group three: "to put him to death"; group four: "and found none."

Ask the groups to stand in sequence and repeat their phrases. Have them repeat this stand-and-quote exercise three or four times. At the end say simply, "And that is the simple and sad truth of today's study."

Into Life

Ask your class to react to each of these "Lessons to Be Learned from Jesus Under Trial." Reactions may be agreement or disagreement, explanation, or editing to "correct." "Lessons": (1) Expect people to lie when they do not like the truth. (2) There is a time to be silent and a time to speak. (3) Some truths simply must be affirmed. (4) Personal humiliation may be necessary to preserve integrity. (5) Unanimity of judgment does not determine truth. (6) Truth is always the best defense. (7) Character is best demonstrated in hard circumstances.

Note to your class that people still make false accusations against the Son and the Father. Such accusations are heard in expressions such as, "If God is truly good, then He would not. . . . " Or, "God abandoned me when I needed Him most." Or, "Jesus was merely a good person who understood much about the happy life." Ask the class to identify other such "accusations," and then suggest that they keep an "Accusations Alert" for the coming week, listening carefully for those who have false ideas about Jesus and His work.

Let's Talk It Over

The questions on this page are designed to promote discussion of the lesson by the class and to encourage application of the lesson Scriptures. The answers provided are only discussion starters. Let your class talk it over from there.

1. Suppose you have been selected by the leadership of the church to join a new ministry effort. Its goal is to identify those church members who follow Jesus "afar off" to encourage them to a closer walk with the Lord. What ideas would you bring to the first ministry-team meeting?

Take notes on this discussion; you may want to implement some of the ideas that come up! Perhaps begin by identifying members whose names are "on the books" but who seldom attend. And what of those who attend but do little else—is their discipleship really wholehearted? Peter was afraid of risking too much (his life); is taking a risk inherent in true discipleship? If your class agrees, then those church members who always "play it safe" may be among the far-off followers.

What will motivate these folks to draw close? Certainly the example of others will help. Discuss times when someone stepped out on faith in some way, thus saying, "Follow me!"

2. Our lesson writer notes, "It is sad that . . . there is no one with enough conscience to denounce" the council's corrupt behavior. How does one develop the strength of conscience required to stand up against powerful forces and denounce injustice? How can our church equip people for such acts of character?

We are prone to avoid conflict, to turn the other way when someone is acting unfairly (unless we ourselves are the victims). We need to cultivate an attitude of support and encouragement so when one of our own takes a stand, he or she will not feel alone. Examples will help. We need to hear stories of people who took a stand. Both Biblical accounts and modern examples will be useful. Whatever we do, we must equip our young people to look for the right path and not the easy path—the two are seldom the same!

3. Surely Jesus knew the council's plan was in trouble. If He just kept quiet, He might even walk! But then He answered with a declaration that He knew would seal His fate. What kind of courage is required to take such a bold action? What was a time when you deliberately put yourself in jeopardy for the sake of a principle you couldn't compromise?

Jesus knew His answer would incite the council's wrath, but He dared not waver on this point. He knew it would lead to His death, but giving His life was the reason He came (Matthew 16:21-23; John 12:27). He knew His purpose, and He did not shy from it. As His followers, we, too, need to know our purpose. Equipping people to fulfill the Great Commission is vital. Our secular and pluralistic culture does not like the "exclusive" nature of the gospel, but we must share it. Allow your learners to tell how they have taken a stand to present the gospel at work, on the university campus, or elsewhere. Encourage those who face strong and/or repeated opposition.

4. The scene in the council chamber is almost more than we can bear. Civilized men (religious leaders!) stoop to the level of mob violence. What causes us to "lose control"? How can we safeguard ourselves from acting from sinful motives in our pursuit of doing what we believe is right?

The council members acted with what Paul called a "zeal . . . not according to knowledge" (Romans 10:2). What made it far worse was the fact that their ignorance was willful. Their power had become more important to them than their mission, and they guarded that power jealously.

We can be guilty of the same sin when our positions, titles, authority, or preferences become more important to us than doing God's will. In such cases, opportunities for frank discussions of different ideas become occasions to "stand our ground" and to defend traditions. It's okay to be zealous for the Lord; we just need to be sure that our zeal does not overrule facts and principles.

5. Sometimes the best answer is no answer at all. When is it best to ignore the accusations of our opponents, and when is an answer appropriate or even imperative?

Jesus knew that there was nothing to gain by answering, and so He kept quiet. In many situations a mob mentality seems to override any hope that reason or truth will get a fair hearing. In such times we may as well save our breath. At other times there are persons present who need to hear what we have to say. If our silence will convey a wrong message, then we must take a stand and declare the truth. Even if we do not persuade many people, we may turn the heart of one or two.

Triumph

DEVOTIONAL READING: Matthew 28:16-20.

BACKGROUND SCRIPTURE: Mark 16.

PRINTED TEXT: Mark 16:1-16.

Mark 16:1-16

1 And when the sabbath was past, Mary Magdalene, and Mary the mother of James, and Salome, had bought sweet spices, that they might come and anoint him.

2 And very early in the morning, the first day of the week, they came unto the sepulchre at the rising of the sun.

3 And they said among themselves, Who shall roll us away the stone from the door of the sepulchre?

4 And when they looked, they saw that the stone was rolled away: for it was very great.

5 And entering into the sepulchre, they saw a young man sitting on the right side, clothed in a long white garment; and they were affrighted.

6 And he saith unto them, Be not affrighted: ye seek Jesus of Nazareth, which was crucified: he is risen; he is not here: behold the place where they laid him.

7 But go your way, tell his disciples and Peter that he goeth before you into Galilee: there shall ye see him, as he said unto you.

8 And they went out quickly, and fled from the sepulchre; for they trembled and were amazed: neither said they any thing to any man; for they were afraid.

9 Now when Jesus was risen early the first day of the week, he appeared first to Mary Magdalene, out of whom he had cast seven devils.

10 And she went and told them that had been with him, as they mourned and wept.

11 And they, when they had heard that he was alive, and had been seen of her, believed not.

12 After that he appeared in another form unto two of them, as they walked, and went into the country.

13 And they went and told it unto the residue: neither believed they them.

14 Afterward he appeared unto the eleven as they sat at meat, and upbraided them with their unbelief and hardness of heart, because they believed not them which had seen him after he was risen.

15 And he said unto them, Go ye into all the world, and preach the gospel to every creature.

16 He that believeth and is baptized shall be saved; but he that believeth not shall be damned.

GOLDEN TEXT: He saith unto them, Be not affrighted: ye seek Jesus of Nazareth, which was crucified: he is risen; he is not here: behold the place where they laid him.—Mark 16:6.

Jesus' Life, Teachings, and Ministry
Unit 1: Jesus' Life
(Lessons 1-4)

Lesson Aims

After participating in this lesson, each student will be able to:

1. Recount the events surrounding the resurrection, including the various reactions, as recorded by Mark.

2. Express his or her own emotional response to the resurrection of Jesus.

3. State some specific plan to share with others his or her faith in the resurrection of Jesus.

Lesson Outline

INTRODUCTION
 A. The Old Curiosity Shop
 B. Lesson Background
I. TRIP TO THE TOMB (Mark 16:1-4)
 A. Women and Mission (vv. 1, 2)
 B. Question and Answer (vv. 3, 4)
II. ENCOUNTER WITH AN ANGEL (Mark 16:5-8)
 A. Alarm (v. 5)
 B. Message (vv. 6, 7)
  Learning from Tombs
 C. Fear (v. 8)
  The Open and Empty Tomb
III. TRUTH AND UNBELIEF (Mark 16:9-13)
 A. Mary Magdalene (v. 9)
 B. Others (vv. 10, 11)
 C. Walkers on the Road (vv. 12, 13)
IV. BELIEF AND UNBELIEF (Mark 16:14-16)
 A. Chastisement (v. 14)
  The Man Who Came Back From the Dead
 B. Charge (vv. 15, 16)
CONCLUSION
 A. The Evidence for the Resurrection
 B. The Significance of the Resurrection
 C. Prayer
 D. Thought to Remember

Introduction

A. The Old Curiosity Shop

Our family turned the corner in anticipation. The London guidebook promised that "The Old Curiosity Shop" was not only a landmark medieval building, but also a great source for the interesting souvenirs that our children loved so much. The shop, we read, was built in 1567 and may have served as the inspiration for a novel of the nineteenth century. Then we saw it, a white two-story building with green trim and a red roof. We could hardly wait to explore its treasures. But when we got to it, we found the Shop was empty. It had a sign that said, "The Old Curiosity Shop immortalized by Charles Dickens," but the door was locked and the shelves were bare. No one was there. We instinctively knew what this meant: although the shop was a well-known tourist attraction, it had failed to be a viable business location.

Today's lesson is about eager visitors who also unexpectedly find an empty place. They are a small group of women who hurried to the tomb of Jesus at dawn to finish their task of preparing His body for burial. They were worried about the mechanics of accessing the tomb and were therefore surprised and terrified to find it open and empty. The body of Jesus was gone. What did this mean?

B. Lesson Background

The events that come just before today's text have been sobering, indeed. Jesus Christ, the King of the universe, had been put to death in an act of judicial murder. One of His closest disciples had betrayed Him for a paltry thirty pieces of silver. His other disciples had deserted Him. The death He suffered was one of the most cruel, agonizing, and humiliating possible. "He came unto his own, and his own received him not" (John 1:11).

Those who first seek Jesus are a group of loyal women followers. It is not a living Jesus they seek, however, but a dead one. A resurrection is the furthest thing from their minds. After (what we can suppose to be) a sleepless night or two, they are in for quite a shock!

I. Trip to the Tomb
(Mark 16:1-4)

A. Women and Mission (vv. 1, 2)

1, 2. And when the sabbath was past, Mary Magdalene, and Mary the mother of James, and Salome, had bought sweet spices, that they might come and anoint him. And very early in the morning, the first day of the week, they came unto the sepulchre at the rising of the sun.

The sabbath had ended at sundown on Saturday night, but darkness prevented the women from visiting the tomb until Sunday dawn. These are women on a mission: they intend to finish a respectful preparation of Jesus' corpse, a process that had been rushed to prevent violation of the Sabbath on Friday afternoon. This should not be seen as anything other than an act of great devotion. They suppose that Jesus' body has been rotting for more than a day and the smell will be disgusting. [See question #1, page 374.]

The women are a curious band, and Mark has mentioned them before (Mark 15:40; two of them in 15:47). *Salome* is the mother of James and John, the wife of Zebedee (see Matthew 4:21; 27:56). She is old, perhaps frail. Tradition records that *Mary Magdalene* had been a prostitute, although this is not confirmed in the New Testament. Jesus had delivered her from great spiritual oppression (Mark 16:9; Luke 8:2) and won her as a devoted follower.

Mary the mother of James (and Joses, see Mark 15:40) is not known to us, but seems to have been well known to Mark's earliest readers. There are several women named Mary in the Gospels, so it's easy to get confused. In any case, she, too, is remarkably committed, having witnessed the crucifixion and burial of Jesus. The women venture out in the early morning, probably as soon as they are able to buy some *sweet spices* with which to *anoint* the body of Jesus.

B. Question and Answer (vv. 3, 4)

3, 4. And they said among themselves, Who shall roll us away the stone from the door of the sepulchre? And when they looked, they saw that the stone was rolled away: for it was very great.

The women apparently have no careful plan. They don't think about how they will gain access to Jesus' body until they are already on the way. Belatedly they recall that *the sepulchre* had been sealed. This was done with a heavy disk-shaped *stone*, carved to fit tightly over the tomb. Rolling the stone back will require several strong men. The issue is resolved when they arrive on the scene: the massive stone already has been removed and the tomb is open.

II. Encounter with an Angel (Mark 16:5-8)

A. Alarm (v. 5)

5. And entering into the sepulchre, they saw a young man sitting on the right side, clothed in a long white garment; and they were affrighted.

It would be easy for us to see these women as weak and easily frightened, but that would be inaccurate. Their devotion and curiosity causes them to venture to the tomb itself, overcoming any fear of dead bodies. But they do not find a dead body. Instead, they are confronted by a *young man* who seems to be waiting for them.

Mark intends that we understand this person to be an angel, a messenger of God. Matthew 28:2-5 tells us specifically that this is an angel. The women are understandably *affrighted*.

B. Message (vv. 6, 7)

6, 7. And he saith unto them, Be not affrighted: ye seek Jesus of Nazareth, which was crucified: he is risen; he is not here: behold the place where they laid him. But go your way, tell his disciples and Peter that he goeth before you into Galilee: there shall ye see him, as he said unto you.

The angel explains everything in three little words: *he is risen!* Jesus is not dead. He is alive! His body is not returning to the dust. Rather, Jesus is on the move back to *Galilee!* [See question #2, page 374.] He does not need to be anointed with spices to combat the stench of death. He emits the sweet aroma of life eternal! The women must tell *Peter.* [See question #3, page 374.]

LEARNING FROM TOMBS

We can learn a lot from tombs. The early inhabitants of Italy were the Etruscans, and almost all that we know of them comes from their tombs. The British have filled Westminster Abbey with tombs. Some of them include a carved image of the one buried there—lying horizontally as in death. When the Greeks carved images, they carved them vertically, as they were in life.

Under the Capuchin Church in Vienna are tombs of Austria's rulers. One holds the remains of Empress Maria Theresa (1717–1780) and her husband Francis Stephen of Lorraine (1708–1765). An image on their double sarcophagus depicts them sitting up, as if they are just awakening on the morning of the resurrection. Is this a testament to their faith in the risen Christ and to their confidence in their own resurrections?

There is a story about a man who was walking in a country cemetery when he saw a stone that read, "Death Is Eternal." He was astounded that anyone would put such a line on a tombstone. He walked over to investigate and discovered

---

How to Say It

BUDDHA. *Boo*-duh.

GALILEE. *Gal*-uh-lee.

JOSES. *Jo*-sez.

MAGDALENE. *Mag*-duh-leen or Mag-duh-*lee*-nee.

NAZARETH. *Naz*-uh-reth.

PROPITIATION. pro-*pih*-she-*ay*-shun (strong accent on *ay*).

SALOME. Suh-*lo*-me.

SEPULCHRE. *sep*-ul-kur.

ZEBEDEE. *Zeb*-eh-dee.

ZECHARIAH. *Zek*-uh-*rye*-uh (strong accent on *rye*).

that his view had been obscured by another tombstone. What the stone really said was, "Death Is Eternal Life." Until Jesus rose from the dead, our view of both death and life was partial and obscured. Now we can see the true nature of both more clearly. —R. C. S.

C. Fear (v. 8)

8. And they went out quickly, and fled from the sepulchre; for they trembled and were amazed: neither said they any thing to any man; for they were afraid.

The result at this point is not understanding but continued fear. This fear results in saying nothing *to any man*. But after they calm down a bit they speak freely (see Mark 16:10; Luke 24:9).

THE OPEN AND EMPTY TOMB

The town of Delft in the Netherlands is famous for its fine china. Not only that, the town is notable for the tomb of William of Orange (1533–1584), the founder of the nation. For an admission fee, you can go in and see his tomb.

But if you can get to Jerusalem, there is no admission charge to see what some think to be the tomb of Jesus. Of course, there is a significant difference: the tomb of Jesus is open and empty! The fullness of the Christian religion depends on that empty tomb. Our forgiveness depends on it. The apostle Paul said that if Christ did not come back from the dead there is no forgiveness and we are still in our sins (1 Corinthians 15:17). Belief in the resurrection is vital (Romans 10:9).

No other tomb is so important to humanity as the empty tomb of Jesus. While a single nation may honor the tomb of William of Orange, people in all nations honor the fact that the tomb of Jesus is empty. He is eternal. He rose from the dead. He sent forth His disciples into all the world. He ascended to the Father. Now we, who know the tomb is empty, must go into our world and take the message everywhere as those first followers did. —R. C. S.

III. Truth and Unbelief
(Mark 16:9-13)

A. Mary Magdalene (v. 9)

9. Now when Jesus was risen early the first day of the week, he appeared first to Mary Magdalene, out of whom he had cast seven devils.

Mary Magdalene has shown her great loyalty to Jesus. She was last at the cross and first at the tomb. Jesus had transformed her life by releasing her from tremendous spiritual bondage. It is entirely fitting that Jesus chose her to be the *first* witness of more than just the empty tomb. She sees the risen Lord!

B. Others (vv. 10, 11)

10, 11. And she went and told them that had been with him, as they mourned and wept. And they, when they had heard that he was alive, and had been seen of her, believed not.

However, when Mary Magdalene shares the truth of the risen Lord, she is rejected. There are two reasons for this rejection. First, a woman is not thought to be a credible witness in the ancient world. Some scholars maintain that a woman's testimony was not considered valid in ancient Jewish courts. This, however, does not seem to be the primary reason Mary's story is rejected. The main reason her story is not *believed* is simply that believing in the resurrection takes a lot of faith, more faith than the disciples have at this point. [See question #4, page 374.]

C. Walkers on the Road (vv. 12, 13)

12, 13. After that he appeared in another form unto two of them, as they walked, and went into the country. And they went and told it unto the residue: neither believed they them.

A second story follows, one that is given fully in Luke 24:13-35. Jesus appears to *two* male disciples as they journey away from the city by foot. These men return to *the residue* who are still in the city, but their testimony is received just like Mary's story—it is not *believed*.

Truth is powerful, but it cannot overcome stubborn unbelief. Mark never tries to hide embarrassing details from us. The fact is that those who first experience the resurrection of Jesus are not believed by the larger group of disciples. This shows how difficult it is to accept that the crucified Jesus, stone cold dead on Friday, is alive and free from His tomb on Sunday. It should give us confidence in the testimony of the early church concerning the resurrection. They do not come to faith quickly or rashly, but slowly and carefully.

IV. Belief and Unbelief
(Mark 16:14-16)

A. Chastisement (v. 14)

14. Afterward he appeared unto the eleven as they sat at meat, and upbraided them with their unbelief and hardness of heart, because they believed not them which had seen him after he was risen.

Mark seems to say that Jesus realizes that no "third party" messenger will be believed. Jesus has to go personally, so He miraculously appears to the eleven chosen disciples while they are having a meal *(at meat)*. He attacks the cause of their unbelief: *hardness of heart*. This defiant spiritual condition is a frequent theme in Mark's

Gospel (see Mark 3:5; 6:52; 8:17). In Mark, the person with the hard heart is spiritually unwilling to repent or to believe. In the Old Testament, the hard heart always results in stubborn disobedience (see Zechariah 7:12). [See question #5, page 374.]

The disciples have no choice but to believe now! By appearing to them personally, Jesus has removed every excuse they may have.

THE MAN WHO CAME BACK FROM THE DEAD

A Christian from America was speaking in a village church in Hungary. After the service the leader of the congregation came to him and said, "Come over here. We want you to meet the man who came back from the dead."

There was a twinkle in the leader's eyes as he led the visitor to an elderly man seated near the back. He then told the man's story. The man had been in the hospital, seriously ill. He was pronounced dead. They were ready to carry him out when someone noticed the flicker of an eyelash. Emergency resuscitation procedures were begun and the man revived. He recovered from this illness and there he was in church, reasonably well and healthy.

Of course, they did not think that he *really* came back from the dead. They knew he had been near death. They knew he had the symptoms of death, but he was not actually dead. They also knew that there was once a man who *really did* come back from the dead. They had met that day to worship Him. They met together on the first day of the week because it was on the first day of the week that He arose.

You may know someone who has had a near-death experience. You may know someone who had all the symptoms of death but was resuscitated. If you are a Christian, you also know Someone who really died and who really came back from the dead. When the apostle Paul summarized the Christian faith, he named three essentials: Christ died, Christ was buried, Christ arose (1 Corinthians 15:3, 4). It was a real death and it was a real resurrection. Will we live this week with these facts directing our thoughts and actions?   —R. C. S.

B. Charge (vv. 15, 16)

15, 16. And he said unto them, Go ye into all the world, and preach the gospel to every creature. He that believeth and is baptized shall be saved; but he that believeth not shall be damned.

Jesus does not allow the disciples to rest in their newfound faith, however. They are to act: to *go* and *preach* the good news of His resurrection. Their target audience is as broad as possible:

Visual for lesson 4. *Use this magnificent image to remind your learners yet again of the central truth: He is risen!*

every creature. This does not mean to evangelize birds or flowers, but all people. The importance of this message is underscored by Jesus. If the hearers reject the message, they will *be damned.* If they do believe and respond by submitting to baptism, they will *be saved.*

We may note that the text says nothing about the status of those who believe but are not baptized. Such persons are unknown in the early church. The idea that baptism is an optional or superfluous part of Christianity is never entertained in the first century.

Conclusion

A. The Evidence for the Resurrection

He is risen. In those three little words rests the central truth of Christianity. Christ is risen and victorious over death!

In the nineteenth and twentieth centuries, many Bible-believing scholars developed elaborate systems to defend the historic and factual reality of the resurrection of Jesus. Some main items mentioned are (1) the empty tomb, which had been guarded by professional soldiers, (2) the inability of Jesus' opponents to produce His body, and (3) the many witnesses to the resurrected Jesus, as many as five hundred at one time (1 Corinthians 15:6).

While all three of these are certainly true, they can be a difficult "sell" to many unbelievers today. Unbelievers can say that the first two are arguments built on a lack of evidence and are therefore very difficult to prove. The third can be dismissed by modern people who are convinced that most information or testimony from the ancient world is inaccurate or unreliable. To use these arguments sometimes puts us in the same position of the three women in today's lesson: we tell the truth, but they don't believe. The idea of resurrection was hard to believe in the first century (see Acts 17:32) and it is difficult today.

There is a fourth argument, however, that still resonates well in the twenty-first century: the willingness of the early Christians to sacrifice their lives for their belief in the resurrection. The book of Acts and the history of the early church are filled with accounts of people who suffered persecution and even death for preaching Jesus as crucified and risen.

Would you die for something that you doubted to be true? No normal person would. It just doesn't make sense to think that average people would be willing to become martyrs on behalf of a "risen Savior" if they knew His body was still in a tomb. When Jesus came alive, walked out, and left the tomb empty, He changed history. Not only that, He changed the lives of many individuals who were committed to Him.

B. The Significance of the Resurrection

Once we have believed that Jesus rose from the dead, what significance does this belief have? The women in our story were terrified and shook physically, and sometimes we, too, should be overwhelmed by the power of the resurrection. Let me suggest three important ways the resurrection affects our lives on a continuing basis.

First, the resurrection shows that God accepted Jesus' death as propitiation for our sins. A propitiation is something that turns away God's wrath. (See Romans 3:25; 1 John 2:2; 4:10.) Paul refers to Jesus as the One "who was delivered for our offenses, and was raised again for our justification" (Romans 4:25). Jesus' death and resurrection were one-time events; they need not be repeated. They give us the assurance of forgiveness and salvation if we place our faith in Him.

Second, the resurrection of Jesus gives us hope for life after death. The longer we live, the more we encounter death. We experience the death of our friends, our grandparents, our mothers, our fathers, our husbands, our wives, even our sons and daughters. The tragic separation from those we love can drive us to despair. Furthermore, we realize our own deaths are inevitable. One author said that a religion that has nothing to say about death has nothing to say. Christianity has everything to say about death. Yes, death is real. Jesus really died! But, as the poet said,

And death's not the end 'neath the cold black sod,
'Tis the inn by the road on the way to God.

Third, the resurrection means that Jesus is alive today and will come again as He promised. Jesus' resurrection and ascension in A.D. 30 means that He has conquered death! He wasn't like Lazarus, who rose only to die again. Jesus wasn't just alive for a few more days or years. He is still alive today, right now!

Think about what this says about Christians and Christianity. We don't just follow the teachings of Jesus from centuries ago like Confucians do with Confucius's teachings. Rather, we make Jesus the active Lord of our lives. We don't just pray the way He taught us like Muslims do with Muhammad. Instead, we pray to the throne of God, where Jesus sits at the right hand. We don't just follow His pathways of spiritual enlightenment like Buddhists follow the Buddha. On the contrary, we allow Jesus to change us through the transforming power of His Word and His Holy Spirit. We don't just admire His courage and integrity, as secularists do with their historical heroes. Rather, we actively look for Jesus to return in power and glory to take us to be with Him forever.

C. Prayer

Mighty God, we frail human beings are terrified by death. It is a curtain we cannot pull back, a darkness we cannot light. But You have shown us that death is not the end. You have proven that death holds no power over You. You have given us hope by allowing Your Son, Jesus Christ, to die, and then raising Him from the dead forevermore. May we live confidently in the strong belief that Jesus left an empty tomb because He came back to life, and that we, too, will share in His resurrection. In His holy name we pray, amen.

D. Thought to Remember

His tomb was empty because Jesus is alive!

Home Daily Bible Readings

Monday, June 20—Jesus' Tomb Is Sealed (Matthew 27:62-66)

Tuesday, June 21—He Is Not Here (Matthew 28:1-6b)

Wednesday, June 22—He Has Been Raised (Mark 16:1-8)

Thursday, June 23—Jesus Appears to the Women (Matthew 28:6c-10)

Friday, June 24—Jesus Appears to Other Followers (Mark 16:9-13)

Saturday, June 25—I Am With You Always (Matthew 28:16-20)

Sunday, June 26—Go into All the World (Mark 16:14-20)

Learning by Doing

This page contains an alternative lesson plan emphasizing learning activities. Classes desiring such student involvement will find these suggestions helpful.

Learning Goals

After participating in this lesson, each student will be able to:

1. Recount the events surrounding the resurrection, including the various reactions, as recorded by Mark.

2. Express his or her own emotional response to the resurrection of Jesus.

3. State some specific plan to share with others his or her faith in the resurrection of Jesus.

Into the Lesson

Hand each learner this list of Bible texts as they enter the classroom: 1 Kings 17:17-24; 2 Kings 4:32-37; 2 Kings 13:21; Mark 5:22-24, 35-43; Luke 7:11-16; John 11:32-44; Acts 9:36-42. Say nothing of the subject matter of these passages or of your intention.

As class begins, ask, "What do the Bible texts on the list I gave to you have in common?" If no one has checked the texts or knows them, give an opportunity to check and wait for a response. The correct response is that all of these texts speak of a person resurrected from the dead. Note that though the resurrections recorded in these texts demonstrate God's ability to restore life to a dead body, only the resurrection described in today's text makes the way for the resurrection of all the godly.

Into the Word

Divide your learners into four groups; label the groups: SOCIAL, EMOTIONAL, PRACTICAL, DOCTRINAL. Once the groups assemble, give a leader in each group one of the following direction cards:

SOCIAL—Look at today's text in Mark 16:1-16 and list the various social relationships and issues seen. For example: three women went to the tomb together, as mutual support at a difficult time (v. 1).

EMOTIONAL—Look at today's text, Mark 16:1-16, and list the various emotions described or implied in the events recorded. For example, the mourning of the followers of Jesus had been so deep as to lead to tears (v. 10).

PRACTICAL—Look at today's text, Mark 16:1-16, and describe the practical elements related to the events. For example, the stone was so large the women knew they could not move it (vv. 3, 4).

DOCTRINAL—Look at today's text, Mark 16:1-16, and list what you consider the key doctrines included. An example is the connection between belief and baptism (v. 16).

Give the groups eight to ten minutes to make their decisions. Then have each group give its report. For reinforcement, write the answers into a four-column graphic on the chalkboard, with appropriate headings. Some possible comments for the four categories are, respectively: "Sometimes even close friends don't believe what their friends tell them" (vv. 11, 13, 14); "Sometimes those whom one loves need to be corrected firmly" (v. 14); "Dead bodies need attention quickly, for decay is quick and inevitable" (v. 1); "Jesus was killed, but He lives bodily anew" (v. 6).

Ending on the DOCTRINAL element will allow you to affirm, "The resurrection of Jesus is at the heart of Bible doctrine." Have a good reader cued to your saying this exact statement and ready to jump up and read 1 Corinthians 15:12-26 with emphasis.

Repeat verses 13 and 14 of that text to lead to the Into Life activity following.

Into Life

Give each learner a copy of a sheet headed **IF—THEN.** Some or all of the following stimulus-response items should be listed below the heading. Feel free to add more if-then statements of your own devising. (This activity is included in the student book.)

If resurrection from the dead has never happened, then . . .

If Jesus had not risen from the dead, then . . .

If I did not believe in God's power to resurrect me from the dead, then . . .

If the current life is all there is, then I will . . .

Some of the key verses in 1 Corinthians 15 should be part of every Christian's "quotable repertoire" for a life of hope and witness. Select one verse and suggest a technique to your class for committing it to memory in the coming week.

One example of a memory technique is copying the verse onto a small card and placing it in a strategic location. This location may be the bathroom mirror, the refrigerator door, the edge of the computer screen, or on a key chain. You could also suggest that the verse be personalized, such as verse 1 Corinthians 15:17: "If Christ be not raised, my faith is vain; [I am] yet in [my] sins." Close with prayer.

Let's Talk It Over

The questions on this page are designed to promote discussion of the lesson by the class and to encourage application of the lesson Scriptures. The answers provided are only discussion starters. Let your class talk it over from there.

1. The women's devotion to their "dead" Master was inspiring. How often do we see the same level of devotion expressed to our *living* Lord? How can we encourage that level of devotion among our fellow Christians?

Of course, there was an urgency for the women that we do not share. They had but a few hours to anoint the body of Jesus. After that, there would be no point. We, however, tend to assume we have lots of time. But that may well be a fallacy. We do not know what each day holds, or how quickly life may change or even cease. Even as "life goes on," there are opportunities that come and go without notice except to those who are alert for them. We want to be like the faithful servants of Jesus' parables, the ones who were alert and watchful. Perhaps your learners can tell of opportunities they have found to honor the Lord with loving deeds or acts of kindness. Their stories will encourage the same kind of alertness among the other class members.

2. The women were looking for Jesus in the wrong place—He was not there! In what wrong places do people today look for Jesus (or any kind of spiritual refreshment)? How can we ensure that those who come to our church do, indeed, find Him?

The younger generation has been described as very "spiritual," but that has nothing to do with the Holy Spirit. It means they are open to non-physical reality. Consequently, they are eager to accept mystical—even mythological—religions, New Age philosophy, and postmodern concepts that often defy reason or historical facts.

The church needs to understand the mind-set of the next generation and seek to address it. This understanding must come to terms with that generation's spiritual hunger. When we do, we can point to Jesus as the only One who can truly fill that void.

3. Peter, of course, had denied Jesus during the trials. Yet it was Peter whom the angel specifically mentioned when he told the women to report to the disciples. What significance do you see in that? What lesson is there for us in this?

The disciples were naturally frightened (John 20:19), and they probably felt guilty about abandoning Jesus in the garden (Mark 14:50). Their hopes had been shattered (Luke 24:21). Surely Peter felt the worst of all. He had failed the Lord.

Perhaps the failure of the kingdom (as Peter perceived it) was his own fault. Assuring Peter of the resurrection says, "The kingdom has not failed; Jesus is victorious!" It also said that the Lord still had a place for Peter in spite of his failure. That is a message we need to repeat continually: the Lord's kingdom has a place for anyone and everyone who has failed! Otherwise, who could be a part of it?

4. Mary Magdalene had seen the risen Lord, but her testimony was rejected. What lesson is there in that for believers today who share their faith with friends and family members?

We are not told how Mary responded when her testimony was rejected. We do not know how much she pleaded for a hearing or whether she wept as the disciples refused to believe her. But we do find her remaining close. Apparently she was patient with the unbelieving disciples. She did not go off in exasperation and start her own group. We, too, need to be patient with friends, family members, and even fellow Christians, whose faith is not where we'd like it to be. It took time and more evidence for the disciples to believe, but they did come to belief. With patience and love and the providence of God, our loved ones may grow in their faith as well.

5. The disciples had followed the Lord, they wanted to do right, and they had ministered in many ways in the Lord's name. Yet they were guilty of hardness of heart! How could that be? How can we tell if we ourselves might be guilty of the same? What can we do to prevent or to cure hardness of heart?

Jesus told the disciples they should have believed those who had given testimony of His resurrection. Hardness of heart elevates one's own thinking and understanding above all others'. When our understanding of a situation is contrary to another's, then we need to be open to the possibility that we do not fully appreciate the situation. We need to examine the facts, including the testimony of those who have something to say. Of course, we need to start with Scripture. If the disciples had done that, they may have come to faith sooner. (See Luke 24:25-27, 32.)

Experiencing True Happiness

DEVOTIONAL READING: Luke 6:17-23.

BACKGROUND SCRIPTURE: Matthew 5:1-16.

PRINTED TEXT: Matthew 5:1-16.

Matthew 5:1-16

1 And seeing the multitudes, he went up into a mountain: and when he was set, his disciples came unto him:

2 And he opened his mouth, and taught them, saying,

3 Blessed are the poor in spirit: for theirs is the kingdom of heaven.

4 Blessed are they that mourn: for they shall be comforted.

5 Blessed are the meek: for they shall inherit the earth.

6 Blessed are they which do hunger and thirst after righteousness: for they shall be filled.

7 Blessed are the merciful: for they shall obtain mercy.

8 Blessed are the pure in heart: for they shall see God.

9 Blessed are the peacemakers: for they shall be called the children of God.

10 Blessed are they which are persecuted for righteousness' sake: for theirs is the kingdom of heaven.

11 Blessed are ye, when men shall revile you, and persecute you, and shall say all manner of evil against you falsely, for my sake.

12 Rejoice, and be exceeding glad: for great is your reward in heaven: for so persecuted they the prophets which were before you.

13 Ye are the salt of the earth: but if the salt have lost his savor, wherewith shall it be salted? it is thenceforth good for nothing, but to be cast out, and to be trodden under foot of men.

14 Ye are the light of the world. A city that is set on a hill cannot be hid.

15 Neither do men light a candle, and put it under a bushel, but on a candlestick; and it giveth light unto all that are in the house.

16 Let your light so shine before men, that they may see your good works, and glorify your Father which is in heaven.

GOLDEN TEXT: Blessed are they which do hunger and thirst after righteousness: for they shall be filled.—Matthew 5:6.

Jesus' Life, Teachings, and Ministry
Unit 2: Jesus' Ministry of Teaching
(Lessons 5-9)

Lesson Aims

After participating in this lesson, each student will be able to:

1. Describe the attitudes and blessings that bring true happiness to the followers of Jesus.

2. Explain how happiness is based not on what one possesses, but on how one's life reflects and glorifies God.

3. Suggest specific ways in which the Beatitudes can correct the distorted goals of contemporary culture.

Lesson Outline

INTRODUCTION
    A. "Enjoy!"
    B. Lesson Background
 I. CHRISTIAN CHARACTER (Matthew 5:1-12)
    A. To Be Lowly and to Mourn (vv. 1-4)
    B. To Be Meek and Hungry (vv. 5, 6)
    C. To Be Pure and Good (vv. 7-9)
    D. To Be Persecuted (vv. 10-12)
       An Unusual Perspective on Persecution
II. CHRISTIAN INFLUENCE (Matthew 5:13-16)
    A. Salt of the Earth (v. 13)
       A Substitute for Salt
    B. Light of the World (vv. 14-16)
CONCLUSION
    A. True Happiness
    B. Prayer
    C. Thought to Remember

Introduction

A. "Enjoy!"

The waiter brings the meals steaming hot from the kitchen and places them dramatically on the table. He looks at each diner expectantly, hoping to see expressions of delight. Before he leaves, he pronounces the inevitable benediction: "Enjoy!"

Many seem to think that's how God should act. He should deliver all the pleasures of "the good life" on a silver platter and say, "Enjoy!" But the more that people try to find happiness in wealth, power, and sensual pleasures, the more they are tortured with inner unrest. With all the trappings of "the good life" around them, why can't people be happy? Why has God failed to deliver the happiness they really want?

When Jesus preached the most famous sermon in history, He laid out the basis of true happiness. In the Beatitudes, the opening verses of the Sermon on the Mount, Jesus turned the usual ways of thinking upside down. Ignoring those who were complacent in their riches, Jesus commended those who knew their spiritual poverty. Spurning the proud and powerful, Jesus congratulated those who were gentle and merciful. Jesus emphasized character traits that have little value in the eyes of the world. But real happiness—eternal happiness—will be found only by those who believe in the values that Jesus taught.

B. Lesson Background

The Sermon on the Mount came perhaps midway in the second year of Jesus' ministry. After beginning in obscurity, Jesus gained a large following among the common people of Galilee and Judea. Great multitudes came out to hear Him and, if possible, to see a miracle. The number of His followers had grown fast. For the apostles and for all His other followers, Jesus needed to explain what kind of people would be seen as heroes in the kingdom of God.

I. Christian Character
(Matthew 5:1-12)

A. To Be Lowly and to Mourn (vv. 1-4)

1. And seeing the multitudes, he went up into a mountain: and when he was set, his disciples came unto him.

Jesus is at the height of His popularity. Large crowds gather to watch Him heal the sick (Matthew 4:23-25). They are also attracted to Jesus because they are "astonished at his doctrine: for he taught them as one having authority, and not as the scribes" (7:28, 29). Jesus speaks like a man who knows what He is talking about.

When Jesus goes *up into a mountain*, it could be any one of many possible locations in the hills of Galilee. The hilly location perhaps weeds out the people who are merely curious, and it provides a natural amphitheater for those who are willing to make the climb.

As Jesus sits down to teach, He adopts the accepted posture of teachers in synagogues or schools (Luke 4:20). The parallel account in Luke 6:17-26 has Jesus standing. Putting together the accounts of Matthew and Luke, we see hints of a multi-day affair. Sometimes Jesus sits, sometimes He stands, depending on a variety of factors. The *disciples* include both the apostles and other followers who are serious about hearing the Master.

2, 3. And he opened his mouth, and taught them, saying, Blessed are the poor in spirit: for theirs is the kingdom of heaven.

It is important to catch the flavor of the word *blessed* in the Beatitudes. In the common language of the day (Greek), the word is used to describe people who are in an enviable position. Jesus is saying, in effect, "How fortunate *are the poor in spirit.*" He is not feeling sorry for them as losers in the game of life; He is congratulating them as the ultimate winners.

Those who are poor in spirit are, in fact, better off than those who are arrogant and smug. People who recognize their own spiritual bankruptcy are much more likely to be ready to turn to God and receive salvation. Only those who humble themselves can enter *the kingdom of Heaven*—both now and in the life to come.

The church is the expression of God's kingdom on earth. After Jesus ascends, the first-century church will be made up of "not many wise men after the flesh, not many mighty, not many noble" (1 Corinthians 1:26). The final expression of the kingdom is Heaven itself. Those who humble themselves will be exalted; they will have a home in Heaven. The best is yet to come!

4. Blessed are they that mourn: for they shall be comforted.

Of all the Beatitudes, this one seems to be the most paradoxical. How can it be fortunate or happy for people to *mourn?* There are two senses in which mourning is good. First, the concept of mourning is found often in the Old Testament when people are expressing sorrow for sin (e.g., Ezra 10:6; Psalms 51:4; 119:136). Those who repent are obviously better off than those who do not. Second, people who are mourning in any kind of tragedy are more likely to learn deep truths than people who live happy but superficial lives. Maybe that is part of the reason why Solomon said, "It is better to go to the house of mourning, than to go to the house of feasting" (Ecclesiastes 7:2). [See question #1, page 382.]

God promises to comfort those who mourn. But the promise of "comfort" does not mean that God will make people "comfortable." It means, rather, that He will stand by them, support them, encourage them, console them (see Isaiah 40:1). Since this is the case, is it not better to mourn and have God near than to feast and have God absent? Is it not better for a nation to humble itself and repent than to abandon God and chase the elusive rainbow of prosperity and "quality of life"? (See also Isaiah 61:2, 3.)

B. To Be Meek and Hungry (vv. 5, 6)

5. Blessed are the meek: for they shall inherit the earth.

A sarcastic bumper sticker says "The meek shall inherit the earth—if that's OK with everyone else!" We should not, however, equate meekness with weakness. Jesus is not commending people for being feeble and spineless. The word *meek* is used in the ordinary society of Jesus' day to describe a trained elephant, a tamed stallion, or a reliable watchdog. These animals have strength, but their strength has been brought under control. Moses and Jesus are two of the most humble men in the Bible (see Numbers 12:3; Matthew 11:29; and 2 Corinthians 10:1). They are examples of strength that was yielded to the control of God. [See question #2, page 382.]

Those who are meek are to be congratulated, for they will have great reward. In the new Heaven and the new earth (Revelation 21:1), when all things are made new, they will dwell in a place prepared for God's own people. They may never have owned a square foot of real estate on this old planet, but in the world to come they will *inherit* a mansion! (Compare Psalm 37:11.)

6. Blessed are they which do hunger and thirst after righteousness: for they shall be filled.

In the physical sense, *hunger and thirst* are appetites that make us desire what is necessary for our very existence. By applying these words to the spiritual realm, Jesus applauds those who have a burning desire to be right with God. (See also Psalm 42:2.)

Righteousness—being seen as innocent in the eyes of God—is not very high on the list of priorities of worldly people. Their goals are wealth (how much can they get) and pleasure (how much can they get away with). Citizens of God's kingdom, on the other hand, long to be more godly than they already are. They long to live in a land where the tempter and his temptations are gone. They hunger for the day when the Lord's rebuilding project in their lives is brought to completion (Philippians 1:6).

How to Say It

COLOSSIANS. Kuh-*losh*-unz.

CORINTHIANS. Ko-*rin*-thee-unz (*th* as in *thin*).

ECCLESIASTES. Ik-*leez*-ee-*as*-teez (strong accent on *as*).

EPHESIANS. Ee-*fee*-zhunz.

EZRA. *Ez*-ruh.

GALATIANS. Guh-*lay*-shunz.

GALILEE. *Gal*-uh-lee.

ISAIAH. Eye-*zay*-uh.

JUDEA. Joo-*dee*-uh.

PHILIPPIANS. Fih-*lip*-ee-unz.

SANHEDRIN. *San*-huh-drun or San-*heed*-run.

John R. W. Stott sees a spiritual progression in these first four Beatitudes. Each step leads to the next and presupposes the one that has gone before. First, we must admit spiritual bankruptcy before God. Second, we must mourn over the cause of it—our sins. Third, we must yield humbly to the Master's control. Fourth, we must hunger for right standing with God. Seen in this light, we cannot pick our favorite Beatitudes and reject the others; the total package is what God desires in our lives.

C. To Be Pure and Good (vv. 7-9)

7. Blessed are the merciful: for they shall obtain mercy.

In a society where people are conditioned to think they have evolved by "survival of the fittest," there seems to be little room for compassion. Big businesses swallow up little businesses; the strong demolish the weak. The world finds revenge sweet, but finds forgiveness tame by comparison.

Jesus commends those who try to reflect the *merciful* nature of God. If we have genuinely made the spiritual pilgrimage that began with admitting our own failure, we certainly will have pity for the failings of others. We will pray with conviction, "Forgive us our debts, as we forgive our debtors" (Matthew 6:12). With the same measure by which we extend *mercy* to others, God's mercy will be extended to us (Mark 4:24). See also Matthew 18:21-35 and James 2:13.

8. Blessed are the pure in heart: for they shall see God.

Purity begins in the *heart*. If the heart is *pure*, right behavior will follow. If the heart is not pure, correct behavior is mere hypocrisy. Therefore, Jesus commends the people whose hearts are pure and good. Such a heart is a place where the seed of the gospel can take root and flourish

Home Daily Bible Readings

Monday, June 27—Jesus Teaches About Discipleship (Luke 6:17-23)

Tuesday, June 28—Instructions on Living the Christian Life (Matthew 5:1-8)

Wednesday, June 29—More Instructions for True Disciples (Matthew 5:9-16)

Thursday, June 30—Love Your Enemies (Matthew 5:43-48)

Friday, July 1—Be Merciful (Luke 6:32-36)

Saturday, July 2—Do Not Judge (Matthew 7:1-5)

Sunday, July 3—On Judging Others (Luke 6:37-42)

(see Luke 8:15). Even though the world sees personal purity as a matter for scorn and mockery, those who are pure in heart will one day *see God.*

At the present time God is invisible to us (1 Timothy 6:16). Scripture promises, however, that in the life to come God's people will see His face (Revelation 22:4). We who long to see God must strive for holiness—to be pure in heart—for without this no one will see the Lord (Hebrews 12:14). See also Psalm 24:3, 4.

9. Blessed are the peacemakers: for they shall be called the children of God.

The Prince of peace commends those who are *peacemakers.* While the gospel will of necessity create division at times (Luke 14:26), believers should never seek conflict. Discord is a work of the flesh; peace is the fruit of the Spirit (Galatians 5:22). To the extent that it is within our control, we are to "live peaceably with all men" (Romans 12:18).

When believers love one another, they are recognized as true disciples of Jesus (John 13:35). When believers live in peace and work to promote peace, they will be recognized as *children of God.*

D. To Be Persecuted (vv. 10-12)

10. Blessed are they which are persecuted for righteousness' sake: for theirs is the kingdom of heaven.

It is not by accident that the Beatitude on being *persecuted* follows the one on making peace, because making peace can be a risky business. The person who steps between warring parties may get shot at from both sides. In fact, all of the Beatitudes put the disciple of Jesus at odds with the world. Recognizing this fact, Jesus commends those whose distinctive difference will bring them persecution.

Not all persecution is undeserved, of course. Sometimes people bring opposition on themselves by their own folly. The one whom God honors is the person who, through no personal fault, suffers the world's wrath. When pursuing righteousness causes a person to be the target of the world's resentment, that persecution is honorably incurred. God will reward the Christian who suffers unjustly. See also 1 Peter 3:14. [See question #3, page 382.]

AN UNUSUAL PERSPECTIVE ON PERSECUTION

During the Communist era in Eastern Europe, Christians often faced persecution. It included surveillance of their lives, interrogations, and sometimes beatings and imprisonment. The viewpoint of those suffering Christians is surprising: they understood that being a Christian always demands sacrifice. While Christians in the West saw prosperity as a sign of God's favor, Christians in Eastern Europe saw suffering in the same way. Suffering to them was proof that one was truly a disciple of Christ. It was something glorious, enabling one to grow in faith and enabling one to share in some way in the suffering of Jesus.

One minister in a former Communist country said, "When I entered the ministry I never expected that I would see a time when we were not persecuted." Those of us who live in the comfort and safety of the West so often complain and whine about some unwelcome experience and wonder if God has forsaken us. Such thoughts did not trouble those who served behind the Iron Curtain. They had no problem understanding the teaching of Jesus that persecution brings blessings. They saw them as unique blessings that might not be received in any other way.

Certainly no one goes out of his or her way to seek persecution; and everyone is glad when he or she does not have to face it. But persecution can bring a unique blessing to those who see it as Jesus did.   —R. C. S.

11. Blessed are ye, when men shall revile you, and persecute you, and shall say all manner of evil against you falsely, for my sake.

In Jesus' eyes the Beatitude on persecution needs to be brought home more forcefully. Changing from "blessed are they" of verse 10, Jesus says, *Blessed are ye, when men shall revile you, and persecute you.* Dedicated disciples should expect to be misunderstood, misrepresented, even reviled by the world. No matter how hard we try to live at peace with some people, sometimes those people refuse to live at peace with us.

Persecution is the inevitable result in the clash of opposite value systems. Those who prefer the darkness will instinctively lash out against the light. When we suffer at the hands of evil people, we can find consolation in the fact that we suffer for Jesus' *sake.* See also Matthew 10:22 and 1 Peter 4:14.

12. Rejoice, and be exceeding glad: for great is your reward in heaven: for so persecuted they the prophets which were before you.

Dietrich Bonhoeffer, who was executed by the Nazis in 1945, said, "Suffering, then, is the badge of true discipleship . . . it is therefore not at all surprising that Christians should be called upon to suffer. In fact, it is a joy and token of God's grace." [See question #4, page 382.]

Just as the prophets were persecuted in the Old Testament, so will the disciples of Jesus be *persecuted* in the New Testament era. The apostles learned this lesson well, for when they were beaten and threatened by the Sanhedrin they rejoiced "that they were counted worthy to suffer shame for his name" (Acts 5:41).

II. Christian Influence
(Matthew 5:13-16)
A. Salt of the Earth (v. 13)

13. Ye are the salt of the earth: but if the salt have lost his savor, wherewith shall it be salted? it is thenceforth good for nothing, but to be cast out, and to be trodden under foot of men.

Salt is a vital substance in the ancient world. It is flavoring to make food palatable; more importantly, it is a preservative to keep meat from putrefying. Just as a little salt can go a long way, even a few Christians can have tremendous influence for good. Christians are the moral disinfectant that keeps a society from going bad.

But what if the salt becomes saltless? Salt from the Dead Sea area is not pure. If the place where it is stored gets wet, the sodium chloride can leach out, leaving only dust-flavored remains. Good for nothing, this "saltless salt" is *cast out.*

Similarly, what if we Christians become indistinguishable from the people around us? What if we no longer mourn over sinfulness or hunger for righteousness? What if we are not pure? It is only as we live out the Beatitudes that we are the influence God intends us to be.

A SUBSTITUTE FOR SALT

Many have been advised to reduce the amount of salt in their diets. This has led to the creation of salt substitutes. Most would agree that many of these substitutes really do not taste much like salt. People on a salt-free diet may adjust to them and use them, but most of us would find them unsatisfactory. The fact is, there just seems to be no substitute for salt. No other substance seems to be as versatile in adding flavor, preserving, and purifying.

Just as there is no substitute for table salt, there is no substitute for those who are spiritually the salt of the earth. Their influence—your influence—cannot be replaced by anything else. If we Christians do not season the world with the grace of Christ, it will not be seasoned.

You have an inescapable influence. You cannot avoid it. You can only determine if that influence will be for good or for bad, will lead people to Christ or will turn them away from Christ. It is a heavy responsibility, but Christ will help us. We need only yield ourselves to Him in obedience and service. He will see to it that we become the salt for life—salt that preserves, that creates a thirst for God, and that heals the spiritual wounds of a broken world.   —R. C. S.

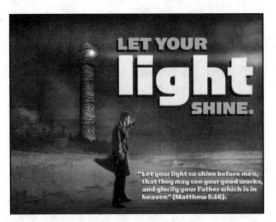

Visual for lesson 5. *This picture of a majestic lighthouse can stimulate a discussion on practical ways for Christians to act as "light."*

B. Light of the World (vv. 14-16)

14. Ye are the light of the world. A city that is set on a hill cannot be hid.

Like salt, just a small *light* can have a large impact. In the spiritual warfare against darkness, Christians shine as lights in *the world* (Philippians 2:15). Even a small light can do a great deal to dispel the darkness.

When Christians go about the business of being Christians, we cannot help but be noticed. Like *a city that is set on a hill*, with lights streaming from its windows at night, we cannot be overlooked. The light we project comes from Jesus (John 1:9; 8:12).

15. Neither do men light a candle, and put it under a bushel, but on a candlestick; and it giveth light unto all that are in the house.

Jesus' words actually refer to olive-oil lamps. In the days when the *King James Version* was translated, the cultural equivalent was the *candle*. Either way, the point is the same. It would be a total waste of perfectly good resources to hide the light *under* a basket.

In the same way, Christians are not intended to be invisible. We have light and truth that people in the world badly need. We should not be ashamed to let our friends and neighbors see what Christ is doing in our lives. See also Luke 8:16; 11:33. [See question #5, page 382.]

16. Let your light so shine before men, that they may see your good works, and glorify your Father which is in heaven.

When we faithfully follow the teachings of Jesus, the world will notice the changes in our lives. We must be careful, however, that we do not do *good works* so that we will gain the praise of people (Matthew 6:1-4). If we do good works with the right attitude, the praise will go to God.

Conclusion

A. True Happiness

Henry David Thoreau (1817–1862) claimed that most people lead lives of "quiet desperation." They want to be happy and successful, but seem to have lost their way. When life is all about self, it becomes stagnated and stale. When people lose sight of their Creator, they also lose sight of the road to happiness.

Long ago, Jesus taught principles that are still the key to true happiness. He taught that people should reflect the image of God in their lives and live for the praise of God. "Be ye therefore perfect," He said, "even as your Father which is in heaven is perfect" (Matthew 5:48). Then people will see our good works and give praise to God.

Jesus not only taught the Beatitudes, He also modeled them. He is the meek and lowly Savior (Matthew 11:29) who wept for the plight of sinful people (Luke 19:41). He hungered for God's Word and God's will (Matthew 4:4; 26:39). He showed mercy from a pure heart; He made peace between us and God by shedding His blood on the cross (Colossians 1:20). He endured persecution, even a cross, because He knew the joy that was set before Him (Hebrews 12:2).

Jesus demonstrated the virtues that bring true happiness. He showed that satisfaction comes from giving, not from getting. He showed that contentment comes from "who you are" before God on the inside, not "what you have" on the outside.

Beyond contentment in this life there is final happiness, eternal bliss in Heaven. Perhaps this final lesson from Jesus is the most important of all. True happiness will finally be gained when we are able to look beyond our present trials and see the ultimate satisfaction that only God can give. When we hear the Savior say, "Well done" (Matthew 25:21), we will know what happiness really is.

B. Prayer

Our Father in Heaven, forgive us for ignoring Your truths and making our own futile attempts to gain happiness. Thank You for caring about us enough to send Your Son, who taught us Your truth and modeled the true life. Help us to be committed to following what He said and how He lived. Help us to be salt and light in the world. May we repent when we fall short. In Jesus' name, amen.

C. Thought to Remember

It is a blessed and happy thing
to be a follower of Jesus.

Learning by Doing

This page contains an alternative lesson plan emphasizing learning activities.
Classes desiring such student involvement will find these suggestions helpful.

Learning Goals

After participating in this lesson, each student will be able to:

1. Describe the attitudes and blessings that bring true happiness to the followers of Jesus.

2. Explain how happiness is based not on what one possesses, but on how one's life reflects and glorifies God.

3. Suggest specific ways in which the Beatitudes can correct the distorted goals of contemporary culture.

Into the Lesson

As a class, create a list of the world's most "successful" people. Form several small groups, each of which is to serve as a selection committee for a "Top 10 People of the Year" award. Designate a different area for each group, such as business, sports, entertainment, and politics.

Have class members select the group they would like to be part of, and then allow about ten minutes for the groups to develop their lists. Have the groups share their results. Make the connection to the lesson by asking your learners to pretend to be someone on their list as they finish the following incomplete sentences. Write each of the three as a separate column across the top of the board:

Happiness is . . . *[Try to define what happiness looks like in terms of money, fame, etc.]*

The road to happiness is . . . *[How do people achieve their dreams for happiness?]*

What I've learned about happiness is . . . *[This could foster discussion about life goals, about pursuing happiness the wrong way, that there is a price to pay to get happiness, that happiness can be lost easily, etc.]*

Do not write the thoughts in brackets on the board. These are provided to help you see the ideas that may surface regarding what many people understand about finding happiness and fulfillment in life.

Into the Word

Say, "Jesus' view of true happiness is quite different from what is observed in contemporary culture and the media." Then discuss the meaning of *blessed* (from page 377), comparing and contrasting this idea with common understandings of happiness. Then start with the middle column entitled, **The road to happiness is** . . . This column that will list those whom the Beatitudes say are blessed (poor in spirit, those who mourn, the meek, those who hunger and thirst for righteousness, the merciful, the pure in heart, peacemakers, and those persecuted for Christ). Place these in the column one at a time, pausing to identify and cross out things that were written previously that this description contradicts. For example, when you write *pure in heart*, you might cross out any comments that refer to inappropriate sexual relationships or lack of integrity in business as a means for finding happiness.

After you write each item in the middle column, follow by writing the description of their blessing in the **Happiness is** . . . column. For example, after writing *poor in spirit* in the middle column, you would then write *theirs is the kingdom of heaven* in this column. Again review and cross out any comments from the "Into the Lesson" exercise that this would contradict.

Finally, discuss personal "life lessons" about happiness. In what ways have your learners seen the truth of Jesus' words confirmed?

Into Life

Say, "While many would claim that they believe the words of Jesus to be true, their lives might contradict them. Each of us has times when our attention and energy are aimed at goals that represent contemporary culture more than the teaching of Jesus." Suggest to your learners that critical questions to consider include (1) What does your life say about what you really believe about true happiness? (2) How do you think your life would be different if the Beatitudes were truly your measure of success? (3) How would your church be different if everyone was committed to helping others live this way? (4) What would it take for that to happen?

Give each learner a blank index card. On this each should write at the top a beatitude that he or she will seek to pursue this week; below that each should write a description of how he or she will pursue that beatitude. On the back of the card, each should then write the opposite of the beatitude; below that, have each write a description what living that way would be like. Encourage each to commit to reading this card (both sides) at least three times each day, asking for God's help in living with Jesus' words in mind.

Let's Talk It Over

The questions on this page are designed to promote discussion of the lesson by the class and to encourage application of the lesson Scriptures. The answers provided are only discussion starters. Let your class talk it over from there.

1. In what ways have you experienced the truth that those who mourn are blessed? What blessings have you received through mourning?

You undoubtedly will have adults in your class who have lost loved ones or have faced serious illnesses and injuries. Let them tell what blessings came about as their brothers and sisters in Christ supported and cared for them. They can tell how they learned to rest on God's presence and His promises. Perhaps they can tell of wonderful examples of providential care as just the right people were present for one specific need or another.

2. If meekness is "strength . . . yielded to the control of God," then what examples of meekness have you seen demonstrated? What situations call for meekness more than others?

It may be easier to recall examples of failures to demonstrate meekness! We all have seen people who thrust themselves forward and seek to get ahead by promoting themselves excessively. But it's the strong yet quiet folk who attract our admiration.

This is especially so in cases of confrontation. When two opinions collide, the one who maintains control—who makes his or her point without launching personal attacks or raising the voice—is more likely to convince others of the rightness of his or her position. The one who loses control in such cases, especially if it is a common occurrence, eventually loses influence with others.

3. If we encounter opposition, how can we tell whether we have invited it by our own folly or if it is the kind of persecution for which Jesus says we are blessed?

Some people almost seem to go out of their way to invite persecution, wearing it as a badge of honor. Others, through immaturity, run frequently into conflict. These are not the kinds of "persecution" Jesus was talking about.

One way to know the difference is to notice who stands with us and who stands against us. If we seem to provoke people whom we generally regard as faithful, mature, and committed Christians, then our positions need a second look! If our support comes from those who need to grow more in their faith or who are generally quick

tempered and controversial, this is another sign that we need to rethink things. We do this by constantly examining our own positions and those of others in light of Scripture. If our positions cannot be supported there, or if we are taking verses out of context to prove a point, then we need to reevaluate our position.

Such an examination requires the meekness described in the third Beatitude. If we are unable to employ such meekness, perhaps we are failing in this area as well.

4. If suffering is, as Bonhoeffer said, "the badge of true discipleship," then what of those Christians who never suffer for their faith? Which of us can truly say we have "suffered" for Jesus? What does this say of our faith?

Bonhoeffer's statement was not original with him. Paul and Barnabas exhorted believers that "we must through much tribulation enter into the kingdom of God" (Acts 14:22).

Yet Western Christians of the past century have known little of real persecution. While believers in other countries have lost their possessions, their families, and even their lives, Western Christians have shared the affluence of their culture. Is it mere coincidence that the influence of the church has diminished in that same period of time?

Societies founded on Christian principles are now referred to as "post-Christian," while Christianity in other countries flourishes. Are we really taking the gospel into the "marketplace" and confronting the secular and materialistic culture to the degree that Christ expects?

5. What is our church doing to equip the members to act as salt and light in the community? What more can we do?

Of course, this is not merely a "church" issue. Every individual believer has an obligation to be salt and light in his or her community. But the church can help to facilitate these efforts.

Together we can often provide help to people in the community that one person could not do alone. The church can organize service projects and ongoing ministry projects in the community that give the members a variety of opportunities to serve in Jesus' name. May God be glorified as we do!

Practicing Genuine Righteousness

DEVOTIONAL READING: Luke 11:5-13.

BACKGROUND SCRIPTURE: Matthew 6:1-34.

PRINTED TEXT: Matthew 6:1-15.

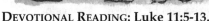

Matthew 6:1-15

1 Take heed that ye do not your alms before men, to be seen of them: otherwise ye have no reward of your Father which is in heaven.

2 Therefore when thou doest thine alms, do not sound a trumpet before thee, as the hypocrites do in the synagogues and in the streets, that they may have glory of men. Verily I say unto you, They have their reward.

3 But when thou doest alms, let not thy left hand know what thy right hand doeth:

4 That thine alms may be in secret: and thy Father which seeth in secret himself shall reward thee openly.

5 And when thou prayest, thou shalt not be as the hypocrites are: for they love to pray standing in the synagogues and in the corners of the streets, that they may be seen of men. Verily I say unto you, They have their reward.

6 But thou, when thou prayest, enter into thy closet, and when thou hast shut thy door, pray to thy Father which is in secret; and thy Father which seeth in secret shall reward thee openly.

7 But when ye pray, use not vain repetitions, as the heathen do: for they think that they shall be heard for their much speaking.

8 Be not ye therefore like unto them: for your Father knoweth what things ye have need of, before ye ask him.

9 After this manner therefore pray ye: Our Father which art in heaven, Hallowed be thy name.

10 Thy kingdom come. Thy will be done in earth, as it is in heaven.

11 Give us this day our daily bread.

12 And forgive us our debts, as we forgive our debtors.

13 And lead us not into temptation, but deliver us from evil: For thine is the kingdom, and the power, and the glory, for ever. Amen.

14 For if ye forgive men their trespasses, your heavenly Father will also forgive you:

15 But if ye forgive not men their trespasses, neither will your Father forgive your trespasses.

GOLDEN TEXT: Take heed that ye do not your alms before men, to be seen of them: otherwise ye have no reward of your Father which is in heaven.—Matthew 6:1.

Jesus' Life, Teachings, and Ministry
Unit 2: Jesus' Ministry of Teaching
(Lessons 5-9)

Lesson Aims

After participating in this lesson, each student will be able to:

1. Identify what is wrong with acts of worship that are performed for others to see.

2. Describe the kinds of giving and praying that please God.

3. Decide what steps are necessary to bring one's own giving and praying into line with the teachings of Jesus.

Lesson Outline

Introduction

A. "Holy, Holy, Holy"?

Simeon the Stylite was a holy man—a very, very holy man. He lived in Syria in the fifth century A.D., amazing the ancient world with his acts of holiness. At the age of thirty-three, he climbed on top of a six-foot wide pillar and did not come down for the next thirty-six years. He would stand for hours reciting Scripture or lifting his hands in prayer. People came by the thousands to watch what they called "this marvel of holiness."

Who is the most holy person you know? Is it a man who prays long and often? Is it a woman who sacrifices her meager income to give more to the church or to the poor? What is the true measure of the holy and righteous person? What is God's measure?

Jesus taught His followers to practice genuine righteousness. This kind of righteousness will not draw big crowds of admirers. It may not seem showy or impressive to the world, but it is far more pleasing to God. In this lesson we will examine how to practice righteousness—the lifestyle of the kingdom of Heaven.

B. Lesson Background

In the Beatitudes of Matthew 5:3-12, Jesus completely reversed the prevailing value systems of society. In the remainder of that chapter, He went on to correct the improper religious teachings of the day. "Ye have heard," Jesus said repeatedly, "but I say unto you . . . " (vv. 21, 22, 27, 28, 33, 34, 38, 39, 43, 44). There were always surprises when Jesus taught.

Jesus insisted that His followers must do better than the scribes and Pharisees had done (5:20). The scribes and Pharisees were widely regarded as experts in carrying out God's laws, but in fact they had missed the point. They kept the externals of the laws, but Jesus insisted that His disciples start on the inside with the heart. When they did they would be ready to practice genuine righteousness—not for people, but for God.

I. Guidelines for Giving (Matthew 6:1-4)

A. Wrong Way to Give (vv. 1, 2)

1. Take heed that ye do not your alms before men, to be seen of them: otherwise ye have no reward of your Father which is in heaven.

The ancient Jews are frequently instructed to give *alms*, which are charitable gifts for poor people (Deuteronomy 15:11). People who have plenty are to share with people in need (e.g., Acts 9:36; 10:2; 24:17; 2 Corinthians 9:6, 7). Handicapped people would lie beside the public thoroughfares, waiting for someone to take pity and give them money (Acts 3:2). In a day with no welfare department or charitable foundations, this one-on-one approach to giving is vital.

It is easy, however, to do the right thing in the wrong way. A very righteous person may innocently think that personal giving should be a good example for others to follow. Such a person may think of himself or herself as simply modeling the godly life. Eventually, however, a person's real reason for public acts of righteousness may be so that he or she can *be seen* by others. People may praise such a person for his or her goodness, but that person will have no congratulations from God.

2. Therefore when thou doest thine alms, do not sound a trumpet before thee, as the hypocrites do in the synagogues and in the streets, that they may have glory of men. Verily I say unto you, They have their reward.

If a very righteous person decides that his or her giving is a good model for less righteous people to follow, then it stands to reason that such a person should call attention to what is being done. (After all, if very righteous deeds go unnoticed, how will others learn?) So the pompous Pharisee perhaps rationalizes to himself that it is appropriate to make ostentatious displays when inviting beggars to receive his generosity.

Jesus ridicules such *trumpet*-blowers as *hypocrites*. A hypocrite is a pretender. People who pretend to be religious but seek the *glory* of other people are phonies in God's eyes. They are nothing but playactors. When they receive the applause of people, they already have all the *reward* they will ever get.

B. Right Way to Give (vv. 3, 4)

3. But when thou doest alms, let not thy left hand know what thy right hand doeth.

Common courtesy should tell the donors that a gift to a needy person should be given quietly. If nothing else, this respects and protects the recipient's dignity. [See question #1, page 390.] This kind of giving also helps to protect the giver's own character and integrity.

By saying that the *left hand* should not know what the *right hand* is doing, Jesus means that the gift should be given without attracting attention. We do not need an audience when we give. We should not even be our own audience, taking smug satisfaction in our righteous act. The audience is not others, nor self—the audience is God.

4. That thine alms may be in secret: and thy Father which seeth in secret himself shall reward thee openly.

There is a certain tension in a Christian keeping his or her charitable giving secret, because

---

How to Say It

BAAL. *Bay*-ul.

COLOSSIANS. Kuh-*losh*-unz.

CORINTHIANS. Ko-*rin*-thee-unz (*th* as in *thin*).

DEUTERONOMY. Due-ter-*ahn*-uh-me.

ELIJAH. Ee-*lye*-juh.

EPHESIANS. Ee-*fee*-zhunz.

EZEKIEL. Ee-*zeek*-ee-ul or Ee-*zeek*-yul.

GETHSEMANE. Geth-*sem*-uh-nee (G as in *get*).

PHARISEES. *Fair*-ih-seez.

Jesus earlier said, "Let your light so shine before men, that they may see your good works, and glorify your *Father* which is in heaven" (Matthew 5:16). It would appear that we are tempted to hide what we ought to show, and to show what we ought to hide. The goal is always to do the right thing without any regard for human praise. God sees what we do *in secret* and does not need us to call it to His attention. He will not fail to *reward* us. [See question #2, page 390.]

II. Guidelines for Praying (Matthew 6:5-8)

A. Wrong Way to Pray (v. 5)

5. And when thou prayest, thou shalt not be as the hypocrites are: for they love to pray standing in the synagogues and in the corners of the streets, that they may be seen of men. Verily I say unto you, They have their reward.

Just as there is a wrong way to give charitably, there is also a wrong way to pray. In Bible times, many different prayer postures are acceptable (see Numbers 16:22; 1 Samuel 1:26; 2 Samuel 7:18; 2 Chronicles 6:13). The problem with the hypocrites is not their *standing* posture in prayer. Rather, the problem is their attitude. Sincere Jews usually stand *to pray* at the three daily times for prayer, sometimes stopping on a street corner to do so. There is nothing wrong with this procedure if their motives are good. However, *hypocrites* love to have people watch them being religious. [See question #3, page 390.]

In Luke 20:47, a similar passage, Jesus accuses the hypocritical Pharisees of making long prayers for a pretense. They do the right things, but for the wrong reason—to be seen by people. They are playactors who think of life as a stage on which they can strut and show their stuff. As a result, the admiration of people will be *their* only *reward*.

PRAYING IN SINCERITY

You can find odd and interesting place names all over the United States. Every state has them. In North Carolina, for example, you can find Friendship, Bridal Veil, Blowing Rock, Kill Devil Hills, and Sincerity. One supposes that people who pray in Sincerity are no more in earnest than those who pray in Raleigh or Charlotte. Wherever we live we should pray in sincerity.

If we are thinking of public prayers, sincerity means that we do not pray to be praised by people for the eloquence of our prayers nor for their length. Lee Carter Maynard once noted that when Jesus prayed in public He was very brief; when He prayed in private He prayed all night. Maynard said, "We usually reverse the process."

If we are thinking of private prayers, sincerity means that we do not pray simply out of habit, but rather pray from our hearts. Certainly we ought to have the habit of prayer. We need a definite time and place to pray. But when that time comes and we go to that place, our prayer must not be routine. To pray in sincerity means that we go beyond some memorized prayer repeated over and over.

Sincerity in prayer also means that we look for ways to enrich our prayer time. The remembered verses of a hymn may help. It may help us to read the printed prayers of others—not to repeat them, but to learn from them new depths of devotion. And, of course, sincerity means we truly believe God hears our prayers and responds to our prayers. We trust that He answers in His own way and in His own time.   —R. C. S.

B. Right Way to Pray (vv. 6-8)

6. But thou, when thou prayest, enter into thy closet, and when thou hast shut thy door, pray to thy Father which is in secret; and thy Father which seeth in secret shall reward thee openly.

Prayer can be spoken in public, of course. See Acts 1:24; 3:1; and 4:24-30. But prayer often is best done in private. To avoid the problem of wrong motives, Jesus tells His disciples to go to an inner room in the house, where there are no windows through which others can see them. After they had *shut* the doors for complete privacy, they could then *pray* to God *in secret* (compare 2 Kings 4:33). Then they can say to God what they truly feel, instead of what sounds good to others. God will hear their prayers and *reward* them *openly*.

Interestingly, the prophet Daniel made a point of leaving the windows to his prayer room

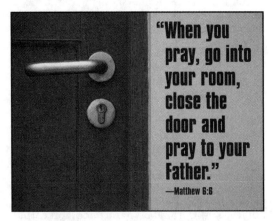

"When you pray, go into your room, close the door and pray to your Father."
—Matthew 6:6

Visual for lesson 6. *Use this image as a starting point to discuss the nature of prayers that God finds acceptable.*

open in Daniel 6:10. But the wider context of that passage shows that he had a godly reason for doing so.

We also can point out that public prayer can be done with a "*closet* mentality." Although there may be a large congregation present, it is still possible to make prayer a personal conversation with God. The more we can tune out everything but God, the more we have the attitude that Jesus is teaching.

7. But when ye pray, use not vain repetitions, as the heathen do: for they think that they shall be heard for their much speaking.

Those who do not know God may use empty *repetitions* to make their prayers impressive, but true disciples do not. An incident in the Old Testament serves as a vivid example of this. At the famous contest on Mount Carmel, the prophets of Baal leaped on their altar and shouted to their god from early morning until noon (see 1 Kings 18:26). But there was no voice from Heaven or anyone that answered.

Then Elijah prayed a brief, private prayer to God and fire fell from Heaven to consume his sacrifice. He was in public, but his prayer was in private. This is the kind of prayer that Jesus instructs His followers to pray.

We should also pause to point out that the phrase *vain repetitions* doesn't mean that we can't be persistent in prayer (Luke 18:1-8). In the Garden of Gethsemane, Jesus repeats His own prayer (Matthew 26:39, 42, 44). It's all the pointless babble that we are to avoid.

8. Be not ye therefore like unto them: for your Father knoweth what things ye have need of, before ye ask him.

Jesus expects His disciples, then and now, to be different. We do not need to try to impress God or even try to inform Him. God already knows our needs, even *before* we ask (see also Matthew 6:32).

Someone may ask, then, "What is the purpose of prayer? If God already knows what we will ask, why bother?" The answer is that God wants us to *ask him*. Perhaps part of the purpose of praying is to remind ourselves how much we depend on God. If we do not take our requests to God, we are taking Him for granted.

III. A Model for Prayer (Matthew 6:9-15)

A. Thinking of God (vv. 9, 10)

9. After this manner therefore pray ye: Our Father which art in heaven, Hallowed be thy name.

Jesus gives a sample prayer to show His disciples how to *pray*. However, if they do no more than memorize His prayer, then they will be no better than the pagans with their empty repetitions. Public recitation of this particular prayer can never take the place of heartfelt, private prayers.

Prayer must focus first on God: *thy name*. All of our self-importance must melt away in the presence of the divine King. Only then are we ready to pray.

Amazingly, the grand Creator of the entire universe is pleased to relate to us as *our Father*. He accepts us as His children and gives us the right to address Him intimately, "Abba, Father" (see Romans 8:15). Our Father reigns in Heaven, but hears our softest prayers on earth. Our earnest desire should be to see His name *hallowed*, that is, treated as a sacred and holy thing. See Ezekiel 36:23. [See question #4, page 390.]

A MODEL TO FOLLOW

Every aspiring artist studies the masters: Raphael and Rembrandt and Michelangelo. Every aspiring composer studies the masters: Beethoven and Brahms, Haydn and Handel. The Twelve noticed that there was something in the prayers of Jesus that they lacked. His prayers had more depth and breadth, and they wanted to pray like that. They were no strangers to prayer. They had prayed all their lives, but they saw in His prayers qualities that theirs did not have. So they said, "Lord, teach us to pray" (Luke 11:1).

In response to that request, He gave them a model by which they could form their own prayers. Is it wrong, then, to recite this prayer? Of course not. It is never wrong to quote Scripture. But the intent of Jesus was that they should learn from this to word their own prayers. The artist may start out copying some great work of art, but eventually composes his own painting. The composer studies closely the music of the masters, not in order to copy them, but that their work may inform, guide, and inspire her own composition. So, in public and in private, we compose our own prayers, using this model as a guide and as inspiration.

We pray remembering that we are children talking to our Father. We want our prayers to be the best that they can be, but we know that the Father accepts our poorest prayer efforts. He does not receive our prayers because of their eloquence, their nicety of expression, or their poetic qualities. He accepts them because He loves His children.   —R. C. S.

10. Thy kingdom come. Thy will be done in earth, as it is in heaven.

Jesus teaches that before we pray for ourselves we should pray for the success of God's *will* and His *kingdom*. God's kingdom is more than just the territory over which He reigns. His kingdom is also His "kingship" over people's lives, beginning with our own.

When we pray *Thy will be done*, we are submitting to that will ourselves. How wonderful it would be if every man and woman were as quick to obey God as the angels *in heaven* are! This is the kind of obedience seen in the total surrender of Jesus Himself in the Garden of Gethsemane (Matthew 26:39; see also Hebrews 5:7, 8).

B. Thinking of Self (vv. 11-13)
11. Give us this day our daily bread.

After giving the first priority to God and His kingship, it is appropriate next to address our own needs. It is right to ask God to provide the things necessary to sustain our lives. This acknowledges that God is the true source of every blessing.

Bread can be understood to refer to food in general. God is the ultimate source of our livelihood (Deuteronomy 8:18; James 1:17). But as we pray for bread we should remember that "man shall not live by bread alone" (Matthew 4:4). We should also think about Jesus who is the bread of life who came down from Heaven to give us eternal life. Just as our bodies need physical food, our souls need spiritual food, or we grow weak and die. [See question #5, page 392.]

12. And forgive us our debts, as we forgive our debtors.

When we pray we must confess our sins and ask for God's forgiveness (1 John 1:9). If we are sincere in our confession and repentance, we will personalize our prayers. If we are praying in secret as Jesus directed, we will naturally confess specific failures; otherwise we have not really admitted to having any sin.

In the same way that we want God to forgive us our shortcomings, we should also be ready to forgive the shortcomings of others. The Parable of the Unmerciful Servant in Matthew 18:21-35 helps us here. If God has forgiven us our enormous sin debt, how can we not forgive others in turn? In fact, if we pray the model prayer of Jesus, then we are inviting God to forgive us only to the extent that we forgive others. This makes genuine prayer a sobering experience.

13. And lead us not into temptation, but deliver us from evil: For thine is the kingdom, and the power, and the glory, for ever. Amen.

God, of course, does not tempt people to sin (see James 1:13). We do not need to beg Him to not do something that is already totally foreign to His nature. Some commentators think that what Jesus means is that we are to ask God to help us not to be led *into temptation* by Satan, as in John

17:15 and 2 Thessalonians 3:3. Other commentators think that our prayer is for God not to allow us to undergo the severe trials and testings of life, as in 2 Timothy 4:18.

The final doxology (although not included in the earliest copies of Matthew) closes the prayer with the same note on which it began: focusing on God. When all is said and done, we must acknowledge that both the temporary kingdoms of this world and the eternal *kingdom* of Heaven belong to God. He has the right to exercise His kingship over all creation.

Likewise, it is proper for us to recognize God's *power* and *glory*. God has the power or strength to do whatever He wants, yet He exercises it only for our good. That is why God deserves to receive glory, both now and *forever*.

C. Thinking of Others (vv. 14, 15)

14. For if ye forgive men their trespasses, your heavenly Father will also forgive you.

It is significant that when Jesus goes back to emphasize one part of the prayer, the part He chooses is about forgiving others for their wrongs against us. When we pray to God, Jesus expects us to get in tune with God. This means that our hearts should be willing to *forgive* people just as God forgives them. We should be encouraged to be more ready to forgive when we consider that God will then extend His forgiveness to us. See also Mark 11:25; Ephesians 4:32; and Colossians 3:13.

15. But if ye forgive not men their trespasses, neither will your Father forgive your trespasses.

On the other hand, if we are unwilling to *forgive* others, then it means that God's nature has not rubbed off on us. How could we dare to approach God and ask for what we refuse to give? (Again, see Matthew 18:21-35.) How can we re-

peatedly enter the throne room in prayer and yet learn nothing about being more like God?

The warning of Jesus is severe: if we will not forgive others, God will not forgive us. Prayer, therefore, involves more than just the petitioner and God. True prayer also involves others and the way we behave toward them.

Conclusion

A. Spotting a Phony

Do you know how to spot counterfeit currency? Businesses that handle large amounts of cash always have to be on the lookout for fake money. Their cashiers are usually given training that enables them to spot the phony bills and reject them. For instance, a cashier may hold a bill up to the light to see if a hidden image (watermark) appears in one area while an embedded stripe appears in another. Being able to spot a counterfeit means saving their company a lot of trouble.

Jesus gave us instructions on how to spot religious phonies. We can hold them up to the light of His teaching and see if their lives are what they claim to be. We can see if the image of their Creator shows up in them. Members of religious cults continue to knock on doors in neighborhoods, and we must remain alert to the false gospels that they bring.

But the lesson today, from the lips of Jesus, is not so much about spotting a phony as it is about not *being* one. He gave warnings about the things that mark a hypocrite so that we, above all, could check ourselves.

Our challenge, then, is to learn to practice genuine righteousness without seeking the praise of people. Since at least some of our giving and praying is done in public, we will have to try all the harder to preserve a sense of privacy in what we do. In the final analysis, the secrecy of giving and the privacy of prayer are more matters of attitude than location. Whether public or private, our "acts of righteousness" must be carried out for the eyes and ears of God.

B. Prayer

Our Father, help us to make Your name, Your kingdom, and Your will the top priorities in our lives. Forgive us for the times we have put our own holiness on display to receive the adulation of others. Teach us not to care so much about what people think and to devote ourselves wholly to pleasing You. In Jesus' name, amen.

C. Thought to Remember

"For if I yet pleased men, I should not be the servant of Christ" (Galatians 1:10).

Home Daily Bible Readings

Monday, July 4—The Importance of Prayer (James 5:13-18)

Tuesday, July 5—Have Faith and Pray (Mark 11:20-25)

Wednesday, July 6—God Answers Prayer (Matthew 7:7-11)

Thursday, July 7—Perseverance in Prayer (Luke 11:5-13)

Friday, July 8—Concerning Almsgiving and Prayer (Matthew 6:1-8)

Saturday, July 9—The Lord's Prayer (Matthew 6:9-15)

Sunday, July 10—Concerning Fasting and Treasures (Matthew 6:16-21)

Learning by Doing

This page contains an alternative lesson plan emphasizing learning activities.
Classes desiring such student involvement will find these suggestions helpful.

Learning Goals

After participating in this lesson, each student will be able to:

1. Identify what is wrong with acts of worship that are performed for others to see.

2. Describe the kinds of giving and praying that please God.

3. Decide what steps are necessary to bring one's own giving and praying into line with the teachings of Jesus.

Into the Lesson

Begin class by asking, "What are some of the classic spiritual disciplines?" Expect answers to include the following: *solitude* (time spent alone for reflection and spiritual focus), *fasting* (abstaining from food, drink, etc.), *frugality* (abstaining from spending money on luxury items), *discreetness* (performing good deeds anonymously), *study* (time spent reading the Word of God, etc.), *prayer* (focused, intentional communication with God), and *journaling* (to focus thoughts on spiritual issues).

Remind your learners that this is only a partial list of the types of things that we can do to foster spiritual growth. While each discipline seems spiritual at first glance, each can be done in a way that does more harm than good. Say, "In today's lesson Jesus gives instructions for how to practice (and how not to practice) two disciplines: the giving of alms and the practice of prayer."

Into the Word

Ask the class to consider the two cases of the lesson (the giving of alms and the practice of prayer) in terms of the following four questions as you write them on the chalkboard: (1) What did the person do? (2) How did the person do it? (3) What was the motive for the actions? (4) What were the results of the actions?

You may find it helpful to divide the class into small groups to discuss the two cases. After ten minutes or so, call for conclusions. Responses will likely include the following.

Case #1—alms: What did the person do? *(gave charitable gifts for the poor)*; How did the person do it? *(called public attention to the charity)*; What was the motive for the actions? *(to receive human accolades)*; What were the results of his actions? *(received what was sought: the attention of people).*

Case #2—prayer: What did the person do? *(prayed publicly)*; How did the person do it? *(prayed with fanfare and repetition)*; What was the motive for the actions? *(to receive human accolades)*; What were the results of the actions? *(received what was sought: the attention of people).* You may add that, "In both cases, by receiving only what was sought, the person actually missed the greater blessing: the pleasure of God."

Ask, "If Jesus were teaching these two illustrations of almsgiving and prayer today, how do you think He would word them differently, based on what we see around us?" Expand the discussion by asking, "What other things do we Christians do that might be improper in God's eyes—things that promote self-attention rather than honoring God? What can we do to help ourselves and each other do these things with the right motives and in a way that truly honors God and prompts spiritual growth?" Allow time for discussion.

Into Life

Draw the attention of your learners to the Daily Disciplines exercise in the student book. (If members of the class do not have the book, they can still follow along with your discussion.) Learners should select two spiritual disciplines they believe will help them grow as they commit themselves to incorporating those disciplines into daily life for the next five weeks. (You can write on the board some of the disciplines from the "Into the Lesson" listing.) Today's passage specifically addresses prayer and charitable giving. Those would be good choices, or other disciplines can be selected.

Encourage each learner to establish a personal standard for each discipline (a certain amount of time, certain things they will do, etc.) and to keep a daily record of his or her practice of the disciplines. Emphasize that this is not a competition. The goal here is not to perform to another person's standard (or even performance at all). The goal is simply to incorporate helpful practices to create an environment that fosters spiritual growth.

Ask for ideas on how learners can practice these disciplines in ways that will foster, rather than inhibit, spiritual growth. Allow time as class ends for people to spend time alone in prayer, asking for God's help in this regard.

Let's Talk It Over

The questions on this page are designed to promote discussion of the lesson by the class and to encourage application of the lesson Scriptures. The answers provided are only discussion starters. Let your class talk it over from there.

1. What measures can the church take to preserve the dignity of recipients of church benevolence funds?

Usually there is some kind of committee, board, or ministry team responsible for administering church benevolence funds. Those who serve on such a group must be committed to the confidentiality of any information they possess. Even records and reports of the group's activities do not need to name the individuals assisted.

Meeting the real need is also important. Sometimes people think they need money when what they really need is help in managing the resources they already have. A wise benevolence team will discreetly but insistently recommend a review of a person's stewardship skills.

2. Jesus says our giving should be secret (Matthew 6:4). But Paul publicly praised the Macedonian believers for their generous giving and told the Corinthians about it in an effort to motivate greater generosity from them (2 Corinthians 8:1-7). How would you resolve this apparent discrepancy?

The whole point is motive. Just as public prayers are appropriate in addition to the teaching about going into one's "closet" to pray, so at times is public giving. If the giving is sincere, done to honor the Lord and not to draw attention to self, then the giving is proper. If this proper gift happens to be known by others, it may serve as a good example and motivation for others to grow in the grace of giving. Thus some churches will have testimonies from people who have learned to be generous and to trust the Lord (and not their own wealth) for their daily provisions. This is appropriate and does not violate Jesus' teaching here.

3. Nearly every worship service has occasions when someone offers a prayer that everyone else can hear. What guidelines, from today's text and others, should such persons follow to be sure they are not falling into the same snare as the Pharisees whom Jesus rebuked?

Sincerity is the key issue. Even a public prayer must be a sincere prayer offered from the worshiper's heart and not an occasion for demonstrating one's spirituality. Some people adopt a special "stained glass prayer voice" or "prayer vo-

cabulary" in an effort to impress others. Others use the occasion to address pet peeves and to lecture the congregation in a way that only remotely resembles a prayer.

Be careful that this discussion does not turn judgmental! Some people use a different "voice" when they pray because they are attempting to be heard by a large group and have no microphone to assist. There is nothing wrong with that. And while it may seem that some prayers employ a vocabulary that is above many of the worshipers who hear, it may be that the person who is praying simply has an impressive vocabulary. Even scholars can be sincere!

4. What can we do to hallow God's name, whether in prayer or otherwise?

To "hallow" is to treat as sacred or holy. Surely, then, the earnest believer will not take the Lord's name in vain, even mildly. Some believers are even careful not to use euphemisms ("socially acceptable" substitutes for God's name) as expletives.

One method of disrespect to avoid is the tendency of some to sprinkle the name "God" or "Lord" or "Father" throughout their prayers in a manner unlike any other kind of communication. The only reason we might address another person that way in conversation is if we think the person is dozing off or otherwise not paying attention. God's name is not a talisman for getting our "wishes" granted; God is not dozing off. We don't have to say His name once for every five or six other words offered in our prayers.

5. Jesus tells us to pray for our "daily" bread. Does this make it wrong to stock our pantries with several days' worth of provisions? Why, or why not?

Depending on God for our daily needs does not preclude our need to work to earn our living (2 Thessalonians 3:6-12). Buying in bulk often offers the best value, so it is an exercise in good stewardship to buy more than one day's worth of provisions. Beside that, it usually requires a drive of several miles to get to the stores that stock the items we need. To drive to these stores once in a while instead of every day is, again, good stewardship. As before, the motives of our hearts is the issue here.

Learning to Listen

DEVOTIONAL READING: Mark 4:10-20.

BACKGROUND SCRIPTURE: Matthew 13:1-23.

PRINTED TEXT: Matthew 13:9-17.

Matthew 13:9-17

9 Who hath ears to hear, let him hear.

10 And the disciples came, and said unto him, Why speakest thou unto them in parables?

11 He answered and said unto them, Because it is given unto you to know the mysteries of the kingdom of heaven, but to them it is not given.

12 For whosoever hath, to him shall be given, and he shall have more abundance: but whosoever hath not, from him shall be taken away even that he hath.

13 Therefore speak I to them in parables: because they seeing see not; and hearing they hear not, neither do they understand.

14 And in them is fulfilled the prophecy of Isaiah, which saith, By hearing ye shall hear, and shall not understand; and seeing ye shall see, and shall not perceive:

15 For this people's heart is waxed gross, and their ears are dull of hearing, and their eyes they have closed; lest at any time they should see with their eyes, and hear with their ears, and should understand with their heart, and should be converted, and I should heal them.

16 But blessed are your eyes, for they see: and your ears, for they hear.

17 For verily I say unto you, That many prophets and righteous men have desired to see those things which ye see, and have not seen them; and to hear those things which ye hear, and have not heard them.

GOLDEN TEXT: Who hath ears to hear, let him hear.—Matthew 13:9.

Jesus' Life, Teachings, and Ministry
Unit 2: Jesus' Ministry of Teaching
(Lessons 5-9)

Lesson Aims

After participating in this lesson, each student will be able to:

1. Describe what parables are and why Jesus used them.

2. Explain why some people could not, or would not, understand the parables.

3. Commit himself or herself to taking the steps necessary to learn to listen to Jesus.

Lesson Outline

INTRODUCTION
    A. "Once Upon a Time . . . "
    B. Lesson Background
  I. THOSE WHO HEAR (Matthew 13:9-12)
    A. Challenge (v. 9)
    B. Question (v. 10)
    C. Promise (vv. 11, 12)
 II. THOSE WHO HEAR NOT (Matthew 13:13-15)
    A. Unnecessary Failure (v. 13)
      Hearing and Doing
    B. Fulfilled Prophecy (v. 14)
    C. Stubborn Refusal (v. 15)
III. THOSE WHO ARE BLESSED (Matthew 13:16, 17)
    A. Blessing for You (v. 16)
      The Right Frequency
    B. Advantage over Prophets (v. 17)
CONCLUSION
    A. Another World
    B. Prayer
    C. Thought to Remember

Introduction

A. "Once Upon a Time . . . "

Everyone loves a good story. Children learn at an early age to perk up their ears at the magic words, "Once upon a time . . . " Stories can carry us to other times, other places, other worlds. Stories can be fun, but they can also carry important lessons.

Jesus told stories called "parables." His stories were interesting and easy to visualize, but they were far more than mere entertainment. Jesus had great spiritual truths to teach, and sometimes His vivid stories were the only way to express them. This was especially true when His listeners were stubborn and hardheaded.

Parables were Jesus' way of transporting His audience to another world—the kingdom of God. It is a world of hidden treasure and pearls of great price. It is a land of sprouting mustard seeds and of grain harvests in astonishing abundance. In this kingdom, beggars go to feasts and rich men go to Hades. It is a world where lost sheep and lost coins are found, where a prodigal son is welcomed home.

K. R. Snodgrass proposes that "parables are best defined as stories with two levels of meaning. . . . In effect, parables are imaginary gardens with real toads in them." Parables express moral or spiritual truths. The parables of Jesus are deceptively simple, but they are packed with an enormous amount of spiritual truth.

A parable may be a brief comparison ("the kingdom of Heaven is like a mustard seed") or a lengthy story ("a certain man had two sons"), but the parable somehow manages to bring a spiritual truth down to earth. Therefore, when parables are told people need to learn to listen. They must learn to hear with their hearts, not just their ears, to understand the spiritual truths of God's kingdom.

Simon Kistemaker has suggested a helpful approach to interpreting parables. First, learn the life setting of the story. Second, note carefully the exact wording that is used, including how the parable is introduced and how it is applied. Third, seek the main lesson. Fourth, compare the teaching of the parable with other Scriptures. Fifth, determine how the parable meets the needs of the twenty-first century church.

When reading a parable, a person should not try to see how creative he or she can be. It serves no purpose to invent special meanings for every detail. Many parables have one main truth. Some parables have two or three main truths. The person who learns to listen carefully to the parables of Jesus will be richly rewarded.

B. Lesson Background

Great crowds gathered on the shore beside the Sea of Galilee. Some of the people were eager disciples, some were hostile enemies, and some were curiosity seekers. In order to allow everyone to hear, Jesus got into a boat and spoke from a short way out into the sea (Matthew 13:1, 2). But the real problem was not just allowing people to hear; it was getting them to listen.

Jesus began His teaching with the Parable of the Sower (Matthew 13:3-8). Later in the same period of teaching, in the verses that follow the text of this lesson, Jesus explained what each part of the parable meant (see Matthew 13:18-23). In between this parable and its explanation, He talks about the issue of parables themselves.

I. Those Who Hear
(Matthew 13:9-12)

A. Challenge (v. 9)

9. Who hath ears to hear, let him hear.

At the end of the Parable of the Sower, Jesus issues a challenge to his audience: whoever has *ears* is commanded *to hear*. Jesus' words go beyond the obvious fact that most everyone has ears and the sense of hearing. Some ears "hear," but do not really "listen." Whoever is willing to use his or her ears to hear and heed the word of Jesus is the subject of His command.

Let him hear does not mean "allow him to hear," as though someone might otherwise prevent a person from hearing. It is, rather, a command addressed to those having ears—hearing ears. Such people are under orders to listen attentively to the words of the Master. [See question #1, page 398.]

Jesus knows that the important truths of eternal life cannot be taught to the crowd in complex, abstract terms. Thus He communicates in ways that common people can comprehend. Even with His use of down-to-earth stories, however, He cannot teach them if they choose not to listen. The prophet Ezekiel ran into this problem (see Ezekiel 33:30-32).

B. Question (v. 10)

10. And the disciples came, and said unto him, Why speakest thou unto them in parables?

The disciples have been with Jesus long enough to recognize the change in Jesus' teaching. Using only *parables* (Matthew 13:34) has not been Jesus' custom to this point. Therefore they ask Jesus *why* He chooses to speak to the crowd in that way. All told, the parables of Jesus make up about one-third of His recorded teachings.

An example from 2 Samuel 11:1–12:14 shows the power of a parable. After David committed adultery with Bath-sheba, he was slow to come to repentance. Even after their baby had been born, David still had not repented. Therefore the Lord sent Nathan to tell David a parable about a poor man whose pet lamb had been taken by a greedy rich man. When David became incensed against the rich man of the story, Nathan replied, "Thou art the man!"

David then immediately recognized his sinful behavior. When a parable is told to someone with listening ears, that person can identify himself or herself in relation to the story.

C. Promise (vv. 11, 12)

11. He answered and said unto them, Because it is given unto you to know the mysteries of the kingdom of heaven, but to them it is not given.

Do you hear His voice?

What things keep you from hearing His voice?

Visual for lesson 7

Use this visual as you ask, "What things keep you from hearing His voice?"

Jesus explains that He speaks in parables because of the diverse nature of those who hear Him. Some, including the disciples, are eager to accept the teachings of Jesus. For true seekers, each parable becomes an exciting moment when they can reach out and embrace the *mysteries of the kingdom of heaven*. In these simple stories they can catch a glimpse of another world.

Others in the crowd, however, do not want to believe. The teachings of Jesus serve only to strengthen their obstinacy. Like the sun that melts the wax but hardens the clay, Jesus' parables either break through to the hearts of the hearers or make them walk away in disgust. Thus the parables of Jesus can both reveal and conceal at the same time. [See question #2, page 398.]

The verse before us has been understood very differently by sincere students of the Bible. Those who believe in "free will" have assigned to the people themselves the blame for their unbelief. Others, equally sincere, think that God in His sovereignty has *given* some people an open heart, but has *not given* a heart of belief to others. If taken by itself, this verse seems to affirm the second view.

In the overall context, however, Jesus calls for people to respond and holds them accountable for their choice. Also, it should not be forgotten that two chapters earlier Jesus had given an open invitation when He said, "Come unto me, all ye that labor and are heavy laden, and I will give you rest" (Matthew 11:28). Jesus draws everyone to Him (John 12:32), but people can resist that drawing if they freely choose.

The promise of Jesus for those who do hear Him is that they will know the mysteries of the kingdom. Another translation of *mysteries* could be "secrets." These are not things that are necessarily complicated and difficult to understand, but are things that are not known until they are revealed. Part of the purpose of the parables is to reveal things in such a way that true seekers can understand them. Those who chose to follow Jesus will soon learn many more things about God and His kingdom.

What Matthew calls *the kingdom of heaven* is called *the kingdom of God* in parallel passages in Mark and Luke. The emphasis of this kingdom is not its location; the emphasis, rather, is the reigning "kingship" of God. People who submit to God's rule are part of His kingdom—both on this present earth and in the future Heaven.

12. For whosoever hath, to him shall be given, and he shall have more abundance: but whosoever hath not, from him shall be taken away even that he hath.

What a blessing it is to be part of God's eternal kingdom! The idea expressed in this verse is so important that Jesus repeats it in Matthew 25:29 as part of the summary of the Parable of the Talents. See also Luke 8:18.

II. Those Who Hear Not
(Matthew 13:13-15)

A. Unnecessary Failure (v. 13)

13. Therefore speak I to them in parables: because they seeing see not; and hearing they hear not, neither do they understand.

When Jesus speaks *in parables,* it brings to light the fact that although the people have eyes capable of normal sight, they do not really *see* God's truths at all. And although they have ears capable of receiving normal auditory input, they do not really absorb or understand what they are *hearing.* If Jesus tells them the will of God plainly, they will reject Him out of hand. By using parables it is possible that the truth will get past their defenses and penetrate their hearts. [See question #3, page 398.]

It should not be necessary for Jesus to use a roundabout approach to teach these people. They should be perfectly able to see and hear, but they are not. Their failure to open their hearts causes them to fail to *understand* God's message.

The parables of Jesus thus serve to separate people into their appropriate categories. First, there are the disciples, the people who have open hearts. They remain with Jesus and go on to learn the deeper truths about God and His kingdom. Then there are the people who are only curious. They soon go home, thinking they have heard only unimportant stories about careless farming practices.

Finally, there are the people who come out to detect false teachings for which they can accuse Jesus. They go home frustrated, since all they hear are harmless stories about everyday life. Soon enough, however, Jesus' enemies will understand that He is using parables against them (see Luke 20:19).

HEARING AND DOING

There once was an executive who would not tolerate disagreement. He had a subordinate who often had to listen to what he, the boss, had to say. In the middle of a monologue, the boss would often pause, and it was obvious that he was waiting for the employee to agree with him.

The employee couldn't be dishonest and lie. Nor could he express disagreement if he wanted to keep his job. So he developed a habit of responding with, "I hear what you're saying." The boss took that to be agreement. Sometimes it was; often it was just a clever way to avoid a heated argument.

We cannot do that with our Lord. We cannot dismiss His words with, "I hear what You are saying." We who *hear* must *do.* To merely acknowledge that we have received the message is not enough. We must put it into action. James, the half-brother of our Lord, also has something to say about hearers and doers. He says that a person who *hears* but doesn't *do* is like a man who sees himself in a mirror and forgets at once what he looks like (James 1:23, 24).

When we hear God's wisdom on any subject, we should respond as did the young Samuel: "Speak; for thy servant heareth" (1 Samuel 3:10). And we should say it with every intention of *doing.*   —R. C. S.

B. Fulfilled Prophecy (v. 14)

14. And in them is fulfilled the prophecy of Isaiah, which saith, By hearing ye shall hear, and shall not understand; and seeing ye shall see, and shall not perceive.

Long ago, the prophet *Isaiah* wrote about the kind of people Jesus is encountering in this narrative (see Isaiah 6:9). The quotation comes at the climax of the well-known vision of Isaiah in which he saw the Lord high and lifted up in His temple. Although Isaiah knew of his own unworthiness, he answered the Lord's call and said, "Here am I; send me."

God told Isaiah to preach to His people, even though they would not accept the message. "Hear ye indeed," Isaiah is to tell them, "but understand not." Even though they would refuse to listen, Isaiah was told to continue calling them to repentance until their cities finally lay wasted and desolate.

Jesus sees in Isaiah's words the parallel to His own situation. Thus the passage has both an immediate application in Isaiah's day and an ultimate fulfillment in Jesus' day. To be honest, should we admit that the words describe many people in our own day as well? Isaiah's words are so important that the apostle Paul repeats them in Acts 28:26, 27. Compare also Jesus' words in John 12:37-41.

C. Stubborn Refusal (v. 15)

15. For this people's heart is waxed gross, and their ears are dull of hearing, and their eyes they have closed; lest at any time they should see with their eyes, and hear with their ears, and should understand with their heart, and should be converted, and I should heal them.

The prophecy of Isaiah continues with a very unflattering picture of the people to whom he was to preach, hundreds of years before Christ. There was a reason that *their ears* did not hear and *their eyes* did not see: it was because their hearts had *waxed gross.* This means that their hearts had become dull and insensitive. Just as King David had been slow to repent following his sin with Bath-sheba, Isaiah's original audience stubbornly refused to face up to their sinfulness and were slow to listen to God.

Like the people in Isaiah's time, many of the people in Jesus' day willfully close their eyes *lest at any time they should see.* They do not want to hear or *understand.* By their refusal to listen, they also signify that they do not want to *be converted* and that they do not want God to *heal them.* Perhaps they think they don't need any spiritual healing. Does any of this sound familiar? [See question #4, page 398.]

The problem is on the part of the people, not on the part of God. God is not willing that any should perish, but that all should come to repentance (2 Peter 3:9). If only the people would listen and turn to Jesus, God would gladly forgive them. But even miraculous signs in abundance do not convince many (see John 12:37).

III. Those Who Are Blessed (Matthew 13:16, 17)

A. Blessing for You (v. 16)

16. But blessed are your eyes, for they see: and your ears, for they hear.

It is truly a blessing for people to be in a position where they are listening to the Word of God! Jesus commends His disciples who have *eyes* that are open to see the truth. He congratulates those who have *ears* that are ready to listen to God's will and obey.

Those who open their hearts to Jesus will be taught many things in parables. Whenever it is needed, Jesus takes the time to explain the parables further to them. When people have open hearts and a receptive attitude, God will help them understand.

As followers of Jesus, we look forward to hearing Him say to us on Judgment Day, "Well done, thou good and faithful servant" (see Matthew 25:21). If we expect to have the commendation of the Lord on that day, we must begin with open eyes and ears. Only after we have learned to listen and obey can we expect to hear Christ's words of approval.

THE RIGHT FREQUENCY

Every radio transmitter has an assigned frequency. Certain frequencies are assigned to shortwave transmitters; others to police, fire, and other emergency services; and still others to commercial radio stations. In order to hear your favorite radio station, you have to tune your radio to the right frequency. If you turn the dial to another frequency, you will not hear what you want to hear or need to hear.

When someone ignores what another is saying, we say, "He tuned her out." We really do decide the things to which we will listen, don't we? We do this physically, and we do this spiritually. Physical hearing is a marvelous gift. Part of our stewardship is to use this gift wisely. But how much more important is "spiritual hearing"! If you keep your spiritual hearing tuned to the divine frequency, you will never be misinformed or led astray. However, if you move the dial of the heart to the devil's frequency, you are certain to be tempted; the longer you stay on that frequency, the more difficult it is to change it.

Our Lord knows what we need to hear. While on earth, Jesus had His own spiritual hearing tuned to the frequency of Heaven. He heard the voice of God. He never tuned His ears to the frequency of evil. We follow His example when we read the Word of God. We do this when we pray. We do this when we listen to Christian music, to sermons, to lessons.

How to Say It

BATH-SHEBA. Bath-*she*-buh.
EPHESIANS. Ee-*fee*-zhunz.
EZEKIEL. Ee-*zeek*-ee-ul or Ee-*zeek*-yul.
GALILEE. *Gal*-uh-lee.
ISAIAH. Eye-*zay*-uh.
MESSIAH. Meh-*sigh*-uh.
NATHAN. *Nay*-thun (*th* as in *thin*).

We are blessed that we live in a time and place where Jesus' message can be heard. To deliberately close our ears to it suggests that we think we know better than God what is best for us. We need to say to ourselves, "Listen up!"

—R. C. S.

B. Advantage over Prophets (v. 17)

17. For verily I say unto you, That many prophets and righteous men have desired to see those things which ye see, and have not seen them; and to hear those things which ye hear, and have not heard them.

The people who hear Jesus speak enjoy a special privilege: they hear things that previously had not been told, even to *prophets and righteous men.* In earlier times God had spoken in veiled prophecies about the messianic age, but He did not fully reveal His ultimate plan to humanity. But with the coming of Jesus Christ, God now reveals what "in other ages was not made known unto the sons of men" (see Ephesians 3:5).

Even the prophets "inquired and searched diligently" into the salvation that they foretold for coming generations (see 1 Peter 1:10-12). The *prophets* searched to learn what events would take place concerning the future sufferings and final glory of the coming Messiah. But God revealed to them that it was not for their own age that certain prophecies were given (e.g., Daniel 12:8, 9).

The ancient prophets were not alone in their yearning to know God's plan. Even the angels longed to look into such things. But neither Old Testament prophets nor angels were told fully the secrets about Jesus and the coming kingdom of God. [See question #5, page 398.]

In a somewhat similar way to the first-century disciples, we are privileged *to hear* the gospel of Christ. We should count it a blessing to know the saving truth and we should live up to the responsibility that this blessing carries with it. God has placed in our hands the task of spreading the gospel to the whole world. If we are faithful to the Great Commission of Matthew 28:19, 20, then people of every tribe and nation can share the blessing—if they have ears to hear.

Conclusion

A. Another World

Mark Twain wrote an amusing book called *A Connecticut Yankee in King Arthur's Court.* The hero of the story goes back in time and amazes the people of King Arthur's realm by doing things as simple as lighting a match. There is much they cannot understand, because he comes from another world, a place far different from their own.

If a person really could go back in time a thousand years, imagine the difficulty he or she would have trying to explain what a computer is and how it works. Such a time traveler would be dealing with people who have never seen a typewriter, have no concept of electricity, and have never even seen a printed book. Imagine further that the people have little or no interest in even listening.

Jesus faced such a situation, only far more difficult. He actually did come from another world—God's eternal kingdom. His task was to explain the things of Heaven to people on earth. What made it even worse was that many of the people in His audience thought they already knew everything about religion. They closed their eyes and shut off their hearing. They had no interest in learning about God's world; therefore Jesus used parables to try to break through their callous hearts.

The parables of Jesus are timeless. His parables still resonate with us because the stories are so true to life. They illustrate the fact that the God of Heaven is also the God of planet Earth, and His principles are true in both worlds.

B. Prayer

Father of Heaven and earth, help us to have open hearts to receive Your truth. Help us cast off anything that would interfere with this communication. Forgive us when our eyes have been turned away and our ears have been tuned out. Teach us to listen and obey. In Jesus' name, amen.

C. Thought to Remember

"Blessed are your eyes, for they see: and your ears, for they hear" (Matthew 13:16).

Home Daily Bible Readings

Monday, July 11—Truth in a Parable (Psalm 78:1-7)

Tuesday, July 12—Keep Looking and Listening (Isaiah 6:1-10)

Wednesday, July 13—The Parable of the Sower (Mark 4:1-9)

Thursday, July 14—The Purpose and Explanation of Parables (Mark 4:10-20)

Friday, July 15—Let Anyone with Ears Listen (Matthew 13:1-9)

Saturday, July 16—Blessed Are Your Eyes and Ears (Matthew 13:10-17)

Sunday, July 17—The Parable of the Sower Explained (Matthew 13:18-23)

Learning by Doing

This page contains an alternative lesson plan emphasizing learning activities.
Classes desiring such student involvement will find these suggestions helpful.

Learning Goals

After participating in this lesson, each student will be able to:

1. Describe what parables are and why Jesus used them.

2. Explain why some people could not, or would not, understand the parables.

3. Commit himself or herself to taking the steps necessary to learn to listen to Jesus.

Into the Lesson

Begin the lesson by having some fun playing a game to introduce the concept of parables. Before class collect several common household items (toothbrush, fork, etc.). You could also include more unusual items, or even a newspaper or magazine headline from a well-known current event. Place each item in a separate paper bag, or wrap each like a Christmas present, and place them in the front of the class.

Next, divide the class into teams of 3-5 members each. Take turns letting each team select one of the wrapped items and then presenting a short lesson about spiritual things using the object as an illustration. This impromptu game can provide much laughter. It will also help explain the format of parables, as ordinary objects or events are used to illustrate a parallel idea about life. This exercise will also increase appreciation for the creativity of Jesus' teaching, as He used very ordinary events and things to explain significant truths in memorable ways.

For the last item, have a small bag of seeds that you will open yourself. Use this as a bridge to share the parable of the sower.

Into the Word

Use Kistemaker's steps to interpreting parables (page 392) as an outline for discussing the Parable of the Sower.

1. Life Setting. Discuss methods of planting. You might want to have an experienced farmer or gardener from your class make a brief presentation on the process of sowing seed by hand and the importance of the soil.

2. Exact Wording. Review the specifics of where the seed fell, the composition of each of the soils, and the resulting harvest (or lack thereof). Compare each of the four soils (beside the road, rocky places, among the thorns, and good soil) and the results.

3. Identify Main Lesson(s). Have each member of the class work with a partner, trying to summarize the main lesson(s) of the parable in a single sentence. Discuss their conclusions. Write on the board some of the ideas and then work together to try to refine the sentence until the explanation is clear.

4. Compare with Other Scriptures. Ask, "How is this parable the same as, and how is it different from, other parables dealing with similar themes?" (For example, we can see a similarity to The Wise and Foolish Builders in Matthew 7:24-27, which illustrates the right response to Jesus' teachings for gaining a firm foundation that will endure through life and its difficulties. On the other hand, The Wheat and the Tares in Matthew 13:24-30 compares the results of good and bad plants growing alongside one another after sowing, with the nature of the soil not being an issue. Although also using sowing as an illustration, the Parable of the Sower, by contrast, is more concerned with the different qualities of soil (receptivity of hearts) involved.

5. Determine Modern Application. Consider each of the four soils and try to describe what type of person that would represent in today's society. What would their lives be like? How would you know if you were that person?

Into Life

Say, "The challenge is to truly 'hear' the parables." Then discuss the difference between just hearing the words and attentively heeding and responding to the message. Note the connection Jesus made between the ears and the heart. Say, "A heart that is hardened and closed to God's message will not listen. Such a person will never truly grasp what Jesus really meant by His teaching. It is only the open and receptive heart (fertile soil) that is truly able to listen and has the ability to truly understand."

Challenge each person to consider which category describes him or her: (1) a *curious listener*, hearing only interesting and confusing stories; (2) a *judgmental listener*, predisposed to refute and discredit Jesus, seeing these parables as distractions; (3) *a disciple*, hearing and eagerly discerning God's Word. Stress that the third type of person is the only one who will truly grasp and obey Jesus' teaching. Close by praying together for tender and receptive hearts.

Let's Talk It Over

The questions on this page are designed to promote discussion of the lesson by the class and to encourage application of the lesson Scriptures. The answers provided are only discussion starters. Let your class talk it over from there.

1. How can you tell "who hath ears" to hear? What is to be gained from noticing who is listening to the Master?

The one who has ears is the one who is listening and putting into practice what Jesus says. Of course, we cannot "listen" to Jesus today with our physical ears as the disciples could. We listen today by reading and meditating on the Word.

One also hears Jesus today by listening to mature followers of the Lord who have learned much through life experiences. We recognize such people by the fact that they are doers of the Word as well as hearers (James 1:22-25). They demonstrate love in action. They model a purity of heart that is worthy of imitation. And that is the reason we can gain from noticing such people. They model for us what it means to listen to Jesus. If we are having trouble hearing His voice, these people can be our "hearing aids"!

2. Jesus told parables so that those who were truly seeking the truth could understand it. Of course, that often meant they had to ask further questions to achieve such learning. How can we identify the true seekers of truth today, and how can we lead them to find it?

True seekers of truth go out of their way to find it. Proverbs 2:1-5 describes the intense search for wisdom that God honors. Such seekers are not going to shrink from the demands of discipleship. Churches can offer classes for such seekers or visits in their homes in order to communicate to them the truths of the gospel.

A "seeker service" that is more entertainment than information may draw crowds, but does it, by itself, truly satisfy the longing of the seeker's heart? Perhaps the church can sponsor events that draw people to its facility in order to find those who are seeking the truth and then set up a follow-up plan to pursue their hearts' real need.

3. Jesus' parables offered a way to get past the people's "defenses" and penetrate their hearts with the truth. What can churches or individual Christians do today to get past people's defenses and share spiritual truth with them?

Today the church is rediscovering the power of storytelling to communicate significant truth. Sometimes it's a true story, a record of someone's personal experience. Other times it may be a made-up story, much like Jesus' parables, that communicate something beyond what the literal words suggest. These stories are told in sermons, but that is not all—for those who are most defensive will not hear sermons. They are told in dramas or in songs; they are shared across the back fence or over a cup of coffee.

Have the class brainstorm some ways to get a hearing for the kind of stories that will communicate the truth of the gospel. Of course, building relationships with neighbors is important for gaining a hearing on that level. Good publicity is important when the church initiates programs aimed at reaching the unchurched.

4. As in Isaiah's time and as in Jesus' time, so it is in our own time that people are reluctant to hear the message even though God is willing to forgive. Why is a message of hope and salvation so often rejected? What can we do about it?

The gospel is good news because the alternative is bad news. Sin is real and must be dealt with. To receive grace, one must admit a need for it, that he or she has indeed sinned. This is what people do not want to accept. They reject salvation because they reject a need of salvation. In a world of "no absolutes," nothing is absolutely wrong or absolutely right, so they think.

The church needs to be creative in addressing this need. Finding areas in which people will question the "no absolutes" philosophy is a start. For example, hardly anyone will disagree that indiscriminate terrorist attacks are wrong. If that is wrong, then wrong (or sin) exists. From there one can go into the concepts of justice and grace.

5. Jesus said that those who heard Him were specially blessed, even more than the prophets of old. In what ways are we especially blessed? How should we respond to such blessings?

"Count your many blessings," the old song says, and surely we ought to. We have heard the gospel; many in the world have not. We have the freedom to express our faith; many in the world—even if they have heard the gospel—are prohibited from expressing faith in Christ. We live in an age of technological wonders, providing opportunities of communication and travel unheard of in earlier generations. Let us put this technology to work to share the gospel!

Receiving and Giving Forgiveness

DEVOTIONAL READING: 2 Corinthians 2:5-11.

BACKGROUND SCRIPTURE: Matthew 18:21-35.

PRINTED TEXT: Matthew 18:21-35.

Matthew 18:21-35

21 Then came Peter to him, and said, Lord, how oft shall my brother sin against me, and I forgive him? till seven times?

22 Jesus saith unto him, I say not unto thee, Until seven times: but, Until seventy times seven.

23 Therefore is the kingdom of heaven likened unto a certain king, which would take account of his servants.

24 And when he had begun to reckon, one was brought unto him, which owed him ten thousand talents.

25 But forasmuch as he had not to pay, his lord commanded him to be sold, and his wife, and children, and all that he had, and payment to be made.

26 The servant therefore fell down, and worshipped him, saying, Lord, have patience with me, and I will pay thee all.

27 Then the lord of that servant was moved with compassion, and loosed him, and forgave him the debt.

28 But the same servant went out, and found one of his fellow servants, which owed him a hundred pence: and he laid hands on him, and took him by the throat, saying, Pay me that thou owest.

29 And his fellow servant fell down at his feet, and besought him, saying, Have patience with me, and I will pay thee all.

30 And he would not: but went and cast him into prison, till he should pay the debt.

31 So when his fellow servants saw what was done, they were very sorry, and came and told unto their lord all that was done.

32 Then his lord, after that he had called him, said unto him, O thou wicked servant, I forgave thee all that debt, because thou desiredst me:

33 Shouldest not thou also have had compassion on thy fellow servant, even as I had pity on thee?

34 And his lord was wroth, and delivered him to the tormentors, till he should pay all that was due unto him.

35 So likewise shall my heavenly Father do also unto you, if ye from your hearts forgive not every one his brother their trespasses.

Jul 24

GOLDEN TEXT: Then the lord of that servant was moved with compassion, and loosed him, and forgave him the debt.—Matthew 18:27.

Jesus' Life, Teachings, and Ministry
Unit 2: Jesus' Ministry of Teaching
(Lessons 5-9)

Lesson Aims

After participating in this lesson, each student will be able to:

1. Relate the essential details in the Parable of the Unforgiving Servant.

2. Explain why receiving forgiveness from God requires passing along that forgiveness to others.

3. Commit himself or herself to identifying the people against whom grievances are held and determine to forgive them.

Lesson Outline

INTRODUCTION
    A. "With Malice Toward None"
    B. Lesson Background
I. QUESTION ABOUT FORGIVENESS (Matthew 18: 21, 22)
    A. Peter's Self-assured Question (v. 21)
    B. Jesus' Surprising Answer (v. 22)
    Keeping Score
II. RECEIVING FORGIVENESS (Matthew 18:23-27)
    A. Unpayable Debt (vv. 23-25)
    How Much Do You Owe?
    B. Undeserved Forgiveness (vv. 26, 27)
III. WITHHOLDING FORGIVENESS (Matthew 18:28-30)
    A. Small Debt (vv. 28, 29)
    B. Improper Penalty (v. 30)
IV. LESSON ABOUT FORGIVENESS (Matthew 18: 31-35)
    A. Sense of Indignation (vv. 31-34)
    B. Call for a Forgiving Heart (v. 35)
    The Heart of Forgiveness
CONCLUSION
    A. To Forgive Is Divine
    B. Prayer
    C. Thought to Remember

Introduction

A. "With Malice Toward None"

At last the terrible Civil War of the United States was nearly over. Abraham Lincoln had won the election to serve a second term as president. He had the daunting task of bringing his nation back together and building a lasting peace. Many in his own political party called for vengeance on the southern states. They thought that those states should pay, and pay dearly!

In his second Inaugural Address, delivered on March 4, 1865, Lincoln spoke words of surprising compassion toward those who had been his enemies: "with malice toward none" and "with charity for all" he called on the people "to bind up the nation's wounds, to care for him who shall have borne the battle and for his widow and his orphan, to do all which may achieve and cherish a just and lasting peace." After Lincoln was assassinated, however, his program of "malice toward none" was not carried out. Forgiveness does not seem to be the human way.

Jesus had much to say about forgiveness. Because the Father forgives us, we should be willing to forgive one another (see also Ephesians 4:32). The Parable of the Unforgiving Servant shows us that forgiveness ought to go both ways: when we have received it, we should also give it. Forgiveness is a beautiful thing, but ingratitude is ugly to the core.

B. Lesson Background

Two specific lessons form the immediate background for the Parable of the Unforgiving Servant, which Jesus taught near the close of the final year of His ministry. The first lesson was about God's eagerness to seek and save His lost sheep (see Matthew 18:12-14). Like a shepherd who rejoices to restore one lost sheep to the ninety-nine that are safe in the fold, God is not willing to see even one of His little ones perish. God is not eager to judge and punish; God would far rather accept a sinner's return. This first lesson established the fact that God loves to extend forgiveness.

The second lesson was about the steps that lead to repentance and reconciliation among people (see Matthew 18:15-17). Jesus taught that every effort should be made to bring about repentance and to offer forgiveness.

I. Question About Forgiveness (Matthew 18:21, 22)

A. Peter's Self-assured Question (v. 21)

21. Then came Peter to him, and said, Lord, how oft shall my brother sin against me, and I forgive him? till seven times?

Peter has heard Jesus teach the principle of forgiveness as early as Matthew 6 in the Sermon on the Mount. At that time Jesus warned, "If ye forgive not men their trespasses, neither will your Father forgive your trespasses" (Matthew 6:15). As Peter hears Jesus teach about forgiveness again (see Matthew 18:15-17), he mulls this over until a question begins to take shape. If, in fact, Peter does agree to *forgive* a person who has wronged him, what should he do if that same person wrongs him again? Will Jesus still want him to be forgiving?

With this in mind, Peter asks a question that seems to answer itself. At least the question includes Peter's answer, indicating what he thinks is obviously an extreme limit. Should he forgive the same person as many as *seven times*? Scripture often views seven as the "complete" number—see Leviticus 26:21; Deuteronomy 28:25; Psalm 79:12; and Proverbs 24:16—and Peter clearly thinks that number will be more than adequate as a limit to the times he should forgive.

It also seems apparent that Peter plans to keep track of the number of times he forgives. Once he reaches the necessary limit, he can turn off the compassion and turn on the revenge. His forgiveness will be "a limited time offer"! [See question #1, page 406.]

B. Jesus' Surprising Answer (v. 22)

22. Jesus saith unto him, I say not unto thee, Until seven times: but, Until seventy times seven.

Drawing on Genesis 4:24, Jesus shows Peter that what he thinks is a generous amount of forgiveness is far too small. Peter must be astonished at what Jesus states as the better number. *Seventy times seven* would be 490—who could forgive that many times? Who could even keep track of that many times?

Jesus' point, of course, is not that 490 times (or 77 times, as some early manuscripts say) is the point at which a person properly stops forgiving. He means that God expects us to keep on forgiving far beyond what we normally do. God Himself has shown boundless forgiveness toward us, so He has every right to expect that we show that kind of forgiveness toward others. [See question #2, page 406.]

KEEPING SCORE

Once there was a lady who took a job where she expected she would be treated unfairly. So she brought along a little notebook and kept it with her at all times. Whenever she experienced what she perceived to be a slight, whenever she encountered anything that could possibly be interpreted as offensive, she wrote it down.

Soon she had a long list that seemed to her to confirm her initial expectations. Of course, many of the things on her list would have gone unnoticed if she had not written them down. Anything that could possibly be seen as offensive was assumed to be intentionally offensive. She was keeping score! If she had begun her job with a different attitude, she would have had very little to write down.

Are you this kind of person, always on the lookout for wrongful deeds done to you? Do you focus so intently on the negative that you interpret every word or deed in the worst possible light?

If you are, consider this: God has forgiven us far more often than we will ever be called upon to forgive someone else. While it may be difficult to forget as well as to forgive, we certainly can put these things away in the back of our minds. We need not dwell on them, and we must not keep score.   —R. C. S.

II. Receiving Forgiveness (Matthew 18:23-27)

A. Unpayable Debt (vv. 23-25)

23. Therefore is the kingdom of heaven likened unto a certain king, which would take account of his servants.

Jesus then goes on to teach a parable to illustrate this principle of being ready to forgive far more often than we usually do. Like all of Jesus' parables, this story has a true-to-life tone with which the audience can easily identify. Life in God's kingdom, lived under God's kingship, will be like the situation of a certain *king* and *his servants*. These servants are actually the king's slaves, and the king is later called their "lord" or "master" (see vv. 25-27). They are not just his workers or hired hands; they are his property.

The time comes for this king to take an inventory of what his servants owe him. As he looks over his *account* with each servant, he reviews what has been borrowed and what has been repaid. He takes action to collect old debts when the situation requires it.

24. And when he had begun to reckon, one was brought unto him, which owed him ten thousand talents.

The king has not gone very far in figuring accounts with each of the servants when he discovers that *one* servant owes *him ten thousand talents*. A talent is a unit of monetary exchange worth six thousand denarii; a single denarius, for its part, is a day's wage for a laborer (see Matthew 20:1-15). So by multiplication we can see that what this servant owes his king is extreme indeed! It is far more than the servant can ever hope to repay.

Jesus' audience probably chuckles at the extreme predicament in which that servant finds himself. The poor fellow will not ever be able to

---

How to Say It

DENARII. dih-*nair*-ee or dih-*nair*-eye.
DENARIUS. dih-*nair*-ee-us.
DEUTERONOMY. Due-ter-*ahn*-uh-me.
LEVITICUS. Leh-*vit*-ih-kus.

repay that kind of money. The amount of money in the story is an obvious exaggeration or hyperbole; no earthly king would lend that kind of money to a mere servant. (See 1 Chronicles 29:3, 4 for a description of King David's personal fortune.) But the principle of the parable is not an exaggeration; Jesus' hearers see it in real life all the time: a man borrows money, gets in over his head, and has no way to pay it back.

HOW MUCH DO YOU OWE?

We are all familiar with debt. It is a part of life. Banking systems would collapse if no one borrowed money. Monetary debt touches all of life.

However, it is probable that you do not know the actual amount of your country's national debt. It is likely that you do not know the exact amount of the debt of your church. It is even possible that you do not know the precise amount of your own personal debt. Neither do we know the magnitude of our debt to God. We know that we have a huge sin debt. But it is possible—indeed, it is likely—that we have committed some sins unaware. An old song says, "Forgive the sins I have confessed to Thee; forgive the secret sins I do not see."

Our debt of sin is so great that it required the sacrifice of Jesus on the cross. The good news is that the debt is now paid. A hymn says, "The old account was settled long ago." Another hymn says, "Jesus paid it all!" No one is going to pay your personal debt for you. It's rare for an individual to pay a church's debt all by himself or herself. We must all participate. No country will come along and pay our national debt. It will be up to us. But the good news is that the sin debt we could never have paid has been paid—in full. "Jesus paid it all. All to Him I owe." —R. C. S.

25. But forasmuch as he had not to pay, his lord commanded him to be sold, and his wife, and children, and all that he had, and payment to be made.

When the king determines that he will not carry such a large debt any longer, he demands immediate payment. When the slave cannot *pay,* the king orders *him* and his whole family *to be sold.* It is a harsh decision, but the king has the legal right to reclaim at least a portion of his loss by whatever means he can.

Slavery to pay debts was common in the ancient world (see 2 Kings 4:1). But economic slavery was strictly and humanely regulated under the Old Testament laws (see Leviticus 25:39-55). Jesus is not approving slavery, of course, but His story tells what a king might do with a man who could not repay a debt. Jesus speaks in images that are understandable to the people of the day.

B. Undeserved Forgiveness (vv. 26, 27)

26. The servant therefore fell down, and worshipped him, saying, Lord, have patience with me, and I will pay thee all.

The servant is distraught at the king's decree. He falls at the feet of the king in the Eastern posture of obeisance, showing his reverence for the king's power and position.

Again, Jesus' audience must chuckle as they hear the servant promise that if the king would just be patient with him, then he would repay the entire amount. A mere servant can never repay such an impossible debt! The servant asks for *patience,* but does he think his master should be patient for the numerous lifetimes it would take to repay that amount? The servant's promise is obviously empty; the servant's doom is certainly sealed. [See question #3, page 406.]

27. Then the lord of that servant was moved with compassion, and loosed him, and forgave him the debt.

Then the story takes a surprising twist. What kind of master is this who is so *moved with compassion* for the slave that he releases him from the hopeless predicament? To freely forgive the man such an incredible sum and ask nothing in return is startling, indeed! *The debt* is canceled; the man is free.

Such generosity rarely happens in the real world, but this story is about the kingdom of Heaven. God is the King in this kingdom, and it is entirely within His nature to show such mercy. When we hear this parable, at some point we begin to recognize not only God as the King, but ourselves as hopeless debtors. We realize that God has forgiven us a sin debt that we can never pay. For this we should be eternally grateful.

III. Withholding Forgiveness (Matthew 18:28-30)

A. Small Debt (vv. 28, 29)

28. But the same servant went out, and found one of his fellow servants, which owed him a hundred pence: and he laid hands on him, and took him by the throat, saying, Pay me that thou owest.

No sooner has the slave been forgiven the huge debt than he goes out to collect a much smaller debt from one of *his fellow servants.* The debt of *a hundred pence* equals a hundred denarii, or a hundred days' wages for an ordinary laborer. This is not "pocket change," but it is certainly miniscule when compared with the ten thousand talents of verse 24! [See question #4, page 406.] Nevertheless, the servant grabs the other man by *the throat,* begins choking him, and insists on immediate payment. Even though the first slave has been shown a beautiful example of how to have a forgiving spirit, he apparently learned nothing from the experience.

Anyone hearing this parable immediately begins to feel the injustice of the situation. How can the forgiven slave show such ingratitude? Why couldn't he show some compassion for a much smaller debt?

29. And his fellow servant fell down at his feet, and besought him, saying, Have patience with me, and I will pay thee all.

The reply of *his fellow servant* is the same as that spoken by the first servant to the king. Jesus intends that the crowd see that the plea for forgiveness is the same. The same result should be expected.

B. Improper Penalty (v. 30)

30. And he would not: but went and cast him into prison, till he should pay the debt.

The unforgiving servant refuses to extend the kind of compassion he has been shown by the king. Instead, he takes his fellow slave and has him thrown into debtor's *prison*. The audience understands that a man thrown into prison has no way to earn money to pay off his debt. (His only hope is that his relatives and friends might care enough to contribute money to his release fund.) Knowing the harsh unfairness of debtor's prison makes their sense of injustice grow.

IV. Lesson About Forgiveness (Matthew 18:31-35)

A. Sense of Indignation (vv. 31-34)

31. So when his fellow servants saw what was done, they were very sorry, and came and told unto their lord all that was done.

When the rest of the master's *servants* find out what has happened, they are distressed. They know a miscarriage of justice when they see one. So they go to their master and report the whole story. [See question #5, page 406.]

Like the servants in the story, we should realize that we are all servants of the same Master in Heaven. Unlike the situation in the story, however, no one needs to go and tell God when a fellow servant is being unfair. God already knows.

32. Then his lord, after that he had called him, said unto him, O thou wicked servant, I forgave thee all that debt, because thou desiredst me.

The forgiving master is a generous man, but he also has a keen sense of what is fair and what is unfair. He summons the *servant* and calls him *wicked*. While the man can protest that he has not broken any laws, the master's accusation is correct. Because the master had forgiven him, the master has every right to expect that the

Visual for lesson 8

Use this visual aid to start a discussion on how the cross relates to person-to-person forgiveness.

slave would share this graciousness with his fellow slave.

We who serve the heavenly Master hope to hear Him greet us one day with the words, "Well done, good and faithful servant!" What a devastating surprise it would be if we are summoned to His throne to hear Him say, "You wicked servant!" We should pay special attention to this parable, therefore, to be sure we hear the words we want to hear on that day.

33. Shouldest not thou also have had compassion on thy fellow servant, even as I had pity on thee?

Doing what is right is sometimes more than merely doing what is legal. What love demands is more than what law requires. When the servant was shown pity, a profound sense of gratitude should have filled his heart. When he went out and attacked his *fellow servant*, he showed that he felt no gratitude at all. He felt no need to extend the master's forgiveness to others.

34. And his lord was wroth, and delivered him to the tormentors, till he should pay all that was due unto him.

The master has a right to be angry. His generosity has been treated with contempt. So he sends the slave to be tortured until he pays everything he owes. Even with contributions from relatives and friends—if the wretched slave still has any!—there is no way he can ever pay enough to escape his torment.

Jesus' parable no doubt stirs several emotions in the crowd. First, they may feel sympathy for the slave in the impossible predicament. Then they feel amazement at the master's compassion. Then comes anger at the slave's ingratitude. Finally, the crowd feels a sense of stern justice when the slave gets exactly what he deserves.

B. Call for a Forgiving Heart (v. 35)

35. So likewise shall my heavenly Father do also unto you, if ye from your hearts forgive not every one his brother their trespasses.

Jesus concludes His parable with a stern warning. Just as the indignant master turned the unforgiving servant over to be tortured, *likewise* shall the *heavenly Father do* to those who do not *forgive.* Jesus does not just recommend forgiveness as a nice thing to do; He says to do it or else!

Furthermore, when we forgive one another it must be more than mere words. Jesus insists that our forgiveness must come from the heart. Even if we have been seriously wronged by another, we must be ready to forgive. God has shown us how to forgive; now He demands that we follow His example when our fellow servant repents (Luke 17:3).

Finally, it is not enough to forgive in the abstract. It costs nothing to forgive vague groups of people for broad, generic offenses. Jesus requires us to extend forgiveness to our *brother* (a specific person) for the *trespasses* (specific wrongs) committed against us. Therefore, the best way to show that we have learned His lesson is for each of us to identify such people as we ought to forgive. Then we should take the appropriate, Biblical steps toward reconciliation.

THE HEART OF FORGIVENESS

At the heart of the word *forgiveness* is the little word *give*. Often we cannot forgive until we *give up* something. Sometimes it is our pride that we must give up. Sometimes it is our delusion that we are always right.

Sometimes we must *give in* so that we may forgive. We cannot always have our own way. We cannot always win. To hold on to power may make it impossible for us to forgive.

Sometimes we must *give over.* We cannot control the lives of others and we should not try. So we give people over to themselves and to God. Controlling persons find forgiveness very difficult.

Sometimes we must *give way.* We must allow others the freedom that God has already given them. That includes the freedom to make choices that may not always be the best choices. It includes the freedom to make mistakes.

But if we would be forgiving we must never *give out.* That is a natural inference of what Jesus is saying. We should not tire of forgiving others. What if God became tired of forgiving us? What if God set a time limit and we would have exhausted His forgiveness after one year or ten or twenty?

We may rest secure in the knowledge that God forgives us without limit upon our sincere repentance. When we forgive others, we, in a way, show them the nature of God. This is not a burden; it is a privilege.   —R. C. S.

Conclusion

A. To Forgive Is Divine

According to Alexander Pope (1688–1744), "To err is human, to forgive divine." People are going to make mistakes; they are going to let each other down. The great heart of God is ready, however, to forgive our trespasses and errors upon our repentance. Forgiveness is one of the most beautiful of all the divine traits. To say, "to forgive is divine" must not, however, mean that we think God ought to do all the forgiving. God expects His children to resemble their Father.

If forgiving is such a good thing, then why are we so reluctant to do it? Perhaps we should reword Pope's proverb: "To err is human; to refuse to forgive is very human, too!" Do we think that an offense against us is more outrageous than an offense against God? Have we somehow earned the right to contradict the character of God and nurse our grudges? Do we fear that by forgiving the offender we let him or her off the hook too easily? Whatever the supposed reason, we need to learn the lesson from Jesus about receiving, then giving, forgiveness.

B. Prayer

Our kind and forgiving Father, we have often failed You by refusing to forgive one another. Help us to open our hearts right now and let Your love fill us. Then let that love be offered freely to those whom we have been slow to forgive. In Jesus' name, amen.

C. Thought to Remember

Forgiveness is not optional.

Home Daily Bible Readings

Monday, July 18—We Sin, But God Forgives (Daniel 9:4-10)

Tuesday, July 19—God Does Forgive Our Sins (Psalm 32:1-5)

Wednesday, July 20—God Is a Forgiving God (Psalm 86:1-7)

Thursday, July 21—You Must Forgive (Luke 17:1-5)

Friday, July 22—Forgive the Offender (2 Corinthians 2:5-11)

Saturday, July 23—About Forgiveness (Matthew 18:21-27)

Sunday, July 24—The Unforgiving Servant (Matthew 18:28-35)

Learning by Doing

This page contains an alternative lesson plan emphasizing learning activities.
Classes desiring such student involvement will find these suggestions helpful.

Learning Goals

After participating in this lesson, each student will be able to:

1. Relate the essential details in the story of the unforgiving servant.

2. Explain why receiving forgiveness from God requires passing along that forgiveness to others.

3. Commit himself or herself to identifying the people against whom grievances are held and determine to forgive them.

Into the Lesson

Begin by taking a pen-and-paper survey of class members. You will be gathering information in a format similar to that used in the television game show, *Family Feud.*

Before class, prepare the surveys on letter-size paper with the following categories (feel free to add additional categories): *Name a well-known case of financial mismanagement. Name an incident of someone not being punished for wrongdoing. Name a well-known case of criminal activity. Name an action or behavior that causes great offense in personal relationships. Name a major problem in personal relationships.*

Collect the papers after five minutes. Discuss the results and list answers on the chalkboard for each of the categories. Consider the topic of forgiveness by discussing the following questions. "If you were a judge, for which of the crimes listed above would you tend to punish most severely?" "Should court systems show forgiveness, or is that only a person-to-person issue? Why?" "For which offenses would you be most likely to show mercy personally?" "Considering the personal offenses, which of those listed would be most difficult to forgive? Why?"

Into the Word

Before class, select three individuals to read the quotations from within the parable that is part of today's text. The quotations are in verses 26b, 28b (man with large debt), verse 29b (man with small debt), and verses 32b, 33 (the king). Encourage participants to read their parts with passion and enthusiasm.

Next, review the story by explaining its major elements: *Setting* (first-century kingdom with financial liability punishable by imprisonment); *Characters* (king, servant with incredibly huge debt, servant with small debt, fellow servants who worked for the king and observed the events); *Plot* (review the order of events, highlighting the elements of surprise); and *Big Idea* (the main point[s] of the story). *Optional:* to explain the theme, have class members work with a partner to summarize the main point(s) of the story. Review their ideas and help refine their statements. Your goal is to help them convey the message of the story clearly and concisely.

Compare and contrast today's parable with Luke 7:36-50. You will note the similarities (two men were in debt and unable to repay) as well as differences (in Luke, both owed their debt to the same moneylender, and both were forgiven). Allow several minutes to discuss the relationship of Luke 7:36-50 with that of the parable from today's lesson.

Into Life

Next, split the class into small groups and give each group the assignment of "rewriting" the parable in order to help them see how this lesson may apply to modern, real-life situations. Remind them that the *Big Idea* must still be the same; this, in turn, demands that the *Plot* be very similar. What would be different are the *Setting* and *Characters.*

Suggest each group go through the following steps to develop their retold parable. First, select a contemporary setting (situation at the office, shop, school, home, etc.). Next, identify the main characters, as appropriate for the setting (supervisor at work and employees, parents and children, etc.).

Next, describe what the offense was. That is, what is the "debt" that is owed? Note that this does not have to be financial, but could simply be a wrong committed that has consequences for another person. The offenses for each of those with "debts" should be very similar in type, but very different in degree (two crimes of embezzlement, but of different amounts of money involved, etc.). Allow time for each group to prepare and present its version to the class.

Challenge class members to consider one situation where they know they should forgive a person who has wronged them. Distribute pieces of paper with the phrase: "Forgiven People Forgive Others" as a reminder of what God has done when forgiving us upon our repentance, and the opportunity (and challenge) that that gives us to forgive others.

Let's Talk It Over

The questions on this page are designed to promote discussion of the lesson by the class and to encourage application of the lesson Scriptures. The answers provided are only discussion starters. Let your class talk it over from there.

1. Probably we all know people who "forgive" but do not forget. What is wrong with this approach? How can we be sure we don't fall into this pattern?

Simply put, forgiveness without forgetfulness is as dead as faith without works. First Corinthians 13 gives us the idea that love does not keep an account of someone's wrongdoings—but that is exactly what Peter wanted to do. It is what many do today. If the wrong is still "on record," then it has not been forgiven.

To be sure, this is not easy. When someone makes a habit of hurting us, we naturally tend to shy away from that person. This illustrates the difference between love as an *action* (as the Bible describes it) and love as a *feeling*. If we act according to how we feel, we will bear a grudge in such a case. If we consciously decide to practice love, we will determine to grant forgiveness and seek reconciliation.

2. Peter must have thought he was being very "righteous" in offering to forgive seven times, but Jesus thought otherwise! Have you ever made what you thought was a generous or righteous gesture, only to find out it was not appropriate or appreciated? How do you handle such a situation? What can you learn from it?

Sometimes our best efforts seem to fall flat. Perhaps we wanted to help a family in need, but we offered milk for a baby who was lactose intolerant. Perhaps we wanted to lead a youth group, but we were unprepared to commit to the number of hours required.

When we misjudge a situation or act inappropriately, we need to be able to swallow our pride and learn from the situation. Maybe we need to learn to ask more questions to size up the situation in advance. Most of all we must remain teachable, ever learning and applying what we have learned to our life situations.

3. Either the servant was lying or he was delusional! He could never repay that debt. When people make promises you know they cannot keep, how can you respond in a way that is in their best interest as well as protecting yourself from being stuck with their unfulfilled promises?

We certainly cannot simply accept the promises and count on their fulfillment. Sometimes we can reason with the person and get him or her to recognize the emptiness of the promise. We can remind the person of the obstacles that would need to be overcome in order for the promise to be kept. Perhaps then we can negotiate a lesser promise that can be kept, allowing the person to save face and still contribute something, even though the original promise is not kept.

4. Sometimes people minimize the second servant's debt, interpreting it as almost pocket change. But it represented more than three months' earnings! How does recognizing this help you to understand what Jesus is demanding in His teaching on forgiveness?

Some people have a hard time applying this parable to themselves. "I am not like the servant who was owed mere pocket change; the debts owed to me are real!" they may say. Jesus did not minimize the servant's debt; His hearers would have recognized it as a matter of significance. Nor does Jesus expect us to shrug off the injustices we suffer as, "Oh, it's nothing," or, "No harm done." True forgiveness does not ignore the infraction. True forgiveness says, "What you did really hurt me, but I value you and our relationship over whatever I have lost: I forgive you." It also recognizes that the sin, while real, was nothing compared with what we have done in sinning against our holy and righteous Lord Jesus Christ. If the Lord can forgive us, we can forgive others.

5. The "fellow servants" in this story "snitched" on the unmerciful servant. When is it right to report an offense, and when ought we to "mind our own business"?

The fellow servants were acting in the spirit of Psalm 82:3: "Defend the poor and fatherless: do justice to the afflicted and needy." (See also Proverbs 31:9.) The debtor servant was afflicted and needy, and the unmerciful servant's treatment of him was not fair considering what a great debt he had been forgiven. Too often we plead for "justice" only when we are the ones being treated unfairly. This can be selfish, as we have a vested interest and may not accurately discern what is really "justice." But to defend others with no hope of personal gain is a selfless act of Christian charity. We ought to look for more opportunities to act in that manner.

Meeting Human Needs

DEVOTIONAL READING: Luke 6:27-31.

BACKGROUND SCRIPTURE: Matthew 25:31-46.

PRINTED TEXT: Matthew 25:31-46.

Matthew 25:31-46

31 When the Son of man shall come in his glory, and all the holy angels with him, then shall he sit upon the throne of his glory:

32 And before him shall be gathered all nations: and he shall separate them one from another, as a shepherd divideth his sheep from the goats:

33 And he shall set the sheep on his right hand, but the goats on the left.

34 Then shall the King say unto them on his right hand, Come, ye blessed of my Father, inherit the kingdom prepared for you from the foundation of the world:

35 For I was ahungered, and ye gave me meat: I was thirsty, and ye gave me drink: I was a stranger, and ye took me in:

36 Naked, and ye clothed me: I was sick, and ye visited me: I was in prison, and ye came unto me.

37 Then shall the righteous answer him, saying, Lord, when saw we thee ahungered, and fed thee? or thirsty, and gave thee drink?

38 When saw we thee a stranger, and took thee in? or naked, and clothed thee?

39 Or when saw we thee sick, or in prison, and came unto thee?

40 And the King shall answer and say unto them, Verily I say unto you, Inasmuch as ye have done it unto one of the least of these my brethren, ye have done it unto me.

41 Then shall he say also unto them on the left hand, Depart from me, ye cursed, into everlasting fire, prepared for the devil and his angels:

42 For I was ahungered, and ye gave me no meat: I was thirsty, and ye gave me no drink:

43 I was a stranger, and ye took me not in: naked, and ye clothed me not: sick, and in prison, and ye visited me not.

44 Then shall they also answer him, saying, Lord, when saw we thee ahungered, or athirst, or a stranger, or naked, or sick, or in prison, and did not minister unto thee?

45 Then shall he answer them, saying, Verily I say unto you, Inasmuch as ye did it not to one of the least of these, ye did it not to me.

46 And these shall go away into everlasting punishment: but the righteous into life eternal.

GOLDEN TEXT: And the King shall answer and say unto them, Verily I say unto you, Inasmuch as ye have done it unto one of the least of these my brethren, ye have done it unto me.—Matthew 25:40.

Jesus' Life, Teachings, and Ministry
Unit 2: Jesus' Ministry of Teaching
(Lessons 5-9)

Lesson Aims

After participating in this lesson, each student will be able to:

1. List some acts of mercy that the Lord expects to be done in His name.

2. Explain why meeting the needs of others is so important in the eyes of Jesus.

3. Decide what specific acts of mercy he or she will to do in the coming week.

Lesson Outline

INTRODUCTION
    A. "All Rise!"
    B. Lesson Background
  I. THE JUDGE (Matthew 25:31-33)
    A. Judge's Glory (v. 31)
    B. Judge's Task (vv. 32, 33)
  II. THE BLESSED (Matthew 25:34-40)
    A. Approval for the Blessed (v. 34)
    B. Deeds of the Blessed (vv. 35, 36)
      A Drink of Water
    C. Surprise of the Blessed (vv. 37-40)
 III. THE CURSED (Matthew 25:41-46)
    A. Condemnation for the Cursed (v. 41)
    B. Failures of the Cursed (vv. 42, 43)
      Take Down the Sign?
    C. Protest of the Cursed (vv. 44-46)
CONCLUSION
    A. Root or Fruit?
    B. Prayer
    C. Thought to Remember

Introduction

A. "All Rise!"

"All rise!" It is a familiar courtroom scene. The spectators suddenly stop their nervous chatter and stand up. The defendant, lawyers, and jurors come to attention. All eyes are fixed on the robed figure who strides importantly into the room. The judge takes a seat at an elevated desk, looking down on the proceedings. In this courtroom the judge is in complete control.

One day the command, "All rise!" will be given for the final time. On that day it will not be addressed to a few dozen spectators in some local court; it will be addressed to the whole world. The dead will rise from their graves; then the liv-ing saints will join them. Together they will meet the Lord in the air (see 1 Thessalonians 4:16, 17).

On the last great day of human history, the Lord Jesus will sit in judgment over all the earth. He will judge in behalf of the Father, and it is the Father's will that the Son exercise this judgment (see John 5:22, 27, 30). When Jesus considers the lives of people, one thing He will be looking for as evidence of faith in Him is how they have treated their fellow humans. Have they cared about the needy? Have they done anything to meet human needs? In today's lesson, the Parable of the Sheep and the Goats, Jesus shows how important He thinks this is. In His eyes, when we do an act of kindness to one of the least of His brethren, we do it unto Him.

B. Lesson Background

Sometime during his final week—probably on Tuesday—Jesus taught in the temple and answered challenges by various religious leaders (see Matthew 21–23). Later, He left the temple and taught His disciples privately at the Mount of Olives. He told them what to expect in the future, both at the fall of Jerusalem (A.D. 70) and at the time of the second coming (see Matthew 24).

Then Jesus told three parables to show His disciples that they needed to be ready for His coming. The first was the Parable of the Ten Virgins. Five were foolish and five were wise (see Matthew 25:1-13). Some were ready when the bridegroom finally arrived; some were not. "Watch therefore," said Jesus, "for ye know neither the day nor the hour wherein the Son of man cometh" (v. 13).

The second story was the Parable of the Talents (see Matthew 25:14-30). When a certain master went away to "a far country," he gave each of his servants a number of talents (money). Upon his return, he summoned the servants to find out what they had accomplished. The faithful and industrious were rewarded, but a "wicked and slothful" servant was cast into the outer darkness, where there would be weeping and gnashing of teeth.

The third parable was the climax of all that Jesus had been teaching about the end times. The Parable of the Sheep and the Goats is a dramatic picture of Judgment Day. Jesus sits as King on a glorious throne and separates the nations into two groups, just as a shepherd separates the sheep from the goats. What will be interesting for our study of this passage is the basis on which Jesus will evaluate and categorize people. We will take note of the importance of meeting human needs, and we will consider how the necessity of good deeds is in harmony with the Bible's teaching of salvation by grace.

I. The Judge
(Matthew 25:31-33)

A. Judge's Glory (v. 31)

31. When the Son of man shall come in his glory, and all the holy angels with him, then shall he sit upon the throne of his glory.

Son of man is Jesus' favorite self-designation. This description emphasizes how completely He identifies with the human race. He lived among us, faced our temptations, and felt our pain. He experienced firsthand what it was like to be hungry, thirsty, homeless, and ignored. The imagery *Son of man* in Daniel 7:13, 14 speaks to His qualifications to sit as our final Judge.

No one knows the day when Jesus will *come,* but the fact that He will return is certain. Unlike His lowly entrance into this world as a baby at Bethlehem, at His second coming He will appear in all His brilliant majesty. The "glory of the Lord" that shone around the shepherds when Jesus was born will be but a faint candle compared with the shining grandeur that will surround Him at that day.

Jesus will be accompanied by all the holy angels of Heaven at His second coming. They who praised Him at His incarnation will rejoice to see His total victory over all evil. He will sit upon a splendid *throne,* surrounded by *glory.* This imagery is repeated in various ways in Zechariah 14:5; Matthew 16:27; 19:28; and Jude 14.

B. Judge's Task (vv. 32, 33)

32. And before him shall be gathered all nations: and he shall separate them one from another, as a shepherd divideth his sheep from the goats.

In the dramatic scene Jesus describes, *all* the *nations* will be summoned to stand trial before Him. People will not be able to go to the god of their choice; they will answer to Jesus. Certain nations will not be excused because of their remoteness; all will be present to answer to the Son of Man. [See question #1, page 414.]

Then, just *as a shepherd* separates *his sheep from the goats,* Jesus will separate the righteous from the wicked. In the same way that a shepherd has no difficulty telling which is which, Jesus will be able to make a clear and correct judgment. As Abraham said of God in the Old Testament (Genesis 18:25), the Judge of all the earth will do right. See also Ezekiel 34:17, 20, 22.

33. And he shall set the sheep on his right hand, but the goats on the left.

To be on the *right hand* is to be on the side of approval and acceptance (for instance, see Psalm 110:1 and Acts 7:55). In the scene described by Jesus, to be *on the left* side represents rejection.

When the shepherd separates *the sheep* and *goats,* the sheep are put on the favored side.

It is interesting that Jesus describes only two groups: sheep and goats. There are no "almost-sheep" or "partly-goat" categories. When Jesus examines the hearts of people on Judgment Day, there will be no middle ground. We are either for Him or against Him (see Matthew 12:30; Mark 9:40). While we may see human behavior in shades of gray, Jesus will be able to pronounce judgment clearly and decisively. Each person will be either saved or lost.

II. The Blessed
(Matthew 25:34-40)

A. Approval for the Blessed (v. 34)

34. Then shall the King say unto them on his right hand, Come, ye blessed of my Father, inherit the kingdom prepared for you from the foundation of the world.

Once the peoples of all nations have been separated and sent to their rightful places on one side or the other, King Jesus will announce His reward for those *on his right.* They are the sheep; they are the ones who have followed the good shepherd. They know the shepherd's voice, and He knows them by name (see John 10:2-4, 12-14). Jesus will call them to His side and confer upon them the blessings of the Father.

Even as God was creating "the heaven and the earth" (Genesis 1:1), He was already preparing a place for His faithful children to spend eternity (compare Luke 12:32). This not only tells us something about Heaven, it also tells us something about God. He has always wanted us to be with Him in Heaven. [See question #2, page 414.]

B. Deeds of the Blessed (vv. 35, 36)

35. For I was ahungered, and ye gave me meat: I was thirsty, and ye gave me drink: I was a stranger, and ye took me in.

King Jesus lists the acts of mercy done to Him by the righteous. They are the ones who gave Him food when He was hungry and something to *drink* when he *was thirsty.* They gave Him shelter when He needed it. The King does not overlook or forget any kindness they have shown.

Such acts are not usually considered as acts of worship or matters of religious devotion. For some people, in fact, giving a little help to needy people is nothing more than a way to get rid of them. But for people who really know God, meeting human needs can be the purest form of religion (see James 1:27). Jesus' parable shows us that meeting human needs is a significant act in the sight of God. See also Isaiah 58:7. [See question #3, page 414.]

A DRINK OF WATER

It has been over forty years since the movie *Ben-Hur* won the Academy Award for "Best Picture." The movie was an adaptation of the book written by Civil War General Lew Wallace (1827 –1905). Many people do not realize that the subtitle of the book is *A Tale of the Christ.*

Two of the most compelling scenes in the movie focus on the giving of drinks of water. Early in the movie, the Romans are leading Judah Ben-Hur on a forced march. He has been denied food and water; he is terribly weak. A man steps forward to offer Ben-Hur a drink of water. We never see the man's face, but it is obvious that it is Jesus. Much later in the story, Ben-Hur has returned to Jerusalem. He follows along as Jesus is led through the streets of the city and out to Golgotha. In one of the cinema's most touching moments, Ben-Hur is able to give a drink of water to Jesus after He has fallen beneath the weight of the cross.

Lew Wallace wrote fiction, but the inclusion of the opportunity for Ben-Hur to return the kindness of Jesus may have been more than a brilliant literary device. It may have been General Wallace's gentle reminder to us that every opportunity to meet the needs of another is an opportunity to minister to Jesus by ministering to someone He loves.   —T. A. C.

36. Naked, and ye clothed me: I was sick, and ye visited me: I was in prison, and ye came unto me.

The King continues to list the ways in which He was served. This much emphasis on service may well make us think Judgment Day will be merely a time for counting up good deeds and merit points. Such a view would contradict all the Scriptures emphasizing that we are saved by God's grace and Jesus' atoning death (e.g., Ephesians 1:7; 2:8, 9). The story of Ebenezer Scrooge is heartwarming to watch at Christmastime. But this tale shows us false doctrine when Scrooge

---

How to Say It

CANA. *Kay*-nuh.
EPHESIANS. Ee-*fee*-zhunz.
EZEKIEL. Ee-*zeek*-ee-ul or Ee-*zeek*-yul.
GALATIANS. Guh-*lay*-shunz.
GOLGOTHA. *Gahl*-guh-thuh.
ISAIAH. Eye-*zay*-uh.
JERUSALEM. Juh-*roo*-suh-lem.
THESSALONIANS. *Thess*-uh-*lo*-nee-unz
    (strong accent on *lo*; *th* as in *thin*).
ZECHARIAH. *Zek*-uh-*rye*-uh (strong accent
    on *rye*).

---

is able to "redeem himself" by his own good works.

On the other hand, we should not think that a lack of good deeds will not matter to God. How shall this tension between grace and good works be resolved? In truth, there is both divine initiative and human response in salvation. Salvation by God's grace must be followed by appropriate good works (see Ephesians 2:10). Salvation based on faith in Jesus Christ must allow that faith to express itself through love (see Galatians 5:6). If a person claims to have saving faith but exhibits no good works, his or her so-called faith is dead (see James 2:26). We are not saved *by* works, but we are saved *for* works.

C. Surprise of the Blessed (vv. 37-40)

37. Then shall the righteous answer him, saying, Lord, when saw we thee ahungered, and fed thee? or thirsty, and gave thee drink?

There is a wonderful innocence in the question asked by *the righteous.* They are completely unaware of ever having done the acts of mercy for their Lord. When they gave food and *drink* to needy people, it was not with any thought of impressing the Master. Their acts of mercy were simply the natural outgrowth of hearts that knew the love of God.

38, 39. When saw we thee a stranger, and took thee in? or naked, and clothed thee? Or when saw we thee sick, or in prison, and came unto thee?

The righteous continue to protest that they have done nothing for their Lord. When they provided shelter and clothing, it was simply for people in need, not for the Lord. When they went to care for the *sick* and the imprisoned, they had no idea they were serving the Master.

When the righteous see needy people, they do not make the usual excuses for doing nothing. They do not accuse the hungry of being lazy; they feed them. They do not let sickness keep them away; they visit them. They do not blame those *in prison* for causing their own predicament; they go to help them. In all of this they have no conscious thought of earning "merit" or impressing anyone. [See question #4, page 414.]

40. And the King shall answer and say unto them, Verily I say unto you, Inasmuch as ye have done it unto one of the least of these my brethren, ye have done it unto me.

Because the King loves His people and identifies with them, anyone who helps them is helping the King. Even serving *one of the least* is not overlooked. No needy person is so insignificant that we can ignore his or her plight. When we give our time and resources to serve the needy, we are serving the Lord (see also Proverbs 19:17).

On an earlier occasion Jesus assured His disciples that even giving a cup of water in His name would not go unnoticed. He promised that whoever would do this "because ye belong to Christ" would not lose his or her reward (see Mark 9:41). It is not the size of the deed but the state of the heart that makes all the difference.

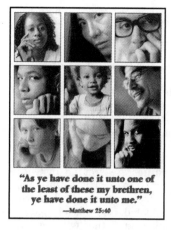

"As ye have done it unto one of the least of these my brethren, ye have done it unto me."
—Matthew 25:40

Visual for lesson 9

III. The Cursed
(Matthew 25:41-46)

A. Condemnation for the Cursed (v. 41)

41. Then shall he say also unto them on the left hand, Depart from me, ye cursed, into everlasting fire, prepared for the devil and his angels.

The penalty for the wicked is stunningly severe. They are banished from the presence of their Master as those who are accursed. They are thrown into a fire that will burn for eternity.

The flames of Hell are the *everlasting fire prepared* in the beginning *for the devil* and his evil helpers. God does not want people to burn in Hell (see 2 Peter 3:9), but people who follow the devil will share his destiny. They will follow him into that same terrible place.

It should not be overlooked that two things are said to be *prepared* by God in this parable. The eternal kingdom has been prepared from the very beginning for God's children to inherit. Hell has been prepared for the devil *and his angels* (demons). See also Matthew 7:23; 2 Peter 2:4; Jude 7; and Revelation 20:10.

B. Failures of the Cursed (vv. 42, 43)

42, 43. For I was ahungered, and ye gave me no meat: I was thirsty, and ye gave me no drink: I was a stranger, and ye took me not in: naked, and ye clothed me not: sick, and in prison, and ye visited me not.

The "goats" in Jesus' parable have totally failed to care about other people. Their complete lack of concern exposes the state of their hearts. Evil hearts and paucity of good deeds go hand in hand. Ignoring people who are hungry, *thirsty*, homeless, ill-clothed, *sick*, and imprisoned shows that the "goats" know nothing of the love of God.

TAKE DOWN THE SIGN?

A car loaded with college students missed a sharp curve on a narrow road and careened into a large tree, seriously injuring one young man. The other young men found themselves in the middle of nowhere—in desperate need of help. One of the students started running to find a house with a phone. To his astonishment, the

Use this visual to ask, "Who does God want you to minister to today?"

first house he found had a sign in the yard: *Doctor's Office.*

The doctor answered the door himself, but explained that he was retired and no longer practiced his profession. The young man angrily responded, "Doctor, if you aren't going to practice medicine, please take down your sign!"

Does the church of Jesus Christ need to take down her signs? We may be very good at planning and executing impressive worship services, but are we busy representing the compassion of Christ to "the least, the last, and the lost"? Do we remember that Jesus seemed to be very comfortable with the poor, the hungry, the sick, and social outcasts?

Have you visited someone in prison, worked in a soup kitchen, or opened your home to someone in need? We often justify our lack of concern for the less fortunate by saying their poor decisions put them in adverse circumstances. Perhaps we should remember that Jesus is the One who looks beyond our situations to see our need. Are your eyes and heart open to "the least of these"?
—T. A. C.

C. Protest of the Cursed (vv. 44-46)

44. Then shall they also answer him, saying, Lord, when saw we thee ahungered, or athirst, or a stranger, or naked, or sick, or in prison, and did not minister unto thee?

When the wicked are bewildered and ignorant about why the Lord is disgusted with them, they show how little they understand God. They admit, in effect, that they have ignored the needs of their fellow humans.

The wicked attempt to defend themselves by implying that if they had known a needy person was actually the Lord, then they would have helped Him. They perhaps assume that helping a needy person who is *not* the Lord is irrelevant and unnecessary. Just before his conversion, Saul of Tarsus learned that persecuting Christians was the same as persecuting Christ (see Acts 9:5).

45. Then shall he answer them, saying, Verily I say unto you, Inasmuch as ye did it not to one of the least of these, ye did it not to me.

The judgment of the Master leaves no doubt about what the problem is: If they do not care about people, then they do not care about Him. Since all human beings are created in God's image and reflect something of His nature, anyone who fails to help them is failing God. If even *the least of these* is slighted, God takes it personally. Anyone who loves the Father will love His children, too. See 1 John 4:20.

46. And these shall go away into everlasting punishment: but the righteous into life eternal.

Jesus describes eternity in only two categories: *everlasting punishment* or *life eternal* (see Daniel 12:2; John 5:29). There is no "in between" place such as a "purgatory" where halfgoats go to get their sins burned away before eventually entering Heaven. The endless punishment of the wicked will be a place where the fire is not quenched and the worm does not die (see Mark 9:48). Hell is an important topic to Jesus in Scripture. See Matthew 5:22, 29, 30; 10:28; 23:33; 25:30; and Luke 16:23-26. [See question #5, page 414.]

While the wicked go away into everlasting punishment, *the righteous* will enter the bliss of eternal life. They will know full well that they have not earned it. All their deeds of mercy for unfortunate people were simply the natural outgrowth of having the Spirit of God in their lives. See you there?

Home Daily Bible Readings

Monday, July 25—God Wants Us to Do Good (Psalm 14)

Tuesday, July 26—Do Not Withhold Good (Proverbs 3:27-33)

Wednesday, July 27—The Golden Rule (Luke 6:27-31)

Thursday, July 28—Do Good, Be Generous, Share (1 Timothy 6:13-19)

Friday, July 29—Help Your Brother or Sister (1 John 3:11-17)

Saturday, July 30—You Did It to Me (Matthew 25:31-40)

Sunday, July 31—You Did It Not to Me (Matthew 25:41-46)

Conclusion

A. Root or Fruit?

As it has been wisely observed, "Good deeds are the fruit, not the root, of the tree of salvation." We dare not think that good deeds produce salvation; instead, it is salvation that produces good deeds. When our faith is real and our hearts are in tune with God, we will naturally reach out to share God's love. On the other hand, if we claim to walk with Jesus but have no concern for the needy, something is seriously wrong. We could say that there is a mismatch between profession and action.

Jesus truly cared about meeting human needs. Even though He came primarily to meet spiritual needs, He took time to meet physical needs as well. The miracles prove it. Look at how He changed water into wine for the wedding at Cana (see John 2:1-11) or when He multiplied loaves and fish to feed the five thousand (see John 6:5-11). The marvel of the great miracles must not cause us to overlook the motive of simple compassion (Matthew 9:36; 14:14; 15:32; and 20:34). When Christ healed the sick and the lepers, it was because He cared. A loving heart cannot help but be moved by human needs.

Jesus said that a tree could be known by its fruit. Bad trees produce bad fruit; good trees produce good fruit (see Matthew 7:16-20). The way we live our lives—specifically the way we treat people in need—is a clear indication of the state of our hearts. Bad, worthless trees are cut down (Luke 13:9.)

The challenge of the Parable of the Sheep and the Goats is not just to force ourselves to do more deeds of mercy. The challenge, rather, is to have our hearts so much in tune with God that we naturally try to relieve human suffering. If we are sincerely motivated by God's Spirit, then whenever we see a need we will reach out in love to help meet it. It will be a natural outgrowth of our Christian love.

B. Prayer

Our kind and compassionate Father, thank You for caring about our needs. Help us to become more aware of the needs of people in our world, and help us to have a more compassionate heart. Lead us to someone whom we can serve in Your name. And as we do, make us realize that the most compassionate thing we can do is to offer the gospel of eternal life. In Jesus' name, amen.

C. Thought to Remember

"For we must all appear before the judgment seat of Christ" (2 Corinthians 5:10).

Learning by Doing

This page contains an alternative lesson plan emphasizing learning activities.
Classes desiring such student involvement will find these suggestions helpful.

Learning Goals

After participating in this lesson, each student will be able to:

1. List some acts of mercy that the Lord expects to be done in His name.

2. Explain why meeting the needs of others is so important in the eyes of Jesus.

3. Decide what specific acts of mercy he or she will to do in the coming week.

Into the Lesson

Before class, arrange the chairs in two groups, with a sign posted telling the men to sit on one side and the women on the other. Play a brief game to introduce today's lesson. Tell the class that you are going to ask two questions that you want them to discuss privately within their groups and predict how the other group will answer. (It will be interesting to see who best understands how members of the opposite sex think!)

Ask each of the questions one at a time, allowing a few minutes for the group to discuss and write down their answers to each. (1) *When getting ready for company, the five most important things that have to be done are . . .* (2) *If unexpected company showed up at my door, I would be most embarrassed if . . .*

Make a transition to today's parable by saying, "I was just using a fun way to get you thinking about preparing for company, because that's related to today's lesson. In modern society, people prepare for the arrival of guests much more precisely than in the times of Jesus (or in many parts of the world today). Without telephone or e-mail, advance notice of a visit would have been rarer. When transportation was by foot or animal, it was much more difficult to predict arrival times than it is today. Hosts might look for guests during an extended period of time or might simply have guests arrive unexpectedly at the door."

Next, say, "The guest arriving in today's parable is more important than any person for whom we may be cleaning our home. The guest whose arrival we are anticipating is Jesus Himself. It is a clean life that He expects when He arrives."

Into the Word

Begin by providing a brief overview of Matthew 25. Note that the parable you will examine in this lesson is actually one of three related parables. You can demonstrate this by presenting verbally each of the first two parables, and then concisely summarizing the main point of each. Demonstrate the logical way Jesus developed His argument by saying the following:

"First, the Parable of the Ten Virgins in Matthew 25:1-13 tells us to be ready and waiting for the return of Jesus. Jesus, the Son of Man, is our bridegroom. Our love for Him and anticipation of His return should prompt us to prepare wisely for His return. For those who are ready there will be great reward; for those who are not ready, there is judgment.

"Second, the Parable of the Talents in Matthew 25:14-30 tells us that when Jesus returns there will be judgment. An important basis of that judgment will be the way that those waiting for Him have used the resources He provided to accomplish His business in His absence. Preparing for the return of Jesus involves wisdom and diligence. This fact sets the stage for the parable we will examine more closely in today's lesson.

"Today's lesson involves a third parable, which we call the Parable of the Sheep and the Goats from Matthew 25:31-46. Here we will see that an important basis of the final judgment will be how we have used the Master's resources to meet human needs. Our true motives will be publicly revealed on that Judgment Day, showing whether we have truly been serving Jesus or merely serving ourselves."

As you move to discussing the lesson verse by verse, make sure to highlight that an important aspect of "the business of the kingdom" is providing for the needy, in the name of Jesus.

Into Life

Move to application by asking, "Who would be the hungry, thirsty, and strangers in our society today?" Allow discussion. *(Just two possible answers are elderly shut-ins and the homeless.)*

Prior to class, research several local organizations that minister to various needs. Provide contact information for members to begin the process of getting involved. If your church has a working relationship established with one of these ministries, this may be a great opportunity to have a representative from that organization come and speak to your class. Ask him or her to emphasize ways for people to get involved, either individually or as a class project.

Let's Talk It Over

The questions on this page are designed to promote discussion of the lesson by the class and to encourage application of the lesson Scriptures. The answers provided are only discussion starters. Let your class talk it over from there.

1. Jesus says "all" nations will be gathered before Him in judgment. What does this say about the imperative of missions? How would you answer those who say people who do not have an opportunity to accept the gospel cannot be judged as if they rejected it?

Jesus makes it clear that every person of every nation will stand at the judgment seat of Christ. There is no hint that some will get a free pass because they did not hear the gospel—otherwise we'd be doing people a disservice to take the gospel to them and risk their rejection of it. Jesus said we are to preach the gospel to "every creature" (Mark 16:15) of "all nations" (Matthew 28:19). If we do not, we are not giving anyone a free pass; we are sitting by silently as they perish! While they will be judged for their own sinfulness, we will bear the responsibility as silent watchmen if we do not make an attempt to reach them with the gospel. (See Ezekiel 33:1-9.)

2. What significance do you see in the King's statement that the kingdom inherited by those on the right was "prepared for you from the foundation of the world"?

It says much about God's eternal purpose for people. We are meant for eternity—an eternity in fellowship with God. Even as God created the heaven and the earth, it was not His intent that we exist here forever.

Satan did not catch God by surprise in tempting Adam and Eve! God saw it coming and He already had a plan for its remedy. And why? Because all along He has wanted to spend eternity with us!

3. Suppose a visitor to the class today said, "I belong to the Brothers of Fraternity lodge, and we do more to help the hungry and sick and homeless than your church does! Why should I join the church? It sounds to me like I've already done my part!" How would you respond?

Anyone who sees these acts of charity as works meriting salvation has not taken into consideration the rest of the New Testament's teaching on salvation. Benevolent works will, on the whole, accompany those who are saved because they respond to their salvation with love.

Jesus said His disciples would be recognized by their love for one another, and these acts cited by the King at judgment are acts of love. But these acts do not merit salvation; they accompany salvation (see Hebrews 6:9, 10). Others will do some of these things, but that is no proof that they are saved. It may be that they are expressing love in some measure, or it may be that they think their good deeds will in some way merit salvation. If it's the latter, they are sadly mistaken.

4. The righteous did not accuse the needy of being lazy or bringing their problems on themselves. Instead, they gave help. But aren't there some needy who are lazy or have brought their problems on themselves? How should we respond to their needs?

The response of love is to address real needs. Giving money may temporarily assist the poor, but assistance in money management or help in finding employment may better address the root need. Giving help and comfort to the sick is one way to help, but giving assistance in good nutrition and instruction about a healthy lifestyle may do more good in the long run.

Seeing the big picture is important in addressing human needs. Giving only short-term fixes may actually reinforce unhealthy life choices and do more harm than good. At the same time, a short-term fix is often necessary as part of an overall approach that includes some kind of help for the long term as well. Taking into account the whole counsel of Scripture requires us to consider 2 Thessalonians 3:10 as well.

5. Many people, even among believers, question the existence of Hell. "How could a loving God consign people to eternal torment?" they reason. How would you respond?

The clear teaching of Scripture is that Hell is real and that it is eternal. The contrast between "everlasting punishment" and "life eternal" makes it clear that if we make the eternal nature of Hell a mere figure of speech, then we have to do the same with eternal life.

The prospect of an eternity spent in torment is frightening to be sure. It should teach us just how awful sin really is. If we are uncomfortable with the idea of eternal punishment, then we are too comfortable with sin. We apparently do not have God's view of sin. If we did, we would take God's view on the punishment that sin is due.

Called to a Mission

DEVOTIONAL READING: Matthew 13:53-58.

BACKGROUND SCRIPTURE: Luke 4:14-30.

PRINTED TEXT: Luke 4:16-24, 28-30.

Luke 4:16-24, 28-30

16 And he came to Nazareth, where he had been brought up: and, as his custom was, he went into the synagogue on the sabbath day, and stood up for to read.

17 And there was delivered unto him the book of the prophet Isaiah. And when he had opened the book, he found the place where it was written,

18 The Spirit of the Lord is upon me, because he hath anointed me to preach the gospel to the poor; he hath sent me to heal the brokenhearted, to preach deliverance to the captives, and recovering of sight to the blind, to set at liberty them that are bruised,

19 To preach the acceptable year of the Lord.

20 And he closed the book, and he gave it again to the minister, and sat down. And the eyes of all them that were in the synagogue were fastened on him.

21 And he began to say unto them, This day is this Scripture fulfilled in your ears.

22 And all bare him witness, and wondered at the gracious words which proceeded out of his mouth. And they said, Is not this Joseph's son?

23 And he said unto them, Ye will surely say unto me this proverb, Physician, heal thyself: whatsoever we have heard done in Capernaum, do also here in thy country.

24 And he said, Verily I say unto you, No prophet is accepted in his own country.

. . . .

28 And all they in the synagogue, when they heard these things, were filled with wrath,

29 And rose up, and thrust him out of the city, and led him unto the brow of the hill whereon their city was built, that they might cast him down headlong.

30 But he, passing through the midst of them, went his way.

Aug 7

GOLDEN TEXT: The Spirit of the Lord is upon me, because he hath anointed me to preach the gospel to the poor; he hath sent me to heal the brokenhearted, to preach deliverance to the captives, and recovering of sight to the blind, to set at liberty them that are bruised, to preach the acceptable year of the Lord.—Luke 4:18, 19.

Jesus' Life, Teachings, and Ministry
Unit 3: Jesus' Ministry of Compassion
(Lessons 10-13)

Learning Aims

After participating in this lesson, each student will be able to:

1. Explain how Jesus described His call to ministry as fulfillment of prophecy.

2. Recognize contemporary ministries that continue Jesus' ministry of compassion.

3. Become an active participant in Jesus' continuing ministry.

Lesson Outline

INTRODUCTION
    A. "You'll Never Come Home Again!"
    B. Lesson Background
  I. JESUS COMES HOME (Luke 4:16, 17)
    A. Worshiping on the Sabbath (v. 16)
    B. Reading from the Scripture (v. 17)
 II. JESUS FULFILLS PROPHECY (Luke 4:18-21)
    A. Holy Spirit–inspired Ministry (vv. 18, 19)
      Fulfilling Our Mission
    B. Jesus' Dramatic Proclamation (vv. 20, 21)
      Leaving a Legacy
III. JESUS IS REJECTED (Luke 4:22-24, 28-30)
    A. Crowd Wonders (v. 22)
    B. Crowd Is Warned (vv. 23, 24)
    C. Crowd Wants Murder (vv. 28-30)
CONCLUSION
    A. Rejected by His Own
    B. Prayer
    C. Thought to Remember

Introduction

A. "You'll Never Come Home Again!"

My older brother helped me pack the car as I left home to go to college. He said, "Look around, because you'll never come home again." I thought he didn't know what he was talking about. But he was right. Things had changed when I returned two weeks later. The family dynamics were different from what I was used to as I was growing up. I was no longer the "kid," but rather someone out on his own. The way I viewed people and the way they viewed me had changed.

B. Lesson Background

Today's lesson puts us in Jesus' first year of public ministry—His so-called "year of inaugura-

tion." We will see Jesus returning to His hometown of Nazareth, the city in Galilee where Joseph and Mary lived before they were married (Luke 1:26-28). Jesus, of course, was born in Bethlehem.

Except for the record of Luke 2:41-52, Jesus lived the first thirty years of His life in relative obscurity. Joseph was a carpenter, and Jesus Himself was also known for the same occupation (Mark 6:3). A Jewish rabbi of the second century A.D. said, "Anyone who does not teach his or her child a trade it is as though the child has been taught to be a thief." As Jesus began His ministry, the hometown folks naturally still thought of Him by His occupation to that point.

Not only was Jesus known primarily by His occupation at this somewhat early point in His ministry, He also carried a stigma of His hometown. Nazareth did not have an especially good reputation. Just like certain cities today can have a reputation—for example, San Francisco with its vocal homosexual population—Nazareth was not known to be a particularly pious town. One of Jesus' early disciples, Nathanael, asked the question, "Can there any good thing come out of Nazareth?" (John 1:46).

Yet there Jesus will speak, and His audience will listen intently. They will initially speak well of this man they had watched grow up, but they will quickly turn into a mob intent on his murder. They will have missed the lesson that Jesus sought to teach them that day. The text will show how God has a concern for everyone. The Lord is abundantly able to meet the needs of all people. We will also see that each person has a responsibility to respond in faith to the offer that Jesus makes.

I. Jesus Comes Home
(Luke 4:16, 17)

A. Worshiping on the Sabbath (v. 16)

16. And he came to Nazareth, where he had been brought up: and, as his custom was, he went into the synagogue on the sabbath day, and stood up for to read.

Jesus is returning to His hometown of *Nazareth*, a fact that sets an interesting "stage" for what follows. Part of this stage is the *synagogue*, which carries the idea of an "assembly place." The synagogue has a variety of usages, depending on location. Most importantly, it is a place of religious instruction, the usage with which we are most familiar (Acts 15:21).

We learn something about the character of Jesus in this verse. Jesus is a man with regular habits and customs. And it is *his custom* to go to the synagogue. He is regular in His worship, prayer, and study. How much more so should His followers be today! Jesus is not slack in His worship; neither should His disciples be remiss in their attendance. It is no small wonder that the Hebrew writer said, "Not forsaking the assembling of ourselves together, as the manner of some is; but exhorting one another: and so much the more, as ye see the day approaching" (Hebrews 10:25). [See question #1, page 422.]

B. Reading from the Scripture (v. 17)

17. And there was delivered unto him the book of the prophet Isaiah. And when he had opened the book, he found the place where it was written.

The book of the prophet Isaiah is in the form of a scroll. It does not have a front and back cover with the pages bound in the middle such as we see today. The text that Jesus reads is from Isaiah 61:1, 2, most likely from the Greek translation of the Hebrew Scriptures, called the Septuagint. We can wonder how much trouble Jesus has in finding just the right passage He wants to read. Scrolls are cumbersome, the book of Isaiah is quite long, and there are no chapter and verse divisions as we have today! But Jesus knows exactly what He wants to read.

II. Jesus Fulfills Prophecy (Luke 4:18-21)

A. Holy Spirit–inspired Ministry (vv. 18, 19)

18, 19. The Spirit of the Lord is upon me, because he hath anointed me to preach the gospel to the poor; he hath sent me to heal the brokenhearted, to preach deliverance to the captives, and recovering of sight to the blind, to set at liberty them that are bruised, to preach the acceptable year of the Lord.

Paul tells us that "when the fulness of the time was come, God sent forth his Son, made of a woman, made under the law" (Galatians 4:4). God had been working throughout the Old Testament to make the conditions favorable for the Messiah to be born at the best possible time. From as early as Genesis 3:15 when God spoke to Adam and Eve, to the promise made to Abraham in Genesis 12:1-3, and throughout God's dealings with the Jews, He was preparing a people and a world to receive His Son, Jesus.

The Holy *Spirit* is an important part of Jesus' ministry. When Jesus was baptized, the Holy Spirit descended as a dove upon Him (Luke 3:21, 22). In Luke 4:1 we are told that Jesus was "full of the Holy Ghost," and that it was the Spirit who led Him into the wilderness to be tempted by the devil. Accompanied with the testimony of the Father—both at Jesus' baptism and His trans-

figuration—that Jesus is His Son, there can be little doubt that Jesus is full of the Holy Spirit, prepared and empowered to do the work of God.

The two verses before us clearly lay out the nature of Jesus' ministry. He is to (1) *preach the gospel* (the good news) *to the poor,* (2) *heal the brokenhearted,* (3) *preach deliverance to the captives,* (4) help with the *recovering of sight to the blind,* (5) *set at liberty them that are bruised,* and (6) *preach the acceptable year of the Lord.* Jesus' ministry is for all people! The gospel is the power of God unto salvation to everyone who believes—to the Jew and to the Greek (see Romans 1:16). [See question #2, page 422.]

The first item in the list should remind us that Jesus said, "Blessed are the poor in spirit: for theirs is the kingdom of heaven" (Matthew 5:3). Once we recognize our spiritual poverty, we can make ourselves dependent upon God for our salvation. We cannot save ourselves. God, being rich in mercy and grace, provides salvation for us through Jesus.

Jesus is the One who sees the great need of people who are distressed and downcast and like sheep without a shepherd (see Matthew 9:36). People today likewise have a great number of "stresses" and "stressors" in their lives. Depression always seems to be on the rise, and people continue to search for answers, security, and hope. Jesus offers these things in abundance. To those who are brokenhearted and bruised Jesus comes with a message of hope and forgiveness. To those who are blind He returns sight. Yes, Jesus physically healed the blind (see Mark 10:46-52), but more importantly He also gave new "vision" to those blinded by the darkness of sin. As the old song says, "The whole world was lost in the darkness of sin; the Light of the world is Jesus"!

How to Say It

ABRAHAM. *Ay*-bruh-ham.
BETHLEHEM. *Beth*-lih-hem.
CANA. *Kay*-nuh.
CAPERNAUM. Kuh-*per*-nay-um.
ELIJAH. Ee-*lye*-juh.
ELISHA. E-*lye*-shuh.
GALILEE. *Gal*-uh-lee.
GENTILES. *Jen*-tiles.
MESSIAH. Meh-*sigh*-uh.
NAAMAN. *Nay*-uh-mun.
NATHANAEL. Nuh-*than*-yull (*th* as in *thin*).
NAZARETH. *Naz*-uh-reth.
SEPTUAGINT. Sep-*too*-ih-jent.
SYNAGOGUE. *sin*-uh-gog.
ZAREPHATH. *Zair*-uh-fath.

Sin holds people captive. It is a yoke of slavery that we cannot break by our own power. Yet Jesus sets the prisoner of sin free!

FULFILLING OUR MISSION

What are you called upon to do at your job? Are you an accountant, reconciling financial records and keeping up with tax laws? Are you a mom, doing laundry, cooking meals, and taking care of kids all day long? Perhaps you are a teacher, imparting knowledge and wisdom to classrooms full of eager students.

Tim McCarthy was a man just doing his job—fulfilling his mission. He was on duty outside the Ambassador Hotel in Washington, DC, on a cloudy afternoon in March 1981. Suddenly, gunfire rang out. McCarthy reacted instinctively and did what he had been trained to do. He turned toward the sound of the gunfire and spread himself out to make the largest possible obstruction. Tim McCarthy was a Secret Service agent, and his mission was to protect the President of the United States. On that terrible day, Tim McCarthy was wounded protecting Ronald Reagan. Television sets across the world replayed his reaction to that first shot.

How many of us are doing exactly what we're supposed to do for God? God may not write out an exact, individualized job description and mail it to us. But Matthew 28:19, 20 gives us a clear idea of what the church's main task is. Most of us have an idea of how we can best serve Him in that capacity. Do we make excuses? Do we say that others could do it better? Do we simply resist? Every Christian should be working toward a level of maturity that leads him or her to act instinctively to answer God's call. Jesus knew His mission, and we must know ours.   —T. A. C.

Visual for lesson 10. *Compassion has many expressions. Use this visual to help your learners think of people who need help.*

B. Jesus' Dramatic Proclamation (vv. 20, 21)

20. And he closed the book, and he gave it again to the minister, and sat down. And the eyes of all them that were in the synagogue were fastened on him.

Have you ever sat through a sermon or a lesson that so fascinated you that you no longer paid attention to the time? Did it seem as if time just flew by because you were so intent on what you were hearing or reading at the time? It is likely that these people have heard this passage read from Isaiah before, but now something is very different! Is it in the way Jesus speaks that captures their attention? Is it in the pronunciation or the elocution? Does He emphasize certain words as He reads the passage from Isaiah? We are not told.

One thing is certain, however: His reading completely captivates His audience. They apparently want more and are hanging on His every word. There probably is absolute silence as they wait to hear what Jesus has to say about this passage.

This is not the first time that the teaching of Jesus makes an impact on people. There are many rabbis (teachers) in the Jerusalem temple and the synagogues, yet there is something about Jesus and His words that puts Him in a different class altogether. Some clues can be found from Mark 1:22: "And they were astonished at his doctrine: for he taught them as one that had authority, and not as the scribes." The Jewish rabbis quote the scholars who came before them as a basis for their teaching. Jesus needs no such help. His word stands on its own authority. It sounds very different to those who listen, as we see next.

21. And he began to say unto them, This day is this Scripture fulfilled in your ears.

Imagine being an eyewitness to a fulfillment of prophecy! How did Simeon feel when he held the Christ-child in his arms, knowing that God had promised that he wouldn't see death until his eyes beheld the coming of the Messiah? (See Luke 2:26-32.) Imagine being present on the Day of Pentecost (Acts 2).

This audience in Nazareth has just heard Jesus read a prophecy that Isaiah made over seven hundred years before. As Jesus sits down, everyone continues to look at him. He then calmly informs them that they are witnessing prophecy being *fulfilled* at that very minute. The One whom Isaiah refers to is seated in their presence. They can see, touch, and speak to the One upon whom the Holy Spirit had descended. He is the One who will do the things mentioned in the ancient prophecy. What a privilege it is to be there at that very hour!

LEAVING A LEGACY

Alfred Nobel (1833–1896) had the opportunity to read his own obituary! His brother Ludvig died in 1888, and a newspaper mistakenly printed Alfred's obituary instead. Alfred Nobel had made his mark on the world up to that point by inventing dynamite. The obituary read, "The merchant of death is dead." The newspaper's mistake changed the Swedish chemist's life. He realized that that was not the kind of legacy he wanted to leave.

You probably will not have the opportunity to read your own obituary, but you can still ask yourself this question: When I am gone, what will people think my mission in life had been? Alfred Nobel apparently asked himself that kind of question, and he did not like the answer. He had become very wealthy, and he decided to use his wealth to encourage people to make the world a better place. Today the Nobel Peace Prize is one of the world's most prestigious awards. His awards also honor people in many areas of the arts and sciences. Alfred Nobel succeeded in changing his legacy. Today, if you ask people about Nobel, they know about his awards. Very few people know how his great wealth was attained.

So the question remains: When you are gone, what will people think your mission in life had been? Will they know that you were a servant of Jesus Christ? What evidence would they have seen to draw that conclusion? Perhaps you, like Alfred Nobel, need to do some things to change your legacy. When we look at Jesus, we see a total focus on His mission. Perhaps we could use a bit of that focus ourselves. Thinking of the kind of legacy we may leave can help.   —T. A. C.

III. Jesus Is Rejected (Luke 4:22-24, 28-30)

A. Crowd Wonders (v. 22)

22. And all bare him witness, and wondered at the gracious words which proceeded out of his mouth. And they said, Is not this Joseph's son?

Many apparently do not sense the privilege they have at this moment in time. Their ears have heard the *words* Jesus read, but their minds have not caught up to the significance of those words. They must be wondering how these things can be, and who is Jesus to say that He is the fulfillment of this prophecy. Their question is, *Is not this Joseph's son?* In other words they are saying, "We know this boy! We've watched him grow up! He's not anything more special than any other resident of Nazareth, is he?" (See also John 6:42.)

Jesus was reared in the home of Joseph, but Jesus is not that man's biological son. What those gathered need to be convinced of is the fact that Jesus is God's Son!

This will prove to be a very difficult truth for the residents of Nazareth to accept. It is difficult even for the half-brothers of Jesus to accept Him as the Messiah. They don't do so until after the resurrection. (See John 7:5; Acts 1:14.) [See question #3, page 422.]

B. Crowd Is Warned (vv. 23, 24)

23. And he said unto them, Ye will surely say unto me this proverb, Physician, heal thyself: whatsoever we have heard done in Capernaum, do also here in thy country.

The growing reputation of Jesus in other places as a miracle worker has not escaped the notice of the residents of Nazareth. They have no doubt heard about water being changed into wine at a wedding feast of Cana of Galilee (John 2:1-11). They are familiar with the healing of an official's son *in Capernaum* (John 4:46-54). Jesus anticipates that those gathered will now want to see their hometown son do something miraculous for them.

Yet Jesus will not do many miracles in Nazareth for one simple reason: there is a lack of faith. In Mark 6:5, 6 we are told regarding a later visit there that, "he could there do no mighty work, save that he laid his hands upon a few sick folk, and healed them. And he marveled because of their unbelief."

24. And he said, Verily I say unto you, No prophet is accepted in his own country.

Jesus recognizes that "familiarity breeds contempt." There is an arrogance among the residents of Nazareth that says, "Who does this man think he is?" They are convinced that they are just as good as Jesus and are not willing to accept the claims that He is making. [See question #4, page 422.]

A teacher may have no difficulties being accepted by others, but may not be respected by his or her own family members. A preacher who establishes a reputation for credibility and wisdom in congregations far from home may not be accepted in the same way back in his home church. There is a great truth contained in this simple proverb: sometimes you have to get away from the hometown folks to be *accepted*. It is certainly true in Jesus' case!

B. Crowd Wants Murder (vv. 28-30)

28. And all they in the synagogue, when they heard these things, were filled with wrath.

In verses 25-27 (not in today's text), Jesus gives illustrations of God's dealings with Gentiles *vs.*

His dealings with His chosen people, the Jews. Jesus mentions how Elijah went to the widow from Zarephath (and not to the people of Israel) to make sure she had provisions during the years of famine. He also mentions how it was Naaman the Syrian whom Elisha provided healing from leprosy, and not the many lepers that were in Israel. This enrages those in the synagogue.

How quickly they go from being fascinated by what Jesus is teaching into a murderous rage against Him! Jesus has seen through their unbelief and will not perform a miracle for them. He has rightly said that a prophet is not honored among his own people. The illustrations from the miraculous work of Elijah and Elisha demonstrate that fact. God works where there is faith!

There is nothing that requires God to work among people who reject Him. The apostle John tells us that "he came unto his own, and his own received him not. But as many as received him, to them gave he power to become the sons of God, even to them that believe on his name" (John 1:11, 12).

29. And rose up, and thrust him out of the city, and led him unto the brow of the hill whereon their city was built, that they might cast him down headlong.

The public ministry of Jesus is barely several months old and already people are trying to kill Him—people in His hometown! Some today mistakenly think that the only time anyone ever tried to kill Jesus was when He was crucified. Yet Jesus experienced opposition and murderous intent from the beginning of His ministry. In John 5:18 we read of the Jews seeking to kill Him because He not only healed on the Sabbath but He also called God His Father, making Himself equal to God. In John 8:59 we see the crowds picking up stones to throw at Jesus because of what He was teaching.

Opposition is not a rare thing for Christ. He knows from the very beginning of His ministry that there will be those who will reject Him and seek to kill Him. He also knows that He will rise from the dead when they do kill Him! (See John 2:19-22.)

The actions of the residents of Nazareth show how far from faith they are. They want to throw Him off a cliff! They aren't interested in discussing, learning, or asking questions. Perhaps they want to be amazed or entertained apart from coming to faith in Him as the Savior of the world. The purpose of miracles is to confirm the message and the messenger as being from God. Miracles are not used as entertainment or conversation starters. They have an intended purpose in their day. See John 14:11.

30. But he, passing through the midst of them, went his way.

Is it with a piercing look that Jesus stops the crowd from carrying out their intent? Does He wave His hand and the crowds part so He can leave them on that hill? We are not told. The point is not *how* Jesus escaped and went about His business, but rather that He can just walk away—one man against a mob! Jesus is in control of His ministry and His timetable from the beginning. Others will not exert their will over Him. He has goals in mind to accomplish and will not allow anything to keep Him from doing what He intends. The same is true of Jesus today! [See question #5, page 422.]

Conclusion

A. Rejected by His Own

Jesus did not reject the people of Nazareth; they rejected him. He was in their midst, and they "drove him out." We must realize that the same thing can happen today. We can choose either to accept His good news and carry it to others or to reject Him and leave Him no place in our hearts and lives. What's *your* choice?

B. Prayer

Father, it's easy for us to criticize the people of Nazareth until we pause to think how much we have been like them at times. Jesus is in our midst today, but how often we treat Him casually or with contempt by our thoughts and actions. Deliver us ever more closely into the arms of Christ this day! In Jesus' name, amen.

C. Thought to Remember

"He that believeth not the Son shall not see life" (John 3:36).

Home Daily Bible Readings

Monday, Aug. 1—The Year of the Lord's Favor (Leviticus 25:8-12)

Tuesday, Aug. 2—Elijah Revives the Widow's Son (1 Kings 17:17-24)

Wednesday, Aug. 3—Jesus Is Rejected in Nazareth (Matthew 13:54-58)

Thursday, Aug. 4—Jesus Teaches in His Hometown (Mark 6:1-6)

Friday, Aug. 5—Jesus Reads Isaiah's Words (Luke 4:14-19)

Saturday, Aug. 6—Today This Scripture Has Been Fulfilled (Luke 4:20-24)

Sunday, Aug. 7—All in the Synagogue Were Enraged (Luke 4:25-30)

Learning by Doing

This page contains an alternative lesson plan emphasizing learning activities.
Classes desiring such student involvement will find these suggestions helpful.

Learning Goals

After participating in this lesson, each student will be able to:

1. Explain how Jesus described His call to ministry as fulfillment of prophecy.

2. Recognize contemporary ministries that continue Jesus' ministry of compassion.

3. Become an active participant in Jesus' continuing ministry.

Into the Lesson

Begin the lesson by asking your learners to consider the motivations people have. Say, "If we did a survey of your neighbors, coworkers, and family members, what would they say is the purpose of their life?" Another way to ask this is, "What is the primary motivation for the things that people do?"

You probably will get answers about pleasure, family life, accumulating wealth, preparing for retirement (and freedom), etc. Write answers on the chalkboard as they are suggested.

After a few minutes, point out that a person's behavior often contradicts what is said about the main purpose for living. Discuss this question: "How can you tell what really motivates a person?" *(Answers might include how people spend their time, the ways they spend their money, and the things that entertain and excite them.)*

Next, ask class members to consider what would happen if they evaluated their own lives the same way. Ask, "Considering the categories of time, treasure, and pleasure, what is the primary motivating force or agenda for your life?" Point out that today's lesson features Jesus teaching a group of people who would express their agenda for life in religious terms, possibly a lot like the members of your class. They were in attendance at the synagogue when Jesus was teaching, and they highly valued their Jewish heritage and beliefs.

Next say, "As you consider today's lesson text, it will be evident that the agenda of Jesus was very different from that of those who were listening to Him teach. This difference will raise the following critical questions: What is the agenda of Jesus? What is the agenda for your life? What would have to change for you to align your agenda with Jesus' agenda? Are you willing to put aside your agenda and commit yourself to following Jesus and His agenda for life?" (It will be helpful to write these questions on the board as you present them.)

Into the Word

Before class begins, select an empty chair in the front row and "mark it off" so nobody sits there. After discussing the questions in the "Into the Lesson" segment, pass out small slips of blank paper and ask your learners to write the name of a respected member of your church or community.

Next, collect the papers and read aloud the names that are written. Select one of the names and place the paper on the empty chair. Say, "As I read the following text, pretend that this person is sitting in this chair and will be teaching class." Then read Luke 4:14-21 aloud. Ask the class what would happen if the person you selected made the claim that Jesus did. Remind the class that Jesus claimed to be the fulfillment of ancient promises from God. Ask, "How would knowing the person well affect the way you would respond to that claim? What would make the claims of Jesus different?" *(Ability to support the claim by being able to perform miracles.)* Also ask, "What does the passage say about Jesus' agenda for His life?" *(Emphasis on fulfilling the commission of the Father, with a repeated focus on ministry to others with great need.)*

Now read aloud Jesus' response in Luke 4:23-27. Ask, "What is the significance of the Old Testament stories that Jesus included?" *(They were examples of God's message and miracles being received by Gentiles but not by Jews.)* "Why would this anger Jesus' audience?" *(Jesus confronted them with a history of rejecting God's message while claiming to be His people.)*

Read the rest of the story in Luke 4:28-30. Discuss other times Jesus faced opposition, as noted in the verse-by-verse commentary.

Into Life

Review the ideas shared during the beginning of the lesson. Ask, "How would the personal agendas of people have to change if the teaching of Jesus were to be accepted and followed?" Challenge class members to daily consider the agenda that is being demonstrated by their time, treasures, and pleasures in the week ahead. Consider steps that could be taken to commit themselves to the agenda of Jesus.

Let's Talk It Over

The questions on this page are designed to promote discussion of the lesson by the class and to encourage application of the lesson Scriptures. The answers provided are only discussion starters. Let your class talk it over from there.

1. What excuses do people give today for not being faithful in attendance when the church meets together? How does Jesus' example challenge these excuses?

Some say, "It's just the same old thing—there's never anything new." While we do not want our worship services to become boring or routine, this is no excuse. What "new" thing would Jesus have heard in the synagogue? He was the author of Scripture; could any rabbi teach Him something He didn't already know?

Others say, "I just don't get anything out of the services," or, "I don't think the worship service has the right feel to it—it's too loud [or quiet or something else]. It's just not like what I'm used to." Again, what could Jesus "get out of" a worship service? Surely He was there to *contribute* in worship much more than He would receive. And after He had been in Heaven, where God is worshiped perfectly, how could any earthly worship service measure up to what He was used to?

2. Consider each aspect of what Isaiah said was the mission of the Messiah—and thus of His church. How are we doing in each area? Suggest some ministry we are involved in or could be involved in to fulfill each aspect.

There are six aspects: (1) Preach the gospel [the good news] to the poor; (2) heal the broken-hearted; (3) preach deliverance to the captives; (4) provide recovery of sight to the blind; (5) set at liberty those who were bruised; and (6) preach the acceptable year of the Lord. Each congregation will be involved in its own unique ministries, and the more creative among your students may come up with some innovative ideas for expanding these ministries.

Of course, many of these areas have spiritual as well as physical dimensions: the "blind" and "bruised" may be perfectly healthy from a physical standpoint, but be blind to the truth or beaten up by stress and turmoil. How can the church minister to these?

3. The people of Nazareth could not accept Jesus as anyone more than an ordinary human —"Joseph's son," as they put it. Many today have the same problem. How can we convince skeptical people that Jesus is more than an ordinary human, that He is the Son of God?

If your learners are slow to respond, you could try a similar question: "What convinced you that Jesus is more than an ordinary human?" What has convinced us will also be convincing to others. It may be the impact Jesus' life has had on the world that is convincing to some. The disciples' timidity turned to unflinching boldness. The calendar itself measures time from the days of Jesus. Fulfilled prophecy is another convincing reason for many.

Of course, the resurrection remains the linchpin of any convincing argument for the identity of Jesus. The empty tomb, the failure of Jesus' enemies to disprove the resurrection, the willingness of the disciples to die for their testimony, and other proofs still testify loud and clear of the resurrection of Christ. Only the Son of God could have done that!

4. The people of Nazareth were prevented from accepting Jesus by their own pride. What obstacles prevent people from accepting Jesus today? How can we overcome these obstacles?

Pride, of course, remains an obstacle for many. Admitting they are sinners in need of a Savior is more than some people can muster. Others are prevented from accepting Jesus because they have been deceived. Scientific or some other evidence has been misinterpreted to lead people to believe the Biblical accounts of the origin of the universe and of life are false—blocking them from accepting anything else the Bible has to say. The more clearly we can demonstrate that the facts of science do not contradict Scripture (it is the *interpretation* of those facts by some scientists that is at odds), the better equipped we will be to help such people.

5. The people were angry with Jesus, to the point of violence. Jesus responded by simply walking away. What makes it so hard to remain calm and walk away from a hostile environment?

Discussions here can move easily from issues to personalities. When we are personally attacked, we react with a "fight or flight" response. Adrenaline flows into our blood and emotions become unstable. It takes determination and self-control to keep our emotions in check. A brief prayer can bring the calmness of the Holy Spirit.

Healing the Incurable

August 14
Lesson 11

DEVOTIONAL READING: Matthew 9:18-26.

BACKGROUND SCRIPTURE: Luke 8:40-56.

PRINTED TEXT: Luke 8:40-56.

Luke 8:40-56

40 And it came to pass, that, when Jesus was returned, the people gladly received him: for they were all waiting for him.

41 And, behold, there came a man named Jairus, and he was a ruler of the synagogue; and he fell down at Jesus' feet, and besought him that he would come into his house:

42 For he had one only daughter, about twelve years of age, and she lay a dying. But as he went the people thronged him.

43 And a woman having an issue of blood twelve years, which had spent all her living upon physicians, neither could be healed of any,

44 Came behind him, and touched the border of his garment: and immediately her issue of blood stanched.

45 And Jesus said, Who touched me? When all denied, Peter and they that were with him said, Master, the multitude throng thee and press thee, and sayest thou, Who touched me?

46 And Jesus said, Somebody hath touched me: for I perceive that virtue is gone out of me.

47 And when the woman saw that she was not hid, she came trembling, and falling down before him, she declared unto him before all the people for what cause she had touched him, and how she was healed immediately.

48 And he said unto her, Daughter, be of good comfort: thy faith hath made thee whole; go in peace.

49 While he yet spake, there cometh one from the ruler of the synagogue's house, saying to him, Thy daughter is dead; trouble not the Master.

50 But when Jesus heard it, he answered him, saying, Fear not: believe only, and she shall be made whole.

51 And when he came into the house, he suffered no man to go in, save Peter, and James, and John, and the father and the mother of the maiden.

52 And all wept, and bewailed her: but he said, Weep not; she is not dead, but sleepeth.

53 And they laughed him to scorn, knowing that she was dead.

54 And he put them all out, and took her by the hand, and called, saying, Maid, arise.

55 And her spirit came again, and she arose straightway: and he commanded to give her meat.

56 And her parents were astonished: but he charged them that they should tell no man what was done.

Aug 14

GOLDEN TEXT: He said unto her, Daughter, be of good comfort: thy faith hath made thee whole; go in peace.—Luke 8:48.

Learning Aims

After participating in this lesson, each student will be able to:

1. Explain the role of faith in the miracles performed by Jesus in the accounts of the hemorrhaging woman and Jairus's daughter.

2. Identify situations in his or her life that call for healing and wholeness.

3. Demonstrate faith in Jesus Christ when facing those situations.

Lesson Outline

INTRODUCTION
    A. See the Specialist
    B. Lesson Background
 I. FATHER'S URGENT REQUEST (Luke 8:40-42)
    A. Jesus' Return (v. 40)
    B. Jairus's Request (v. 41)
      A Humble Hero
    C. Jairus's Dilemma (v.42)
II. WOMAN'S URGENT NEED (Luke 8:43-48)
    A. Weakened by Illness (v. 43)
    B. Emboldened by Desperation (v. 44)
    C. Discovered by Inquiry (vv. 45-47)
    D. Healed by Faith (v. 48)
      Too High a Price
III. JESUS' TIMELY RESPONSES (Luke 8:49-56)
    A. Sad News (v. 49)
    B. Encouraging Words (v. 50)
    C. Astonishing Miracle (vv. 51-56)
CONCLUSION
    A. Amazing!
    B. Prayer
    C. Thought to Remember

Introduction

A. See the Specialist

Have you ever had to see a specialist? You went to see your regular physician, and, for whatever reason, he or she sent you on to a specialist—someone better trained or with more experience for your situation. When the need is critical, you want the very best help.

Jesus is the ultimate specialist! He specializes in the critical needs of the body and of the soul. As one needs confidence in a physician's knowledge and skills to treat our needs, so our text challenges us to put our faith in Christ, even in the darkest hours. When no one else can help, Jesus still can!

B. Lesson Background

Today's lesson finds Jesus late in the second year of His public ministry. His popularity is very high. Before we reach the point of today's lesson, we notice that crowds seek Him relentlessly (Luke 8:4, 19). But opposition presents itself as well (Luke 8:37). And yet as Jesus deals with both enthusiastic and hostile crowds, He never loses sight of the individual. That's how we see Jesus in today's lesson—taking time to minister to individuals as crowds swirl about. Matthew 9:18-26 and Mark 5:21-34 offer us parallel accounts.

I. Father's Urgent Request
(Luke 8:40-42)

A. Jesus' Return (v. 40)

40. And it came to pass, that, when Jesus was returned, the people gladly received him: for they were all waiting for him.

Jesus has just *returned* from the region of the Gadarenes (or Gerasenes) where He had cast out the legion of demons from the man who was living in the tombs. This region (on the eastern side of the Sea of Galilee) has more of a Gentile population than Galilee or Judea. Jesus' occasional trips to these largely Gentile areas demonstrate that His ministry is for all people, even as the gospel is the power of God to everyone who believes—both Jew and Greek (Romans 1:16).

This is a time in Christ's ministry when the crowds make it difficult for Jesus to have any solitary moments or time He can spend solely with the Twelve preparing them for future ministry. Wherever Jesus goes, there seems to be a crowd pressing against Him for an opportunity to hear Him speak or to receive a miracle. Now that Jesus is back in Galilee, the crowds again swarm around Him. They are glad to have Him back.

B. Jairus's Request (v. 41)

41. And, behold, there came a man named Jairus, and he was a ruler of the synagogue; and he fell down at Jesus' feet, and besought him that he would come into his house.

Not only is the average citizen excited to have Jesus back in Capernaum, Jesus' arrival also catches the notice of *Jairus*. As *a ruler of the synagogue*, he oversees the day-to-day operations of all that happens there. He is an important official. It is unusual for someone of prominence to come and fall at another's *feet* in Jesus' day. It is more typical for someone to come and bow.

Even the idea of bowing would itself suggest an attitude of humility in the presence of someone greater than you. This is the heart of submission. No one is immune from great personal needs. As important as Jairus may be in the eyes of the community—or even his own eyes—he still recognizes that he has a need that he is unable to meet on his own. So he humbly comes before Jesus, pleading with Him to *come into his house.* [See question #1, page 430.]

A HUMBLE HERO

John Bradley was a funeral director from Appleton, Wisconsin. His children knew he had done something special in World War II, but Bradley would not speak of the event that made him famous. He was nearing the end of his life when he finally consented to tell his son James about the events of February 23, 1945.

Bradley was a Navy medical corpsman at the battle on Iwo Jima. He was on Mount Suribachi when a flag was to be raised to signal the capture of the highest point on the island. Joe Rosenthal photographed Bradley and several others hoisting Old Glory. That photograph became one of the most famous in American history. When John Bradley came home, people wanted to make him a hero. He refused, thinking instead of the nearly seven thousand Americans who died on Iwo Jima. He said, "The real heroes of Iwo Jima are the guys who didn't come back." Such humility!

Jairus was a man of credentials as well. He was a synagogue ruler, but he humbled himself to come to Jesus and ask for help. Humility—once considered a foundation of character—is now often seen as a sign of weakness. But Jairus had a desperate need. He also had a proper attitude. We, too, have desperate needs. Do we have the proper attitude? If pride is your problem, remember the cross. The Son of God—the King of Heaven—humbled Himself to bear our sins. How can your pride remain?   —T. A. C.

C. Jairus's Dilemma (v. 42)

42. For he had one only daughter, about twelve years of age, and she lay a dying. But as he went the people thronged him.

What motivates Jairus's urgent request of Jesus is now apparent: his *only daughter,* perhaps his only child, is sick and is becoming steadily worse. Any loving father will do whatever he can to save the life of his little girl, and one can almost see Jairus pushing his way through the crowds that are pressing in on Jesus. When the need is most urgent, you will go to extreme measures to have that need met (compare Luke 5:19). It is apparently not easy for him to get close to Christ. Muscling and elbowing his way through

the crowd undoubtedly draws dirty looks. But Jairus is focused. He does not stop until he has the Lord's attention and can make his plea on his daughter's behalf. [See question #2, page 430.]

II. Woman's Urgent Need (Luke 8:43-48)

A. Weakened by Illness (v. 43)

43. And a woman having an issue of blood twelve years, which had spent all her living upon physicians, neither could be healed of any.

The story now becomes more complex. While on His way to perform one miracle, the Lord is "interrupted" and performs another. Picture Jairus and Jesus leading this mass of humanity through narrow, rough streets. Unbeknownst to everyone else, a woman with a great need also is seeking out Jesus.

An issue of blood is what we would call "hemorrhaging." This is likely a condition associated with gynecological problems. This situation is difficult enough as a permanent physical ailment, but there is another ramification: this woman is ceremonially unclean. Leviticus 15:19-33 gives regulations concerning a woman's monthly cycle. A woman is considered "unclean" for as long as she continues to bleed. During this time she is to be excluded from religious activities, and those whom she touches are unclean as well. (See Numbers 19:22.)

It is an interesting coincidence that Jesus is on His way to help a sick twelve-year-old girl. Now this woman, who has been ill in her own right for *twelve years,* desires to *be healed* as well. Luke, a physician himself according to Colossians 4:14, tells us that she has spent all her money on *physicians.* Mark adds something to our understanding when he says, "And had suffered many things of many physicians, and had spent all that she had, and was nothing bettered, but rather grew worse" (Mark 5:26). We may

---

How to Say It

COLOSSIANS. Kuh-*losh*-unz.

CORINTHIANS. Ko-*rin*-thee-unz (*th* as in *thin*).

GADARENES. *Gad*-uh-reens.

GALILEE. *Gal*-uh-lee.

GENTILES. *Jen*-tiles.

GERASENES. *Gur*-uh-seenz.

JAIRUS. *Jye*-rus or *Jay*-ih-rus.

JUDEA. Joo-*dee*-uh.

LAZARUS. *Laz*-uh-rus.

THESSALONIANS. *Thess*-uh-*lo*-nee-unz (strong accent on *lo;* *th* as in *thin*).

smile as we wonder why Luke the physician leaves that part out!

B. Emboldened by Desperation (v. 44)

44. Came behind him, and touched the border of his garment: and immediately her issue of blood stanched.

Imagine jostling against dozens of people who surround the person you wish to meet. There is the roar of the crowd, a crowd impelled by its own desire to press ever closer to hear and see what the person at the center of attention may say. A woman weakened by sickness will have great difficulty managing to get through all of those people in order to have her need met.

Yet, somehow, perhaps finding the right angle to get her arm out far enough, she manages to touch the hem of Jesus' *garment.* When she does, a miracle takes place!

Another word for *stanched* is *stopped.* So often with sicknesses there is a recovery period from the time the diagnosis is made to the time a procedure is performed or medications are given. It takes time for the desired results to occur. Such is not the case here. The supernatural results are instant, perfect, and complete.

She is now free from her disease. She is no longer under a cloud of being unclean, where she will have to be excluded from participation in religious services and even careful about who or what she touches. These are the results she has desperately hoped for, and her faith is what set Jesus' healing power in motion.

C. Discovered by Inquiry (vv. 45-47)

45. And Jesus said, Who touched me? When all denied, Peter and they that were with him said, Master, the multitude throng thee and press thee, and sayest thou, Who touched me?

Is *Jesus* aware of what is going on around Him? Does He have power over the ability to heal and to withhold healing? Or is He a source of power that anyone can just "plug in to"?

One thing is sure: He certainly knows that power has gone out from Him. So He stops and asks the question, *Who touched me?* Typically, it is *Peter* who has something to say when no one steps forward. Peter in effect says, "Lord, are you serious? You see all these people pressing around you and yet you ask *who touched* you? How can you even ask such a question?" [See question #3, page 430.]

At first glance, it does seem like a foolish question. Yet Jesus seems determined to have His question answered. The phrase *When all denied* seems to imply that even the woman who received healing said at first, "Not me!" or at least she tried to be inconspicuous.

46. And Jesus said, Somebody hath touched me: for I perceive that virtue is gone out of me.

Jesus responds to Peter and others who are listening that the touch is not some inadvertent, casual, or accidental contact. Something happened when the hem of Jesus' garment was *touched.* Jesus knows that *virtue* (or power) has *gone out of* Him. Jesus is indicating that He knows someone had a distinct purpose for touching Him. He wants that person to speak up. The reason why will be clear in the next two verses.

47. And when the woman saw that she was not hid, she came trembling, and falling down before him, she declared unto him before all the people for what cause she had touched him, and how she was healed immediately.

The joy this *woman* felt at her instant, miraculous healing is now changed to fear. She had sought to obtain this benefit from Christ without any notice—now she is caught! Perhaps she makes her admission as Jesus' piercing yet gentle eyes go from person to person, finally landing on her. Jesus' purpose is not to humiliate her or to retract the healing. Rather, it is to allow her the high privilege of offering a testimony of faith to the crowd of people who press in.

Are you able to picture her now choking back the tears as she recalls to Jesus and to others who are listening the story of her suffering? No doubt this touches even the most callous of hearts who hear her desperate story. She describes how she had come to believe that Jesus was her last hope. Perhaps her tears from fear of discovery turn to tears of joy as she is able to say with confidence that her body is whole and healthy again, and that it is Jesus who has provided this blessing to her. The crowds hear her testify that for twelve long, difficult years she has suffered; but with one touch of Jesus' garment the suffering has come to an end. Her body is free from the sickness, and her heart is made glad again.

D. Healed by Faith (v. 48)

48. And he said unto her, Daughter, be of good comfort: thy faith hath made thee whole; go in peace.

Before the woman touched the hem of Jesus' garment, He was on His way to attend to Jairus's daughter. Now having heard this woman's testimony of faith, He sends her home and uses the word *daughter* as a term of endearment for her. No doubt this woman is a child of God, who has put her complete faith and trust in God as the only One who can lift her physical agony and spiritual separation.

Imagine the joy she experiences after twelve long years of misery—to finally have peace. Only Jesus could have provided that for her. And Jesus credits the woman's faith. The Bible teaches that without faith it is impossible to please God (Hebrews 11:6). The woman has faith, and she confesses it to others as well. [See question #4, page 430.]

TOO HIGH A PRICE

Two old prospectors wandered the desert for many years, searching for a silver mine. They had spent a long time in the desert, and their attitude toward matters of life and death was rather casual. That changed one afternoon when one of the prospectors disturbed a rattlesnake. He would not show any fear in the presence of his friend, so he cavalierly said he could kiss the rattler before the snake could strike. He bent forward to plant his lips on the snake and was promptly bitten. The "kiss" had been successful! The snake's fangs struck both his upper and lower lips.

The prospector panicked and sent his friend to the nearest town to get a doctor. The other prospector found the doctor, but he could not accompany the prospector back into the desert. He told him he could save his friend's life by using his own lips to suck the poison out of the wounds. As the friend rode back, he thought about what he would have to do to save his friend's life. When he finally arrived back at his friend's side, the natural question was, "What did the doc say?" The old prospector took off his hat and somberly answered, "He said you're gonna die!"

What a corny story! But it has a point: Are there times when we consider "the price of healing" to be too high? We are God's representatives in the world. We are, in the words of a missionary doctor, God's hands to heal. You may not be a physician, but you are God's messenger of healing to a world that has been poisoned and is dying. And the great physician still makes house calls! —T. A. C.

III. Jesus' Timely Responses (Luke 8:49-56)

A. Sad News (v. 49)

49. While he yet spake, there cometh one from the ruler of the synagogue's house, saying to him, Thy daughter is dead; trouble not the Master.

From the joy of the woman who was healed comes now the devastating news that the little girl has died. What further need is there for Jesus to come? This messenger thinks that all hope is gone and that preparations now need to be made for the funeral and burial. The great excitement and joy of the crowd must turn to silence as the

Visual for lessons 2 and 11. *Display this poster again to review the quarter and to tie in today's lesson with the overall theme.*

news spreads about the death of this young girl. Jairus is no doubt devastated by the announcement. Perhaps there is even some anger about the delay of Jesus caused by this woman (compare John 11:21). Jairus now probably believes he will never again see his *daughter* alive.

B. Encouraging Words (v. 50)

50. But when Jesus heard it, he answered him, saying, Fear not: believe only, and she shall be made whole.

Jesus' response may seem somewhat mysterious. Just moments before, a woman confessed her faith to Jesus after having been *made whole* herself. But that woman is still alive, and Jairus's daughter lies dead. How can there be any hope? The healing of the woman's issue of blood after twelve years of suffering should be reason to believe that Jesus can do something about the death of Jairus's daughter.

The faith that saved the woman is the type of faith that Jairus now needs. [See question #5, page 430.] When Lazarus dies a bit later, Jesus will tell Martha that her brother will rise again (John 11:23). Martha will state her faith that she expects Lazarus to rise on the last day. Before He raises Lazarus, Jesus will respond, "I am the resurrection, and the life: he that believeth in me, though he were dead, yet shall he live" (John 11:25).

C. Astonishing Miracle (vv. 51-56)

51. And when he came into the house, he suffered no man to go in, save Peter, and James, and John, and the father and the mother of the maiden.

Jesus has twelve apostles, but on several occasions He allows only three of them to witness something special. These three apostles—*Peter, and James, and John*—have been called "the inner circle." They are now the only apostles allowed to see the raising of Jairus's daughter. They are the only apostles allowed to see the transfiguration. And while eight of the apostles are left near the gate of the Garden of Gethsemane, Peter, James, and John are the ones Jesus takes a bit farther into the garden before He falls in sorrowful prayer (Matthew 26:36).

52, 53. And all wept, and bewailed her: but he said, Weep not; she is not dead, but sleepeth. And they laughed him to scorn, knowing that she was dead.

When Jesus and His inner circle arrive at the home of Jairus, the place is already filled with mourners (Matthew 9:23; Mark 5:38). While it certainly isn't unusual for there to be mourning at the passing of a loved one, what makes this unusual to us is that in the first century some are paid to mourn! To have people making a loud commotion at her passing shows just how loved the deceased person is. What demonstrates that the "carrying on" of these people is something less than sincere is the fact that they so quickly go from wailing to laughing when Jesus says the child is asleep. They know a lifeless body when they see one. Yet Jesus indicates that this condition is a temporary one, something these mourners cannot yet comprehend.

Jesus introduces the word *sleep* for physical death. And it is appropriate. As one expects the body to awaken from a nap or a night of sleep, so, too, may a believer expect his or her body to rise to renewed life after physical death. God is able to restore life to the body again. Death will not have the last word; it is a temporary situation that God will reverse. Jesus uses the term *sleep* at the death of Lazarus in John 11:1-14. Paul uses the

term in 1 Corinthians 15:51 as well as 1 Thessalonians 4:13.

54, 55. And he put them all out, and took her by the hand, and called, saying, Maid, arise. And her spirit came again, and she arose straightway: and he commanded to give her meat.

Jesus does not take the time to explain His figurative meaning of sleep for physical death to those mourners. Rather, He just sends *them all out!* Seven people including the daughter are in the room when Jesus calls her back to life (Mark 5:40). The God who created all life in the first place is more than able to restore life. Jesus calls the child's spirit back into her body and she revives.

56. And her parents were astonished: but he charged them that they should tell no man what was done.

The *astonished* reaction of *her parents* is certainly understandable. They, too, know that she was dead, but now can see that she is full of life. Shocked and stunned would certainly be apt ways of describing them. Yet Jesus makes a surprising command of them: *tell no man!*

How can they hide the fact that their daughter who was dead is now very much alive? Are they able to keep her locked in her room? Obviously the Lord would not command such a thing. But He is telling them not to broadcast the news to everyone they meet, as hard as that will be. Their natural inclination is to tell everyone. The Lord does not come primarily to heal the sick and raise the dead. Rather, He comes to seek and save the lost. That's where He wants attention given to His ministry.

Conclusion

A. Amazing!

Jesus is truly amazing. He taught with great authority. He commanded demons and they obeyed. He healed the sick and raised the dead. With God all things are possible!

But Jesus is more than a great teacher, an authority over demons, and a healer of physical disease. Jesus is the One who voluntarily leaves His throne of glory to walk among sinners and die at their hands. His death pays the price for our sins. His resurrection proves, once again, who He really is. Now *that's* amazing!

B. Prayer

Father, may we never cease to be amazed at the One who died for our sins. Help us to share our amazement with others. In Jesus' name, amen.

C. Thought to Remember

Seek spiritual healing above all else.

Home Daily Bible Readings

Monday, Aug. 8—A Centurion's Servant Is Healed (Luke 7:1-10)

Tuesday, Aug. 9—A Girl Restored, A Woman Healed (Matthew 9:18-26)

Wednesday, Aug. 10—Two Blind Men Healed by Faith (Matthew 9:27-31)

Thursday, Aug. 11—A Hemorrhaging Woman Is Healed (Mark 5:24b-34)

Friday, Aug. 12—A Girl Is Restored to Life (Mark 5:35-43)

Saturday, Aug. 13—A Sick Woman Is Healed (Luke 8:40-48)

Sunday, Aug. 14—Jairus's Daughter Is Alive (Luke 8:49-56)

Learning by Doing

This page contains an alternative lesson plan emphasizing learning activities.
Classes desiring such student involvement will find these suggestions helpful.

Learning Goals

After participating in this lesson, each student will be able to:

1. Explain the role of faith in the miracles performed by Jesus in the accounts of the hemorrhaging woman and Jairus's daughter.

2. Identify situations in his or her life that call for healing and wholeness.

3. Demonstrate faith in Jesus Christ when facing those situations.

Into the Lesson

Bring to class several headlines (current or historical) of famous people who have faced great difficulties in life. The difficulties should be ones that were not a result of their actions (criminal charges, etc.). Rather, they should be ones that they are powerless to change on their own (illness, etc.). The people you select could include politicians, entertainers, or religious leaders. Also bring articles describing the stories of "ordinary" people facing similar situations (these are people who are not famous, or are famous only because of their tragedy).

As you mention several of these situations to the class, note how tragedy comes to everyone, regardless of social class, wealth, or fame. Social status, wealth, fame, etc. often cannot "solve" a crisis. Say, "In today's lesson we will see two people facing terrible situations that they were powerless to overcome. We will see their responses and watch what happened when they had an encounter with Jesus."

Into the Word

Next, say, "As you consider this story, watch closely for three things: the setting, the response of the powerless, and the result."

The Setting. Read Luke 8:40-56 aloud. Ask class members to compare and contrast Jairus with the sick woman. You can let them work with a partner to make lists of similarities and differences. *(Differences may include: male/female; upper-class socially/unclean outcast from society; influential position in society/ordinary person; loved one was sick/facing illness personally. A similarity would be that both faced situations over which they were entirely powerless.)*

Read aloud the portions of the passage that demonstrate that these people were really sick or deceased *(eyewitnesses, the doctors who tried to*

heal the woman, the mourners who mocked Jesus when He said the girl wasn't dead, etc.). Remind them of the conclusions from the "Into the Lesson" section: situations over which everyone is powerless do not differentiate based on issues such as social class or wealth.

The Responses of the Powerless. Say, "Look again at the passage and focus on the faith responses of Jairus and the woman. What were those responses?" *(The woman responded in faith with humility as she silently touched Jesus' robe, then fell at His feet; Jairus demonstrated faith with humility in coming publicly to Jesus and asking for help, thus opening himself up to ridicule from the religious leaders who opposed Jesus.)*

The Result. Say, "Look closely at the descriptions of the woman's healing. Luke, a doctor himself, describes these events in ways that leave no doubt that it was truly a miracle performed by Jesus. The little girl came back to life in front of her own parents."

Into Life

Make a transition to application by saying, "Today's passage clearly demonstrates the power of God over disease and even death. But Jesus commanded the parents not to tell anyone what had happened. Why would Jesus do this?" *(He demonstrates that the ultimate focus is not on the healing, but on the way it confirms the person and message of Jesus).*

Continue by noting that, "Although the lesson clearly demonstrates the power of God over disease and death, Paul describes a personal situation where God chose not to heal, to allow a greater purpose to be accomplished through suffering (see 2 Corinthians 12:7-10). Physical death is a temporary situation that will be reversed someday by God. This should provide great hope for those who believe in Jesus Christ, providing comfort and encouragement, as well as a challenge to live life with eternity in view."

Ask class members to estimate how often they pray for spiritual healing in comparison with prayers for physical healing. The answer may be surprising! Allow time for them to pray for those who are facing difficult situations. Encourage prayers for the ability to trust God. Challenge class members to offer at least one prayer for spiritual issues for every prayer that involves physical needs.

Let's Talk It Over

The questions on this page are designed to promote discussion of the lesson by the class and to encourage application of the lesson Scriptures. The answers provided are only discussion starters. Let your class talk it over from there.

1. How can we help people recognize that Jesus is the answer to their deepest need?

Spiritual need is not easily discerned by the carnal mind. Usually something has to happen to make the person question his or her belief system. Perhaps it is a personal or family health crisis, as in Jairus's case. Perhaps it is a financial issue or a loss of a friend or family member.

Many people face crises, however, and never turn to the Lord. They need someone to show the way. That is the reason it is critical that believers establish relationships with their unbelieving neighbors and associates. When one of these unbelievers finds that he or she is ill-equipped to handle a crisis, it is the caring attitude of the believer, in addition to his or her faith, that can lead the unbeliever to seek the truth.

2. We imagine Jairus abandoning social etiquette as he pushes his way through the crowd to Jesus. For what would you abandon social etiquette or risk upsetting people? Why do we not demonstrate greater boldness in rescuing people from eternal damnation?

For Jairus, a life was at stake—his daughter's life. Most of us would risk virtually any opposition to rescue the life of a loved one. Certainly we would not be thwarted by a little social ire in such a case. Point out the irony that we don't care what people think or say about us when a loved one's life or health is at stake, but we are afraid to rescue a soul because we don't want people to think we are fanatics or something of the sort. What makes the difference? Could it be we do not love the potential rescued soul as much as we love the security of our reputations?

3. Peter thought the Lord's question was beyond belief—how could Jesus ask, "Who touched me?" in that throng of people? When have you felt the Lord's requirements were "beyond belief"? How do you come to terms with it and accept it in faith and submission even when it does not seem rational?

How about the command to love your enemies? How does one do that? Perhaps students can tell of times they have prayed for someone who might be called an enemy, or of times they went out of their way to be helpful to someone who had been antagonistic.

Related to that, what does it mean to turn the other cheek? How does a person accept abuse or hostility without fighting back? Can a person put the interests of others ahead of his or her own sense of dignity in order to suffer such indignities? Remembering how Jesus faced His trials and crucifixion without fighting back will help.

4. Jesus described the woman's new condition as *whole*. She was not just *healed* and merely *well*—she was *whole*, complete. Her faith had ministered to both her spiritual and physical conditions. To what extent do our ministries lead people to wholeness? How can we improve?

People are very complex, consisting of physical, mental, spiritual, and social components. To be whole is to be healthy in each area. Some are mentally sound but socially stunted. Some are physically fit but spiritually sick. In some way the church is meant to minister to all of these. The fellowship of the believers adds a social dimension that some fail to appreciate. Conversely, some see the social benefit but fail to take advantage of the greater spiritual blessings available.

Some churches focus on spiritual needs, especially the need to accept Christ, but they do not minister to physical needs. At the other end of the spectrum are churches that do a great deal of good on the social level but have abandoned the disciple-making mission of the church. Tying all these together to minister to people's needs at every level is imperative.

5. Jairus's worst fears had come to pass. But Jesus challenged him to rise above his fear on the wings of faith. How do we "fear not" but "believe only" when we face distressing circumstances? Tell of a time when your faith carried you above your fear in a difficult situation.

Faith is the ability to see the unseen (see Hebrews 11:1). We build our faith in the quiet times, when we are not being tested. We see the evidence of Scripture and the evidence in the lives of faithful people around us, and our faith grows. If we wait until we are in a difficult situation to try to "fear not: believe only," we will surely fail. We must equip ourselves in advance.

If we have done that, then we can be part of God's plan to develop faith in others. Our stories will help them.

Being a Good Neighbor

August 21
Lesson 12

DEVOTIONAL READING: Matthew 22:34-40.

BACKGROUND SCRIPTURE: Luke 10:25-37.

PRINTED TEXT: Luke 10:25-37.

Luke 10:25-37

25 And, behold, a certain lawyer stood up, and tempted him, saying, Master, what shall I do to inherit eternal life?

26 He said unto him, What is written in the law? how readest thou?

27 And he answering said, Thou shalt love the Lord thy God with all thy heart, and with all thy soul, and with all thy strength, and with all thy mind; and thy neighbor as thyself.

28 And he said unto him, Thou hast answered right: this do, and thou shalt live.

29 But he, willing to justify himself, said unto Jesus, And who is my neighbor?

30 And Jesus answering said, A certain man went down from Jerusalem to Jericho, and fell among thieves, which stripped him of his raiment, and wounded him, and departed, leaving him half dead.

31 And by chance there came down a certain priest that way; and when he saw him, he passed by on the other side.

32 And likewise a Levite, when he was at the place, came and looked on him, and passed by on the other side.

33 But a certain Samaritan, as he journeyed, came where he was; and when he saw him, he had compassion on him,

34 And went to him, and bound up his wounds, pouring in oil and wine, and set him on his own beast, and brought him to an inn, and took care of him.

35 And on the morrow when he departed, he took out two pence, and gave them to the host, and said unto him, Take care of him: and whatsoever thou spendest more, when I come again, I will repay thee.

36 Which now of these three, thinkest thou, was neighbor unto him that fell among the thieves?

37 And he said, He that showed mercy on him. Then said Jesus unto him, Go, and do thou likewise.

GOLDEN TEXT: And he answering said, Thou shalt love the Lord thy God with all thy heart, and with all thy soul, and with all thy strength, and with all thy mind; and thy neighbor as thyself.—Luke 10:27.

Aug
21

Jesus' Life, Teachings, and Ministry
Unit 3: Jesus' Ministry of Compassion
(Lessons 10-13)

Learning Aims

After participating in this lesson, each student will be able to:

1. Explain the meaning of the Parable of the Good Samaritan in light of the historical context in which it was taught.

2. Compare himself or herself with the main characters in the story, determining whom they most resemble.

3. Commit to sacrificially meeting the needs of a specific person.

Lesson Outline

INTRODUCTION
  A. Too Busy to Help!
  B. Lesson Background
 I. WHAT MUST I DO? (Luke 10:25-28)
  A. Knowing What to Do (vv. 25-27)
  B. Doing What You Know (v. 28)
II. WHO IS MY NEIGHBOR? (Luke 10:29-35)
  A. Question Asked (v. 29)
  B. Story Told (vv. 30-35)
    Get Mad—In a Good Way
III. GO AND DO LIKEWISE! (Luke 10:36, 37)
  A. What Do You Think? (v. 36)
  B. Do What You Think! (v. 37)
    "Let Them Up Easy"
CONCLUSION
  A. Helping Those in Need
  B. Prayer
  C. Thought to Remember

Introduction

A. Too Busy to Help!

"I can't help people because I am too busy, and besides, it can be dangerous." What a statement! We no longer stop and help people stranded alongside the road because of the *potential* risk involved. We might like to lend a helping hand to an elderly person, but we just have so many other commitments.

Of course we love the Lord and would do anything for Him, but finding the time to help people is just too hard anymore. After all, I have my problems as well, and I don't ask anyone to help me! So why should anyone expect that I would help them? And how about all those government

social programs that I support with my taxes? Can't they "help" like they're supposed to?

Does any of this sound familiar? Are we too busy, too self-involved, too wary of possible dangers, too much given to rationalizing that we no longer see the needs around us? Have we forgotten that as we show acts of kindness to people, we are doing it as unto the Lord? Remember what Jesus said: "Verily I say unto you, Inasmuch as ye have done it unto one of the least of these my brethren, ye have done it unto me" (Matthew 25:40).

B. Lesson Background

Today's text reminds us of the importance of loving God and loving others. The very familiar story of the Good Samaritan encourages us to see the needs of others, take the time to become personally involved, and demonstrate our love for God through love for others. As Jesus spoke these words, He was modeling the very principles He was advocating.

I. What Must I Do?
(Luke 10:25-28)

A. Knowing What to Do (vv. 25-27)

25. And, behold, a certain lawyer stood up, and tempted him, saying, Master, what shall I do to inherit eternal life?

A certain lawyer, or what we could call an expert in religious law, attempts to trap Jesus. He wants to see if he can ask a question so difficult that Jesus will become confused or perhaps say something that would put Him in trouble with the religious authorities. Instead, the lawyer stumbles across life's most important question: *What shall I do to inherit eternal life?*

This lawyer is not the only person in the pages of Scripture to ask this essential question. In Mark 10:17 a young man comes to Jesus and asks, "Good Master, what shall I do that I may inherit eternal life?" A jailer in Philippi asks Paul and Silas the question, "Sirs, what must I do to be saved?" (Acts 16:30). Knowing and then following the answer to this question is the difference between eternal life and eternal damnation. [See question #1, page 438.]

26. He said unto him, What is written in the law? How readest thou?

Jesus answers the lawyer's question with a question of His own. In effect, the Lord says to him, "What do you think is the answer to your own question?"

The lawyer seems to come to Jesus with an agenda. He's convinced that he does indeed know the answer, but he wants to find out if Jesus agrees with him! In the next verse, the lawyer will proceed to give Jesus his best understanding of how to be saved. [See question #2, page 438.]

27. And he answering said, Thou shalt love the Lord thy God with all thy heart, and with all thy soul, and with all thy strength, and with all thy mind; and thy neighbor as thyself.

The lawyer goes to the Old Testament for his answer. First, he makes reference to Deuteronomy 6:4, 5. These verses are called the *shema,* which means "to hear." Paraphrased, these verses say to *love* God with everything you have—heart, *soul,* and all your might. With every part of our beings we are to love God. We cannot be divided in our affections—saying one thing but doing another. It is hypocrisy to say we love God and then proceed to disobey Him. If we love God in our *heart,* it will be demonstrated by how we live and the things that we do.

The second part of the lawyer's answer is originally found in Leviticus 19:18: "Thou shalt not avenge, nor bear any grudge against the children of thy people, but thou shalt love *thy neighbor as thyself:* I am the Lord." The lawyer's answer could be summed up simply as, "Love God and then love others."

B. Doing What You Know (v. 28)

28. And he said unto him, Thou has answered right: this do, and thou shalt live.

To paraphrase a response from a TV game show, Jesus tells the lawyer, "Good answer!" Jesus does not disagree with the lawyer in the least bit. He tells him that he is exactly right. If he loves God and others, he shall *live.*

It is interesting to note that Jesus comes back to these two concepts again in His teaching. During the final week of the Lord's ministry, another lawyer will seek to test Him by asking what is the greatest commandment. Jesus will quote Deuteronomy 6:4, 5 as the greatest commandment and Leviticus 19:18 as the second greatest (see Matthew 22:34-40). The apostle Paul picks up on this theme at least twice. In Romans 13:8 he says, "For he that loveth another hath fulfilled the law." And in Galatians 5:14 Paul writes, "For all the law is fulfilled in one word, even in this; Thou shalt love thy neighbor as thyself."

Replying to the lawyer's Old Testament frame of reference, Jesus commends him for getting it exactly right: If he wants to be saved, he needs to love God and then love others. When the Holy Spirit is given on the Day of Pentecost, the answer will need to be expanded (see Acts 2:37-39).

II. Who Is My Neighbor?
(Luke 10:29-35)
A. Question Asked (v. 29)

29. But he, willing to justify himself, said unto Jesus, And who is my neighbor?

The lawyer is not quite satisfied. He may be feeling more than a little bit uncomfortable. Jesus has affirmed that loving God and then loving others are keys in salvation. How well has the lawyer done these two things? Perhaps he is selective in his love, but he doesn't want to look bad in front of Jesus or others who may be listening to this conversation. He apparently wants to make himself look as good as possible, not having any doubt or suspicion cast upon him. [See question #3, page 438.]

Thus he attempts *to justify himself,* that is, to make himself appear completely free from wrongdoing in regard to loving God or neighbor. After all, he is talking about how to be saved, and he certainly wouldn't want to put himself in a light that would make him appear lost! So he asks the question, *Who is my neighbor?*

That, too, is an important question. Whom should we help? Whom should we love? Are my neighbors only those who live next door to me? Are they also the people I see at work whom I know and like? Certainly strangers are not my neighbors, are they? Should we be "nice" only to people who are nice and helpful (neighborly) to us? The lawyer probably feels like he has done at least that much, thus he is safe. Yet Jesus will seize on his question and seek to open his eyes (and ours) as to who a neighbor really is!

B. Story Told (vv. 30-35)

30. And Jesus answering said, A certain man went down from Jerusalem to Jericho, and fell among thieves, which stripped him of his raiment, and wounded him, and departed, leaving him half dead.

This is the beginning of what is called the Parable of the Good Samaritan. Jesus offers sev-

---

How to Say It

ASSYRIAN. Uh-*sear*-e-un.
DENARII. dih-*nair*-ee or dih-*nair*-eye.
DEUTERONOMY. Due-ter-*ahn*-uh-me.
EZEKIEL. Ee-*zeek*-ee-ul or Ee-*zeek*-yul.
EZRA. *Ez*-ruh.
JERICHO. *Jair*-ih-co.
JERUSALEM. Juh-*roo*-suh-lem.
LEVITE. *Lee*-vite.
LEVITICUS. Leh-*vit*-ih-kus.
NEHEMIAH. *Nee*-huh-*my*-uh (strong accent on *my*).
SAMARITANS. Suh-*mare*-uh-tunz.
SHEMA (Hebrew). shih-*mah*.

eral specifics in this story, including an interesting point of Bible geography. *Jericho* is approximately twenty miles northeast of *Jerusalem.* Typically, when we speak of directions we'll say we're going "up" when we mean north, and going "down" when we mean south.

The text says the man was going *down from Jerusalem to Jericho.* The Scriptures are consistent in noting that one always goes "up" to Jerusalem, and "down" when departing from that city. The reason for this is that Jerusalem is built on a hill. It does not matter from what direction you approach the city—you are going to go up to get there. The reverse is naturally true as well: you always go down as you leave the city.

As this man made his way from Jerusalem to Jericho, he was attacked. Traveling alone by foot or by donkey in the open countryside is dangerous. What happened was much more than just having a wallet stolen. The *thieves* took his clothing along with whatever valuables he may have possessed. They beat him up and left *him half dead.* The thieves may have intended to murder him. Perhaps they assumed that he was indeed dead as he lay there unconscious.

The thieves had a mentality that still is with us today. It's a mind-set of "what's yours is ours and we'll take it because we're stronger." This man was easy prey. Life was of no value to the thieves. They cared only for what they could get from him. If he died, that was no concern of theirs. Obviously, this is not a godly attitude! This is about as far away from love and concern as you can get!

The injured man presents the issue that Jesus wants to address. Here is a man with a tremendous need. His personal possessions are gone, he is beaten and bloodied, and perhaps he will die without the intervention from a "neighbor." Who will rescue this man and love him as he does his own self?

31, 32. And by chance there came down a certain priest that way; and when he saw him, he passed by on the other side. And likewise a Levite, when he was at the place, came and looked on him, and passed by on the other side.

When needs take place within the church today, our first inclination is often to "call the preacher." If he's not available, we call for an elder or a deacon! It is just typical to expect that these men of God will be the first to offer help and assistance in a time of need. That may be our expectation, but as Jesus tells the story we will have our expectation challenged.

After the thieves made their getaway, a *priest* came by and later *a Levite.* The priest, being a man of God, served in the temple, where he offered sacrifices. A Levite likewise had duties in the temple services—see Ezekiel 44:10-14. Both certainly had read Leviticus 19:18 many times, but they had not made the personal application of what they had read. Why did they not stop and render assistance to the man?

There is a possible answer to this question: they may have been so concerned about "serving God" that they were unwilling to help this man in need. Temple service demands that those who officiate be clean from any sort of defilement. If the priest and Levite became unclean, they would be disqualified from serving in the temple until they were again considered clean. One thing that makes an individual unclean is coming into contact with a dead body (see Leviticus 21:11; Numbers 5:2; 9:6; 19:11, 13).

However, the priest was going *down* on that road, in other words *away* from the temple in Jerusalem. He should have been less concerned about ceremonial defilement if his service in the temple had concluded. Yet he walked by *on the other side* as if to say, "There is no way I will become defiled by you." The Levite likewise offered no assistance to the man. How callous could so-called "men of God" be not to at least investigate if the distressed man were alive or dead?

While the thieves had the attitude of "what's yours is ours and we'll take it," the priest and the Levite had the attitude of, "what's ours is ours, and we'll keep it." They saw a man with problems but had no concern for him. They obviously cannot see any connection between love for God and love for others. [See question #4, page 438.]

33. But a certain Samaritan, as he journeyed, came where he was; and when he saw him, he had compassion on him.

Jesus has a way of introducing unexpected elements into His teaching. This story is no exception. The word *Samaritan* would definitely make the listeners pay special attention. And when the word *compassion* is used in association with the Samaritan, that certainly causes even greater surprise. The reason for the shock would be the hatred and distrust that Jews and Samaritans have for each other. In John 4:9 we are given the note that "Jews have no dealings with the Samaritans."

We know that racial and religious tensions are severe in our era. But racial and religious problems have existed for many centuries, and the divisions they caused were just as severe (or more so) in other times. After the Assyrian conquest of northern Israel in 722 B.C., the Jews remaining in that land intermarried with people from other nations. Thus their descendants were not "pure blood" Jews. These Samaritans wanted to help rebuild the temple after the Babylonian captivity ended in 538 B.C., but the Jews refused their help (Ezra 4:1-5; Nehemiah 2:10, 19; 4:1-8).

What is striking, then, is that this Samaritan looked beyond racial and religious differences, saw a man with a tremendous need, and knew he had the ability to help. And he didn't just have the resources to help, he also had the willingness to actually do something. He didn't just wring his hands and say, "My, what a shame; someone really should do something." Rather, he stopped, got involved, and helped his neighbor—a man whom he had never met. The following verses describe the ways he helped.

34. And went to him, and bound up his wounds, pouring in oil and wine, and set him on his own beast, and brought him to an inn, and took care of him.

The priest and Levite were unwilling to touch this stripped and beaten man, and they went by on the other side of the road. The Samaritan demonstrated his love and concern by "getting his hands dirty" and treating the man's injuries. He used his own resources—*oil and wine*—to help clean the man's *wounds*. He bandaged the cuts.

The Samaritan has invested his time, personal resources, and also his comfort. But the help doesn't stop there. He put the injured man on his *beast* and took *him to an inn* for recuperation. This Samaritan had started his day like any other day. He was traveling on his business. But his business suddenly took second place to the more immediate and urgent needs of an injured man. He sacrifices much for a person whom he had never seen until that day. But he does even more.

35. And on the morrow when he departed, he took out two pence, and gave them to the host, and said unto him, Take care of him: and whatsoever thou spendest more, when I come again, I will repay thee.

It is one thing to sacrifice a little time, another thing to sacrifice a little comfort, but now this Samaritan has sacrificed money! He has already used his oil and wine on the man's wounds, but now he is putting a significant amount of financial resources into the man's care as well. *Two pence* in the original language is two denarii, or two days' wages. We are not talking about just a couple of pennies or dollars!

The Samaritan then does still more: he makes a legally binding agreement to pay extra, if need be. The injured man was someone he had never met, and he could have said, "That's all I'm able to do right now."

This Samaritan is rightly described as a man having concern, compassion, and love for peo-

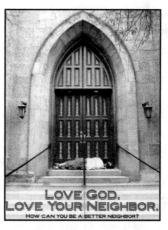

Visual for lesson 12

Use this image to introduce the question, "Who will experience God's love through me?"

ple. His attitude can be described as, "What's mine is yours, and I'll share it." This is far different from the robbers who stole and the priest and Levite who would not get involved. The Samaritan demonstrated by his actions the compassion that lived in his heart.

GET MAD—IN A GOOD WAY

Can anger cause you to do something good? We usually think of anger in negative terms, as an emotion that causes us to lose control and do things we later regret. There is no mention of anger in Jesus' Parable of the Good Samaritan. Yet when one reads it one cannot help but be angry at the thieves who left the man dying and at the "religious" people who passed him by without helping.

When Chrysler Corporation Chairman Lee Iacocca addressed a college graduating class in 1983, he reportedly told them to get mad at things that were wrong in the world—mad enough to do something to change things. He wanted the graduates to get mad about the state of things. The United States of America was born when several dozen patriots got mad enough to sign the Declaration of Independence. The U.S. put a man on the moon because Sputnik made the country mad at being number two in the space race. Getting mad in a constructive way is good for the soul.

Righteous anger is a valid emotion and a powerful motivator. It moves people to join causes that make the world a better place by combating abortion, hunger, illiteracy, poverty, injustice, and other societal ills. When we add the compassion of the good Samaritan to our justifiable anger, there will be no stopping the work of Christ!   —T. A. C.

III. Go and Do Likewise!
(Luke 10:36, 37)

A. What Do You Think? (v. 36)

36. Which now of these three, thinkest thou, was neighbor unto him that fell among the thieves?

The lawyer is probably wishing he had never asked the question, "Who is my neighbor?" Jesus' question provides a tremendous opportunity to expose the hypocrisy and unsympathetic attitude of the religious leaders. It also demonstrates that love reaches across cultural boundaries. We learn that our *neighbor* is whomever we have occasion to help. A neighbor is not only someone who lives in geographical proximity to us, but rather anyone who needs our assistance. [See question #5, page 438.]

B. Do What You Think! (v. 37)

37. And he said, He that showed mercy on him. Then said Jesus unto him, Go, and do thou likewise.

To his credit, the lawyer does not try to slip out of the question by "blaming the victim." This would be something like, "Well, that beaten man should have known better than to be on a road that is well traveled by robbers."

Instead, the lawyer answers forthrightly. It is apparent that the priest and the Levite were not neighbors to the injured man. It is only the Samaritan who demonstrated the qualities of a good neighbor that we should display. Jesus challenges the lawyer—and He also speaks to our generation—when He says *Go, and do thou likewise.* Each day we will encounter neighbors whom we can assist. We must look beyond those people we know well and see others that still need the help we can supply.

Home Daily Bible Readings

Monday, Aug. 15—The Great Commandment (Deuteronomy 6:1-9)

Tuesday, Aug. 16—Love Your Neighbor (Leviticus 19:11-18)

Wednesday, Aug. 17—The Greatest Commandment (Matthew 22:34-40)

Thursday, Aug. 18—The First Commandment (Mark 12:28-34)

Friday, Aug. 19—Love Your Neighbor as Yourself (Luke 10:25-29)

Saturday, Aug. 20—The Parable of the Good Samaritan (Luke 10:30-37)

Sunday, Aug. 21—Love Fulfills the Law (Romans 13:8-14)

"LET THEM UP EASY"

On April 9, 1865, soldiers of the Confederacy waited outside the house that was the site of Lee's surrender to Grant. While they waited, they probably wondered about the terms of the surrender. The American Civil War had been a bitter contest, and it would have been easy for the victorious army to demand harsh terms of their vanquished foe.

President Abraham Lincoln already had thought about what would happen when the war was over and the nation needed to heal. He realized that this had been a war among neighbors, and it would need to be followed by a peace among neighbors. "Let them up easy" is a famous phrase attributed to Lincoln after the fall of Richmond. Lincoln's understanding of "neighbors" helped heal a nation.

There are various facets to the Parable of the Good Samaritan. At its heart, however, it is an illustration of being a godly neighbor. What kind of neighbor are you? "Neighbor" is not limited to the person or family next door. It means anyone who is in need. How do you respond to those in need? How do you respond to someone who has wronged you and is now in need? Your answer to those questions may reveal far more about your Christian character than the number of church services you attend!   —T. A. C.

Conclusion

A. Helping Those in Need

John wrote, "If a man say, I love God, and hateth his brother, he is a liar: for he that loveth not his brother whom he hath seen, how can he love God whom he hath not seen? And this commandment have we from him, That he who loveth God love his brother also" (1 John 4:20, 21). The lawyer wanted to know how to be saved. In his mind he knew the correct answer: Love God and love others.

Unfortunately, the lawyer had much to learn about loving his neighbor. The old chorus says, "And they'll know we are Christians by our love." Our faith in God our Savior is demonstrated as we love our neighbors. We must be willing to help those neighbors we find in need.

B. Prayer

Father, we confess that we have not always been Your hands and feet in our love for others. Convict our hearts that we will be a "good Samaritan" to someone today. In Jesus' name, amen.

C. Thought to Remember

Put hands and feet to your love.

Learning by Doing

This page contains an alternative lesson plan emphasizing learning activities.
Classes desiring such student involvement will find these suggestions helpful.

Learning Goals

After participating in this lesson, each student will be able to:

1. Explain the meaning of the Parable of the Good Samaritan in light of the historical context in which it was taught.

2. Compare himself or herself with the main characters in the story, determining whom they most resemble.

3. Commit to sacrificially meeting the needs of a specific person.

Into the Lesson

Bring several newspapers and current news magazines to class. Place them around the room on chairs before class members arrive. This may prompt conversations about current events as people arrive.

Begin by asking your learners to find examples of people in need from the articles and pictures. Cut them out and affix them to the wall or poster board. The heading should read *Needs in the World Today*. Say, "Today's lesson will consider a very familiar and straightforward story: the Parable of the Good Samaritan. A major focus today will be on how the lesson applies, as we hear Jesus' answer to the question, 'Who is my neighbor?'"

Into the Word

Begin by reading Luke 10:25-29 aloud to review the background and context for this parable. Using three poster boards, write on top of the first, "Reaction #1"; the second, "Reaction #2"; and the third, "Reaction #3"; place them on the wall beside the collection of articles and pictures you have posted.

One by one, discuss the reaction of each of the three main characters in the parable (priest, Levite, and Samaritan), asking the following questions for each: "Who is this? How did he react? Why do you think he responded this way? What does this reveal about his love for another? What does this reveal about his love for God?"

Next, write responses to the following additional questions on the corresponding poster board: "What people today would correspond to the characters in the parable? That is, if Jesus were telling this story today, what characters could He have used?" For the first two characters, some suggestions may include a preacher, missionary, or elder in place of the priest; in place of the Levite may be a deacon, a leader in a parachurch organization, or a Christian author.

After placing several suggestions on the board, ask, "What reason could each of these give for doing nothing to help someone they see in need?" For the part of the Samaritan, ask the class to list people today who would be considered outcasts. Again, write the ideas on poster board.

Next, ask someone to come up and retell the story while walking across the room and selecting items from the lists on the poster board. For example, the story might sound like this:

A family was homeless, with the mother hospitalized, after their house burned. A minister heard about it, but was too busy preparing his sermon to help. The chairman of the missionary society at the church thought it was more important to attend a committee meeting, so he didn't help either. A man/woman from *[fill in with an appropriate description of a "despised" group]* went to the hospital, volunteered to house the children, and brought money saved for vacation to buy meals.

Repeat this process several times. Each time before a person retells the story in modern terms, ask, "Who is my neighbor?" After the story is retold each time, stop and ask the class, "Who was a neighbor to the one in need?"

This process should help emphasize the way Jesus showed that the lawyer was actually asking the wrong question. The lawyer asked the question, "Who is my neighbor?" (Luke 10:29). Jesus showed him that the real question should be, "To whom can I be a neighbor?"

Into Life

Next, have class members identify situations where they have been confronted with people in need over the last year. Ask them to consider how they responded. Say, "If Jesus were telling the story with you as one of the characters, who would you be?"

Discuss specific ways members of the class can become more effective at seeing and sensitively meeting the needs of others. Also discuss the importance of doing this in Jesus' name. Pray as a class for the right heart and courage to act when seeing others in need.

Let's Talk It Over

The questions on this page are designed to promote discussion of the lesson by the class and to encourage application of the lesson Scriptures. The answers provided are only discussion starters. Let your class talk it over from there.

1. The lawyer was not sincere; he was trying to trap Jesus! The Master would have been perfectly justified in refusing to answer. But He did answer—and we are glad. How do you decide whether or not to answer a question when the person asking is not sincere? Tell of an experience either way, if you can.

These are hard situations. We are afraid that if we don't answer then our position will appear untenable. But we're afraid that if we do answer then our words will be twisted and used against us. As much as possible, we need to prepare ourselves to answer hard questions. "Be ready always to give an answer to every man that asketh you a reason of the hope that is in you with meekness and fear" (1 Peter 3:15). Still, there are times to remain silent. Jesus refused to answer in some of His trials (compare Matthew 27:12-14), and sometimes we also may be better off to answer nothing. (See also Amos 5:13.)

2. Why do you suppose Jesus answered the lawyer's question with a question? When would you find it appropriate to respond that way?

The lawyer was not sincere in asking about eternal life; he wanted to trap Jesus. Perhaps Jesus knew that forcing the lawyer to answer his own question would thwart that attempt.

On the other hand, Jesus often used questions. Questions force people to think, and Jesus wanted the lawyer to give this issue some thought. Sometimes people who ask us questions need to give the issues on their mind some thought. Thinking through the matter may help them understand the issue better than if we simply give them an answer. At the same time, even in His question Jesus gave some information. He pointed the lawyer to the law. Sometimes people who ask us questions just need a nudge in the right direction. Then they can sort things out for themselves.

3. From trying to trap Jesus, the lawyer finds himself on the verge of being trapped. He needs to "justify himself." What difficulties have you seen arise as a result of someone's trying to "justify himself"? What should one do instead?

Trying to justify ourselves distorts our perspective. We diminish our faults and exaggerate those of others. We attempt to manipulate the system or the law to find an advantage. We make our own welfare more important than anything else—even the truth. Instead of justifying ourselves, we need to seek the truth and align ourselves with it. Remaining objective as much as possible, we can even arrange to have a friend help us "see ourselves as others see us."

4. What makes us reluctant to help someone in need? What can break down barriers to make us willing to help?

Like the lawyer who raised the question, we are often quite willing to help those whom we like—those whom we see as our "neighbors." But it's easy to make excuses for not helping strangers or people with whom we don't get along well. We may be "too busy," or the situation might be dangerous. "Surely there are others more qualified," we think. It all comes down to the issue Jesus was trying to teach: love. Those whom we love we help.

Of course, there are times when giving help may not be the proper thing to do. Sometimes what looks like help is really enabling a destructive lifestyle. For example, giving money to one who has not learned to budget and live within his or her means is probably only enabling the person to continue to practice poor stewardship. We need to consider the situation and potential outcomes of our actions before we offer to help in some way.

5. To whom are we being good neighbors? Who has a "neighbor" who is not being helped? How can we do better?

If you can get a report from your benevolence or missions ministry before class, that will help you seed this discussion. Does your church sponsor a mission that provides food and/or clothing to people in need? Are individuals in your church involved in similar activities beyond the scope of church-sponsored ministries? This is a good opportunity to promote those efforts and encourage others to get involved.

At the same time, members of your class may be aware of people in need who are not currently being helped. Explore the possibility of initiating a class project to be "good Samaritans." Don't forget that a person's greatest need is forgiveness of sins through Jesus Christ.

Accepting the Invitation

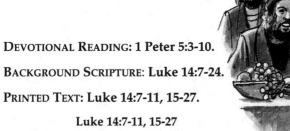

DEVOTIONAL READING: **1 Peter 5:3-10.**

BACKGROUND SCRIPTURE: **Luke 14:7-24.**

PRINTED TEXT: **Luke 14:7-11, 15-27.**

Luke 14:7-11, 15-27

7 And he put forth a parable to those which were bidden, when he marked how they chose out the chief rooms; saying unto them,

8 When thou art bidden of any man to a wedding, sit not down in the highest room; lest a more honorable man than thou be bidden of him;

9 And he that bade thee and him come and say to thee, Give this man place; and thou begin with shame to take the lowest room.

10 But when thou art bidden, go and sit down in the lowest room; that when he that bade thee cometh, he may say unto thee, Friend, go up higher: then shalt thou have worship in the presence of them that sit at meat with thee.

11 For whosoever exalteth himself shall be abased; and he that humbleth himself shall be exalted.

. . . .

15 And when one of them that sat at meat with him heard these things, he said unto him, Blessed is he that shall eat bread in the kingdom of God.

16 Then said he unto him, A certain man made a great supper, and bade many:

17 And sent his servant at supper time to say to them that were bidden, Come; for all things are now ready.

18 And they all with one consent began to make excuse. The first said unto him, I have bought a piece of ground, and I must needs go and see it: I pray thee have me excused.

19 And another said, I have bought five yoke of oxen, and I go to prove them: I pray thee have me excused.

20 And another said, I have married a wife, and therefore I cannot come.

21 So that servant came, and showed his lord these things. Then the master of the house being angry said to his servant, Go out quickly into the streets and lanes of the city, and bring in hither the poor, and the maimed, and the halt, and the blind.

22 And the servant said, Lord, it is done as thou hast commanded, and yet there is room.

23 And the lord said unto the servant, Go out into the highways and hedges, and compel them to come in, that my house may be filled.

24 For I say unto you, That none of those men which were bidden shall taste of my supper.

25 And there went great multitudes with him: and he turned, and said unto them,

26 If any man come to me, and hate not his father, and mother, and wife, and children, and brethren, and sisters, yea, and his own life also, he cannot be my disciple.

27 And whosoever doth not bear his cross, and come after me, cannot be my disciple.

GOLDEN TEXT: And the lord said unto the servant, Go out into the highways and hedges, and compel them to come in, that my house may be filled.
—Luke 14:23.

Jesus' Life, Teachings, and Ministry

Unit 3: Jesus' Ministry of Compassion
(Lessons 10-13)

Learning Aims

After participating in this lesson, each student will be able to:

1. Explain the lesson from Jesus' parables in Luke 14.

2. Understand the relationship between humility and being a disciple of Jesus.

3. Accept the call of Jesus to follow Him humbly, gratefully, and wholeheartedly.

Lesson Outline

INTRODUCTION
   A. "I Must Be in the Front Row!"
   B. Lesson Background
 I. WHERE SHOULD I SIT? (Luke 14:7-11)
   A. Proud Are Humbled (vv. 7-9)
   B. Humble Are Promoted (vv. 10, 11)
II. INEXCUSABLE EXCUSES (Luke 14:15-24)
   A. Invitation (vv. 15-17)
   B. Property Inspection Excuse (v. 18)
   C. Yoke of Oxen Excuse (v. 19)
   D. New Wife Excuse (v. 20)
   E. Invitation Broadened (vv. 21-23)
     The Unexpected Invitation
     The Place of No Exclusions
   F. Invitation Revoked (v. 24)
III. GOD FIRST! (Luke 14:25-27)
   A. First in Love (v. 25, 26)
   B. First in Sacrifice (v. 27)
CONCLUSION
   A. Humility and Sacrifice
   B. Prayer
   C. Thought to Remember

Introduction

A. "I Must Be in the Front Row!"

You may remember the television commercial from the 1980s featuring sports celebrity Bob Uecker. He would enter a stadium and declare, "I must be in the front row!" Next, you saw him way up in the "cheap seats." In this spoof, Uecker thought he was more of an honored celebrity than he actually was. He felt in his pretended arrogance that he deserved the place of honor.

Today's text will illustrate the importance of humility in a way that modern celebrities rarely do. Make no mistake: we, too, can be guilty of as-

suming that we are more important than others and deserve great recognition. Yet Jesus taught that the first shall be last and the last shall be first. As we learn humility, we may also learn discipleship.

B. Lesson Background

Luke 14 finds Jesus well on His way to Jerusalem and the crucifixion that awaits (compare Luke 13:22). It is a time for more teaching and more miracles as opposition steadily rises (Luke 13:31). The time is short, and Jesus has much left to say and do. Today's lesson finds Him at "the house of one of the chief Pharisees" for a Sabbath Day meal (Luke 14:1a). There's an old saying: "Keep your friends close and your enemies even closer." The Pharisees intend to do just that (Luke 14:1b)!

I. Where Should I Sit?
(Luke 14:7-11)

A. Proud Are Humbled (vv. 7-9)

7. And he put forth a parable to those which were bidden, when he marked how they chose out the chief rooms; saying unto them.

People are selecting their seats *(rooms)* for the banquet just ahead. One wonders what goes through the Lord's mind as He observes them. Does He shake His head or even roll His eyes as He sees people posture for recognition? Does it grieve Him to observe how they step across one another in an attempt to appear more important than their counterparts? Perhaps He sighs as He recognizes that in order for His disciples to be effective they will have to change their way of thinking and develop a genuine humility in their hearts and lives.

Jesus thus tells *a parable* that illustrates the folly of pomposity. It is fairly easy to see how we find ourselves with the same attitudes at times. [See question #1, page 446.]

8. When thou art bidden of any man to a wedding, sit not down in the highest room; lest a more honorable man than thou be bidden of him.

Imagine that you've heard that an important elected official is coming to town for an event followed by a meal. Somehow you assume that he will want you to be seated next to him at the head table. You put on your best clothes and proceed to make your way to the front. Moments later his security detail comes and forcibly removes you from the building! This scenario is both frightening and humiliating.

Jesus teaches that we should not assume that we are the most honored guest or the most important person in any situation. How embarrassing it would be to have someone of an even higher status show up unexpectedly. The next verse illustrates the type of embarrassment that can come when we assume that we are more important than what we truly are.

9. And he that bade thee and him come and say to thee, Give this man place; and thou begin with shame to take the lowest room.

One can picture that uncomfortable, awkward moment! Someone has assumed a place at the head table and sits down as if it were reserved for him. Unfortunately, someone comes along, taps him on the shoulder, and says, "I'm sorry, you're going to have to move. This is not your seat. You'll have to find another table, and I think there's one in the back!"

To the snickering of the other invited guests, this once self-important person shrinks back to the less-honored seat. Such a foolish error! Arrogance is his downfall. Had he not assumed a certain level of importance, such humiliation would have been avoided. Next, Jesus suggests a strategy to save a person from this type of *shame*.

B. Humble Are Promoted (vv. 10, 11)

10. But when thou art bidden, go and sit down in the lowest room; that when he that bade thee cometh, he may say unto thee, Friend, go up higher: then shalt thou have worship in the presence of them that sit at meat with thee.

Go back to the previous illustration of the elected official coming to town. You've come into the convention hall and have seated yourself in the farthest corner of the building, perhaps more distant from the official than anyone else.

Next, you see him stand and begin peering through the crowd. Perhaps he asks for assistance in finding *you!* When he finally sees you, he smiles and begins waving to you and motioning for you to come up front. He's expecting you to sit with him. In full view of all, you make your way to the front where you are now seated in a place of high honor. You started at the back and found your way up front! How much better this is than to assume a place at the front, only to be sent to the back in shame.

Jesus tells us to not make false assumptions about personal importance. Start by sitting in the back and being thankful for even being asked to come in the first place. Then the one who invited you may give you a great honor by escorting you from the back table up to the head table. That would be tremendous, so much better than having to be told to move because someone more important than you needs that good seat.

All through this parable the application to servanthood and humility is seen. It is a high honor to be a disciple of the Lord. As the servant does

Visual for lesson 13

Display this poster and have it read aloud as you begin your study of question #2 on page 446.

the bidding of the master, so also should we view ourselves as servants of Christ. One should not assume that he or she is indispensable or favored more than another servant. Rather, God's servants should do the assigned work gratefully. There remains a day when the Lord shall judge the work of His servants. Those who have served faithfully shall hear the words, "Well done."

11. For whosoever exalteth himself shall be abased; and he that humbleth himself shall be exalted.

Jesus now provides the key point of the parable. Disaster comes when we think we are more important than we are. "Pride goeth before destruction, and a haughty spirit before a fall" (Proverbs 16:18). Those who exalt themselves—presuming that they are more important than others or are deserving of special treatment—will be surprised to find themselves *abased*, that is, brought down lower or humiliated.

Yet Jesus also teaches that there is a counterpart to this. Those who do not make such false assumptions, who faithfully serve without desire of recognition, and who have an attitude of lowliness will *be exalted*. It is better to start low and be promoted, than to assume you're starting high and get demoted! [See question #2, page 446.]

The Lord's disciples must understand that pride and arrogance are counterproductive to the tasks that the Lord has given (compare Mark 10:35-37). If an attitude of pride and feelings of superiority exist, this will negatively affect our witness and productivity in kingdom work. Many times we are too good at pointing out the shortcomings of others in an attempt to make ourselves look good. There's truth in that old saying that when we point our finger at someone then there are three more pointing right back at us! We recognize that there is a job for each disciple. The Lord will evaluate the work (Romans 14:4). The task for the Christian is to be concerned with his or her own work, not that of others. God will reward as He sees fit.

II. Inexcusable Excuses
(Luke 14:15-24)

A. Invitation (vv. 15-17)

15. And when one of them that sat at meat with him heard these things, he said unto him, Blessed is he that shall eat bread in the kingdom of God.

Those who are assembled with Jesus understand that it is a high privilege to be invited into the Lord's *kingdom* and enjoy fellowship with Him. It will indeed be a high privilege to be in the presence of the Lord as it is to be called into His service.

16, 17. Then said he unto him, A certain man made a great supper, and bade many: and sent his servant at supper time to say to them that were bidden, Come; for all things are now ready.

In the first-century culture, an invitation is a significant thing. It is a social blunder to receive an invitation then fail to honor it when the time comes. If someone goes to the trouble of preparing a meal, it is expected that the one who is invited will honor the invitation at the appropriate time. This *certain man* has prepared a sumptuous feast and is *ready* for his guests. He even goes to the additional trouble of sending a *servant* out to remind people that it is time for them to arrive and enjoy the meal. All they have to do is show up! They had been invited previously, and the servant now encourages them to come and dine.

B. Property Inspection Excuse (v. 18)

18. And they all with one consent began to make excuse. The first said unto him, I have bought a piece of ground, and I must needs go and see it: I pray thee have me excused.

As the servant goes out to remind people of the dinner to which they were invited, he begins to hear one excuse after another. Employers often hear excuses about why an employee is late or doesn't complete a job. Teachers often get excuses for why a student is absent or why assignments are not completed. We are quick to make excuses, but not so quick to accept responsibility for our actions! Excuses will not hold water with God. He has been very gracious to invite us into His kingdom, even as the man said in verse 15. Yet many who are invited to the Lord's kingdom make one poor excuse after another as to why they just cannot honor the invitation.

Think about the first excuse: *I have bought a piece of ground.* Would this property disappear in the time that it will take to go and enjoy the meal the man has prepared? Would that much really be lost? It seems that the person's priorities are somewhat misguided. To this man, checking out his newly acquired land is more important than the fellowship he would enjoy with the friend who has invited him to dinner.

C. Yoke of Oxen Excuse (v. 19)

19. And another said, I have bought five yoke of oxen, and I go to prove them: I pray thee have me excused.

Likewise, this second individual has something more pressing on his mind, something of a higher priority to him than his friend's banquet. He chooses to go and work with his new *oxen* to see how productive they will be for him. One wonders if that really is such a pressing need right then. It also suggests that the man would rather spend time with his oxen than with his friend—someone who has gone to time and expense to prepare a banquet and invite him to attend. [See question #3, page 446.]

D. New Wife Excuse (v. 20)

20. And another said, I have married a wife, and therefore I cannot come.

The third man also has other things on his mind, namely enjoying time with his new bride. It is very possible that this banquet is a "men only" event, so she is probably not invited. Single men often lament that their married buddies no longer have time to "hang out with the guys." This newlywed's priorities have changed. He, too, declines to honor the invitation to dinner.

This man, however, has the rest of his life to spend with his new wife! Will one evening away from her really be such a burden to honor a friend? Misplaced priorities will keep people from experiencing the blessings of a relationship with God. Jesus tells us, "Seek ye first the kingdom of God, and his righteousness; and all these things shall be added unto you" (Matthew 6:33).

God is not fooled by the excuses that we make today. The Lord is most definitely aware that people are telling Him that other things or other people are more important to them than He is. God deserves to be in first place, and He expects it.

E. Invitation Broadened (vv. 21-23)

21. So that servant came, and showed his lord these things. Then the master of the house being angry said to his servant, Go out quickly into the streets and lanes of the city, and bring in hither the poor, and the maimed, and the halt, and the blind.

The master of the house has gone to considerable trouble and expense. The meal was declared "all ready," and there is no one to enjoy it! He is both offended and angered at the lack of regard that his honored, invited guests have shown him. So now he changes his thinking and tells *his servant* to find anyone he can and bring them in!

Those who are included in this new invitation are not the high and noble—the ones who had turned him down. Rather, these are on the lower end of society's ladder. The servant is sent to the streets and lanes, the places where the homeless and the beggars are to be found. Among these there will be those who are dirty, sick, lame, and *blind.* These are not the ones who normally find themselves invited to "society events." But now they are invited to come and share in the prepared feast.

THE UNEXPECTED INVITATION

Every U.S. president knows that his selection of cabinet officers may determine the success or failure of his administration. In 1862 Abraham Lincoln had to appoint a new Secretary of War, a position of great importance during the American Civil War.

Lincoln extended an invitation to an old political enemy: Edwin M. Stanton (1814–1869). Stanton was of a different political party. He had snubbed Lincoln earlier, calling him a "gawky, long-armed ape" during the McCormick-Manny legal case of 1855. Stanton had publicly expressed his doubts about Lincoln's ability to serve as president.

Imagine how Stanton must have felt when Lincoln asked him to serve in the most crucial cabinet office in his administration! Imagine what others thought about Lincoln for extending that invitation. Many undoubtedly thought it was political suicide. Yet, when Lincoln died on the morning of April 15, 1865, it was Stanton who wept and said, "Now he belongs to the ages."

Some people have a difficult time understanding God's invitation to be part of His kingdom. That invitation, offered to His enemies, is extended by the power of grace available through the cross and empty tomb. The invitation is God's—not ours. We do not determine the invitation list; it is God who extends the invitation to all, even to His worst enemies. We only decide if we shall accept it or not.   —T. A. C.

How to Say It

EPHESIANS. Ee-*fee*-zhunz.
PHARISEES. *Fair*-ih-seez.

22, 23. And the servant said, Lord, it is done as thou hast commanded, and yet there is room. And the lord said unto the servant, Go out into the highways and hedges, and compel them to come in, that my house may be filled.

This man will not be satisfied until his banquet room is *filled* to capacity. That word *compel* is a stronger word than *invited.* His so-called friends had spurned the invitation. Now others are told to come and enjoy a meal.

It would seem that Jesus is making clear what He taught in the previous parable. The ones who were humbled had the opportunity to be exalted. And the ones who thought themselves to be too important and too busy are now being disdained. The next verse makes this clearer still.

THE PLACE OF NO EXCLUSIONS

The Tomb of the Unknowns in Arlington National Cemetery is one of America's most "sacred" sites. It houses remains of service members from World Wars I and II and Korea. In 1999 it was announced that there probably would be no more remains interred there. It would be nice to think that it meant there would be no more wars. But there was a different reason: the U.S. armed services were now to use DNA samples for identification. Americans will still be killed in wars, but their remains always will be identifiable, thanks to modern technology.

In some respects, America has been defined by the Tomb of the Unknowns. The remains there, "known but to God," may have been the bodies of officers or enlisted, black or white, rich or poor, educated or illiterate. None of that matters. America is not a nation of kings and peasants, gentry and serfs, aristocrats and riffraff. The Tomb of the Unknowns does not reflect station in life at time of death.

When you look at your congregation on Sunday morning, what kind of people do you see? Mostly of one race? Mostly middle class? If the lack of diversity is intentional, something is terribly wrong! The church is not a body in which station in life should matter. The invitation to God's great banquet is extended to all. —T. A. C.

F. Invitation Revoked (v. 24)

24. For I say unto you, That none of those men which were bidden shall taste of my supper.

The original group, first invited to share in the man's banquet, are now "uninvited." They had their chance but lost it because other things had become more important to them. They had been invited the first time, and a servant had come and invited them again. They turned down the gracious invitation. They now have no one to blame but themselves for losing their places. The friendships are (we may safely assume) permanently damaged! By their own choices, the "uninvited" have lost a relationship with someone who cared for them. [See question #4, page 446.]

III. God First!
(Luke 14:25-27)
A. First in Love (vv. 25, 26)

25, 26. And there went great multitudes with him: and he turned, and said unto them, If any man come to me, and hate not his father, and mother, and wife, and children, and brethren, and sisters, yea, and his own life also, he cannot be my disciple.

Jesus' ministry continues to experience great growth and excitement. People still flock to Him. They are both observing and receiving great miracles that He performs. They thrill to hear Him teach and preach. They must enjoy watching Him debate with the religious leaders and humiliate them for their arrogance and sinful attitudes (Luke 13:17). Yet Jesus now has a word for the people who are following Him. They, too, have to make sure that they have the right priorities.

A person can be materialistic whether as a millionaire or as one beneath the poverty level. It is possible to put many things in a place of higher prominence than a relationship with the Lord. Some do it with entertainment, sports, leisure, or business dealings. Some even put their earthly family as a higher priority than their Heavenly Father.

But doesn't the idea of "hating" your *father and mother and wife and children* and brothers and *sisters,* and even one's *own life* seem extreme? Doesn't Exodus 20:12 teach that we are to honor our father and mother? Are we not told that in 1 Timothy 5:8 that if we don't take care of the needs of our family we are worse than an infidel? Is verse 26 a contradiction to Ephesians 5:25 that tells us the importance of husbands loving their wives as Christ loved the church?

Jesus grabs the audience's attention by using that strong word *hate!* He uses it to illustrate the importance of having God first in one's life—a higher priority than any other thing or person. Our relationship with God must be such a passion that by comparison it would appear that we do hate everything else. Obviously, Jesus does not intend *hate* to be taken in an absolute sense. In a relative sense, our love for God must be greater than even that of our beloved family.

B. First in Sacrifice (v. 27)

27. And whosoever doth not bear his cross, and come after me, cannot be my disciple.

We sing songs about the old rugged *cross* and ask, "Must Jesus Bear the Cross Alone?" In the first century the cross is not beautiful or something in which people glory. Before Jesus' death and resurrection, no one would have worn a cross as jewelry.

There is only one reason a person ever takes up a cross: to die upon it. As Jesus will be made to carry His own cross, so also is there a task for us. Jesus will not refuse His cross, but because of His devotion to His Father's will and because of His love for us, He will be nailed to that cross for our sins. [See question #5, page 446.]

No one will die for a cause in which he or she does not believe. All of the bold statements of what we would do for Christ are empty if He is not actually first in our lives. Do we believe someone who says, "I'd die for Jesus," but won't do small things that serve and honor the Lord?

Conclusion
A. Humility and Sacrifice

The answer to the songwriter's question, "Must Jesus bear the cross alone, And all the world go free?" is this: "No; there's a cross for ev'ryone, And there's a cross for me" (Thomas Shepherd, 1665–1739).

Those who are self-important and believe they deserve the very best have not made God their priority. Many reject the Lord's invitation to His kingdom because other things are more important. Humility and sacrifice are what the Lord seeks.

B. Prayer

Father, show us our crosses this week. Give us strength to carry them. In Jesus' name, amen.

C. Thought to Remember

Accept and honor the Lord's invitation.

Home Daily Bible Readings

Monday, Aug. 22—Bear with One Another in Love (Ephesians 4:1-6)

Tuesday, Aug. 23—Imitate Christ's Humility (Philippians 2:1-8)

Wednesday, Aug. 24—Clothe Yourself with Humility (1 Peter 5:3-10)

Thursday, Aug. 25—Parable of the Wedding Banquet (Matthew 22:1-10)

Friday, Aug. 26—Jesus Heals the Man with Dropsy (Luke 14:1-6)

Saturday, Aug. 27—Humility and Hospitality (Luke 14:7-14)

Sunday, Aug. 28—Parable of the Great Dinner (Luke 14:15-24)

Learning by Doing

This page contains an alternative lesson plan emphasizing learning activities.
Classes desiring such student involvement will find these suggestions helpful.

Learning Goals

After participating in this lesson, each student will be able to:

1. Explain the lesson from Jesus' parables in Luke 14.

2. Understand the relationship between humility and being a disciple of Jesus.

3. Accept the call of Jesus to follow Him humbly, gratefully, and wholeheartedly.

Into the Lesson

Before class, prepare invitations for a formal dinner party, leaving the significant details blank. For example: "You are cordially invited to a party hosted by *[name of host]* to celebrate *[occasion of celebration]* on *[time and date]* at *[location of party]*. RSVP." Begin class by putting your learners into small groups. Have each group plan an imaginary party by filling in the blanks of the invitations. They should also comment on other details of the party, such as appropriate attire, entertainment, and menu.

After a few minutes, ask each group to read its invitation and describe the event they have planned. Say, "Having these settings in mind sets the stage for understanding the two parables of Jesus we will examine, both of which occur in a banquet context."

Into the Word

Banquet Attendance Etiquette. Read Luke 14:7-11 aloud. Review the parable several times by describing the story in the context of the imaginary events that have been planned by your small groups. (For example, "While at the Lincoln Center, a guest took a seat next to the President of the United States, at which point security ushered him to a small adjoining room where he could only observe the event on closed-circuit TV.") After repeating this for several of the situations created by your class members, ask, "What lessons do we learn about pride and humility?" Conclude this discussion by reading aloud the summary in Luke 14:11.

Banquet Invitation Etiquette. Say, "So far we have learned something about banquet 'attendance etiquette,' but there's also something to learn about 'invitation etiquette.'" Then pass out small slips of paper (several to each learner) with the following phrase written on the top: *"I'm sorry, but I will not be able to attend because . . . "*

Inform your learners that you are now having a "Lame Excuse" contest. You want them to write the reason they could express to the host for not attending the event to which they have been invited. Remind them of the important galas that they previously had created. Say, "I will be looking for the lamest excuses based on how humorous or ridiculous they are." (You could even offer prizes!)

After a few minutes of small-group discussions, you can either have class members read aloud their lame excuses or you can collect them to read several aloud yourself. After reading these (and laughing together), ask, "How would you feel if you were the host who received such responses from the guests you had invited?" Next, read aloud Luke 14:15-20. After each excuse is given in the parable itself, pause to discuss how well it would do in your "Lame Excuse" contest.

Discuss what the excuses in the text might sound like today. Begin by saying, "Jesus extends an invitation for everyone to follow Him. His offer of forgiveness and grace is free. However, people often respond by providing lame excuses. These show pride rather than humility. These excuses may indicate preoccupation with money, or success, or many other things. Ultimately, however, this attitude reflects a pride that says, 'I don't need Jesus.' It is an insult to Him and His gracious offer. So how do any of our excuses *really* sound to Him?"

Conclude this part of the discussion by reading aloud Luke 14:21-24. After you reach the end of verse 23, pause and tell your learners that you want everyone to join in as you read verse 24 aloud together, then do so. For dramatic effect, you can go around the room and have each person read verse 24 aloud separately.

Into Life

Distribute "invitations" that read as follows: "You are cordially invited by Jesus Christ to participate in a celebration of forgiveness and freedom beginning today and lasting for all eternity. RSVP." (Make these up ahead of time, preferably using some kind of "fancy" font as commonly found in word processing software.) Encourage students to use the invitation as a bookmark, reminding them to consider daily their response to this invitation. Close with a prayer for this.

Let's Talk It Over

The questions on this page are designed to promote discussion of the lesson by the class and to encourage application of the lesson Scriptures. The answers provided are only discussion starters. Let your class talk it over from there.

1. How do people today posture for position, seeking to make themselves appear important in the eyes of others?

Keep this discussion focused on issues—not people. Finger-pointing at people present or just known to those in your class will not be helpful. But an honest self-analysis of ways we sometimes push ourselves forward will help us to deal with the attitude that drives such behavior. Sometimes we do it by the way we dress. Perhaps we spend more on a car than we can afford because we want a car that suggests prestige or success. Do we refuse to speak to certain people at social occasions because of who might see us?

Sometimes being recognized is important. Police or security personnel wear uniforms and badges for that purpose. But in most cases we can get more accomplished if we are willing to don the servant's towel (John 13:4) and seek to meet needs instead.

2. When have you seen demonstrated the truth "whosoever exalteth himself shall be abased; and he that humbleth himself shall be exalted"? Tell about the event.

Probably every church has a corps of faithful workers who shun the spotlight and simply pitch in to get a job done. Perhaps they are craftsmen who do a beautiful job on a church remodeling project, making the facility more attractive to visitors and more useful in ministry. How appropriate it is for the church to recognize these folks when the task is complete! (They are usually embarrassed to be "fussed over," but they truly are pleased, and it is appropriate to recognize them.)

Unfortunately, there seem always to be certain ones in every church who expect more recognition than their efforts warrant. Like the "hypocrites" Jesus condemned in Matthew 6, they do their good deeds to be noticed. If there is no notice, don't expect to find them on hand. (Again, be sure this discussion stays focused on issues, not personalities!)

3. What excuses do people offer for not getting more involved in church ministries? What priorities do these excuses reveal? What is the difference between an *excuse* and a *reason*, if any?

The most common excuse must be, "I'm too busy." Each of the excuses in the text was essentially, "I'm too busy"—busy with business, busy with chores at home, busy with family.

These are the same misplaced priorities we see today. People spend so much time with work that they are unable to play meaningful roles in ministry. Others always have home projects but never have time for work in the church. Even family, which is important, can become an excuse for not being involved in ministry. Often those who use this as an excuse have actually shorted the family of their time as well, spending too much time at the office or shop.

What drives this is often materialism. We have committed ourselves to so much consumer debt in order to have things that we are forced to spend more and more time at work to pay for it. Are we really seeking first the kingdom when that happens?

4. In the parable, those who were too busy to accept the host's invitation were excluded from his fellowship. What blessings do we miss out on when we are too busy for the Lord's service?

If we are "too busy" to accept the Lord's offer of salvation, then we miss out on that—eternal life with the Lord! Many believers who will share in eternal life, however, will miss out on many blessings because they fail to be as involved in ministry as they could be.

Jesus said it is more blessed to give than to receive. He did not enumerate on the blessings, but your learners can suggest many. There is the joy of seeing needs met. Sometimes there is recognition that comes—even when it is not the reason one gets involved in ministry. Often the ministry itself is its own reward.

5. In what ways do we bear the cross today?

Too often people cheapen the concept of cross-bearing to include minor inconveniences. Yet, the cross was an instrument of death. To bear the cross, then, must signify dying to a certain way of life. Perhaps some of your students went against generations of family tradition to come to faith in Christ. They have "died" in the eyes of their family! Others have given up a lifestyle and/or a host of "friends" in coming to the Lord. Paul's admonition to give ourselves as living sacrifices (Romans 12:1, 2) is completely consistent with this issue.

Ready, Aim, Teach

The Importance of Lesson Aims in Teaching

by Jonathan Underwood

DO YOU EVER WONDER whether you are doing any good as the teacher of your class? Does it ever seem you are just passing time in class instead of accomplishing anything meaningful? If so, perhaps you need to take a second look at the lesson aims (also called learning goals) included in each lesson. These aims are carefully crafted to get you started on the right path and to keep you focused on your goal.

Where Are You Going?

Someone has said, "If you don't know where you are going, then any road will take you there." To know which is the right road, or the right way, one must know where it is he or she wants to be. The same is true in your teaching. Unless you have a clear idea of what you want to accomplish by the end of the class session—where you want your students to be, if you please—then there is no way to know just what you ought to spend your time doing in the class session.

What is your goal in teaching? Surely it is more than providing sixty minutes worth of diversion; you're not just filling time. And you're not just trying to cover a particular portion of Scripture. No, you want more. You want your students to know something they may not have known before they came into your classroom. More than that, you want them to understand the truths and principles of Scripture that the lesson text presents.

Finally, you want the students to apply to their lives those things they have come to know and understand. For these reasons, the editors of the *Standard Lesson Commentary* and *The NIV® Standard Lesson Commentary* spend much time in formulating the lesson aims that appear in each lesson.

The Content Aim

"What Does the Text Say?"

There are three aims for every lesson. The first is a *content* aim. This aim addresses the issue of what facts the student should know as a result of having participated in the study of the assigned lesson text. Verbs like *recount, tell,* and *identify* will frequently introduce such aims. Knowledge of Bible content is foundational.

The Concept Aim

"What does the text mean?"

The second aim might be called a *concept* aim. This goal probes beneath the surface of the material to find the timeless principles underlying the facts reported in the Scripture text.

This aim takes the learner beyond the knowledge of facts toward understanding. This is a necessary link to bring the historical truth about events of centuries gone by to relevance to learners in our own day. Verbs like *relate, compare,* and *explain* will be more common in introducing these aims.

The Conduct Aim

"What does the text demand of me?"

The third aim is what we might call a *conduct* aim. This is the goal that addresses the issue of application: How will the students' conduct change as a result of participating in this study? Such aims may challenge the learner to make a commitment or to suggest a specific action that he or she can take in the coming week.

Putting It Together

So, are any of the three aims more important than the other two? Or are all three equally important? What you as the teacher choose to stress depends on the nature of the lesson you're teaching.

The concept aims are especially important, for example, in studying the historical narratives in Scripture. It is not enough to know the facts about the story of David's killing the giant Goliath. We must also understand the principles of faith and courage that moved David to action. Only then can we move on from the content aim, knowing the facts, to the conduct aim: applying this lesson to how we face the giants in our own lives. In some passages, especially in the epistles, the content may be more exposition than narration, more conceptual than historical. In these cases we may find that to know the content of the passage is almost the same as knowing the concept.

Thus, starting your lesson preparation with a clear understanding of what you want to accomplish is vital! Knowing where you want to end up will determine which aim or aims you will stress.

COMPANION DEVOTIONS
for Standard Lesson Commentary® Users

Understand and personalize lessons from the
Standard Lesson Commentary with the new
Companion Devotions.

With daily facts and comments, readers' hearts will be
prepared for the coming week's lesson.

2004-2005

STANDARD LESSON
COMMENTARY®

COMPANION
DEVOTIONS

The LORD is my shepherd; I shall not want.
He maketh me to lie down in green pastures: he leadeth me beside the still waters.
He restoreth my soul: he leadeth me in the paths of righteousness for his name's sake.
– Psalm. 23:3

Daily Bible readings & meditations to support the weekly
International Sunday School Lessons